17th Conference on Natural Language Processing/Konferenz zur Verarbeitung naturlicher Sprache (KONVENS 2021)

Dusseldorf, Germany
6-9 September 2021

ISBN: 978-1-7138-3697-1

Printed from e-media with permission by:

Curran Associates, Inc.
57 Morehouse Lane
Red Hook, NY 12571

Association for Computational Linguistics
209 N. Eighth Street
Stroudsburg, Pennsylvania 18360

Phone: 1-570-476-8006
Fax: 1-570-476-0860

acl@aclweb.org

Additional copies of this publication are available from:

Curran Associates, Inc.
57 Morehouse Lane
Red Hook, NY 12571 USA
Phone: 845-758-0400
Fax: 845-758-2633
Email: curran@proceedings.com
Web: www.proceedings.com

KONVENS 2021

Proceedings of the 17th Conference on Natural Language Processing/Konferenz zur Verarbeitung natürlicher Sprache (KONVENS)

6–9 September, 2021
Heinrich Heine University Düsseldorf
Düsseldorf, Germany

Introduction

The papers of these proceedings have been presented at the 17th edition of KONVENS (Konferenz zur Verarbeitung natürlicher Sprache/Conference on Natural Language Processing). KONVENS is a conference series on computational linguistics established in 1992 that was held biennially until 2018 and has been held annually since. KONVENS is organized under the auspices of the German Society for Computational Linguistics and Language Technology, the Special Interest Group on Computational Linguistics of the German Linguistic Society and the Austrian Society for Artificial Intelligence.

The 17th KONVENS took place from September 6 to September 9, 2021 at Heinrich Heine University Düsseldorf. Due to the COVID-19 pandemic situation, KONVENS was held as a hybrid event in order to allow both speakers and regular participants to attend the conference either on-site or online. The special theme of this year's meeting was *Deep Linguistic Modeling*. The KONVENS main conference was accompanied by two workshops, three shared task meetings, and a 'PhD Day'.

Many thanks to all who submitted their work to KONVENS and to our board of reviewers for supporting us greatly with evaluating the submissions. Moreover we would like to thank Heinrich Heine University Düsseldorf for providing the conference rooms and all people from the CL department in Düsseldorf who made the conference possible. Our special thanks go to Tobias Koch from the 'Multimediazentrum' for his generous technical support.

Kilian Evang
Laura Kallmeyer
Rainer Osswald
Jakub Waszczuk
Torsten Zesch

People

Local Organization:

Tatiana Bladier, Rafael Ehren, Kilian Evang, Laura Kallmeyer, Rainer Osswald, Esther Seyffarth

Program Chairs:

Laura Kallmeyer, Rainer Osswald, Jakub Waszczuk, Torsten Zesch

Program Committee:

Adrien Barbaresi, Felix Bildhauer, Marcel Bollmann, Ernst Buchberger, Stephan Busemann, Miriam Butt, Mark Cieliebak, Berthold Crysmann, Stefanie Dipper, Sarah Ebling, Kilian Evang, Stefan Evert, Diego Frassinelli, Abhijeet Gupta, Anke Holler, Laura Kallmeyer, Manfred Klenner, Roman Klinger, Valia Kordoni, Brigitte Krenn, Udo Kruschwitz, Sandra Kübler, Gabriella Lapesa, Ekaterina Lapshinova-Koltunski, Anke Lüdeling, Alexander Mehler, Günter Neumann, Rainer Osswald, Sebastian Pado, Simone Paolo Ponzetto, Simon Petitjean, Hannes Pirker, Ines Rehbein, Georg Rehm, Michael Roth, Josef Ruppenhofer, Younes Samih, Felix Sasaki, Roland Schäfer, Yves Scherrer, Helmut Schmid, Gerold Schneider, Roman Schneider, Sabine Schulte im Walde, Marcin Skowron, Manfred Stede, Ludovic Tanguy, Jakub Waszczuk, Thomas Weskott, Magdalena Wolska, Torsten Zesch, Heike Zinsmeister

Invited Speakers:

Afra Alishahi, Tilburg University
Milica Gašić, Heinrich Heine University Düsseldorf
Mirella Lapta, University of Edinburgh
Johann-Mattis List, Max Planck Institute for the Science of Human History Jena

Satellite Events

1st Workshop on Computational Linguistics for Political Text Analysis

Organizers: Ines Rehbein, Goran Glavaš, Simone Ponzetto, Gabriella Lapesa

Workshop on Multimodal and Multilingual Hate Speech Detection

Organizers: Özge Alaçam, Seid Muhie Yimam

Shared Task on Scene Segmentation (STSS)

Organizers: Albin Zehe, Leonard Konle, Lea Dümpelmann, Evelyn Glus, Svenja Guhr, Andreas Hotho, Fotis Jannidis, Lucas Kaufmann, Markus Krug, Frank Puppe, Nils Reiter, Annekea Schreiber

GermEval 2021 Shared Task on the Identification of Toxic, Engaging, and Fact-Claiming Comments

Organizers: Julian Risch, Anke Stoll, Lena Wilms, Michael Wiegand

Shared Task on the Disambiguation of German Verbal Idioms

Organizers: Rafael Ehren, Laura Kallmeyer, Timm Lichte, Jakub Waszczuk

PhD Day

Organizers: Esther Seyffarth, Oliver Deck, Jannis Pagel, Ronja Laarmann-Quante, Stefan Grünewald

Invited Talks

Afra Alishahi: Decoding what deep, grounded neural models learn about language

Humans learn to understand speech from weak and noisy supervision: they extract structure and meaning from speech by simply being exposed to utterances situated and grounded in their daily sensory experience. Emulating this remarkable skill has been the goal of numerous studies; however, researchers have often used severely simplified settings where either the language input or the extralinguistic sensory input, or both, are small-scale and symbolically represented.

Recently, deep neural network models have been successfully used for visually grounded language understanding, where representations of images are mapped to those of their written or spoken descriptions. Despite their high performance, these architectures come at a cost: we know little about the type of linguistic knowledge these models capture from the input signal in order to perform their target task.

I present a series of studies on modelling visually grounded language learning and analyzing the emergent linguistic representations in these models. Using variations of recurrent neural networks to model the temporal nature of spoken language, we examine how form and meaning-based linguistic knowledge emerges from the input signal.

Mirella Lapata: Summarization and Paraphrasing in Quantized Transformer Spaces

Deep generative models with latent variables have become a major focus n of NLP research over the past several years. These models have been used both for generating text and as a way of learning latent representations of text for downstream tasks. While much previous work uses continuous latent variables, discrete variables are attractive because they are more interpretable and typically more space efficient. In this talk we consider learning discrete latent variable models with Quantized Variational Autoencoders, and show how these can be ported to two NLP tasks, namely opinion summarization and paraphrase generation for questions. For the first task, we provide a clustering interpretation of the quantized space and a novel extraction algorithm to discover popular opinions among hundreds of reviews, while for the second task we show that a principled information bottleneck leads to an encoding space that separately represents meaning and surface from, thereby allowing us to generate syntactically varied paraphrases.

Johann-Mattis List: Chances and Challenges for Computational Comparative Linguistics in the 21st Century

The quantitative turn at the beginning of the 21st century has drastically changed the field of comparative linguistics. Had individual genious and expert insights dominated historical linguistics in the past, we now find many studies by interdisciplinary teams who use complex computational techniques to investigate the history of invididual language families based on large amounts of data. Had the identification of linguistic universals in hand-crafted language samples dominated linguistic typology for a long time, scholars now use large cross-linguistic databases to investigate dependencies among linguistic and non-linguistic variables with the help of complex statistical models.

However, despite a period of more than two decades in which quantitative approaches have been increasingly used in comparative linguistics, gaining constantly more popularity even among predominantly qualitatively oriented linguists, we still find many problems, which have only sporadically been addressed. In the talk, I will present three of these so far unsolved problems, which I find particularly important for the future of the field of comparative linguistics. These are: (1) the problem of modeling and comparing sound change patterns across the languages of the world; (2) the problem of identifying cross-linguistic patterns of semantic change, and (3) the problem of estimating the borrowability of linguistic traits across languages and times.

While none of these problems has been solved so far, I will argue that substantial progress on their solution can be made by improving the integration of cross-linguistic data and by developing dedicated problem-solving strategies in computational linguistics which take the specifics of cross-linguistic data and language evolution into account.

Table of Contents

Long Papers

Short Papers

The Impact of Word Embeddings on Neural Dependency Parsing

Benedikt Adelmann
Wolfgang Menzel
Fachbereich Informatik
Universität Hamburg
adelmann@informatik.uni-hamburg.de
menzel@informatik.uni-hamburg.de

Heike Zinsmeister
Institut für Germanistik
Universität Hamburg
heike.zinsmeister@uni-hamburg.de

Abstract

Using neural models to parse natural language into dependency structures has improved the state of the art considerably. These models heavily rely on word embeddings as input representations, which raises the question whether the observed improvement is contributed by the learning abilities of the network itself or by the lexical information captured by means of the word embeddings they use. To answer this question, we conducted a series of experiments on German data from three different genres using artificial embeddings intentionally made uninformative in different ways. We found that without the context information provided by the embeddings, parser performance drops to that of conventional parsers, but not below. Experiments with domain-specific embeddings, however, did not yield additional improvements in comparison to large-scale general-purpose embeddings.

1 Introduction

In recent years, using neural models has notably improved the accuracy of dependency parsing, compared to non-neural or 'conventional' statistical parsers. However, while typical non-neural parsers normally have to extract all knowledge encoded in their models, including lexical information, from the training data, i. e. a dependency treebank, neural dependency parsers are usually endowed with word embeddings in addition to the treebank, not only at training, but also at test time. Given that embeddings are highly informative about distributional properties of the embedded entities (words in this case), which probably correlate with the possibility or plausibility of syntactic relationships, and that they are generally trained on corpora orders of magnitude larger than the dependency treebanks available for any language, this can be seen as an additional external source of information that conventional parsers do not have at their disposal.

This raises the question of how much of the reported difference, if any, is due to the neural model being better at modelling syntax and how much is just due to the information in the embeddings. On the one hand, one could argue that this distinction is irrelevant because the comparison reflects the way the systems would be used in practice. On the other hand, however, it is scientifically unsound to derive claims about capability differences of models or formalisms from experiments where more than just the model or formalism changes with respect to a control setting.

Furthermore, insight into the individual influence of model parts on the overall output (or at least its quality) can be seen as a step towards (some kind of) interpretability. Understanding the influence of embeddings is especially useful in language processing, where most knowledge is symbolic while neural networks necessarily operate on continuous representations. As it is embeddings of some kind that bridge this gap, systems should not be too dependent on their quality.

To gain more insight into this dependence of dependency parsing on embeddings, we have conducted experiments with a neural dependency parser provided with deterministically uninformative as well as random word embeddings and we report on the results.

2 Related Work

To our knowledge, the mechanisms leading to neural parsers exhibiting better performance than conventional ones have not yet been investigated. It has been shown that recurrent neural networks are able to capture syntactic structures such as nesting in practice as long as the depth is bounded (Bhattamishra et al., 2020), but this does not make a statement about whether or why they are better at it than conventional parsers, and it remains unclear what influence the input embeddings have on this capability.

The question how a model output changes when trained and evaluated on different input embeddings, specifically word embeddings, has been addressed by Rios and Lwowski (2020). They train numerous word embeddings using Word2Vec, GloVe or fastText, each with various different initialization seeds and on different corpora, and compare the performance of models when using these different embeddings as input. We take a similar approach, except that we use 'artificial' embeddings, and while their focus is on the consequences of embedding differences due to algorithm and initialization, we are interested in the impact of the (distributional) semantics available through the embedding in the first place.

For a short period in time there were even some neural parsing architectures without (external) embeddings, such as the ISBN parser by Titov and Henderson (2007). Its reported performance was well below what current parsers (with external embeddings) achieve, similar indeed to that of non-neural parsers.

Within a more recent apporach, parsing performance with and without external word embeddings has been compared by Kiperwasser and Goldberg (2016), who mention a counter-intuitive finding that external word embeddings *degraded* the performance of one of their parsers. In the small ablation study they report, however, the addition of external embeddings was accompanied by a change in parsing strategy (from graph-based to greedy transition-based), not allowing for conclusions about the impact of the embeddings alone.

More generally, there has been growing interest in the relationship between embeddings and downstream tasks in recent years, usually with a focus on the knowledge possibly encoded in the embedding, but also on how this knowledge and its representation affect further processing to which it is used as input. Much work on this topic has been concerned with sentence embeddings; for example, Miaschi et al. (2020) find a correlation between the amount of linguistic knowledge represented in a sentence embedding and its ability to solve a specific downstream task. They also provide evidence that fine-tuning the embedding makes it represent more task-specific knowledge at the expense of general knowledge.

A popular method for assessing what linguistic knowledge an embedding represents is *probing tasks* (a term that seems to have been coined by Conneau et al., 2018, based on Adi et al., 2017, and Shi et al., 2016), classifiers trained to reconstruct known explicit linguistic properties from embeddings. In one sense, dependency parsing can be seen as a probing task where the linguistic property to be extracted is the dependency structure of a sentence, and has indeed been used as a probing task (Miaschi et al., 2020; Kunz and Kuhlmann, 2020). However, 'viewing probing results in isolation can lead to overestimating the linguistic capabilities of a model' (Mosbach et al., 2020, p. 780), and Kunz and Kuhlmann (2020) point out that in such scenarios, it is generally unknown to what extent the output is indeed present in and extracted from the embedding, as opposed to being learned by the model ('probe') built on top of it. They consider embeddings to most likely lie between two extremes: no useful information being represented at all, or the information already being represented in a human-readable way. Apart from restricting the probing classifier to limited expressiveness, one possibility of distinguishing embedding from classifier power is therefore the comparison with the results of probing baseline embeddings lacking *any* linguistic information content, a common choice being random ones. We too use randomness as one way to create such embeddings.

A study relating word-level probing tasks to higher-level processing for several languages, including dependency parsing for German, can be found in Şahin et al. (2020). They report significant correlations between dependency parsing and morphosyntactic probing performance, suggesting that not only semantic, but also morphosyntactic information encoded in a word embedding can be influential. Note though that neural dependency parsing based on word embeddings is different from probing sentence embeddings for dependencies of the encoded sentence. One could say that the situation is the converse: In the probing scenario, the embedding is the result of a procedure and is probed to investigate its dependence on the original input. In our case, the embeddings are the input, and we want to investigate the dependence of the procedure on it. There are similar findings to the above for word embeddings, due to Köhn (2016), attesting the choice of embeddings a noticeable impact on parser performance.

3 Experimental Setup

As we cannot directly inspect what the neural architecture learns and whether it is indeed better than 'conventional' (non-neural) architectures at learning the syntactic knowledge needed for parsing, we employ a proxy question instead and ask how the output of a neural parser changes when depriving it of the knowledge encoded in the input word embeddings, as these embeddings are an additional input that most conventional parsers do not have at their disposal. If the neural parser performs significantly better than conventional parsers when provided with the same input, its neural architecture is obviously a better learner of syntax than the architectures of the conventional parsers. On the other hand, if the neural parser needs more input (i. e. the embeddings) than the conventional parsers to outperform them, the comparison is inherently unfair as it is hardly surprising that a system with more input can yield better predictions. While this does not necessarily rule out the possibility that the neural architecture is superior, the performance impact of eliminating a source of information sheds light on the dependence on that information. Such a dependence may be undesirable in certain contexts, such as low-resource settings where high-quality word embeddings are unavailable.

Another common scenario is that of *domain adaptation*, where only a generic treebank of considerable size is available for training, but specific embeddings can be obtained in an unsupervised[1] way from in-domain data (possibly the same data one wishes to parse later), which may be much smaller than the data employed for training general-purpose embeddings. We complement our experiments on the impact of uninformative embeddings by also providing the parser with embeddings trained on the corpora from which we draw our test data.

3.1 Parser

The parser we experiment with is **Sticker** (de Kok and Pütz, 2020), a recent neural dependency parser treating parsing as a sequence labelling problem: Every token is assigned a complex tag encoding where to attach it. In the case of Sticker, the tags indicate the attachment point as its relative position among tokens with a part of speech (e. g. 'the second finite verb to the left') and are computed by a neural network. (From the different architectural options we chose the LSTM architecture, which had turned out to work best on our data.) The only information that the neural network is provided with as input are embedding vectors of the tokens (words) in the sentence and of their part-of-speech (POS) tags. At training time, the parser trains the network based on these inputs (and the gold dependency structure and labels), but it does not alter the embeddings provided nor save any other lexical information about words in the training data; in particular, there is no attempt to obtain semantic knowledge about words not covered by the embedding.[2] This implies a substantial dependence on those embeddings.

As a conventional baseline we employ the five non-neural parsers from Adelmann et al. (2018a), excluding JWCDG, but only report the performance of the best parser per test text as reference. In all cases this was either Malt[3] (Nivre, 2003) with the 'Covington non-projective' algorithm (Covington, 2001) or Mate[4] (Bohnet, 2010).

3.2 Uninformative Embeddings

As Sticker cannot be run without word embeddings as input, we cannot entirely turn off this input, but we can substitute artificially created pseudo (or 'dummy') embeddings that are 'uninformative' in the sense that they do not encode any properties of the words beyond the word form identity (in particular, no semantics at all). We experiment with such uninformative embeddings created in different ways, two of them deterministic and four random (sampled with respect to different distributions, thus having different properties):

empty: an embedding not containing any words at all. This will make any word form encountered by the parser out-of-vocabulary (just like rare word forms simply not covered by a 'normal' embedding).

zero: an embedding mapping every word to the zero vector (the vector containing only zeroes). The out-of-vocabulary words are therefore the same as for the informative control embedding (see further below), but as all of them are assigned the same vector, they are entirely indistinguishable when processing them only by means of their word vectors.

cube: an embedding mapping every word to a vector with stochastically independent components all uniformly distributed in the unit interval [0, 1). In contrast to the previous embedding, words now have different vectors and are therefore

[1] Or 'self-supervised', referring to the fact that manual annotation effort is unnecessary.

[2] Details given here that are not from the cited paper are from personal communication with Daniël de Kok.

[3] http://www.maltparser.org/

[4] https://code.google.com/archive/p/mate-tools/

distinguishable, but as the vectors are chosen at random, they are highly unlikely to correlate with any linguistic relation: They do not carry any semantic information whatsoever.

ccube: like *cube*, but shifted into the origin, i. e. with components drawn from $[-0.5, 0.5)$.

gauss: an embedding mapping every word to a standard normal random vector, i. e. a vector with stochastically independent components all following a standard normal ('Gaussian') distribution.

sphere: an embedding mapping every word to a vector of length one (i. e. on the Euclidean unit sphere, hence the name), with every such vector having equal probability. In this embedding, any word vector can be separated from every other word vector by some hyperplane, so distinguishing words should be especially easy.

As an informative control embedding we use the German word embedding released with the pre-trained Sticker models.[5] Except for 'empty', which does not contain any vectors at all, all artificially created embeddings share dimension (300) and vocabulary with the control embedding.

For testing the influence of domain-specific embeddings, we train additional embeddings on texts sampled from the test corpora (see Section 3.4).

As mentioned above, the parser also requires an embedding of the part-of-speech (POS) tags present in the input. The control embedding here is based on one released with the pre-trained Sticker models which embeds the STTS (Schiller et al., 1999).[6] Additionally we created uninformative embeddings of the same six types as above, again with vocabulary (tag inventory; except for 'empty') and dimension (50) the same as in the control embedding.

However, we do not provide the parser with *both* uninformative word *and* uninformative POS embedding, as the only input that the parser receives are embedded words and POS tags, so making both embeddings uninformative would actually decouple the parser from its input.[7] We have not tried combining the uninformative POS embeddings with the domain-specific word embeddings either.

This leaves us with four types of neural parser configuration: With control word and control POS embedding (baseline), with uninformative word and control POS embedding, with control word and uninformative POS embedding, and with domain-specific word and control POS embedding.

For every artificial embedding we train one model for the parser and the respective embedding on the first 91,999 sentences of part A of the *Hamburg Dependency Treebank* (Foth et al., 2014), with the remaining 10,000 sentences (9.8 %) as validation set.

3.3 Test Data

To obtain test data, three annotators manually annotated randomly drawn sentences from three different corpora. The first one is a corpus of 636 modern dystopias written by German writers. The second one is the *d-Prose* corpus (Gius et al., 2020) containing 2,529 literary German prose texts from between 1870 and 1920. The third one consists of 8,788 documents downloaded from the internet, selected by the appearance of German keywords related to telemedicine (Franken and Adelmann, 2021). The sentences sampled from each corpus were combined with the annotated sentences of the respective texts from Adelmann et al. (2018b). The three test sets comprise around 7,500 tokens and 450 sentences each, with similar sentence length distributions (for details see Table 5; this, as well as some other tables, can be found in the appendix).

These datasets can be expected to notably differ both stylistically and thematically from the training data and between each other, without being intrinsically hard to annotate (and parse) like spoken or Twitter data.

The three annotators annotated the texts with dependency relations following the guidelines of Foth (2006), obtaining an overall inter-annotator reliability of Fleiss' $\kappa = 0.89$ for unlabelled attachment accuracy and Fleiss' $\kappa = 0.93$ for labelled attachment accuracy on a balanced subset of about 20 % of the test data. The remaining data

[5] German word embeddings, trained on TüBa-D/DP (de Kok and Pütz, 2019), quantized using optimized product quantization: https://github.com/stickeritis/sticker-models/releases/tag/de-structgram-20190426-opq (September 16, 2019, last retrieved April 14, 2021)

[6] With PAV instead of PROAV; source of the original embedding: https://blob.danieldk.eu/sticker-models/de-structgram-tags-20190426.fifu (last retrieved May 14, 2021)

[7] As a sanity check we did try that, obtaining UAS values between 17 % and 22 % and LAS values between 10 % and 16 %. Note that even in this scenario the parser still has access to sentence lengths, and POS tags are available when determining the attachment point based on the complex tag being predicted by the neural network, which itself does not have this information.

was distributed among the annotators (so that sentences were annotated by only one annotator each) and subsequently post-edited based on some heuristics for checking consistency.

The annotators only annotated dependencies. POS tags (required by all parsers as input), lemmata and morphological features (required by the non-neural parsers) were predicted by a tagger ensemble.[8] This is in contrast to training time, where gold POS tags from the treebank were used.[9]

3.4 Domain-Specific Embeddings

To obtain domain-specific embeddings we trained word embeddings on samples of similar total token count as part A of the *Hamburg Dependency Treebank* (approx. 1,872,622 tokens) from each of our test corpora, a reasonable order of magnitude for domain-specific data. The samples were chosen at random from the test corpora, taking care that no sentences used as test data were also selected as training data for the embeddings. Additionally, we sampled a collection of sentences, again of roughly the same total token count, from the union of all three test corpora.

4 Results

We assess performance differences by comparing unlabelled and labelled attachment accuracy (also known as unlabelled and labelled attachment score, or UAS and LAS) with respect to our test data between the best conventional (non-neural) parser, the neural parser with the ('informative') control embeddings, and the neural parser with our manipulated (i. e. uninformative or domain-specific) embeddings. For the webcrawling data, the best-performing conventional parser was Malt; for the other test sets, it was Mate.

Usually, such attachment accuracies are computed *excluding punctuation* since punctuation attachment and labelling is considered trivial. This, however, may not be the case if uninformative embeddings make it hard for the parser to determine which tokens are in fact punctuation. For this reason, we treat punctuation like any other tokens and report attachment accuracies *including punctuation*. Between 12 % and 17 % of the tokens in our test data are punctuation (according to automatic POS tagging), so they also increase the effective amount of test data, and when excluding them, attachment accuracies are about 2 percentage points lower than those we report, for both the neural and the conventional baseline.

4.1 Uninformative Word Embeddings

With the control embedding, the neural parser has a UAS 3 to 4 percentage points higher than the best conventional parser and an LAS 5 to 6 percentage points higher; this is a considerable baseline difference. With uninformative word embeddings, this margin decreases by 1 to 3 percentage points in the case of UAS and by 1 to 7 percentage points for LAS, depending on test set and the type of uninformative embedding. For instance, on the modern dystopias data with the 'cube' embedding, the UAS decreases from 0.93 to 0.90, and the LAS decreases from 0.91 to 0.84, the UAS reducing to and the LAS even falling short of Mate's performance (cf. Table 1). The other uninformative embeddings have less dramatic effects, giving values generally still above the conventional baseline. For all test sets, the embedding with the highest UAS and LAS is 'sphere', and the 'cube' embedding is among those with the smallest UAS and LAS. The other embeddings do not differ much from each other, their accuracies being mostly closer to those of the conventional than those of the neural baseline. Performance differences between test sets are similar for the baseline models (both conventional and neural) and the models with uninformative embeddings.

As the UAS and LAS differences are small, we also tested for statistical significance, using the randomization test of Yeh (2000) (with 100,000 samples) because theoretical distributions are not known. Except for the 'sphere' embedding tested on webcrawling data or the combination of all three, the p-value for the hypothesis that the model performs as well as the *neural* baseline is below 5 %; in the vast majority of cases, it is even below the stricter significance threshold of 0.25 % proposed by Søgaard et al. (2014), so we can be confident that the models do indeed perform *worse* than the neural baseline. On the other hand, the p-value for the hypothesis that the model performs as well as the *conventional* baseline is mostly not below the strict threshold, but below 5 % in more than half of the cases (see Table 4). The hypothesis cannot be rejected for the UAS of the 'cube' embedding (i. e. this embedding makes the neural parser perform no better than the best conventional parser, at least not with respect to

[8] See https://github.com/benadelm/hermA-Pipeline (last retrieved August 7, 2021).

[9] Again, with PAV instead of PROAV.

text	traditional			normal		empty		zero		cube		ccube		gauss		sphere	
	Parser	UAS	LAS	UAS	LAS	UAS	LAS	UAS	LAS	UAS	LAS	UAS	LAS	UAS	LAS	UAS	LAS
dystopias	Mate	0.90	0.85	0.93	0.91	0.91	0.87	0.91	0.87	0.90	0.84	0.91	0.86	0.90	0.86	0.92	0.88
19th century	Mate	0.88	0.83	0.91	0.88	0.89	0.84	0.89	0.84	0.88	0.83	0.89	0.84	0.88	0.84	0.90	0.85
webcrawling	Malt	0.87	0.83	0.91	0.88	0.88	0.85	0.88	0.85	0.88	0.84	0.89	0.86	0.88	0.86	0.90	0.87
all three	Mate	0.88	0.83	0.92	0.89	0.90	0.85	0.89	0.85	0.89	0.84	0.90	0.85	0.89	0.85	0.91	0.87

Table 1: Attachment accuracies for the uninformative word embeddings, including punctuation

text	traditional			normal		empty		zero		cube		ccube		gauss		sphere	
	Parser	UAS	LAS	UAS	LAS	UAS	LAS	UAS	LAS	UAS	LAS	UAS	LAS	UAS	LAS	UAS	LAS
dystopias	Mate	0.90	0.85	0.93	0.91	0.91	0.87	0.91	0.87	0.92	0.89	0.93	0.90	0.93	0.90	0.93	0.90
19th century	Mate	0.88	0.83	0.91	0.88	0.89	0.85	0.90	0.86	0.91	0.86	0.91	0.88	0.91	0.88	0.91	0.88
webcrawling	Malt	0.87	0.83	0.91	0.88	0.89	0.87	0.89	0.87	0.91	0.88	0.91	0.88	0.91	0.88	0.91	0.88
all three	Mate	0.88	0.83	0.92	0.89	0.90	0.87	0.90	0.87	0.91	0.88	0.92	0.89	0.92	0.89	0.92	0.89

Table 2: Attachment accuracies for the uninformative POS embeddings, including punctuation

text	traditional			normal		dystopias		19th century		webcrawling		total	
	Parser	UAS	LAS	UAS	LAS	UAS	LAS	UAS	LAS	UAS	LAS	UAS	LAS
dystopias	Mate	0.90	0.85	0.93	0.91	0.93	0.90	0.93	0.90	0.93	0.90	0.93	0.90
19th century	Mate	0.88	0.83	0.91	0.88	0.90	0.87	0.91	0.88	0.91	0.87	0.91	0.87
webcrawling	Malt	0.87	0.83	0.91	0.88	0.90	0.88	0.91	0.88	0.91	0.88	0.90	0.87
all three	Mate	0.88	0.83	0.92	0.89	0.91	0.88	0.91	0.89	0.91	0.88	0.91	0.88

Table 3: Attachment accuracies for the domain-specific word embeddings, including punctuation

head attachments), but it can be rejected (even with the stricter threshold) for the 'sphere' embedding (i. e. this embedding makes the neural parser still perform better than the best conventional parser). For the other embeddings, the picture is mixed. Even where the p-value is below 5 %, it is not much lower, so one should be cautious about rejecting the null hypothesis.

4.2 Uninformative POS Embeddings

For the uninformative POS embeddings, UAS and LAS values are higher than for the uninformative word embeddings. The 'ccube', 'gauss', and 'sphere' embedding even result in the same UAS as the control embedding (and so does the 'cube' embedding on the 19th century and web-crawling data). This is not very surprising since there are substantially fewer POS tags than words, and consequently, uninformative POS embeddings mean less information loss than uninformative word embeddings. Still, performance decreases with respect to the baseline can be observed over all test sets for the 'empty' and 'zero' embeddings, and for the other uninformative embeddings, there seems to be a tendency towards reductions in LAS (see Table 2). The increase in UAS from uninformative word to uninformative POS embeddings is smaller (1.6 percentage points on average) than the increase in LAS (2.6 percentage points on average), suggesting that there are in comparison more label errors when word embeddings are uninformative than when only POS embeddings are. Additionally, all values across the board are better now than those of the conventional parsers.

Correspondingly, p-values (Table 9) do clearly not permit rejection of the hypothesis that the uninformative 'ccube', 'gauss', or 'sphere' embedding makes the neural parser perform worse than with the control embedding, and the hypothesis that the performance is only as good as that of the conventional baseline can be rejected to the strict significance level of 0.25 %. The latter is even true for the 'cube' embedding, while the p-value for the test against the neural baseline LAS is also below 0.25 % for the dystopias and still below 5 % for the 19th century novels. The 'empty' and 'zero' embeddings exhibit mixed values. The p-values are below 5 % when testing against either baseline (but mostly not below 0.25 % for the neural baseline), with values below the stricter threshold appearing mostly for the LAS against the conventional parsers. Hence, here the assertion that the neural parser yields a better LAS than the conventional ones even with uninformative POS embeddings is more likely true than the corresponding one about the UAS. Apparently uninformative word embeddings have a stronger negative impact on LAS than uninformative POS embeddings.

4.3 Domain-Specific Word Embeddings

A difference between the neural parser's performance with domain-specific word embeddings and

text	empty		zero		cube		ccube		gauss		sphere	
	UAS	LAS	UAS	LAS	UAS	LAS	UAS	LAS	UAS	LAS	UAS	LAS
dystopias	***0.0430***	***0.0010***	***0.0170***	***0.0010***	***0.0010***	***0.0010***	***0.1360***	***0.0010***	***0.0010***	***0.0010***	*3.0180*	***0.0190***
19th century	***0.0960***	***0.0010***	***0.1520***	***0.0010***	***0.0110***	***0.0010***	*0.7470*	***0.0010***	***0.0130***	***0.0010***	*3.1170*	***0.0910***
webcrawling	***0.0200***	***0.0080***	***0.0040***	***0.0010***	***0.0040***	***0.0010***	*0.4580*	*0.3800*	***0.0160***	***0.0840***	7.0029	*3.3850*
all three	*0.7350*	***0.0210***	*0.5000*	***0.0150***	***0.0570***	***0.0010***	*2.5480*	***0.0410***	***0.2090***	***0.0100***	10.1369	*1.8220*

(a) p-values for the hypothesis that the results are not worse than Sticker's performance

text	empty		zero		cube		ccube		gauss		sphere	
	UAS	LAS	UAS	LAS	UAS	LAS	UAS	LAS	UAS	LAS	UAS	LAS
dystopias	*4.5430*	*1.4080*	8.9129	*2.0470*	26.1857	*2.8720*	*2.4620*	10.8949	44.2846	35.8266	***0.1020***	***0.0020***
19th century	*4.8630*	10.7799	*3.7090*	9.4529	17.6328	38.7696	*1.3280*	12.4229	14.2029	21.2568	*0.3060*	***0.0840***
webcrawling	*1.5910*	*0.3840*	*3.4910*	*1.8410*	6.4879	*3.0440*	***0.1160***	***0.0120***	*1.8230*	***0.0450***	***0.0040***	***0.0020***
all three	5.8059	*3.7340*	7.2999	*4.9590*	25.4797	41.4556	*2.2270*	*3.7790*	15.4428	8.3229	*0.3610*	***0.0740***

(b) p-values for the hypothesis that the results are not better than the performance of the respective best conventional parser (see Table 1)

Table 4: p-values (in %) for Yeh's randomized permutation test on performance differences between the uninformative word embeddings and the two baselines. Values below the significance threshold of 5 % are marked in italics; values below the stricter threshold of 0.25 % are additionally marked in bold. Values for the combination of all three corpora were computed on a subset of 461 sentences so that p-values are comparable.

with the control embedding is almost nonexistent, and the p-values are never below the significance threshold either. Conversely, they are always below the strict threshold for the hypothesis that the performance is not better than that of the conventional parser. While it is notable that even 'little' data the size of a dependency treebank (embeddings are usually trained on much bigger corpora) are sufficient to create an embedding sufficiently informative for the parser,[10] this does so far not facilitate insight into the role the embedding may play in domain adaptation. We did not test for effects of the embeddings being used cross-domain (e. g. the embedding trained on 19th century novels being used for parsing web-crawling data) as the performance differences among the different embeddings for the same test set are small where present at all, so we expect differences between test sets to be largely due to other parser-challenging aspects (such as general sentence complexity).

4.4 Label-Specific Evaluation

Finally, we take a brief look at some individual dependency labels. As pointed out in Adelmann et al. (2018a), overall attachment accuracies are skewed towards the performance on frequent phenomena such as determiner attachment, obfuscating issues with dependency relations that are of interest to content analyses, but appear less often. This evaluation only refers to the combination of all three test sets in the hope that as many labels as possible will be frequent enough there to be meaningfully evaluated.

For a number of labels, attachment precision and recall changed by more than 10 percentage points when parsed with uninformative embeddings, compared to parsing with the control embedding. Out of those, eleven appear more than 100 times in our test data; Table 11 shows their attachment precision and recall. Similarly great or in some cases even greater differences can also be observed for eleven other labels, but those are less frequent, some of them indeed very infrequent (e. g. there are only four occurrences of OBJG), so their values are probably unreliable. Among the frequent labels, heavy losses (up to 56 percentage points) can be observed for OBJD (dative object) and OBJP (prepositional object), mainly for the 'empty', 'zero' and 'cube' embeddings. OBJA (accusative object), PRED (predicative) and GMOD (genitive modifier) show losses mainly for these three embeddings, too, albeit not as big. With the 'ccube', 'gauss' and 'sphere' embeddings, losses are generally smaller, and for KOM (comparison), recall even *rises* with the 'ccube', 'gauss' and 'sphere' embedding.

There are also three labels where almost no difference in precision and recall can be observed for the deterministically uninformative embeddings ('empty' and 'zero'), but for the other (the random) embeddings: APP (apposition), ROOT and S. The latter two are especially interesting as S denotes the root node of sentences (in HDT, this is usually the finite verb) and ROOT is the label used exclusively for punctuation. While the precision of ROOT is

[10] We have not tested how well the domain-specific embeddings capture relationships between the embedded words.

always 1.00 (when the parser assigns this label, it is always correct), recall drops from almost 1.00 by 13 to 14 percentage points for the 'cube', 'ccube' and 'gauss' embeddings, that is, with those embeddings the parser fails to correctly identify about 13 to 14 % of the punctuation tokens. This is strange and remarkable given that punctuation is trivially identified by its POS. The decrease does not occur for the deterministic embeddings, nor for 'sphere'. S exhibits a similar phenomenon, but there it is precision that drops while recall remains, meaning that the parser mis-identifies something as a sentence root.

Table 12 shows precision and recall when parsing with uninformative POS embeddings, for the same labels as above. As with UAS and LAS, differences are less pronounced here, except for three labels when parsing with the deterministic embeddings: KOM shows a considerable increase in recall and OBJI (object infinitive) in precision, while ROOT decreases, again by 13 percentage points. This is complementary to the situation with uninformative word embeddings, where ROOT does not decrease for these two embeddings.

For the sake of completeness we note that there were no particularly interesting label performance differences when parsing with the domain-specific embeddings (Table 13).

5 Conclusion and Future Work

The main motivation for this paper was the question of whether neural networks are better than conventional, non-neural architectures at learning the syntactic knowledge needed for parsing, as opposed to just having the advantage of being provided with extra information in the form of word embeddings, and we approached this using the proxy question of how the output of a neural parser changes when depriving it of this extra information. The answer to this question from our results can be framed in two ways, depending on the perspective: Even without access to the knowledge encoded in a word embedding, the neural parser still performs (at least) as well as the best non-neural parser, so this lack of knowledge does not impair it so much that a conventional tool would be clearly preferable. Or alternatively: Without access to the knowledge encoded in a word embedding, the neural parser performs only about as well as the best non-neural parser, implying that it may indeed very well be the knowledge in the embedding that enables superior performance, not a superiority of the architecture.[11]

The results further suggest that a lack of word embedding knowledge abets label errors, while a lack of POS embeddings abets attachment errors, with a general tendency towards an increase in label errors in both cases. This could mean that knowledge about the co-occurrence of POS tags is more useful for predicting the correct head and knowledge about the co-occurrence of words is more useful for choosing the correct dependency label, which would not be implausible from a linguistic point of view. More dedicated experiments are necessary, however, to corroborate this hypothesis.

We also found that not all dependency labels are affected equally, the losses being concentrated mainly at 'content-related' labels such as OBJA (accusative object), with the especially vexing observation that uninformative word embeddings hinder the correct labelling of punctuation even though POS information should be sufficient to do so. A qualitative analysis of the label errors could be illuminative; possible reasons for this oddity would have to be investigated in greater depth.

The experiment with domain-specific embeddings was inconclusive, at least with the limited amount of domain-specific data used; the differences in vocabulary and in word semantics between the corpora were possibly too small to have a noticeable impact on parsing. We do observe, though, that even embeddings trained on little data make the parser perform almost as well as the control embeddings trained on big data.

Given this finding, subsequent research would have to dig further into the relationship between the size of the data used for training word embeddings and parser performance when using them.

We conducted our experiments with only one single parser. To assess how well our results apply to neural dependency parsing in general, future work would have to examine other parsers as well, particularly ones built on other parsing paradigms such as transition-based or graph-based parsing. It could furthermore be insightful to draw a comparison with conventional parsers able to use word embeddings (e. g. RBGParser).

[11] Of course, the mere ability to utilize word embeddings can be seen as an architectural superiority. This is not restricted to neural networks, though: RBGParser (Lei et al., 2014), too, can use word embeddings (cf. Köhn, 2016).

Acknowledgements

This work has been funded by 'Landesforschungsförderung Hamburg' in the context of the *hermA* project (LFF-FV 35). We would like to thank the reviewers for their thorough comments, Lea Röseler and Emily Roose for their invaluable annotation effort and Piklu Gupta for improving our English. All remaining errors are ours.

References

Benedikt Adelmann, Melanie Andresen, Wolfgang Menzel, and Heike Zinsmeister. 2018a. Evaluation of Out-of-Domain Dependency Parsing for its Application in a Digital Humanities Project. In *Proceedings of the 14th Conference on Natural Language Processing (KONVENS 2018)*, pages 121–135.

Benedikt Adelmann, Melanie Andresen, Wolfgang Menzel, and Heike Zinsmeister. 2018b. Manual Dependency Annotation of Three German Text Extracts from the Project hermA (Gold Standard Data). doi:10.5281/zenodo.1324079.

Yossi Adi, Einat Kermany, Yonatan Belinkov, Ofer Lavi, and Yoav Goldberg. 2017. Fine-grained Analysis of Sentence Embeddings Using Auxiliary Prediction Tasks. In *Proceedings of ICLR Conference Track*, Toulon, France.

Satwik Bhattamishra, Kabir Ahuja, and Navin Goyal. 2020. On the Practical Ability of Recurrent Neural Networks to Recognize Hierarchical Languages. In *Proceedings of the 28th International Conference on Computational Linguistics*, pages 1481–1494.

Bernd Bohnet. 2010. Very High Accuracy and Fast Dependency Parsing is not a Contradiction. In *Proceedings of the 23rd International Conference on Computational Linguistics*, pages 89–97.

Alexis Conneau, German Kruszewski, Guillaume Lample, Loïc Barrault, and Marco Baroni. 2018. What you can cram into a single $&!#* vector: Probing sentence embeddings for linguistic properties. In *Proceedings of the 56th Annual Meeting of the Association for Computational Linguistics (Volume 1: Long Papers)*, pages 2126–2136.

Michael Covington. 2001. A Fundamental Algorithm for Dependency Parsing. In *Proceedings of the 39th Annual ACM Southeast Conference*, pages 95–102.

Kilian Foth. 2006. Eine umfassende Constraint-Dependenz-Grammatik des Deutschen. Technical report, Universität Hamburg.

Kilian Foth, Arne Köhn, Niels Beuck, and Wolfgang Menzel. 2014. Because Size Does Matter: The Hamburg Dependency Treebank. In *Proceedings of the Language Resources and Evaluation Conference 2014*. European Language Resources Association (ELRA).

Lina Franken and Benedikt Adelmann. 2021. Webcrawling zu Akzeptanzproblematiken der Telemedizin. doi:10.5281/zenodo.4557100.

Evelyn Gius, Svenja Guhr, and Benedikt Adelmann. 2020. d-Prose 1870–1920. doi:10.5281/zenodo.4315208.

Eliyahu Kiperwasser and Yoav Goldberg. 2016. Simple and Accurate Dependency Parsing Using Bidirectional LSTM Feature Representations. *Transactions of the Association for Computational Linguistics*, 4:313–327.

Daniël de Kok and Sebastian Pütz. 2019. TüBa-D/DP Stylebook. Technical report, Seminar für Sprachwissenschaft, University of Tübingen.

Daniël de Kok and Tobias Pütz. 2020. Self-distillation for German and Dutch dependency parsing. In *Computational Linguistics in the Netherlands Journal*, volume 10, pages 91–107.

Jenny Kunz and Marco Kuhlmann. 2020. Classifier Probes May Just Learn from Linear Context Features. In *Proceedings of the 28th International Conference on Computational Linguistics*, pages 5136–5146.

Arne Köhn. 2016. Evaluating Embeddings using Syntax-based Classification Tasks as a Proxy for Parser Performance. In *Proceedings of the 1st Workshop on Evaluating Vector Space Representations for NLP*, pages 67–71.

Tao Lei, Yu Xin, Yuan Zhang, Regina Barzilay, and Tommi Jaakkola. 2014. Low-rank Tensors for Scoring Dependency Structures. In *Proceedings of the 52nd Annual Meeting of the Association for Computational Linguistics*, volume 1, pages 1381–1391.

Alessio Miaschi, Dominique Brunato, Felice Dell'Orletta, and Giulia Venturi. 2020. Linguistic Profiling of a Neural Language Model. In *Proceedings of the 28th International Conference on Computational Linguistics*, pages 745–756.

Marius Mosbach, Stefania Degaetano-Ortlieb, Marie-Pauline Krielke, Badr Abdullah, and Dietrich Klakow. 2020. A Closer Look at Linguistic Knowledge in Masked Language Models: The Case of Relative Clauses in American English. In *Proceedings of the 28th International Conference on Computational Linguistics*, pages 771–787.

Joakim Nivre. 2003. An efficient algorithm for projective dependency parsing. In *Proceedings of the 8th International Workshop on Parsing Technologies (IWPT)*, pages 149–160.

Anthony Rios and Brandon Lwowski. 2020. An Empirical Study of the Downstream Reliability of Pre-Trained Word Embeddings. In *Proceedings of the 28th International Conference on Computational Linguistics*, pages 3371–3388.

Anne Schiller, Simone Teufel, Christine Stöckert, and Christine Thielen. 1999. Guidelines für das Tagging deutscher Textcorpora mit STTS. Technical report, Institut für maschinelle Sprachverarbeitung, Seminar für Sprachwissenschaft, Stuttgart, Tübingen.

Xing Shi, Inkit Padhi, and Kevin Knight. 2016. Does String-Based Neural MT Learn Source Syntax? In *Proceedings of the 2016 Conference on Empirical Methods in Natural Language Processing*, pages 1526–1534.

Anders Søgaard, Anders Johannsen, Barbara Plank, Dirk Hovy, and Hector Martinez. 2014. What's in a p-value in NLP? In *Proceedings of the Eighteenth Conference on Computational Language Learning*, pages 1–10.

Ivan Titov and James Henderson. 2007. Fast and Robust Multilingual Dependency Parsing with a Generative Latent Variable Model. In *Proceedings of the 2007 Joint Conference on Empirical Methods in Natural Language Processing and Computational Natural Language Learning (EMNLP-CoNLL)*, pages 947–951.

Alexander Yeh. 2000. More accurate tests for the statistical significance of result differences. In *Proceedings of the 18th International Conference on Computational Linguistics*, pages 947–953.

Gözde Gül Şahin, Clara Vania, Ilia Kuznetsov, and Iryna Gurevych. 2020. LINSPECTOR: Multilingual Probing Tasks for Word Representations. *Computational Linguistics*, 46(2):335–385.

Appendix

text	overall tokens	sentences count	token count avg	token count m	token count stddev
dystopias	7,474	470	15.90	13	11.23
19th century	7,662	459	16.69	14	12.11
webcrawling	7,082	454	15.60	12	14.53
total	22,218	1,383	16.065	13	12.684

Table 5: Total number of tokens as well as sentence count and average, median and standard deviation of the number of tokens per sentence in our test sets

text	traditional			normal		empty		zero		cube		ccube		gauss		sphere	
	Parser	UAS	LAS	UAS	LAS	UAS	LAS	UAS	LAS	UAS	LAS	UAS	LAS	UAS	LAS	UAS	LAS
dystopias	Mate	0.88	0.82	0.92	0.89	0.89	0.84	0.89	0.84	0.89	0.84	0.91	0.87	0.90	0.86	0.91	0.87
19th century	Mate	0.85	0.80	0.89	0.86	0.87	0.81	0.87	0.81	0.87	0.82	0.88	0.84	0.88	0.83	0.88	0.83
webcrawling	Malt	0.85	0.80	0.90	0.87	0.87	0.83	0.86	0.82	0.87	0.83	0.89	0.85	0.88	0.85	0.89	0.85
all three	Mate	0.86	0.80	0.90	0.87	0.88	0.83	0.87	0.82	0.88	0.83	0.89	0.85	0.88	0.85	0.89	0.85

Table 6: attachment accuracies for the uninformative word embeddings (like Tab. 1), ignoring punctuation

text	traditional			normal		empty		zero		cube		ccube		gauss		sphere	
	Parser	UAS	LAS	UAS	LAS	UAS	LAS	UAS	LAS	UAS	LAS	UAS	LAS	UAS	LAS	UAS	LAS
dystopias	Mate	0.88	0.82	0.92	0.89	0.91	0.88	0.91	0.88	0.91	0.88	0.91	0.89	0.91	0.88	0.91	0.88
19th century	Mate	0.85	0.80	0.89	0.86	0.89	0.85	0.89	0.85	0.89	0.85	0.89	0.86	0.89	0.85	0.89	0.85
webcrawling	Malt	0.85	0.80	0.90	0.87	0.89	0.86	0.88	0.86	0.90	0.87	0.90	0.87	0.90	0.86	0.90	0.87
all three	Mate	0.86	0.80	0.90	0.87	0.89	0.87	0.89	0.87	0.90	0.87	0.90	0.87	0.90	0.86	0.90	0.87

Table 7: attachment accuracies for the uninformative POS embeddings (like Tab. 2), ignoring punctuation

text	traditional			normal		dystopias		19th century		webcrawling		total	
	Parser	UAS	LAS	UAS	LAS	UAS	LAS	UAS	LAS	UAS	LAS	UAS	LAS
dystopias	Mate	0.88	0.82	0.92	0.89	0.91	0.88	0.91	0.88	0.91	0.88	0.91	0.88
19th century	Mate	0.85	0.80	0.89	0.86	0.89	0.85	0.89	0.85	0.89	0.85	0.89	0.85
webcrawling	Malt	0.85	0.80	0.90	0.87	0.89	0.86	0.89	0.86	0.89	0.86	0.89	0.86
all three	Mate	0.86	0.80	0.90	0.87	0.90	0.86	0.90	0.86	0.90	0.86	0.90	0.86

Table 8: attachment accuracies for the domain-specific word embeddings (like Tab. 3), ignoring punctuation

text	empty		zero		cube		ccube		gauss		sphere	
	UAS	LAS	UAS	LAS	UAS	LAS	UAS	LAS	UAS	LAS	UAS	LAS
dystopias	***0.0050***	***0.0010***	***0.0200***	***0.0010***	6.5989	***0.0670***	27.6917	34.9537	20.3168	14.8269	25.7857	21.0308
19th century	*0.9970*	***0.1160***	*2.4010*	***0.1450***	29.1617	*3.3620*	49.0645	46.4145	43.1016	36.6626	47.5075	40.9466
webcrawling	*0.3660*	7.1739	*0.3280*	5.7079	26.5617	25.0447	44.1776	45.7915	42.6606	35.2796	45.0225	47.3175
all three	*1.2110*	*0.7660*	*1.8830*	*0.7500*	25.9947	8.0109	46.2675	48.6785	39.1796	33.5217	42.4446	39.6556

(a) p-values for the hypothesis that the results are not worse than Sticker's performance

text	empty		zero		cube		ccube		gauss		sphere	
	UAS	LAS	UAS	LAS	UAS	LAS	UAS	LAS	UAS	LAS	UAS	LAS
dystopias	20.1508	*0.8100*	8.9059	*0.8490*	***0.0380***	***0.0010***	***0.0010***	***0.0010***	***0.0020***	***0.0010***	***0.0010***	***0.0010***
19th century	*1.0150*	***0.0550***	*0.4340*	***0.0460***	***0.0030***	***0.0010***	***0.0010***	***0.0010***	***0.0010***	***0.0010***	***0.0010***	***0.0010***
webcrawling	***0.2430***	***0.0010***	*0.3280*	***0.0010***	***0.0010***	***0.0010***	***0.0010***	***0.0010***	***0.0010***	***0.0010***	***0.0010***	***0.0010***
all three	*4.1960*	***0.1660***	*2.5450*	***0.1890***	***0.0330***	***0.0050***	***0.0080***	***0.0010***	***0.0090***	***0.0010***	***0.0080***	***0.0010***

(b) p-values for the hypothesis that the results are not better than the performance of the respective best conventional parser (see Table 2)

Table 9: p-values (in %) for Yeh's randomized permutation test on performance differences between the uninformative POS embeddings and the two baselines. Values below the significance threshold of 5 % are marked in italics; values below the stricter threshold of 0.25 % are additionally marked in bold. Values for the combination of all three corpora were computed on a subset of 461 sentences so that p-values are comparable.

text	dystopias		19th century		webcrawling		total	
	UAS	LAS	UAS	LAS	UAS	LAS	UAS	LAS
dystopias	15.4958	12.1299	19.7578	13.7949	18.7668	6.8609	22.4608	10.3269
19th century	26.1267	20.1548	36.5816	33.2397	34.4367	14.9089	45.3085	26.7537
webcrawling	15.7938	17.4818	27.3167	31.9647	23.1158	21.8738	11.2789	12.4249
all three	25.5267	22.8208	33.2327	31.5717	31.0637	20.3748	30.1267	21.8918

(a) p-values for the hypothesis that the results are not worse than Sticker's performance

text	dystopias		19th century		webcrawling		total	
	UAS	LAS	UAS	LAS	UAS	LAS	UAS	LAS
dystopias	***0.0050***	***0.0010***	***0.0050***	***0.0010***	***0.0040***	***0.0010***	***0.0020***	***0.0010***
19th century	***0.0090***	***0.0010***	***0.0020***	***0.0010***	***0.0020***	***0.0010***	***0.0010***	***0.0010***
webcrawling	***0.0010***	***0.0010***	***0.0010***	***0.0010***	***0.0010***	***0.0010***	***0.0010***	***0.0010***
all three	***0.0350***	***0.0010***	***0.0150***	***0.0010***	***0.0160***	***0.0010***	***0.0210***	***0.0010***

(b) p-values for the hypothesis that the results are not better than the performance of the respective best conventional parser (see Table 3)

Table 10: p-values (in %) for Yeh's randomized permutation test on performance differences between the domain-specific embeddings and the two baselines. Values below the significance threshold of 5 % are marked in italics; values below the stricter threshold of 0.25 % are additionally marked in bold. Values for the combination of all three corpora were computed on a subset of 461 sentences so that p-values are comparable.

label	gold count	normal P	normal R	empty P	empty R	zero P	zero R	cube P	cube R	ccube P	ccube R	gauss P	gauss R	sphere P	sphere R
APP	704	0.75	0.88	0.73	0.86	0.72	0.85	**0.62**	0.87	0.65	0.87	**0.62**	0.87	0.71	0.87
GMOD	384	0.95	0.96	**0.79**	**0.85**	**0.78**	**0.84**	0.88	0.90	0.90	0.91	0.89	0.91	0.91	0.90
KOM	110	0.89	0.72	0.88	0.68	0.89	0.70	0.87	0.69	0.88	**0.89**	0.87	**0.90**	0.86	0.73
NEB	224	0.84	0.83	0.76	**0.72**	0.81	**0.66**	0.79	0.78	0.86	0.79	0.88	0.81	0.82	0.79
OBJA	928	0.88	0.90	**0.70**	**0.77**	**0.69**	**0.76**	**0.73**	0.82	0.80	0.85	0.78	0.85	0.84	0.85
OBJD	163	0.78	0.77	**0.39**	**0.17**	**0.36**	**0.21**	**0.64**	**0.37**	**0.62**	**0.64**	**0.64**	**0.64**	**0.63**	0.67
OBJI	109	0.72	0.82	0.70	0.78	0.71	0.80	0.68	0.75	0.70	0.80	0.71	0.77	0.74	0.81
OBJP	114	0.51	0.28	**0.25**	**0.02**	0.50	**0.06**	**0.32**	**0.05**	**0.38**	0.24	**0.34**	0.18	0.41	0.22
PRED	277	0.83	0.85	**0.71**	**0.69**	0.73	**0.67**	**0.70**	**0.66**	0.81	0.75	0.77	**0.74**	0.77	0.77
ROOT	3466	1.00	0.99	1.00	0.99	1.00	0.99	1.00	**0.86**	1.00	**0.85**	1.00	**0.85**	1.00	0.95
S	1726	0.91	0.86	0.90	0.86	0.90	0.86	**0.78**	0.84	**0.76**	0.85	**0.79**	0.85	0.86	0.85

Table 11: Precision and recall for selected labels when parsing with the uninformative word embeddings. The 'gold count' column gives the number of occurrences of the label in our test data. Values differing by more than 10 percentage points from the baseline are marked in bold.

label	gold count	normal P	normal R	empty P	empty R	zero P	zero R	cube P	cube R	ccube P	ccube R	gauss P	gauss R	sphere P	sphere R
APP	704	0.75	0.88	0.69	0.93	0.70	0.92	0.75	0.88	0.76	0.86	0.76	0.88	0.74	0.88
GMOD	384	0.95	0.96	0.92	0.96	0.95	0.96	0.96	0.96	0.95	0.95	0.95	0.95	0.95	0.95
KOM	110	0.89	0.72	0.89	**0.89**	0.90	**0.91**	0.88	0.68	0.89	0.68	0.87	0.67	0.86	0.68
NEB	224	0.84	0.83	0.84	0.85	0.86	0.86	0.83	0.80	0.84	0.81	0.85	0.82	0.81	0.80
OBJA	928	0.88	0.90	0.86	0.92	0.86	0.91	0.86	0.90	0.89	0.90	0.86	0.89	0.89	0.90
OBJD	163	0.78	0.77	0.81	0.76	0.80	0.80	0.76	0.79	0.75	0.83	0.75	0.79	0.77	0.82
OBJI	109	0.72	0.82	**0.90**	0.85	**0.91**	0.86	0.69	0.80	0.73	0.79	0.74	0.81	0.72	0.80
OBJP	114	0.51	0.28	0.47	0.25	0.52	0.30	0.46	0.28	0.45	0.29	0.42	0.24	0.46	0.29
PRED	277	0.83	0.85	0.79	0.83	0.79	0.82	0.84	0.84	0.80	0.84	0.83	0.86	0.80	0.83
ROOT	3466	1.00	0.99	1.00	**0.86**	1.00	**0.86**	1.00	0.91	1.00	0.99	1.00	0.99	1.00	0.99
S	1726	0.91	0.86	0.83	0.87	**0.80**	0.87	0.83	0.85	0.90	0.86	0.90	0.86	0.90	0.86

Table 12: Precision and recall for selected labels when parsing with the uninformative POS embeddings. The 'gold count' column gives the number of occurrences of the label in our test data. Values differing by more than 10 percentage points from the baseline are marked in bold.

label	gold count	normal P	normal R	dystopias P	dystopias R	19th century P	19th century R	webcrawling P	webcrawling R	total P	total R
APP	704	0.75	0.88	0.73	0.88	0.74	0.89	0.73	0.88	0.73	0.88
GMOD	384	0.95	0.96	0.94	0.93	0.94	0.94	0.93	0.94	0.94	0.92
KOM	110	0.89	0.72	0.88	0.69	0.90	0.71	0.88	0.71	0.88	0.71
NEB	224	0.84	0.83	0.86	0.82	0.88	0.80	0.88	0.82	0.81	0.81
OBJA	928	0.88	0.90	0.87	0.88	0.86	0.89	0.85	0.87	0.85	0.88
OBJD	163	0.78	0.77	0.70	0.79	0.75	0.74	**0.67**	0.72	0.72	0.78
OBJI	109	0.72	0.82	0.69	0.82	0.69	0.82	0.74	0.81	0.72	0.82
OBJP	114	0.51	0.28	0.46	0.25	0.46	0.28	0.49	0.29	0.41	0.27
PRED	277	0.83	0.85	0.81	0.81	0.82	0.83	0.81	0.81	0.81	0.79
ROOT	3466	1.00	0.99	1.00	0.99	1.00	0.99	1.00	0.99	1.00	0.99
S	1726	0.91	0.86	0.91	0.86	0.91	0.86	0.91	0.86	0.91	0.85

Table 13: Precision and recall for selected labels when parsing with the domain-specific word embeddings. The 'gold count' column gives the number of occurrences of the label in our test data. Values differing by more than 10 percentage points from the baseline are marked in bold.

Benchmarking down-scaled (not so large) pre-trained language models

Matthias Aßenmacher♠ **Patrick Schulze**♣ **Christian Heumann**♠

Department of Statistics
Ludwig-Maximilians-Universität
Ludwigstr. 33, D-80539 Munich, Germany
♠{matthias,chris}@stat.uni-muenchen.de, ♣pa.schulze@campus.lmu.de

Abstract

Large Transformer-based language models are pre-trained on corpora of varying sizes, for a different number of steps and with different batch sizes. At the same time fundamental components, such as the pre-training objective or architectural hyperparameters, are modified. In total, it is therefore difficult to ascribe changes in performance to specific factors. Since searching the hyperparameter space over the full systems is too costly, we pre-train down-scaled versions of several popular Transformer-based architectures on a common pre-training corpus and benchmark them on a subset of the GLUE tasks (Wang et al., 2018). Specifically, we systematically compare three pre-training objectives for different shape parameters and model sizes, while also varying the number of pre-training steps and the batch size. In our experiments MLM + NSP (BERT-style) consistently outperforms MLM (RoBERTa-style) as well as the standard LM objective. Furthermore, we find that additional compute should be mainly allocated to an increased model size, while training for more steps is inefficient. Based on these observations, as a final step we attempt to scale up several systems using compound scaling (Tan and Le, 2019) adapted to Transformer-based language models.

1 Introduction

The introduction of the Transformer (Vaswani et al., 2017) together with the application of transfer learning (Thrun and Pratt, 1998) has led to major advances in Natural Language Processing (NLP). While many different lines of research exist, most attention is generally paid to the largest systems which often reach new state-of-the-art (SOTA) results. The current trend is to scale up such systems to ever new orders of magnitude: 213M parameters in the Transformer, 300M parameters in BERT (Devlin et al., 2019), 1.5B parameters in GPT-2 (Radford et al., 2019) and 175B in GPT-3 (Brown et al., 2020). Since these models are pre-trained on corpora of widely varying sizes, for a different number of training steps and with different batch sizes, comparability suffers (Aßenmacher and Heumann, 2020). At the same time, new systems often apply fundamentally different methods, such as using a different pre-training objective or modified architectural hyperparameters. While altering multiple components simultaneously can help achieve new SOTA results, which is an important endeavor, it is difficult to disentangle the effects of the various factors. Though there exist various ablation studies, these often show only a small excerpt from the broad spectrum of experimental opportunities and can thus not provide a comprehensive picture. In this work, we conduct a systematic study of three Transformer-based architectures with respect to several pre-training hyperparameters.

2 Related work

One line of research empirically derives generalization results for large neural NLP systems. Rosenfeld et al. (2019) study how the generalization error of language models (LMs) depends on model and data set size. Regarding model size, they provide an approximation of the test loss, assuming that a LM is scaled with respect to a pre-defined scheme, such as increasing solely the embedding dimension. A related but more comprehensive study was conducted by Kaplan et al. (2020), examining power laws of the test loss when scaling large neural LMs with respect to a broad variety of different dimensions. These dimensions include architectural hyperparameters, model size, data set size, number of training steps and batch size. A central question in their work is how these factors can be combined to attain an optimal performance given a fixed amount of compute.

Compute efficient training is also investigated by Li et al. (2020), recognizing that an optimal allocation of computational resources is crucial for improving model performance. Considering Masked Language Modeling (MLM) pre-training, Li et al. (2020) examine the optimal choice of number of training steps and batch size in the relation to the model size. In a large-scale study, Raffel et al. (2019) cover an even broader variety of modeling scenarios than Kaplan et al. (2020), but train a much smaller number of systems per scenario. For instance, they include several variants of the Transformer, different pre-training objectives and various fine-tuning strategies in their analysis. Finally, based on their observations, Raffel et al. (2019) also scale-up a system to 11B parameters.

3 Materials and Methods

Pre-training data We pre-train all models on WikiText-103[1] (Merity et al., 2016), a large-scale text corpus for training and evaluating language models on long-range contexts, which has served as an evaluation data set (Radford et al., 2019; Dai et al., 2019; Shoeybi et al., 2019) as well as for pre-training (Howard and Ruder, 2018). We pre-train all models on the training set of WikiText-103, which allows for learning long-range dependencies (Rae et al., 2019). The validation set is employed to compare different architectures by their validation loss during pre-training. WikiText-103 is much smaller than most pre-training corpora of modern language models. For instance, Devlin et al. (2019) trained BERT on a $3,300$M words corpus, which is approximately 32x the size of WikiText-103. Aside from this, pre-training data sets of different models often vary considerably in size, which makes fair comparisons difficult (Aßenmacher and Heumann, 2020). Pre-training on the same corpus allows us to exclude the amount and quality of pre-training data as confounding factors when evaluating the different model components.

Models We compare three different model types: BERT (Devlin et al., 2019), RoBERTa (Liu et al., 2019) and GPT-2 (Radford et al., 2019). BERT is a bidirectional Transformer encoder which is trained with both MLM as well as Next Sentence Prediction (NSP). Its direct successor RoBERTa relies on the exact same architecture and differs from BERT solely in the pre-training procedure. Amongst other changes, Liu et al. (2019) abandoned the NSP objective and introduced a dynamic masking[2] procedure for the MLM objective[3]. GPT-2 is a Transformer decoder, and thus a unidirectional model, trained with the standard LM objective.

Since we train a multitude of down-scaled versions for each model type, thus modifying the specifications of the original models, we introduce the following conventions: We label models trained with MLM & NSP as *BERT-style*, models trained with MLM as *RoBERTa-style*, and models trained with LM as *GPT-2-style*. Alongside with the pre-training objectives, we also use the respective tokenizers of the different models. This means using byte-level BPE (Radford et al., 2019) for *RoBERTa-* and *GPT-2-style* and the WordPiece algorithm (Schuster and Nakajima, 2012) for *BERT-style* models, all of them exhibiting a uniform vocabulary size of 30,000 tokens

Fine-tuning data We fine-tune and evaluate our systems on GLUE (Wang et al., 2018). We mainly compare performances on MNLI (Williams et al., 2017), QQP (Shankar et al., 2017) and QNLI (Wang et al., 2018), which are the three largest GLUE tasks, since the results on these tasks are the most reliable. In particular, we therefore calculate the average score over the validation set performances of the three tasks, which we denote by *GLUE-Large*. For MNLI, we consider only the matched validation set when calculating this score. Whenever meaningful results for the two next largest data sets SST-2 (Socher et al., 2013) and CoLa (Warstadt et al., 2019) were achieved[4], those will also be reported.

Training details Hyperparameters and the pre-training/fine-tuning procedure are largely adopted from the original models (cf. Appendix A and B).

4 Experiments

4.1 Comparison of different Shapes[5]

In computer vision it has been observed that the performance of a neural network strongly depends on the choice of architectural hyperparameters, such

[1] www.salesforce.com/products/einstein/ai-research/the-wikitext-dependency-language-modeling-dataset/

[2] We also use dynamic masking throughout this study.

[3] There were further alterations, none of which are crucial for our experiments since we are using fixed pre-training data sets, batch sizes, learning rates, etc. for better comparability.

[4] For the smaller model sizes the performance on these smaller data sets did not significantly differ from zero.

[5] There exist several other choices, but examining the entire spectrum of possible shapes is out of the scope of this study.

as width or depth (Tan and Le, 2019). In contrast, Kaplan et al. (2020) observed a similar LM test loss over a wide range of shape parameters. Similarly, for MLMs, Li et al. (2020) found that the validation loss does not depend strongly on the model shape. This holds true also for the MNLI validation accuracy of fine-tuned systems.

In this study, we examine the impact of three different architectural hyperparameters in Transformer-based models: *depth*, *width* and the *number of attention heads*. Depth is given by the number of layers L. Stacking many layers in Transformer-based systems can be somewhat inefficient and does not always lead to a considerable increase in performance (Lan et al., 2019). Width corresponds to the embedding dimension H. Increasing H has in general produced slightly better results than increasing L in Transformer-based systems (Lan et al., 2019; Raffel et al., 2019; Li et al., 2020). Attention Heads are used to discriminate between different regions of the embedding space. In most applications of the Transformer, the number of attention heads A is set in fixed relation to H, such as $H = 64 \times A$. Decreasing performance has been reported for larger ratios (Vaswani et al., 2017; Brown et al., 2020).

4.2 Model Size, Training Steps and Batch size

Several recent studies have investigated the problem of compute efficient training of Transformer-based systems (Raffel et al., 2019; Li et al., 2020; Kaplan et al., 2020). The consensus among these studies is that, under a restricted budget, optimal performance is achieved by training very large models and stopping training well before convergence. Furthermore, additional compute should rather be used to increase the batch size instead of training for more steps. To examine convergence characteristics, we monitor the pre-training validation loss of several systems and test how this loss corresponds to different model sizes and shapes. Additionally, we conduct experiments regarding the effect of the batch size and the number of training steps. In particular, we evaluate how the training time and the model performance depend on both factors.

4.3 Definition of the Model Size

We follow Kaplan et al. (2020) and use the approximate number of non-embedding parameters to define the model size, which we denote as N_{model}. Since the share of embedding parameters decreases for larger models, similarly to Kaplan et al. (2020) we expect that discarding the number of embedding parameters allows for better generalization of our results to large models. Another advantage of defining the model size as the number of non-embedding parameters is that it is closely linked to the number of (non-embedding related) floating point operations (FLOPs) per input token (Kaplan et al., 2020). This enables us to design benchmarking scenarios by training different models of comparable size, which at the same time require roughly similar amounts of computation.

Omitting biases and other sub-leading terms, the number of non-embedding parameters is given by

$$N_{\text{model}} = 12LH^2, \tag{1}$$

assuming that queries, keys and values are all transformed to dimension $\frac{H}{A}$ and the feed-forward dimension is $4H$. For a more in-depth explanation, please see Appendix E.

5 Results[6]

We start by evaluating how varying single shape dimensions affects the performance on GLUE-Large for the three different pre-training objectives (cf. Sec. 5.1). This aims at investigating whether the performance gain diminishes after a certain level, comparing how the performance changes when scaling different dimensions, and examining whether models with different pre-training objectives respond differently to single-dimension scaling. Subsequently in Section 5.2, we change multiple shape dimensions simultaneously to investigate whether the different dimensions depend on each other. In Sections 5.3 and 5.4 we study how to train efficiently by varying the model size, the number of training steps and the batch size. In Section 5.5 we put together our observations from the previous sections and scale networks to different sizes.

5.1 Scaling Single Shape Dimensions

In this section, we separately scale L and H, while holding all other dimensions constant. As shown in Figure 1, BERT-style systems perform significantly better than GPT-2-style and RoBERTa-style systems on GLUE-Large, contrary to the results of Liu et al. (2019) and in line with the original findings of Devlin et al. (2019).

Observation 1 *The pre-training objective has a large impact on the performance of a fine-tuned*

[6]Source code: https://github.com/PMSchulze/NLP-benchmarking

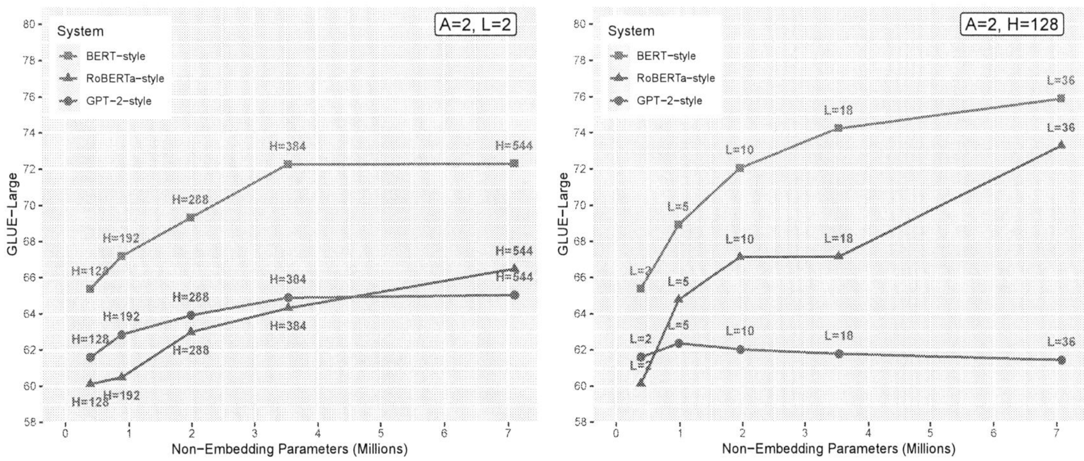

Figure 1: Average score on GLUE-Large, when varying H (left) vs. when varying L (right). For detailed performance values on the single tasks, see Table 5 and Table 6 in Appendix C.

system. Pre-training with the combination of MLM & NSP achieves the best results on sentence-pair tasks[7]*, while pre-training with the unidirectional LM objective shows in general the worst performance.*

Furthermore, for BERT-style systems the average performance is a relatively smooth function of the model size. Scaling up H results in an increasing performance, which saturates at approximately 72%, while for L we cannot clearly see this saturation (even not at 75%). For RoBERTa-style systems, the difference between scaling L and H individually is much larger. Furthermore, a saturation (as for BERT-style systems) can not be observed.[8] For GPT-2-style systems, the average score slightly increases when scaling the embedding size, but interestingly, stacking more layers shows no positive effect at all. This suggests that GPT-2-style systems require more pre-training data compared to BERT-style and RoBERTa-style systems.

Observation 2 *In most cases, the performance of a fine-tuned system increases up to a certain level when scaling either width or depth, but the progression depends strongly on the pre-training objective.*

5.2 Scaling Multiple Shape Dimensions

We next examine whether the performance can be improved by scaling multiple dimensions at the same time. First, we increase both H and L and compare the performance with the results from Section 5.1. Fig. 2 shows that for RoBERTa-style and BERT-style systems, scaling both dimensions significantly improves the performance on GLUE-Large.

Observation 3 *Scaling multiple shape dimensions can lead to a better performance than scaling single dimensions.*

Therefore, we conclude that the shape dimensions are not independent of each other. For GPT-2-style systems, however, we do not observe a performance increase, as shown in Table 1.

BERT-Style				**Validation Set Performance**
A	H	L	N_{model}	GLUE-Large
2	204	7	3,495,744	77.1
2	256	9	7,077,888	78.6
8	544	2	7,102,464	78.4
GPT-2-Style				**Validation Set Performance**
A	H	L	N_{model}	GLUE-Large
2	204	7	3,495,744	63.6
2	256	9	7,077,888	63.8
8	544	2	7,102,464	66.0
RoBERTa-Style				**Validation Set Performance**
A	H	L	N_{model}	GLUE-Large
2	204	7	3,495,744	72.9
2	256	9	7,077,888	75.0
8	544	2	7,102,464	70.9

Table 1: Performance on GLUE-Large when increasing multiple shape dimensions at the same time.

So far, we did not increase A when scaling H and observed that, without using more attention heads, wide systems perform worse than deep systems (cf. Fig. 1). To evaluate whether a larger num-

[7]Note that this does not necessarily generalize to other languages or other types of tasks.

[8]Note that the relatively low average score for the 18-layer RoBERTa-style system, shown in the right plot of Figure 1, is due to a weak performance on the QNLI task.

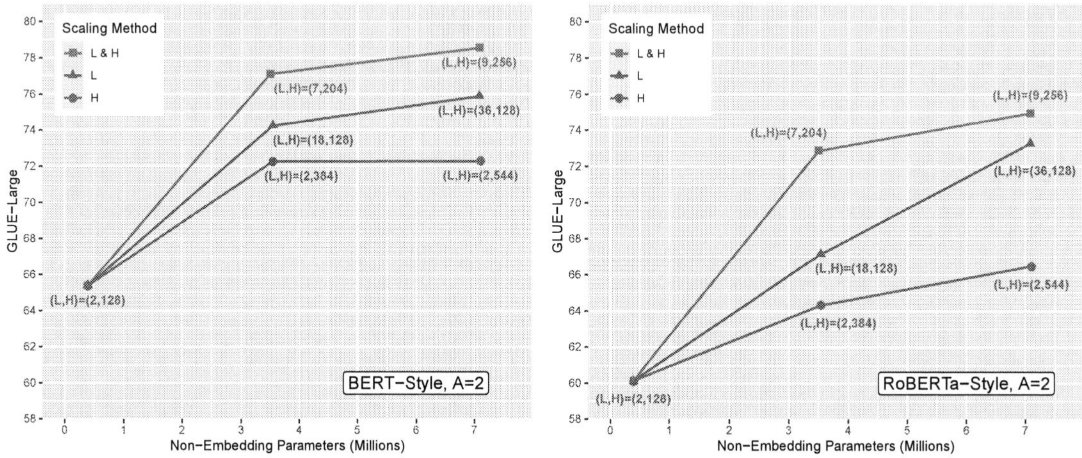

Figure 2: Performance on GLUE-Large when increasing multiple shape dimensions.

ber of attention heads can boost the performance of wide systems, we re-implement our widest systems with $A = 8$ attention heads, which corresponds to $\frac{H}{A} = 68$. We observe that the score of the widest system on GLUE-Large improved substantially by doing so (cf. Fig. 1 and Tab. 1). In particular, when using $A = 8$ instead of $A = 2$, the wide BERT-style system ($A = 8, H = 544, L = 2$) performs even better than the deep BERT-style system of comparable size ($A = 2, H = 128, L = 36$). Furthermore, as also shown in Table 1, the wide BERT-style system (with increased A) performs close to the balanced one ($A = 2$, $H = 256$, $L = 9$).

Observation 4 *The fine-tuning performance can be similar over a wide range of shapes. For BERT-style systems, wide systems perform slightly better than deep systems, if the number of attention heads is adapted to the embedding dimension.*

In contrast to BERT-style systems, deep RoBERTa-style systems still perform better than wide systems, even when increasing the number of attentions heads. For GPT-2-style systems, adding more attention heads hardly increases the performance.

5.3 Monitoring the Validation Loss

In the previous sections, different models were made comparable by their number of non-embedding parameters. As stated in section 4.3, this number is related to the computational cost when evaluated as the number of FLOPs per token. Reporting the computational cost in FLOPs neglects, however, that some operations can be run in parallel, while others cannot. In order to assess the speed of convergence, following Li et al. (2020), we therefore directly report the wall-clock time in seconds.

Figure 3 shows the validation loss for BERT-style systems of different shape, when pre-trained on the short sequences.[9]. The left plot depicts several pre-training loss curves corresponding to the single-dimension scaling experiments from Section 5.1. Interestingly, when comparing the validation loss with the GLUE-Large results (cf. Fig. 1), we find that, although increasing H (while holding A fixed) results in a lower validation loss than increasing L, the GLUE-Large score shows a higher increase in the latter case.

Observation 5 *The pre-training validation loss is not necessarily a good indicator for the performance of a fine-tuned system.*

Dependent on the downstream task some architectures presumably favor fine-tuning more than others, which can offset a relatively worse initialization point. This finding suggests that, although Kaplan et al. (2020) observe similar test losses for different shapes, benchmarking the corresponding fine-tuned versions may present a different picture.

In the left plot of Figure 3 we furthermore observe that shape has a significant effect on the pre-training time. In particular, stacking many layers requires much longer pre-training. It is also evident that increasing the size does not lead to a proportionate increase in the pre-training time. This holds true especially when scaling multiple dimensions, as depicted in the right plot of Figure 3. When doubling the number of pre-training parameters, the

[9]We do pre-training on short and long sequences. For a detailed description, see Appendix A and Appendix F.

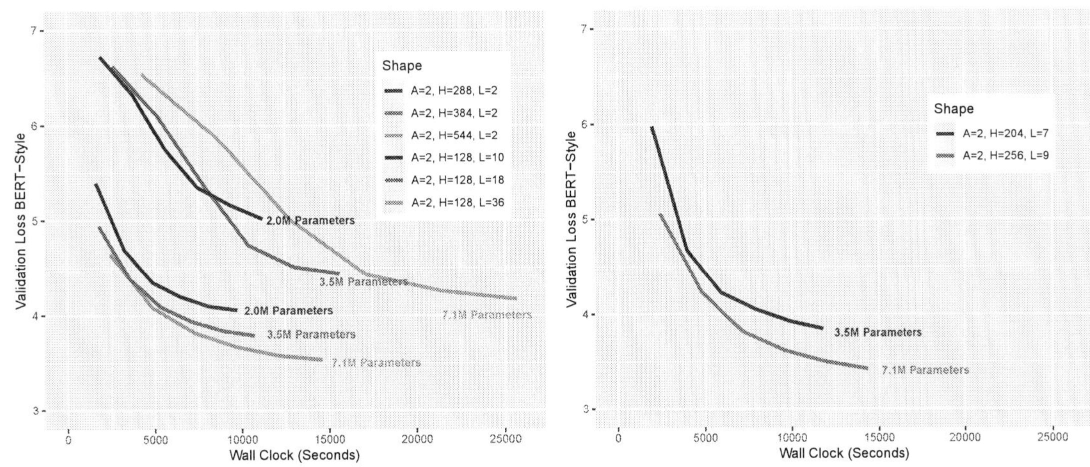

Figure 3: Loss curves of BERT-Style systems of different shape. All loss curves are associated with the first stage of pre-training, where we train on short sequences with a of 128 tokens (For the loss curves for the subsequent training on the long sequences, see Appendix D). The depicted parameter counts refer to the model size N_{model}.

training time only increases from approximately $11,800$ seconds to approximately $14,400$ seconds. In particular, the loss of the larger system is smaller at any measured point in time.

Observation 6 *Given a fixed time budget, training large systems for a relatively small number of steps is more efficient than training small systems for a large number of steps.*

The 9-layer system in the right plot of Figure 3 achieves a notably lower validation loss than the 7-layer system after $10,000$ seconds, which corresponds to approximately $65,800$ and $79,800$ steps, respectively. Li et al. (2020) made a similar observation by showing that larger Transformer-based systems generally reach a lower pre-training validation perplexity in shorter time. A point of concern might be that larger systems overfit more easily during fine-tuning. However, Li et al. (2020) showed that, when stopping models of different size at the same pre-training validation perplexity, large systems generally achieve comparable downstream task performances to small systems, which contradicts the overfitting argument.

5.4 Number of Training Steps and Batch Size

The amount of processed data can be increased by increasing either the number of trainig steps or the batch size. In Table 2 we compare how halving the number of steps vs. halving the batch size impacts model performance. As baseline we use our best performing system thus far ($A = 2, H = 256, L = 9$), pre-trained RoBERTa- and BERT-style.

In both cases we find that reducing the number of training steps is more detrimental to the performance than reducing the batch size. Conversely, it follows that when scaling up a system, a better model performance can be achieved when doubling the amount of training steps than when doubling the batch size, which is consistent with the results of Raffel et al. (2019). On the other hand, we observe that the systems with the smaller batch size were trained for a significantly longer time than the systems with the reduced number of training steps. Therefore, increasing the batch size may result in a more favorable training duration than increasing the number of training steps. The modest drop in GLUE-Large performance, when halving the number of training steps is consistent with our findings from Section 5.3 and provides additional evidence that training for a large number of steps is inefficient.

Observation 7 *Doubling the number of training steps marginally increases the downstream task performance, whereas doubling the batch size significantly reduces the average training time of an input sequence.*

As stated, several other studies have shown that using a larger batch size is in general more efficient than training for more steps (Kaplan et al., 2020). This means that the reduction of training time by using larger batches dominates the marginal performance gains resulting from an increased number of training steps. However, for each specific model and training configuration there exists a critical batch size, after which the performance hardly im-

BERT-Style		Validation Set Performance				
Training Strategy	Total Time	GLUE-Large	MNLI-(m/mm)	QQP	QNLI	SST-2
Baseline	21,358s	78.6	72.0/72.7	81.2	82.5	83.4
$\frac{1}{2}$x steps, 1x batch	10,736s	77.4	70.2/71.2	80.5	81.5	82.5
1x steps, $\frac{1}{2}$x batch	14,575s	78.2	71.5/71.9	80.9	82.3	83.9
RoBERTa-Style		**Validation Set Performance**				
Training Strategy	Total Time	GLUE-Large	MNLI-(m/mm)	QQP	QNLI	SST-2
Baseline	19,760s	75.0	68.4/70.9	78.2	78.3	75.0
$\frac{1}{2}$x steps, 1x batch	9,906s	73.7	67.0/69.0	76.7	77.4	83.5
1x steps, $\frac{1}{2}$x batch	13,101s	75.6	68.2/70.0	79.5	78.9	84.4

Table 2: GLUE results and total pre-training time when halving batch size vs. number of training steps.

proves, if at all (Kaplan et al., 2020; Li et al., 2020). Our results suggest that this critical size is very small in our experiments, which we believe is due to the small size of the pre-training data set, as also observed by Kaplan et al. (2020).

5.5 Systematic Scaling

In this section we apply a modified version of the compound scaling method that was used to scale up EfficientNet (Tan and Le, 2019), a model that achieved a notably better accuracy on ImageNet (Deng et al., 2009) than previous approaches using less compute. For scaling, we only consider BERT-style systems and propose the following compound scaling method for Transformer-based systems:

$$\begin{aligned} &L = \alpha^{\phi}, \qquad H = \beta^{\phi}, \qquad A \approx H/64, \\ &\text{s.t. } \alpha\beta^2 \approx 2, \quad \text{with} \quad \alpha \geq 1, \beta \geq 1. \end{aligned} \tag{2}$$

For suitable values of α and β, a system is scaled up by increasing the *compound coefficient* ϕ. Doubling L doubles N_{model}, while H leads to a fourfold increase. Since N_{model} dominates the amount of compute in a Transformer, the constraint $\alpha\beta^2 \approx 2$ thus ensures that when scaling the network from ϕ_{old} to ϕ_{new}, the amount of compute (which is approx. independent of A) approximately increases by the factor $2^{\phi_{\text{new}}-\phi_{\text{old}}}$. Following existing approaches and using Observation 4, we therefore set the number of attention heads to $A \approx H/64$.

Grid search To determine α and β, we follow Tan and Le (2019) and perform a grid search over a set of nine small networks of comparable size trained only on the short sequences. Subsequently, we select the three systems with the lowest validation loss. Based on Observation 5, we then fine-tune and evaluate these three systems on GLUE-Large, which leads to the best performing system having $L = 3$ and $H = 104$ (cf. Tab. 7 in Appendix C). From the constraint in Eq. (2) it follows that the size of this system corresponds to a compound coefficient of $\phi = \log_2(LH^2) = 14.99 \approx 15$, such that we obtain $\alpha = 3^{\frac{1}{15}} \approx 1.076$, $\beta = 104^{\frac{1}{15}} \approx 1.363$. Note that the resulting coefficients favor scaling width over depth. In general, we believe that this is reasonable, especially in light of the much longer training times of deep networks compared to wide networks (cf. Fig. 3). However, we also want to emphasize that further research is needed, whether these scaling coefficients are suitable for BERT-style systems. For GPT-2-style systems, Kaplan et al. (2020) proposed to scale such that width/depth remains fixed. Importantly, however, Kaplan et al. (2020) did not study the effect of shape parameters on the GLUE-Large performance, but instead only monitored the LM test loss. In machine translation, on the other hand, Transformer-based systems are scaled preferably by increasing width (Shazeer et al., 2018; Li et al., 2020). Other approaches focus on increasing depth, while making modifications to the Transformer to allow for more efficient training (Al-Rfou et al., 2019).

Scaling Based on Observation 6, we successively increase the compound coefficient to scale three systems to larger sizes than all previously trained systems, but train for less steps. For our smallest system, we train for 5 epochs on both the long and the short sequences.[10] The results are listed in Table 4. Furthermore, Table 3 shows a comparison of the smallest of the three systems to the best performing system so far, as well as to a modification of this system which fulfills the requirement

[10]Since validation loss on the long sequences did not further decrease after 3 epochs, the two larger systems were only trained for 3 epochs on these sequences (cf. Appendix D).

BERT-Style							Validation Set Performance	
ϕ	A	H	L	N_{model}	Total Time	Epochs	GLUE-Large	Final Loss
NA	2	256	9	7,0778,88	21,358s	6	78.6	3.24
NA	4	256	9	7,0778,88	21,703s	6	78.9	3.29
19.865	7	469	4	10,558,128	**20,873s**	5	**79.4**	**3.13**

Table 3: Verification of the scaling method: The proposed modifications lead to a better GLUE score and a lower validation loss, while requiring less training time compared to previous best performing models.

BERT-Style					Validation Set Performance					
ϕ	A	H	L	N_{model}	GLUE-Large	MNLI-(m/mm)	QQP	QNLI	SST-2	CoLA
20.578	9	585	5	20,553,500	80.7	75.3/75.5	83.5	83.4	85.1	16.5
21.716	13	832	5	41,553,440	**81.4**	**75.6/75.9**	**84.1**	**84.4**	**85.8**	**21.3**

Table 4: GLUE results of BERT-style systems, scaled up based on the observations made in the previous sections.

$A \approx H/64$. As can be observed, both the performance on the large GLUE-Large tasks and the final validation loss are improved, while requiring less training time. For the two larger systems, each obtained by approximately doubling the model size, downstream performance and validation loss are further improved (cf. Tab. 4). Note that these systems are rather large compared to the amount of pre-training data. This demonstrates the remarkable robustness of these systems with respect to overfitting on the pre-training data, which is in line with the results of Kaplan et al. (2020).

6 Conclusion & Future work

Limitations The most severe limitation is the small pre-training data set. Based on the observations of Kaplan et al. (2020), systems train faster if more training examples are used. The small size of the pre-training data set might also be the cause of overfitting on smaller tasks. Therefore, for further experiments, we suggest to expand the amount of pre-training data. Furthermore, we did no hyperparameter tuning, but instead adopted the configurations from the original models. It would be advisable to adjust the hyperparameters accordingly (Li et al., 2020), especially since we used different batch sizes as the original models.

Directions for Further Research Kaplan et al. (2020) studied the effect of the amount of pre-training data, however, not with regard to downstream task performance. Due to the fact that current NLP systems are trained on vastly different amounts of pre-training data, we believe that this relationship should be explored further.

Although attempts have been made to study the relationship between different pre-training objectives and the performance on downstream tasks (Arora et al., 2019), this relation is yet not well understood. Empirically, contrastive pre-training objectives, such as replaced token detection (Clark et al., 2020) have shown very promising results. It would be interesting to extend the study to such contrastive objectives. Since we observed that the NSP task is beneficial for learning sentence-pair relationships, comparing it to ALBERT's SOP task (Lan et al., 2019) could yield further insights.

Finally, by fine-tuning on a larger variety of tasks we could break down in more detail how different modeling choices affect the performances on different tasks. We believe that further investigation of such relationships will open many opportunities for future research.

Conclusion In our experiments, BERT-style systems consistently outperform RoBERTa-style and GPT-2-style systems. We therefore conclude that, at least in case of a relatively small pre-training data set, the combination of MLM & NSP is preferable to MLM or LM. Although our experiments were conducted on a much smaller scale than other studies, we were able to reproduce many previous findings. For instance, we observed that, provided multiple dimensions are scaled, systems with very different shapes can achieve similar performances.

Consistent with previous studies (Kaplan et al., 2020; Li et al., 2020) we found that it is in general inefficient to train until convergence and that training for more steps improves the performance rather marginally. Instead, in accordance with Kaplan et al. (2020), we believe that increasing the batch size is more beneficial than training for more steps.

More importantly, also consistent with the results of Kaplan et al. (2020) and Li et al. (2020), we conclude that the model size is the key factor in Transformer-based systems. We observed that even for rather large systems, both the final pre-training validation loss and the GLUE performance benefit from further increasing the size. At the same time, the total pre-training time increases at a rather low rate. In particular, given a fixed time budget, large systems reach a lower loss than small systems. Therefore, we believe that additional compute should be allocated mainly to increase the model size.

Acknowledgements We would like to thank the three anonymous reviewers for their insightful comments and their feedback on our work.

References

Rami Al-Rfou, Dokook Choe, Noah Constant, Mandy Guo, and Llion Jones. 2019. Character-level language modeling with deeper self-attention. In *Proceedings of the AAAI Conference on Artificial Intelligence*, volume 33, pages 3159–3166.

Sanjeev Arora, Hrishikesh Khandeparkar, Mikhail Khodak, Orestis Plevrakis, and Nikunj Saunshi. 2019. A theoretical analysis of contrastive unsupervised representation learning. *arXiv preprint arXiv:1902.09229*.

Matthias Aßenmacher and Christian Heumann. 2020. On the comparability of pre-trained language models. In *Proceedings of the 5th Swiss Text Analytics Conference and 16th Conference on Natural Language Processing*, Zurich, Switzerland (Online). CEUR Workshop Proceedings.

Tom B Brown, Benjamin Mann, Nick Ryder, Melanie Subbiah, Jared Kaplan, Prafulla Dhariwal, Arvind Neelakantan, Pranav Shyam, Girish Sastry, Amanda Askell, et al. 2020. Language models are few-shot learners. *arXiv preprint arXiv:2005.14165*.

Kevin Clark, Minh-Thang Luong, Quoc V Le, and Christopher D Manning. 2020. Electra: Pre-training text encoders as discriminators rather than generators. *arXiv preprint arXiv:2003.10555*.

Zihang Dai, Zhilin Yang, Yiming Yang, Jaime Carbonell, Quoc V Le, and Ruslan Salakhutdinov. 2019. Transformer-xl: Attentive language models beyond a fixed-length context. *arXiv preprint arXiv:1901.02860*.

Jia Deng, Wei Dong, Richard Socher, Li-Jia Li, Kai Li, and Li Fei-Fei. 2009. Imagenet: A large-scale hierarchical image database. In *2009 IEEE conference on computer vision and pattern recognition*, pages 248–255. Ieee.

Jacob Devlin, Ming-Wei Chang, Kenton Lee, and Kristina Toutanova. 2019. BERT: Pre-training of deep bidirectional transformers for language understanding. In *Proceedings of the 2019 Conference of the North American Chapter of the Association for Computational Linguistics: Human Language Technologies, Volume 1 (Long and Short Papers)*, pages 4171–4186, Minneapolis, Minnesota. Association for Computational Linguistics.

Dan Hendrycks and Kevin Gimpel. 2016. Bridging nonlinearities and stochastic regularizers with gaussian error linear units. *OpenReview.net*.

Jeremy Howard and Sebastian Ruder. 2018. Universal language model fine-tuning for text classification. *arXiv preprint arXiv:1801.06146*.

Jared Kaplan, Sam McCandlish, Tom Henighan, Tom B Brown, Benjamin Chess, Rewon Child, Scott Gray, Alec Radford, Jeffrey Wu, and Dario Amodei. 2020. Scaling laws for neural language models. *arXiv preprint arXiv:2001.08361*.

Diederik P Kingma and Jimmy Ba. 2014. Adam: A method for stochastic optimization. *arXiv preprint arXiv:1412.6980*.

Zhenzhong Lan, Mingda Chen, Sebastian Goodman, Kevin Gimpel, Piyush Sharma, and Radu Soricut. 2019. Albert: A lite bert for self-supervised learning of language representations. *arXiv preprint arXiv:1909.11942*.

Zhuohan Li, Eric Wallace, Sheng Shen, Kevin Lin, Kurt Keutzer, Dan Klein, and Joseph E Gonzalez. 2020. Train large, then compress: Rethinking model size for efficient training and inference of transformers. *arXiv preprint arXiv:2002.11794*.

Yinhan Liu, Myle Ott, Naman Goyal, Jingfei Du, Mandar Joshi, Danqi Chen, Omer Levy, Mike Lewis, Luke Zettlemoyer, and Veselin Stoyanov. 2019. Roberta: A robustly optimized bert pretraining approach. *arXiv preprint arXiv:1907.11692*.

Stephen Merity, Caiming Xiong, James Bradbury, and Richard Socher. 2016. Pointer sentinel mixture models. *arXiv preprint arXiv:1609.07843*.

Alec Radford, Jeffrey Wu, Rewon Child, David Luan, Dario Amodei, and Ilya Sutskever. 2019. Language models are unsupervised multitask learners. *OpenAI Blog*, 1(8):9.

Jack W Rae, Anna Potapenko, Siddhant M Jayakumar, and Timothy P Lillicrap. 2019. Compressive transformers for long-range sequence modelling. *arXiv preprint arXiv:1911.05507*.

Colin Raffel, Noam Shazeer, Adam Roberts, Katherine Lee, Sharan Narang, Michael Matena, Yanqi Zhou, Wei Li, and Peter J Liu. 2019. Exploring the limits of transfer learning with a unified text-to-text transformer. *arXiv preprint arXiv:1910.10683*.

Jonathan S Rosenfeld, Amir Rosenfeld, Yonatan Belinkov, and Nir Shavit. 2019. A constructive prediction of the generalization error across scales. *arXiv preprint arXiv:1909.12673*.

Mike Schuster and Kaisuke Nakajima. 2012. Japanese and korean voice search. In *2012 IEEE International Conference on Acoustics, Speech and Signal Processing (ICASSP)*, pages 5149–5152. IEEE.

Iyer Shankar, Dandekar Nikhil, and Csernai Kornél. 2017. First quora dataset release: Question pairs. Accessed: 2021-02-01.

Noam Shazeer, Youlong Cheng, Niki Parmar, Dustin Tran, Ashish Vaswani, Penporn Koanantakool, Peter Hawkins, HyoukJoong Lee, Mingsheng Hong, Cliff Young, et al. 2018. Mesh-tensorflow: Deep learning for supercomputers. In *Advances in Neural Information Processing Systems*, pages 10414–10423.

Mohammad Shoeybi, Mostofa Patwary, Raul Puri, Patrick LeGresley, Jared Casper, and Bryan Catanzaro. 2019. Megatron-lm: Training multi-billion parameter language models using gpu model parallelism. *arXiv preprint arXiv:1909.08053*.

Richard Socher, Alex Perelygin, Jean Wu, Jason Chuang, Christopher D Manning, Andrew Y Ng, and Christopher Potts. 2013. Recursive deep models for semantic compositionality over a sentiment treebank. In *Proceedings of the 2013 conference on empirical methods in natural language processing*, pages 1631–1642.

Mingxing Tan and Quoc V Le. 2019. Efficientnet: Rethinking model scaling for convolutional neural networks. *arXiv preprint arXiv:1905.11946*.

Sebastian Thrun and Lorien Pratt. 1998. Learning to learn: Introduction and overview. In *Learning to learn*, pages 3–17. Springer.

Ashish Vaswani, Noam Shazeer, Niki Parmar, Jakob Uszkoreit, Llion Jones, Aidan N Gomez, Łukasz Kaiser, and Illia Polosukhin. 2017. Attention is all you need. In *Advances in neural information processing systems*, pages 5998–6008.

Alex Wang, Amanpreet Singh, Julian Michael, Felix Hill, Omer Levy, and Samuel R Bowman. 2018. Glue: A multi-task benchmark and analysis platform for natural language understanding. *arXiv preprint arXiv:1804.07461*.

Alex Warstadt, Amanpreet Singh, and Samuel R Bowman. 2019. Neural network acceptability judgments. *Transactions of the Association for Computational Linguistics*, 7:625–641.

Adina Williams, Nikita Nangia, and Samuel R Bowman. 2017. A broad-coverage challenge corpus for sentence understanding through inference. *arXiv preprint arXiv:1704.05426*.

Thomas Wolf, Lysandre Debut, Victor Sanh, Julien Chaumond, Clement Delangue, Anthony Moi, Pierric Cistac, Tim Rault, Rémi Louf, Morgan Funtowicz, Joe Davison, Sam Shleifer, Patrick von Platen, Clara Ma, Yacine Jernite, Julien Plu, Canwen Xu, Teven Le Scao, Sylvain Gugger, Mariama Drame, Quentin Lhoest, and Alexander M. Rush. 2020. Transformers: State-of-the-art natural language processing. In *Proceedings of the 2020 Conference on Empirical Methods in Natural Language Processing: System Demonstrations*, pages 38–45, Online. Association for Computational Linguistics.

Appendix

A Pre-training details

Training duration To ensure a fair comparison of the different pre-training objectives, we pre-train RoBERTa-style and GPT-2-style systems for 10 epochs, and BERT-style systems for 6 epochs, which in all cases equates to approximately 137,000 total training steps combined over both partitions.[11] Since the data is duplicated when training with MLM & NSP, it is natural to simply lower the number of epochs in relation to the amount of pre-training data. While the amount of pre-training data of RoBERTa-style and GPT-2-style systems amounts to more than 60% of the data of BERT-style systems, we found that, on the other hand, the average WordPiece token contains slightly more information than the average byte-level BPE token.

Optimization Apart from the experiments in section 5.4, we use a batch size of 64 when training on the short sequences and a batch size of 16 for the long sequences. We optimize all systems with Adam (Kingma and Ba, 2014) using the following parameters: $\beta_1 = 0.9$, $\beta_2 = 0.999$, $\epsilon =$ 1e-6 and L_2 weight decay of 0.01. For BERT-style and RoBERTa-style systems we use a maximum learning rate of 1e-4, and for GPT2-style systems the maximum learning rate is 2.5e-4. In all cases we use a linear warmup for the first 1000 steps, which corresponds to approximately 1% of the total steps. Furthermore, for all systems we employ dropout with a rate of 0.1 on all layers. The activation function of all systems is the GELU (Hendrycks and Gimpel, 2016). The hyperparameters are in general chosen as in the original systems, except for RoBERTa-style systems, because RoBERTa was trained with significantly larger batches, which requires different hyperparameters. For RoBERTa-style systems we therefore choose the same hyperparameters as for BERT-style systems.

Implementation We pre-train all systems on a single NVIDIA 16GB V100 GPU, making use of the Hugging Face transformers library (Wolf et al., 2020). The same also holds true for fine-tuning.

Short and long sequences With our pre-training procedure we follow Devlin et al. (2019): The first 90% of the steps on short sequences (128 tokens), the remaining 10% on long ones (512 tokens). When inspecting the validation loss, we adjust the evaluation sequence lengths to the lengths of the training sequences, so ensure the same distribution for training and validation data. This causes the validation loss on the long sequences to start at a slightly higher point than the final validation loss on the short sequences (cf. Appendix D).

[11] In sections where we do not compare the different objectives the number of epochs may differ.

B Fine-tuning details

We follow Devlin et al. (2019) and train for three epochs on all GLUE tasks. We use a batch size of 16 and a learning rate of 2e-5 for each task. Apart from these hyperparameter configurations, we apply the same fine-tuning procedures that were used by the original systems. For GPT-2-style systems, we implemented the fine-tuning approach of GPT (because GPT-2 was not fine-tuned).

However, we do make one small modification to the original implementations. In contrast to BERT-style systems, the pre-training objective of RoBERTa-style and GPT-2-style systems does not contain a classification task. When performing the NSP task, in the original BERT the contextualized representation of the `CLS` token is obtained by feeding the corresponding final hidden state through a linear layer with dropout and $tanh$ activation. Subsequently, the contextualized representation is fed through another linear layer with dropout, which is the output layer mapping the contextualized representation to the class probabilities. Consequently, when fine-tuning BERT-style systems on a classification task, there are in fact two linear layers between the final hidden state and the output classes. However, RoBERTa and GPT in their original implementation use only one linear layer. In order to be as consistent as possible, in contrast, we use two linear output layers for all systems. The first linear layer is followed by a $tanh$ activation and both layers are implemented with a dropout rate of 0.1. For more information regarding this issue see huggingface's discussion forum.

C Detailed performance values for single shape dimensions and results for the grid search

Performance values on GLUE-Large and SST-2 for scaling H (Tab. 5) and for scaling L (Tab. 6). Table 7 shows the results of the grid search.

BERT-Style				Validation Set Performance				
A	H	L	N_{model}	GLUE-Large	MNLI-(m/mm)	QQP	QNLI	SST-2
2	128	2	393,216	65.4	59.0/60.2	72.3	64.8	78.0
2	192	2	884,736	67.2	62.1/62.8	74.0	65.4	82.6
2	288	2	1,990,656	69.3	63.7/65.2	76.0	68.3	82.0
2	384	2	3,538,944	72.3	65.7/66.6	77.8	73.2	81.1
2	544	2	7,102,464	72.3	66.8/68.1	78.0	72.0	83.3
GPT-2-Style				**Validation Set Performance**				
A	H	L	N_{model}	GLUE-Large	MNLI-(m/mm)	QQP	QNLI	SST-2
2	128	2	393,216	61.6	56.3/56.2	66.1	62.3	79.8
2	192	2	884,736	62.9	58.0/58.4	68.7	61.9	79.7
2	288	2	1,990,656	63.9	58.7/58.7	70.9	62.2	81.7
2	384	2	3,538,944	64.9	59.8/59.6	71.9	63.0	81.2
2	544	2	7,102,464	65.0	59.8/59.7	72.4	62.9	82.5
RoBERTa-Style				**Validation Set Performance**				
A	H	L	N_{model}	GLUE-Large	MNLI-(m/mm)	QQP	QNLI	SST-2
2	128	2	393,216	60.1	53.7/55.1	64.7	61.9	79.2
2	192	2	884,736	60.5	54.4/55.4	65.0	62.0	80.8
2	288	2	1,990,656	63.0	57.5/58.0	68.1	63.4	80.3
2	384	2	3,538,944	64.3	59.4/59.8	69.0	64.6	81.9
2	544	2	7,102,464	66.5	60.2/60.7	72.7	66.5	81.8

Table 5: Performance on GLUE when increasing only the embedding dimension.

BERT-Style				Validation Set Performance				
A	H	L	N_{model}	GLUE-Large	MNLI-(m/mm)	QQP	QNLI	SST-2
2	128	2	393,216	65.4	59.0/60.2	72.3	64.8	78.0
2	128	5	983,040	68.9	62.1/64.2	75.0	68.6	79.8
2	128	10	1,966,080	72.0	65.3/66.9	76.7	74.1	81.8
2	128	18	3,538,944	74.2	67.2/68.6	77.8	77.7	82.2
2	128	36	7,077,888	75.9	69.7/70.4	79.7	78.3	83.3
GPT-2-Style				**Validation Set Performance**				
A	H	L	N_{model}	GLUE-Large	MNLI-(m/mm)	QQP	QNLI	SST-2
2	128	2	393,216	61.6	56.3/56.2	66.1	62.3	79.8
2	128	5	983,040	62.4	57.6/56.1	67.4	62.0	80.5
2	128	10	1,966,080	62.0	56.9/57.0	67.7	61.5	81.4
2	128	18	3,538,944	61.8	56.1/56.4	66.8	62.4	80.6
2	128	36	7,077,888	61.4	56.6/56.7	66.6	61.1	80.7
RoBERTa-Style				**Validation Set Performance**				
A	H	L	N_{model}	GLUE-Large	MNLI-(m/mm)	QQP	QNLI	SST-2
2	128	2	393,216	60.1	53.7/55.1	64.7	61.9	79.2
2	128	5	983,040	64.8	59.5/60.6	70.4	64.4	80.2
2	128	10	1,966,080	67.1	60.9/61.9	72.0	68.5	81.7
2	128	18	3,538,944	67.2	62.9/64.3	74.3	64.3	80.0
2	128	36	7,077,888	73.3	67.6/69.1	77.3	75.0	82.6

Table 6: Performance on GLUE when increasing only the number of layers.

BERT-Style				Validation Loss (WikiText-103)	Validation Performance (GLUE)
A	H	L	N_{model}	BERT-Style Loss	GLUE-Large
2	128	2	393,216	**5.66**	66.6
2	104	3	389,376	**6.34**	**68.2**
2	90	4	388,800	**6.41**	67.1
2	74	6	394,272	6.47	-
2	64	8	393,216	6.50	-
2	58	10	403,680	6.54	-
2	52	12	389,376	6.58	-
2	48	14	387,072	6.62	-
2	46	16	406,272	6.62	-

Table 7: Grid search over nine small BERT-style systems.

D Validation loss for scaled-up models

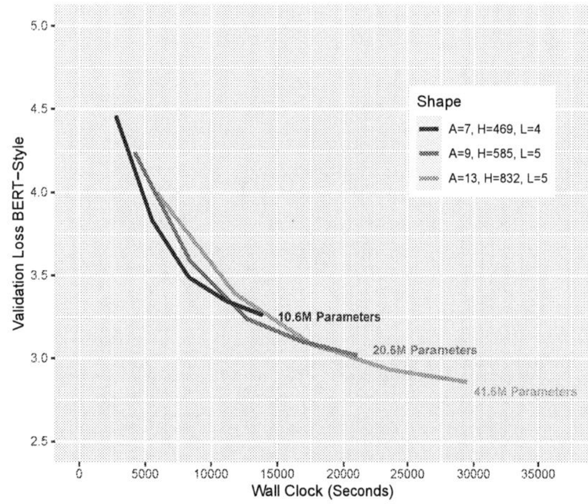

Figure 4: Validation loss of scaled-up BERT-style systems when pre-training on the short sequences. The depicted parameter counts refer to N_{model}.

E Definition of the model size

We follow Kaplan et al. (2020) and use the approximate number of non-embedding parameters to define the model size, which we denote as N_{model}. The embedding parameters consist of all token, position and (if present) segment embeddings. The number of embedding parameters does not depend on the network depth, and when scaling width and/or depth, it is a sub-leading term of the total number of parameters. Furthermore, the number of FLOPs related to embedding (and de-embedding) is also sub-leading term of the total number of FLOPs. Consistent with this is the observation of Kaplan et al. (2020) that discarding the number of embedding parameters when calculating model size and amount of compute results in significantly cleaner scaling laws. Since the share of embedding parameters decreases significantly for larger models, similarly to Kaplan et al. (2020) we expect that discarding the number of embedding parameters allows for a better generalization of our results to large models. Another advantage of defining the model size as the number of non-embedding parameters is that this number is closely linked to the number of (non-embedding related) FLOPs. This enables us to design benchmarking scenarios by training different models of comparable size, which at the same time require roughly similar amounts of computation.

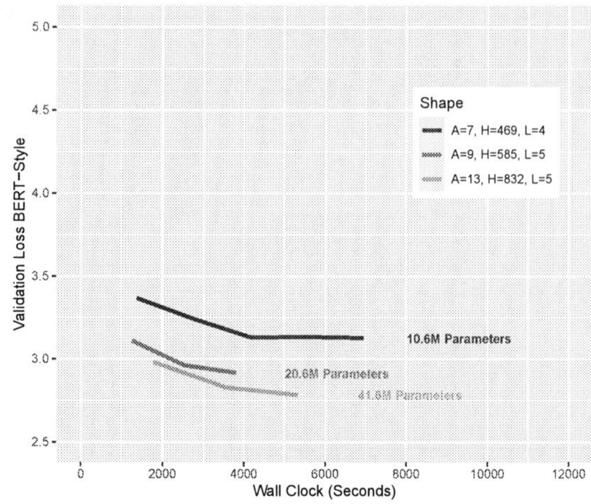

Figure 5: Validation loss of scaled-up BERT-style systems when pre-training on the long sequences. The depicted parameter counts refer to N_{model}.

Number of Non-Embedding Parameters

Omitting biases and other sub-leading terms, the number of non-embedding parameters, which is our definition of the model size, is given by

$$N_{\text{model}} := 12LH^2, \tag{3}$$

where we have assumed that $H_k = H_v = \frac{H}{A}$ and $H_{ff} = 4H$. Therefore, per layer there are approximately $12H^2$ non-embedding parameters. This number can be derived from the following three steps performed in each layer of a Transformer:

1. Input projection For each attention head, the queries, keys and values of dimension $\frac{H}{A}$ are obtained with the three matrices $\boldsymbol{W}_i^Q$, $\boldsymbol{W}_i^K$, and $\boldsymbol{W}_i^V$, which are each of size $H \times \frac{H}{A}$. In total, the input projection thus consists of $3 \cdot A \cdot \frac{H^2}{A} = 3H^2$ parameters.

2. Output projection First, note that performing attention on the projected inputs of dimension $\frac{H}{A}$ involves no additional parameters. The concatenated attention results are projected back to dimension H with the $H \times H$ matrix $\boldsymbol{W}^O$. Therefore, the output projection involves an additional set of H^2 parameters.

3. Feed-forward network The last sub-layer of each layer consists of applying a feed-forward network to the output projections. There exist $H \cdot 4H$ connections between the output projections and the neurons of the inner-layer, and another $4H \cdot H$ connections from the inner-layer to the final output neurons. This step hence involves $8H^2$ parameters.

Note that the feed-forward network accounts for the majority of non-embedding parameters, followed by the input and output projections, respectively.

Relation to FLOPs

As stated, the number of non-embedding parameters is closely linked to the number of non-embedding related FLOPs. We start by deriving the number of FLOPs per token and forward pass for GPT-2-style systems, where sub-leading terms such as biases and layer normalization are again omitted.

1. Input projection The matrix-vector products of each per-layer input with $\boldsymbol{W}_i^Q$, $\boldsymbol{W}_i^K$, and $\boldsymbol{W}_i^V$ involve approximately $3 \cdot 2 \cdot H \cdot \frac{H}{A}$ FLOPs per attention head. Considering all attention heads, the input projection thus requires approximately $6H^2$ FLOPs per token.

2. Attention The computation of the attention operation can be divided into two sub-components:

- **Computation of the weights**: On average, $\frac{N_{ctx}}{2}$ attention weights have to be computed per input token, since on average half of the tokens are masked for each input token. Computation of a dot-product attention weight requires approximately $2\frac{H}{A}$ FLOPs per head. In total, the computation of the attention weights hence involves approximately $N_{ctx}H$ FLOPs per token.

- **Computation of the weighted sum**: Since only half of the tokens are summed on average, given the attention weights, calculation of the weighted sum of the values has an average cost of approximately $N_{ctx}H$ FLOPs for each token.

3. Output projection The vector matrix product of the attention outputs with $\boldsymbol{W}^O$ requires approximately $2H^2$ FLOPs for each token.

4. Feed-forward network The feed-forward network consists of two consecutive matrix multiplications, where each matrix contains $4H^2$ parameters. Thus, the feed-forward network requires approximately $2 \cdot 2 \cdot 4H^2 = 16H^2$ FLOPs per token.

The number of FLOPs per token and forward pass in GPT-2-style systems, which we denote by $C_{forward}$, can hence be approximated as

$$\begin{aligned} C_{forward} &\approx L(6H^2 + N_{ctx}H + N_{ctx}H \\ &\quad + 2H^2 + 16H^2) \\ &= 24LH^2 + 2LN_{ctx}H \\ &= 2N_{\text{model}} + 2LN_{ctx}H. \end{aligned} \tag{4}$$

BERT-style and RoBERTa-style systems require slightly more FLOPs than GPT-2-style systems, because these systems have no autoregressive attention mask. Hence, in both steps of the attention operation above, the computational cost is approximately twice as much, i.e., $2N_{ctx}H$ in each step. Therefore, BERT-style and RoBERTa-style systems require approximately $2N_{\text{model}} + 4LN_{ctx}H$ FLOPs per token and forward pass. As mentioned by Kaplan et al. (2020), if $H > N_{ctx}/12$, the context-dependent term in Eq. (4) only accounts for a relatively small fraction of the compute of GPT-2-style systems. In particular, when increasing H, the importance of the context-dependent term diminishes. For BERT-style and RoBERTa-style systems the context-dependent term becomes small if $H > N_{ctx}/6$. Both constraints are satisfied by a large margin for all our systems, especially since we mainly train on rather short sequences. The backward pass requires approximately twice as much compute as the forward pass (Kaplan et al., 2020), such that the total amount of non-embedding related compute per token and training step can be approximated as

$$C := 6N_{\text{model}}. \tag{5}$$

F Sequence characteristics

The following Table 8 provides an overview on the number of tokens in short and long sequences.

System	Partition	Number of Tokens	
		Total	Average
BERT-Style	Short	110,888,186	110.04
	Long	43,274,856	375.52
RoBERTa-Style	Short	70,025,709	110.31
	Long	27,692,351	457.04
GPT-2-Style	Short	70,564,106	111.16
	Long	27,729,551	457.65

Table 8: Number of tokens for the short and the long sequences as well as the average sequence lengths resulting from the different tokenizers.

ArgueBERT: How To Improve BERT Embeddings for Measuring the Similarity of Arguments

Maike Behrendt
Heinrich Heine University
maike.behrendt@hhu.de

Stefan Harmeling
Heinrich Heine University
harmeling@hhu.de

Abstract

Argumentation is an important tool within human interaction, not only in law and politics but also for discussing issues, expressing and exchanging opinions and coming to decisions in our everyday life. Applications for argumentation often require the measurement of the arguments' similarity, to solve tasks like clustering, paraphrase identification or summarization. In our work, BERT embeddings are pre-trained on novel training objectives and afterwards fine-tuned in a siamese architecture, similar to Reimers and Gurevych (2019b), to measure the similarity of arguments. The experiments conducted in our work show that a change in BERT's pre-training process can improve the performance on measuring argument similarity.

1 Introduction

Since today it is common to share opinions on social media to discuss and argue about all kinds of topics, the interest of research in the field of artificial intelligence in argumentation is constantly rising. Tasks like counter-argument retrieval (Wachsmuth et al., 2018), argument clustering (Reimers et al., 2019a) and identifying the most prominent arguments in online debates (Boltužić and Šnajder, 2015) have been examined and automated in the past. Many of these tasks involve measuring the textual similarity of arguments.

Transformer-based language models such as the bi-directional encoder representations from transformers (BERT) by Devlin et al. (2019) are widely used for different natural language processing (NLP) tasks. Nevertheless, for large-scale tasks like finding the most similar sentence in a collection of sentences, BERT's cross-encoding approach is disadvantageous as it creates a huge computational overhead.

In our work, we focus on exactly these large-scale tasks. We want to train embeddings of arguments in order to measure their similarity, e.g., to automatically recognize similar user entries in ongoing discussions in online argumentation systems. In this way redundancy can be avoided when collecting arguments. We base our approach on Sentence-BERT (SBERT), proposed by Reimers and Gurevych (2019b), which is a bi-encoder, fine-tuning the model's parameters to place similar sentences close to one another in the vector space. This approach yields good results on paraphrase identification tasks, but evaluating it on an argument similarity corpus shows a noticeable drop in performance.

To improve this method, we propose and evaluate three alternative pre-training tasks that replace the next sentence prediction (NSP) in BERT's pre-training process to optimize SBERT for measuring the similarity of arguments. These proposed tasks are *similarity prediction*, *argument order prediction* and *argument graph edge validation*. Being pre-trained on these tasks and fine-tuned in a siamese SBERT architecture, we call these models argueBERT throughout this work.

To examine the models' applicability in practice, we also propose a new evaluation task, which is called similar argument mining (SAM). Solving the task of SAM includes recognizing paraphrases (if any are present) in a large set of arguments, e.g., when a user enters a new argument to an ongoing discussion in some form of argumentation system.

In summary our contributions of this paper are the following:

1. We propose and evaluate new pre-training objectives for pre-training argument embeddings for measuring their similarity.
2. We propose a novel evaluation task for argumentation systems called SAM.

2 Related Work

Alternative Pre-Training Objectives The original BERT model uses two different pre-training objectives to train text embeddings that can be used for different NLP tasks. Firstly masked language modeling (MLM) and secondly next sentence prediction. However, Liu et al. (2019) have shown that BERT's next sentence prediction is not as effective as expected and that solely training on the MLM task can slightly improve the results on downstream tasks. Since then there have been attempts to improve the pre-training of BERT by replacing the training objectives.

Lewis et al. (2020) propose, inter alia, token deletion, text infilling and sentence permutation as alternative pre-training tasks. Their experiments show that the performance of the different pre-training objectives highly depends on the NLP task it is applied to. Inspired by this we want to explore tasks that perform well on measuring the semantic similarity of arguments.

Lan et al. (2020) propose a sentence ordering task instead of the next sentence prediction, which is similar to our argument order prediction. They find that sentence ordering is a more challenging task than predicting if a sentence follows another sentence. Instead of continuous text, we use dialog data from argumentation datasets, as we hope to encode structural features of arguments into our pre-trained embeddings.

Clark et al. (2020) use replaced token detection instead of MLM, where they do not mask tokens within the sentence, but replace some with alternative tokens that also fit into the sentence. In this way they implement a contrastive learning approach into BERT's pre-training, by training the model to differentiate between real sentences and negative samples. Their approach outperforms a model pre-trained on MLM on all tasks.

Argument Embeddings Embeddings of textual input that encode semantic and syntactical features are crucial for NLP tasks. Some research has already been conducted using the BERT model or its embeddings to measure the similarity of arguments. These are described briefly in the following.

Reimers et al. (2019a) use, inter alia, BERT for argument classification and clustering as part of an open-domain argument search. This task involves firstly classification of arguments concerning their topic, and afterwards clustering the arguments in terms of their similarity. They achieve the best results with a fine-tuned BERT model, when incorporating topic knowledge into the network.

In a proximate work Reimers and Gurevych (2019b) introduce SBERT which serves a base for our work. They train a BERT model in a siamese architecture to produce embeddings of textual input for tasks like semantic similarity prediction. The model is described in detail in Section 3.1.

Dumani et al. (2020) build upon the work of Reimers et al. (2019a) and propose a framework for the retrieval and ranking of arguments, which are both sub-tasks of an argument search engine.

Thakur et al. (2020) present an optimized version of SBERT and publish a new argument similarity corpus, which we also use for evaluation in this work. They expand the training data for the SBERT model through data augmentation, using the original BERT model for labeling sentence pairs.

To the best of our knowledge there are currently no contextualized embeddings developed especially for the task of measuring the similarity of arguments.

3 Background

In this section the SBERT (Reimers and Gurevych, 2019b) architecture, the training procedure and characteristics are explained in detail.

3.1 SBERT

We use SBERT, proposed by Reimers and Gurevych (2019b) to fine-tune the BERT models pre-trained with our novel proposed pre-training tasks.

SBERT is a network architecture that fine-tunes BERT in a siamese or triplet architecture to create embeddings of the input sentences to measure their similarity. Unlike the original BERT model, SBERT is a bi-encoder, which means it processes each input sentence individually, instead of concatenating them. The advantage of bi-encoders is their efficiency. Cross-encoders like BERT generate an enormous computational overhead for tasks such as finding the most similar sentence in a large set of sentences, or clustering these sentences.

By connecting both input sequences, handling it as one input, BERT is able to calculate cross-sentence attention. Although this approach performs well on many tasks, it is not always applicable in practice. SBERT is much faster and produces

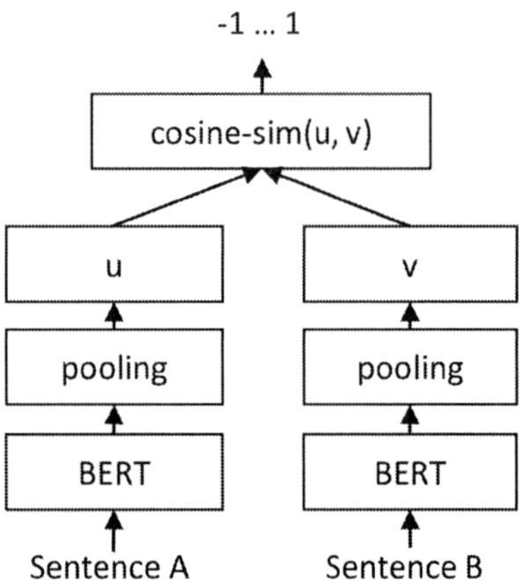

Figure 1: SBERT architecture for measuring sentence similarity.

results that outperform other state-of-the-art embedding methods (Reimers and Gurevych, 2019b).

To fine-tune the model the authors propose different network structures. For regression tasks, e.g., measuring sentence similarity, they calculate the cosine similarity of two embeddings u and v, as shown in Figure 1, and use a mean squared error (MSE) loss as objective function. To calculate the fixed sized sentence embeddings from each input, a pooling operation is applied to the output of the BERT model. The authors experiment with three different pooling strategies, finding that taking the *mean* of all output vectors works best for their model.

In the siamese architecture the weights of the models are tied, meaning that they receive the same updates. In this way the BERT model is fine-tuned to create sentence embeddings that map similar sentences nearby in the vector space.

In the original paper, the model is fine-tuned on the SNLI (Bowman et al., 2015) and the Multi-Genre NLI datasets (Williams et al., 2018) to solve multiple semantic textual similarity tasks, which leads to improved performance in comparison to other state-of-the-art embedding methods. However, evaluating the model on the argument facet similarity (AFS) (Misra et al., 2016) dataset shows a significant drop in accuracy. Different than in our work, the authors do not pursue the measurement of argument similarity in the first place, but rather use the model for general textual similarity tasks. The aim of this work is therefore to optimize BERT's pre-training process to generate argument embeddings that lead to better results on this task.

4 argueBERT

4.1 Pre-Training

We propose and evaluate three new tasks, which should improve the performance of BERT embeddings on measuring the similarity of arguments. The proposed pre-training objectives that are optimized instead of the next sentence prediction are the following:

1. **Similarity prediction**: Given a pair of input sentences s_1 and s_2, predict whether the two sentences have the same semantic meaning. BERT therefore is pre-trained on the Paraphrase Adversaries from Word Scrambling (PAWS) (Zhang et al., 2019) and the Quora Question Pairs (QQP)[1] dataset.

2. **Argument order prediction**: Given an argumentative dialog consisting of a statement and an answer to that statement, predict if the given paragraphs p_1 and p_2 are in the correct order. For this task we train BERT on the Internet Argument Corpus (IAC) 2.0 (Abbott et al., 2016), which contains argumentative dialogues from different online forums. This task is the same as the sentence ordering objective from ALBERT (Lan et al., 2020) but with argument data.

3. **Argument graph edge validation**: Given two arguments a_1 and a_2 from an argument graph, classify if they are adjacent, thus connected through an edge in the graph. For this task we use several argument graph corpora, taken from `http://corpora.aifdb.org/` for pre-training.

The pre-training process of argueBERT is the same as for the original BERT, except that we replace the next sentence prediction task. Our novel proposed pre-training objectives are trained as binary classification tasks.

To compare the new pre-training tasks, we train medium sized BERT models with 8 layers and a hidden embedding size of 512 (Turc et al., 2019). We train the models for a total of $100,000$ training steps. To guarantee comparability we also train a model with the original NSP and MLM objectives for $100,000$ steps on the BookCorpus (Zhu et al., 2015). To examine if the pre-training tasks also

[1] `https://www.kaggle.com/c/quora-question-pairs/data`

perform on a larger scale, we additionally train a $\text{BERT}_{\text{BASE}}$ model (12 layers, hidden embedding size 768) on our best performing pre-training task for $1,000,000$ steps. All hyperparameters we used for pre-training can be found in Table 5 in the Appendix.

4.2 Fine-Tuning

For fine-tuning argueBERT, we use SBERT (Reimers and Gurevych, 2019b). The model fine-tunes the weights of the pre-trained BERT model in a siamese architecture, such that the distance between embeddings of similar input sentences is minimized in the corresponding vector space. Therefore, $\hat{y}$ is calculated as the cosine similarity between two input embeddings u and v and then the MSE loss

$$\text{MSE} = \frac{1}{n}\sum_{i=1}^{n}(y_i - \hat{y}_i)^2 \tag{1}$$

is optimized. Here n is the batch size and y the true label. We fine-tune each model on every evaluation dataset for a total of five epochs with a batch size of 16 and a learning rate of 2e-5. All hyperparameters used for fine-tuning can be found in Table 6 in the Appendix.

4.3 Similar Argument Mining (SAM)

The main idea of proposing argueBERT as an improved version of SBERT on measuring argument similarity is in particular to use it for identifying and mining similar arguments in online argumentation systems. In order to evaluate language models for this purpose, we propose a new evaluation task which we call SAM. It is defined as follows.

Task definition. Given a query argument q, match the argument against all arguments of an existing set $S = \{a_1, a_2, \ldots, a_n\} \setminus \{q\}$ to predict, if S contains one or more paraphrased versions of q and find the paraphrased sentences in the set.

For the evaluation on SAM, the model is given a set of arguments of which some are paraphrased argument pairs and some are unpaired arguments that are not considered equivalent to any other argument in the set. The model then encodes all arguments into vector representations and calculates the pairwise cosine similarities. If the highest measured similarity score for an argument exceeds a pre-defined threshold, the argument is classified as being a paraphrase. We calculate the accuracy and the F_1 score of the models on this task.

5 Experiments

5.1 Datasets

We use the following datasets for the evaluation of our embeddings.

- The Microsoft Research Paraphrase Corpus[2] (MSRP) (Dolan and Brockett, 2005), which includes $5,801$ sentence pairs for paraphrase identification with binary labeling (0: *"no paraphrase"*, 1: *"paraphrase"*), automatically extracted from online news clusters.

- The Argument Facet Similarity Dataset[3] (AFS) (Misra et al., 2016), consisting of $6,000$ argument pairs taken from the Internet Argument Corpus on three controversial topics (*death penalty*, *gay marriage* and *gun control*), annotated with an argument facet similarity score from 0 (*"different topic"*) to 5 (*"completely equivalent"*).

- The BWS Argument Similarity Dataset[4] (BWS) (Thakur et al., 2020), which contains $3,400$ annotated argument pairs on 8 controversial topics from a dataset collected from different web sources by Stab et al. (2018b). Labeled via crowd-sourcing with similarity scores between 0 and 1.

- The UKP Argument Aspect Similarity Corpus[5] (UKP) (Reimers et al., 2019a) with a total of $3,595$ argument pairs, annotated with four different labels *"Different topic/ can't decide"*, *"no similarity"*, *"some similarity"* and *"high similarity"* on a total of 28 topics, which have been identified as arguments by the ArgumenText system (Stab et al., 2018a).

As baselines we use (i) a medium sized SBERT, pre-trained with the standard BERT pre-training procedure, fine-tuned in a siamese architecture, and (ii) average word2vec[6] (Mikolov et al., 2013) vec-

[2] https://www.microsoft.com/en-us/download/details.aspx?id=52398

[3] https://nlds.soe.ucsc.edu/node/44

[4] https://tudatalib.ulb.tu-darmstadt.de/handle/tudatalib/2496

[5] https://tudatalib.ulb.tu-darmstadt.de/handle/tudatalib/1998

[6] https://code.google.com/archive/p/word2vec/

Model	MSRP r	MSRP ρ	UKP r	UKP ρ	AFS r	AFS ρ
average word2vec	18.17	17.96	22.29	17.44	11.25	5.22
SBERT	47.12	44.54	32.04	30.89	38.02	35.92
argueBERT sim. pred. (ours)	**48.33**	**46.34**	**35.33**	**34.77**	37.57	35.83
argueBERT order pred. (ours)	45.08	43.15	28.41	28.11	**38.25**	**36.80**
argueBERT edge val. (ours)	40.88	40.03	28.36	26.64	36.89	34.04

Table 1: Pearson's correlation r and Spearman's rank correlation $\rho \times 100$ on the MSRP, UKP and AFS corpora.

tors with vector-size 300, pre-trained on part of the Google News dataset.

To be able to fine-tune the models, the discrete labels of the AFS and UKP corpus are transformed into similarity scores between 0 and 1. The labels of the AFS corpus, which range from 0 to 5, are normalized by dividing it through the maximum value of 5. For the UKP corpus, the labels *"different topic/ can't decide"* and *"no similarity"* are assigned the value 0, *"some similarity"* is translated into a similarity score of 0.5 and for all pairs with label *"high similarity"* we assign a similarity score of 1. The labels for the MSRP corpus remain unchanged.

We perform two different evaluations. Firstly on the task of similarity prediction. Therefore we evaluate the models by calculating the Pearson's and Spearman's rank correlation for the predicted cosine similarities. Secondly we calculate the accuracy and F_1 score on the novel proposed task of SAM.

For the AFS corpus, which contains arguments for three different controversial topics, we use the same cross-topic evaulation strategy as suggested by Reimers and Gurevych (2019b). The models are fine-tuned on two of the three topics and evaluated on the third one, taking the average of all possible cross-topic scenarios as overall model performance score.

The UKP corpus, including arguments on 28 different topics, is evaluated with a 4-fold cross-topic validation as done by Reimers et al. (2019a). Out of the 28 topics, 21 are chosen for fine-tuning the model and 7 are used as test set. The evaluation result is the averaged result from all folds.

The BWS argument similarity dataset incorporates 8 different controversial topics. For evaluation we fine-tune the models on a fixed subset ($T_1 - T_5$), validate them on another unseen topic (T_6) and use the remaining two topics as test set ($T_7 - T_8$), as suggested by Thakur et al. (2020).

6 Results

First of all, we evaluate how well our models can predict the similarity of a given argument pair by calculating the cosine similarity between the two embeddings. Table 1 shows the Pearson correlation r and Spearman's rank correlation ρ on this task for the MSRP, AFS and UKP datasets.

On the MSRP dataset, the model pre-trained with a similarity prediction objective performs slightly better than the baseline that is trained with the next sentence prediction objective. The argueBERT order prediction model only performs a little worse on this dataset, than the next sentence prediction model, while the model trained on edge validation can not compete with the aforementioned models.

On the UKP dataset the performance increase by the model that used the similarity prediction objective for pre-training is even more significant. It outperforms the traditionally pre-trained SBERT model by 3 points for Pearson correlation and almost 4 points for the Spearman rank correlation.

Surprisingly, the order prediction model is able to outperform the similarity prediction task on the AFS corpus. But it has to be noticed that there is not much difference in the performance of all models on this dataset. Only the averaged word2vec vectors perform notably worse than all other evaluated models.

Out of all evaluated datasets, the recently published BWS corpus is the only one whose similarity values are quantified on a continuous scale. Table 2 shows the evaluation results for all models for three different distance measures. We chose the cosine similarity as default distance measure for evaluation. But in the case of the BWS corpus it is striking that both Manhattan and Euclidean distance result in a higher Pearson correlation as well as Spearman rank correlation. The embeddings of argueBERT pre-trained with a similarity prediction objective achieve the highest correlation for all distance measures. The model outperforms the SBERT model by 4 points. The argument order prediction model also performs better than the model

Model	Cosine		Manhattan		Euclidean	
	r	ρ	r	ρ	r	ρ
average word2vec	8.98	3.46	41.67	43.61	41.73	43.54
SBERT	38.55	38.72	42.33	42.02	42.35	42.09
argueBERT sim. pred. (ours)	**43.44**	**43.76**	**46.84**	**46.94**	**46.56**	**46.70**
argueBERT order pred. (ours)	38.97	38.02	44.20	43.39	44.14	43.30
argueBERT edge val. (ours)	33.72	33.22	39.49	38.79	39.74	39.17

Table 2: Pearson's correlation r and Spearman's rank correlation ρ ×100 on the **BWS** Argument Similarity Dataset (Thakur et al., 2020) for three different distance measures.

Model	ρ
average word2vec	43.54
$\text{SBERT}_{\text{BASE}}$ (Thakur et al., 2020)	58.04
$\textbf{argueBERT}_{\text{BASE}}$ sim. pred. (ours)	62.44
$\text{BERT}_{\text{BASE}}$ (Thakur et al., 2020)	**65.06**

Table 3: Spearman's rank correlation ρ ×100 on the **BWS** argument similarity dataset.

Model	Acc.	F_1
average word2vec	35.49	45.68
SBERT	44.92	52.54
argueBERT sim. pred. (ours)	**64.09**	**69.80**
argueBERT order pred. (ours)	38.14	46.81
argueBERT edge val. (ours)	48.10	49.08
$\text{SBERT}_{\text{BASE}}$	**66.88**	**71.45**
$\textbf{argueBERT}_{\text{BASE}}$ sim. pred. (ours)	65.92	70.76

Table 4: Accuracy and F_1 score on SAM for the **MSRP** corpus for a threshold of 0.8.

pre-trained with next sentence prediction, only the edge validation argueBERT model does not lead to an improvement and even performs worse than the word2vec baseline approach for both Manhattan and Euclidean distance measures.

To see how well the pre-training works for larger models, we also trained an $\text{argueBERT}_{\text{BASE}}$ model on the task of similarity prediction for 1, 000, 000 training steps on the PAWS and QQP datasets. The evaluation results for the BWS dataset are shown in Table 3. For comparison we also list the evaluation result of the standard $\text{BERT}_{\text{BASE}}$ model on this dataset. Even though $\text{argueBERT}_{\text{BASE}}$ was trained on a comparably small dataset, it outperforms SBERT on the BWS argument similarity prediction task and almost reaches the level of the $\text{BERT}_{\text{BASE}}$ cross-encoder.

Lastly, Table 4 shows the results on the MSRP dataset on the task of SAM for both the small and large pre-trained models. The small argueBERT model, pre-trained with the similarity prediction objective, by far achieves the highest accuracy, as well as the highest F_1 value for a threshold of 0.8. This reflects the evaluation results of the sentence embeddings on this dataset, showing that the similarity prediction argueBERT model is able to recognize paraphrases in the dataset quite well. The second best performing models, which are the argueBERT model trained on the task of edge validation and the baseline, trained on next sentence prediction, are almost more than 16 points behind. This shows the great potential of incorporating similarity prediction in the pre-training process of BERT. Looking at the results for the larger models, the $\text{argueBERT}_{\text{BASE}}$ model does not perform as well as the SBERT model on this dataset.

The remaining argument similarity datasets were found to be unsuitable for the task of SAM as they do not only contain dedicated paraphrased argument pairs, but rather present all increments of similarity. This means that very similar arguments are not necessarily matched as argument pairs in the data. Therefore, for future research new datasets that suit the task of SAM are required.

7 Discussion

Our conducted experiments show that the new proposed pre-training tasks are able to improve the SBERT embeddings on argument similarity measurement, compared to the next sentence prediction objective. Nevertheless, our presented approach has some limitations that should be addressed in the following.

First of all, the proposed models were pre-trained and fine-tuned on a single GPU. Due to the limited resources, a BERT model in medium size was chosen as basis for all pre-trained models. The models were trained only for a total of 100, 000 training steps, which is just a small fraction of the conducted training of the original BERT model. The achieved results have to be regarded as comparative values on how much an adaptation of the pre-training process can improve the performance. However, training a larger model for 1, 000, 000 steps on the task of similarity prediction indicates that the adapted pre-training also works for larger models and is able to compete with a pre-trained cross-encoder.

Another point is that the corpora we used for pre-training have quite different characteristics. The IAC (Abbott et al., 2016) for example consists of posts from different online forums. The used language is colloquial and the posts strongly vary in length and linguistic quality. The same applies to the QQP corpus. In contrast, the PAWS dataset consists of paraphrases extracted from Wikipedia articles, implying a formal language without misspellings. Training models on informal datasets can be advantageous, depending on the application of the trained model. In our case the differences of the used datasets rather constitute a disadvantage, as it may affect the comparability of the resulting models.

Additionally to having different characteristics, the few available datasets on paraphrase identification, argument similarity and also the argument graph corpora are relatively small, compared to the corpora the original BERT model is trained on. For the task of argument similarity prediction only the recently published BWS corpus (Thakur et al., 2020) includes argument pairs annotated with continuous scaled similarity scores. It can be said that there is still a lack of high-quality annotated argumentation corpora for this task.

8 Conclusion

In our work, we proposed and evaluated different pre-training tasks to improve the performance of SBERT embeddings on the task of argument similarity measurement. We call the new pre-trained model variants argueBERT. Evaluation of the models shows that adapting the pre-training process of BERT has an impact on the resulting embeddings and can improve the models' results. ArgueBERT trained with a similarity prediction objective led to a performance improvement up to 5 points Spearman's rank correlation on the evaluated BWS argument similarity corpus, compared to the model trained with the classic NSP pre-training task and also showed the best results on our new proposed evaluation task SAM on the MSRP corpus.

A larger argueBERT$_{\text{BASE}}$ pre-trained with the similarity prediction task could improve the evaluated embeddings compared to SBERT and almost reaches the results of the cross-encoding BERT$_{\text{BASE}}$ model.

For future research, the new proposed task of SAM can be used to evaluate models on the ability to identify paraphrases from a large collection of sentences. Fields of application are, for example, online argumentation tools, where users can interchange arguments on certain topics. Newly added arguments can be compared to existing posts and duplicate, paraphrased entries can be avoided. A trained model that is good at measuring argument similarity is also advantageous for tasks like argument mining and argument clustering.

References

Rob Abbott, Brian Ecker, Pranav Anand, and Marilyn Walker. 2016. Internet argument corpus 2.0: An sql schema for dialogic social media and the corpora to go with it. In *Proceedings of the Tenth International Conference on Language Resources and Evaluation (LREC'16)*, pages 4445–4452, Portorož, Slovenia. European Language Resources Association (ELRA).

Filip Boltužić and Jan Šnajder. 2015. Identifying prominent arguments in online debates using semantic textual similarity. In *Proceedings of the 2nd Workshop on Argumentation Mining*, pages 110–115, Denver, CO. Association for Computational Linguistics.

Samuel R. Bowman, Gabor Angeli, Christopher Potts, and Christopher D. Manning. 2015. A large annotated corpus for learning natural language inference. In *Proceedings of the 2015 Conference on Empirical Methods in Natural Language Processing*, pages 632–642, Lisbon, Portugal. Association for Computational Linguistics.

Kevin Clark, Minh-Thang Luong, Quoc V. Le, and Christopher D. Manning. 2020. Electra: Pre-training text encoders as discriminators rather than generators. In *International Conference on Learning Representations*.

Jacob Devlin, Ming-Wei Chang, Kenton Lee, and Kristina Toutanova. 2019. BERT: Pre-training of deep bidirectional transformers for language understanding. In *Proceedings of the 2019 Conference of the North American Chapter of the Association for Computational Linguistics: Human Language Technologies, Volume 1 (Long and Short Papers)*, pages 4171–4186, Minneapolis, Minnesota. Association for Computational Linguistics.

William B. Dolan and Chris Brockett. 2005. Automatically constructing a corpus of sentential paraphrases. In *Proceedings of the Third International Workshop on Paraphrasing (IWP2005)*.

Lorik Dumani, Patrick J. Neumann, and Ralf Schenkel. 2020. A framework for argument retrieval - ranking argument clusters by frequency and specificity.

In *Advances in Information Retrieval - 42nd European Conference on IR Research, ECIR 2020, Lisbon, Portugal, April 14-17, 2020, Proceedings, Part I*, volume 12035 of *Lecture Notes in Computer Science*, pages 431–445. Springer.

Zhenzhong Lan, Mingda Chen, Sebastian Goodman, Kevin Gimpel, Piyush Sharma, and Radu Soricut. 2020. Albert: A lite bert for self-supervised learning of language representations. In *International Conference on Learning Representations*.

Mike Lewis, Yinhan Liu, Naman Goyal, Marjan Ghazvininejad, Abdelrahman Mohamed, Omer Levy, Veselin Stoyanov, and Luke Zettlemoyer. 2020. BART: Denoising sequence-to-sequence pretraining for natural language generation, translation, and comprehension. In *Proceedings of the 58th Annual Meeting of the Association for Computational Linguistics*, pages 7871–7880, Online. Association for Computational Linguistics.

Yinhan Liu, Myle Ott, Naman Goyal, Jingfei Du, Mandar Joshi, Danqi Chen, Omer Levy, Mike Lewis, Luke Zettlemoyer, and Veselin Stoyanov. 2019. Roberta: A robustly optimized bert pretraining approach.

Tomas Mikolov, Ilya Sutskever, Kai Chen, Greg Corrado, and Jeffrey Dean. 2013. Distributed representations of words and phrases and their compositionality. In *Proceedings of the 26th International Conference on Neural Information Processing Systems - Volume 2*, NIPS'13, page 3111–3119, Red Hook, NY, USA. Curran Associates Inc.

Amita Misra, Brian Ecker, and Marilyn Walker. 2016. Measuring the similarity of sentential arguments in dialogue. In *Proceedings of the 17th Annual Meeting of the Special Interest Group on Discourse and Dialogue*, pages 276–287, Los Angeles. Association for Computational Linguistics.

Nils Reimers and Iryna Gurevych. 2019b. Sentence-BERT: Sentence embeddings using Siamese BERT-networks. In *Proceedings of the 2019 Conference on Empirical Methods in Natural Language Processing and the 9th International Joint Conference on Natural Language Processing (EMNLP-IJCNLP)*, pages 3982–3992, Hong Kong, China. Association for Computational Linguistics.

Nils Reimers, Benjamin Schiller, Tilman Beck, Johannes Daxenberger, Christian Stab, and Iryna Gurevych. 2019a. Classification and clustering of arguments with contextualized word embeddings. In *Proceedings of the 57th Annual Meeting of the Association for Computational Linguistics*, pages 567–578, Florence, Italy. Association for Computational Linguistics.

Christian Stab, Johannes Daxenberger, Chris Stahlhut, Tristan Miller, Benjamin Schiller, Christopher Tauchmann, Steffen Eger, and Iryna Gurevych. 2018a. ArgumenText: Searching for arguments in heterogeneous sources. In *Proceedings of the 2018 Conference of the North American Chapter of the Association for Computational Linguistics: Demonstrations*, pages 21–25, New Orleans, Louisiana. Association for Computational Linguistics.

Christian Stab, Tristan Miller, Benjamin Schiller, Pranav Rai, and Iryna Gurevych. 2018b. Cross-topic argument mining from heterogeneous sources. In *Proceedings of the 2018 Conference on Empirical Methods in Natural Language Processing*, pages 3664–3674, Brussels, Belgium. Association for Computational Linguistics.

Nandan Thakur, Nils Reimers, Johannes Daxenberger, and Iryna Gurevych. 2020. Augmented sbert: Data augmentation method for improving bi-encoders for pairwise sentence scoring tasks. *arXiv preprint arXiv:2010.08240*.

Iulia Turc, Ming-Wei Chang, Kenton Lee, and Kristina Toutanova. 2019. Well-read students learn better: On the importance of pre-training compact models. *arXiv preprint arXiv:1908.08962v2*.

Henning Wachsmuth, Shahbaz Syed, and Benno Stein. 2018. Retrieval of the best counterargument without prior topic knowledge. In *Proceedings of the 56th Annual Meeting of the Association for Computational Linguistics (Volume 1: Long Papers)*, pages 241–251, Melbourne, Australia. Association for Computational Linguistics.

Adina Williams, Nikita Nangia, and Samuel Bowman. 2018. A broad-coverage challenge corpus for sentence understanding through inference. In *Proceedings of the 2018 Conference of the North American Chapter of the Association for Computational Linguistics: Human Language Technologies, Volume 1 (Long Papers)*, pages 1112–1122, New Orleans, Louisiana. Association for Computational Linguistics.

Yuan Zhang, Jason Baldridge, and Luheng He. 2019. PAWS: paraphrase adversaries from word scrambling. In *Proceedings of the 2019 Conference of the North American Chapter of the Association for Computational Linguistics: Human Language Technologies, NAACL-HLT 2019, Minneapolis, MN, USA, June 2-7, 2019, Volume 1 (Long and Short Papers)*, pages 1298–1308. Association for Computational Linguistics.

Yukun Zhu, Ryan Kiros, Rich Zemel, Ruslan Salakhutdinov, Raquel Urtasun, Antonio Torralba, and Sanja Fidler. 2015. Aligning books and movies: Towards story-like visual explanations by watching movies and reading books. In *Proceedings of the 2015 IEEE International Conference on Computer Vision (ICCV)*, ICCV '15, page 19–27, USA. IEEE Computer Society.

A Appendix

Pre-Training and fine-tuning settings

Table 5 shows the used settings for pre-training all proposed BERT models in this work.

BERT model	BERT medium uncased, BERT base uncased
learning_rate	1e-4, 2e-5
do_lower_case	True
max_seq_length	128
max_predictions_per_seq	5
masked_lm_prob	0.15
random_seed	12345
dupe_factor	10

Table 5: Settings for creating the pre-training data.

Table 6 shows the settings for fine-tuning SBERT on the evaluated datasets, using the sentence-transformers library[7] published by the UKPLab on GitHub.

learning_rate	2e-5
train_batch_size	16
num_epochs	5
optimizer_class	transformers.AdamW
weight_decay	0.01

Table 6: Settings for fine-tuning.

[7] https://github.com/UKPLab/sentence-transformers

How Hateful are Movies? A Study and Prediction on Movie Subtitles

Niklas von Boguszewski * nvboguszewski@googlemail.com

Sana Moin * moinsana77@gmail.com

Anirban Bhowmick * anirbanbhowmick88@gmail.com

Seid Muhie Yimam seid.muhie.yimam@uni-hamburg.de

Chris Biemann christian.biemann@uni-hamburg.de

Language Technology Group
Universität Hamburg, Germany

Abstract

In this research, we investigate techniques to detect hate speech in movies. We introduce a new dataset collected from the subtitles of six movies, where each utterance is annotated either as hate, offensive or normal. We apply transfer learning techniques of domain adaptation and fine-tuning on existing social media datasets, namely from Twitter and Fox News. We evaluate different representations, i.e., Bag of Words (BoW), Bi-directional Long short-term memory (Bi-LSTM), and Bidirectional Encoder Representations from Transformers (BERT) on 11k movie subtitles. The BERT model obtained the best macro-averaged F1-score of 77%. Hence, we show that transfer learning from the social media domain is efficacious in classifying hate and offensive speech in movies through subtitles.

Cautionary Note: The paper contains examples that many will find offensive or hateful; however, this cannot be avoided owing to the nature of the work.

1 Introduction

Nowadays, hate speech is becoming a pressing issue and occurs in multiple domains, mostly in the major social media platforms or political speeches. Hate speech is defined as verbal communication that denigrates a person or a community on some characteristics such as race, color, ethnicity, gender, sexual orientation, nationality, or religion (Nockleby et al., 2000; Davidson et al., 2017). Some examples given by Schmidt and Wiegand (2017) are:

- Go fucking kill yourself and die already a useless ugly pile of shit scumbag.
- The Jew Faggot Behind The Financial Collapse.
- Hope one of those bitches falls over and breaks her leg.

Several sensitive comments on social media platforms have led to crime against minorities (Williams et al., 2020). Hate speech can be considered as an umbrella term that different authors have coined with different names. Xu et al. (2012); Hosseinmardi et al. (2015); Zhong et al. (2016) referred it by the term *cyberbully-ing*, while Davidson et al. (2017) used the term *offensive language* to some expressions that can be strongly impolite, rude or use of vulgar words towards an individual or group that can even ignite fights or be hurtful. Use of words like f**k, n*gga, b*tch is common in social media comments, song lyrics, etc. Although these terms can be treated as obscene and inappropriate, some people also use them in non-hateful ways in different contexts (Davidson et al., 2017). This makes it challenging for all hate speech systems to distinguish between hate speech and offensive content. Davidson et al. (2017) tried to distinguish between the two classes in their Twitter dataset.

These days due to globalization and online media streaming services, we are exposed to different cultures across the world through movies. Thus, an analysis of the amount of hate and offensive content in the media that we consume daily could be helpful.

Two research questions guided our research:

1. **RQ 1.** What are the limitations of social media hate speech detection models to detect hate speech in movie subtitles?
2. **RQ 2.** How to build a hate and offensive speech classification model for movie subtitles?

To address the problem of hate speech detection in movies, we chose three different models. We have used the BERT (Devlin et al., 2019) model, due

* Equal contribution

to the recent success in other NLP-related fields, a Bi-LSTM (Hochreiter and Schmidhuber, 1997) model to utilize the sequential nature of movie subtitles and a classic Bag of Words (BoW) model as a baseline system.

The paper is structured as follows: Section 2 gives an overview of the related work in this topic and Section 3 describes the research methodology and the annotation work, while in Section 4 we discuss the employed datasets and the pre-processing steps. Furthermore, Section 5 describes the implemented models while Section 6 presents the evaluation of the models, the qualitative analysis of the results and the annotation analysis followed by Section 7, which covers the threats to the validity of our research. Finally, we end with the conclusion in Section 8 and propose further work directions in Section 9.

2 Related Work

Some of the existing hate speech detection models classify comments targeted towards certain commonly attacked communities like gay, black, and Muslim, whereas in actuality, some comments did not have the intention of targeting a community (Borkan et al., 2019; Dixon et al., 2018). Mathew et al. (2021) introduced a benchmark dataset consisting of hate speech generated from two social media platforms, Twitter and Gab. In the social media space, a key challenge is to separately identify hate speech from offensive text. Although they might appear the same way semantically, they have subtle differences. Therefore they tried to solve the bias and interpretability aspect of hate speech and did a three-class classification (i.e., hate, offensive, or normal). They reported the best macro-averaged F1-score of 68.7% on their BERT-HateXplain model. It is also one of the models that we use in our study, as it is one of the 'off-the-shelf' hate speech detection models that can easily be employed for the topic at hand.

Lexicon-based detection methods have low precision because they classify the messages based on the presence of particular hate speech-related terms, particularly those insulting, cursing, and bullying words. Davidson et al. (2017) used a crowdsourced hate speech lexicon to identify tweets with the occurrence of hate speech keywords to filter tweets. They then used crowdsourcing to label these tweets into three classes: hate speech, offensive language, and neither. In their dataset, the more generic racist and homophobic tweets were classified as hate speech, whereas the ones involving sexist and abusive words were classified as offensive. It is one of the datasets we have used in exploring transfer learning and model fine-tuning in our study.

Due to global events, hate speech also plagues online news platforms. In the news domain, context knowledge is required to identify hate speech. Lei and Ruihong (2017) conducted a study on a dataset prepared from user comments on news articles from the Fox News platform. It is the second dataset we have used to explore transfer learning from the news domain to movie subtitles in our study.

Several other authors have collected the data from different online platforms and labeled them manually. Some of these data sources are: Twitter (Xiang et al., 2012; Xu et al., 2012), Instagram (Hosseinmardi et al., 2015; Zhong et al., 2016), Yahoo! (Nobata et al., 2016; Djuric et al., 2015), YouTube (Dinakar et al., 2012) and Whisper (Silva et al., 2021) to name a few. Most of the data sources used in the previous studies are based on social media, news, and micro-blogging platforms. However, the notion of the existence of hate speech in movie dialogues has been overlooked. Thus in our study, we first explore how the different existing ML (Machine Learning) models classify hate and offensive speech in movie subtitles and propose a new dataset compiled from six movie subtitles.

3 Research Methodology

To investigate the problem of detecting hate and offensive speech in movies, we used different machine learning models trained on social media content such as tweets or discussion thread comments from news articles. Here, the models in our research were developed and evaluated on an in-domain 80% train and 20% test split data using the same random state to ensure comparability.

We have developed six different models: two Bi-LSTM models, two BoW models, and two BERT models. For each pair, one of them has been trained on a dataset consisting of Twitter posts and the other on a dataset consisting of Fox News discussion threads. The trained models have been used to classify movie subtitles to evaluate their performance by domain adaptation from social media content to movies. In addition, another state-of-the-art BERT-based classification model called *HateXplain* (Mathew et al., 2021) has been used to classify the movies out of the box. While it is also possible to further fine-tune the HateXplain model, we are restricted in reporting the result of the 'off-the-shelf' classification system to new domains, such as movie subtitles.

Furthermore, the movie dataset we have collected (see Section 4) is used to train domain-specific BoW, Bi-LSTM, and BERT models using 6-fold cross-validation, where each movie was selected as a fold and report the averaged results. Finally, we have identified the best model trained on social media content based on macro-averaged F1-score and fine-tuned it with the movie dataset using 6-fold cross-validation on that particular model, to investigate fine-tuning and transfer learning capabilities for hate speech on movie subtitles.

3.1 Annotation Guidelines

In our annotation guidelines, we defined hateful speech as a language used to express hatred towards a targeted individual or group or is intended to be derogatory, to humiliate, or to insult the members of the group, based on attributes such as race, religion, ethnic origin, sexual orientation, disability, or gender. Although the meaning of hate speech is based on the context, we provided the above definition agreeing to the definition provided by Nockleby et al. (2000); Davidson et al. (2017). Offensive speech uses profanity, strongly impolite, rude, or vulgar language expressed with fighting or hurtful words to insult a targeted individual or group (Davidson et al., 2017). We used the same definition also for offensive speech in the guidelines. The remaining subtitles were defined as normal.

3.2 Annotation Task

For the annotation of movie subtitles, we have used Amazon Mechanical Turk (MTurk) crowdsourcing. Before the main annotation task, we have conducted an annotation pilot study, where 40 subtitles texts were randomly chosen from the movie subtitle dataset. Each of them has included 10 hate speech, 10 offensive, and 20 normal subtitles that are manually annotated by experts. In total, 100 MTurk workers were assigned for the annotation task. We have used the built-in MTurk qualification requirement (HIT approval rate higher than 95% and number of HITs approved larger than 5000) to recruit workers during the Pilot task. Each worker was assessed for accuracy and the 13 workers who have completed the task with the highest annotation accuracy were chosen for the main study task. The rest of the workers were compensated for the task they have completed in the pilot study and blocked from participating in the main annotation task. For each HIT, the workers are paid 40 cents both for the pilot and the main annotation task.

Dataset	normal	offensive	hate	# total
Twitter	0.17	0.78	0.05	24472
Fox News	0.72	-	0.28	1513
Movies	0.84	0.13	0.03	10688

Table 1: Class distribution for the different datasets

For the main task, the 13 chosen MTurk workers were first assigned to one movie subtitle annotation to further look at the annotator agreement as will be described in Section 6.3. Two annotators were replaced during the main annotation task with the next-best workers from the identified workers in the pilot study. This process was repeated after each movie annotation for the remaining five movies. One batch consists of 40 subtitles which were displayed in chronological order to the worker. Each batch has been annotated by three workers. In Figure 1, you can see the first four questions of a batch out of the movie American History X 1998.

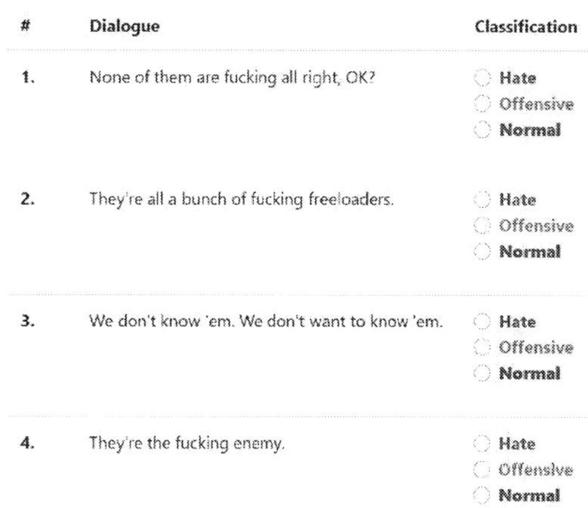

Figure 1: Annotation template containing a batch of the movie American History X

Name	normal	offensive	hate	#total
Django Unchained	0.89	0.05	0.07	1747
BlacKkKlansman	0.89	0.06	0.05	1645
American History X	0.83	0.13	0.03	1565
Pulp Fiction	0.82	0.16	0.01	1622
South Park	0.85	0.14	0.01	1046
The Wolf of Wall Street	0.81	0.19	0.001	3063

Table 2: Class distribution on each movie

4 Datasets

The publicly available Fox News corpus[1] consists of 1,528 annotated comments compiled from ten discussion threads that happened on the Fox News website in 2016. The corpus does not differentiate between offensive and hateful comments. This corpus has been introduced by Lei and Ruihong (2017) and has been annotated by two trained native English speakers. We have identified 13 duplicates and two empty comments in this corpus and removed them for accurate training results. The second publicly available corpus we use consists of 24,802 tweets[2]. We identified 204 of them as duplicates and removed them again to achieve accurate training results. The corpus has been introduced by Davidson et al. (2017) and was labeled by CrowdFlower workers as hate speech, offensive, and neither. The last class is referred to as *normal* in this paper. The distribution of the normal, offensive, and hate classes can be found in Table 1.

The novel movie dataset we introduce consists of six movies. The movies have been chosen based on keyword tags provided by the IMDB website[3]. The tags *hate-speech* and *racism* were chosen because we assumed that they were likely to contain a lot of hate and offensive speech. The tag *friendship* was chosen to get contrary movies containing a lot of normal subtitles, with less hate speech content. In addition, we excluded movie genres like documentations, fantasy, or musicals to keep the movies comparable to each other. Namely we have chosen the movies BlacKkKlansman (2018) which was tagged as *hate-speech*, Django Unchained (2012), American History X (1998) and Pulp Fiction (1994) which were tagged as *racism* whereas South Park (1999) as well as The Wolf of Wall Street (2013) were tagged as *friendship* in December 2020. The detailed distribution of the normal, offensive, and hate classes, movie-wise, can be found in Table 2.

[1] `https://github.com/sjtuprog/fox-news-comments`

[2] `https://github.com/t-davidson/hate-speech-and-offensive-language/`

[3] `https://www.imdb.com/search/keyword/`

4.1 Pre-processing

The goal of the pre-processing step was to make the text of the Tweets and conversational discussions as comparable as possible to the movie subtitles since we assume that this will improve the transfer learning results. Therefore, we did not use pre-processing techniques like stop word removal or lemmatization.

4.2 Data Cleansing

After performing a manual inspection, we applied certain rules to remove the textual noise from our datasets. The following was the noise observed in each dataset, which we removed for the Twitter and Fox News datasets: (1) repeated punctuation marks, (2) multiple username tags, (3) emoticon character encodings, and (4) website links. For the movie subtitle text dataset: (1) sound expressions, e.g [PEOPLE CHATTERING], [DOOR OPENING], (2) name header of the current speaker, e.g. "DIANA: Hey, what's up?" which refers to Diana is about to say something, (3) HTML tags, (4) non-alpha character subtitle, and (5) non-ASCII characters.

4.3 Subtitle format conversion

The downloaded subtitle files are provided by the website *www.opensubtitles.org*[4] and are free to use for scientific purposes. The files are available in the SRT-format[5] that have a time duration along with a subtitle, which while watching appears on the screen in a given time frame. We performed the following operations to create the movie dataset: (1) Converted the SRT-format to CSV-format by separating start time, end time, and the subtitle text, (2) Fragmented subtitles which were originally single appearances on the screen and spanned across multiple screen frames were combined, by identifying sentence-ending punctuation marks, (3) Combined single word subtitles with the previous subtitle because single word subtitles tend to be expressions to what has been said before.

[4] `https://www.opensubtitles.org/`

[5] `https://en.wikipedia.org/wiki/SubRip`

Model	Class	F1-Score	Macro AVG F1
HateXplain	normal	0.93	
HateXplain	offensive	0.27	0.66
HateXplain	hate	0.77	

Table 3: Prediction results using the HateXplain model on the movie dataset (domain adaptation)

5 Experimental Setup

The Bi-LSTM models are built using the Keras and the BoW models are built using the PyTorch library while both are trained with a 1e-03 learning rate and categorical cross-entropy loss function.

For the development of BERT-based models, we rely on the *TFBERTForSequenceClassification* algorithm, which is provided by HuggingFace[6] and pre-trained on *bert-base-uncased.* Learning rate of 3e-06 and sparse categorical cross-entropy loss function was used for this. All the models used the Adam optimizer (Kingma and Ba, 2015). We describe the detailed hyper-parameters for all the models used for all the experiments in the Appendix A.1.

6 Results and Annotation Analysis

In this section, we will discuss the different classification results obtained from the various hate speech classification models. We will also briefly present a qualitative exploration of the annotated movie datasets. The model referred in the tables as LSTM refers to Bi-LSTM models used.

6.1 Classification results and Discussion

We have introduced a new dataset of movie subtitles in the field of hate speech research. A total of six movies are annotated, which consists of sequential subtitles.

First, we experimented on the *HateXplain* model (Mathew et al., 2021) by testing the model's performance on the movie dataset. We achieved a macro-averaged F1-score of 66% (see Table 3). Next, we tried to observe how the different models (BoW, Bi-LSTM, and BERT) perform using transfer learning and how comparable are those results to this state-of-the-art model's results.

We trained and tested the BERT, Bi-LSTM, and BoW model by applying an 80:20 split on the social media datasets (see Table 4). When applied to the Fox News dataset, we observed that BERT performed better than both BoW and Bi-LSTM with a small margin in terms of macro-averaged F1-score. Hate is detected close to 50% whereas normal is detected close to 80% for all three models on F1-score.

[6] `https://huggingface.co/transformers`

Dataset	Model	Class	F1-Score	Macro AVG F1
Fox News	BoW	normal	0.83	0.63
		hate	0.43	
	BERT	normal	0.86	**0.68**
		hate	0.51	
	LSTM	normal	0.77	0.62
		hate	0.46	
Twitter	BoW	normal	0.78	
		offensive	0.93	0.66
		hate	0.26	
	BERT	normal	0.89	
		offensive	0.95	**0.76**
		hate	0.43	
	LSTM	normal	0.76	
		offensive	0.91	0.66
		hate	0.31	

Table 4: In-domain results on Twitter and Fox News with 80:20 split

When applied on the Twitter dataset, results are almost the same for the BoW and Bi-LSTM models, whereas the BERT model performed close to 10% better by reaching a macro-averaged F1-score of 76%. All the models have a high F1-score of above 90% for identifying offensive class. This goes along with the fact that the offensive class is the dominant one in the Twitter dataset (Table 1).

Hence, by looking at the macro-averaged F1-score values, BERT performed best in the task for training and testing on social media content on both datasets.

Next, we train on social media data and test on the six movies (see Table 5) to address RQ 1.

When trained on the Fox News dataset, BoW and Bi-LSTM performed similarly by poorly detecting hate in the movies. In contrast, BERT identified the hate class more than twice as well by reaching an F1-score of 39%.

When trained on the Twitter dataset, BERT performed almost double in terms of macro-averaged F1-score than the other two models. Even though

Dataset	Model	Class	F1-Score	Macro AVG F1
Fox News	BoW	normal	0.86	0.51
		hate	0.15	
	BERT	normal	0.89	**0.64**
		hate	0.39	
	LSTM	normal	0.83	0.51
		hate	0.18	
Twitter	BoW	normal	0.62	0.37
		offensive	0.32	
		hate	0.15	
	BERT	normal	0.95	**0.77**
		offensive	0.74	
		hate	0.63	
	LSTM	normal	0.66	0.38
		offensive	0.34	
		hate	0.16	

Table 5: Prediction results using the models trained on social media content to classify the six movies (domain adaptation)

the detection for the offensive class was high on the Twitter dataset (see Table 4) the models did not perform as well on the six movies, which could be due to the domain change. However, BERT was able to perform better on the hate class, even though it was trained on a small proportion of hate content in the Twitter dataset. The other two models performed very poorly.

To address RQ 2, we train new models from scratch on the six movies dataset using 6-fold cross-validation (see Table 6). In this setup, each fold represents one movie that is exchanged iteratively during evaluation.

Compared to the domain adaptation (see Table 5), the BoW and Bi-LSTM models performed better. Bi-LSTM distinguished better than BoW among hate and offensive while maintaining a good identification of the normal class resulting in a better macro-averaged F1-score of 71% as compared to 64% for the BoW model. BERT performed best across all three classes resulting in 10% better results compared to the Bi-LSTM model on macro-averaged F1-score, however, it has similar results when compared to the domain adaptation (see Table 5) results.

Furthermore, the absolute amount of hateful subtitles in the movies The Wolf of Wall Street (3), South Park (10), and Pulp Fiction (16) are very

Dataset	Model	Class	F1-Score	Macro AVG F1
Movies	BoW	normal	0.95	0.64
		offensive	0.59	
		hate	0.37	
	BERT	normal	0.97	**0.81**
		offensive	0.76	
		hate	0.68	
	LSTM	normal	0.95	0.71
		offensive	0.63	
		hate	0.56	

Table 6: In-domain results using models trained on the movie dataset using 6-fold cross-validation

minor, hence the cross-validation on these three movies as test set is very sensible of only predicting a few of them wrong since a few of them will already result in a high relative amount.

We have also tried to improve our BERT model trained on social media content (Table 4) by fine-tuning it via 6-fold cross-validation using the six movies dataset (see Table 7).

The macro-averaged F1-score increased compared to the domain adaptation (see Table 5) from 64% to 89% for the model trained on the Fox News dataset. For the Twitter dataset the macro-averaged F1-score is comparable to the domain adaptation (see Table 5) and in-domain results (see Table 6). Compared to the results of the HateXplain model (see Table 3) the identification of the normal utterances are comparable whereas the offensive class was identified by our BERT model much better, with an increment of 48%, but the hate class was identified by a decrement of 18%.

The detailed results of all experiments is given in Appendix A.2.

6.2 Qualitative Analysis

In this section, we investigate the unsuccessfully classified utterances (see Figure 2) of all six movies by the BERT model trained on the Twitter dataset and fine-tuned with the six movies via 6-fold cross-validation (see Table 7) to analyze the model addressing RQ 2.

The majority of unsuccessfully classified utterances (564) are offensive classified as normal and vice versa resulting in 69%. Hate got classified as offensive in 5% of all cases and offensive as hate in 8%. The remaining misclassification is between

Dataset	Model	Class	F1-Score	Macro AVG F1
Movies	BERT (Fox News)	normal	0.97	0.89
		hate	0.82	
	BERT (Twitter)	normal	0.97	**0.77**
		offensive	0.75	
		hate	0.59	

Table 7: Prediction results using BERT models trained on the Twitter and Fox News datasets and fine-tuned them with the movie dataset by applying 6-fold cross-validation (fine-tuning)

normal and hate resulting in 18%, which we refer to as the most critical for us to analyze further.

We looked at the individual utterances of the hate class misclassified as normal (37 utterances). We observed that most of them were sarcastic and those did not contain any hate keywords, whereas some could have been indirect or context-dependent, for example, the utterance *"It's just so beautiful. We're cleansing this country of a backwards race of chimpanzees"* indirectly and sarcastically depicts hate speech which our model could not identify. We assume that our model has shortcomings in interpreting those kinds of utterances correctly.

Furthermore, we analyzed the utterances of the class normal which were misclassified as hate (60 utterances). We observed that around a third of them were actual hate but were misclassified by our annotators as normal, hence those were correctly classified as hate by our model. We noticed that a fifth of them contain the keyword *"Black Power"*, which we refer to as normal whereas the BERT model classified them as hate.

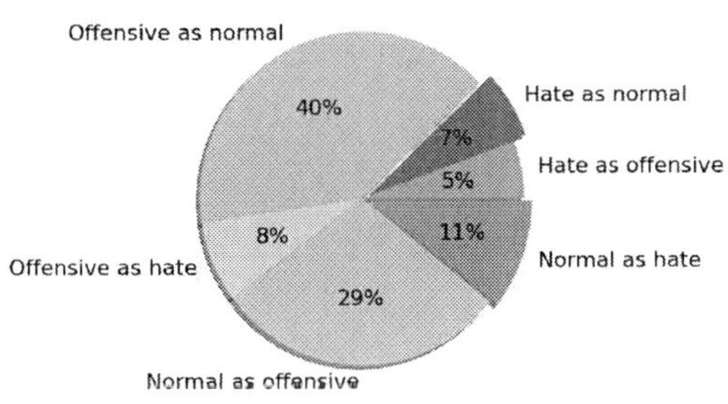

Figure 2: Label misclassification on the movie dataset using the BERT model of Table 7 trained on the Twitter dataset

6.3 Annotation Analysis

Using the MTurk crowdsourcing, a total of 10,688 subtitles (from the six movies) are annotated. For each of the three workers involved, 81% agreed to the same class. Out of the total annotations, only 0.7% received disagreement on the classes (where all the three workers chose a different class for each subtitle).

To ensure the quality of the classes for the training, we chose majority voting. In the case of disagreement, we took the offensive class as the final class of the subtitle. One reason why workers do disagree might be that they do interpret a scene differently. We think that providing the video and audio clips of the subtitle frames might help to disambiguate such confusions.

Let us consider an example from one of the annotation batches that describes a scene where the shooting of an Afro-American appears to happen. Subtitle 5 in that batch reads out *"Shoot the nigger!"*, and subtitle 31 states *"Just shit. Got totally out of control."*, which was interpreted as normal by a worker who might not be sensible to the word *shit*, as offensive speech by a worker who is, in fact, sensible to the word *shit* or as hate speech by a worker who thinks that the word *shit* refers to the Afro-American.

The movie Django Unchained 2012 was tagged as *racism* and has been annotated as the most hateful movie (see Table 2) followed by BlacKkKlansman 2018 and American History X 1998 which where tagged as *racism* or *hateful*. This indicates that hate speech and racist comments often go along together. As expected, movies tagged by *friendship* like The Wolf of Wall Street 2013 and South Park 1999 were less hateful. Surprisingly the percentage of offensive speech increases when the percentage of hate decreases making the movies tagged by *friendship* most offensive in our movie dataset.

7 Threats to Validity

1. The pre-processing of the movies or the social media datasets could have deleted crucial parts which would have made a hateful tweet normal, for example. Thus the training on such datasets could impact the training negatively.

2. Movies are not real, they are more like a very good simulation. Thus, for this matter, hate

speech is simulated and arranged. Maybe documentation movies are better suited since they tend to cover real-case scenarios.

3. The annotations could be wrong since the task of identifying hate speech is subjective.

4. Movies might not contain a lot of hate speech, hence the need to detect them is very minor.

5. As the annotation process was done batch-wise, annotators might lose crucial contextual information when the batch change happens, as it misses the chronological order of the dialogue.

6. Only textual data might not provide enough contextual information for the annotators to correctly annotate the dialogues as the other modalities of the movies (audio and video) are not considered.

8 Conclusion

In this paper, we applied different approaches to detect hate and offensive speech in a novel proposed movie subtitle dataset. In addition, we proposed a technique to combine fragments of movie subtitles and made the social media text content more comparable to movie subtitles (for training purposes).

For the classification, we used two techniques of transfer learning, i.e., domain adaptation and fine-tuning. The former was used to evaluate three different ML models, namely Bag of Words for a baseline system, transformer-based systems as they are becoming the state-of-the-art classification approaches for different NLP tasks, and Bi-LSTM-based models as our movie dataset represents sequential data for each movie. The latter was performed only on the BERT model and we report our best result by cross-validation on the movie dataset.

All three models were able to perform well for the classification of the normal class. Whereas when it comes to the differentiation between offensive and hate classes, BERT achieved a substantially higher F1-score as compared to the other two models.

The produced artifacts could have practical significance in the field of movie recommendations. We will release the annotated datasets, keeping all the contextual information (time offsets of the subtitle, different representations, etc.), the fine-tuned and newly trained models, as well as the python source code and pre-processing scripts, to pursue research on hate speech on movie subtitles.[7]

9 Further Work

The performance of hate speech detection in movies can be improved by increasing the existing movie dataset with movies that contain a lot of hate speech. Moreover, multi-modal models can also improve performance by using speech or image. In addition, some kind of hate speech can only be detected through the combination of different modals, like some memes in the hateful meme challenge by Facebook (Kiela et al., 2020) e.g. a picture that says *look how many people love you* whereas the image shows an empty desert.
Furthermore, we also did encounter the widely reported sparsity of hate speech content, which can be mitigated by using techniques such as data augmentation, or balanced class distribution. We intentionally did not perform shuffling of all six movies before splitting into k-folds to retain a realistic scenario where a classifier is executed on a new movie.

Another interesting aspect that can be looked at is the identification of the target groups of the hate speech content in movies and to see the more prevalent target groups. This work can also be extended for automated annotation of movies to investigate the distribution of offensive and hate speech.

References

1994. Movie: Pulp Fiction. Last visited 23.05.2021.

1998. Movie: American History X. Last visited 23.05.2021.

1999. Movie: South Park: Bigger, Longer & Uncut. Last visited 23.05.2021.

2012. Movie: Django Unchained. Last visited 23.05.2021.

2013. Movie: The Wolf of Wall Street. Last visited 23.05.2021.

2018. Movie: BlacKkKlansman. Last visited 23.05.2021.

Daniel Borkan, Lucas Dixon, Jeffrey Sorensen, Nithum Thain, and Lucy Vasserman. 2019. Nuanced Metrics for Measuring Unintended Bias with Real Data for Text Classification. In *Companion of The 2019*

[7] `https://github.com/uhh-lt/hatespeech`

World Wide Web Conference, WWW, pages 491–500, San Francisco, CA, USA.

Thomas Davidson, Dana Warmsley, Michael Macy, and Ingmar Weber. 2017. Automated Hate Speech Detection and the Problem of Offensive Language. In *Proceedings of the 11th International AAAI Conference on Web and Social Media*, pages 512–515, Montréal, QC, Canada.

Jacob Devlin, Ming-Wei Chang, Kenton Lee, and Kristina Toutanova. 2019. BERT: Pre-training of Deep Bidirectional Transformers for Language Understanding. In *Proceedings of the 2019 Conference of the North American Chapter of the Association for Computational Linguistics: Human Language Technologies, Volume 1 (Long and Short Papers)*, pages 4171–4186, Minneapolis, MN, USA. Association for Computational Linguistics.

Karthik Dinakar, Birago Jones, Catherine Havasi, Henry Lieberman, and Rosalind Picard. 2012. Common Sense Reasoning for Detection, Prevention, and Mitigation of Cyberbullying. *ACM Trans. Interact. Intell. Syst.*, 2(3):18:1–18:30.

Lucas Dixon, John Li, Jeffrey Sorensen, Nithum Thain, and Lucy Vasserman. 2018. Measuring and Mitigating Unintended Bias in Text Classification. In *Proceedings of the 2018 AAAI/ACM Conference on AI, Ethics, and Society. Association for Computing Machinery*, pages 67–73, New Orleans, LA, USA.

Nemanja Djuric, Jing Zhou, Robin Morris, Mihajlo Grbovic, Vladan Radosavljevic, and Narayan Bhamidipati. 2015. Hate Speech Detection with Comment Embeddings. In *Proceedings of the 24th International Conference on World Wide Web*, pages 29–30, Florence, Italy.

Sepp Hochreiter and Jürgen Schmidhuber. 1997. Long Short-Term Memory. *Neural Comput.*, 9(8):1735–1780.

Homa Hosseinmardi, Sabrina Arredondo Mattson, Rahat Ibn Rafiq, Richard Han, Qin Lv, and Shivakant Mishra. 2015. Detection of Cyberbullying Incidents on the Instagram Social Network. *CoRR*, abs/1503.03909.

Douwe Kiela, Hamed Firooz, Aravind Mohan, Vedanuj Goswami, Amanpreet Singh, Pratik Ringshia, and Davide Testuggine. 2020. The Hateful Memes Challenge: Detecting Hate Speech in Multimodal Memes. *CoRR*, abs/2005.04790.

Diederik P. Kingma and Jimmy Ba. 2015. ADAM: A Method for Stochastic Optimization. In *3rd International Conference on Learning Representations, ICLR 2015*, pages 1–15, San Diego, CA, USA.

Gao Lei and Huang Ruihong. 2017. Detecting Online Hate Speech Using Context Aware Models. In *Proceedings of the International Conference Recent Advances in Natural Language Processing, RANLP*, pages 260–266, Varna, Bulgaria.

Binny Mathew, Punyajoy Saha, Seid Muhie Yimam, Chris Biemann, Pawan Goyal, and Animesh Mukherjee. 2021. HateXplain: A Benchmark Dataset for Explainable Hate Speech Detection. *Proceedings of the AAAI Conference on Artificial Intelligence*, 35(17):14867–14875.

Chikashi Nobata, Joel Tetreault, Achint Thomas, Yashar Mehdad, and Yi Chang. 2016. Abusive Language Detection in Online User Content. In *Proceedings of the 25th International Conference on World Wide Web.*, pages 145–153, Montréal, QC, Canada.

John T. Nockleby, Leonard W. Levy, Kenneth L. Karst, and Dennis J. Mahoney editors. 2000. *Encyclopedia of the American Constitution.* Macmillan, 2nd edition.

Anna Schmidt and Michael Wiegand. 2017. A Survey on Hate Speech Detection using Natural Language Processing. In *Proceedings of the Fifth International Workshop on Natural Language Processing for Social Media*, pages 1–10, Valencia, Spain. Association for Computational Linguistics.

Leandro Silva, Mainack Mondal, Denzil Correa, Fabrício Benevenuto, and Ingmar Weber. 2021. Analyzing the targets of hate in online social media. In *Proceedings of the International AAAI Conference on Web and Social Media*, pages 687–690, Cologne, Germany.

Matthew L. Williams, Pete Burnap, Amir Javed, Han Liu, and Sefa Ozalp. 2020. Hate in the Machine: Anti-Black and Anti-Muslim Social Media Posts as Predictors of Offline Racially and Religiously Aggravated Crime. *The British Journal of Criminology*, 60(1):93–117.

Guang Xiang, Bin Fan, Ling Wang, Jason Hong, and Carolyn Rose. 2012. Detecting Offensive Tweets via Topical Feature Discovery over a Large Scale Twitter Corpus. In *Proceedings of the 21st ACM international conference on Information and knowledge management*, pages 1980–1984, Maui, HI, USA.

Jun-Ming Xu, Kwang-Sung Jun, Xiaojin Zhu, and Amy Bellmore. 2012. Learning from Bullying Traces in Social Media. In *Proceedings of the 2012 Conference of the North American Chapter of the Association for Computational Linguistics: Human Language Technologies*, pages 656–666, Montréal, QC, Canada. Association for Computational Linguistics.

Haoti Zhong, Hao Li, Anna Squicciarini, Sarah Rajtmajer, Christopher Griffin, David Miller, and Cornelia Caragea. 2016. Content-Driven Detection of Cyberbullying on the Instagram Social Network. In *Proceedings of the Twenty-Fifth International Joint Conference on Artificial Intelligence (IJCAI-16)*, IJCAI'16, pages 3952–3958, New York, NY, USA.

A Appendix

A.1 Hyperparameter values for experiments

All the models used the Adam optimizer (Kingma and Ba, 2015). Bi-LSTM and BoW used the cross-entropy loss function whereas our BERT models used the sparse categorical and cross-entropy loss function. Further values for the hyperparameters for each experiment are shown in Table 8.

A.1.1 Bi-LSTM

For all the models except for the model trained on the Twitter dataset, the architecture consists of an embedding layer followed by two Bi-LSTM layers stacked one after another. Finally, a Dense layer with a softmax activation function is giving the output class.

For training with Twitter (both in-domain and domain adaptation), a single Bi-LSTM layer is used.

A.1.2 BoW

The BoW model uses two hidden layers consisting of 100 neurons each.

A.1.3 BERT

BERT uses TFBertForSequenceClassification model and BertTokenizer as its tokenizer from the pretrained model bert-base-uncased.

A.2 Additional Performance Metrics for Experiments

We report precision, recall, F1-score and macro averaged F1-score for every experiment in Table 9.

Model	Train-Dataset	Test-Dataset	Learning Rate	Epochs	Batch Size
BoW	Fox News	Fox News	1e-03	8	32
BoW	Twitter	Twitter	1e-03	8	32
BoW	Fox News	Movies	1e-03	8	32
BoW	Twitter	Movies	1e-03	8	32
BoW	Movies	Movies	1e-03	8	32
BERT	Fox News	Fox News	3e-06	17	32
BERT	Twitter	Twitter	3e-06	4	32
BERT	Fox News	Movies	3e-06	17	32
BERT	Twitter	Movies	3e-06	4	32
BERT	Movies	Movies	3e-06	6	32
BERT	Fox News and Movies	Movies	3e-06	6	32
BERT	Twitter and Movies	Movies	3e-06	6	32
Bi-LSTM	Fox News	Fox News	1e-03	8	32
Bi-LSTM	Twitter	Twitter	1e-03	8	32
Bi-LSTM	Fox News	Movies	1e-03	8	32
Bi-LSTM	Twitter	Movies	1e-03	8	32
Bi-LSTM	Movies	Movies	1e-03	8	32

Table 8: Detailed setups of all applied experiments

Model	Train-Dataset	Test-Dataset	Category	Precision	Recall	F1-Score	Macro AVG F1
BoW	Fox News	Fox News	normal	0.81	0.84	0.83	0.63
BoW	Fox News	Fox News	hate	0.45	0.41	0.43	0.63
BoW	Twitter	Twitter	normal	0.79	0.78	0.78	0.66
BoW	Twitter	Twitter	offensive	0.90	0.95	0.93	0.66
BoW	Twitter	Twitter	hate	0.43	0.18	0.26	0.66
BoW	Fox News	Movies	normal	0.84	0.87	0.86	0.51
BoW	Fox News	Movies	hate	0.16	0.13	0.15	0.51
BoW	Twitter	Movies	normal	0.96	0.46	0.62	0.37
BoW	Twitter	Movies	offensive	0.20	0.82	0.32	0.37
BoW	Twitter	Movies	hate	0.11	0.24	0.15	0.37
BoW	Movies	Movies	normal	0.93	0.97	0.95	0.64
BoW	Movies	Movies	offensive	0.65	0.56	0.59	0.64
BoW	Movies	Movies	hate	0.56	0.28	0.37	0.64
BERT	Fox News	Fox News	normal	0.84	0.87	0.86	0.68
BERT	Fox News	Fox News	hate	0.57	0.46	0.51	0.68
BERT	Twitter	Twitter	normal	0.88	0.91	0.89	0.76
BERT	Twitter	Twitter	offensive	0.94	0.97	0.95	0.76
BERT	Twitter	Twitter	hate	0.59	0.34	0.43	0.76
BERT	Fox News	Movies	normal	0.88	0.90	0.89	0.64
BERT	Fox News	Movies	hate	0.40	0.37	0.39	0.64
BERT	Twitter	Movies	normal	0.98	0.92	0.95	0.77
BERT	Twitter	Movies	offensive	0.63	0.90	0.74	0.77
BERT	Twitter	Movies	hate	0.63	0.63	0.63	0.77
BERT	Movies	Movies	normal	0.97	0.98	0.97	0.81
BERT	Movies	Movies	offensive	0.80	0.76	0.78	0.81
BERT	Movies	Movies	hate	0.79	0.68	0.68	0.81
BERT	Fox News and Movies	Movies	normal	0.97	0.97	0.97	0.89
BERT	Fox News and Movies	Movies	hate	0.83	0.81	0.82	0.89
BERT	Twitter and Movies	Movies	normal	0.97	0.97	0.97	0.77
BERT	Twitter and Movies	Movies	offensive	0.76	0.76	0.75	0.77
BERT	Twitter and Movies	Movies	hate	0.57	0.73	0.59	0.77
Bi-LSTM	Fox News	Fox News	normal	0.83	0.72	0.77	0.62
Bi-LSTM	Fox News	Fox News	hate	0.39	0.55	0.46	0.62
Bi-LSTM	Twitter	Twitter	normal	0.74	0.78	0.76	0.66
Bi-LSTM	Twitter	Twitter	offensive	0.91	0.91	0.91	0.66
Bi-LSTM	Twitter	Twitter	hate	0.31	0.31	0.31	0.66
Bi-LSTM	Fox News	Movies	normal	0.85	0.81	0.83	0.51
Bi-LSTM	Fox News	Movies	hate	0.17	0.20	0.18	0.51
Bi-LSTM	Twitter	Movies	normal	0.96	0.50	0.66	0.38
Bi-LSTM	Twitter	Movies	offensive	0.22	0.79	0.34	0.38
Bi-LSTM	Twitter	Movies	hate	0.10	0.33	0.16	0.38
Bi-LSTM	Movies	Movies	normal	0.94	0.97	0.95	0.71
Bi-LSTM	Movies	Movies	offensive	0.67	0.60	0.63	0.71
Bi-LSTM	Movies	Movies	hate	0.73	0.49	0.56	0.71
HateXplain	-	Movies	normal	0.88	0.98	0.93	0.66
HateXplain	-	Movies	offensive	0.62	0.17	0.27	0.66
HateXplain	-	Movies	hate	0.89	0.68	0.77	0.66

Table 9: Detailed results of all applied experiments

Emotion Recognition under Consideration of the Emotion Component Process Model

Felix Casel[*]**, Amelie Heindl**[*]**, and Roman Klinger**
Institut für Maschinelle Sprachverarbeitung, University of Stuttgart
Pfaffenwaldring 5b, 70569 Stuttgart, Germany
{firstname.lastname}@ims.uni-stuttgart.de

Abstract

Emotion classification in text is typically performed with neural network models which learn to associate linguistic units with emotions. While this often leads to good predictive performance, it does only help to a limited degree to understand how emotions are communicated in various domains. The emotion component process model (CPM) by Scherer (2005) is an interesting approach to explain emotion communication. It states that emotions are a coordinated process of various subcomponents, in reaction to an event, namely the subjective feeling, the cognitive appraisal, the expression, a physiological bodily reaction, and a motivational action tendency. We hypothesize that these components are associated with linguistic realizations: an emotion can be expressed by describing a physiological bodily reaction ("he was trembling"), or the expression ("she smiled"), etc. We annotate existing literature and Twitter emotion corpora with emotion component classes and find that emotions on Twitter are predominantly expressed by event descriptions or subjective reports of the feeling, while in literature, authors prefer to describe what characters do, and leave the interpretation to the reader. We further include the CPM in a multitask learning model and find that this supports the emotion categorization. The annotated corpora are available at `https://www.ims.uni-stuttgart.de/data/emotion`.

1 Introduction

The task of emotion classification from written text is to map textual units, like documents, paragraphs, or sentences, to a predefined set of emotions. Common class inventories rely on psychological theories such as those proposed by Ekman (1992) (*anger*, *disgust*, *fear*, *joy*, *sadness*, *surprise*) or Plutchik (2001). Often, emotion classification is tackled as an end-to-end learning task, potentially informed by lexical resources (see the SemEval Shared Task 1 on Affect in Tweets for an overview of recent approaches (Mohammad et al., 2018)).

While end-to-end learning and fine-tuning of pretrained models for classification have shown great performance improvements in contrast to purely feature-based methods, such approaches typically neglect the existing knowledge about emotions in psychology (which might help in classification and to better understand how emotions are communicated). There are only very few approaches that aim at combining psychological theories (beyond basic emotion categories) with emotion classification models: We are only aware of the work by Hofmann et al. (2020), who incorporate the cognitive appraisal of events, and Buechel et al. (2020), who jointly learn affect (valence, arousal) and emotion classes; next to knowledge-base-oriented modelling of events by Balahur et al. (2012) and Cambria et al. (2014).

An interesting and attractive theory for computational modelling of emotions that has not been used in natural language processing yet is the emotion component process model (Scherer, 2005, CPM). This model states that emotions are a coordinated process in five subsystems, following an event that is relevant for the experiencer of the emotion, namely a *motivational action tendency*, the *motor expression* component, a *neurophysiological, bodily symptom*, the *subjective feeling*, and the *cognitive appraisal*. The cognitive appraisal has been explored in a fine-grained manner by Hofmann et al. (2020), mentioned above. The subjective feeling component is related to the dimensions of affect.[1]

[*]The first two authors contributed equally to this work.

[1]There exists other work that has been motivated by appraisal theories, but that is either rule-based (Shaikh et al., 2009; Udochukwu and He, 2015) or does not explicitly model appraisal or component dimensions (Balahur et al., 2012;

We hypothesize (and subsequently analyze) that emotions in text are communicated in a variety of ways, and that these different stylistic means follow the emotion component process model. The communication of emotions can either be an explicit mention of the emotion name ("I am angry"), focus on the motivational aspect ("He wanted to run away."), describe the expression ("She smiled.", "He shouted.") or a physiological bodily reaction ("she was trembling", "a tear was running down his face"), the subjective feeling ("I felt so bad."), or, finally, describe a cognitive appraisal ("I wasn't sure what was happening.", "I am not responsible.").

With this paper, we study how emotions are communicated (following the component model) in Tweets (based on the Twitter Emotion Corpus TEC, by Mohammad (2012)) and literature (based on the REMAN corpus by Kim and Klinger (2018)). We post-annotate a subset of 3041 instances with the use of emotion component-based emotion communication categories, analyze this corpus, and perform joint modelling/multi-task learning experiments. Our research goals are (1) to understand if emotion components are distributed similarly across emotion categories and domains, and (2) to evaluate if informing an emotion classifier about emotion components improves their performance (and to evaluate various classification approaches). We find that emotion component and emotion classification prediction interact and benefit from each other and that emotions are communicated by means of various components in literature and social media. The corpus is available at `https://www.ims.uni-stuttgart.de/data/emotion`.

2 Background and Related Work

2.1 Emotion Models

Emotion models can be separated into those that consider a discrete set of categories or those that focus on underlying principles like affect. The model of basic emotions by Ekman (1992) considers anger, disgust, fear, joy, sadness, and surprise. According to his work, there are nine characteristics that a basic emotion fulfills: These are (1) distinctive universal signals, (2) presence in other primates, (3) distinctive physiology, (4) distinctive universals in antecedent events, (5) coherence among emotional response, (6) quick onset, (7) brief duration, (8) automatic appraisal, and (9) unbidden occurrence. His model of the six universal emotions constitutes one of the most popular emotion sets in natural language processing. Yet it might be doubted if this set is sufficient. Plutchik (2001) proposed a model with eight main emotions, visualized on a colored wheel. In this visualization, opposites and distance of emotion names are supposed to correspond to their respective relation.

Rashkin et al., 2018).

A complementary approach to categorizing emotions in discrete sets is advocated by Russell and Mehrabian (1977). Their dimensional affect model corresponds to a 3-dimensional vector space with dimensions for pleasure-displeasure, the degree of arousal, and dominance-submissiveness (VAD). Emotion categories correspond to points in this vector space. A more expressive alternative to the VAD model of affect is motivated by the cognitive appraisal process that is part of emotions. The model of Smith and Ellsworth (1985) introduces a set of variables that they map to the principle components of pleasantness, responsibility/control, certainty, attention, effort, and situational control. They show that these dimensions are more powerful to distinguish emotion categories than VAD.

Appraisals are also part of the emotion component process model by Scherer (2005), which is central to this paper. The five components are *cognitive appraisal*, *neurophysiological bodily symptoms*, *motor expressions*, *motivational action tendencies*, and *subjective feelings*. *Cognitive appraisal* is concerned with the evaluation of an event. The event is assessed regarding its relevance to the individual, the implications and consequences it might lead to, the possible ways to cope with it and control it, and its significance according to personal values and social norms. The component of *neurophysiological symptoms* regards automatically activated reactions and symptoms of the body, like changes in the heartbeat or breathing pattern. The *motor expression* component contains all movements, facial expressions, changes concerning the speech, and similar patterns. Actions like attention shifts and movement with respect to the position of the event are part of the *motivational action tendencies* component. Finally, the component of *subjective feelings* takes into account how strong, important, and persisting the felt sensations are. Scherer (2005) argues that it is possible to infer the emotion a person is experiencing by analyzing the set of changes in the five components. Scherer (2009) also points out that computational models must not ignore emotion components.

2.2 Emotion Analysis in Text

The majority of modelling approaches focuses on the analysis of fundamental emotions (see Alswaidan and Menai, 2020; Mohammad et al., 2018; Bostan and Klinger, 2018) or on the recognition of valence, arousal, and dominance (Buechel and Hahn, 2017). Work with a focus on other aspects of emotions is scarce.

Noteworthy, though this has not been a computational study, is the motivation of the ISEAR project (Scherer and Wallbott, 1994), from which a textual corpus originated, which is frequently used in NLP. It consists of event descriptions and is therefore relevant for appraisal theories. Further, participants in that study have not only been asked to report on events they experienced, but they also report additional aspects, including the existence of bodily reactions. However, their work does not focus on the *linguistic realization* of emotion components, but on the *existence* in the described event.

Similarly, Troiano et al. (2019) asked crowdworkers to report on events that caused an emotion. This resource has then been postannotated with appraisal dimensions (Hofmann et al., 2020). This is the only recent work we are aware of that models appraisal as a component of the CPM to predict emotion categories, next to the rule-based classification approach by Shaikh et al. (2009), who built on top of the work by Clore and Ortony (2013). Another noteworthy related work is SenticNet, which models event properties including people's goals, for sentiment analysis (Cambria et al., 2014).

The only work we are aware of that studies emotion components (though not following the CPM, and without computational modelling), is the corpus study by Kim and Klinger (2019). They analyze if emotions in fan fiction are communicated via facial descriptions, body posture descriptions, the appearance, look, voice, gestures, subjective sensations, or spatial relations of characters. This set of variables is not the same as emotion components, however, it is related. They find that some emotions are preferred to be described with particular aspects by authors. Their work was motivated by the linguistic study of van Meel (1995).

In contrast to their work, our study compares two different domains (Tweets and Literature), and follows the emotion component process model more strictly. Further, we show the use of that model for computational emotion classification through multi-task learning.

3 Corpus Annotation

3.1 Corpus Selection

To study the relation between emotion components and emotions, we annotate subsets from two different existing emotion corpora from two different domains, namely literature and social media.

For literature, we use the REMAN corpus (Kim and Klinger, 2018), which consists of fiction written after the year 1800. It is manually annotated with text spans related to emotions, as well as their experiencers, causes, and targets. Emotion cue spans are annotated with the emotions of anger, fear, trust, disgust, joy, sadness, surprise, and anticipation, as well as 'other emotion'. From the 1720 instances, we randomly sample a subset of 1000. Each instance comprises a sentence triple and may contain any number of annotated spans. We map the emotions associated to spans to the text instances as the union of all labels, which leads to a multi-label classification task. Instances without emotion annotations are considered 'neutral'.

For the social media domain, we choose the Twitter Emotion Corpus (TEC) (Mohammad, 2012). The emotion categories are anger, disgust, fear, joy, sadness, and surprise. TEC consists of approximately 21,000 posts from Twitter that have a hashtag at the end which states one of the six mentioned emotions. According to the authors, the validity of hashtags as classification labels is commensurable to the inter-annotator agreements of human annotators. We randomly sample 2041 instances with the emotion hashtags as labels for the creation of our corpus. Each instance equals one post and has exactly one emotion label.

3.2 Annotation Procedure and Inter-Annotator Agreement

We annotate the emotion component dimensions independently: The existence of a CPM label means that this component is mentioned somewhere in the text, independent of its function to communicate one of the emotions. This is a simplification due to the fact that it turned out to be difficult to infer from the limited context of an instance if an emotion category and an emotion component mention are actually in relation. Further, this procedure also ensures that there is no information leak introduced in the annotation process (e.g., that components are only annotated if they indeed inform the emotion, and that a model could learn from its sheer presence).

Component	Explanation of Example	Example
Cognitive appraisal	evaluation of the pleasantness of an event.	Thinks that @melbahughes had a great 50th birthday party
Neurophysiol. symptoms	change in someone's heartbeat.	Loves when a song makes your heart race [...]
Motiv. Action tendencies	urge to attack a person or object.	sometimes when i think bout you i want to beat the shit out of your face so everyone can see how ugly you are inside and out
Motor expressions	facial expression.	@TheBodyShopUK when I walk in the room and my 9month old nephew recognises me and his face lights up with the biggest smile thats 100%
Subjective feelings	internal feeling state.	Feelin a bit sad tonight

Table 1: Excerpt of the final annotation guidelines including examples from TEC.

Component	round 1	round 2
Cognitive appraisal	0.288	0.777
Neurophysiological symptoms	0.459	–
Motiv. Action tendencies	0.444	0.732
Motor expressions	0.643	0.617
Subjective feelings	0.733	0.793

Table 2: Inter-annotator agreement after the different annotation rounds during the guideline creation process measured with Cohen's κ. In the second round, no annotator detected the neurophysiological component in the sample instances.

We refined the annotation guidelines in an iterative process with two annotators. Annotator 1 is a 23 year-old female undergraduate computer science student, Annotator 2 is a 28 year-old male graduate student of computational linguistics. We first defined a list of guidelines for each emotion component, then let each annotator label 40 randomly sampled instances (20 each in two iterations) out of each corpus and measured the inter-annotator agreement. Based on instances with disagreement, we refined the guidelines. The achieved inter-annotator agreement scores are displayed in Table 2. We observe that particularly the concepts of cognitive appraisal and motivational action tendencies have been clarified. During this process, for example, the discussion of the instance *"He did so, and to his surprise, found that all the bank stock had been sold, and transferred"* lead to the addition of a rule stating that the explicit mention of a feeling has to be annotated with subjective feeling. A rule for the annotation of tiredness as neurophysiological symptoms was created due to the instance *"Here he remained the whole night, feeling very tired and sorrowful."*. Concerning the annotation of verbal communication as motor expression, we decided to only annotate instances with verbal communications that address an emotional reaction or instances with interjections as for example 'oh' or 'wow'. With this clarification, the instance *"'Jolly rum thing about that boat,' said the spokesman of the party, as the boys continued their walk. 'I expect it got adrift somehow,' said another. 'I don't know,' said the first."* should not be annotated, whereas *"'Sounds delightful.' 'Oh, it was actually pretty cool.'"* should (this aspect has particularly appeared in the second annotator training round, which lead to a slight decrease in agreement). We make the annotation guidelines available together with our corpus. Table 1 shows a short excerpt.

After the refinement process concluded, Annotator 1 annotated the subsample of TEC and Annotator 2 annotated the subsample of REMAN.

3.3 Corpus Statistics

We show corpus statistics in Table 3 to develop an understanding how emotions are communicated in the two domains. For both corpora, we observe that cognitive appraisal is most frequent. In TEC, the second most dominant component is subjective feeling, while in REMAN it is the motor expression. The amount of subjective feeling descriptions is substantially lower for literature than for social media – which is in line with the show-don't-tell paradigm which is obviously not followed in social media as it is in literature.

Components are not distributed equally across emotions. Particularly noteworthy is the co-occurrence of disgust with neurophysiological symptoms in social media, but not in literature where this component dominates the emotion of fear. We also observe a particularly high co-occurrence of the subjective feeling component with fear for social media, which is not the case for literature. In literature, the motivational action tendency component co-occurs with anger (and anticipation) more frequently than with all other emotions. This is not the case for the social media do-

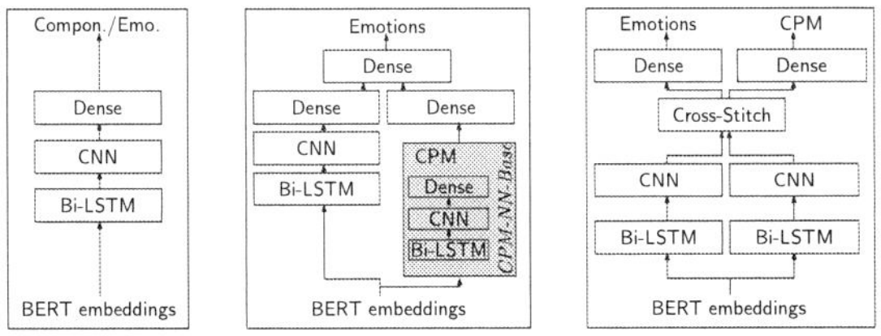

(a) *Emo/CPM-NN-Base* (b) *Emo-Cpm-NN-Pred* (c) *MTL-XS*

Figure 1: Neural Model Architectures (subset)

main. On the REMAN corpus, components occur least frequently when there is no emotion across all components. For both corpora, neurophysiological symptoms make up the smallest share of components, even more so in the case of TEC than REMAN.

In a comparison of social media and literature, we observe that emotions are distributed more uniformly in literature. The relative number of co-occurrences of CPM components with emotions varies more for REMAN than for the TEC corpus.

4 Methods

We will now turn to the computational modelling of emotion components and evaluate their usefulness for emotion classification. We evaluate a set of different feature-based and deep-learning based classification approaches to join the tasks of emotion classification and component classification.

4.1 Emotion Classifier

As baseline emotion classification models which are not particularly informed about components, we use two models: ***Emo-ME-Base*** is a maximum entropy (ME) classifier with TF-IDF-weighted bag-of-words unigram and bigram features. As preprocessing, we convert all words to lowercase, and stem them with the PorterStemmer. On TEC, with its single-label annotation, *Emo-ME-Base* consists of one model, while on REMAN with multi-label annotation, we use 10 binary classifiers.

Our neural baseline ***Emo-NN-Base*** uses pretrained BERT sentence embeddings[2] (Devlin et al., 2019) as input features. Inspired by Chen and Wang (2018); Sosa (2017), the network architecture consists of a bidirectional LSTM layer (Hochreiter and Schmidhuber, 1997), followed by a convolutional layer with kernel sizes 2, 3, 5, 7, 13, and 25. The outputs of the convolutional layer are max-pooled over the dimension of the input sequence, inspired by Collobert et al. (2011). Stacked on top of the pooling layer is a fully connected layer. Its outputs are finally fed into an output layer with a sigmoid activation function (see Figure 1a).[3]

We use dropout regularization after each layer. The network uses a weighted cross-entropy loss function, whereby the loss of false negatives is multiplied by 4 to increase recall. The model is trained using an Adam optimizer (Kingma and Ba, 2015). All network parameters of this model and subsequent neural models are determined using a subset of the training data as development set for the REMAN corpus and using 10-fold cross-validation for the TEC corpus. Details of the resulting hyperparameters are listed in the Appendix.

4.2 Component Classifier

The emotion component classifiers predict which of the five CPM components occur in a text instance. Our ***Cpm-ME-Base*** baseline models (one for each component) only use bag-of-words features in the same configuration as *Emo-ME-Base*.

In the model ***Cpm-ME-Adv***, we add task-specific features, namely features derived from manually crafted small dictionaries with words associated with the different components. Those dictionaries were developed without considering the corpora and with inspiration from Scherer (2005) and contain on average 26 items. Further, we add part-of-speech tags (calculated with spaCy[4], Honnibal et al. (2020)) and glove-twitter-100 embeddings[5] (Pennington et al., 2014). Additionally, only for the cognitive appraisal component, we run the appraisal classifier developed by Hofmann et al. (2020) and use the predictions as features.[6] For each component individually, the best-performing combination of these features is chosen.

The ***Cpm-NN-Base*** is configured analogously to *Emo-NN-Base*. The primary reason for using an equivalent setup is to facilitate a multi-head architecture as joint model for both tasks in the next step.

[2] https://tfhub.dev/google/experts/bert/wiki_books/sst2/1

[3] We selected this architecture based on preliminary experiments on the validation data. We evaluated it against LSTM-Dense Layer and CNN-LSTM architectures.

[4] https://spacy.io/usage/linguistic-features#pos-tagging

[5] https://nlp.stanford.edu/projects/glove/

[6] http://www.ims.uni-stuttgart.de/data/appraisalemotion

	Emotion	Cognitive		Phys.		Motiv. Action		Motor Exp.		Subject.		Total
TEC	Anger	127	(75%)	8	(5%)	30	(18%)	20	(12%)	49	(29%)	169
	Disgust	65	(83%)	11	(14%)	6	(8%)	17	(22%)	19	(24%)	78
	Joy	606	(71%)	59	(7%)	176	(21%)	95	(11%)	233	(27%)	848
	Sadness	323	(87%)	13	(3%)	58	(16%)	53	(14%)	142	(38%)	373
	Fear	196	(74%)	9	(3%)	37	(14%)	27	(10%)	130	(49%)	266
	Surprise	219	(71%)	2	(1%)	55	(18%)	55	(18%)	83	(27%)	307
	Total.	1536	(75%)	102	(5%)	362	(18%)	267	(13%)	656	(32%)	
REMAN	Anger	66	(67%)	7	(7%)	40	(41%)	61	(62%)	25	(26%)	98
	Anticip.	69	(59%)	6	(5%)	50	(43%)	63	(54%)	19	(16%)	117
	Disgust	81	(86%)	5	(5%)	21	(22%)	33	(35%)	16	(17%)	94
	Fear	96	(67%)	33	(23%)	35	(24%)	70	(49%)	34	(24%)	143
	Joy	121	(57%)	11	(5%)	28	(13%)	117	(55%)	66	(31%)	213
	Neutral	39	(34%)	0	(0%)	13	(11%)	22	(19%)	3	(3%)	116
	Other	64	(57%)	11	(10%)	21	(19%)	53	(47%)	21	(19%)	113
	Sadness	94	(69%)	19	(14%)	22	(16%)	66	(49%)	42	(31%)	136
	Surprise	103	(74%)	11	(8%)	21	(15%)	83	(60%)	22	(16%)	139
	Trust	94	(82%)	2	(2%)	17	(15%)	34	(30%)	27	(23%)	115
	Total	610	(61%)	76	(8%)	190	(19%)	440	(44%)	174	(17%)	

Table 3: Total/relative counts of CPM components and emotions in our reannoted TEC and REMAN subsamples. Note that the CPM categorization is a multi-label task, with 1000 instances in REMAN and 2041 instances reannotated in TEC.

4.3 Joint Modelling and Multi-Task Learning of Emotions and Components

To analyze if emotion classification benefits from the component prediction (and partially also vice versa), we set up several model configurations.

In ***Emo-Cpm-ME-Pred***, we predict the emotion with *Cpm-ME-Adv* and use these predictions as features. Other than that, *Emo-Cpm-ME-Pred* corresponds to *Emo-ME-Base*. In ***Emo-Cpm-ME-Gold***, we replace the predictions by gold component annotations to analyze error propagation.

Emo-Cpm-NN-Pred and ***Emo-Cpm-NN-Gold*** are configured analogously and follow the same architecture as *Emo-NN-Base* with the following differences: A binary vector with the CPM annotations is introduced as additional input feature, feeding into a fully connected layer. Its outputs are concatenated with the outputs of the penultimate layer and passed to another fully connected layer, followed by the output layer.

Emo-Cpm-NN-Pred uses *Cpm-NN-Base* to obtain component predictions, but the weights of *Cpm-NN-Base* are frozen. The basic network architecture resembles that of the *Emo-Cpm-NN-Gold* model, replacing the additional CPM input vector with the *Cpm-NN-Base* model (see Figure 1b). Its outputs are, again, fed into a fully connected layer which is connected to the output layer.

Next to the models that make use of the output of the CPM classifiers for prediction, we use two multi-task learning models which predict emotions and components based on shared latent variables. For a multi-head variant (***MTL-MH***), the basic architectures of the individual models for both tasks remain the same. Outputs of the CNN layer are fed to two separate, task-specific, fully connected layers. This model has two output layers, one for emotion classification and one for CPM component classification. Both tasks use the weighted cross entropy loss function to increase recall.

Based on the model proposed by Misra et al. (2016), we use cross-stitch units in our model ***MTL-XS***. This model employs two separate parallel instances of the *Cpm-NN-Base* architecture introduced above, one for the CPM classification task and one for emotion classification. The model additionally employs one cross-stitch unit after the respective CNN layers. This sharing unit learns a linear combination of the pooled task-specific CNN activation maps which is then passed to the task-specific fully connected layers. The cross-stitch unit learns during training which information to share across tasks (see Figure 1c).

5 Results

For our experiments, we use our reannotated subsample of TEC and REMAN (not all instances available in TEC and REMAN). We split the corpora into 90% for training and 10% to test.

		Cpm-ME-Base			*Cpm-ME-Adv*			*Cpm-NN-Base*			*MTL-XS*			*MTL-MH*		
	Component	P	R	F_1	P	R	F_1	P	R	F_1	P	R	F_1	P	R	F_1
REMAN	Cognitive appraisal	60	98	**75**	60	98	**75**	60	98	**75**	60	98	**75**	59	96	73
	Neurophysiological symp.	50	20	29	50	40	**44**	20	20	20	25	20	22	0	0	0
	Motiv. action tendencies	36	47	41	46	68	**55**	42	26	32	29	42	34	25	68	36
	Motor expressions	67	56	61	76	65	**70**	92	53	68	76	60	68	81	60	69
	Subjective feelings	38	32	34	45	53	49	58	37	45	48	53	**50**	35	32	33
	Macro avg.	50	51	48	56	65	**59**	54	47	48	48	55	50	40	51	42
	Micro avg.			61			**67**			63			63			57
TEC	Cognitive appraisal	72	99	84	76	98	**86**	76	88	81	77	90	83	75	91	82
	Neurophysiological sympt.	17	17	17	15	33	21	25	17	20	17	17	17	100	17	**29**
	Motiv. action tendencies	42	57	48	50	74	**60**	46	51	49	48	57	52	45	54	49
	Motor expressions	47	52	49	41	61	49	55	58	**56**	50	48	49	62	32	43
	Subjective feelings	63	70	66	63	70	66	74	81	**77**	61	81	69	57	80	67
	Macro avg.	48	59	53	49	67	56	55	59	**57**	51	59	54	68	55	54
	Micro avg.			70			71			**73**			71			70

Table 4: Performance of the emotion component detection models (multiplied by 100).

5.1 Component Prediction

We start the discussion of the results with the component classification, a classification task that has not been addressed before and for which our data set is the first that becomes available to the research community. Table 4 shows the results.

The model performances are acceptable. Macro-average F_1 scores on REMAN range from .42 of *MTL-MH* to .59 for *Cpm-ME-Adv*, and from .53 (*Cpm-ME-Base*) to .57 (*Cpm-NN-Base*) on TEC. There are, however, differences for the components: On TEC, there are difficulties in predicting neurophysiological symptoms. The addition of task-specific features in *Cpm-ME-Adv* shows a clear improvement across all components.

The neural baseline *Cpm-NN-Base* outperforms *Cpm-ME-Adv* on TEC, and does so without feature engineering. On REMAN, the feature-based model is superior which might be due to the engineered features being more commonly represented in the literature domain than in social media. This is partially leveraged in the *MTL-XS* model on REMAN.

The components are not equally difficult to predict; the relations between the components are comparable across models. The lowest performance scores are observed for neurophysiological symptoms. This holds across models and corpora. For the neurophysiological component on the literature domain, however, the engineered features in *Cpm-ME-Adv* show substantial improvement, yielding an F_1 score of 0.44. Cognitive appraisal shows best prediction performances, with F_1 between .73 and .86. For TEC, we observe a correlation between performance and class size for all components.

For REMAN, *Cpm-ME-Adv* is the best-performing model. *Cpm-ME-Adv*'s macro average F_1 of 0.59 is 9pp higher than the second best F_1-score. For TEC, the best results are achieved by *Cpm-NN-Base* with a macro F_1 of 0.57.

5.2 Emotion Classification

In this section, we discuss the performance of our emotion classification models across different configurations. One question is how providing component information to them helps most. Table 5 shows the results for all experiments.

The comparison of *Emo-ME-Base* and *Emo-NN-Base* reveals that a pure word-based model is not able to categorize emotions in REMAN, due to the imbalancedness in this multilabel classification setup. This observation is in line with previous results (Kim and Klinger, 2018). The use of BERT's contextualized sentence embeddings leads to a strong improvement of 43pp (against a 0 F_1 for *Emo-ME-Base*). The performance of the ME models is comparably limited also on TEC, though this is less obvious on the micro-averaged F_1 due to the imbalancedness of the resource (.35 macro, .54 micro F_1).

Our main research question is if emotion components help emotion classification. In our first attempt to include this information as features, we see some improvement. On REMAN, *Emo-Cpm-ME-Pred* "boosts" from 0 to 6 F_1, on TEC we

	Model	Anger	Anticip	Disgust	Fear	Joy	Neutral	Other	Sadness	Surpr.	Trust	Macavg.	Micavg.
REMAN	*Emo-ME-Base*	0	0	0	0	0	0	0	0	0	0	0	0
	Emo-Cpm-ME-Gold	18	0	0	25	16	62	0	0	0	0	12	14
	Emo-Cpm-ME-Pred	0	0	0	12	15	0	0	0	0	14	4	6
	Emo-NN-Base	36	18	29	41	59	46	14	36	**71**	50	40	43
	Emo-Cpm-NN-Gold	56	22	28	37	68	71	15	39	50	60	45	45
	Emo-Cpm-NN-Pred	32	0	**33**	34	**71**	40	17	**52**	58	42	38	43
	MTL-MH	35	16	24	39	62	49	22	48	67	**56**	42	42
	MTL-XS	**38**	**24**	26	**47**	64	**54**	**37**	48	64	55	**46**	**47**
TEC	*Emo-ME-Base*	11		0	53	64			43	38		35	54
	Emo-Cpm-ME-Gold	11		0	59	66			40	43		36	55
	Emo-Cpm-ME-Pred	11		0	59	67			43	43		37	55
	Emo-NN-Base	**41**		44	56	69			51	39		50	57
	Emo-Cpm-NN-Gold	52		33	67	72			60	47		55	62
	Emo-Cpm-NN-Pred	32		0	59	70			53	44		43	56
	MTL-MH	17		**57**	53	**76**			53	**45**		50	58
	MTL-XS	34		50	**60**	73			**57**	44		**53**	**61**

Table 5: F_1 (/100) results across models and emotion categories. (empty cells denote that this category is not available in the respective corpus. The best scores (except the gold setting) are printed bold face.

observe an improvement by 1pp, to .55 F_1. The inclusion of predicted component information as features in the neural network model shows no improvement on REMAN or on TEC.

To answer the question if this limited improvement is only due to a limited performance of the component classification model, we compare these results to a setting, in which the predicted values are replaced by gold labels from the annotation. This setup does show an improvement with *Emo-Cpm-ME-Gold* to .14 F_1 on REMAN, which is obviously still very low; and no improvement on TEC. However, with our neural model *Emo-Cpm-NN-Gold*, we see the potential of gold information increasing the score for emotion classification to .45 F_1 on REMAN and .62 F_1 on TEC.

This is an unrealistic setting – the classifier does not have access to annotated labels in real world applications. However, in the (realistic) cross-stitch multi-task learning setting of *MTL-XS*, we observe further improvements: On REMAN, we achieve .47 F_1 (which is even slightly higher than with gold component labels), which constitutes an achieved improvement by 4pp to the emotion classifier which is not informed about components. On TEC, we achieve .61 F_1, which is close to the model that has access to gold components (.62). This is an improvement of 4pp as well in comparison to the model that has no access to components but follows the same architecture.

Particularly, we observe that models with component information perform better across all emotions, with the exception of surprise on the REMAN corpus and anger on the TEC corpus. We can therefore conclude that emotion component information does contribute to emotion classification; the best-performing combination is via a cross-stitch model.

A detailed discussion based on example predictions of the various models is available in the Appendix.

6 Conclusion and Future Work

We presented the first data sets (based on existing emotion corpora) with emotion component annotation. While Hofmann et al. (2020) has proposed to use the cognitive appraisal for emotion classification, they did not succeed to present models that actually benefit in emotion classification performance. That might be due to the fact that cognitive appraisal classification itself is challenging, and that they did not compare multiple multi-task learning approaches.

With this paper we moved to another psychological theory, namely the emotion component process model, and make the first annotations available that closely follow this theory. Based on this resource, we have shown that, even with a comparably limited data set size, emotion components contribute to emotion classification. We expect that with a larger corpus the improvement would be more substantial than it is already now. A manual introspection of the data instances also shows that the components indeed help. Further, we have seen that emotions are communicated quite differently in the two domains, which is an explanation why emotion classification systems (up-to-today) need to be developed particularly for domains of interest. We propose that future work analyzes further which information is relevant and should be shared across these tasks in multi-task learning models.

Further, we propose that larger corpora should be created across more domains, and also that multitask learning is not only performed individually, but also across corpora. Presumably, the component information in different domains is not the same, but might be helpful across them.

Acknowledgments

This work was supported by Deutsche Forschungsgemeinschaft (project CEAT, KL 2869/1-2).

Ethical Considerations

We did not collect a new data set from individuals, but did reannotate existing and publicly available resources. Therefore, this paper does not pose ethical questions regarding data collection.

However, emotion analysis has the principled potential to be misused, and researchers need to be aware that their findings (though they are not in themselves harmful) might lead to software that can do harm. We assume that sentiment and emotion analysis are sufficiently well-known that users of social media might be aware that their data could be automatically analyzed. However, we propose that no automatic system ever does report back analyses of individuals and instead does aggregate data of anonymized posts. We do not assume that analyzing literature data poses any risk.

One aspect of our work we would like to point out is that, in contrast to other and previous emotion analysis research, we focus and enable particularly the analysis of implicit (and perhaps even unconcious) communication of emotions. That might further mean that authors of posts in social media are not aware that their emotional state could be computationally analyzed, potentially, they are not even fully aware of their own affective state. We would like to point out that automatically analyzing social media data without the explicit consent of the users is unethical at least when the user can be identified or identify themselves, particularly if they might not be aware of the details of an analysis system.

References

Nourah Alswaidan and Mohamed Menai. 2020. A survey of state-of-the-art approaches for emotion recognition in text. *Knowledge and Information Systems*, 62:2937–2987.

Alexandra Balahur, Jesus M. Hermida, and Andrew Montoyo. 2012. Building and exploiting emotinet, a knowledge base for emotion detection based on the appraisal theory model. *IEEE Transactions on Affective Computing*, 3(1):88–101.

Laura-Ana-Maria Bostan and Roman Klinger. 2018. An analysis of annotated corpora for emotion classification in text. In *Proceedings of the 27th International Conference on Computational Linguistics*, pages 2104–2119, Santa Fe, New Mexico, USA. Association for Computational Linguistics.

Sven Buechel and Udo Hahn. 2017. EmoBank: Studying the impact of annotation perspective and representation format on dimensional emotion analysis. In *Proceedings of the 15th Conference of the European Chapter of the Association for Computational Linguistics: Volume 2, Short Papers*, pages 578–585, Valencia, Spain. Association for Computational Linguistics.

Sven Buechel, Luise Modersohn, and Udo Hahn. 2020. Towards a unified framework for emotion analysis.

Erik Cambria, Daniel Olsher, and Dheeraj Rajagopal. 2014. Senticnet 3: A common and common-sense knowledge base for cognition-driven sentiment analysis. In *Proceedings of the AAAI*.

Nan Chen and Peikang Wang. 2018. Advanced combined LSTM-CNN model for Twitter sentiment analysis. In *2018 5th IEEE International Conference on Cloud Computing and Intelligence Systems (CCIS)*, pages 684–687.

Gerald L. Clore and Andrew Ortony. 2013. Psychological construction in the OCC model of emotion. *Emotion Review*, 5(4):335–343.

Ronan Collobert, Jason Weston, Léon Bottou, Michael Karlen, Koray Kavukcuoglu, and Pavel Kuksa. 2011. Natural language processing (almost) from scratch. *Journal of machine learning research*, 12:2493–2537.

Jacob Devlin, Ming-Wei Chang, Kenton Lee, and Kristina Toutanova. 2019. BERT: Pre-training of deep bidirectional transformers for language understanding. In *Proceedings of the 2019 Conference of the North American Chapter of the Association for Computational Linguistics: Human Language Technologies, Volume 1 (Long and Short Papers)*, pages 4171–4186, Minneapolis, Minnesota. Association for Computational Linguistics.

Paul Ekman. 1992. An argument for basic emotions. *Cognition & emotion*, 6(3-4):169–200.

Sepp Hochreiter and Jürgen Schmidhuber. 1997. Long short-term memory. *Neural Computation*, 9(8):1735–1780.

Jan Hofmann, Enrica Troiano, Kai Sassenberg, and Roman Klinger. 2020. Appraisal theories for emotion classification in text. In *Proceedings of the 28th International Conference on Computational Linguistics*, pages 125–138, Barcelona, Spain (Online). International Committee on Computational Linguistics.

Matthew Honnibal, Ines Montani, Sofie Van Landeghem, and Adriane Boyd. 2020. spaCy: Industrial-strength Natural Language Processing in Python.

Evgeny Kim and Roman Klinger. 2018. Who feels what and why? annotation of a literature corpus with semantic roles of emotions. In *Proceedings of the 27th International Conference on Computational Linguistics*, pages 1345–1359. Association for Computational Linguistics.

Evgeny Kim and Roman Klinger. 2019. An analysis of emotion communication channels in fan-fiction: Towards emotional storytelling. In *Proceedings of the Second Workshop on Storytelling*, pages 56–64, Florence, Italy. Association for Computational Linguistics.

Diederik P. Kingma and Jimmy Ba. 2015. Adam: A method for stochastic optimization. In *International Conference on Learning Representations (ICLR Poster)*.

Jacques M. van Meel. 1995. Representing emotions in literature and paintings: A comparative analysis. *Poetics*, 23(1):159 – 176. Emotions and Cultural Products.

Ishan Misra, Abhinav Shrivastava, Abhinav Gupta, and Martial Hebert. 2016. Cross-stitch networks for multi-task learning. In *Proceedings of the IEEE Conference on Computer Vision and Pattern Recognition*, pages 3994–4003.

Saif Mohammad. 2012. #emotional tweets. In **SEM 2012: The First Joint Conference on Lexical and Computational Semantics – Volume 1: Proceedings of the main conference and the shared task, and Volume 2: Proceedings of the Sixth International Workshop on Semantic Evaluation (SemEval 2012)*, pages 246–255, Montréal, Canada. Association for Computational Linguistics.

Saif Mohammad, Felipe Bravo-Marquez, Mohammad Salameh, and Svetlana Kiritchenko. 2018. SemEval-2018 task 1: Affect in tweets. In *Proceedings of The 12th International Workshop on Semantic Evaluation*, pages 1–17, New Orleans, Louisiana. Association for Computational Linguistics.

Jeffrey Pennington, Richard Socher, and Christopher Manning. 2014. GloVe: Global vectors for word representation. In *Proceedings of the 2014 Conference on Empirical Methods in Natural Language Processing (EMNLP)*, pages 1532–1543, Doha, Qatar. Association for Computational Linguistics.

Robert Plutchik. 2001. The nature of emotions: Human emotions have deep evolutionary roots, a fact that may explain their complexity and provide tools for clinical practice. *American scientist*, 89(4):344–350.

Hannah Rashkin, Maarten Sap, Emily Allaway, Noah A. Smith, and Yejin Choi. 2018. Event2Mind: Commonsense inference on events, intents, and reactions. In *Proceedings of the 56th Annual Meeting of the Association for Computational Linguistics (Volume 1: Long Papers)*, pages 463–473, Melbourne, Australia. Association for Computational Linguistics.

James Russell and Albert Mehrabian. 1977. Evidence for a three-factor theory of emotions. *Journal of Research in Personality*, 11(3):273–294.

Klaus R. Scherer. 2005. What are emotions? and how can they be measured? *Social Science Information*, 44(4):695–729.

Klaus R. Scherer. 2009. Emotions are emergent processes: they require a dynamic computational architecture. *Philosophical Transactions of the Royal Society B*, 364(1535):3459–3474.

Klaus R. Scherer and Harald G. Wallbott. 1994. Evidence for universality and cultural variation of differential emotion response patterning. *Journal of personality and social psychology*, 66(2):310.

Mostafa Al Masum Shaikh, Helmut Prendinger, and Mitsuru Ishizuka. 2009. A linguistic interpretation of the OCC emotion model for affect sensing from text. *Affective Information Processing*, pages 45–73.

Craig A. Smith and Phoebe C. Ellsworth. 1985. Patterns of cognitive appraisal in emotion. *Journal of personality and social psychology*, 48(4):813.

Pedro M. Sosa. 2017. Twitter sentiment analysis using combined LSTM-CNN models. *Eprint Arxiv*, pages 1–9.

Enrica Troiano, Sebastian Padó, and Roman Klinger. 2019. Crowdsourcing and validating event-focused emotion corpora for German and English. In *Proceedings of the 57th Annual Meeting of the Association for Computational Linguistics*, pages 4005–4011, Florence, Italy. Association for Computational Linguistics.

Orizu Udochukwu and Yulan He. 2015. A rule-based approach to implicit emotion detection in text. In *Natural Language Processing and Information Systems*, pages 197–203, Cham. Springer International Publishing.

A Ablation Study for Feature Based Maximum Entropy Classification Model of Emotion Components

Table 6 shows the performance scores if just one additional feature is enabled (while bag-of-words always remains available). It can be seen, that the most advantageous feature are word embeddings. On REMAN, *Cpm-ME-Adv* achieves a macro F1-score of 0.59 and a micro F_1-score of 0.67. On TEC, we have respective values of 0.56 and 0.71, with the high micro score resulting from cognitive appraisal being the best performing class while also being more than twice as frequent as any other component.

		Emo-ME-Base			Dictionaries			POS-tags			Embeddings			Appraisal prediction		
	Component	P	R	F_1	P	R	F_1	P	R	F_1	P	R	F_1	P	R	F_1
REMAN	Cognitive appraisal	60	98	75	60	98	75	57	73	64	60	88	72	60	98	75
	Neurophysiological symptoms	50	20	29	25	20	22	00	00	00	40	40	40	50	20	29
	Action tendencies	36	47	41	38	42	40	28	47	35	45	68	54	36	47	41
	Motor expressions	67	56	61	68	58	63	61	63	62	76	65	70	67	56	61
	Subjective feelings	38	32	34	44	37	40	32	37	34	45	53	49	38	32	34
	Macro avg.	50	51	48	47	51	48	36	44	39	53	63	57	50	51	48
	Micro avg.			61			62			52			65			61
TEC	Cognitive appraisal	72	99	84	72	99	83	74	98	84	76	97	85	72	99	84
	Neurophysiological symptoms	17	17	17	11	17	13	00	00	00	12	33	17	17	17	17
	Action tendencies	42	57	48	40	51	45	42	63	50	45	66	53	42	57	48
	Motor expressions	47	52	49	43	48	45	34	45	39	40	61	48	47	52	49
	Subjective feelings	63	70	66	62	68	65	62	65	64	58	65	61	63	70	66
	Macro avg.	48	59	53	46	57	50	42	54	47	46	64	53	48	59	53
	Micro avg.			70			69			68			69			70

Table 6: Overview over the single feature's impact in classification with *Cpm-ME-Adv*. Each column displays the classification results if only this column's feature is additionally to bag-of-words features, enabled. In the last column, the additional feature is only used for the prediction of cognitive appraisal, due to the classification assumption that the components can appear individually of each other in text.

B Detailed Emotion Results for Emotion Classification

The results table in the main paper did, for space reasons, only show F_1 scores. Table 7 present the complete results for the neural network, including precision and recall values.

		Emo-NN-Base			*Emo-Cpm-NN-Gold*			*Emo-Cpm-NN-Pred*			*MTL-MH*			*MTL-XS*		
	Emotion	P	R	F_1	P	R	F_1	P	R	F_1	P	R	F_1	P	R	F_1
REMAN	Anger	28	50	36	47	70	**56**	33	30	32	31	40	35	31	50	38
	Anticipation	18	18	18	19	27	22	0	0	0	12	27	16	17	36	**24**
	Disgust	20	56	29	20	44	28	24	56	**33**	16	56	24	18	44	26
	Fear	35	50	41	25	71	37	33	36	34	28	64	39	40	57	**47**
	Joy	47	77	59	74	64	68	70	73	**71**	65	59	62	57	73	64
	Neutral	40	55	46	100	55	**71**	29	64	40	35	82	49	38	91	54
	Other	33	9	14	50	9	15	17	18	17	15	45	22	29	55	**37**
	Sadness	27	53	36	31	53	39	50	53	**52**	37	67	48	44	53	48
	Surprise	65	79	**71**	41	64	50	53	64	58	55	86	67	47	100	64
	Trust	39	69	50	86	46	**60**	67	31	42	43	77	56	50	62	55
	Macro avg.	35	52	40	49	50	45	38	42	38	34	60	42	37	62	**46**
	Micro avg.			43			45			43			42			**47**
TEC	Anger	50	35	41	57	47	**52**	30	35	32	29	12	17	42	29	34
	Disgust	40	50	44	50	25	33	0	0	0	67	50	**57**	50	50	50
	Fear	65	50	56	86	55	**67**	73	50	59	48	59	53	54	68	60
	Joy	60	82	69	68	78	72	67	72	70	79	74	**76**	66	82	73
	Sadness	57	47	51	61	58	**60**	61	47	53	66	44	53	61	53	57
	Surprise	48	32	39	45	50	**47**	40	50	44	36	62	45	60	35	44
	Macro avg.	53	49	50	61	52	**55**	45	42	43	54	50	50	55	53	53
	Micro avg.			57			**62**			56			58			61

Table 7: Performance of the neural network emotion classifiers. The highest F_1 scores are printed bold face.

C Neural Network Parameters

Table 8 shows the network parameters that were determined during the development process of the neural models.

	Parameter	*Cpm-NN-Base*	*Emo-NN-Base*	*Emo-Cpm-NN-Gold*	*Emo-Cpm-NN-Pred*	*MTL-XS*	*MTL-MH*
REMAN	Bi-LSTM units	24	24	24	24	32 / 24	24
	CNN filters	10	10	16	16	12 / 10	16
	FC neurons (cpm)	128	—	96	64	128	128
	FC neurons (emo)	—	128	128	128	128	128
	FC neurons (comb.)	—	—	128	96	—	—
	Loss weight (emo)	—	4.0	6.0	4.0	7.8	7.8
	Loss weight (cpm)	1.5	—	—	—	1.5	1.5
	Task weight (emo)	—	1.0	1.0	1.0	0.75	0.75
	Task weight (cpm)	1.0	—	—	—	0.5	0.35
	Minibatch size	60	50	50	50	25	25
TEC	Bi-LSTM units	24	24	24	24	32/24	24
	CNN filters	32	32	32	32	24/24	32
	FC neurons (cpm)	32	—	—	64	128	32
	FC neurons (emo)	—	128	128	128	128	128
	FC neurons (comb.)	—	—	256	256	—	—
	Loss weight (emo)	—	1.0	1.0	1.0	1.0	1.0
	Loss weight (cpm)	1.0	—	—	—	1.0	1.0
	Task weight (emo)	—	1.0	1.0	1.0	0.75	0.5
	Task weight (cpm)	1.0	—	—	—	0.5	0.5
	Minibatch size	40	80	80	80	80	80

Table 8: Neural network parameters. In cases where multiple values are displayed, the first value refers to the emotion detection part of the network, while the second value refers to CPM detection.

D Discussion of Instances

We show examples in Table 9 where component information is helpful for emotion classification. Regarding the neural classifiers, *MTL-XS* generally tends to predict fewer false positives when there are no strong correlations among the potential emotions to the predicted CPM, like in (1). Similarly, in (2) the model predicts only 'fear', which is more likely to occur together with the 'subjective feeling' component than 'anger' or 'disgust', according to Table 3 in the paper. Additionally, CPM information helps to solve ambiguities: In (3), the model predicts 'anticipation' rather than 'sadness', presumably because of the stronger correlation to the predicted CPM component 'action tendency'.

In the two TEC examples (4–5), the baseline detects 'joy', while *MTL-XS* correctly detects 'sadness'. The cross-stitch model predicts a 'subjective feeling' component in both instances and a 'cognitive appraisal' component in one instance. Both components are more strongly correlated with 'sadness' than with 'joy' (see Table 3 in main paper).

We also show some examples that exemplify differences in prediction of the ME-based models (6–8). Generally, the CPM information leads to little improvement in emotion detection on TEC. Nevertheless, there are some cases in which the correct emotion was predicted by at least one of *Emo-Cpm-ME-Gold* and *Emo-Cpm-ME-Pred*, whereas it was not detected by *Emo-ME-Base*. In both examples (6–7), the correct emotions 'surprise' and 'sadness' have not been found by *Emo-ME-Base* (predicting 'joy' and 'surprise' respectively). *Emo-Cpm-ME-Gold* and *Emo-Cpm-ME-Pred* both correctly predicted 'surprise' for (6) and 'sadness' for (7). There are indications of 'subjective feeling' in the second and of 'motor expression' and 'cognitive appraisal' in both examples, that were also predicted by *Cpm-ME-Adv*, which might have helped assigning the correct emotion class. On REMAN, the ME models were able to classify a small fraction of the instances correctly, which is still an improvement compared to the miserably failing baseline. An example with improved prediction for REMAN is (8), where the emotion 'joy' was correctly identified by *Emo-Cpm-ME-Gold* and *Emo-Cpm-ME-Pred*, while not being detected by *Emo-ME-Base*.

(1) As for the hero of this story, 'His One Fault' was absent-mindedness. He forgot to lock his uncle's stable door, and the horse was stolen. In seeking to recover the stolen horse, he unintentionally stole another. (REMAN)	
Emotion *Emo-NN-Base*	disgust, other, sadness
CPM, *MTL-XS*	**cognitive appraisal**
Emotion, *MTL-XS*	**neutral**
CPM Gold	**cognitive appraisal**, action tendency
Emotion Gold	**neutral**
(2) In that fatal valley, at the foot of that declivity which the cuirassiers had ascended, now inundated by the masses of the English, under the converging fires of the victorious hostile cavalry, under a frightful density of projectiles, this square fought on. It was commanded by an obscure officer named Cambronne. At each discharge, the square diminished and replied. (REMAN)	
Emotion *Emo-NN-Base*	anger, disgust, **fear**
CPM, *MTL-XS*	**cognitive appraisal**, subjective feeling
Emotion, *MTL-XS*	**fear**
CPM Gold	**cognitive appraisal**
Emotion Gold	**fear**
(3) If sleep came at all, it might be a sleep without waking. But after all that was but one chance in a hundred: the action of the drug was incalculable, and the addition of a few drops to the regular dose would probably do no more than procure for her the rest she so desperately needed.... She did not, in truth, consider the question very closely–the physical craving for sleep was her only sustained sensation. Her mind shrank from the glare of thought as instinctively as eyes contract in a blaze of light–darkness, darkness was what she must have at any cost. (REMAN)	
Emotion *Emo-NN-Base*	sadness, **fear**
CPM, *MTL-XS*	**cognitive appraisal**, **action tendency**
Emotion, *MTL-XS*	**fear**, **anticipation**
CPM Gold	**cognitive appraisal**, neurophysiological symptoms, **action tendencies**
Emotion Gold	**fear**, **anticipation**
(4) @justinbieber nocticed a girl the first day she got a twitter! :((TEC)	
Emotion *Emo-NN-Base*	joy
CPM, *MTL-XS*	**cognitive appraisal**, **subjective feeling**
Emotion, *MTL-XS*	**sadness**
CPM Gold	**cognitive appraisal**, **subjective feeling**
Emotion Gold	**sadness**
(5) when the love of your life is half way acrosss the world (TEC)	
Emotion *Emo-NN-Base*	joy
CPM, *MTL-XS*	**subjective feeling**
Emotion, *MTL-XS*	**sadness**
CPM Gold	**cognitive appraisal**
Emotion Gold	**sadness**
(6) My sister is home! YAY. VISIT (TEC)	
CPM *Cpm-ME-Adv*	**cognitive appraisal, motor expression**
Emotion *Emo-ME-Base*	joy
Emotion *Emo-Cpm-ME-Pred*	**surprise**
Emotion *Emo-Cpm-ME-Gold*	**surprise**
CPM Gold	**cognitive appraisal, motor expression**
Emotion Gold	**surprise**
(7) @lauren_frost It was?!?! What the heck, man! I always miss it! Haha. - You guys need another reunion!! :) (TEC)	
CPM *Cpm-ME-Adv*	**cognitive appraisal, motor expression, subjective feeling**
Emotion *Emo-ME-Base*	surprise
Emotion *Emo-Cpm-ME-Pred*	**sadness**
Emotion *Emo-Cpm-ME-Gold*	**sadness**
CPM Gold	**cognitive appraisal, motor expression, subjective feeling**
Emotion Gold	**sadness**
(8) And if this was a necessary preparation for what, should follow, I would be the very last to complain of it. We went to bed again, and the forsaken child of some half-animal mother, now perhaps asleep in some filthy lodging for tramps, lay in my Ethelwyn's bosom. I loved her the more for it; though, I confess, it would have been very painful to me had she shown it possible for her to treat the baby otherwise, especially after what we had been talking about that same evening. (REMAN)	
CPM *Cpm-ME-Adv*	**cognitive appraisal**, action tendency, **subjective feeling**
Emotion *Emo-ME-Base*	/
Emotion *Emo-Cpm-ME-Pred*	**joy**
Emotion *Emo-Cpm-ME-Gold*	**joy**
CPM Gold	**cognitive appraisal, subjective feeling**
Emotion Gold	disgust, **joy**, sadness, trust

Table 9: Examples in which components support emotion classification.

Identifikation von Vorkommensformen der Lemmata in Quellenzitaten frühneuhochdeutscher Lexikoneinträge

Stefanie Dipper
Sprachwissenschaftliches Institut
Fakultät für Philologie
Ruhr-Universität Bochum
stefanie.dipper@rub.de

Jan Christian Schaffert
Georg-August-Universität Göttingen &
Akademie der Wissenschaften zu Göttingen
jan.schaffert@phil.uni-goettingen.de

Abstract

In dieser Arbeit werden zwei Ansätze vorgestellt, die die Quellenzitate innerhalb eines Wörterbucheintrags im Frühneuhochdeutschen Wörterbuch analysieren und darin die Vorkommensform identifizieren, d. h. die Wortform, die dem Lemma dieses Eintrags entspricht und als historische Schreibform in verschiedenen Schreibvarianten vorliegt. Die Evaluation zeigt, dass schon auf Basis kleiner Trainingsdaten brauchbare Ergebnisse erzielt werden können.

1 Einleitung

Wörterbücher erschließen Sprachen, deren Dialekte, Sprachstufen und Fachwortschätze über die strukturierte Präsentation sprachbezogener Informationen. Die Ausdifferenzierung kann dabei sehr unterschiedlich sein und zeigt sich schon in den Namen der Wörterbücher (Deutsches Rechtswörterbuch, Wörterbuch der schweizerdeutschen Sprache, Wörterbuch der deutschen Pflanzennamen). Eine besondere Position nehmen die allgemeinen Wörterbücher ein, die den Gesamtwortschatz einer Sprache diachron oder synchron erfassen. Wird eine historische Sprachstufe bearbeitet, kommt den Werken zudem eine kulturpädagogische Funktion zu, da sie die diachronen Unterschiede zu der jeweiligen Standardsprache herausarbeiten müssen, um entsprechende sprachbezogene Informationen adäquat zu vermitteln (Reichmann, 1986).

Natürlich wurden während des Digital Turns neben den historischen Quellen auch die Wörterbücher digitalisiert, sodass deren Informationsangebot nun überall abrufbar, durchsuchbar und vielfältig auswertbar ist. Eine Verknüpfung der Quellen mit den Wörterbüchern fand jedoch nicht statt. Die historischen Quellen bieten daher aktuell nur rudimentäre Möglichkeiten der Nachnutzbarkeit (Klaffki et al., 2018). So mangelt es ihnen an jener semantischen Erschließungstiefe, die über ein passendes Wörterbuch erreicht werden könnte und maßgeblich zum Verständnis beitragen würde.

Im nachfolgenden Beitrag stellen wir auf Basis des Frühneuhochdeutschen Wörterbuches (im Folgenden FWB) zwei Ansätze vor, die dies möglich machen sollen, indem sie durch die Lemmatisierung frühneuhochdeutscher Wörter die Basis einer Semantisierung schaffen.

Der eine Ansatz wendet ein existierendes System zur Normalisierung historischer Schreibungen an, der andere nutzt ein künstliches neuronales Netzwerk.[1] Ausgangspunkt ist die Identifikation der Lemmata und deren Wortbildungen in den Quellenzitaten des FWBs. Langfristiges Ziel ist die möglichst umfassende automatische Lemmatisierung digitaler frühneuhochdeutscher Texte.

Der Artikel ist wie folgt aufgebaut: Zunächst stellen wir die Daten des FWBs vor (Kap. 2). Kap. 3 erklärt, wie unser genereller Ansatz aussieht. In Kap. 4 und 5 beschreiben wir die beiden Systeme zur Identifikation der Vorkommensform. Kap. 6 enthält die Resultate, gefolgt von einem Ausblick in Kap. 7.

2 Das Frühneuhochdeutsche Wörterbuch (FWB)

Das FWB ist ein semantisches Bedeutungswörterbuch mit kulturwissenschaftlichem Schwerpunkt, dessen Ziel es ist, den Gesamtwortschatz des Frühneuhochdeutschen synchron in seiner Heterogenität zu präsentieren (Reichmann, 1986). Um dessen Varietätenspektrum bestmöglich zu erfassen, bildet das FWB die drei wichtigsten frühneuhochdeutschen Heterogenitätsdimensionen Zeit

[1]Unser Dank gilt insbesondere Herrn Dr. Matthias Schütze, der das FWB seit vielen Jahren technisch begleitet und in diesem Zusammenhang auch das künstliche neuronale Netz entwickelt hat.

(1350 bis 1650), Raum (Thüringisch, Elsässisch, Alemannisch, etc.) und Textsorte (erbauliche, literarische, rechtsgeschichtliche, etc. Texte) möglichst ungewichtet in seinen Quellen und sprachbezogenen Informationen ab. Pro Lemma, bei polysemen Lemmata pro Einzelsemantik, bietet das FWB eine Vielzahl qualitativ hochwertiger, heuristisch kompetent überprüfter, semantischer und pragmatischer Informationen und belegt diese mit Zitaten.

Da das Frühneuhochdeutsche weder eine normativ geregelte Orthographie noch eine überdachende Leitvarietät aufweist, belegt das FWB pro Lemma zudem eine z. T. erhebliche Anzahl von Vorkommensformen (kurz: VKF) pro Lemma. Da diese seit 2017 manuell ausgezeichnet werden, ergibt sich ein unschätzbares Potenzial: Aktuell werden 13.178 VKF eindeutig 4.674 Lemmata zugeordnet. Dieses Verhältnis deutet die Problematiken der Lemmatisierungsansätze jener VKF an, die nicht ausgezeichnet sind.

Exemplarisch ist das Lemma *abenteuer*, das in den Quellenzitaten u. a. in folgenden VKF belegt ist: *aventevre*, *auffentür*, *abenteür*, *aventúre*, *abentewr*, *abentur*, *ofentúre*, *obentewer*, *aubentúr*, *aubenteur*, usw. (s. Abbildung 8 im Appendix mit einem Ausschnitt des FWB-Eintrags zu diesem Lemma). Wie kann in allen diesen Vorkommensformen (insgesamt 36 unterscheidbare) automatisch und möglichst eindeutig das Lemma erkannt werden?

Die in diesem Beitrag genutzten Daten des FWB stehen online z. T. frei zur Verfügung oder werden in den kommenden Jahren freigeschaltet.[2]

3 Identifikation von Vorkommensformen durch Lemmatisierung

In diesem Beitrag soll es also noch nicht um die Lemmatisierung beliebiger Texte des Frühneuhochdeutschen gehen, sondern zunächst um eine einfachere Aufgabe: Gegeben ein Lemma wie *abenteuer*, identifiziere die zugehörige Vorkommensform (VKF) innerhalb der Quellenzitate. (1) zeigt ein Beispiel für ein Quellenzitat für dieses Lemma aus einem nordoberdeutschen Text. Das Lemma ist in standardisierter Form vorgegeben, während die VKF eine flektierte Wortform sein kann, die zudem in der historischen Originalschreibung vorliegt. Ziel ist es also, in (1) die VKF *obentewern* zu identifizieren.

(1) *das die frembden in [. . .] wirtshewser geen mit iren obentewern.*

Wir fassen die Aufgabe als Lemmatisierungsaufgabe auf: Gegeben ein Kandidat für eine VKF, lässt sich dieser Kandidat auf das vorgegebene Lemma lemmatisieren? Dabei gehen beide Ansätze so vor, dass sie sämtliche historischen Wortերformen w_i innerhalb eines Belegs mit dem vorgegebenen Lemma l paaren: $< w_i, l >$ und für jedes Paar überprüfen, ob l das Lemma von w_i sein könnte. Im Beispiel (1) wären das also die Paare *<das, abenteuer>*, *<die, abenteuer>*, *<frembden, abenteuer>* etc.

Ein möglicher Ansatz wäre es, für diese Aufgabe einen vorhandenen Lemmatisierer zu nutzen. Das ist allerdings aus verschiedenen Gründen nicht ohne Weiteres möglich:

Viele der Ziel-Lemmata aus dem FWB haben keine moderne Entsprechung, z. B. lauten die ersten zehn Lemmata einer Zufallsauswahl *sünde, *quatembergeld, *entspanen, erzeigen, *erbholde, *abtilgen, abschlagen, *äfern, streuen, abtun*[3] – für fünf davon (mit Stern markiert) gibt es keinen Eintrag in einem Standardwörterbuch wie dem Duden[4]. Damit lassen sich moderne Lemmatisierer nicht ohne Weiteres sinnvoll auf diese Daten anwenden, da die Zahl der ungesehenen Lemmata ungewöhnlich hoch ist. Auch lassen sich vorhandene Korpora wie z. B. das Anselm-Korpus[5], das RIDGES-Korpus[6] oder das Referenz-Korpus Frühneuhochdeutsch[7] nicht als Trainingsdaten verwenden, da diese moderne Lemmata verwenden.

Außerdem basieren viele moderne Lemmatisierer auf Wortart-Information (und integrieren gegebenenfalls einen entsprechenden Tagger), so z. B. Liebeck and Conrad (2015); Konrad (2019). Für unsere Daten liegen aber keine entsprechenden Wortart-Annotationen vor.

Ein weiteres Problem ist, dass die VKF-Kandidaten nicht in einer standardisierten Form vorliegen, sondern stark variieren können. Daher lässt sich beispielsweise der Ansatz von Wartena

[2]`https://fwb-online.de/` (letzter Zugriff: 5.5.2021)

[3]Die Daten stammen aus dem Mittleren Ostoberdeutsch (moobd.), vgl. Abschnitt 4.

[4]`https://www.duden.de/`

[5]`https://www.linguistics.rub.de/comphist/projects/anselm/`

[6]`https://www.linguistik.hu-berlin.de/de/institut/professuren/korpuslinguistik/forschung/ridges-projekt`

[7]`https://www.linguistics.ruhr-uni-bochum.de/ref/`

(2019) nicht umsetzen, der von markierten Morphemgrenzen innerhalb der Trainingsdaten ausgeht.

Schließlich liegen in unserem Szenario nur wenig Trainingsdaten vor: Im Ansatz mit Norma (s. Abschnitt 4) stehen jeweils nur 500 Wörter als Trainingsdaten zur Verfügung – eine der Stärken von Norma ist es, mit solch geringen Datenmengen bereits gute Ergebnisse zu liefern. Dem künstlichen neuronalen Netz (s. Abschnitt 5) stehen mit ca. 170.000 Wörtern zwar mehr, aber ebenfalls vergleichsweise wenige Trainingsdaten zur Verfügung. Zum Vergleich: das neuronale Modell von Schmid (2019) nutzt zwei Millionen Wörter zum Trainieren.

4 Identifikation durch Norma

Im ersten Ansatz verwenden wir ein existierendes System, das frei verfügbar ist: Norma[8] (Bollmann 2012). Norma wurde entwickelt für eine automatische Normalisierung von (historischen) Schreibvarianten und wird auf Trainingspaaren der Form <original, normalisiert> trainiert. Norma integriert drei verschiedene Arten von Lernkomponenten (für Details, s. Bollmann (2012)):

1. Mapper: Diese Komponente stellt eine Liste der Paare <original, normalisiert> bereit, die in den Trainingsdaten gesehen wurden. Mapper kann also nur bekannte Schreibungen per Lexikon Lookup normalisieren.

2. RuleBased: Diese Komponente lernt kontextsensitive Ersetzungsregeln, die einen Buchstaben bzw. eine Buchstabensequenz durch eine andere ersetzen. Die Regeln sind nach Frequenz ihrer Anwendung geordnet.

3. WLD (weighted Levenshtein distance): Diese Komponente wendet gewichtete LD an, um Buchstaben-Ngramme aufeinander abzubilden.[9]

RuleBased und WLD benötigen außerdem ein Lexikon mit normalisierten Schreibungen, gegen das die generierten Kandidaten abgeglichen werden. Bei der Normalisierung wendet Norma die drei Komponenten der Reihe nach an. Sobald eine Komponente eine normalisierte Form generiert, wird abgebrochen. Norma generiert allerdings nur Kandidaten, die sich nicht mehr als eine gewisse Distanz vom Ausgangswort unterscheiden. Gibt es keinen solchen Kandidaten, bleibt der Output leer.

Norma wurde für die Normalisierung flektierter Wortformen entwickelt. In einer ersten Evaluation testeten wir daher, ob sich Norma prinzipiell auch für die Lemmatisierung eignet. Eine Crossvalidierung ergab Durchschnittswerte zwischen 56,8-69,8% Genauigkeit pro Teilkorpus, was Norma für die (wesentlich leichtere) Aufgabe der VKF-Identifikation als mögliches Tool erscheinen lässt. (Details zu dieser Evaluation im Appendix.)

Norma als Tool für die VKF-Identifikation Für die VKF-Identifikation lemmatisiert Norma zunächst jeden VKF-Kandidaten aus einem Beleg. Anschließend werden die generierten Lemmata mit dem vorgegebenen Lemma abgeglichen und die VKF wird ausgewählt, deren Lemma mit dem vorgegebenen übereinstimmt. Gegebenenfalls kann auch kein oder mehrere Kandidaten zum vorgegebenen Lemma lemmatisiert werden.

Für diese Anwendung trainieren wir Norma auf Paaren der Form <historische Wortform, FWB-Lemma>.[10] Entsprechend besteht das Lexikon zum Abgleich aus Lemmata. Wir nutzen zwei unterschiedliche Lexika für den Abgleich:

1. Norma-full: das Lexikon besteht aus einer Liste von rund 78.000 Lemmata des FWB ("full lexicon")

2. Norma-small: das Lexikon besteht nur aus dem vorgegebenen Lemma ("small lexicon")

Das Szenario Norma-full entspricht dem üblichen Vorgehen und könnte beispielsweise bei der Lemmatisierung von Freitext (ohne vorgegebenes Lemma) Anwendung finden. Das Szenario Norma-small ist auf die aktuelle Aufgabenstellung zugeschnitten: Da das Ziel-Lemma schon bekannt ist, kann Normas Hypothesenraum extrem auf genau diese Form eingeschränkt werden. Das hat folgende Konsequenzen:

Norma-full generiert die Kandidaten sehr viel unrestriktiver als Norma-small. Daher kommt es

[8] `https://github.com/comphist/norma` (letzter Zugriff: 5.5.2021)

[9] Norma markiert nur bei der Komponente RuleBased die Wortgrenzen explizit (mit "#"). Die Wortgrenzen stellen eine wichtige Information für die Lemmatisierung dar: Am Wortende müssen andere Ersetzungen gelernt werden als in der Wortmitte. Daher fügen wir "#" für WLD am Wortanfang und -ende an.

[10] Sonderzeichen in den Wortformen innerhalb der Belege wie Satzzeichen (! ? , etc.) oder Anführungszeichen und Klammern werden gelöscht.

hier öfters vor, dass Norma-full bei keiner der Input-Formen die vorgegebene Lemma-Form generiert. D. h. Norma-full hat eine geringere Abdeckung als Norma-small.

Im Fall von sehr kurzen Wortformen und Lemmata kann Norma-small (zu) viele der Input-Wortformen auf das vorgegebene Lemma abbilden, da alle innerhalb der Abbruch-Schwelle liegen. (2) zeigt ein solches Beispiel. Das vorgegebene Lemma ist *öl* und der dazugehörige Beleg enthält viele sehr kurze Wortformen. (3) zeigt die Liste der Wortformen aus (2), die Norma-small auf das Lemma *öl* abbilden konnte. Die Liste ist nach einem Score geordnet, den Norma ausgibt. *öl* (der erste VKF-Kandidat) ist demnach der "beste" Kandidat, den Norma generiert (was hier auch die korrekte Form ist). In der Evaluation (Kap. 6) wird jeweils nur die erste Form berücksichtigt.

(2) *chümpt dann ain gast mit öl vnd wil zemarcht damit sten vnd gibet es von hant hin, als oft er ain lagel öls auf tuet, so geit er ain pfunt öls, als oft er die verchauffet.*

(3) *öl, als, als, wil, oft, oft, lagel, von, sten, es, er, er, er, hin, ain, ain, ain, so, die, geit, mit, vnd, vnd, auf, pfunt, hant, gast, dann, tuet*

Wir führen eine sechsfache Crossvalidierung durch und trainieren Norma auf jeweils 500 Paaren aus drei verschiedenen Sprachräumen (Nordoberdeutsch/nobd, Mittleres Ostoberdeutsch/moobd, Elsässisch/els) und evaluieren auf jeweils 100 Paaren.

5 Identifikation durch ein künstliches neuronales Netz

Im zweiten Ansatz verwenden wir ein künstliches neuronales Netz, um den Herausforderungen, die aus den FWB-Daten erwachsen können, zu begegnen. Neben ihrem geringem Umfang sind die Daten auch unvollständig und sehr spezifisch: derzeit liegen Trainingsdaten nur für die e-, q-, r- und st-Strecken vor. In unserer Evaluation zeigte es sich allerdings, dass hieraus keine größeren Nachteile entstehen: Das über die r-Strecke trainierte Netz generalisiert gut und ergibt für die anderen Strecken F-Scores, die mit denen der Trainingsdaten vergleichbar oder sogar besser sind (vgl. Tabelle 4). Dies ist von besonderer Bedeutung, da das FWB aktuell erst zu ca. 75% abgeschlossen ist und das Netz in Zukunft beliebige Texte lemmatisieren soll.

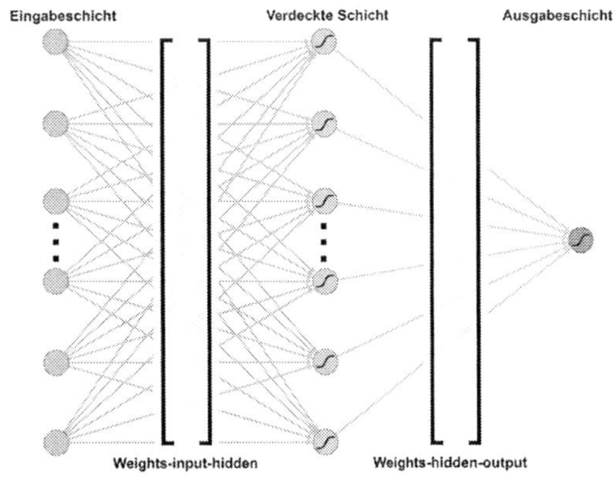

Abbildung 1: Schematische Darstellung der Topologie des Netzes

Da über das FWB nur eingeschränkte Trainingsdaten zu Verfügung stehen, wurden einige manuell erstellte Normalisierungsregeln in das Netz aufgenommen, um spezielle Fälle, die für einen relativ großen Prozentsatz von Fehlern verantwortlich sind, schnell zu entschärfen (Ernst-Gerlach and Fuhr, 2006; Pilz et al., 2007). Dieses Vorgehen erwies sich als erfolgreich, da schon wenige manuelle Regeln (vgl. Regeln 12–15 in Tabelle 1) den F-Score des Netzes signifikant anheben. Aktuell handelt es sich nur um Normalisierungsregeln im Sinne der Lemmazeichengestalt (Reichmann, 1986), in Zukunft sollen auch sprachraumspezifische Regeln implementiert werden.[11]

Die Topologie ist basal und empirisch unterstützt. Das Netz entspricht einem typischen dreischichtigen feedforward-Netz mit einfacher verborgener Schicht, angewendeter Sigmoid-Funktion und zwei Gewichtsmatrizes (Goodfellow et al., 2018), vgl. Abb. 1. Das Netz selbst ist in Python programmiert, orientiert sich in seinem Framework an Rashid (2017) sowie Steinwendner and Schwaiger (2019) und lernt gemäß der Aufgabenstellung überwacht und parametrisch. Die Matrizenmultiplikation wird mit NumPy[12] realisiert.

Die Eingabe- und verdeckte Schicht sind gleich mächtig, da die Verringerung von verdeckten Neu-

[11] Ein vergleichbares Vorgehen wurde für des Referenzkorpus Althochdeutsch genutzt, für dessen Lemmatisierer über 700 Regeln manuell aufgestellt wurden, die pro Zeit und Raum gewissen Lautständen mehr oder weniger statistische Bedeutsamkeit zuweisen und somit die Metadaten eines Textes produktiv in die Analyse einfließen lassen (Mittmann, 2016). Da das Frühneuhochdeutsche jedoch wesentlich umfassender und somit zwangsläufig diverser überliefert ist, gestaltet sich ein vergleichbarer Ansatz als unlösbar komplexe Aufgabe. In Zukunft sollen entsprechende Regeln daher erlernt werden.

[12] `https://numpy.org/` (letzter Zugriff: 02.06.2021)

ronen zu erheblichen Schwankungen der Fehlerquote während des Trainings geführt hat. Die Ausgabeschicht besteht nur aus einem Neuron, da das Netz anhand des Scores nur eine Voraussage darüber trifft, ob ein Wort als Lemma erkannt wird oder nicht. Je höher der Score, desto sicherer wird das betreffende Lemma erkannt. Hierbei wird analog zu Norma mit Paaren der Form $< w_i, l >$ gearbeitet.

Die Paarung von historischen Wortformen mit den Lemmata des FWB $< w_i, l >$ ergeben die Daten, die als Bewertungsvektor formalisiert werden. Dieser Vektor bildet die Eingabeschicht, deren Werte gewichtet und auf der verdeckten Schicht propagiert werden. Nach einer weiteren Gewichtung gibt das Netz auf der Ausgabeschicht einen Score an, der determiniert, ob lemmatisiert wird oder nicht. Diese Lemmatisierung wird anschließend anhand der bereits ausgezeichneten Strecken evaluiert und das Netz so trainiert. Diese Aspekte werden im Folgenden genauer erläutert.

Bewertungsvektoren Da das FWB und die meisten maschinenlesbaren historischen Quellen nicht getaggt sind, kann nur auf jene Informationen zurückgegriffen werden, die sich aus dem Vergleich der VKF mit den Lemmata des FWB ergeben. Darüber hinaus werden Metadaten zum jeweiligen Sprachraum berücksichtigt, da diese genutzt werden, um sprachraumspezifische Normalisierungen in das Netz einfließen zu lassen.

Um z. B. die VKF *Refftrager* im Quellenzitat (4) als das Lemma *refträger* zu identifizieren, werden insgesamt neun Bewertungsvektoren für sämtliche Paarungen <*secht, refträger*>, [...], <*Refftrager, refträger*> erstellt. Der Bewertungsvektor für die VKF *Refftrager* entspricht der vierten Spalte von Tabelle 1.

(4) *secht recht wie ein Hundsschlager | Oder ein alter Refftrager*

Alle Informationen müssen für das Netz in numerische Werte transformiert werden, damit sie als Features der Eingabeneuronen dienen können. Die Features und deren Werte ergeben sich aus Tests-Trainings. Es wurden stets die Werte gewählt, für die sich die beste Entwicklung des Fehlerquotienten ergab (vgl. hierzu Abb. 2). Die Anhebung des F-Scores wurde erst ansatzweise durch die Implementierung der Regeln 12–15 angegangen.

Die Länge von Lemma und Wortform ergibt sich als Verhältnis zur maximalen Wortlänge von

	Merkmal	Erläuterung	Wert
1	LLemma	Länge Lemma	0,36
2	LOriginal	Länge Originalschreibung	0,4
3	Durchsn.L	Differenz Längen	0,05
4	Subst.	Substantiv	0,5
5	Adj.	Adjektiv/Adverb	0
6	Verb	Verb	0
7	Unbekannt	Unbekannt	0
8	JW	Jaro-Winkler-Distanz	0,93
9	phon	phonetische Distanz	1
10	JW-norm	JW-Distanz mit Normierung	0,984
11	phon-norm	ph-Distanz mit Normierung	1
12	JW-fwb-allg	JW-Distanz mit FWB-Norm.	0,93
13	JW-kw-qu	JW-Distanz kw-qu	0,93
14	JW-ai-ei	JW-Distanz ai-ei	0,93
15	JW-ich-ig	JW-Distanz auslautendes ich-ig	0,93
16	nrdnieders.	Niedersächsisch	0
...			
39	orfrk.	Ostfränkisch	1
...			
45	balt.	Baltisch	0

Tabelle 1: Bewertungsmatrix für die Wortform *Refftrager*

25 Buchstaben. Die Jaro-Winkler-Distanz wird entsprechend (Winkler, 1990), die phonetische Distanz gemäß der Kölner Phonetik (Postel, 1969) berechnet. Alle weiteren Distanzen ergeben sich aus den Normierungen, die Nichtbuchstaben aus dem Lemma entfernen, Diakritika und Ligaturen auflösen und die Originalschreibung gemäß der Richtlinien für die FWB-Lemmazeichengestalt normalisieren (Reichmann, 1986). Insofern folgt das Netz dem etablierten Ansatz, Vorkommensformen zu normalisieren, ermöglicht jedoch die Inklusion von Metadataden und händisch erstellten Regeln, die sich für vergleichbare Ansätze als hilfreich erwiesen haben.

Da für die Zukunft abzusehen ist, dass Informationen zu den Wortarten zwar hilfreich, aber nicht nutzbar sein werden, ist geplant, nach den sprachraumspezifischen Regelsätzen auch spezielle FLexions- und Deklinationsregeln zu implementieren, die generelle Prinzipien erfassen, jedoch nicht auf Informationen zur Wortart angewiesen sind. Der Defaultwert für die Wortarten ist 0, das Feature für die entsprechende Wortart (unter Sonstige subsummiert das FWB Artikel, Interjektionen, etc.) ist 0,5.

Insgesamt deckt das FWB vom Niederpreußischen bis zum Alemannischen 31 Sprachräume ab. Der Default-Wert der entsprechenden Neuronen ist wiederum 0. Je nachdem welchem Sprachraum das jeweilige Wort zugeordnet ist, müssen ggf. mehrere Neuronen aktiviert werden, da sowohl über-als auch untergeordnete Sprachräume existieren. *Refftrager* ist z. B. in einer Nürnberger, d. h. einer oberfränkischen Quelle belegt (für Städte wird immer der Sprachraum gewählt, in dem sie liegen). Da sich der oberfränkische Sprachraum aus keinen untergeordneten zusammensetzt, wird nur dessen Neuron aktiviert und der Wert 1 eingetragen. Bei einer rheinfränkischen Quelle müssten hingegen mehrere Sprachräume berücksichtigt werden, weil dieser Sprachraum aus dem hessischen und pfälzischen besteht. Für solche Fälle wird der Wert nach der auf dem Kehrwert der Gebietszahl basierenden Formel Feature = 0,3 + 0,5/x für x = Anzahl aktivierte Sprachräume berechnet.

Lemmatisierung Das Netz identifiziert ein Wort als Lemma über den Score. Ist dieser größer als der aktuell noch willkürlich gewählte Wert von 0,58, wird lemmatisiert. Zentrales Element der Berechnung des Scores sind neben den Werten des Bewertungsvektors zwei Gewichtsmatrizes, die zwischen Eingabeschicht und verdeckter (Weights-input-hidden) sowie verdeckter und Ausgabeschicht (Weights-hidden-output) positioniert sind. Die Values der Eingabeschicht werden wie üblich per Matrixmultiplikation propagiert und auf der verdeckten Ebene mit einer Sigmoidfunktion auf das Intervall [0, 1] beschränkt und so der Rechenaufwand zu minimiert, ohne Präzision einzubüßen. Derart können auch verdeckte Neuronen deaktiviert werden und kann das Netz verschiedene Eingaben korrelieren und nichtlinear arbeiten.

Training Das Training des Netzes erfolgt auf ursprünglich randomisierten Gewichtsmatrizes entsprechend des hot cold learning. Ziel ist eine gleichbleibende, möglichst geringe Fehlerquote. Da unser Netz simpel aufgebaut ist, können wir mit einer sehr geringen Lernrate arbeiten und so das Minimum der Fehlerquote genau bestimmen, was zu einem robusten Netz führen sollte.

Die Kurve in Abb. 2 beschreibt die Entwicklung des Fehlerquotienten beim Training über der r-Strecke, die in 173.379 Wörtern 11.187 Vorkommensformen von 1.819 Lemmata enthält. Der lokale Anstieg des Fehlerquotieten weist auf eine zu hohe Lernrate hin, die den statistischen Gradientenabstieg in zu großen Schritten über das Minimum der Fehler-Gewichts-Kurven hinausschießen lässt. Es ist zu erkennen, dass noch ca. 2000 Fehler existieren.

Im Folgenden einige beispielhafte Analysen: Im Quellenzitat (5) hat die Vorkommensform *abethewer* einen Score von 0,79, wird also korrekt lemmatisiert. Wir prüfen jedoch auch, ob zwei auf einander folgende Wörter einem getrennt geschriebenen Lemma entsprechen, damit erhalten wir für die aufeinander folgenden Wörter *aber einer* einen Score von 0,67 und somit einen false positive.

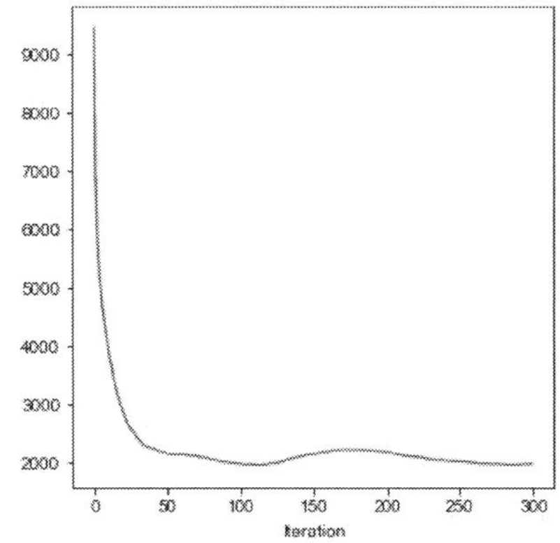

Abbildung 2: Lernkurve des Netzes

Im Quellenzitat (6) hingegen ermittelt das Netz für *avonture* einen Score, der kleiner als 0,58 ist. Die Vorkommensform wird also nicht erkannt, es liegt ein false negative vor.

(5) *sucht aber einer awßflucht, so sten einer seyn abethewer*

(6) *also uns die avonture und ouch daz buch noch seit*

6 Resultate

6.1 Ergebnisse von Norma

Als Baseline verwenden wir ein einfaches System, das jeweils die vorliegende Wortform als Lemma vorhersagt. Die Baseline entspricht damit dem Anteil der Stichworte, die formal mit dem Lemma übereinstimmen. In den drei Korpora liegt die Baseline zwischen 15,0–18,2% Genauigkeit.

Insgesamt ergeben sich durchschnittliche Genauigkeiten von 84,3% mit Norma-small und 60,8% mit Norma-full. Der Großteil der Fehlerrate von Norma-full ergibt sich aus den Fällen, bei denen Norma kein passendes Lemma generiert. Schaut man sich die Genauigkeit bei den generierten Lemmata allein an (d. h. die Precision), so ergibt sich bei Norma-small 88,6% und bei Norma-full 91,9%.

Von den Korpora ist nobd das schwierigste, mit Genauigkeiten von 82,5% (Norma-small) und

	–	Mapper	Rules	WLD
# Lemmata				
Norma-small	88	417	276	1.019
Norma-full	609	422	256	513
Precision				
Norma-small	0	81,3	97,8	89,1
Norma-full	0	80,3	98,0	98,2

Tabelle 2: Verteilung der erzeugten Lemmata über die Normalisierer sowie die jeweilige Genauigkeit (Durchschnitt in Prozent)

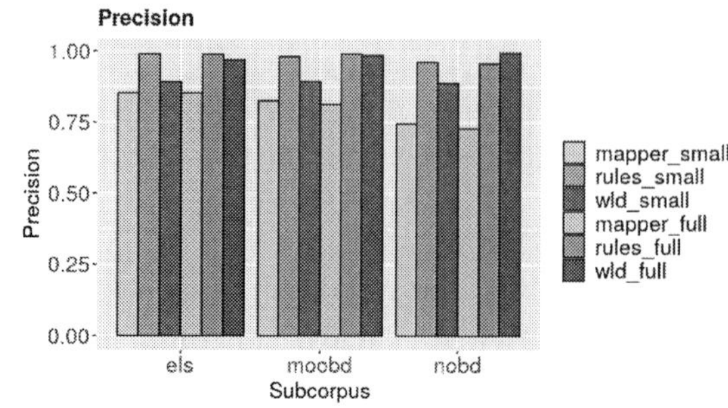

Abbildung 3: Precision der einzelnen Normalisierer

52,8% (Norma-full), gegenüber rund 85% bzw. 65% bei den beiden anderen Korpora.

Tabelle 2 zeigt, von welchen Normalisierern die erzeugten Lemmata in den beiden Szenarien stammen. "–" sind die Fälle, in denen Norma keinen Kandidaten generiert. Man sieht deutlich, dass ein Großteil der WLD-Lemmata, die im Szenario Norma-small dank des minimalen Ziellexikons erzeugt werden, im Szenario Norma-full nicht generiert werden und zu einer großen Anzahl von unanalysierten Fällen führen (33,8%) . Gleichzeitig zeigt es sich, dass die Precision von WLD bei Norma-small deutlich abfällt gegenüber Norma-full (89,1% vs. 98,2%). D. h. von den rund 500 Lemmata, die Norma-small zusätzlich generiert, sind nur rund 400 korrekt.

In Tabelle 2 fällt zudem auf, dass der Mapper in beiden Szenarien deutlich abfällt gegenüber den anderen Normalisierern. Das ist zunächst überraschend, da der Mapper nur bei bereits bekannten Paaren aktiv wird. Die Fehleranalyse unten zeigt, dass die schlechte Performanz zu großen Teilen auf Eigenschaften der Evaluationsdaten zurückgeführt werden kann.

Abb. 3 zeigt die Precision der einzelnen Normalisierer. Rules schneidet hier am besten ab (mit Werten von 95.6–99.0%). Im Szenario Norma-full liefert WLD vergleichbar gute Ergebnisse (96.9–99.3%).

Fehleranalyse Wie schon erwähnt, machen die fehlenden Lemmatisierungen einen wesentlichen Teil der Fehlerrate aus: bei Norma-small sind es 31,1%, bei Norma-full sogar 86,3%.

Kritischer sind allerdings die Fälle, in denen Norma eine VKF identifiziert, diese aber nicht die richtige ist (false positives). Das ist in 195 (Norma-small) bzw. 97 (Norma-Full) Fällen der Fall. Eine manuelle Analyse dieser Fälle ergab:

Bei Norma-Full sind nur zwei dieser Fälle tatsächlich echte (wenn auch nachvollziehbare) Fehler. Dabei identifizierte Norma als VKF des Lemmas *osterwind* einmal *westerwint* und einmal *oberwind* statt *oster(wint)* im Quellenzitat in (7). In allen anderen Fällen wurde als VKF entweder ein (korrekter) Bestandteil eines komplexen Wortes erkannt oder umgekehrt, oder es kamen im Quellenzitat mehrere mögliche VKFs vor und Norma wählte eine andere VKF als in den Testdaten vorgegeben. Einige Beispiele werden in Tabelle 3 gezeigt.

(7) *Oster- und westerwint, den man ober und nider nent, wäen dick und oft und gegen denen pflegt man nit zu pauen; der oberwind pringt gern regen und ungewitter.*

Von Norma-Small wurden die ersten 100 Fälle manuell analysiert. Davon waren 75 eigentlich korrekt. Dabei handelte es sich z. T. um die gleichen Fälle wie bei Norma-Full. Zusätzlich kommt es hier zu echten Fehlern wie in der unteren Hälfte von Tabelle 3 illustriert. Z. B. wird für das Lemma *erbe* als VKF *brief* identifiziert. Der Grund dafür ist, dass der Mapper kein Ziellexikon nutzt und als erste Komponente die (eigentlich gesuchte) Wortform *erben* auf das Lemma *erben* lemmatisiert hat, so dass die weiteren Normalisierer gar nicht mehr auf diese Wortform angewendet wurden. Rules und WLD hätten sonst die VKF korrekt identifiziert. Dasselbe passiert im Fall von *straff*, das der Mapper auf *strafe* statt auf *strafen* lemmatisiert. Es wäre hier also zu überlegen, den Output des Mappers zusätzlich mit dem Ziellexikon abzugleichen.

6.2 Ergebnisse des Netzes

Schon jetzt ergibt das noch unfertige künstliche neuronale Netz vielversprechende Ergebnisse, s. Tabelle 4. Auf Basis des aktuellen Trainings erhalten wir einen durchschnittlichen F-Score von 0,931. Da die einzelnen F-Scores über die analysierten

Gold-Lemma	Gold-VKF	System-VKF	System
abschlagen	ab	schlueg	Nfl/Nsm
anheben	hueb	an	Nfl/Nsm
straus	straussen	strauß	Nfl/Nsm
entblössen	entblotzet	entblotzest	Nfl/Nsm
erbe	erben	brief	Nsm
strafen	straff	spricht	Nsm

Tabelle 3: False Positives von Norma-full (Nfl) und Norma-small (Nsm)

	r-Strecke	e-Str.	q-Str.	st-Str.
TN	153.687	10.876	71.132	67.953
TP	9.806	646	4.648	4.326
FN	715	52	310	285
FP	800	33	315	436
Precision %	92,5	95,1	93,7	90,08
Recall %	93,2	92,55	93,75	93,12
F-Score	0.928	0.938	0.937	0.923

Tabelle 4: Ergebnisse für das Netz: r-Strecken: Trainingsdaten; Rest: Testdaten. (TN: True Negatives, TP: True Positives, FN: False Negatives, FP: False Positives)

Strecken hinweg recht konstant sind, können wir davon ausgehen, dass das Netz weder über- noch unterangepasst ist. Um die Treffsicherheit des Netz zu verbessern, sollen in Zukunft gemischtere Trainingsdaten aus allen manuell getaggten Strecken erstellt werden. Zudem scheint es sinnvoll, den Score, über den lemmatisiert wird, nach oben zu korrigieren, das Netz so kritischer zu gestalten und false positives auszuschließen. Das damit einhergehende vermehrte Auftreten von false negatives ist zu verkraften, da diese, wenn das Netzwerk weiter trainiert wird, zurückgehen sollten.

Die folgenden Analysen basieren auf der a- und b-Strecke.

Hinsichtlich der Wortarten entfällt der Großteil der Fehler auf flektierte Verben, vgl. Abb. 4. Ein besonderes Problem stellen Partikelverben da, die getrennt geschrieben nur dann lemmatisiert werden können, wenn die betreffenden Teilstücke direkt aufeinander folgen. Adjektive/Adverbien und Sonstige werden durchschnittlich bzw. unterdurchschnittlich gut erkannt, fallen aufgrund ihres relativ geringen Anteils von ca. 12% Adjektive/Adverbien und nur ca. 1,7% Sonstige weniger ins Gewicht. Für die Verbesserung des Netzes ist daher zunächst sowohl die Implementierung von Flexionsregeln angedacht, die flektierte Formen zur Infinitivform hin normalisieren, als auch ein Mechanismus zum

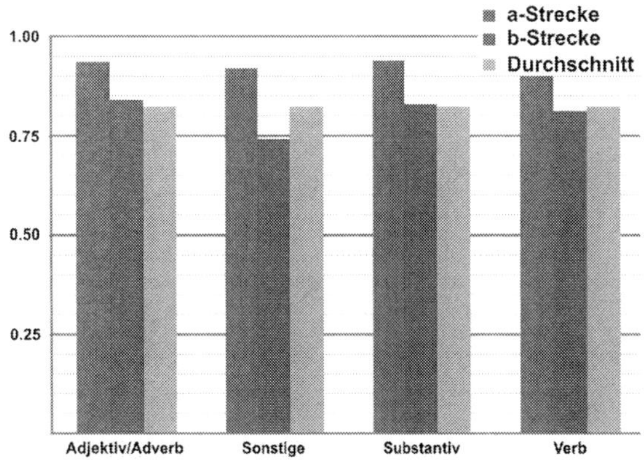

Abbildung 4: F-Scores nach Wortarten auf Basis der a- und b-Strecke

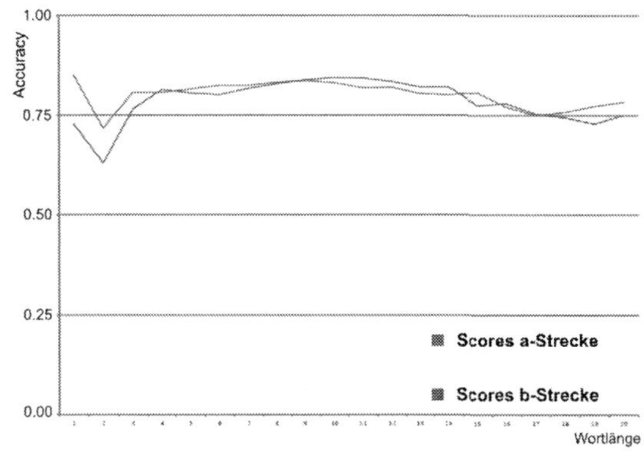

Abbildung 5: F-Scores in Abhängigkeit zur Wortlänge. Wörter mit mehr als 20 Buchstaben wurden ausgeklammert, da sie nur punktuell auftreten

Erfassen von nicht adjazent geschriebenen Partikelverben.

Hinsichtlich der Wortlänge werden VKF mit einer Länge von 5–12 Buchstaben überdurchschnittlich gut erkannt, vgl. Abb. 5. Dies ist erfreulich, da sie mit 62,5% (a-Strecke) und 72,2% (b-Strecke) den Großteil der zu lemmatisierenden VKF ausmachen.

Besonders interessant ist, dass Wörter, die nur aus einem Buchstaben bestehen, gut erkannt werden. Dies ist darauf zurückzuführen, dass es sich hierbei nur um Buchstabennamen handelt, die entsprechend gut zugeordnet werden können. Analog sollte dieser Mechanismus auch für besonders lange Wörter geltend gemacht werden, weswegen die Kurve nach dem zweiten lokalen Minimum nochmals ansteigt. Kurze Wörter werden erst dann problematisch, wenn sie, wie oben in (2) und (3) für Norma belegt, auch für das Netz zu false positives führen. Dies erklärt auch die vergleichsweise

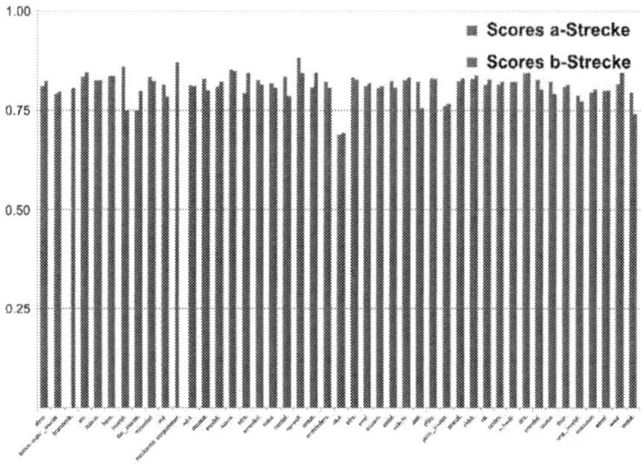

Abbildung 6: F-Scores nach Sprachraum

schlechten Scores der Sonstigen, da es sich hierbei generell um eher kurze Wörter handelt. Hier sollte die Korrektur des Scores nach oben false positives ausschließen. Eventuell ist zu überlegen, ob es unterschiedliche Limits für den Score geben könnte, die von der Wortlänge abhängig sind. Schlechter erkannte längere Wörter fallen aufgrund ihrer geringen Frequenz weniger ins Gewicht.

Über die Analyse der Sprachräume lassen sich einzelne herausarbeiten, die unterdurchschnittliche Werte aufweisen, wie z. B. das Oberdeutsche oder Preußische (s. Abb. 6).[13] Dies weist auf Sprachräume hin, deren VKF erheblich von der Gestalt des Lemmazeichens im FWB abweichen (Preußisch). Es könnte sich jedoch auch um Sprachräume handeln, die weniger belegt sind (Oberdeutsch mit nur durchschnittlich 0,1% aller VKF) und deren Systematiken daher nicht in genügendem Umfang vom Netz erlernt worden sind. Eine Lösung für beide Problematiken könnten Regelsets sein, die sprachraumspezifische Normalisierungen durchführen und über die entsprechenden Features der Sprachraum-Neuronen aktiviert werden. Solche Regelsets lassen sich mit Norma generieren und sollten für das Netz produktiv gemacht werden können. Daneben sollten die Trainingsdaten so gewählt werden, dass alle Sprachräume möglichst gleich stark vertreten sind.

7 Ausblick

Wir haben in diesem Beitrag zwei Ansätze beschrieben, die für die Identifikation von Vorkommensformen genutzt werden können. Beide erreichen noch keine perfekte Abdeckung. Norma erreicht mit extrem wenig Trainingsdaten bereits gute Ergebnisse: die Präzision liegt z. B. bei Norma-full bei nahezu 100%, bei einer Abdeckung von 66.2%. Das Netz wurde auf einer größeren Datenmenge trainiert, die allerdings weniger spezifisch waren. Es erreicht eine Abdeckung von 86,66% und hinsichtlich der Sprachräume wesentlich homogenere Ergebnisse.

Die hier umrissene Lemmatisierung stellt eine notwendige Grundlage für eine geplante Semantisierung frühneuhochdeutsche Texte dar. Ist ein genügend großer Anteil der entsprechenden Quellen lemmatisiert, kann, z. B. über Kollokationsanalysen und vektorbasierte Verfahren damit begonnen werden, die Lesarten der erkannten Lemmata zu disambiguieren. Eine solche Semantisierung würde z. B. Wortformen von *gnade* nicht mehr nur auf den entsprechenden Artikel verlinken, sondern auf eine der 20 verschiedene Lesarten, die im FWB notiert sind und von 1. "unverdiente, unerwartete, rettende, helfende Zuwendung des liebenden Gottes zum Menschen" über 10. "Gabe, die eine höhergestellte Person aufgrund einer wohlwollenden Gesinnung an einen in der Hierarchie Niedrigeren verteilt" bis hin zu 17. "Teil einer Begrüßungs- und Segensformel" reichen. Allein dies zeigt, welchen Mehrwert eine zukünftige Semantisierung frühneuhochdeutscher Texte haben könnte, der sich u. A. im Erkenntnisgewinn während der Lektüre niederschlagen würde oder tiefergehende semantische Analysen wie beispielsweise eine Methaphernanalyse unterstützen würde.

Bibliographie

Marcel Bollmann. 2012. (Semi-)automatic normalization of historical texts using distance measures and the Norma tool. In *Proceedings of the Workshop on Annotating Corpora for Research in the Humanities (ACRH-2)*, Lisbon.

Andrea Ernst-Gerlach and Norbert Fuhr. 2006. Generating search term variants for text collections with historic spellings. In *Proceedings of the 28th European Conference on Information Retrieval Research (ECIR 2006)*, München.

Ian Goodfellow, Yoshua Bengio, and Aaron Courville. 2018. *Deep Learning: Das umfassende Handbuch. Grundlagen, aktuelle Verfahren und Algorithmen, neue Forschungsansätze*. MIT Press.

Lisa Klaffki, Stefan Schmunk, and Thomas Stäcker. 2018. *Stand der Kulturgutdigitalisierung in Deutschland: Eine Analyse und Handlungsvorschläge des DARIAH-DE Stakeholdergremiums "Wissenschaftliche Sammlungen"*. DARIAH-DE working papers 26. Göttingen.

[13] In Ermangelung von geeigneten Sprachkürzeln gemäß ISO 639 werden die im FWB verwendeten Sprachkürzel verwendet.

Markus Konrad. 2019. GermaLemma: A lemmatizer for German language text. https://github.com/WZBSocialScienceCenter/germalemma.

Matthias Liebeck and Stefan Conrad. 2015. IWNLP: Inverse Wiktionary for natural language processing. In *Proceedings of the 53rd Annual Meeting of the Association for Computational Linguistics and the 7th International Joint Conference on Natural Language Processing (Short Papers)*, pages 414–418, Beijing, China.

Roland Mittmann. 2016. Automatisierter Abgleich des Lautstandes althochdeutscher Wortformen. *Journal for Language Technology and Computational Linguistics*, 31(2):17–24. Special issue on Corpora and Resources for (Historical) Low Resource Languages.

Thomas Pilz, Andrea Ernst-Gerlach, Sebastian Kempken, and Paul Rayson. 2007. The identification of spelling variants in English and German historical texts: Manual or automatic? *Literary and Linguistic Computing*, 23(1).

Hans Joachim Postel. 1969. *Die Kölner Phonetik. Ein Verfahren zur Identifizierung von Personennamen auf der Grundlage der Gestaltanalyse*. IBM-Nachrichten, 19. Jahrgang. Stuttgart.

Tariq Rashid. 2017. *Neuronale Netze selbst programmieren. Ein verständlicher Einstieg mit Python*. O'Reilly, Heidelberg.

Oskar Reichmann. 1986. *Frühneuhochdeutsches Wörterbuch. Band 1: Einführung, a - äpfelkern*. Berlin, New York. Herausgeber: Robert R. Anderson [für Band 1], Ulrich Goebel, Anja Lobenstein-Reichmann [Einzelbände] & Oskar Reichmann [Bände 3 und 7 in Verbindung mit dem Institut für deutsche Sprache; ab Band 9, Lieferung 5 im Auftrag der Akademie der Wissenschaften zu Göttingen].

Helmut Schmid. 2019. Deep learning-based morphological taggers and lemmatizers for annotating historical texts. In *Proceedings of the 3rd International Conference on Digital Access to Textual Cultural Heritage (DATeCH2019)*, page 133–137. Association for Computing Machinery.

Joachim Steinwendner and Roland Schwaiger. 2019. *Neuronale Netze programmieren mit Python*. Rheinwerk, Bonn.

Christian Wartena. 2019. A probabilistic morphology model for German lemmatization. In *Proceedings of the 15th Conference on Natural Language Processing (KONVENS 2019)*, pages 40–49.

William E. Winkler. 1990. String comparator metrics and enhanced decision rules in the Fellegi-Sunter model of record linkage. In *Proceedings of the Section on Survey Research Methods*, Göttingen.

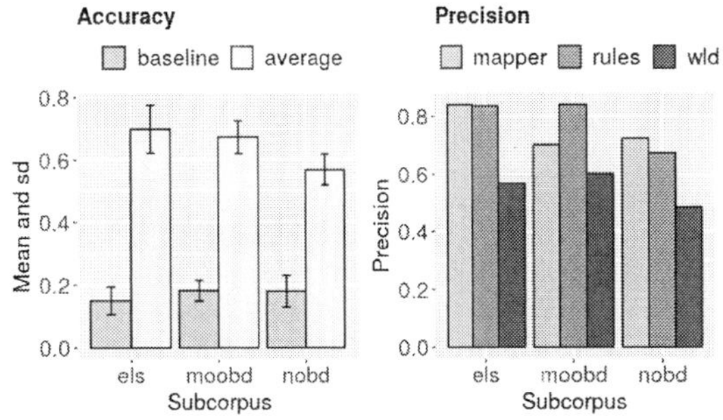

Abbildung 7: Genauigkeit (links) und Precision der einzelnen Normalisierer (rechts) in der ersten Evaluation von Norma

Appendix

Norma als Lemmatisierer Norma wurde für die Normalisierung flektierter Wortformen entwickelt. Für die VKF-Identifikation setzen wir Norma abweichend dafür ein, VKF-Kandidaten aus Belegen zu lemmatisieren. In einer ersten Evaluation untersuchten wir daher zunächst, wie gut Norma flektierte Originalschreibungen auf standardisierte Lemmata abbilden kann. Dazu führten wir eine sechsfache Crossvalidierung durch und trainierten Norma auf jeweils 500 Paaren aus drei verschiedenen Sprachräumen (Nordoberdeutsch/nobd, Mittleres Ostoberdeutsch/moobd, Elsässisch/els) und evaluierten auf jeweils 100 Paaren. Dieselben Splits wurden in Kap. 6 für die Evaluation der VKF-Identifikation durch Norma genutzt.

Als Baseline verwendeten wir ein einfaches System, das jeweils die vorliegende Wortform als Lemma vorhersagt.

Abb. 7 zeigt die Ergebnisse. Die Baseline der Genauigkeit liegt zwischen 15,0–18,2%, die Durchschnittswerte ("average") zwischen 56,8-69,8% pro Teilkorpus, was Norma für die (wesentlich leichtere) Aufgabe der VKF-Identifikation als mögliches Tool erscheinen lässt. Die Normalisierer Mapper und Rules erreichen gute Precision-Werte (Mapper: 70,1–84,0%, Rules: 67,3–84,0%). WLD schneidet am schlechtesten ab (48,3–60,1%), allerdings muss hier berücksichtigt werden, dass WLD als letzte Komponente die "schwierigen" Fälle übernimmt und insgesamt die meisten Wortformen lemmatisiert (gesamt: 1.800; WLD: 1.013; Mapper: 453; Rules: 333; ohne Analyse: 1). In allen Fällen sind die Werte für das Korpus nobd am niedrigsten.

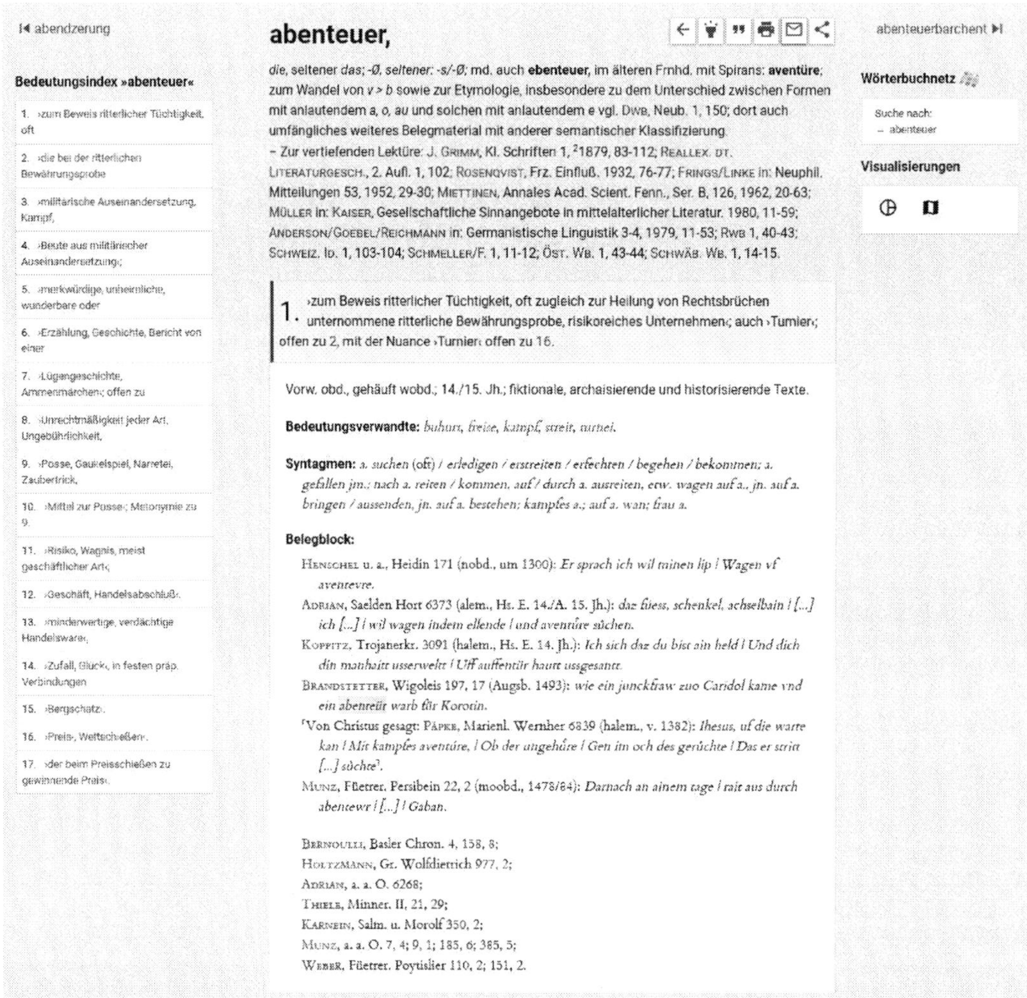

Abbildung 8: Beispielhafter Bedeutungsansatz 1 des Lemmas *abenteuer* in der Online-Ausgabe des FWB (`http://fwb-online.de/go/abenteuer.s.1fn_1619637065`, letzter Zugriff: 03.06.2021)

Emotion Stimulus Detection in German News Headlines

Bao Minh Doan Dang, Laura Oberländer, and **Roman Klinger**
Institut für Maschinelle Sprachverarbeitung, University of Stuttgart, Germany
st117194@stud.uni-stuttgart.de,
{laura.oberlaender, roman.klinger}@ims.uni-stuttgart.de

Abstract

Emotion stimulus extraction is a fine-grained subtask of emotion analysis that focuses on identifying the description of the cause behind an emotion expression from a text passage (e.g., in the sentence "I am happy that I passed my exam" the phrase "passed my exam" corresponds to the stimulus.). Previous work mainly focused on Mandarin and English, with no resources or models for German. We fill this research gap by developing a corpus of 2006 German news headlines annotated with emotions and 811 instances with annotations of stimulus phrases. Given that such corpus creation efforts are time-consuming and expensive, we additionally work on an approach for projecting the existing English GoodNewsEveryone (GNE) corpus to a machine-translated German version. We compare the performance of a conditional random field (CRF) model (trained monolingually on German and cross-lingually via projection) with a multilingual XLM-RoBERTa (XLM-R) model. Our results show that training with the German corpus achieves higher F1 scores than projection. Experiments with XLM-R outperform their respective CRF counterparts.

1 Introduction

Emotions are a complex phenomenon that play a central role in our experiences and daily communications. Understanding them cannot be accounted by any single area of study since they can be represented and expressed in different ways, e.g., via facial expressions, voice, language, or gestures. In natural language processing, most models build on top of one out of three approaches to study and understand emotions, namely basic emotions (Ekman, 1992; Strapparava and Mihalcea, 2007; Aman and Szpakowicz, 2007), the valence-arousal model (Russell, 1980; Buechel and Hahn, 2017) or cognitive appraisal theory (Scherer, 2005; Hofmann et al., 2020, 2021). Emotion classification in text has received abundant attention in natural language processing research in the past few years. Hence, many studies have been conducted to investigate emotions on social media (Stieglitz and Dang-Xuan, 2013; Brynielsson et al., 2014; Tromp and Pechenizkiy, 2015), in literary and poetry texts (Kim and Klinger, 2019; Haider et al., 2020) or for analysing song lyrics (Mihalcea and Strapparava, 2012; Hijra Ferdinan et al., 2018; Edmonds and Sedoc, 2021). However, previous work mostly focused on assigning emotions to sentences or text passages. These approaches do not allow to identify which event, object, or person caused the emotion (which we refer to as the *stimulus*).

Emotion stimulus detection is the subtask of emotion analysis which aims at extracting the stimulus of an expressed emotion. For instance, in the following example from FrameNet (Fillmore et al., 2003) "Holmes is happy having the freedom of the house when we are out" one could assume that *happiness* or *joy* is the emotion in the text. One could also highlight that the term "happy" indicates the emotion, "Holmes" is the experiencer and the phrase "having the freedom of the house when we are out" (underlined) is the stimulus for the perceived emotion. Detecting emotion stimuli provides additional information for a better understanding of the emotion structures (e.g., semantic frames associated with emotions). More than that, the fact that stimuli are essential in understanding the emotion evoked in a text is supported by research in psychology; Appraisal theorists of emotions seem to agree that emotions include a cognitive evaluative component of an event (Scherer, 2005). Therefore emotion stimulus detection brings the field of emotion analysis in NLP closer to the state of the art in psychology.

To the best of our knowledge, there are mostly corpora published for Mandarin (Lee et al., 2010b;

Gui et al., 2014, 2016; Gao et al., 2017) and English (Ghazi et al., 2015; Mohammad et al., 2014; Kim and Klinger, 2018; Bostan et al., 2020). We are not aware of any study that created resources or models for identifying emotion stimuli in German. We fill this gap and contribute the GERSTI (GERman STImulus) corpus with 2006 German news headlines. The headlines have been annotated for emotion categories, for the mention of an experiencer or a cue phrase, and for stimuli on the token level (on which we focus in this paper). News headlines have been selected as the domain because they concisely provide concrete information and are easy to obtain. Additionally, unlike social media texts, this genre avoids potential privacy issues (Bostan et al., 2020). Given that annotating such a corpus is time-consuming, we propose a heuristic method for projecting an annotated dataset from a source language to a target language. This helps to increase the amount of training data without manually annotating a huge dataset. Within this study, the GoodNewsEveryone corpus (GNE, Bostan et al., 2020) is selected as an English counterpart.

Our contributions are therefore: (1) the creation, publication, and linguistic analysis of the GERSTI dataset to understand the structure of German stimulus mentions;[1] (2), the evaluation of baseline models using different combinations of feature sets; and (3) comparison of this in-corpus training with cross-lingual training via projection and with a pre-trained cross-lingual language model with XLM-RoBERTa (Conneau et al., 2020).

2 Related Work

We now introduce previous work on emotion analysis and for detecting emotion stimuli.

2.1 Emotion Analysis

Emotion analysis is the task of understanding emotions in text, typically based on psychological theories of Ekman (1992), Plutchik (2001), Russell (1980) or Scherer (2005). Several corpora have been built for emotion classification such as Alm and Sproat (2005) with tales, Strapparava and Mihalcea (2007) with news headlines, Aman and Szpakowicz (2007) with blog posts, Buechel and Hahn (2017) with various domains or Li et al. (2017) with conversations. Some datasets were created using crowdsourcing, for instance Mohammad et al. (2014) , Mohammad and Kiritchenko (2015) or Bostan et al. (2020), that have been annotated with tweets, or news headlines, respectively. Some resources mix various annotation paradigms, for example Troiano et al. (2019) (self-reporting and crowd-sourcing) or Haider et al. (2020) (experts and crowdworkers).

Emotion analysis also includes other aspects such as emotion intensities and emotion roles (Aman and Szpakowicz, 2007; Mohammad and Bravo-Marquez, 2017; Bostan et al., 2020) including experiencers, targets, and stimuli (Mohammad et al., 2014; Kim and Klinger, 2018).

2.2 Stimulus Detection

Emotion stimulus detection received substantial attention for Chinese Mandarin (Lee et al., 2010b; Li and Xu, 2014; Gui et al., 2014, 2016; Cheng et al., 2017, i.a.). Only few corpora have been created for English (Neviarouskaya and Aono, 2013; Mohammad et al., 2014; Kim and Klinger, 2018; Bostan et al., 2020). Russo et al. (2011) worked on a dataset for Italian news texts and Yada et al. (2017) annotated Japanese sentences from news articles and question/answer websites.

Lee et al. (2010b,a) developed linguistic rules to extract emotion stimuli. A follow-up study developed a machine learning model that combines different sets of such rules (Chen et al., 2010). Gui et al. (2014) extended these rules and machine learning models on their Weibo corpus. Ghazi et al. (2015) formulated the task as structured learning.

Most methods for stimulus detection have been evaluated on Mandarin. Gui et al. (2016) propose a convolution kernel-based learning method and train a classifier to extract emotion stimulus events on the clause level. Gui et al. (2017) treat emotion stimulus extraction as a question answering task. Li et al. (2018) use a co-attention neural network. Chen et al. (2018) explore a joint method for emotion classification and emotion stimulus detection in order to capture mutual benefits across these two tasks. Similarly, Xia et al. (2019) evaluate a hierarchical recurrent neural network transformer model to classify multiple clauses. They show that solving these subtasks jointly is beneficial for the model's performance.

Xia and Ding (2019) redefine the task as emotion/cause pair extraction and intend to detect potential emotions and corresponding causes in text.

[1] The data is available at `https://www.ims.uni-stuttgart.de/data/emotion`.

Xu et al. (2019) tackle the emotion/cause pair extraction task by adopting a learning-to-rank method. Wei et al. (2020) also argue for the use of a ranking approach. They rank each possible emotion/cause pair instead of solely ranking stimulus phrases. Fan et al. (2020) do not subdivide the emotion/cause pair detection task into two subtasks but propose a framework to detect emotions and their associated causes simultaneously.

Oberländer and Klinger (2020) studied whether sequence labeling or clause classification is appropriate for extracting English stimuli. As we assume that these findings also hold for German, we follow their finding that token sequence labeling is more appropriate.

3 Corpus Creation

To tackle German emotion stimulus detection on the token-level, we select headlines from various online news portals, remove duplicates and irrelevant items, and further subselect relevant instances with an emotion dictionary. Two annotators then label the data. We describe this process in detail in the following.

3.1 Data Collection

We select various German news sources and their RSS feeds based on listings at a news overview website[2] and add some regional online newspapers.[3] The collected corpus consists of headlines between September 30, 2020 and October 7, 2020 and between October 22 and October 23, 2020 with 9000 headlines, spread across several domains including *politics*, *sports*, *tech and business*, *science* and *travel*.

3.2 Data Preprocessing and Filtering

Short headlines, for instance "Verlobung!" or "Krasser After-Baby-Body" do not contain sufficient information for our annotation, therefore we omit sentences that have less than 5 words. Further, we remove generic parts of the headline, like "++ Transferticker ++", "+++ LIVE +++" or "News-" and only keep the actual headline texts.

We also remove headlines that start with particular key words which denote a specific event which would not contribute to an understanding of

No.	Linguistics Rules
1.	Stimuli can be described by verbal or nominal phrases
2.	Subjunctions like "because of" belong to the sequence
3.	Conjunctions like "and", "or" and "but" connect main clauses. They can therefore belong to a stimulus sequence.
4.	Antecedents, if present, are annotated as stimuli
5.	If antecedent is not present, an anaphora may be annotated instead
6.	Composites with "-" are considered a single word
7.	Stimuli can include one or multiple words
8.	Punctuation (e.g. ,.-:;“”!?) should not be labeled as stimulus

Table 1: Linguistics rules for annotating stimuli.

emotions or stimuli, such as "Interview", "Kommentare", "Liveblog", "Exklusive", as well as visual content like "Video", "TV" or "Pop". Additionally, we discard instances which include dates, like "Lotto am Mittwoch, 30.09.2020" or "Corona-News am 05.10".[4]

After filtering, we select instances that are likely to be associated with an emotion with the help of an emotion lexicon (Klinger et al., 2016). For this purpose, we accept headlines which include at least one entry from the dictionary.

3.3 Annotation

The annotation of the 2006 headlines which remain after preprocessing and filtering consists of two phases. In the first phase, emotion cues, experiencers and emotion classes are annotated, while stimuli are addressed in the second phase only for those instances which received an emotion label. Table 8 in the Appendix shows the questions to be answered during this annotation procedure. Each headline in the dataset is judged by two annotators. One of them is female (23 years old) while the other annotator is male (26 years old). The first annotator has a background in digital humanities and linguistics, while the second has a background in library and information management. After each phase, we combine overlapping stimulus annotations by choosing the parts annotated by both annotators, and discuss the cases where the annotations do not overlap until a consensus is reached.

Guidelines. We created an initial version of guidelines motivated by Lee et al. (2010b,a); Gui et al. (2014); Ghazi et al. (2015). Based on two batches of 25 headlines, and one with 50 headlines,

[2] `https://www.deutschland.de/de/topic/wissen/nachrichten`, accessed on April 27, 2021

[3] The list of RSS feeds is available in the supplemental material.

[4] Details in Supplementary Material.

					F_1	
		κ			tok.	span
Iteration	Cue	Exp.	Emo.		Stim.	
Prelim. 1	.22	.43	.25	—	—	—
Prelim. 2	.71	.49	.47	—	—	—
Prelim. 3	.46	.69	.44	—	.65	—
Final	.56	.57	.51	.68	.72	.56

Table 2: Inter-annotator agreement for the binary tasks of annotating the existance of cue mentions, experiencer mentions, the multi-label annotation of emotion labels, and the token-level annotation of stimulus spans. The F_1-span value for stimuli is an exact match value for the whole span.

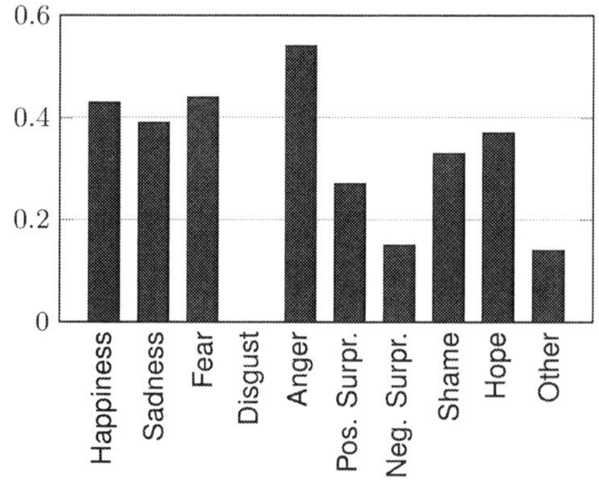

Figure 1: κ for all emotion classes.

we refined the guidelines in three iterations. After each iteration, we calculated inter-annotator agreement scores and discussed the annotator's results. It should be noted that we only considered annotating emotions in the first two iterations. The sample annotation of emotion stimuli on the token-level has been performed in the third round, i.e., after two discussions and guideline refinements. During these discussions, we improved the formulation of the annotation task, provided more detailed descriptions for each predefined emotion and clarified the concept of sequence labeling using the IOB scheme. Additionally, we formulated several linguistic rules that help annotating stimuli (see Table 1).

Details. The goal of Phase 1 of the annotation procedure is to identify headlines with an emotional connotation. Those which do then receive stimulus annotations in Phase 2.

We annotated in a spread sheet application. In Phase 1a both annotators received 2006 headlines. They were instructed to annotate whether a headline expresses an emotion by judging if cue words or experiencers are mentioned in the text. Further, only one, the most dominant, emotion is to be annotated (*happiness*, *sadness*, *fear*, *disgust*, *anger*, *positive surprise*, *negative surprise*, *shame*, *hope*, *other* and *no emotion*). In Phase 1b we aggregated emotion annotations and jointly discussed non-overlapping labels to a consensus annotation.

In Phase 2a, annotators were instructed to label pretokenized headlines with the IOB alphabet for stimulus spans – namely those which received an emotion label in Phase 1 (811 instances). In Phase 2b, we aggregated the stimulus span annotations to a gold standard by accepting all overlapping tokens of both annotators in cases where they partially matched. For the other cases where the stimulus annotations did not overlap, we discussed the annotations to reach an agreement.

Agreement Results. Table 2 presents the inter-annotator agreement scores for the preliminary annotation rounds and for the final corpus. We observe that the results are moderate across classes. Figure 1 illustrates the agreement for each emotion class. The emotions *anger*, *fear*, and *happiness* show the highest agreement, while *surprise*, *other*, and particularly *disgust* show lower scores.

For the stimulus annotation, we evaluate the agreement via token-level Cohen's κ, via token-level F_1, and via exact span-match F_1 (in the first two cases, B and I labels are considered to be different). The token-level result for the final corpus is substantial with κ =.68, F_1 =.72 and moderate for the exact span match, with F_1 =.56 (see Table 2).

4 Corpus Analysis

4.1 Quantitative Analysis

Our corpus consists of 2006 headlines with 20,544 tokens and 6,763 unique terms. From those, 811 instances were labeled with an emotion category and received stimulus annotations on the token-level. The shortest headline consists of five words, while the longest has 20 words. The headlines are on average short with nine words. The stimulus spans range from one to eleven tokens and have four words on average.

Table 3 summarizes the corpus statistics of GERSTI. For aggregating emotion cue and experiencer we accept instances for which the mention of these emotion roles has been annotated by one annotator. For all emotions, most instances include the mention of an emotion cue (likely biased by our sam-

Emotion	# inst.	w/ cue	w/ exp	w/ stimulus	avg. |stimulus|
Happiness	80	80	77	76	3.72
Sadness	65	65	54	59	4.07
Fear	177	117	138	167	3.83
Disgust	3	3	2	3	4.00
Anger	226	226	195	208	3.86
Pos. Surprise	51	51	45	44	4.11
Neg. Surprise	142	140	125	130	3.96
Shame	9	9	9	8	3.75
Hope	20	19	16	19	4.05
Other	38	37	26	34	3.71
No Emo.	1195	930	109	-	-
All	2006	1737	796	748	3.9

Table 3: Corpus statistics. Columns show the amount of annotated instances for emotion cue, experiencer, stimulus and the average length of all stimulus spans within each respective dominant emotion. For aggregating cue and experiencer, cases where one of the annotators annotated with a *yes* have been accepted.

Emotion	News Sources
Happiness	Bild, Welt, Stuttgarter Zeitung
Sadness	Bild, Spiegel, Stuttgarter Z.
Fear	Stuttgarter Z., Bild, Welt
Disgust	T-Online, Welt, Spiegel
Anger	Bild, Stuttgarter Z., Spiegel
Pos. Surprise	Welt, Focus, Bild
Neg. Surprise	Bild, Stuttgarter Z., Spiegel
Shame	Stuttgarter Z., Bild, Welt
Hope	T-Online, Bild, Stuttgarter Z.
Other	Bild, Stuttgarter Z., Welt

Table 4: Top three most observed media sources for each dominant emotion sorted by frequency.

pling procedure). Further, the number of headlines with mentions of a stimulus and an experiencer is also high for those instances which are labeled to be associated with an emotion.

Table 4 presents the most common sources, sorted by their frequencies, for each aggregated emotion during Phase 1b. Not surprisingly, *Bild-Zeitung* is to be found in the top three for almost all emotion classes, followed by *Stuttgarter-Zeitung* and *Welt*. In particular, in five out of ten of the emotions, *Bild-Zeitung* takes the first place. As Table 3 demonstrates, *disgust* is relatively rare, we therefore list all available sources for this emotion category. Furthermore, four in five most frequently annotated emotions are negative (*anger*, *fear*, *negative surprise*, *happiness*, *sadness*).

Note that this analysis does not necessarily reflect the actual quality of chosen news sources. The findings we report here might strongly be biased by the data collection time span.

4.2 Qualitative Analysis of Stimuli

To obtain a better understanding of stimuli in German, we analyse which words together with their preferred grammatical realizations are likely to indicate a stimulus phrase. For this purpose, we examine the parts of speech[5] of terms that are directly left positioned to stimulus phrases, inside the stimulus phrases and right after it (see Table 5). We further compare our findings with Mandarin (Lee et al., 2010a) and English (Bostan et al., 2020).

Our analysis shows that for GERSTI common nouns, proper nouns, punctuation, and verbs are most frequently located directly to the left of stimulus mentions (common nouns ≈26%, punctuation ≈28%, verbs ≈22%, proper nouns ≈0.09%). Often, these words are emotionally connotated, for instance as in the nouns "Streit", "Angst", "Hoffnung" or "Kritik" or the verbs "warnen", "kritisieren", "bedrohen", "beklagen" or "kämpfen".

There are discrepancies between German and Mandarin stimuli. Lee et al. (2010a,b) state that prepositions or conjunctions mostly indicate stimulus phrases in Mandarin, while this is not the case for German due to our predefined annotation rules (Rule 2 from Table 1). Furthermore, indicator words for Chinese stimulus events do not cover common nouns or proper nouns. However, verbs seem to emphasize emotion causes in both languages.

Compared to GNE, we also notice some differences: English stimuli do not begin with prepositions, but prepositions are most likely to be included in the stimulus span ((ADP) ≈0.14% in GNE vs ≈0.03% in GERSTI). Further, by looking at the part of speech tags that were relevant in indicating the stimuli for GERSTI we see that they are dominating for GNE as well. However, there are far more proper nouns than common nouns and quite fewer verbs that occur right before the stimulus phrase (common nouns≈11%, punctuation ≈21%, verbs ≈0.09%, proper nouns ≈0.25%).

[5]We use spaCy, `https://spacy.io/usage/linguistic-features`, accessed on April 29, 2021

	GERSTI				GNE			
POS	All	Inside	Before@1	After@1	All	Inside	Before@1	After@1
NOUN	.28	.33 (1.17×)	.26 (0.93×)	.00 (0.01×)	.16	.17 (1.09×)	.11 (0.69×)	.17 (1.05×)
ADP	.15	.22 (1.48×)	.03 (0.19×)	.23 (1.54×)	.10	.12 (1.12×)	.14 (1.37×)	.20 (1.95×)
PROPN	.14	.09 (0.65×)	.09 (0.68×)	.01 (0.04×)	.30	.26 (0.89×)	.25 (0.86×)	.25 (0.83×)
PUNCT	.13	.02 (0.16×)	.28 (2.23×)	.49 (3.87×)	.09	.07 (0.82×)	.21 (2.40×)	.08 (0.91×)
VERB	.09	.09 (0.91×)	.22 (2.32×)	.16 (1.68×)	.11	.12 (1.06×)	.09 (0.80×)	.09 (0.85×)
DET	.05	.08 (1.47×)	.00 (0.09×)	.01 (0.16×)	.04	.05 (1.03×)	.04 (0.81×)	.03 (0.63×)
ADJ	.05	.07 (1.44×)	.00 (0.03×)	.01 (0.29×)	.05	.05 (1.09×)	.02 (0.42×)	.03 (0.53×)
ADV	.05	.05 (1.04×)	.04 (0.87×)	.04 (0.93×)	.02	.02 (1.07×)	.02 (0.80×)	.03 (1.47×)
AUX	.02	.01 (0.75×)	.04 (2.34×)	.03 (1.68×)	.03	.03 (1.01×)	.03 (1.16×)	.03 (1.11×)
PRON	.01	.01 (0.71×)	.02 (1.02×)	.00 (0.19×)	.03	.03 (1.14×)	.01 (0.45×)	.02 (0.63×)
NUM	.01	.02 (1.49×)	.00 (0.00×)	.00 (0.00×)	.02	.02 (1.15×)	.01 (0.27×)	.01 (0.34×)
CCONJ	.01	.01 (0.97×)	.01 (0.55×)	.01 (0.77×)	.01	.01 (1.21×)	.00 (0.64×)	.02 (3.82×)

Table 5: Relative frequencies of POS tags of all tokens in GERSTI and GNE datasets (All) vs relative frequencies of POS tags inside the stimuli spans (Inside), before and after the stimuli spans (Before@1, After@1). For all the columns that show frequencies of the spans related to the stimuli we show the factor (×) of how much it differs to the global frequencies in All.

Often, these indicator words of English stimuli do not as directly evoke an emotion. For instance, "say", "make", "woman", "people" or "police" are often observed to be directly left located words of English stimuli. Nevertheless, similar to GERSTI, stimuli from GNE corpus are not indicated by conjunctions, numerals or pronouns.

The positioning of the stimuli is only similar to a limited degree in German and English: 53% of the instances in GERSTI end with the stimulus (86% in English GNE) and 13% begin with the stimulus (11% in GNE).

5 Experiments

In the following, we explain how we project annotation from an English stimulus corpus to a machine-translated counterpart. Based on this, we evaluate how well a linear-chain conditional random field (Lafferty et al., 2001) performs with the projected dataset in comparison to the monolingual setup. We compare that result to the use of the pre-trained language model *XLM-RoBERTa* (XLM-R) (Conneau et al., 2020).

5.1 Annotation Projection

We use the GNE dataset (Bostan et al., 2020) which is a large English annotated corpus of news headlines. Stimulus sequences in this dataset are comparatively longer with eight tokens on average.

We translate the GNE corpus via *DeepL*[6] and perform the annotation projection as follows: We first translate the whole source instance $\mathbf{t}_{\text{en}}$ to the translation $\mathbf{t}_{\text{de}}$ (from English to German). We further translate the stimulus token sequence $\mathbf{stim}_{\text{en}}$ to $\mathbf{stim}_{\text{de}}$. We assume the stimulus annotation for $\mathbf{t}_{\text{de}}$ to correspond to all tokens in $\mathbf{stim}_{\text{de}}$, heuristically corrected to be a consecutive sequence.

5.2 Experimental Setting

5.2.1 Models

CRF. We implement the linear-chain conditional random field model via the CRF-suite in Scikit-learn[7] and extract different features. What we call *corpus-based features* contains the frequency of a current word in the whole corpus, position label for first (*begin*), last (*end*) and remaining (*middle*) words of the headline, if the current word is capitalized, or entirely in upper or lowercase, if the token is a number, a punctuation symbol, or in the list of 50 most frequent words in our corpus.

We further include *linguistic features*, namely the part-of-speech tag, the syntactic dependency between the current token and its head, if it is a stopword or if it has a named entity label (and which one it is).

We further add a feature which specifies whether the token is part of an emotion-word dictionary (Klinger et al., 2016). Additionally, we combine the feature vector of the preceding and succeeding token (we add the prefixes *prev* and *next* to each feature name) with the current token to get information about surrounding words. We mark the first and last token with additional features.

[6] `https://www.deepl.com/en/translator`, accessed on May 20, 2021

[7] `https://sklearn-crfsuite.readthedocs.io/en/latest/`, accessed on April 30, 2021

RoBERTa. We use the pre-trained *XLM-RoBERTa* base model with the *HuggingFace*[8] library from Wolf et al. (2020). In addition to the pre-trained transformer, we add a linear layer which outputs a sequence of IOB tags for each input sentence. We fine-tune the language model in five epochs and use a batch size of 16 during training, a dropout rate of 0.5, and the Adam optimizer with weight decay (Loshchilov and Hutter, 2019), with a learning rate of 10^{-5} and a maximum gradient norm of 1.0.

Setup. For our experiments, we only use the 811 instances from the GERSTI dataset that received annotations for emotion stimuli. We split them into a train and validation subset (80 %/20 %) and perform experiments in three different settings. In the *in-corpus training*, we train with the GERSTI training data and test on the test corpus. In the *projection* setting, we train on the english GNE data and test on the German GERSTI test data (either with the CRF via projection or directly with the XLM-R model). In the *aggregation* setting, we use both the English train data and the German train data for training.

5.2.2 Evaluation Metrics

We evaluate the stimuli prediction as follows (following Ghazi et al. (2015) and Oberländer and Klinger (2020)): *Exact* match leads to a true positive for an exactly correct span prediction. *Partial* accepts a predicted stimulus as true positive if at least one token overlaps with a gold standard span. A variation is *Left/Right*, where the left/right boundary needs to perfectly match the gold standard.

5.3 Results

Table 6 reports the results for our experiments. The top four blocks compare the importance of the feature set choice for the CRF approach.

In nearly all combinations of model and evaluation measure, the in-corpus evaluation leads to the best performance – adding data from the GNE corpus only slightly improves for the *Partially* evaluation setting when the CRF is limited to corpus features. The projection-based approach, where the model does not have access to the GERSTI training data consistently shows a lower performance, with approximately a drop by 50 % in F_1 score.

Model	F_1	in-corp.	proj.	aggre.
CRF with corpus features	Exact	**.38**	.19	.33
	Partial	.49	.43	**.52**
	Left	**.42**	.22	.38
	Right	**.51**	.41	**.51**
CRF with linguistic features	Exact	**.42**	.16	.35
	Partial	***.58***	.41	.54
	Left	**.52**	.19	*.43*
	Right	***.57***	.40	*.53*
CRF with corp.+lingu. features	Exact	***.45***	.19	.35
	Partial	**.57**	*.48*	.53
	Left	***.53***	.24	.41
	Right	**.56**	*.47*	.52
CRF with all features	Exact	**.42**	*.20*	*.36*
	Partial	**.56**	*.48*	*.55*
	Left	**.50**	*.25*	*.43*
	Right	**.55**	.46	*.53*
RoBERTa XLM-R	Exact	**.47**	.25	.45
	Partial	**.75**	.61	.70
	Left	**.68**	.35	.58
	Right	.71	.59	**.72**

Table 6: Results for the CRF models with different feature sets and the XLM-R model. Highest F_1-scores in each row printed with **bold face**, highest score in column/per evaluation measure is underlined, highest score in each column and per evaluation measure in the CRF is printed *italics*.

The linguistic features particularly help the CRF in the *Exact* evaluation setting, but all feature set choices are dominated by the results of the XLM-RoBERTa model. This deep learning approach shows the best results across all models, and is particularly better in the *Partial* evaluation setting, with 19pp, 13pp and 15pp improvement.

Both projection and aggregation models indicate that extracting the beginning of a stimulus span is challenging. We assume that both models have learned English stimulus structures and therefore could not generalize well on the German emotion stimuli (also see Section 4.2).

5.4 Error Analysis

We now discuss the model's quality (see Table 7) based on various error types, namely *Early Start*, *Late Start*, *Early Stop*, *Late Stop*, *Surrounding* (*Early Start* & *Late stop*) and *Consecutive* error.

Both CRF and XLM-R with projection settings have largely generated *Early Start* and *Late Stop* errors. These models tend to detect longer stimulus segments than annotated in the gold data. This might be a consequence of English stimuli being longer than in German. Despite the fact that a CRF does not have an understanding of the length

[8] `https://huggingface.co/xlm-roberta-base`, accessed on April 30, 2021

Err. Type	Example	Setup
Early start	Hof in Bayern: 21-Jähriger [nach tödlichem Autounfall zu Court in Bavaria : 21-year-old after deadly car-accident to Bewährungsstrafe verurteilt] probation convicted *Court in Bavaria: 21-year-old sentenced to probation after fatal car accident*	projection
Late start	Peter Madsen in Dänemark: Kim Walls Mörder [scheitert bei Peter Madsen in Denmark : Kim Wall's murderer fails by Fluchtversuch aus Gefängnis] escape-attempt from prison *Peter Madsen from Denmark: Kim Wall's killer fails in escape attempt from prison*	in-corpus
Early stop	Noch mehr Eltern erzählen [von den unheimlichen Dingen, die ihr Even more parents tell about the scary things , that their Kind mal gesagt hat] child once said has *More parents share creepy things their kid once said*	in-corpus
Late stop	In Paris: [Lauter Knall] schreckt Menschen auf - Ursache schnell In Paris : Loud bang scares people on - Cause quickly gefunden found *In Paris: Loud bang startles people - cause quickly found*	aggregation
Surrounding	EU-Gipfel: Streit[über Linie zur Tükei] - Erdogan reagiert mit Häme EU-summit : Dispute about line to Turkey - Erdogan reacts with gloat *EU-summit: Dispute over line on Turkey - Erdogan responds with gloating*	projection
Consecutive	Niederlage für Autohersteller: [Betriebsratswahl bei Daimler Defeat for car-manufacturer : work-council-election by Daimler ungültig] invalid *Defeat for car manufacturer: Daimler's work council election invalid*	aggregation

Table 7: Example headlines for examined error types. Gold annotations correspond to tokens between [ ]. Predicted stimulus segments are highlighted as follows: red (B tag), blue (I tag). English translations for each sample are written in *italics*. All examples stem from the CRF models except the last one.

of span due to the Markov property, it has a bias weight for transitions between I labels. An example for such a case is the first instance from Table 7 the projection setting also extracted the token "21-Jähriger" as the start of the stimulus sequence. This explains the difference between partial and exact F_1 scores in Table 6.

The *Surrounding* exemplifies that the models tend to predict the beginning of a stimulus span directly after a colon. In contrast, in the in-corpus experiments (particularly with XLM-R), models tend to generate *Late Start* and *Early Stop* errors more often. For example the second headline from Table 7 shows a missing prediction of the verb "scheitert". Instead, the preposition "bei" is found as the start of the stimulus phrase. Further, in the subsequent example, this model setting does not cover the phrase "die ihr Kind mal gesagt hat" in the stimulus segment. Both sample headlines demonstrate that in-corpus models tend to label prepositions as the start of stimulus sequences.

In the XML-R experiments, we opted against the use of a Viterbi-decoded output layer (like a CRF output) – this leads to errors of the *Consecutive* type, as shown in the last example: start and end of the stimulus are correctly found, but tokens in between have been missed.

6 Conclusion and Future Work

We introduced the first annotated German corpus for identifying emotion stimuli and provided baseline model results for various CRF configurations and an XLM-R model. We additionally proposed a data projection method.

Our results show training and testing the model in the same language outperforms cross-lingual models. Further, the XLM-R model that uses a multilingual distributional semantic space outperforms the projection. However, based on partial matches, we see that, when approximate matches are sufficient projection and multilingual methods show an acceptable result.

Previous work has shown that the task of stimulus detection can be formulated as token sequence labeling or as clause classification (Oberländer and Klinger, 2020). In this paper we limited our analysis and modeling on the sequence labeling approach. Thus, we leave to future work the comparison with the clause-classification approach. However, from the results obtained, we find sequence labeling an adequate formulation in German.

For further future work, we suggest experimenting with the other existing corpora in English to examine whether the cross-lingual approach would work well on other domains. Regarding this, one could also train and improve models not only for language change but also to extract stimuli across different domains. Subsequently, another aspect that should be investigated is the simultaneous recognition of emotion categories and stimuli.

Acknowledgements

This work was supported by Deutsche Forschungsgemeinschaft (project CEAT, KL 2869/1-2). Thanks to Pavlos Musenidis for fruitful discussions and feedback on this study.

References

Cecilia Ovesdotter Alm and Richard Sproat. 2005. Emotional sequencing and development in fairy tales. In *Affective Computing and Intelligent Interaction*, pages 668–674, Berlin, Heidelberg. Springer Berlin Heidelberg.

Saima Aman and Stan Szpakowicz. 2007. Identifying expressions of emotion in text. In *Text, Speech and Dialogue*, pages 196–205. Springer Berlin Heidelberg.

Laura Ana Maria Bostan, Evgeny Kim, and Roman Klinger. 2020. GoodNewsEveryone: A corpus of news headlines annotated with emotions, semantic roles, and reader perception. In *Proceedings of the 12th Language Resources and Evaluation Conference*, pages 1554–1566, Marseille, France. European Language Resources Association.

Joel Brynielsson, Fredrik Johansson, Carl Jonsson, and Anders Westling. 2014. Emotion classification of social media posts for estimating people's reactions to communicated alert messages during crises. *Security Informatics*, 3(1):1–11.

Sven Buechel and Udo Hahn. 2017. EmoBank: Studying the impact of annotation perspective and representation format on dimensional emotion analysis. In *Proceedings of the 15th Conference of the European Chapter of the Association for Computational Linguistics: Volume 2, Short Papers*, pages 578–585, Valencia, Spain. Association for Computational Linguistics.

Ying Chen, Wenjun Hou, Xiyao Cheng, and Shoushan Li. 2018. Joint learning for emotion classification and emotion cause detection. In *Proceedings of the 2018 Conference on Empirical Methods in Natural Language Processing*, pages 646–651, Brussels, Belgium. Association for Computational Linguistics.

Ying Chen, Sophia Yat Mei Lee, Shoushan Li, and Chu-Ren Huang. 2010. Emotion cause detection with linguistic constructions. In *Proceedings of the 23rd International Conference on Computational Linguistics (Coling 2010)*, pages 179–187, Beijing, China. Coling 2010 Organizing Committee.

Xiyao Cheng, Ying Chen, Bixiao Cheng, Shoushan Li, and Guodong Zhou. 2017. An emotion cause corpus for chinese microblogs with multiple-user structures. *ACM Transactions on Asian and Low-Resource Language Information Processing*, 17(1).

Alexis Conneau, Kartikay Khandelwal, Naman Goyal, Vishrav Chaudhary, Guillaume Wenzek, Francisco Guzmán, Edouard Grave, Myle Ott, Luke Zettlemoyer, and Veselin Stoyanov. 2020. Unsupervised cross-lingual representation learning at scale. In *Proceedings of the 58th Annual Meeting of the Association for Computational Linguistics*, pages 8440–8451, Online. Association for Computational Linguistics.

Darren Edmonds and João Sedoc. 2021. Multi-emotion classification for song lyrics. In *Proceedings of the Eleventh Workshop on Computational Approaches to Subjectivity, Sentiment and Social Media Analysis*, pages 221–235, Online. Association for Computational Linguistics.

Paul Ekman. 1992. An argument for basic emotions. *Cognition and Emotion*, 6(3-4):169–200.

Chuang Fan, Chaofa Yuan, Jiachen Du, Lin Gui, Min Yang, and Ruifeng Xu. 2020. Transition-based directed graph construction for emotion-cause pair extraction. In *Proceedings of the 58th Annual Meeting of the Association for Computational Linguistics*, pages 3707–3717, Online. Association for Computational Linguistics.

Charles J. Fillmore, Miriam R. L. Petruck, Josef Ruppenhofer, and Abby Wright. 2003. Framenet in action: The case of attaching. *International Journal of Lexicography*, 16:297–332.

Qinghong Gao, Hu Jiannan, Xu Ruifeng, Gui Lin, Yulan He, Kam-Fai Wong, and Quin Lu. 2017. Overview of ntcir-13 eca task. In *Proceedings of the 13th NTCIR Conference on Evaluation of Information Access Technologies*, pages 361–366, Tokyo, Japan. National Institute of Informatics Test Collection for Information Resources.

Diman Ghazi, Diana Inkpen, and Stan Szpakowicz. 2015. Detecting emotion stimuli in emotion-bearing sentences. In *Computational Linguistics and Intelligent Text Processing*, pages 152–165, Cham. Springer.

Lin Gui, Jiannan Hu, Yulan He, Ruifeng Xu, Qin Lu, and Jiachen Du. 2017. A question answering approach for emotion cause extraction. In *Proceedings of the 2017 Conference on Empirical Methods in Natural Language Processing*, pages 1593–1602, Copenhagen, Denmark. Association for Computational Linguistics.

Lin Gui, Dongyin Wu, Ruifeng Xu, Qin Lu, and Yu Zhou. 2016. Event-driven emotion cause extraction with corpus construction. In *Proceedings of the 2016 Conference on Empirical Methods in Natural Language Processing*, pages 1639–1649, Austin, Texas. Association for Computational Linguistics.

Lin Gui, Li Yuan, Ruifeng Xu, Bin Liu, Qin Lu, and Yu Zhou. 2014. Emotion cause detection with linguistic construction in chinese weibo text. In *Natural Language Processing and Chinese Computing*, pages 457–464, Berlin, Heidelberg. Springer Berlin Heidelberg.

Thomas Haider, Steffen Eger, Evgeny Kim, Roman Klinger, and Winfried Menninghaus. 2020. PO-EMO: Conceptualization, annotation, and modeling of aesthetic emotions in German and English poetry. In *Proceedings of the 12th Language Resources and Evaluation Conference*, pages 1652–1663, Marseille, France. European Language Resources Association.

Afif Hijra Ferdinan, Andrew Brian Osmond, and Casi Setianingsih. 2018. Emotion classification in song lyrics using k-nearest neighbor method. In *2018 International Conference on Control, Electronics, Renewable Energy and Communications (ICCEREC)*, pages 63–69.

Jan Hofmann, Enrica Troiano, and Roman Klinger. 2021. Emotion-aware, emotion-agnostic, or automatic: Corpus creation strategies to obtain cognitive event appraisal annotations. In *Proceedings of the Eleventh Workshop on Computational Approaches to Subjectivity, Sentiment and Social Media Analysis*, pages 160–170, Online. Association for Computational Linguistics.

Jan Hofmann, Enrica Troiano, Kai Sassenberg, and Roman Klinger. 2020. Appraisal theories for emotion classification in text. In *Proceedings of the 28th International Conference on Computational Linguistics*, pages 125–138, Barcelona, Spain (Online). International Committee on Computational Linguistics.

Evgeny Kim and Roman Klinger. 2018. Who feels what and why? annotation of a literature corpus with semantic roles of emotions. In *Proceedings of the 27th International Conference on Computational Linguistics*, pages 1345–1359, Santa Fe, New Mexico, USA. Association for Computational Linguistics.

Evgeny Kim and Roman Klinger. 2019. Frowning Frodo, wincing Leia, and a seriously great friendship: Learning to classify emotional relationships of fictional characters. In *Proceedings of the 2019 Conference of the North American Chapter of the Association for Computational Linguistics: Human Language Technologies, Volume 1 (Long and Short Papers)*, pages 647–653, Minneapolis, Minnesota. Association for Computational Linguistics.

Roman Klinger, Surayya Samat Suliya, and Nils Reiter. 2016. Automatic Emotion Detection for Quantitative Literary Studies – A case study based on Franz Kafka's "Das Schloss" and "Amerika". In *Digital Humanities 2016: Conference Abstracts*, pages 826–828, Kraków, Poland. Jagiellonian University and Pedagogical University.

John D. Lafferty, Andrew McCallum, and Fernando C. N. Pereira. 2001. Conditional random fields: Probabilistic models for segmenting and labeling sequence data. In *Proceedings of the Eighteenth International Conference on Machine Learning*, page 282–289, San Francisco, CA. Morgan Kaufmann Publishers Inc.

Sophia Yat Mei Lee, Ying Chen, and Chu-Ren Huang. 2010a. A text-driven rule-based system for emotion cause detection. In *Proceedings of the NAACL HLT 2010 Workshop on Computational Approaches to Analysis and Generation of Emotion in Text*, pages 45–53, Los Angeles, CA. Association for Computational Linguistics.

Sophia Yat Mei Lee, Ying Chen, Shoushan Li, and Chu-Ren Huang. 2010b. Emotion cause events: Corpus construction and analysis. In *Proceedings of the Seventh International Conference on Language Resources and Evaluation (LREC'10)*, Valletta, Malta. European Language Resources Association (ELRA).

Weiyuan Li and Hua Xu. 2014. Text-based emotion classification using emotion cause extraction. *Expert Systems with Applications*, 41(4):1742–1749.

Xiangju Li, Kaisong Song, Shi Feng, Daling Wang, and Yifei Zhang. 2018. A co-attention neural network model for emotion cause analysis with emotional context awareness. In *Proceedings of the 2018 Conference on Empirical Methods in Natural Language*

Processing, pages 4752–4757, Brussels, Belgium. Association for Computational Linguistics.

Yanran Li, Hui Su, Xiaoyu Shen, Wenjie Li, Ziqiang Cao, and Shuzi Niu. 2017. DailyDialog: A manually labelled multi-turn dialogue dataset. In *Proceedings of the Eighth International Joint Conference on Natural Language Processing (Volume 1: Long Papers)*, pages 986–995, Taipei, Taiwan. Asian Federation of Natural Language Processing.

Ilya Loshchilov and Frank Hutter. 2019. Decoupled weight decay regularization. In *International Conference on Learning Representations*.

Rada Mihalcea and Carlo Strapparava. 2012. Lyrics, music, and emotions. In *Proceedings of the 2012 Joint Conference on Empirical Methods in Natural Language Processing and Computational Natural Language Learning*, pages 590–599, Jeju Island, Korea. Association for Computational Linguistics.

Saif Mohammad and Felipe Bravo-Marquez. 2017. Emotion intensities in tweets. In *Proceedings of the 6th Joint Conference on Lexical and Computational Semantics (*SEM 2017)*, pages 65–77, Vancouver, Canada. Association for Computational Linguistics.

Saif Mohammad and Svetlana Kiritchenko. 2015. Using hashtags to capture fine emotion categories from tweets. *Computational Intelligence*, 31(2):301–326.

Saif Mohammad, Xiaodan Zhu, and Joel Martin. 2014. Semantic role labeling of emotions in tweets. In *Proceedings of the 5th Workshop on Computational Approaches to Subjectivity, Sentiment and Social Media Analysis*, pages 32–41, Baltimore, Maryland. Association for Computational Linguistics.

Alena Neviarouskaya and Masaki Aono. 2013. Extracting causes of emotions from text. In *Proceedings of the Sixth International Joint Conference on Natural Language Processing*, pages 932–936, Nagoya, Japan. Asian Federation of Natural Language Processing.

Laura Ana Maria Oberländer and Roman Klinger. 2020. Token sequence labeling vs. clause classification for English emotion stimulus detection. In *Proceedings of the Ninth Joint Conference on Lexical and Computational Semantics*, pages 58–70, Barcelona, Spain (Online). Association for Computational Linguistics.

Robert Plutchik. 2001. The nature of emotions: Human emotions have deep evolutionary roots, a fact that may explain their complexity and provide tools for clinical practice. *American Scientist*, 89(4):344–350.

James A. Russell. 1980. A circumplex model of affect. *Journal of personality and social psychology*, 39(6):1161–1178.

Irene Russo, Tommaso Caselli, Francesco Rubino, Ester Boldrini, and Patricio Martínez-Barco. 2011. EMOCause: An easy-adaptable approach to extract emotion cause contexts. In *Proceedings of the 2nd Workshop on Computational Approaches to Subjectivity and Sentiment Analysis (WASSA 2.011)*, pages 153–160, Portland, Oregon. Association for Computational Linguistics.

Klaus R. Scherer. 2005. What are emotions? And how can they be measured? *Social Science Information*, 44(4):695–729.

Stefan Stieglitz and Linh Dang-Xuan. 2013. Emotions and information diffusion in social media-sentiment of microblogs and sharing behavior. *Journal of management information systems*, 29(4):217–248.

Carlo Strapparava and Rada Mihalcea. 2007. Semeval-2007 task 14: Affective text. In *Proceedings of the Fourth International Workshop on Semantic Evaluations (SemEval-2007)*, pages 70–74. Association for Computational Linguistics.

Enrica Troiano, Sebastian Padó, and Roman Klinger. 2019. Crowdsourcing and validating event-focused emotion corpora for German and English. In *Proceedings of the 57th Annual Meeting of the Association for Computational Linguistics*, pages 4005–4011, Florence, Italy. Association for Computational Linguistics.

Erik Tromp and Mykola Pechenizkiy. 2015. Pattern-based emotion classification on social media. In *Advances in social media analysis*, pages 1–20. Springer.

Penghui Wei, Jiahao Zhao, and Wenji Mao. 2020. Effective inter-clause modeling for end-to-end emotion-cause pair extraction. In *Proceedings of the 58th Annual Meeting of the Association for Computational Linguistics*, pages 3171–3181, Online. Association for Computational Linguistics.

Thomas Wolf, Lysandre Debut, Victor Sanh, Julien Chaumond, Clement Delangue, Anthony Moi, Pierric Cistac, Tim Rault, Remi Louf, Morgan Funtowicz, Joe Davison, Sam Shleifer, Patrick von Platen, Clara Ma, Yacine Jernite, Julien Plu, Canwen Xu, Teven Le Scao, Sylvain Gugger, Mariama Drame, Quentin Lhoest, and Alexander Rush. 2020. Transformers: State-of-the-art natural language processing. In *Proceedings of the 2020 Conference on Empirical Methods in Natural Language Processing: System Demonstrations*, pages 38–45, Online. Association for Computational Linguistics.

Rui Xia and Zixiang Ding. 2019. Emotion-cause pair extraction: A new task to emotion analysis in texts. In *Proceedings of the 57th Annual Meeting of the Association for Computational Linguistics*, pages 1003–1012, Florence, Italy. Association for Computational Linguistics.

Rui Xia, Mengran Zhang, and Zixiang Ding. 2019. Rthn: A rnn-transformer hierarchical network for emotion cause extraction. In *Proceedings of the Twenty- Eighth International Joint Conference on Artificial Intelligence (IJCAI-19)*, pages 5285–5291, Macao. International Joint Conferences on Artificial Intelligence.

Bo Xu, Hongfei Lin, Yuan Lin, Yufeng Diao, Liang Yang, and Kan Xu. 2019. Extracting emotion causes using learning to rank methods from an information retrieval perspective. *IEEE Access*, 7:15573–15583.

Shuntaro Yada, Kazushi Ikeda, Keiichiro Hoashi, and Kyo Kageura. 2017. A bootstrap method for automatic rule acquisition on emotion cause extraction. In *2017 IEEE International Conference on Data Mining Workshops (ICDMW)*, pages 414–421, New Orleans, LA. Institute of Electrical and Electronics Engineers.

A Appendix

Question	Annotation	Labels
Phase 1: Emotion Annotation		
1. Are there terms in the headline which could indicate an emotion?	Cue word	0, 1
2. Does the text specify a person or entity experiencing an emotion?	Experiencer	0, 1
3. Which emotion is most provoked within the headline?	Emotion	Emotions
Phase 2: Stimuli		
4. Which token sequence describes the trigger event of an emotion?	Stimulus	BIO

Table 8: Questions for the annotation.

Lexicon-based Sentiment Analysis in German: Systematic Evaluation of Resources and Preprocessing Techniques

Jakob Fehle
Media Informatics Group
University of Regensburg
Regensburg, Germany
jakob.fehle@ur.de

Thomas Schmidt
Media Informatics Group
University of Regensburg
Regensburg, Germany
thomas.schmidt@ur.de

Christian Wolff
Media Informatics Group
University of Regensburg
Regensburg, Germany
christian.wolff@ur.de

Abstract

We present the results of an evaluation study in the context of lexicon-based sentiment analysis resources for German texts. We have set up a comprehensive compilation of 19 sentiment lexicon resources and 20 sentiment-annotated corpora available for German across multiple domains. In addition to the evaluation of the sentiment lexicons we also investigate the influence of the following preprocessing steps and modifiers: stemming and lemmatization, part-of-speech-tagging, usage of emoticons, stop words removal, usage of valence shifters, intensifiers, and diminishers. We report the best performing lexicons as well as the influence of preprocessing steps and other modifications on average performance across all corpora. We show that larger lexicons with continuous values like *SentiWS* and *SentiMerge* perform best across the domains. The best performing configuration of lexicon and modifications considering the f1-value and accuracy averages across all corpora achieves around 67%. Preprocessing, especially stemming or lemmatization increases the performance consistently on average around 6% and for certain lexicons and configurations up to 16.5% while methods like the usage of valence shifters, intensifiers or diminishers rarely influence overall performance. We discuss domain-specific differences and give recommendations for the selection of lexicons, preprocessing and modifications.

1 Introduction

Sentiment analysis (also often referred to as opinion mining) is a sub-field of *affective computing*, which deals with the detection and analysis of human sentiment and emotions in various application areas like game design (Halbhuber et al., 2019), health (Hartl et al., 2019) and human-computer interaction (Ortloff et al., 2019). Sentiment analysis focuses on text as modality and refers to the task of classifying texts of various lengths concerning polarity (or valence) expressed in the text, meaning whether the sentiment of a text is rather positive or negative (Liu, 2015). Application areas for sentiment analysis in natural language processing (NLP) are social media content (Mäntylä et al., 2018), social sciences (Schmidt et al., 2020b), health (Moßburger et al., 2020), user-generated content (Schmidt et al., 2020a) , digital humanities (Kim and Klinger, 2018a), and human-computer interaction (Schmidt et al., 2020c) to name just a few examples.

Methods for performing sentiment analysis can be divided into two major branches: lexicon-based (also often referred to as rule-based or dictionary-based methods; Taboada et al., 2011) and machine learning (ML)-based approaches. Lexicon-based sentiment analysis uses lexicons consisting of words that are pre-annotated concerning their sentiment expression, which we refer to as sentiment bearing words (SBWs). There are multiple ways to create and acquire such lexicons like crowdsourcing, expert annotations or semi-automatic approaches (cf. Ribeiro et al., 2016). Values of SBWs can either be binary, e.g. +1 (positive) and -1 (negative) (Waltinger, 2010; Mohammad and Turney, 2013) or continuous (e.g. between -3 and + 3) (Remus et al., 2010; Vo et al., 2009; Emerson and Declerck, 2014) to represent differences in sentiment expression across words more precisely. A text can be assigned with an overall polarity by summing up the values of the positively assigned words and subtracting the values of the negative ones. A negative end result points towards a negative and a positive result towards a positive sentiment; a value of 0 is interpreted as neutral (Taboada et al., 2011).

However, developments in ML in the last decade and especially in recent years have led to a dominance of ML-based methods for most NLP-tasks. Current state-of-the-art sentiment analysis regards sentiment analysis oftentimes as text sequence classification task with three classes (neutral, positive, negative). Current approaches are based on large transformer-based models like BERT and achieve accuracies up to 95% in standardized evaluation settings for English (Nazir et al., 2020; Jindal and Aron, 2021; Dang et al., 2020; González-Carvajal and Garrido-Merchán, 2021) and around 80-90% in German (Wojatzki et al., 2017; Struß et al., 2019; Chan et al., 2020). ML-based methods are dependant of sentiment-annotated corpora and especially for English, an increasing number of sentiment-annotated data-sets that can be used to train algorithms can be found for various domains (Ribeiro et al., 2016; Balazs and Velásquez, 2016; Singh et al., 2020). When compared to each other, modern ML-based methods usually outperform lexicon-based methods, which more recently only serve as baseline for performance comparisons (Dhaoui et al., 2017; Kim and Klinger, 2018b; Khoo and Johnkhan, 2018; Khan et al., 2017; Kharde et al., 2016). Nevertheless, many languages and also special domains lack large annotated corpora necessary for state-of-the art ML-based sentiment analysis. Since lexicon-based methods are not bound to quality and quantity of training data, they are still a common approach for languages (Mukhtar et al., 2018; Al-Ayyoub et al., 2019) and areas (Aung and Myo, 2017) with fewer resources. Furthermore, lexicon-based methods are fast to apply and easy to comprehend which has also led to their popularity in research areas like digital humanities (Kim and Klinger, 2018a; Schmidt et al., 2018b) and especially the sub-field of computational literary studies (Alm and Sproat, 2005; Reagan et al., 2016; Schmidt and Burghardt, 2018a,b; Schmidt, 2019; Schmidt et al., 2019b,c, 2021). For the English language, various research exists evaluating the performance of sentiment lexicons and modifications on multiple corpora (Khan et al., 2017; Ribeiro et al., 2016) or evaluating and surveying lexicons in a context of larger studies including ML-methods (Tsytsarau and Palpanas, 2012; Medhat et al., 2014; Kharde et al., 2016; Singh et al., 2020). Thus, researchers can build upon recommendations and best practices based on this research when selecting sentiment lexicons, preprocessing steps and other modifications. However, to the best of our knowledge, there are no similar resources that provide an exhaustive and systematic listing and evaluation of lexicon-based methods across various sentiment-annotated corpora for the German language. In the following paper we want to address this gap and systematically evaluate lexicon-based techniques for sentiment analysis for German to provide recommendations for the selection of lexicons, preprocessing steps and further configurations. The contributions of this paper are as follows: (1) a comprehensive listing of datasets of sentiment lexicons and sentiment-annotated corpora in German, (2) an in-depth evaluation of resources and methods of lexicon-based sentiment analysis for German, and (3) a discussion of validated recommendations concerning the selection of sentiment lexicons, preprocessing steps and other modifications.

2 Resources

To acquire an exhaustive list of relevant corpora and lexicons for German sentiment analysis we searched in various digital libraries and search engines with appropriate search terms. The most important platforms we investigated are the ACM Digital Library[1], ACL Anthology[2], IEEE[3], Springer Verlag[4] and, on the other hand, more specific platforms such as the Conference on Natural Language Processing[5] (KONVENS). Other sources we referred to are the publications related to the regularly held GermEval[6] competitions or publications of the Interest Group on German Sentiment Analysis[7] (IGGSA). Please note that we do not include resources in the context of German-based emotion analysis. While this research area certainly neighbours sentiment analysis, it is out of scope of this paper. Before discussing the different preprocessing and modification steps, we present an overview of corpora as well as lexicons that we have found for German sentinment analysis.

2.1 Corpora

First, we present all German sentiment annotated corpora we managed to find and that were publicly available or accessible per request (see Table 1). The corpora are of varying quantity and quality. Major differences concern, among other things, the

[1] `https://dl.acm.org/`
[2] `https://www.aclweb.org/anthology/`
[3] `https://www.ieee.org/`
[4] `https://www.springer.com/de`
[5] `https://konvens.org/site/`
[6] `https://germeval.github.io/`
[7] `https://sites.google.com/site/iggsahome/`

Abbrevation	Corpus name (if reported)	Reference	#Pos	#Neg
LT01-Zehe	German Novel Dataset	Zehe et al., 2017	75	89
LT02-Schmidt		Schmidt et al., 2019a	202	370
LT03-Schmidt		Schmidt et al., 2018a	61	139
MI01-Clematide	MLSA	Clematide et al., 2012	69	110
MI02-Wojatzki	GermEval 2017	Wojatzki et al., 2017	1,537	6,887
MI03-Rauh		Rauh, 2018	333	475
NA01-Butow	GerSEN	Bütow et al., 2016	372	485
NA02-Ploch	GerOM	Ploch, 2015	71	38
NA03-Schabus	One Million Posts Corpus	Schabus et al., 2017	43	1,606
RE01-Klinger	USAGE	Klinger and Cimiano, 2014	506	50
RE02-Sänger	SCARE	Sänger et al., 2016	418,9 k	185,7 k
RE03-Du	SentiLitKrit	Du and Mellmann, 2019	718	290
RE04-Guhr		Guhr et al., 2020	39.6 k	15.4 k
RE05-Prettenhofer		Prettenhofer and Stein, 2010	159,3 k	136,8 k
SM01-Cieliebak	SB10k	Cieliebak et al., 2017	1.717	1.130
SM02-Sidarenka	PotTS	Sidarenka, 2016	3,349	1,510
SM03-Narr		Narr et al., 2012	350	237
SM04-Mozetič		Mozetič et al., 2016	16,5 k	11,7 k
SM05-Siegel	German Irony Corpus	Siegel et al., 2017	49	107
SM06-Momtazi		Momtazi, 2012	278	191

Table 1: Listing of all corpora included in the evaluation. Pos and Neg mark the number of respective annotated text units, acronyms are explained in the text. More information can be found in the appendix (Table 4).

size of the corpora, the granularity of the annotated polarity, the text domain, and also the quality of the annotations. The corpora were classified into five different domains based on the text units they contained: literary and historical texts, texts from or related to news articles, product reviews, social media, and mixed corpora with text units from different domains. For more details about the corpora please refer to Table 4 in the appendix or the specific papers of the corpora. The corpora are further referenced with abbreviations, which are composed of a domain assignment and the primary author of the respective publication (see Table 1). We include three corpora containing literary texts (LT01-LT03), three with mixed types (MI01-MI03), three containing news articles (NA01-NA03), five reviews (RE01-RE05) and six social media content (SM01-SM06). Some of the most well-known corpora of our list are SB10k (SM01-Cieliebak), PotTS (SM02-Sidarenka), USAGE (RE01-Klinger), and the GermEval 2017 corpus (MI02-Wojatzki).

2.2 Lexicons

Table 2 illustrates all lexicons we gathered for this evaluation study. For more details concerning the lexicons please refer to the appendix (Table 5). Please note that some of the lexicons share common word entries or are based in part on other resources. The lexicons are referenced with abbreviations, which are composed of a numeration and the primary author of the respective publication since many lexicons have no explicit names given by the authors. The order of numbers has no specific meaning. There are different versions for some lexicons: 05-Siegel-p and 06-Siegel-m, which focus on words from the *Pressrelations* (Scholz et al., 2012) and *MLSA* (Clematide et al., 2012) datasets, and 08-Takamura-c and 09-Takamura-d, respectively, for continuous and dichotomous sentiment values. Several well-known and often used lexicons are also included, such as *SentiWS* (01-Remus), *BAWL-R* (03-Võ), *GermanPolarityClues* (13-Waltinger), and *LIWC-De* (14-Wolf). Our general calculation of sentiment values is as follows: For a text unit, we count the positive and negative matches and subtract the sum of positive words by the negative ones. A positive end result is counted as positive polarity, a negative as a negative one. Across chapter 3 we detail some further methods to adjust this calculation.

Abbrevation	Lexicon name (if reported)	Reference	Tokens
01-Remus	SentiWS	Remus et al., 2010	34,238
02-Clematide		Clematide et al., 2010	9,239
03-Võ	BAWL-R	Vo et al., 2009	2,902
04-Emerson	SentiMerge	Emerson and Declerck, 2014	96,420
05-Siegel-p		Siegel and Diwisch, 2014	2,917
06-Siegel-m		Siegel and Diwisch, 2014	2,917
07-Rill	SePL	Rill et al., 2012	14,395
08-Takamura-c	GermanSentiSpin	Takamura et al., 2005	105,560
09-Takamura-d	GermanSentiSpin	Takamura et al., 2005	88,925
10-Rauh		Rauh, 2018	37,080
11-Du	SentiLitKrit	Du and Mellmann, 2019	3,620
12-Asgari	UniSent	Asgari et al., 2019	1,384
13-Waltinger	GermanPolarityClues	Waltinger, 2010	38,901
14-Wolf	LIWC-De	Wolf et al., 2008	4,894
15-Klinger	USAGE Sentiment Lexicon	Klinger and Cimiano, 2014	4,743
16-Wilson	GermanSubjectivityClues	Wilson et al., 2009	9,827
17-Mohammad	NRC Emotion Lexicon	Mohammad and Turney, 2013	10,617
18-Ruppenhofer		Ruppenhofer et al., 2017	9,544
19-Chen	Multilingual Sentiment Lexicon	Chen and Skiena, 2014	3,973

Table 2: Listing of all lexicons included in our evaluation. Lexicons 1-8 include two versions: dichotomous and continuous sentiment values. The rest is solely dichotomous. More information can be found in the appendix (Table 5).

3 Methods

3.1 General Data Cleaning

We perform the following steps to clean the texts of all corpora before evaluation:

- Removing non-alphabetic characters (numbers, special characters, etc.) as well as leading, trailing and multiple spaces (Haddi et al., 2013).
- The removal of URL links, Twitter usernames, and Twitter-specific words such as "RT" (Pak and Paroubek, 2010).

All of the above steps showed no relevant influence on SBWs or lexicon-based sentiment analysis and serve only normalization purposes.

3.2 Preprocessing and other Modifications

In addition to the evaluation of lexicon resources, we also investigate the influence on performance by various preprocessing steps and other configurations which are frequently used when preparing the application of sentiment lexicons. The following techniques are evaluated: The assignment and use of part-of-speech (POS) information, lemmatization and stemming, emoticon processing, stop words removal, lowercasing and the application of valence-changing words. We will refer to these techniques in the following as *modifiers* or *modifications*. Most modifiers are either on or off, meaning they are performed or not, except for POS-tagging, stemming and lemmatization for which multiple approaches are evaluated as well as on and off. In order to identify the best combination of modifiers in the context of the chosen lexicon, the different methods are cross-evaluated and compared based on classification metrics.

3.2.1 Part-of-Speech-Tagging

In sentiment analysis, POS information can be used to solve the problem of word ambiguity since words with the same spelling can have a different valence dependent of the POS (Taboada et al., 2011). Knowledge of the correct POS can support the resolving of this kind of ambiguity. It is necessary to perform POS-tagging on the text and on the lexicon (few of our lexicons already do contain POS information). We evaluate and use two of the most well-known POS-taggers for German: *TreeTagger* (Schmid, 2013) which has shown good performance in evaluation studies (Gleim et al., 2019; Horsmann et al., 2015) and *Stanza* (Qi et al., 2020), a novel POS-tagger for German. Sentiment lexicons consist almost exclusively of nouns, adjectives, verbs and adverbs, which are mainly responsible for the polarity of a text unit (Pak and Paroubek, 2010). Therefore, all POS information was normalized to these four categories. When we apply POS-tagging in our sentiment analysis pipeline, after finding matching words between text and lexicon, we also test if the POS matches or refers to the word with the correct POS before including it in the calculation.

3.2.2 Stemming or Lemmatization

While some sentiment lexicons contain various inflections of words (Remus et al., 2010), the vocabulary of these lexicons mostly consist of base forms. To enable the mapping of words in texts and in the lexicon, base form reduction via lemmatization or stemming is often applied (Taboada et al., 2011). Stemming refers to algorithms that attempt to reduce the word to the base form by truncating suffixes and affixes based on predefined rules. Lemmatization, on the other hand, often takes sentence order and surrounding words into account or works with large dictionaries to reduce a word to its true base form, the lemma, which is necessary for languages with complex morphology like German. In this study, we evaluate the usage of the following two lemmatizers for German: *TreeTagger* (Schmid, 2013), and *Inverse Wiktionary for Natural Language Processing* (IWNLP) (Liebeck and Conrad, 2015). In terms of stemming, two established stemming algorithms are evaluated: *Cistem* (Weissweiler and Fraser, 2017) and *Snowball Porter* (Porter, 1980). Please note that we do not evaluate the lemmatizers or stemming approaches for their intended task but only with respect to the influence on sentiment analysis (the same holds true for POS-tagging). For a review of base form reduction in German we recommend Gleim et al. (2019). We evaluate these methods by applying stemming/lemmatization to the text and lexicon before looking for the matches.

3.2.3 Lowercasing

Unlike English, German does not only capitalize the beginning of sentences and proper names, but also nouns or nominalizations. Thus, for certain cases, it is important to differ between cased and uncased versions of words in German to disambiguate sentiment (e.g. "würde" (*would*, auxiliary verb) has no sentiment, "Würde" (*dignity*, noun) is positive in some lexicons). However, written text in general and in social media in particular includes a lot of spelling errors and incorrect capitalization hindering correct sentiment calculations. Therefore, we evaluate how lowercasing of the lexicon and the texts influences performance.

3.2.4 Emoticons

Emoticons are representations of body language in text, very frequently connected to sentiment expressions (Ptaszynski et al., 2011). Since emoticons are common on the social web, several papers show the benefits of including emoticons in the calculation of the sentiment value of a text unit (Hogenboom et al., 2015; Gonçalves et al., 2013). To translate emoticons to sentiment values, we used a 232-entry list of emoticons from the SCARE dataset by Sänger et al. (2016). Positive or negative emoticons are treated as additional entries to the lexicon vocabulary (positive as +1, negative as -1).

3.2.5 Stop Words Removal

The removal of stop words, i.e. common words (like function words) that occur with high frequency in a language, is a common practice in NLP pipelines, predominantly to improve computation performance. In this process, the individual words of a text unit are matched against a list of words and removed from the text unit if they match any of the entries. Common stop words in language are articles, prepositions, conjunctions, and pronouns and they usually bear no sentiment. While stop words usually have no influence on calculations via lexicon-based methods, sentiment lexicons that are created automatically or semi-automatically can contain stop words which can skew sentiment calculations, e.g. "dieser, jetzt, ihnen, ihrer, ihm" in the lexicon 08-Takamura-d. Such entries are not considered further by removing stop words. Indeed, in some settings the removal of stop words has been shown to be beneficial for sentiment analysis (Saif et al., 2014). We evaluate the application of the German stop words list provided by the information retrieval framework *Solr.*[8]. The list is rather conservative with a length of 231 entries. If we use the modification stop words list, words of this list are ignored in the text as well as in the lexicon that is used.

3.2.6 Valence Shifters

Depending on the surrounding of a SBW, the sentiment value of a word can be influenced, for exam-

[8]`https://solr.apache.org/`

ple the word "glücklich" (happy), usually positive, turns negative with the negation "nicht" (not) right before. Such words and phrases are referred to as valence shifters (Mohammad, 2016). It is recommended to include valence shifters into the calculation process for lexicon-based sentiment analysis (Pröllochs et al., 2015). The following parameters are important for dealing with valence shifters: (1) the window size, meaning how close a valence shifter has to be to a SBW to influence calculations and (2) the position, meaning if the valence shifter is left or right of the SBW (Pang et al., 2002; Kennedy and Inkpen, 2006). For this work, we used a two-sided window with a fixed length of 4 words, which achieved the best results in a wider comparison of methods on German-language datasets by Pröllochs et al. (2015). If a valence shifter occurs in the text, the sentiment values of all words within the context window are reversed. We use a list of 22 German negations collected by various lists (Clematide et al., 2010; Ruppenhofer et al., 2017; Tymann et al., 2019).

3.2.7 Valence Intensifiers and Diminishers

Similar to valence shifters, words can also act as valence intensifiers or diminishers e.g. "sehr" (very) or "wenig" (little). As with valence shifters, a variety of possible implementation approaches exist regarding the context window and position of these words (Taboada et al., 2011; Klenner et al., 2009. We chose to use the approach of Taboada et al. (2011): given a context window of 2 words before the SBW, the sentiment values of all SBWs within the window are multiplied by the value of the diminishers or intensifier. We use a list of 78 German intensifiers and diminishers by Clematide et al. (2010) and Ruppenhofer et al. (2017).

3.2.8 Usage of Lexicon-specific continuous Sentiment Values

While most lexicons have sentiment values in dichotomous (positive, negative) or trichotomous (positive, negative, neutral) expressions, some lexicons contain sentiment values with continuous values, for example between +3 and -3. Thus, if a lexicon offers continuous metrics, we evaluate both approaches: the usage of these continuous values in the calculation and the binary representation via +1 and -1. This is the case for the lexicons 1-8.

4 Results

We evaluate the lexicons and modifiers regarding sentiment analysis as binary classification tasks with positive and negative values, ignoring all neutral information. If a calculation produces 0 (neutral) as output, this is counted as false prediction. In chapter 4.1 we first present the lexicon performance without using modifiers to investigate the general performance of lexicons, corpora and domains. In chapter 4.2 we present modifier-based results before we take a closer look at the best lexicon-modifier combinations in chapter 4.3.

Due to the high class imbalances of certain corpora, we primarily report macro f1 measure. When we report averages across corpora we do not account for size imbalances of the corpora. Instead we calculate the mean average of f1 measures over all corpora.[9]

4.1 Lexicon Performance without modifiers

First, we present the results of cross-evaluations when using the sentiment lexicons on the corpora without any modifiers via a heatmap (see Fig. 1). Please note that the random and majority baselines of the corpora fluctuate around 50-70% for most corpora (see 4 in the appendix). The average f1 measure of all lexicons across all corpora is 45%. A few lexicons achieve an average f1 measure above 50% across all corpora. The best performing lexicons are, on average, 13-Waltinger with 60%, 10-Rauh with 57%, 19-Chen with 53%, 01-Remus with 52% and 04-Emerson with 51%. However, multiple lexicons do perform way below 50%. Considering differences on the corpora of various domains, we have identified the following findings: On average, the lexicons perform best on corpora from the product review domain with f1 scores between 46 to 58%. Corpora based on social media content lead to rather low f1 values between 36-46%. The f1 scores do however vary a lot, for certain lexicons around 10-20% showing that the selection of the corpus-lexicon combination is important. The best result is achieved by lexicons designed specifically for the task on certain corpora e.g. 15-Klinger on corpus RE01-Klinger with

[9] We limit the result report to the most important results. However, we publish a GitHub repository including all results for all lexicon-modifier combination across all corpora for multiple performance metrics and further overview data like heat maps and domain specific result tables. The repository can be found at `https://github.com/JakobFehle/Lexicon-based-SentA-German`

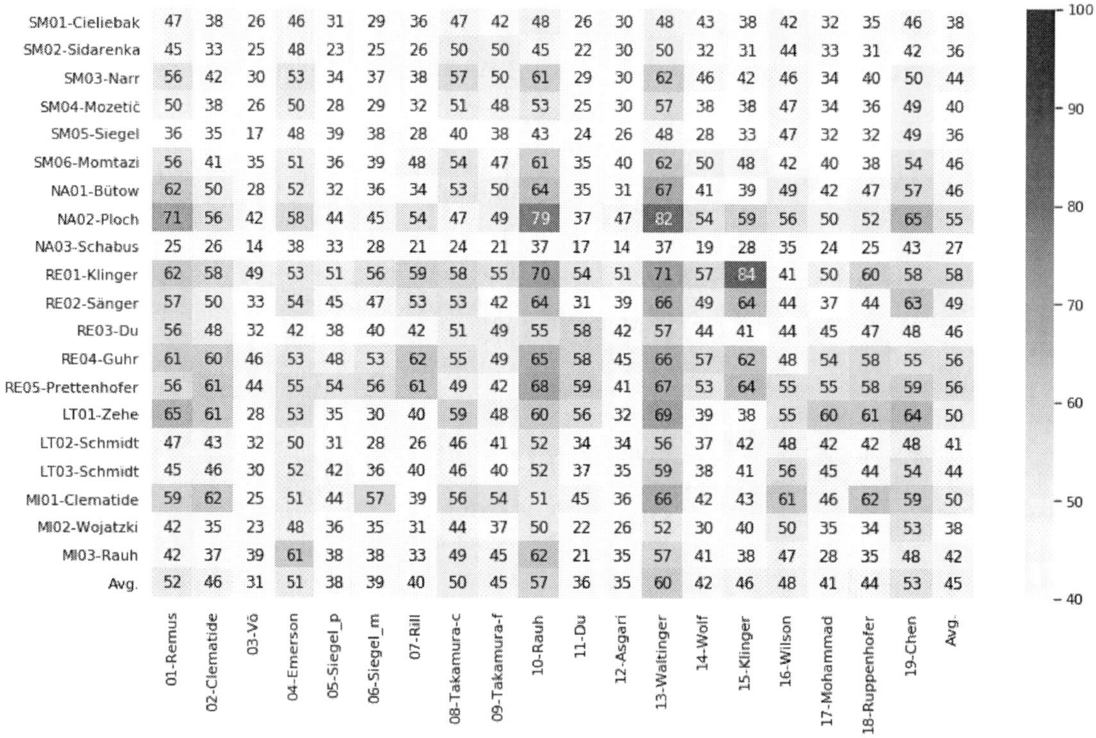

Figure 1: Heatmap for the cross-evaluation of lexicons and corpora including overall averages with no modifications. Values are given as f1 measure and rounded. X-axis are the lexicons, y-axis the corpora.

84%. Other good performances are found with 13-Waltinger and 10-Rauh on NA02-Ploch with 82% and 79%, respectively.

4.2 Modifications

To evaluate the effects of the respective modifiers, they are examined in two ways: (1) We regard the average performance of all lexicons and corpora without modifiers as baseline (f1 measure of 44.8%) and compare it with the average of the isolated use of a single modifier turned on (all other modifiers off) across all corpora and lexicons. We refer to the difference of the baseline f1 measure (44.8%) and the average across all corpora and lexicons with just this modifier turned on as *f1-raw-delta*. A positive value shows an improvement, a negative value a decrease of performance. (2) We measure every possible on/off configuration for all modifiers across all corpora and lexicons once with the specific examined modifier on and once off. We then take the multiple differences between modifier on and off for all of this runs and build an average. We refer to this value as *f1-combination-delta*. Please refer to Table 6 in the appendix for a detailed overview of the results.

Concerning POS-tagging, stemming and lemmatization, the different tools show very low differences. Therefore, we always refer to the best-performing tool as representative of the method. POS-tagging leads to a small decrease of the f1 measure compared to not applying it (f1-raw-delta = -1.7%) and also on average combined with other modifiers (f1-combination-delta = -1.5%). Stemming and lemmatization however improves f1 measures and is the most consistent and strongest improvement. F1-raw-delta shows an improvement by 6.3% for the best stemming-method and 5.6% for the best lemmatizer. This result stays consistent for f1-combination-delta with 5% and 5.1% respectively.

Lowercasing shows a smaller positive influence (f1-raw-delta = 2.8; f1-combination-delta = 0.2). Including emoticons in the calculation process improves the performance similarly but also consistent in combination with other modifiers (f1-raw-delta = 2.9; f1-combination-delta = 1.7). The increase of the f1 measure is connected to the corpora of the social media domain. The processing of emoticons improves the f1 measure actually by 8.8% points when we reduce the results on the social media corpora. The removal of stop words before performing calculation does actually decrease the average f1 measure by 0.3% when no other methods are applied. Intertwined with other methods, this decrease is also marginal (f1-combination-delta = -0.2). Integrating valence shifters into calculation does actually barely show an influence on performance according to our evaluations (f1-raw-delta = 0.0; f1-combination-delta = -0.2). The same holds true for intensifiers and diminushers (f1-raw-delta = 0.5; f1-combination-delta = 0.4).

For the modifier of continuous sentiment values, we limit the calculation of f1-raw-delta to the 8 lexicons containing such values, thus the baseline is 43.3%. The application of continuous values improves the f1-score by 3.4%. Indeed an improvement can be found for every lexicon compared to their dichotomous equivalent.

Please note however that the values given above are averaged overall results. Several methods do actually have much higher positive influence depending on the specific corpus-lexicon combination. The following sub-chapter will highlight some of these interaction effects.

4.3 Lexicon Performance with Modifications

In the following chapter, we present the best result achieved with various modifier combinations for each lexicon (see Table 3). Next to the highest f1 measure, we also report the average performance (averaging the result of all method combinations). For the lexicons 1-8 we differ between the continuous and the dichotomous calculation (the latter in brackets in Table 3). More information about the precise combination of methods can be found in the appendix in Table 7.

Lexicon 04-Emerson achieves both the highest average performance with an f1 measure of 62.0% over all method combinations and the best specific combination with 67.3% in regards to all lexicons and all method combinations. The modifiers are lemmatization (IWNLP lemmatizer), lowercasing, removing stop words, using emoticons as well as continuous sentiment values; all other modifiers are turned off. This value is 16.5% higher than the baseline of 04-Emerson using no modifier showing that in contrast to the overall results in chapter 4.1, certain modifier combinations can highly boost performance.

The f1 values for all lexicons range between 52 and 67% for the best methods. Overall, the best performing lexicons with no modifications are mostly

Lexicon Performance		
Lexicon	Average-f1	Best-Method-f1
04-Emerson	*62.0* (55.1)	67.3
01-Remus	*60.1* (55.1)	63.6
10-Rauh	58.5	63.6
02-Clematide	*56.5* (54.6)	61.9
08-Takamura-c	*56.3* (52.3)	60.6
19-Chen	55.8	60.5
13-Waltinger	55.2	63.4
18-Ruppenhofer	53.5	59.2
16-Wilson	52.2	56.0
07-Rill	*51.4* (48.7)	56.2
03-Võ	*49.3* (45.0)	54.9
09-Takamura-d	48.8	52.7
14-Wolf	48.6	53.9
06-Siegel_m	*47.7* (45.9)	53.8
17-Mohammad	47.4	51.6
15-Klinger	46.8	53.4
05-Siegel_p	*46.8* (45.9)	54.3
11-Du	46.7	53.2
12-Asgari	43.9	52.0

Table 3: Lexicon performance in combination with modifiers. Best method is the value for the best modifier combination for each lexicon. Average is the overall average for all modifier combinations of this lexicon. Values in brackets are results for dichotomous equivalents for lexicons 1-8.

the same as with modifications (see chapter 4.1, 4.3 and Fig. 1) but modifiers increase the performance by 5-17%. The best combination for each lexicon consistently includes emoticons and stemming or lemmatizing. Four of the best five performing lexicons work with continuous values. Considering lowercasing, stop words removal, valence shifters, intensifier and diminushers, the usage is rather inconsistent among the best lexicon-modifier combinations. POS-tags are only part of the best combination for 10-Rauh (see Table 7 in the appendix).

5 Discussion

In the following chapter, we summarize the results and formulate recommendations and best practices for the usage of German general purpose sentiment lexicons. We have evaluated, to our knowledge, all relevant and publicly available corpora and lexicons for the German language. The six best performing lexicons without preprocessing and modifications but also with such methods are: *SentiMerge (04-Emerson)* (Emerson and Declerck, 2014), *Sen-*

tiWS (*01-Remus*) (Remus et al., 2010), 10-Rauh (Rauh, 2018), the *Multilinguial Sentiment Lexicon* (19-Chen) (Chen and Skiena, 2014), 02-Clematide (Clematide et al., 2010) and *GermanSentiSpin* (08-Takamura-c) (Takamura et al., 2005). Performance can vary a lot depending of domain and corpus, however these lexicons perform, on average, well on all domains compared to the other evaluated lexicons. Therefore, we recommend the usage of these lexicons. *SentiMerge* (04-Emerson) achieves the best result with a specific modifier setting (f1 measure = 67.3%), thus we especially encourage the usage of this lexicon. On average, larger lexicons (that consist of more entries) perform better. Indeed, 04-Emerson is the second largest resource in our evaluation, although there are exceptions. Lexicons performing rather good but which are small: e.g. 02-Clematide and 19-Chen. It is striking that 04-Emerson is actually a lexicon derived by fusing multiple other lexicons to increase items size (Emerson and Declerck, 2014). We recommend exploring this idea further in future work. Another pattern that emerges is that on average lexicons with continuous sentiment values outperform dichotomous annotations, which has also been shown in other studies for English (Taboada et al., 2011). Based on these result we conclude that continuous representations of sentiment expressions fit human language more.

Considering modifications and preprocessing, we have identified that the application of one single modifier rarely helps, and we recommend the combination of multiple modifications and preprocessing steps. The most consistent and supportive modifier is the application of stemming or lemmatization of lexicon and text which solves the problem of complex inflections matching in the sentiment analysis pipeline. We did not identify a large difference between these two methods or between specific tools implementing them. POS-tagging, on the other hand showed no significant improvement.

Another consistent boost is the integration of emoticons into the calculation, especially for tasks in the social media area (Hogenboom et al., 2013; Pozzi et al., 2013). The removal of stop words and lowercasing produced inconsistent results. Overall, the modifications are not necessary or beneficial based on our results. In contrast to previous research on German (Pröllochs et al., 2015), we could not identify an improvement by integrating valence shifters, intensifiers and diminishers into our calculation. This result is counter-intuitive; we assume that the specific selection of a larger window size and position (see chapter 3.2.6) might be a reason for this. We plan to investigate this phenomenon in future work in more detail, but cannot recommend the application of these modifiers the way we did in this evaluation.

With regard to corpora and domains, we identified that, as expected, lexicons that are designed for specific corpora or domains perform best on these corpora. Overall, the evaluated lexicons perform best on product reviews while social media corpora are more challenging. We encourage to address these problems in future work in sentiment analysis.

Summing up, we must note that compared to English lexicon-based resources which can achieve f1 measures above 70% (Khan et al., 2017; Ribeiro et al., 2016) the German resources perform rather poorly. German resources often lack size and suffer from strong class imbalances resulting in the sometimes fairly poor results reported here. This accounts for lexicons as well as for corpora and influences performance negatively. The rise of ML-based methods and their better performance compared to lexicon-based methods will certainly hinder the further development and improvement of sentiment lexicons. However, as the popularity of resources like VADER (Hutto and Gilbert, 2014) for English language shows, there is still an interest by certain communities for fast and easy-to-use sentiment lexicons to perform sentiment analysis. Thus, we not just want to support decision-making for German resources with the presented evaluation study, but give impulses for future developments for German sentiment analysis resources.

References

Mahmoud Al-Ayyoub, Abed Allah Khamaiseh, Yaser Jararweh, and Mohammed N Al-Kabi. 2019. A comprehensive survey of arabic sentiment analysis. *Information processing & management*, 56(2):320–342.

Cecilia Ovesdotter Alm and Richard Sproat. 2005. Emotional Sequencing and Development in Fairy Tales. In *Affective Computing and Intelligent Interaction*, Lecture Notes in Computer Science, pages 668–674, Berlin, Heidelberg. Springer.

Ehsaneddin Asgari, Fabienne Braune, Benjamin Roth, Christoph Ringlstetter, and Mohammad RK Mofrad. 2019. Unisent: Universal adaptable sentiment lexica for 1000+ languages. *arXiv preprint arXiv:1904.09678*.

Khin Zezawar Aung and Nyein Nyein Myo. 2017. Sentiment analysis of students' comment using lexicon based approach. In *2017 IEEE/ACIS 16th international conference on computer and information science (ICIS)*, pages 149–154. IEEE.

Jorge A Balazs and Juan D Velásquez. 2016. Opinion mining and information fusion: a survey. *Information Fusion*, 27:95–110.

Florian Bütow, Andreas Lommatzsch, and Danuta Ploch. 2016. Creation of a german corpus for internet news sentiment analysis.

Branden Chan, Stefan Schweter, and Timo Möller. 2020. German's Next Language Model. *arXiv:2010.10906 [cs]*. ArXiv: 2010.10906.

Yanqing Chen and Steven Skiena. 2014. Building sentiment lexicons for all major languages. In *Proceedings of the 52nd Annual Meeting of the Association for Computational Linguistics (Volume 2: Short Papers)*, pages 383–389.

Mark Cieliebak, Jan Milan Deriu, Dominic Egger, and Fatih Uzdilli. 2017. A twitter corpus and benchmark resources for german sentiment analysis. In *Proceedings of the Fifth International Workshop on Natural Language Processing for Social Media*, pages 45–51.

Simon Clematide, Stefan Gindl, Manfred Klenner, Stefanos Petrakis, Robert Remus, Josef Ruppenhofer, Ulli Waltinger, and Michael Wiegand. 2012. Mlsa—a multi-layered reference corpus for german sentiment analysis.

Simon Clematide, Manfred Klenner, A Montoyo, P Martínez-Barco, A Balahur, and E Boldrini. 2010. Evaluation and extension of a polarity lexicon for german.

Nhan Cach Dang, María N. Moreno-García, and Fernando De la Prieta. 2020. Sentiment analysis based on deep learning: A comparative study. *Electronics*, 9(3):483.

Chedia Dhaoui, Cynthia M Webster, and Lay Peng Tan. 2017. Social media sentiment analysis: lexicon versus machine learning. *Journal of Consumer Marketing*.

Keli Du and Katja Mellmann. 2019. Sentimentanalyse als instrument literaturgeschichtlicher rezeptionsforschung. ein pilotprojekt.

Guy Emerson and Thierry Declerck. 2014. Sentimerge: Combining sentiment lexicons in a bayesian framework. In *Proceedings of Workshop on Lexical and Grammatical Resources for Language Processing*, pages 30–38.

Rüdiger Gleim, Steffen Eger, Alexander Mehler, Tolga Uslu, Wahed Hemati, Andy Lücking, Alexander Henlein, Sven Kahlsdorf, and Armin Hoenen. 2019. A practitioner's view: a survey and comparison of lemmatization and morphological tagging in german and latin. *Journal of Language Modelling*, 7.

Pollyanna Gonçalves, Matheus Araújo, Fabrício Benevenuto, and Meeyoung Cha. 2013. Comparing and combining sentiment analysis methods. In *Proceedings of the first ACM conference on Online social networks*, pages 27–38.

Santiago González-Carvajal and Eduardo C. Garrido-Merchán. 2021. Comparing bert against traditional machine learning text classification.

Oliver Guhr, Anne-Kathrin Schumann, Frank Bahrmann, and Hans Joachim Böhme. 2020. Training a broad-coverage german sentiment classification model for dialog systems. In *Proceedings of The 12th Language Resources and Evaluation Conference*, pages 1627–1632.

Emma Haddi, Xiaohui Liu, and Yong Shi. 2013. The role of text pre-processing in sentiment analysis. *Procedia Computer Science*, 17:26–32.

David Halbhuber, Jakob Fehle, Alexander Kalus, Konstantin Seitz, Martin Kocur, Thomas Schmidt, and Christian Wolff. 2019. The mood game - how to use the player's affective state in a shoot'em up avoiding frustration and boredom. In *Proceedings of Mensch Und Computer 2019*, MuC'19, page 867–870, New York, NY, USA. Association for Computing Machinery.

Philipp Hartl, Thomas Fischer, Andreas Hilzenthaler, Martin Kocur, and Thomas Schmidt. 2019. Audiencear - utilising augmented reality and emotion tracking to address fear of speech. In *Proceedings of Mensch Und Computer 2019*, MuC'19, page 913–916, New York, NY, USA. Association for Computing Machinery.

Alexander Hogenboom, Daniella Bal, Flavius Frasincar, Malissa Bal, Franciska De Jong, and Uzay Kaymak. 2015. Exploiting emoticons in polarity classification of text. *J. Web Eng.*, 14(1&2):22–40.

Alexander Hogenboom, Daniella Bal, Flavius Frasincar, Malissa Bal, Franciska de Jong, and Uzay Kaymak. 2013. Exploiting emoticons in sentiment analysis. In *Proceedings of the 28th annual ACM symposium on applied computing*, pages 703–710.

Tobias Horsmann, Nicolai Erbs, and Torsten Zesch. 2015. Fast or accurate?-a comparative evaluation of pos tagging models. In *GSCL*, pages 22–30.

Clayton Hutto and Eric Gilbert. 2014. Vader: A parsimonious rule-based model for sentiment analysis of social media text. In *Proceedings of the International AAAI Conference on Web and Social Media*, volume 8.

Kanika Jindal and Rajni Aron. 2021. A systematic study of sentiment analysis for social media data. *Materials Today: Proceedings*.

Alistair Kennedy and Diana Inkpen. 2006. Sentiment classification of movie reviews using contextual valence shifters. *Computational Intelligence*, 22(2):110–125.

Farhan Hassan Khan, Usman Qamar, and Saba Bashir. 2017. Lexicon based semantic detection of sentiments using expected likelihood estimate smoothed odds ratio. *Artificial Intelligence Review*, 48(1):113–138.

Vishal Kharde, Prof Sonawane, et al. 2016. Sentiment analysis of twitter data: a survey of techniques. *arXiv preprint arXiv:1601.06971*.

Christopher SG Khoo and Sathik Basha Johnkhan. 2018. Lexicon-based sentiment analysis: Comparative evaluation of six sentiment lexicons. *Journal of Information Science*, 44(4):491–511.

Evgeny Kim and Roman Klinger. 2018a. A survey on sentiment and emotion analysis for computational literary studies. *arXiv preprint arXiv:1808.03137*.

Evgeny Kim and Roman Klinger. 2018b. Who feels what and why? annotation of a literature corpus with semantic roles of emotions. In *Proceedings of the 27th International Conference on Computational Linguistics*, pages 1345–1359, Santa Fe, New Mexico, USA. Association for Computational Linguistics.

Manfred Klenner, Angela Fahrni, and Stefanos Petrakis. 2009. Polart: A robust tool for sentiment analysis. In *Proceedings of the 17th Nordic Conference of Computational Linguistics (NODALIDA 2009)*, pages 235–238.

Roman Klinger and Philipp Cimiano. 2014. The usage review corpus for fine-grained, multi-lingual opinion analysis. In *Proceedings of the Ninth International Conference on Language Resources and Evaluation (LREC'14)*.

Matthias Liebeck and Stefan Conrad. 2015. Iwnlp: Inverse wiktionary for natural language processing. In *Proceedings of the 53rd Annual Meeting of the Association for Computational Linguistics and the 7th International Joint Conference on Natural Language Processing (Volume 2: Short Papers)*, pages 414–418.

Bing Liu. 2015. Sentiment analysis: mining opinions, sentiments, and emotions.

Mika V Mäntylä, Daniel Graziotin, and Miikka Kuutila. 2018. The evolution of sentiment analysis—a review of research topics, venues, and top cited papers. *Computer Science Review*, 27:16–32.

Walaa Medhat, Ahmed Hassan, and Hoda Korashy. 2014. Sentiment analysis algorithms and applications: A survey. *Ain Shams engineering journal*, 5(4):1093–1113.

Saif M Mohammad. 2016. Sentiment analysis: Detecting valence, emotions, and other affectual states from text. In *Emotion measurement*, pages 201–237. Elsevier.

Saif M Mohammad and Peter D Turney. 2013. Crowdsourcing a word–emotion association lexicon. *Computational intelligence*, 29(3):436–465.

Saeedeh Momtazi. 2012. Fine-grained german sentiment analysis on social media. In *LREC*, pages 1215–1220. Citeseer.

Luis Moßburger, Felix Wende, Kay Brinkmann, and Thomas Schmidt. 2020. Exploring online depression forums via text mining: A comparison of Reddit and a curated online forum. In *Proceedings of the Fifth Social Media Mining for Health Applications Workshop & Shared Task*, pages 70–81, Barcelona, Spain (Online). Association for Computational Linguistics.

Igor Mozetič, Miha Grčar, and Jasmina Smailović. 2016. Multilingual twitter sentiment classification: The role of human annotators. *PloS one*, 11(5):e0155036.

Neelam Mukhtar, Mohammad Abid Khan, and Nadia Chiragh. 2018. Lexicon-based approach outperforms supervised machine learning approach for urdu sentiment analysis in multiple domains. *Telematics and Informatics*, 35(8):2173–2183.

Sascha Narr, Michael Hulfenhaus, and Sahin Albayrak. 2012. Language-independent twitter sentiment analysis. *Knowledge discovery and machine learning (KDML), LWA*, pages 12–14.

Ambreen Nazir, Yuan Rao, Lianwei Wu, and Ling Sun. 2020. Issues and challenges of aspect-based sentiment analysis: A comprehensive survey. *IEEE Transactions on Affective Computing*.

Anna-Marie Ortloff, Lydia Güntner, Maximiliane Windl, Thomas Schmidt, Martin Kocur, and Christian Wolff. 2019. Sentibooks: Enhancing audiobooks via affective computing and smart light bulbs. In *Proceedings of Mensch Und Computer 2019*, MuC'19, page 863–866, New York, NY, USA. Association for Computing Machinery.

Alexander Pak and Patrick Paroubek. 2010. Twitter as a corpus for sentiment analysis and opinion mining. In *LREc*, volume 10, pages 1320–1326.

Bo Pang, Lillian Lee, and Shivakumar Vaithyanathan. 2002. Thumbs up? sentiment classification using machine learning techniques. *arXiv preprint cs/0205070*.

Danuta Ploch. 2015. Intelligent news aggregator for german with sentiment analysis. In *Smart information systems*, pages 5–46. Springer.

Martin F Porter. 1980. An algorithm for suffix stripping. *Program*.

Federico Alberto Pozzi, Elisabetta Fersini, Enza Messina, and Daniele Blanc. 2013. Enhance polarity classification on social media through sentiment-based feature expansion. *WOA@ AI* IA*, 1099:78–84.

Peter Prettenhofer and Benno Stein. 2010. Cross-language text classification using structural correspondence learning. In *Proceedings of the 48th annual meeting of the association for computational linguistics*, pages 1118–1127.

Nicolas Pröllochs, Stefan Feuerriegel, and Dirk Neumann. 2015. Enhancing sentiment analysis of financial news by detecting negation scopes. In *2015 48th Hawaii International Conference on System Sciences*, pages 959–968. IEEE.

Michal Ptaszynski, Rafal Rzepka, Kenji Araki, and Yoshio Momouchi. 2011. Research on emoticons: review of the field and proposal of research framework. *Proceedings of 17th Association for Natural Language Processing*, pages 1159–1162.

Peng Qi, Yuhao Zhang, Yuhui Zhang, Jason Bolton, and Christopher D Manning. 2020. Stanza: A python natural language processing toolkit for many human languages. *arXiv preprint arXiv:2003.07082*.

Christian Rauh. 2018. Validating a sentiment dictionary for german political language—a workbench note. *Journal of Information Technology & Politics*, 15(4):319–343.

Andrew J. Reagan, Lewis Mitchell, Dilan Kiley, Christopher M. Danforth, and Peter Sheridan Dodds. 2016. The emotional arcs of stories are dominated by six basic shapes. *EPJ Data Science*, 5(1):31. ArXiv: 1606.07772.

Robert Remus, Uwe Quasthoff, and Gerhard Heyer. 2010. Sentiws-a publicly available german-language resource for sentiment analysis. In *LREC*. Citeseer.

Filipe N Ribeiro, Matheus Araújo, Pollyanna Gonçalves, Marcos André Gonçalves, and Fabrício Benevenuto. 2016. Sentibench-a benchmark comparison of state-of-the-practice sentiment analysis methods. *EPJ Data Science*, 5(1):1–29.

Sven Rill, Jörg Scheidt, Johannes Drescher, Oliver Schütz, Dirk Reinel, and Florian Wogenstein. 2012. A generic approach to generate opinion lists of phrases for opinion mining applications. In *Proceedings of the first international workshop on issues of sentiment discovery and opinion mining*, pages 1–8.

Josef Ruppenhofer, Petra Steiner, and Michael Wiegand. 2017. Evaluating the morphological compositionality of polarity.

Hassan Saif, Miriam Fernandez, Yulan He, and Harith Alani. 2014. On stopwords, filtering and data sparsity for sentiment analysis of Twitter. In *Proceedings of the Ninth International Conference on Language Resources and Evaluation (LREC'14)*, pages 810–817, Reykjavik, Iceland. European Language Resources Association (ELRA).

Mario Sänger, Ulf Leser, Steffen Kemmerer, Peter Adolphs, and Roman Klinger. 2016. Scare—the sentiment corpus of app reviews with fine-grained annotations in german. In *Proceedings of the Tenth International Conference on Language Resources and Evaluation (LREC'16)*, pages 1114–1121.

Dietmar Schabus, Marcin Skowron, and Martin Trapp. 2017. One million posts: A data set of german online discussions. In *Proceedings of the 40th International ACM SIGIR Conference on Research and Development in Information Retrieval*, pages 1241–1244.

Helmut Schmid. 2013. Probabilistic part-ofispeech tagging using decision trees. In *New methods in language processing*, page 154.

Thomas Schmidt. 2019. Distant reading sentiments and emotions in historic german plays. In *Abstract Booklet, DH_Budapest_2019*, pages 57–60. Budapest, Hungary.

Thomas Schmidt and Manuel Burghardt. 2018a. An Evaluation of Lexicon-based Sentiment Analysis Techniques for the Plays of Gotthold Ephraim Lessing. In *Proceedings of the Second Joint SIGHUM Workshop on Computational Linguistics for Cultural Heritage, Social Sciences, Humanities and Literature*, pages 139–149, Santa Fe, New Mexico. Association for Computational Linguistics.

Thomas Schmidt and Manuel Burghardt. 2018b. Toward a Tool for Sentiment Analysis for German Historic Plays. In *COMHUM 2018: Book of Abstracts for the Workshop on Computational Methods in the Humanities 2018*, pages 46–48, Lausanne, Switzerland. Laboratoire laussannois d'informatique et statistique textuelle.

Thomas Schmidt, Manuel Burghardt, and Katrin Dennerlein. 2018a. Sentiment annotation of historic german plays: An empirical study on annotation behavior. In Sandra Kübler and Heike Zinsmeister, editors, *annDH 2018, Proceedings of the Workshop on Annotation in Digital Humanities 2018 (annDH 2018), Sofia, Bulgaria, August 6-10, 2018*, pages 47–52. RWTH Aachen, Aachen.

Thomas Schmidt, Manuel Burghardt, Katrin Dennerlein, and Christian Wolff. 2019a. Sentiment annotation for lessing's plays: Towards a language resource for sentiment analysis on german literary texts. In Thierry Declerck and John P. McCrae, editors, *2nd Conference on Language, Data and Knowledge (LDK 2019)*, pages 45–50. RWTH Aachen, Aachen.

Thomas Schmidt, Manuel Burghardt, and Christian Wolff. 2018b. Herausforderungen für Sentiment Analysis-Verfahren bei literarischen Texten. In *INF-DH-2018*, Berlin, Germany. Gesellschaft für Informatik e.V.

Thomas Schmidt, Manuel Burghardt, and Christian Wolff. 2019b. Toward Multimodal Sentiment Analysis of Historic Plays: A Case Study with Text and Audio for Lessing's Emilia Galotti. In *Proceedings of the Digital Humanities in the Nordic Countries 4th Conference*, volume 2364 of *CEUR Workshop Proceedings*, pages 405–414, Copenhagen, Denmark. CEUR-WS.org.

Thomas Schmidt, Johanna Dangel, and Christian Wolff. 2021. Senttext: A tool for lexicon-based sentiment analysis in digital humanities. In Thomas Schmidt and Christian Wolff, editors, *Information Science and its Neighbors from Data Science to Digital Humanities. Proceedings of the 16th International Symposium of Information Science (ISI 2021)*, volume 74, pages 156–172. Werner Hülsbusch, Glückstadt.

Thomas Schmidt, Philipp Hartl, Dominik Ramsauer, Thomas Fischer, Andreas Hilzenthaler, and Christian Wolff. 2020a. Acquisition and analysis of a meme corpus to investigate web culture. In *Digital Humanities Conference 2020 (DH 2020.*

Thomas Schmidt, Florian Kaindl, and Christian Wolff. 2020b. Distant reading of religious online communities: A case study for three religious forums on reddit. In *Proceedings of the Digital Humanities in the Nordic Countries 5th Conference*, pages 157–172, Riga, Latvia.

Thomas Schmidt, Miriam Schlindwein, Katharina Lichtner, and Christian Wolff. 2020c. Investigating the relationship between emotion recognition software and usability metrics. *i-com*, 19(2):139–151.

Thomas Schmidt, Brigitte Winterl, Milena Maul, Alina Schark, Andrea Vlad, and Christian Wolff. 2019c. Inter-rater agreement and usability: A comparative evaluation of annotation tools for sentiment annotation. In *INFORMATIK 2019: 50 Jahre Gesellschaft für Informatik – Informatik für Gesellschaft (Workshop-Beiträge)*, pages 121–133, Bonn. Gesellschaft für Informatik e.V.

Thomas Scholz, Stefan Conrad, and Lutz Hillekamps. 2012. Opinion mining on a german corpus of a media response analysis. In *International Conference on Text, Speech and Dialogue*, pages 39–46. Springer.

Uladzimir Sidarenka. 2016. Potts: the potsdam twitter sentiment corpus. In *Proceedings of the Tenth International Conference on Language Resources and Evaluation (LREC'16)*, pages 1133–1141.

Melanie Siegel and Kerstin Diwisch. 2014. Opm. `https://sites.google.com/site/iggsahome/downloads`. Last access: 05.12.2020.

Melanie Siegel, Katharina Emig, Nikola Ihringer, Serhat Kesim, and Tamer Yilmaz. 2017. Sentiment analysis. ressources for sentiment analysis of german language. `https://github.com/hdaSprachtechnologie/Sentiment-Analysis`. Last access: 10.12.2020.

Nikhil Kumar Singh, Deepak Singh Tomar, and Arun Kumar Sangaiah. 2020. Sentiment analysis: a review and comparative analysis over social media. *Journal of Ambient Intelligence and Humanized Computing*, 11(1):97–117.

Julia Maria Struß, Melanie Siegel, Josef Ruppenhofer, Michael Wiegand, Manfred Klenner, et al. 2019. Overview of germeval task 2, 2019 shared task on the identification of offensive language.

Maite Taboada, Julian Brooke, Milan Tofiloski, Kimberly Voll, and Manfred Stede. 2011. Lexicon-based methods for sentiment analysis. *Computational linguistics*, 37(2):267–307.

Hiroya Takamura, Takashi Inui, and Manabu Okumura. 2005. Extracting semantic orientations of words using spin model. In *Proceedings of the 43rd Annual Meeting of the Association for Computational Linguistics (ACL'05)*, pages 133–140.

Mikalai Tsytsarau and Themis Palpanas. 2012. Survey on mining subjective data on the web. *Data Mining and Knowledge Discovery*, 24(3):478–514.

Karsten Tymann, Matthias Lutz, Patrick Palsbröker, and Carsten Gips. 2019. Gervader-a german adaptation of the vader sentiment analysis tool for social media texts. In *LWDA*, pages 178–189.

Melissa LH Vo, Markus Conrad, Lars Kuchinke, Karolina Urton, Markus J Hofmann, and Arthur M Jacobs. 2009. The berlin affective word list reloaded (bawl-r). *Behavior research methods*, 41(2):534–538.

Ulli Waltinger. 2010. Germanpolarityclues: A lexical resource for german sentiment analysis. In *LREC*, pages 1638–1642. Citeseer.

Leonie Weissweiler and Alexander Fraser. 2017. Developing a stemmer for german based on a comparative analysis of publicly available stemmers. In *International Conference of the German Society for Computational Linguistics and Language Technology*, pages 81–94. Springer.

Theresa Wilson, Janyce Wiebe, and Paul Hoffmann. 2009. Recognizing contextual polarity: An exploration of features for phrase-level sentiment analysis. *Computational linguistics*, 35(3):399–433.

Michael Wojatzki, Eugen Ruppert, Sarah Holschneider, Torsten Zesch, and Chris Biemann. 2017. Germeval 2017: Shared task on aspect-based sentiment in social media customer feedback. *Proceedings of the GermEval*, pages 1–12.

Markus Wolf, Andrea B Horn, Matthias R Mehl, Severin Haug, James W Pennebaker, and Hans Kordy. 2008. Computergestützte quantitative textanalyse: äquivalenz und robustheit der deutschen version des linguistic inquiry and word count. *Diagnostica*, 54(2):85–98.

Albin Zehe, Martin Becker, Fotis Jannidis, and Andreas Hotho. 2017. Towards sentiment analysis on german literature. In *Joint German/Austrian Conference on Artificial Intelligence (Künstliche Intelligenz)*, pages 387–394. Springer.

A Appendix

Abbreviation	Domain	Corpus	Reference	Pos	Neg	Total
LT01-Zehe	Literary Texts	German Novel Dataset	(Zehe et al., 2017)	75	89	164
LT02-Schmidt	Literary Texts		(Schmidt et al., 2019a)	202	370	572
LT03-Schmidt	Literary Texts		(Schmidt et al., 2018a)	61	139	200
MI01-Clematide	Mixed Domains	MLSA	(Clematide et al., 2012)	69	110	179
MI02-Wojatzki	Mixed Domains	GermEval 2017	(Wojatzki et al., 2017)	1,537	6,887	8,424
MI03-Rauh	Mixed Domains		(Rauh, 2018)	333	475	808
NA01-Bütow	News Articles	GerSEN	(Bütow et al., 2016)	372	485	857
NA02-Ploch	News Articles	GerOM	(Ploch, 2015)	71	38	109
NA03-Schabus	News Articles	One Million Posts Corpus	(Schabus et al., 2017)	43	1,606	1,649
RE01-Klinger	Product Reviews	USAGE	(Klinger and Cimiano, 2014)	506	50	556
RE02-Sänger	Product Reviews	SCARE	(Sänger et al., 2016)	418,880	185,666	604,546
RE03-Du	Product Reviews	SentiLitKrit	(Du and Mellmann, 2019)	718	290	1,008
RE04-Guhr	Product Reviews		(Guhr et al., 2020)	39,623	15,436	55,059
RE05-Prettenhofer	Product Reviews		(Prettenhofer and Stein, 2010)	159,315	136,757	296,072
SM01-Cieliebak	Social Media	SB10k	(Cieliebak et al., 2017)	1,717	1,130	2,847
SM02-Sidarenka	Social Media	PotTS	(Sidarenka, 2016)	3,349	1,510	4,859
SM03-Narr	Social Media		(Narr et al., 2012)	350	237	587
SM04-Mozetič	Social Media		(Mozetič et al., 2016)	16,502	11,693	28,195
SM05-Siegel	Social Media	German Irony Corpus	(Siegel et al., 2017)	49	107	156
SM06-Momtazi	Social Media		(Momtazi, 2012)	278	191	469

Table 4: List of corpora with information about the respective domain of the texts, information about the size of the corpora, an abbreviation for further identification, and optionally, a corpus name if given by the authors. Pos and Neg illustrate the number of text units for the respective sentiment class in the corpus.

Abbreviation	Lexicon	Reference	Pos. Tokens	Neu. Token	Neg. Tokens	Total Tokens	Cont. Val.
01-Remus	SentiWS	(Remus et al., 2010)	16,385	0	17,853	34,238	x
02-Clematide		(Clematide et al., 2010)	3,378	608	5,253	9,239	x
03-Võ	BAWL-R	(Vo et al., 2009)	1,576	60	1,266	2,902	x
04-Emerson	SentiMerge	(Emerson and Declerck, 2014)	45,301	221	50,898	96,420	x
05-Siegel-p		(Siegel and Diwisch, 2014)	1,142	365	1,410	2,917	x
06-Siegel-m		(Siegel and Diwisch, 2014)	1,104	396	1,417	2,917	x
07-Rill	SePL	(Rill et al., 2012)	11,015	1,442	1,938	14,395	x
08-Takamura-c	GermanSentiSpin	(Takamura et al., 2005)	50,084	235	55,241	105,560	x
09-Takamura-d	GermanSentiSpin	(Takamura et al., 2005)	42,276	1	46,648	88,925	
10-Rauh		(Rauh, 2018)	17,330	0	19,750	37,080	
11-Du	SentiLitKrit	(Du and Mellmann, 2019)	1,800	0	1,820	3,620	
12-Asgari	UniSent	(Asgari et al., 2019)	656	0	728	1,384	
13-Waltinger	GermanPolarityClues	(Waltinger, 2010)	17,627	1,312	19,962	38,901	
14-Wolf	LIWC-De	(Wolf et al., 2008)	2,210	0	2,684	4,894	
15-Klinger	USAGE Sentiment Lexicon	(Klinger and Cimiano, 2014)	3,164	101	1,478	4,743	
16-Wilson	GermanSubjectivityClues	(Wilson et al., 2009)	3,336	749	5,742	9,827	
17-Mohammad	NRC Emotion Lexicon	(Mohammad and Turney, 2013)	1,550	6,728	2,339	10,617	
18-Ruppenhofer		(Ruppenhofer et al., 2017)	2,874	2,038	4,632	9,544	
19-Chen	Multilingual Sentiment Lexicon	(Chen and Skiena, 2014)	1,509	0	2,464	3,973	

Table 5: List of lexicons with information regarding the size of each polarity class of a lexicon, an abbreviation for further identification, the presence or absence of continuous sentiment values, and optionally, a lexicon name if given by the authors. X in column Cont. Val. marks that the lexicon contains continuous sentiment values.

Modifier	Baseline	f1	f1-delta	f1-combination-delta
POS with Treetagger	44.8	43.1	-1.7	-1.5
POS with Stanza	44.8	43.1	-1.8	-1.8
Stemming with Cistem	44.8	51.2	6.3	5.0
Stemming with Snowball	44.8	50.8	6.0	4.7
Lemmatization with Treetagger	44.8	50.4	5.5	5.1
Lemmatization with IWNLP	44.8	50.5	5.6	5.0
Lowercasing	44.8	47.6	2.8	0.2
Emoticons	44.8	47.8	2.9	1.7
Stop Words List	44.8	44.5	-0.3	-0.2
Valence Shifter	44.8	44.9	0.0	-0.2
Valence Intensifier and Diminusher	44.8	45.4	0.5	0.4

Table 6: Results of the modifier evaluation. Baseline is average f1 value without any modification across all corpora and lexicons. F1 the new value when only the specific modifier is added. F1-delta the difference between f1 and the baseline. F1-combination-delta is the average of all differences of all configuration with modifier turned on and off.

Lexicon Abbr.	f1	Selected Modifications								
		Lemmatization	Stemming	Cont. Sent.-Values	Emoticons	POS	Lowercasing	Stop Words Removal	Val.-Sh.	Int. & Dim.
04-Emerson	67.3	X		X	X		X	X		
01-Remus	63.6		X	X	X					X
10-Rauh	63.6		X		X	X				
13-Waltinger	63.4		X		X					
02-Clematide	61.9		X	X	X			X		
08-Takamura-c	60.6	X		X	X		X	X		
19-Chen	60.5	X			X		X	X		
18-Ruppenhofer	59.2		X		X			X		
07-Rill	56.2			X	X				X	X
16-Wilson	56.0		X		X			X		
03-Võ	54.9		X	X	X					X
15-Klinger	54.3		X		X					
14-Wolf	53.9	X			X		X		X	X
06-Siegel-m	53.8		X	X	X					
05-Siegel-p	53.4	X		X	X		X	X		
11-Du	53.2		X		X				X	X
09-Takamura-d	52.7	X			X		X	X		X
12-Asgari	52.0		X		X					X
17-Mohammad	51.6		X		X				X	X

Table 7: Best modifier combination for each lexicon sorted by f1 values. For stemming, lemmatization and POS-tagging the results with the respective best tool are shown. X in the column marks that this modifier is used.

Definition Extraction from Mathematical Texts on Graph Theory in German and English

Theresa Kruse
University of Hildesheim
Universitätsplatz 1
31141 Hildesheim, Germany
kruset@uni-hildesheim.de

Fritz Kliche
University of Hildesheim
Universitätsplatz 1
31141 Hildesheim, Germany
kliche@uni-hildesheim.de

Abstract

We extract definitions from text books and scientific publications on mathematics in both, German and English, from the sub-domain of graph theory. Mathematical texts differ from other domains because sentences which appear as definitions from a linguistic perspective are not necessarily definitions in the mathematical sense. For the English texts we train a neural network on existing training data (Vanetik et al., 2020). For the German texts we semi-automatically generate training data using patterns for the extraction of definitions. We show that this is a feasible approach for the domain of mathematical texts which generally makes extensive use of formalized language patterns. We measure precision and recall on a random sample to evaluate our results. The F-Score is similar for both languages but precision and recall are closer to each other for the German data. Further comparisons are made with a term list automatically extracted from the data. We conclude that our approach can be used to extract candidate sentences for further postprocessing.

1 Introduction

In this paper, we combine two domains where definitions play a significant role: lexicography and mathematics. In lexicography, definitions provide dictionary users with information about a term. In mathematics, definitions are crucial to ensure a common understanding of the domain's concepts. We extract definitions from texts on graph theory to use them in a domain-specific dictionary. In Section 2, we give an overview of related work on types and forms of definitions and on extraction methods. In Section 3.1, we describe our data. Sections 3.2 and 3.3 present our method for the extraction of definitions from the English and the German data. Section 4.1 gives a qualitative analysis of the results and Section 4.2 a quantitative evaluation. We conclude in Section 5.

2 Background and Related Work

2.1 Definitions in Mathematical Texts

Mathematical texts consist of corollaries, lemmas, propositions, theorems, proofs and definitions (Solow, 1990). Usually, a numbering indicates the types (e.g. *Theorem 2.1*) but this is not necessarily the case for definitions. Some authors include them in the numbering and others simply give them in the text. Some authors highlight defined terms, e.g. by means of italics. Kruse and Heid (2020) analyze mathematical definitions for lexicographic purposes. They conclude that *analytical definitions* (or *logical definitions* as they are also called) in the Aristotelian scheme are mostly used. *Single-clause when-definitions* appear to define adjectives and verbs, contrary to usual practice in dictionaries for general language, as Dziemianko and Lew (2006) proposed. For definition extraction, however, it is more relevant to distinguish a definition from a non-definition rather than paying attention to the different types of definitions. Nevertheless, some sentences are definitions from a linguistic perspective but not from a mathematical perspective in content. This constitutes a special challenge for automatic definition extraction.

Different kinds of sentences may be regarded as definitions in mathematics: The first kind defines a term which is used in the rest of the text. Often, one finds similar definitions for the same terms in different works of a sub-domain. Definition 1 is an example of such a definition from the sub-domain of graph theory. It defines the term *semiregular* as a property of *bipartite graphs*. We want to find such definitions in our extraction experiments. They follow the Aristotelian scheme with a definiendum (the term defined) and the definiens (the part defining, cf. e.g. Meyer, 2001, p. 283).

The second kind of definitions follows the Aristotelian scheme on a syntactic level but requires anaphora resolution to be comprehensible as it refers to something mentioned earlier or later in the text. For this kind, the context is indispensable to understand its meaning. Definition 2 constitutes such an example. These definitions are not useful for our dictionary project because they do not contain any relevant semantic information.

The third kind of definitions defines a variable which also cannot be used for the dictionary. Even if some variables often refer to the same objects (e.g. G for *graph*) they are not considered as terminology in our dictionary project as they rather resemble named entities. For example, Definition 3 formally defines $A(G)$ but is only relevant in the context of the particular paragraph, i.e., a proof or a construction, and not for the conceptual sphere of the domain.

We thus aim to find definitions following the scheme of Definition 1. However, the structure of Definition 1 is ambiguous between definition and non-definition. As an example consider Definition 4. It appears to be a definition with *tree* as the definiendum and the subject as the definiens. This example is taken from Saha Ray (2013) where it actually is a theorem which requires a proof as *tree* has been defined before (cf. Definition 5). It is not obvious that a graph meets the criteria from Definition 5 if it already has the properties from Definition 4. We do not expect our system to differentiate between these two kinds of definitions because this would require an analysis of the context beyond sentence level.

Which aspects are used in a definition and which aspects are left to be proven depends on the author's preferences for introducing a concept. The decision seems arbitrary at first sight but depends on the author's intended target group of the text (Rey, 1995; Solow, 1990; van Dormolen and Arcavi, 2000). Some general aspects can be considered for the decision because a mathematical definition should meet certain criteria (van Dormolen and Zaslavsky, 2003): *Hierarchy, existence, equivalence* and *axiomatization* are necessary, whereas *minimality, elegance* and *degeneration* are common but not required.

A *hierarchy* between the defined terms is inherent to the Aristotelian scheme. Further, a definition is only meaningful if the term defined does actually *exist*. *Equivalence* refers to the above-mentioned aspect that different definitions may exist for the same concept. It has to be shown that they are actually equivalent. The criterion of *axiomatization* is related to *hierarchy*: It is possible to define more and more general hypernyms. In order to stop this chain at one point axioms are needed, usually related to set theory.

The following criteria are not mandatory: *minimality* requires that only necessary properties are mentioned in a definition without redundancies. *Elegance* is hardly an objective property but can be taken into consideration when deciding which of several possible definitions is to be taken and which is left to be proven. "*Degenerations* are instances of a concept which are not expected to be included when defining the concept. They are a logical consequence from the definition. One might not want the occurrence of such instances and therefore change the definition in order to exclude them. Describing an instance as a degeneration is, of course, highly subjective and there is no objective criterion for this decision" (van Dormolen and Zaslavsky, 2003). These criteria combined with the individual preferences and ideas of concepts sum up to the final definitions which a mathematician writes.

Mathematical definitions are usually unambiguous within a certain sub-domain. Nevertheless, homonymy may occur between different subdomains. For example, the German *Körper* is translated into English as *solid figure* in geometry but as *field* in algebra. Another example is the adjective *complete* used as an attribute to *metric spaces* or *graphs*. The definitions differ considerably in both cases, although the same mental concept underlies both. As we work only with one mathematical sub-domain we can neglect homonymy.

Examples of definitions

1. We call a bipartite graph semiregular if it has a proper 2-colouring such that all vertices with the same colour have the same valency.

2. We call the above procedure branching-search.

3. Let $A(G)$ be an incidence matrix of a connected graph G with n vertices.

4. A connected graph with n vertices and $n-1$ edges is a tree.

5. A tree is a connected acyclic graph.

6. The floor function $\lfloor x \rfloor$, also called the greatest integer function or integer value, gives the largest integer less than or equal to x.

7. Similarly, define the points A_c, B_c, B_a, C_a, C_b so that the points A_c and B_c lie on the extended segment AB, the points B_a and C_a lie on the extended segment BC, and the point C_b lies on the extended segment CA, and we have $AA_c = a$, $BB_c = b$, $BB_a = b$, $CC_a = c$ and $CC_b = c$.

2.2 Definition extraction

Definition extraction originally started with pattern-based approaches. The patterns were then combined with a grammar analysis for e.g. apposition and anaphora resolution or syntactic features. These methods have been applied to several languages like English (Klavans and Muresan, 2001), German (Storrer and Wellinghoff, 2006), Spanish (Alarcón et al., 2009) and Dutch (Fahmi and Bouma, 2006). Examples for such patterns in English texts are *is called, is the term used to describe, is defined as, is the term for*. In German, the following patterns can be indicative for definitions: *bedeuten, begreifen als, bekannt als, benennen, beschreiben, bestehen aus, bezeichnen als, charakterisieren als, definieren als, gebrauchen, heißen, nennen, sein, spezifizieren als, sprechen von, Terminus einführen, verstehen unter, verwenden als, vorstellen als*[1].

Pattern-based approaches have been used in a wide range of applications. They were among others used by Meyer et al. (1999), Meyer (2001), or Pearson (1998) and are still applied today (Christensen, 2019). Barbaresi et al. (2018) extract "definitory contexts" for words from a broad range of domains (e.g. *Auseinandersetzungsbilanz* or *Pelletheizung*) in the context of lexicography using patterns such as *a* X_1 *is a* X_2. In line with this approach, definitions in mathematical texts can be regarded as knowledge-rich contexts which can be used in pattern-based approaches for information extraction. (Meyer, 2001; Meyer et al., 1999). Cramer (2011, 183 ff.) analyzes linguistic features of definitions. Schumann (2014) describes (corpus-)linguistic analyses for the detection of text passages containing description (thus not explicitly definitions) of terminologically relevant concepts.

Other approaches combine pattern-based extraction and machine learning (e.g., Westerhout, 2009). Boella and Di Caro (2013) combine syntactic dependencies with a Support Vector Machine classifier without using patterns. Fišer et al. (2010) combine morphosyntactic patterns, automatic terminology recognition and semantic tagging with WordNet senses for their work on Slovene Wikipedia texts.

Today, learning algorithms and neural networks are frequently used for definition extraction. Borg et al. (2010) use genetic programming and genetic algorithms to train their system on grammatical rules. Navigli and Velardi (2010) introduce Word-Class Lattices, an approach based on word lattices generalizing over lexico-syntactic definitional patterns which outperforms traditional extraction methods. Reiplinger et al. (2012), however, compare two methods, one based on bootstrapping lexico-syntactic patterns and the other based on deep analysis, and do not find major differences in the performances. Espinosa-Anke et al. (2015) use a weakly supervised bootstrapping approach and Espinosa-Anke and Schockaert (2018) combine Convolutional and Recurrent Neural Networks for definition extraction.

Del Gaudio and Branco (2009) suggest that definition extraction is language and domain independent. But Vanetik et al. (2020) show that this does not hold for definition extraction from mathematical texts. They work on a corpus crawled from *Wolfram MathWorld*[2] and indicate whether a certain sentence is a definition.[3] They conclude "that mathematical definitions require special treatment, and that using cross-domain learning for detection of mathematical definitions is inefficient".

3 Experiments

3.1 Data preprocessing

Our work is based on two comparable corpora, one in German, one in English, with texts from the mathematical sub-domain of graph theory. The German corpus contains about 700,000 tokens with about 30,000 types and consists of lecture notes and (parts of) nine text books. Parts of books, as opposed to the entire book, were used when only some chapters cover graph theory. The English

[1]Engl. *mean, understand as, known as, designate, describe, consist of, refer to as, characterize as, define as, use, be called, state, be, specify as, speak of, introduce a term, understand by, use as, conceive as*

[2]https://mathworld.wolfram.com

[3]The data of Vanetik et al. (2020) is publicly available on GitHub https://github.com/uplink007/FinalProject/tree/master/data/wolfram

corpus consists of eight text books and 26 scientific papers, totaling about one million tokens with about 30,000 types.

Our goal was to create corpora of a similar size. The exact number of tokens depends on how formulas are counted. We chose material from text books and literature students at our institution work with, as students are the target group of our dictionary. The choice of texts was based on a survey we carried out with the students (Kruse and Giacomini, 2019). Although many students indicated that they use Wikipedia for their studies we decided against including it into our corpus because we have less control on its quality from an academic perspective. Due to copyright restrictions we cannot make our corpus publicly available but in can be reproduced as we used published material.

Our source files are machine-readable PDF documents, scans and plain texts. As the data is not homogeneous, we had to use different workflows to integrate them into the corpus depending on the source file. We used inftyreader[4] and Tesseract (Smith, 2007) to convert PDF documents into plain text. The mathematical formulas produced some obstacles, e.g., Tesseract had difficulties to convert fractions into plain text as it works line by line. Inftyreader is specialized in processing mathematical texts and converts formulas according to the W3C standard MathML[5] but has difficulties with low quality scans. In the latter cases we used Tesseract which ignored the formulas. Thus, some errors remain in the texts due to errors in the optical character recognition (OCR). Afterwards, we did some semi-manual post-processing to eliminate the most common errors but could not cover all of them. Thus, some errors remain as can be seen in Examples 8 and 9.

We remove Latex commands for typesetting and document layout, while commands for mathematical formulas (e.g. `\sum`) are kept to preserve parts of the formulas in the input for the classifier. We split the data into sentences using the tokenizer described by Schmid (2000). Some issues with the automatic split into sentences remain, e.g., the exclamation mark is used for calculating factorials, or sentences with the following structure appear: *We can say that G is bipartite (why?) and continue the following way...*, where *(why?)* should motivate the reader to realize the truth of the given statement. As it would cost too much effort to go through these cases manually we leave them unchanged but they should be kept in mind when discussing quantitative results such as the number of sentences in the corpus because a different tokenizer might yield different results.

3.2 Definition Extraction from the English Corpus

We use the training data compiled by Vanetik et al. (2020) for the extraction of definitions in the English corpus. The training data consists of 1,793 sentences of which 811 are definitions. We count the sentences with domain-specific definition patterns in the training data using the following pattern indicators: *abbreviate, termed, determine, definition, refer, name, the term, associate, consist, said to be, then .* is, denote, known as, given by, is a(n), define, call, is the*. 72.87 % of the definition sentences and 28.21 % of the non-definition sentences contain at least one of the patterns. This legitimates our workflow to semi-automatically create the German training data by extracting sentences containing definition patterns.

We further analyze the training data and find definitions in which none of the patterns appears. They often contain the verbs *is/are*, *has/have* not followed by an article and thus deviate from the standard pattern. We exclude these verbs in our set of defining verbs to avoid too many false positives.

As mentioned above, some non-definitions also contain the patterns. One of these cases is the verb *call* which in the non-definitions is frequently combined with *also*, as in Definition 6 where it is followed by a synonym but not an actual definition. In our lexicographic application, synonyms are dealt with separately from definitions. Similar reasons hold for the other definition patterns in the non-definitions. We give an example for the indicator *define* in Definition 7 which constitutes a typical example of defining a variable, as described in Section 2 (cf. Definition 3).

After the pre-processing as described in Section 3.1, our corpus contains 56,978 English sentences to be classified. We use the SimpleTransformers implementation[6] of BERT (Devlin et al., 2019)[7] with one epoch. 11,936 (20.95 %) of the sentences were classified as definitions and 45,042 sentences

[4] https://www.inftyreader.org

[5] https://www.w3.org/TR/MathML3/

[6] https://github.com/ThilinaRajapakse/simpletransformers

[7] https://huggingface.co/bert-base-cased

(79.05 %) as non-definitions.

Again, we count the sentences containing at least one definition pattern: 51.42 % of the sentences classified as definitions contain a pattern but only 15.98 % of those classified as non-definitions. Like in the training data, more sentences classified as definitions contain one of the patterns. Yet, this holds for only half of the sentences unlike the 72.87 % in the training data. The amount of sentences classified as non-definitions containing a pattern is significantly lower which might be also a consequence of noise in the data.

We measure precision and recall on an exemplary random sample.[8] We manually collect 100 definitions and 100 non-definitions from our data set. To that end, we randomly sequence the sentences in the corpus and find definition sentences with help of patterns. For the non-definitions we randomly extract 200 sentences from the corpus and manually annotate if they are definitions. We take the first 100 of them for the evaluation. Thus, we have a random sample of 100 definitions and 100 non-definitions.

We measure precision and recall for the labels these 200 sentences were assigned with by the BERT classifier. The results for the definition sentences are given in Table 1. If we evaluate, in turn, the classification of non-definitions we get a precision of 0.8857 and a recall of 0.62 resulting in an F-Score of 0.7229. The higher precision of the non-definitions can probably be explained with the much higher number of non-definitions in the data compared to the number of definitions. Likewise, the high recall for the definitions can be explained by the fact that we calculate the values on a balanced random sample. We would get more realistic results if we would select 200 sentences completely random for this evaluation but in that case we run the risk of having almost no definitions in the sample which would not give reliable results.

3.3 Definition Extraction from the German Corpus

For the German corpus we create our own training data. To that end, we collect sentences containing at least one form for the following lemmas: *bestehen, bezeichnen, definieren, heißen, nennen, sagen, sprechen, verstehen.*[9] We randomly extract a maximum of 100 sentences for each indicator verb and manually annotate them as definitions or non-definitions following the criteria detailed in Section 2. Additionally, we manually search the corpus for examples of definitions which do not contain an indicator verb, e.g., because they contain the verb *sein* (engl. *be*). Again, we did not include all sentences containing *sein* to avoid false positives. Further, non-definitions without any indicator verbs are added to the data set. In sum, we collect 799 sentences of which 256 are definitions.

We use the pre-trained model `bert-based-german-cased`[10] from the Hugging Face library and one epoch of training. All results are summarized in Table 1. 90.54 % of the sentences are labeled as non-definitions and 9.46 % as definitions. 47.79 % of the sentences labeled as definitions contain at least one of the patterns whereas this is the case for only 4.75 % of the sentences labeled as non-definitions which matches the expectation as this percentage is higher for definitions. For measuring precision, recall and F-Scores we evaluate again a random sample of 100 sentences for each category. We yield a similar F-Score as for the English data. But precision and recall for German are closer to each other, i.e., the precision is slightly higher and the recall slightly lower. This might be explained by the fact that the percentage of sentences labeled as definitions is lower in the German data set. However, this comparison is only valid if we expect the same percentage of definitions in both corpora.

4 Discussion

4.1 Qualitative Analysis

Both, the English and German results have lower values for precision but higher values for recall. Thus, the definitions are usually found but false positives need to be filtered. We take a closer look at the false negatives in our evaluation samples. The German sample contains nine and the English sample only 15 false negatives (cf. Examples 8 to 11). Example 8 repeats the distributive law which is not defined in this sentence. Example 9 states that two already defined terms describe the same concept. This is another example where definitions and theorems are not distinguishable. The same holds for Example 10. Four of the nine false negatives in

[8]We thank the anonymous reviewers for their useful comments on the evaluation and discussion sections.

[9]Engl. *consist, denote, define, call, name, (to) name, say, speak, understand*

[10]`https://huggingface.co/bert-base-german-cased`

		German	English
Number...	...of sentences	$36,103$	$56,978$
	...classified as definition	$3,417$ (9.46 %)	$11,936$ (20.95 %)
	...classified as non-definition	$32,686$ (90.54 %)	$45,042$ (79.05 %)
Patterns in sentences...	...classified as definitions	47.79 %	51.42 %
	...classified as non-definitions	4.75 %	15.98 %
Evaluation of random sample	precision	0.7522	0.7054
	recall	0.8500	0.9100
	F-Score	0.7981	0.7948

Table 1: Overview of extraction results

the random sample contain the phrase *we say that*. We searched for this phrase in the training data and found that no example containing this phrase is included. This might be because the data was extracted from *Wolfram MathWorld* and not from scientific publications or textbooks. This might hint at differences in the "language for definitions" in different resources.

Examples 12 to 14 are false positives. Example 12 contains tokens which could also occur in definitions (e.g. *ist eine Zahl*, Engl. *is a number*). Example 13 is a similar case (*nennt man*, Engl. *is called*). Example 14 is an example from the English evaluation sample. It contains the expression *is defined* which is also indicative for a definition. Furthermore, the English sample includes several false positives beginning with *If*. In the whole data set, $2,719$ sentences contain this feature; 66.50 % of them are classified as a definition. This ratio may be a result from the training data which contains 52 sentences with an initial *If* which are labeled in 78.85 % of the cases as definitions.

Examples

8. Es gilt das Distributivgesetz: a-(b +c) = (a-b) + (a-c) für alle a, b, c eK.
   The distributive law holds: a-(b +c) = (a-b) + (a-c) for all a, b, c eK.

9. Damit beschreiben die Ausdrücke { Ecken)-3-panzyklisch und { Ecken)-panzyklisch den gleichen Sachverhält.
   Thus, the expressions { node)-3-pancyclic and { node)-pancyclic describe the same state of affairs.

10. Die einzigen 3-kritischen Graphen sind Kreise ungerader Länge.
    The only 3-critical graphs are circles of odd length.

11. We say that a graph G is reconstructible if every reconstruction of G ' is isomorphic to G, in other words, if G can be ' reconstructed up to isomorphism from its vertex-deleted subgraphs.

12. Jeder Buchstabe ist eine Zahl zwischen 1 und n.
    Each letter is a number between 1 and n.

13. In diesem speziellen Fall nennt man die Menge {x,y} auch das ungeordnete Paar von x und y.
    In this particular case, the set {x,y} is also called the unordered pair of x and y.

14. The matrix Miq is defined dually.

4.2 Quantitative Analysis

For a quantitative analysis we extract 1,000 keywords and 1,000 multiword terms from our data for each language using the corpus web tool *Sketch Engine* (Kilgarriff et al., 2014) which includes a function for keyword extraction. One rater evaluates in two rounds if these automatically found "keywords" are terminologically relevant. In the German list, 0.4705% of the keywords were relevant in this sense, and 0.5350% in the English list. These values are quite similar. Most of the false positives are variables and multiword expressions like *following graph*.

The chosen terms are manually divided into nine semantic categories:

- ACTIVITY: events which can be performed in graph theory, mostly verbs, e.g. *connect*

- ALGORITHM: domain-specific algorithms having a given name, e.g. *Dijkstra's algorithm*
- GENERAL: mathematical terminology which is not particularly attributed to the domain of graph theory, e.g. *disjoint*
- MAPPING: mappings in the mathematical sense, e.g. *edge contraction*
- PART: elements a graph is composed of, e.g. *edges*
- PERSON: mathematicians who worked in graph theory and related areas, e.g. *Dijkstra*
- PROBLEM: mathematical problems having a given name, e.g. *Traveling Salesman Problem*
- PROPERTY: descriptions of a graph, mostly adjectives, e.g. *regular*
- THEOREM: mathematical theorems having a given name, e.g. *Kirchhoff's matrix tree theorem*
- TYPE: names for special kinds of graphs, e.g. *Petersen graph*

We expect to find definitions for ACTIVITIES, GENERAL TERMS, MAPPINGS, PARTS, PROPERTIES and TYPES. ALGORITHMS, PERSONS, PROBLEMS and THEOREMS are usually not defined in mathematics. Thus, we analyze the terms in the sentences considered as definitions.

Table 2 shows the percentage of lemmas in the sentences classified as definitions. The value is higher for the English data which can be explained with the higher amount of definition sentences and the slightly lower precision indicated by the random sample. Thus, the probability to find a word in this set is generally higher. Figures 1 and 2 show which lemmas are found grouped by category. This matches our hypothesis that definitions mostly lack for the categories PERSON, PROBLEM, THEOREM and ALGORITHM. The results are much clearer for the German data which matches the results for precision and recall (cf. Table 1). We conclude that the definition extraction worked well for the majority of sentences which is reflected by the values for recall.

Still, some aspects affect the results, e.g., we did not exclude variants in our simple search. So, there is for example a definition for *1-Faktor-Satz* but not for *1-Faktorsatz*; and some multiword terms appear in the lemma list as a compound but are separated in the definition.

5 Conclusion and future work

Our approach yields higher values for recall but lower values for precision. We conclude that our semi-automatic approach can be used for finding candidates for mathematical definitions but they require a subsequent manual or automatic post-processing in order to distinguish definitions from sentences with a similar syntactic structure and vocabulary. An active learning approach in which parts of the results are evaluated in order to increase the training data iteratively could improve the approach.

We get different results for the English and the German data. We see several reasons for that: The German training data was semi-automatically generated using sentences from the sample on which the trained model was subsequently applied. Therefore, the same rules for annotating definitions were used for the generation of training data and for the evaluation of the results. For our English training data provided by Vanetik et al. (2020) we only had few indications of the annotation guidelines. Furthermore, the German training data contained only half as many sentences as the English data. In combination with the fact that the training data and evaluation data stem from the same corpus, there might be some over-specification to the data set. It might be interesting to train a network on this data and to apply the model on mathematical texts from different sub-domains.

About 20 % of the English sentences are classified as a definition, but only about 10 % of the German sentences. A reason for this difference may be the number of sources: The German corpus comprises of only ten texts while the English corpus contains 34 texts which are shorter. A reason for the different lengths are the text types as we used more text books for German and more scientific papers for English. The number of definitions in a mathematical text also depends on its type. In general, we would expect scientific papers to contain less definitions when compared to textbooks because they can pick up prior knowledge of their readers whereas textbooks are mostly targeted at learners with less prior domain knowledge. However, our results do not confirm this hypothesis as there are more sentences classified as definitions in

	German Data	English Data
number of definitions	3,417	11,936
number of lemmas	1,070	933
percentage of lemmas found in definitions	70.63%	90.47%

Table 2: Amount of lemmas in data

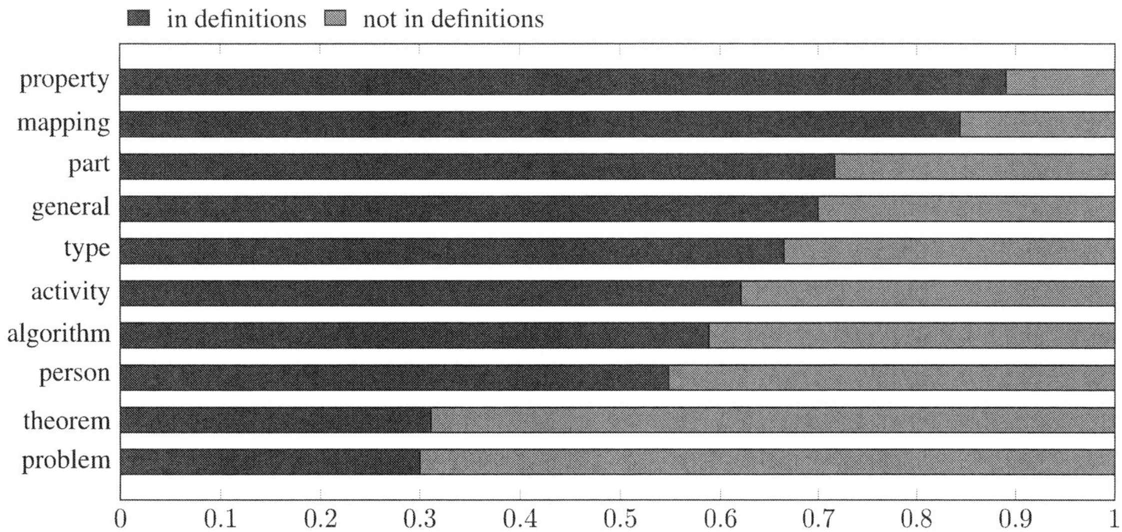

Figure 1: Distribution of German lemmas in definitions over categories

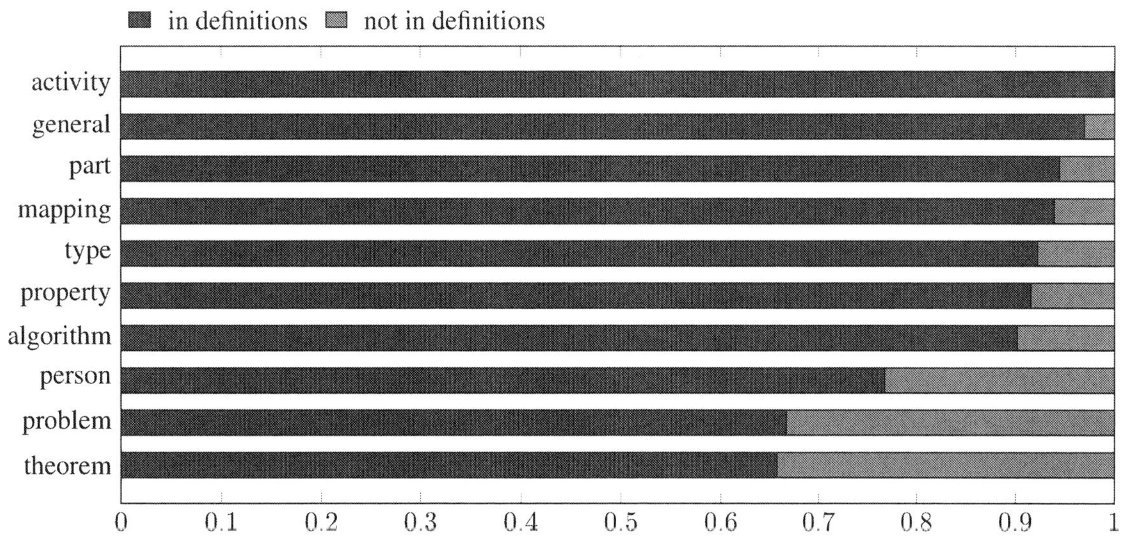

Figure 2: Distribution of English lemmas in definitions over categories

the English data than in the German. This might be related to the lower precision for the experiments on English texts. It would be interesting to investigate empirically if the percentage of definitions varies across different mathematical text types.

Furthermore, for our English corpus we had to rely more on OCR than for the German data. This may result in more mistakes which cause difficulties for the classifier. Interesting further research would be to analyze if the English extraction results differ when the training data is taken from the same corpus or from a corpus of the same sub-domain or type of resource. Maybe the results of Vanetik et al. (2020) can be interpreted in the more general way that the quality of definition extraction increases with the similarity between training data and evaluation data even for a highly formalized language like mathematics.

We can conclude that patterns are good indicators for mathematical definitions in German and English and can be used to generate training data. Nevertheless, automatic solutions are still needed for definition extraction in mathematics as some sentences are definitions from a linguistic perspective but not intended as such by their author.

References

Rodrigo Alarcón, Gerardo Sierra, and Carme Bach. 2009. Description and evaluation of a pattern based approach for definition extraction. In *Proceedings of the 1st Workshop on Definition Extraction*, pages 7–13, Borovets, Bulgaria. Association for Computational Linguistics.

Adrien Barbaresi, Lothar Lemnitzer, and Alexander Geyken. 2018. A database of German definitory contextsfrom selected web sources. In *Proceedings of the Eleventh International Conference on Language Resources and Evaluation (LREC'10)*, Miyazaki, Japan.

Guido Boella and Luigi Di Caro. 2013. Extracting definitions and hypernym relations relying on syntactic dependencies and support vector machines. In *Proceedings of the 51st Annual Meeting of the Association for Computational Linguistics (Volume 2: Short Papers)*, pages 532–537, Sofia, Bulgaria.

Claudia Borg, Mike Rosner, and Gordon J. Pace. 2010. Automatic grammar rule extraction and ranking for definitions. In *Proceedings of the Seventh International Conference on Language Resources and Evaluation (LREC'10)*, Valletta, Malta.

Lotte Weilgaard Christensen. 2019. Danish knowledge patterns and word sketches for semi-automatic extraction of terminological information. In Ingrid Simonnæs, Øivin Andersen, and Klaus Schubert, editors, *New challenges for Research on Language for Special Purposes. Selected Proceedings from the 21st LSP-conference 28-30 June 2017 Bergen, Norway*, pages 173–189. Frank & Timme, Berlin.

Irene Cramer. 2011. *Definitionen in Wörterbuch und Text: Zur manuellen Annotation, korpusgestützten Analyse und automatischen Extraktion definitorischer Textsegmente im Kontext der computergestützten Lexikographie.* Dissertation, Technische Universität Dortmund, Dortmund.

Rosa Del Gaudio and António Branco. 2009. Language independent system for definition extraction: First results using learning algorithms. In *Proceedings of the 1st Workshop on Definition Extraction*, pages 33–39, Borovets, Bulgaria. Association for Computational Linguistics.

Jacob Devlin, Ming-Wei Chang, Kenton Lee, and Kristina Toutanova. 2019. BERT: Pre-training of deep bidirectional transformers for language understanding. In *Proceedings of the 2019 Conference of the North American Chapter of the Association for Computational Linguistics: Human Language Technologies, Volume 1 (Long and Short Papers)*, pages 4171–4186, Minneapolis, Minnesota. Association for Computational Linguistics.

Joop van Dormolen and Abraham Arcavi. 2000. What is a circle? *Mathematics in School*, 29(5):15–19.

Anna Dziemianko and Robert Lew. 2006. When you are explaining the meaning of a word: The effect of abstract noun definition format on syntactic class identification. In *Proceedings of the 12th EURALEX International Congress*, pages 857–863, Torino, Italy. Edizioni dell'Orso.

Luis Espinosa-Anke, Horacio Saggion, and Francesco Ronzano. 2015. Weakly supervised definition extraction. In *Proceedings of the International Conference Recent Advances in Natural Language Processing*, pages 176–185, Hissar, Bulgaria. INCOMA Ltd. Shoumen.

Luis Espinosa-Anke and Steven Schockaert. 2018. Syntactically aware neural architectures for definition extraction. In *Proceedings of the 2018 Conference of the North American Chapter of the Association for Computational Linguistics: Human Language Technologies, Volume 2 (Short Papers)*, pages 378–385, New Orleans, Louisiana.

Ismail Fahmi and Gosse Bouma. 2006. Learning to identify definitions using syntactic features. In *Proceedings of the Workshop on Learning Structured Information in Natural Language Applications*, pages 64–71.

Darja Fišer, Senja Pollak, and Špela Vintar. 2010. Learning to mine definitions from slovene structured and unstructured knowledge-rich resources. In *Proceedings of the Seventh International Conference on Language Resources and Evaluation (LREC'10)*, Valletta, Malta.

Adam Kilgarriff, Vìt Baisa, Jan Bušta, Miloš Jakubíček, Vojtěch Kovář, Jan Michelfeit, Pavel Rychlý, and Vìt Suchomel. 2014. The sketch engine: ten years on. *Lexicography*, pages 7–36.

Judith L. Klavans and Smaranda Muresan. 2001. Evaluation of the definder system for fully automatic glossary construction. In *Proceedings AMIA Symposium*, pages 324–328.

Theresa Kruse and Laura Giacomini. 2019. Planning a domain-specific electronic dictionary for the mathematical field of graph theory: definitional patterns and term variation. In *Electronic lexicography in the 21st century. Proceedings of the eLex 2019 conference*, pages 676–693, Brno. Lexical Computing CZ, s.r.o.

Theresa Kruse and Ulrich Heid. 2020. Lemma selection and microstructure: Definitions and semantic relations of a domain-specific e-dictionary of the mathematical domain of graph theory. In *Euralex Proceedings*, volume 1, pages 227–233.

Ingrid Meyer. 2001. Extracting knowledge-rich contexts for terminography: A conceptual and methodological framework. In Didier Bourigault, Christian Jacquemin, and Marie-Claude L'Homme, editors, *Recent Advances in Computational Terminology*, volume 2 of *Natural Language Processing*, pages 279–302. John Benjamins, Amsterdam/Philadelphia.

Ingrid Meyer, Kristen Mackintosh, Caroline Barrière, and Tricia Morgan. 1999. Conceptual sampling for terminographical corpus analysis. In *Terminology and Knowledge engineering*, pages 256–267, Vienna. TermNet.

Roberto Navigli and Paola Velardi. 2010. Learning word-class lattices for definition and hypernym extraction. In *Proceedings of the 48th Annual Meeting of the Association for Computational Linguistics*, pages 1318–1327, Uppsala, Sweden.

Jennifer Pearson. 1998. *Terms in Context*, volume 1 of *Studies in Corpus Linguistics*. John Benjamins, Amsterdam / Philadelphia.

Melanie Reiplinger, Ulrich Schäfer, and Magdalena Wolska. 2012. Extracting glossary sentences from scholarly articles: A comparative evaluation of pattern bootstrapping and deep analysis. In *Proceedings of the ACL-2012 Special Workshop on Rediscovering 50 Years of Discoveries*, pages 55–65, Jeju Island, Korea.

Alain Rey. 1995. *Essays on Terminology*, volume 9 of *Benjamins Translation Library*. John Benjamins, Amsterdam.

Santanu Saha Ray. 2013. *Graph Theory with Algorithms and its Applications. In Applied Science and Technology*. Springer India, New Delhi/Heidelberg/New York/Dordrecht/London.

Helmut Schmid. 2000. Unsupervised learning of period disambiguation for tokenisation. Technical report, IMS, University of Stuttgart.

Anne-Kathrin Schumann. 2014. *Linguistische Analyse und korpusbasierte Extraktion deutscher und russischer wissenshaltiger Kontexte*. Dissertation, Universität Wien, Wien.

Ray Smith. 2007. An overview of the tesseract ocr engine. In *Ninth International Conference on Document Analysis and Recognition*, pages 629–633, Parana, Brasilien.

Daniel Solow. 1990. *How to read and do proofs. An introduction to mathematical thought processes*, second edition edition. John Wiley & sons, New York.

Angelika Storrer and Sandra Wellinghoff. 2006. Automated detection and annotation of term definitions in german text corpora. In *Proceedings of The 5th Language Resources and Evaluation Conference*, pages 2373–2376.

Joop van Dormolen and Orit Zaslavsky. 2003. The many facets of a definition: The case of periodicity. *The Journal of Mathematical Behavior*, 22(1):91 – 106.

Natalia Vanetik, Marina Litvak, Sergey Shevchuk, and Lior Reznik. 2020. Automated discovery of mathematical definitions in text. In *Proceedings of the 12th Language Resources and Evaluation Conference*, pages 2086–2094, Marseille, France. European Language Resources Association.

Eline Westerhout. 2009. Definition extraction using linguistic and structural features. In *Proceedings of the 1st Workshop on Definition Extraction*, pages 61–67, Borovets, Bulgaria. Association for Computational Linguistics.

Extraction and Normalization of Vague Time Expressions in German

Ulrike May[1, 2], **Karolina Zaczynska**[1], **Julián Moreno-Schneider**[1], **and Georg Rehm**[1]

[1]DFKI Gmbh, Berlin, Germany
[2]Linguistics Department, University of Potsdam, Germany
ulrike.may@hotmail.de, {karolina.zaczynska, julian.moreno_schneider, georg.rehm}@dfki.de

Abstract

Existing datasets and methods that aim at the identification of time expressions in natural language text do not pay particular attention to expressions that are imprecise and that cannot be easily represented on a timeline. We call these vague time expressions (VTEs). We present an analysis of existing time extraction approaches and steps towards a novel scheme for the annotation of VTEs, developed using a corpus of German news articles. To the best of our knowledge, this work is the first to suggest an extension of the ISO standard TimeML with the goal of enabling the annotation of VTEs. In addition, we present a collection of 339 German VTEs as well as classification experiments on the news corpus with results from 60 up to 77 macro-avg. F1 score.

1 Introduction

Time is critical to the meaning of language, for understanding events, cause-effect relations and narratives, etc. In NLP, temporal expression analysis is a key issue which has been receiving a lot of attention in recent years, especially for English news texts (e. g., UzZaman et al., 2013; Caselli and Vossen, 2017; Strötgen et al., 2018). Existing approaches mostly focus on time expressions which can be more or less easily and specifically represented on a timeline with an accuracy of different granularity levels. Given an expression like *at 6 'o clock*, the hour can be pinpointed, *this Sunday* or *tomorrow* refer to a specific day. Such time expressions can be annotated using standardized machine-readable expressions. This process is typically referred to as normalization.

Nevertheless, there is a large proportion of time expressions that are inherently *vague* – they are neither exact nor precise and, i. e., they cannot be readily normalized. Examples for vague time expressions (VTEs) are *in the future* or *lately*. VTEs are typically not taken into account by existing annotation schemes; some simply normalize them as a reference to the past or future. According to Tissot et al. (2019), around 13% of time expressions in news articles can be considered vague. In our German corpus, almost 30% of all time expressions are VTEs (Section 3). The annotation of time expressions in TimeML (Saurí et al., 2006), arguably the most well known scheme, is possible only if we can fully and precisely interpret the expression (Mazur and Dale, 2011). As VTEs cannot be fully and precisely interpreted, we are unable to represent them using TimeML, which is why an annotation scheme needs to be developed that is able to capture VTEs. Given that a large number of time expressions tend to be overlooked or oversimplified, our goal is the annotation and normalization of VTEs by extending TimeML; we concentrate on German documents and the German extension for TimeML. According to our research, no corpora exist that cover VTEs in a substantial way, neither for English nor for German.

While VTEs cannot be easily normalized and expressed on a timeline (Schilder and Habel, 2001), we argue that, based on our analysis, it is possible to describe their meaning systematically by their semantic and syntactic properties, which enables us to normalize VTEs more precisely than existing annotation schemes. Our main contributions are:

- We provide an overview of schemes for time expressions and their ability to express VTEs.
- We present a list of over 300 categorized German VTEs.[1]
- Building upon Tissot et al. (2019) and Mazur and Dale (2011), we develop a study about

[1]The full list is available under: https://live.european-language-grid.eu/catalogue/lcr/7975 (last access: 2021-08-13)

the possibilities of normalizing and classifying VTEs by expressing the closest or most precise meaning. To the best of our knowledge, we are the first to present such a study on VTEs for German. Our methods can be adapted to other languages.

- We present an annotated sample dataset and preliminary classification experiments.

2 Background and Related Work

Our approach is primarily based on the categorization of precise time expressions according to TimeML and LTIMEX (Section 2.1) as well as on the categorization of VTEs provided by Tissot et al. (2019) (Section 2.2). Channell (1983) and Dinu et al. (2017) describe approaches on vague expressions in domains other than time.

2.1 Categories of Precise Time Expressions

The ISO standard for the annotation of time expressions is TimeML (Pustejovsky et al., 2010). Temporal expressions are marked up using TimeML's TIMEX3 tag to capture their meaning. Important attributes of this tag are *type* and *value*: *Type* records whether the expression is a *duration*, a point in time (either a specific *date*, or a *time* of the day) or a *set* of points in time (Saurí et al., 2006). The *type* of an expression determines how the expression is normalised in the *value* attribute. Temporal expressions with a modifier that cannot be expressed using the value attribute, e. g., "in *about* 3 days" are handled by the optional attribute *mod*, which was adapted from TIDES (Ferro et al., 2001).

With LTIMEX, Mazur and Dale (2011) attempted to modularise the normalization process of a temporal expression. This annotation scheme extends TIDES to capture partial meanings of time expressions. It differentiates between local and global meaning. The local meaning is the same for each occurrence of a word and determining this meaning requires no contextual information. For example, "yesterday" has the local meaning "the day before today" (Mazur and Dale, 2011). The global meaning, on the other hand, is gained through the context about the utterance time of the expression and, based on the local meaning, the date of what is referred to as "yesterday" can be concluded.

LTIMEX distinguishes 12 categories of time expressions. Similar to TimeML, they include *points*, *durations* and *sets*. Additionally, *offsets* are functions that normalize a time expression relative to the document creation time (dct) or a given reference time (ref). An example for an offset would be "in 3 days" meaning "3 days after the *dct*". Another class is *ordinally specified*, which are expressions based on numbers, like "the *first*|*last*|*every second* Monday in July". The categories that indicate VTEs are *modified point* and *modified duration*. The annotation scheme provides no other methods for normalising VTEs.

2.2 Categories of Vague Time Expressions

Using the definition of the word *vague* from Devos (2003), a time expression is vague, when it is not clear which date the expression refers to or which dates limit the referenced time period. Even an expression like "in 2010" can be used without referring to the whole year 2010 but to a specific, yet unknown point or period (Strötgen, 2015). Only few approaches or schemes deal with VTEs in more detail (e. g., Devos et al., 1994; Rong et al., 2017), from which Tissot et al. are the only ones to present a classification especially for VTEs (Tissot et al., 2019).[2] The six categories are based on an evaluation of clinical corpora. The first category, *present reference*, includes temporal references related to the present, such as "now", "recently" and "currently". Modified precise time expressions, like "in *approximately* 10 days", belong to the category *modified value*. *Imprecise value* refers to expressions built up around an imprecise period of time, such as "*a few* days" or "*several* weeks". This category also contains expressions with an indefinite period of time, in which the granularity is usually represented in plural form without numeric values.[3] An example would be "years" in "It took years to finish the job.". The fourth category, *range of values*, describes time spans defined by limits, such as "every 3 to 4 months". *Partial period* covers time spans that are part of a larger time frame, such as "mid-January". The last class, *generic expressions*, includes a general period or duration, like "this time" or "at the same time". Although these categories are relevant, Tissot et al. do not present further methods for normalization. We adapt and extend the classes for our own categorization (Sec-

[2]Instead of "vague", Tissot et al. use the term "imprecise".

[3]The granularity describes how precise a time expression is. It can, for example, be one of the values *millennium*, *century*, *decade*, *year*, *month*, *day*, *hour*, *minute* or *second* (Caselli and Sprugnoli, 2015).

tion 4).

3 Dataset

Part of the dataset we used for our primary annotation experiments including the annotations for VTEs is taken from KRAUTS (Strötgen et al., 2018). KRAUTS is a German corpus consisting of 50 articles from the newspaper *Die Zeit*, annotated using the TimeML guidelines by Minard et al. (2017). We also incorporate 1037 documents we call, for the remainder of this work, *Short_News* because they consist of short articles from various news media.[4] The Short_News articles consist, on average, of fewer tokens than the articles in KRAUTS and only briefly and factually state the most important facts. One news document can contain several short articles on various topics while in KRAUTS, one document always covers exactly one topic. The KRAUTS articles are more detailed and explain the background of events or an opinion on a subject. The corpus includes comments, opinion pieces, reports, interviews, reviews, and excerpts from a book or film but also fictional types of texts, such as short stories and poems.

To narrow down the size of the dataset for the scope of this work, we selected 100 articles from Short_News with about every tenth text being chosen. We filtered near-duplicate articles which left us with 69 documents with 96 721 tokens in total.[5] Table 1 shows key corpus statistics.

Articles	Sentences per file	Sentences in total	Tokens per file	Tokens in total
KRAUTS	52.2	2 609	1 005.0	50 250
Short_News	22.3	1 536	673.5	46 471
Both	37.2	4 145	839.2	96 721

Table 1: Key data set statistics (after reducing Short_News to 100 articles).

4 Data Annotation

The category adaptations and resulting TimeML extensions are described in Sections 4.1 and 4.2, respectively. Based on a list of German VTE (Section 4.3) we developed the attribute *meaning* which enables a more precise normalization of VTEs. The categories postulated by Tissot et al. (2019) indicate a variation in the level of precision and vagueness, which we utilize for our normalization of VTEs (Section 4.4). While the normalization was adapted to each of these categories, the categories themselves do not appear in the annotation. Furthermore, Section 4.5 describes additional vague time expressions, while Section 4.6 presents statistics about the annotated dataset.

4.1 Inferring a Classification

Tissot et al. (2019) do not describe the category *modified value* in much detail, which is why we interpret it as described in TimeML, where a (precise) temporal expression is modified by a modifier. Since *partial period* also includes modified time expressions, like "mid-January", we decided to merge it into the *modified value* category. As mentioned, time expressions of the *modified value* category are precise time expressions that are made vague using a modifier, such as "*approximately* 10 days". Here, the intended time span can be narrowed down to a few days. The category *range of values* contains expressions that give specific boundaries, like "in 2-3 days". The exact point in time or time period is unknown yet somewhere in between. Expressions in the *imprecise value* category still reveal their granularity. For example, "in a few days" most likely refers to days after the utterance time and not weeks or months. Nevertheless, Tissot et al. (2019) do not distinguish between points in time, time periods or sets. We, therefore, took the categories *modified value*, *imprecise value* and *range of values* and subdivided them respectively for normalization according to the TimeML types *date*, *time*, *duration* and *set*. The categories that could not be subdivided according to TimeML types (*present reference* and *generic expression*) were not included in our annotation scheme.

4.2 TimeML Extensions

Our annotation scheme for VTEs builds upon TimeML and ensures compatibility. We realise TimeML-compliant normalization of precise time expressions by keeping the attribute *value* and by adding the new attribute *meaning* to cover the interpretation of VTEs.

4.2.1 Normalising the Attribute "meaning"

The mechanisms for capturing normalizations in the attribute *meaning* is based on the *type* of the VTE. We used the formalizations for the *offset* in

[4] We thank our project partner Condat AG for providing the documents (https://condat.de/ (last access: 2021-08-13)).

[5] Since these documents are copyrighted material, we are unable to make them available publicly. However, we present annotated examples in Appendix A.

the LTIMEX-scheme of Mazur and Dale (2011) as a starting point. Similar to Mazur and Dale (2011), a $+$ or a $-$ in the normalization means that the expression describes a point in time that lies before or after a reference point. For example, "+0000-00-0X" means "in einigen Tagen" (*in a few days*). The $+$ indicates that the referenced point in time is after the *dct*, while "0000-00-0X" represents the number of years, month and days that are between the *dct* and the described point in time. The "X" placeholder indicates, in this case, a number of days between 1 and 9. In contrast to Mazur and Dale (2011), we included $<$ and $>$ as comparison operators. $A_1 < A_2$ means that an expression A_1 is temporally before an expression A_2, and $A_1 <= A_2$, that A_1 happens before or at the same time as A_2. One of the placeholders A_1 or A_2 can be replaced by *dct* or *ref* to refer to the document creation time (dct) or another reference point (ref). While dct is important for factual text types (e. g., news articles), ref is helpful especially for narrative texts where the utterance time of the text is not necessarily the time when the document was created. *P* stands for period and indicates a normalization of type *duration*, *Y* stands for *years* and can be replaced by *D* (days), *M* (months), *DE* (decades) or by a leading *T* (time) and *h* (hours), *m* (minutes) or *s* (seconds) (Saurí et al., 2006). We expand the use of *X* in our scheme so that it can be used to indicate one or more decimal places. Therefore, in addition to "PXY" (representing at most nine years), it is now also possible to use "PXXY" (representing at most 99 years). The largest range probable in a given context should always be used. We did not further modify the attribute *value* of TIMEX3.

The value of the attribute *meaning* resembles a function. It can take one of two forms. In the first form, it contains *Z* as a symbol for the time expression, see the examples in the rows for *date*, *time*, *duration* and *set* in the *range of values* category in Table 2. The second form is used to describe a expression that refers to a point that lies a specific time before or after ref or dct. In this, a number of units is subtracted from or added to dct or ref to represent a specific point in time. The number of units is specified in ISO format: $YYYY - MM - [WW]DD - Thh : mm : ss$, where zero represents an empty position and *X* represents an unknown position. A digit can be omitted if it is zero and followed only by zeros. For the expression "vor Jahrzehnten" (*decades ago*) in example (1) we derive the meaning $dct - 00XX$, which indicates that the expressed point in time must lie a two-digit number of years before the dct. The hundreds and thousands digits are *0*. All units more specific than the year are left out. Appendix A contains more examples.

(1) Er ist vor Jahrzehnten ausgewandert.
He is before decades emigrated.
'He emigrated decades ago.'

In TimeML (Saurí et al., 2006), only "Jahrzehnten" (*decades*) would be marked as a time expression while ignoring the preposition "vor". We, however, consider prepositions as well as adverbs to be an inherent part of the time expression because they can convert one type of time expression into another one. In this example, the preposition converts a duration into a point in time, so that the *value* changes from "PXDE" to "PAST_REF". The same applies to reverse cases, when a preposition or an adverb converts a point in time into a duration.

4.2.2 Additional Adaptations

In addition, we circumvent empty tags by specifying values directly in the appropriate attributes instead of creating and linking another point in time with the help of references. For example, instead of creating two empty tags to represent the begin and end points of a duration, these times are directly annotated in the *begin* and *end* fields of an expression of type duration. In the sentence "Die Expedition beginnt am 4. April 2022 und dauert ungefähr 10 Tage" (*The expedition starts at April 4, 2022 and takes about 10 days*) the start point will be "2022-04-04" and the end will be "2022-04-14" with the *mod*-value "approx" (see also row 5 in the *modified value* section of Table 2). In addition to numerical values, the normalization of the label *set* for irregular or unclear intervals can also include the values *low*, *normal*, *high*, *increasing* or *decreasing* in the attribute *freq*. For example, "Ich treibe selten Sport" (*I rarely do sports*), yields the value "low" for the attribute *freq*.

We foresee the attribute *vague* to distinguish VTEs from precise time expressions. It is *true* whenever a time expression cannot be normalized to an exact *value*, i. e., whenever *value* contains the placeholder *X* or is *past_ref* or *future_ref*. It is also *true* when a modifier is used. Every example in table 2 has this attribute set to "true".

4.3 Vague Time Expressions in German

We collected 338 German VTEs in total. The seed entries of our inventory were based on an analysis of the KRAUTS corpus (Strötgen et al., 2018) as well as various brainstorming sessions among the authors. The list was expanded using synonyms found in the DWDS[6] and Duden[7] online search. Similar expressions are summarised using placeholders. In "Anfang *Monat*" (*begin month*), "Monat" should be replaced by a specific month, e. g., "Januar" (*January*). Granularity expressions like days, weeks, etc. are indicated by a capitalised "G" (e. g., "in einigen *G*" (*in a few G*)). Additionally, numbers are represented by an *x*. For example"in *x G*" can be replaced by "in 3 Tagen" (*in 3 days*).

We structure the time expressions into different categories (see Section 4.1). Not all expressions were assigned to a category since, as pointed out in Section 4.5, there are other types of time expressions which are challenging to describe with the given categories. Our list served as an initial basis for the development of the normalization approach. Appendix B shows an excerpt of the full list.[8]

4.4 Description of the Classes

Table 2 illustrates our classification (Section 4.1) including the categories *modified value*, *imprecise value* and *range of values* and additional subcategories according to the four types used in TimeML. We included two additional types based on the *offset* category (Mazur and Dale, 2011). These are *offset-like date* and *offset-like time* which use a time interval and a reference point to refer to a date or a time respectively. While *offset-like time* can take a time granularity like seconds, minutes or hours (e. g., "in 5 hours") an *offset-like date* can take any other granularity like days, month or years (e. g., "in 5 days"). Additional example expressions and their normalizations are shown in Table 2. Although the *offset* types are eventually converted to *dates* or *times* when the local representation of LTIMEX is turned into a global annotation, we listed them separately to show the semantic difference between *points* and *offsets*. While *point* expressions, like "Mitte Januar" (*mid January*), consist mostly of nouns, *offset* expressions seem to always contain a preposition, e. g., "in" (*in*) in the expression "in 6 Tagen" (*in* 6 days) or "vor" (*ago*) in "vor 6 Tagen" (*6 days ago*) or an adverb "danach" (*after that*) in the expression "10 Tage danach" (*10 days after that*). At this point, it is important to mention that it might be insufficient to only look at prepositions for distinguishing a duration or an offset-like time expression. The prepostion "in" can be used in German for indicating a point in time but sometimes also a duration: "Anna ruft uns in 10 Tagen an" (*Anna will us call in 10 days*) versus "Er schrieb das Buch in 10 Tagen" (*He wrote the book in 10 days*). Nevertheless, German temporal prepositions in general can be distinguished between indicating a point in time or a duration.

This categorization enables us to distinguish different capturing methods, see column three in Table 2. While the *modified value* category contains enough information, i. e., a more or less specific number of days, to arrive at a date or time, the difference to the other two major categories *imprecise value* and *range of values* becomes more obvious. There, the meaning of an offset expression is described using the dct or ref, and an addition or subtraction of a number of granularities (years, months, weeks, days, hours or minutes). In contrast, the values of *date* and *time* contain no addition or subtraction. The normalization of the three different major types differs from one another. *Modified value* contains specific values and a modifier. *Imprecise value* consists mostly of additions and subtractions from a reference point and of undefined values in form of an uppercase *X*. Also, there are no imprecise dates or times that are not described like an offset. *Range of values* is characterised by the use of comparison operators.

4.5 Other Vague Time Expressions

There are types of time expressions that are difficult to classify in the way described above. In contrast to the examples in Table 2, expressions such as "bald" (*soon*) or "kurz danach" (*shortly afterwards*) do not inherently indicate a specific granularity. For example, "früher" (*back then*) in "früher war alles besser." (*Everything was better in the good old days.*) does not refer to a duration with a certain start and end point, but to an unspecified span in the speaker's past. It is probably valid to assume that a period of time is meant that is at least a decade in the past (depending on the age of the speaker), so that the granularity can be narrowed down to "dct - 00XX". The example shows that for the annotation of VTEs, world knowledge as

[6] https://www.dwds.de (last access: 2021-05-30)

[7] https://www.duden.de (last access: 2021-05-30)

[8] https://live.european-language-grid.eu/catalogue/lcr/7975 (last access: 2021-08-13)

TimeML-Type Subcategory	Example (English)	Example (German)	Normalization
VTE category: *modified value*			
date	mid-January*	Mitte Januar	mod="mid" value="xxxx-01"
offset-like date	after about 10 days	nach ungefähr 10 Tagen	mod="approx" value="2021-05-11"
time	around 1 p.m.	ungefähr 13 Uhr	mod="approx" value="2021-05-01-T13"
offset-like time	after about 10 hours	nach ungefähr 10 Stunden	mod="approx" value="2021-05-01-T22"
duration	about 10 days*	ungefähr 10 Tage	mod="approx" value="P10D"
set	approximately every 3rd day	ungefähr jeden 3. Tag	mod="approx" value="P3D" freq="1x"
VTE category: *imprecise value*			
date	–	–	–
offset-like date	a few days earlier	vor ein paar Tagen	value="future_ref" meaning="dct + 0000-00-0X"
time	–	–	–
offset-like time	a few hours earlier	vor ein paar Stunden	value="future_ref" meaning="dct + 0000-00-00-T0X"
duration	a few days*	ein paar Tage	value="PXD"
set	every few days	alle paar Tage	value="PXD" freq="1x"
VTE category: *range of values*			
date	between August 13th and 15th	zwischen dem 13. und 15. August	meaning="2021-08-13 $\leq$ Z $\leq$ 2021-08-15"
offset-like date	5 to 6 days later	5 bis 6 Tage später	value="future_ref" meaning="dct + 0000-00-05 $\leq$ Z $\leq$ dct + 0000-00-06"
time	between 1 p.m. and 3 p.m.	zwischen 13 und 15 Uhr	meaning="2021-05-01-T13 $\leq$ Z $\leq$ 2021-05-01-T15"
offset-like time	5 to 6 hours later	5 bis 6 Stunden später	value="future_ref" meaning="dct + 0000-00-00-T05 $\leq$ Z $\leq$ dct + 0000-00-00-T06"
duration	between 8 and 10 years*	zwischen 8 und 10 Jahren	meaning="P8Y $\leq$ Z $\leq$ P10Y"
set	every 3-4 months*	alle 3-4 Monate	meaning="P3M $\leq$ Z $\leq$ P4M" freq="1x"

Table 2: VTE categories (taken from Tissot et al., 2019) with TimeML-type extensions and examples. Where possible, examples from Tissot et al. (2019) were used and marked with *.

The assumed document creation time (dct) is 2021-05-01-T12:00. Like Mazur and Dale (2011), a lowercase *x* represents a value that has to be determined from the context of an expression.

well as additional contextual knowledge are crucial and that the meaning cannot always be determined unambiguously and directly from the text.

A VTE can also be used anaphorically[9] when another time expression is provided as context. In "2003 bin ich 6 geworden. Damals war die Welt noch in Ordnung." (*I turned 6 in 2003. Back then, the world was still alright.*), "damals" receives the value *2003*. With regard to future tense, in "Ina wird in zwei Jahren 18. Dann kann sie ihren Führerschein machen." (*Ina will turn 18 in two years. Then, she can get her driver's license.*) "dann" (*then*) gets the (local) meaning *in two years* which would, depending on ref/dct, result in a specific year. In both cases, the date of the otherwise vague time expression can be identified as such.

Expressions such as "künftig" (*in future*) and "in letzter Zeit" (*lately*) refer to a period of time anchored in the utterance time and facing towards the future or the past. The example "Ich werde künftig vorsichtiger sein." (*I'll be more careful in the future.*) suggests that the proposition "Ich bin vorsichtiger" (*I will be more careful*) applies to the speaker at any point after the utterance time. The expression is of type *duration* and receives the meaning "PXXY" with a *beginpoint* "dct" and an *endpoint* "future_ref". In "Peter hat in letzter Zeit sehr hart gearbeitet." (*Peter has been working very hard lately.*), "in letzter Zeit" (*lately*) refers to a time span from a point in time in the near past to the utterance time. This period of time can be days, weeks, or months, depending on the context.

There are some idiomatic expressions or phrases in German (as well as in English) which contain a precise time expression but are used for expressing an undefined short time duration, and should be therefore regarded as VTEs, like "Hast du eine

[9] We use this term following Mazur and Dale (2011) who describe a deictic and *anaphoric* use of time expressions in the *offset* category, where *anaphoric offset* includes another time expression as a reference point.

Minute?" (*Do you have a minute?*) or "Eine Sekunde!" (*Just a second!*).

For expressions like "inzwischen" (*meanwhile*), in the example "Inzwischen hat es Rücktrittsforderungen gegen sie [...] gegeben." (*In the meantime, there have been calls for her resignation [...].*) (Strötgen et al., 2018) we define the following framework. There is a given time in the past from which an implicit time span is drawn up to the utterance time. We reason that the expression is of type *date* because a call for resignation is an event that takes place at a specific time and/or date and is within a specified period. In the example, the starting point of the implicit time span is a police operation on an unspecified day, but probably several days prior to the dct. Between the operation and the statement, there has been at least one call for resignation. The expression can therefore be normalised to "dct - 0000-00-XX < Z < dct".

4.6 Dataset Statistics after Annotation

The annotation, performed by one of the authors, shows that the corpus includes 1 910 time expressions, of which 568 are VTEs, i. e., about 29.74% of the time expressions can be considered vague, with 44.15% in KRAUTS and 18.09% in Short_News. The majority is of types *date* and *duration*. The highest ratio of VTEs to all time expressions has a book review (from KRAUTS) with 87.5% VTEs. The highest ratio in a Short_News article is 50%. The largest total number of time expressions (11.3%) as well as VTEs in one article can be found in a weather report with 5 300 tokens and 49 VTEs (Short_News). The largest total number of time expressions in KRAUTS is 46 and can be found in a report (2.43% of tokens) and in a newspaper column (2% of tokens).

Table 3 shows a summary of the annotation results. The statistics show that texts with a narrative structure, which appear more frequently in KRAUTS, contain more VTEs than texts limited to the most important facts, like the articles in Short_News. A possible reason for the increased use of VTEs in columns, comments or fictional texts in KRAUTS is that an exact point in time is neither relevant nor known, or that VTEs fit better into the flow of the text. The fact that there are more precise time expressions on average in the Short_News articles than in KRAUTS suggests that precise time expressions are more suitable to support the facts in short articles.

Table 4 presents the number of classes for each label and reveils a class imbalance in the corpus. The most striking imbalance can be observed for the labels *vague* and *anchorType* in Short_News. The labels *type* of Short_News and *vague* of KRAUTS are the ones with the most similar distribution of classes.

5 Experiments

For our classification experiments, all tested labels should have at least a limited number of values. This excludes labels like *value* and *meaning* because their values are not limited to a fixed set. The labels we tested are *type*, *anchorType* and *vague*.

We used the classifiers *RandomForest*, *DecisionTree*, *softVoting* and *ExtraTrees* from scikit-learn.[10] The *softVoting* classifier uses the highest probability from the sum of the predicted probabilities. It combines the classifiers *DecisionTree*, *RandomForest* and *LinearSupportVectorClassifier*. Two types of classification tasks were tested. On the one hand, we used *multiclass* algorithms that can predict a label with multiple classes. For example, *type* can be predicted, which contains *date*, *time*, *duration* and *set*. On the other hand, there are *multitask* algorithms that can predict several classes, as well as several labels, i. e., predictions for *type*, *vague* and *anchorType* as well as their values can be made at the same time instead of one after the other.

6 Results and Discussion

The results for the full dataset show scores from 0.6 up to 0.75 for the soft voting classifier and up to 0.77 for Extra Trees for the binary classification of *vague*. Given the size of the corpus and the amount of classes and labels, we consider these results decent. *RandomForest* and *DecisionTree*, respectively for *multiclass* and *multitask*, achieved slightly lower scores (with up to 0.02 difference for KRAUTS and 0.003 for Short_News). There are no strong deviations between the *multiclass* and the *multitask* algorithms. We utilized a macro-averaged F1-score metric to weigh our metric towards the smallest class. Due to the label imbalance, this slightly lowers our score but more precisely represents the results of the experiments.

Table 5 shows the results for each label for the two best algorithms. The classifiers achieve better results on Short_News than KRAUTS. *ExtraTrees* performs best for two of three labels.

[10]https://scikit-learn.org (last access: 2021-05-12)

	TE Tokens	%TE of Tokens	VTE Tokens	%VTE of Tokens	%VTE of TE
KRAUTS	854	1.7	7.5	0.75	44.15
Short_News	1 056	2.27	2.8	0.41	18.09
Both	1 910	1.97	5.2	0.59	29.74

Table 3: Overview of the annotation results (TE = time expression) – almost 30% of all TE are vague TE.

Label	Class	KRAUTS	Short_News
type	date	506	431
	time	13	212
	duration	247	234
	set	80	29
vague	true	375	190
	false	471	716
anchor-Type	ref	80	70
	dct	441	615

Table 4: Distribution of classes and labels in the corpus.

Model	Dataset	type	vague	anchor-Type
soft-voting	**Both**	0.60	0.75	**0.62**
	KRAUTS	0.48	0.73	0.58
	Short_News	0.60	0.70	0.58
Extra-Trees	**Both**	**0.68**	**0.77**	0.61
	KRAUTS	0.47	0.73	0.58
	Short_News	0.58	0.72	0.58

Table 5: Macro F1-scores for the two best performing algorithms.

On KRAUTS, the algorithms achieve low results on *type*, mainly because its class *set* has a low accuracy of 0.22 F1-score for the full dataset because there are only 80 annotated labels in KRAUTS and 29 in Short_News (Table 4). The same problem appears for *anchorType* with the infrequent *ref* label. The macro-averaged F1-score clearly demonstrates this because it weighs each class equally so the smaller classes with lower scores equally count to the overall score. In future work, we need to annotate additional data to achieve reasonable classification results. The remaining classes with more samples for *type* are slightly better with F1-scores from 0.42 for *time* up to 0.71 for *date*.

The results show that classifiers with small training sets are capable of achieving F1-scores of up to 0.77. We can assume that more sophisticated approaches will yield better results. In terms of future work, we plan to combine such machine learning-based and rule-based systems, such as Heideltime (Strötgen and Gertz, 2010), which achieves an F1-score of 93.8 on German narrative texts (Strötgen and Gertz, 2015) for precise time expressions. It remains to be explored if a rule-based system can provide similar results for VTEs.

7 Conclusion

We concentrate on the annotation of vague time expressions, borrowing especially from Tissot et al. (2019), whose categorization we modified and adapted to classify and normalise VTEs. We describe methods for the normalization of VTEs and annotated a data set of German news documents. Determining the meaning of a VTE proved to be difficult, because it is context-dependent and may require empirical knowledge if no temporal granularity (year, day, hour, etc.) is given. Although our annotation scheme was developed using German documents, we believe it to be applicable to English, too, because English VTE work in a similar way. Finally, we carried out preliminary classification experiments.

In terms of future work, we plan to label the data set with additional annotators to determine the inter-annotator agreement, to expand the data set and to improve the classification results. Another aspect for expanding our work would be to include an evaluation of time span representation of our normalizations. We also plan to explore additional possibilities of classifying different categories of VTE automatically, which are, as of now, only implicitly included. In that regard, it is worth exploring if a regular expression-based approach, like HeidelTime (Strötgen and Gertz, 2010), is able to derive normalised values of VTEs.

Acknowledgments

The work presented in this paper has received funding from the German Federal Ministry of Education and Research (BMBF) through the project QURATOR (Wachstumskern no. 03WKDA1A).

References

Tommaso Caselli and Rachele Sprugnoli. 2015. It-TimeML, TimeML Annotation Guidelines for Italian. Technical report.

Tommaso Caselli and Piek Vossen. 2017. The Event StoryLine Corpus: A New Benchmark for Causal and Temporal Relation Extraction. In *Proceedings of the Events and Stories in the News Workshop*, pages 77–86,. ACL.

Joanna Mary Channell. 1983. *Vague language: some vague expressions in English*. Ph.D. thesis, University of York.

Filip Devos. 2003. Semantic Vagueness and Lexical Polyvalence. *Studia Linguistica*, 3(57):121–141.

Filip Devos, Nancy Van Gyseghem, Ria Vandenberghe, and Rita De Caluwe. 1994. Modelling vague lexical time expressions by means of fuzzy set theory. *Journal of Quantitative Linguistics*, 1(3):189–194.

Anca Dinu, Walther v Hahn, and Cristina Vertan. 2017. On the annotation of vague expressions: a case study on Romanian historical texts. *Proceedings of the LT4DHCSEE in conjunction with RANLP*, pages 24–31.

Lisa Ferro, Inderjeet Mani, Laurie Gerber, Beth Sundheim, and George Wilson. 2001. TIDES Temporal Annotation Guidelines. Technical Report MTR 01W0000041, The MITRE Corporation.

Paweł Mazur and Robert Dale. 2011. LTIMEX: representing the local semantics of temporal expressions. In *2011 Federated Conference on Computer Science and Information Systems*, pages 201–208. Institute of Electrical and Electronics Engineers (IEEE).

Anne-Lyse Minard, Manuela Speranza, Sara Baino, and Martina Coser. 2017. Examples and Guidelines for Annotation of Temporal Expressions (<TIMEX3>) in German.

James Pustejovsky, Kiyong Lee, Harry Bunt, and Laurent Romary. 2010. ISO-TimeML: An International Standard for Semantic Annotation. In *Proceedings of the Seventh International Conference on Language Resources and Evaluation (LREC'10)*, pages 394–397.

Xin Rong, Adam Fourney, Robin N. Brewer, Meredith Ringel Morris, and Paul N. Bennett. 2017. Managing Uncertainty in Time Expressions for Virtual Assistants. In *Proceedings of the 2017 CHI Conference on Human Factors in Computing Systems*, page 568–579. Association for Computing Machinery.

Roser Saurí, Jessica Littman, Bob Knippen, Robert Gaizauskas, Andrea Setzer, and James Pustejovsky. 2006. *TimeML annotation guidelines*.

Frank Schilder and Christopher Habel. 2001. From Temporal Expressions to Temporal Information: Semantic Tagging of News Messages. In *Proceedings of the Workshop on Temporal and Spatial Information Processing*. ACL.

Jannik Strötgen. 2015. *Domain-sensitive Temporal Tagging for Event-centric Information Retrieval* . Ph.D. thesis, Heidelberg University.

Jannik Strötgen and Michael Gertz. 2010. HeidelTime: High quality rule-based extraction and normalization of temporal expressions. In *Proceedings of the 5th International Workshop on Semantic Evaluation*, pages 321–324. ACL.

Jannik Strötgen and Michael Gertz. 2015. A baseline temporal tagger for all languages. In *Proceedings of the 2015 Conference on Empirical Methods in Natural Language Processing*, pages 541–547.

Jannik Strötgen, Anne-Lyse Minard, Lukas Lange, Manuela Speranza, and Bernardo Magnini. 2018. KRAUTS: A German Temporally Annotated News Corpus. In *Proceedings of the Eleventh International Conference on Language Resources and Evaluation (LREC 2018)*, Miyazaki, Japan. European Language Resources Association (ELRA).

Hegler Tissot, Marcos Didonet Del Fabro, Leon Derczynski, and Angus Roberts. 2019. Normalisation of imprecise temporal expressions extracted from text. *Knowledge and Information Systems*, 61(3):1361–1394.

Naushad UzZaman, Hector Llorens, Leon Derczynski, James Allen, Marc Verhagen, and James Pustejovsky. 2013. SemEval-2013 task 1: TempEval-3: Evaluating time expressions, events, and temporal relations. In *Second Joint Conference on Lexical and Computational Semantics (*SEM), Volume 2: Proceedings of the Seventh International Workshop on Semantic Evaluation (SemEval 2013)*, pages 1–9. ACL.

A Annotation examples

The assumed *document creation time* (dct) is 2021-05-31.

1. Wir haben uns zuletzt bei unserer Abschlussfeier getroffen. <Timex3 type="date" anchorType="dct" value="past_ref" meaning="dct - 000X < Z < dct" vague="true"> Inzwischen </Timex3> habe ich mir ein Auto gekauft.[11]

2. Er ist <Timex3 type="date" anchorType="dct" value="past_ref" meaning="dct - 00XX" vague="true"> vor Jahrzehnten </Timex3> ausgewandert.

3. Die Kampagne startet <Timex3 type="date" anchorType="dct" value="2021-06" mod="mid" vague="true"> Mitte Juni</Timex3>.

4. Das Gesetz wird <Timex3 type="date" anchorType="dct" value="2021-08" meaning="2021-08-12 <= Z <= 2021-08-15" vague="true"> zwischen dem 12. und 15. August </Timex3> verabschiedet.

5. Die Lebensspanne dieser Schmetterlingsart beträgt <Timex3 type="duration" value="P10D" mod="approx" vague="true"> circa 10 Tage </Timex3>

6. Der Umbau dauert nur noch <Timex3 type="duration" value="PXD" vague="true" beginPoint="dct" endPoint="dct + 0000-00-0X"> wenige Tage </Timex3>

7. Die Post kommt hier nur <Timex3 type="set" value="PXD" freq="1x" vague="true"> alle paar Tage </Timex3>

8. <Timex3 tid="t1" type="date" value="2003" vague="false"> 2003 </Timex3> bin ich 6 geworden. <Timex3 tid="t2" type="date" anchorType="ref" anchorTimeID="t1" value="2003" vague="false"> Damals </Timex3> war die Welt noch in Ordnung.

9. Es tut mir leid, dass ich dich verletzt habe. Ich werde <Timex3 type="duration" value="future_ref" anchorType="dct" meaning="PXXY" beginPoint="dct" endPoint="future_ref" vague="true"> künftig </Timex3> besser aufpassen.

B List of Vague Time Expressions

Table 6 is an excerpt from the list of over 300 VTEs which can be found in:
https://live.european-language-grid.eu/catalogue/lcr/7975 (last access: 2021-08-13).

Time Expression	Type	Vague Type	Informal Meaning	Example
Pi mal Daumen	depends on the context	MV	approximately	Pi mal Daumen 1,5 Jahre
überschlägig	depends	MV	approximately	überschlägig 1,5 Jahre
annähernd	depends	MV	approximately	annähernd 1,5 Jahre
ca.	depends	MV	approximately	ca. 1,5 Jahre
circa	depends	MV	approximately	circa 1,5 Jahre
in etwa	depends	MV	approximately	in etwa 1,5 Jahre
praktisch	depends	MV	approximately	praktisch 2 Jahre
rund	depends	MV	approximately	rund 1,5 Jahre
schätzungsweise	depends	MV	approximately	schätzungsweise 1,5 Jahre
so ziemlich	depends	MV	approximately	so ziemlich 1,5 Jahre
um	depends	MV	approximately	um die 1,5 Jahre; um 1 Uhr

[11]The meaning of this syntax becomes more apparent when the < macros are expanded: meaning="dct - 000X < Z < dct".

den einen Tag	date	GE	undefined reference	Den einen Tag auf der Bühne, den anderen vor der Kamera, dann noch auf den Kabarettbrettern, wo sie Lieder ihres geliebten [...].
einst	date	not defined	undefined reference	Einst war das anders bei uns.
dereinst	date	not defined	past-ref, distant	Ich weiß nur mehr: ich küßte es [das Gesicht] dereinst.
einstmals	date	not defined	undefined reference	Einstmals war das anders bei uns.
vordem	date	not defined	<anaphoric point	Das Bild hatte vordem im Zimmer seiner Großmutter gehangen.
dann	date	not defined	anaphoric point	In einem Jahr steht die Abstimmung über die Abspaltung Schottlands vom Vereinigten Königreich an, spätestens dann muss sich die EU Gedanken machen, ob ein so wichtiger Teil Europas wie Schottland ausgeschlossen werden kann [...].
nunmehr	date	not defined	dct	Der Streik dauert nunmehr schon einen Monat.
sofort	date	not defined	future-ref, approx. reference point	Ich habe dich sofort erkannt, als du aus dem Zug stiegst.
umgehend	date	not defined	future-ref, approx. reference point	einer Behörde, Instanz umgehend von etw. Mitteilung machen
hinterher	date	not defined	future-ref, anaphoric	Die Bedeutung dieser Worte wurde ihm erst hinterher klar.
Jahreszeit-monate	duration	GE	date-like	Am meisten liebe ich die Herbstmonate, wegen der vielen Farben.
warme|kalte Jahreszeit	duration	GE	date-like	Die warme Jahreszeit ist in dieser Region wirklich schön.
in diesen Tagen	duration	IV	anaphoric	Er hat in diesen Tagen viel gelacht.
G-lang	duration	IV	PXG	Er musste stundenlang darauf warten
all diese G	duration	IV	PXG	All diese Tage gehören der Vergangenheit an.
innerhalb von G	duration	IV	PXG / ref <Z <ref + G	Er hat sich innerhalb von Wochen davon erholt.
den ersten G	duration	IV	ordinal specified	In den ersten Tagen wird sie noch Probleme damit haben.
die nächsten G	duration	IV	DCT/ref + XG	Es wird die nächsten Tage weh tun.
in den nächsten G	duration	IV	duration, ordinal specified, future-ref, G	In den nächsten Jahren wird sie viel lernen.
die damaligen G	duration	IV	duration, past-ref, distant	Die damaligen Wochen waren wunderschön.
spätestens in x G	offset	MV	dct <Z <= dct + X G	Wir sehen uns spätestens in 3 Stunden wieder.
frühestens in x G	offset	MV	>= number G	frühestens in einem Monat
tags drauf	offset	not defined	anaphoric point +1	Er geht nie weg, wenn er tags drauf arbeitet.

alsbaldig	offset	not defined	future-ref, relatively close	Die Ware ist zum alsbaldigen Verbrauch bestimmt.
später	offset	not defined	future-ref, relatively distant	Wie soll das erst einmal später werden?
zeitnah	offset	not defined	future-ref, relatively close	Es gab zeitnah vor und nach dem Brief [von Dr. R.] Gespräche mit Dr. R[. . .]«, daher hielt man eine schriftliche Antwort nicht für nötig.
alsbald	offset	not defined	future-ref, relatively close	Narziß wendete sich zu ihm um, und alsbald fühlte er sich erlöst.
alsobald	offset	not defined	future-ref, relatively close	veraltet; wie alsbald
schnellstmöglich	offset	not defined	future-ref, very close	Der Chef drängt auf eine schnellstmögliche Erledigung der Arbeit.
gleich	offset	not defined	future-ref, very close	Ich komme gleich.
alle paar G	set	IV	set, irregular G	Die Haut sollte alle paar Tage gründlicher gereinigt werden, um Ablagerungen zu entfernen Beim Haare waschen mit Shampoo [...].
gelegentlich	set	not defined	set, irregular, rarely	Heute soll es nur gelegentlich Niederschläge geben.
alltäglich	set	not defined	everyday	[...] und Vokabular, sondern altersgemäß intuitiv durch den alltäglich stattfindenden Gebrauch der englischen Sprache im Betreuungskontext.
regelmäßig	set	not defined	set, regularly	regelmäßige Mahlzeiten
turnusmäßig	set	not defined	set, regularly	eine turnusmäßige Sitzung, Kontrolle
zyklisch	set	not defined	set, regularly	etw. läuft zyklisch ab, verläuft zyklisch
periodisch	set	not defined	set, undef	Die Beschwerden kehrten periodisch wieder.
zwischendurch	set	not defined	set, undef	Der vor längerer Zeit errichtete und zwischendurch verfallene Zaun ist jetzt repariert.
unregelmäßig	set	not defined	set, irregularly	Er lebt unregelmäßig.
öfters	set	not defined	set, irregularly, often	man muß das öfters üben, sagen
sporadisch	set	not defined	set, irregularly, rarely	Wir sehen uns nur ganz sporadisch.
vor x Uhr	time	MV	<number o'clock	[...] an der in der jeweiligen Prospektergänzung angegebenen Adresse vor 12 Uhr (irische Ortszeit) an dem dem betreffenden Handelstag vorangegangenen [...].
spätestens x Uhr	time	MV	<= number o'clock	die Arbeit muss bis spätestens 12 Uhr fertig sein
nach x Uhr	time	MV	>number o'clock	Darüber hinaus sind Personen, die sich nach 20 Uhr auf dem DESY-Gelände aufhalten, verpflichtet, sich auf Verlangen den [...]

mindestens x Uhr	time	MV	>= number o'clock	Die SBB RailCities bieten täglich bis mindestens 23.00 Uhr
bis maximal x Uhr	time	MV	until <= number o'clock	25. Juni 2012 Abbauende - ein verlängerter Abbau bis maximal 12.00 Uhr am Dienstag, den 26. Juni 2012 kann in Ausnahmefällen bis zum [...].
ca. x Uhr	time	MV	approx. number o'clock	Ab 16:30 Uhr gibt es ein buntes Animationsprogramm und ab ca. 18:30 Uhr wird ein Filmhit nach Besucherwünschen gezeigt.
gleich x Uhr	time	MV	approx. number o'clock (<)	Es ist gleich 12 Uhr.
eben	time	not defined	past-ref, very close	Eben hat es fünf Uhr geschlagen.

Table 6: Excerpt of the list of VTE. *Type* values are taken from TimeML, *Vague Type* borrows from the categories described by Tissot et al. (2019) (without Partial Period). G means granularity and $G + 1$ means one granularity lever higher. For example, if $G = month$, then $G + 1 = year$. X represents a number.

Automatic Phrase Recognition in Historical German

Katrin Ortmann
Department of Linguistics
Fakultät für Philologie
Ruhr-Universität Bochum
ortmann@linguistics.rub.de

Abstract

Due to a lack of annotated data, theories of historical syntax are often based on very small, manually compiled data sets. To enable the empirical evaluation of existing hypotheses, the present study explores the automatic recognition of phrases in historical German. Using modern and historical treebanks, training data for a neural sequence labeling tool and a probabilistic parser is created, and both methods are compared on a variety of data sets. The evaluation shows that the unlexicalized parser outperforms the sequence labeling approach, achieving F_1-scores of 87%–91% on modern German and between 73% and 85% on different historical corpora. An error analysis indicates that accuracy decreases especially for longer phrases, but most of the errors concern incorrect phrase boundaries, suggesting further potential for improvement.

1 Introduction

In recent years, the availability of ever-larger data sets and increasing computational power have led to major changes in the way language is analyzed. Today, NLP tools can automatically enrich large amounts of text quickly and accurately with linguistic annotations needed for commercial or research purposes. When it comes to non-standard data like historical language, though, the availability of models and annotated corpora is still limited compared to modern language and hypotheses are often based on qualitative analyses of very small data sets. For example, Speyer (2011) investigates object order in the middle field of Early New High German sentences based on a total of 70 pairs of direct and indirect objects from three centuries. Similarly, Light (2012) grounds her study of extraposition, i.e. the movement of elements behind the clause-final verb, on 115 cases of extraposed subjects in one Early New High German bible translation, while Sapp (2014) analyzes 683 extraposed phrases spread over texts from five centuries. Although data-driven qualitative analyses like these provide valuable insights for linguistic research, they require a lot of manual effort and cannot achieve the same statistical significance as studies of modern language.

Recently, there have been several attempts to address the lack of annotated historical data and provide a basis for the empirical evaluation of existing hypotheses by automatically identifying relevant syntactic units in historical text (e.g. Chiarcos et al., 2018; Ortmann, 2020, 2021). The present paper takes a similar approach and looks explicitly at the units targeted by the qualitative studies mentioned above, namely phrases.

In the context of this study, phrases are understood as continuous, non-overlapping constituents from a sentence's parse tree. Since the concrete definition of constituents may vary depending on the annotation scheme and not all constituents are equally relevant for linguistic studies like the ones mentioned above, this paper focuses on four main phrase types: noun phrases (`NP`), prepositional phrases (`PP`), adjective phrases (`AP`), and adverb phrases (`ADVP`). For each sentence, only the highest non-terminal nodes of the given types are considered, ignoring the internal structure of phrases. This means that phrases may dominate other phrases of the same or different types, but the dominated phrases are not evaluated here. Example (1) shows an annotated sentence from a 1731 theological text.

(1) [$_{NP}$ Der kråftigfte Bewegungs-Grund] nimmt [$_{NP}$ seinen Urfprung] [$_{PP}$ aus einer zårtlichen Leydenfchaft meines Gemůhts].
The most powerful motive takes its origin from a tender passion of my heart.

To enable research on phenomena like extraposition, phrases may not cross topological field boundaries.[1] For example, a prepositional phrase in the middle field is considered separate from an adjacent modifying relative clause in the post-field, as shown in example (2) from a chemistry essay (field boundaries are indicated by vertical pipes). Also, discontinuous structures as they exist in some German corpora are not allowed here.

(2) Erhebt | [$_{NP}$ es] [$_{NP}$ fich] [$_{PP}$ mit dem Wafferftoffgas], | [$_{NP}$ welches] | [$_{NP}$ die Moråfte] [$_{PP}$ in Ueberfluß] | ausdunften?
Does it rise with the hydrogen gas that the swamps evaporate in abundance?

The goal of this study is to automatically recognize phrases that meet the aforementioned requirements in historical German texts. The remainder of the paper is structured as follows: Section 2 presents related work on the syntactic analysis of (historical) German before Section 3 introduces the data sets used in this study. In Section 4, two different methods for the automatic recognition of phrases are selected based on the findings of previous studies and their performance is evaluated in Section 5. The paper concludes with a discussion in Section 6.

2 Related Work

The recognition of phrases as defined in the previous section is related to chunking as well as (constituency) parsing and can be located somewhere in between the two tasks regarding its complexity.

Chunking refers to the identification of non-overlapping, non-recursive phrases from a sentence's parse tree, ending with the head token (Sang and Buchholz, 2000). As a consequence, chunks are often shorter than phrases because post-modifying elements form separate chunks. For simple cases without pre- or post-modifying elements, however, the definitions of chunks and phrases overlap and methods that are successful at chunking may also be useful for phrase recognition.

Parsing, on the other hand, aims at a complete syntactic analysis of the sentence. Hence, the resulting constituency tree includes more information than just the phrase annotation, e.g. dominance relations, which are not considered in this study. As a result, phrase annotations can be derived from the more complex parse output, but the complexity of the task may also reduce overall accuracy.

[1]For an overview of the topological field model, see e.g. Cheung and Penn (2009) or Wöllstein (2018, in German)

While studies on chunking observe F_1-scores >95% for modern German (cf. Müller, 2005; Ortmann, 2021), the highest F_1-scores for constituency parsing of German are reported with approx. 90%, compared to 95% for English (Kitaev et al., 2019). In general, parsing results heavily depend on the selected treebank and the inclusion of grammatical functions (Dakota and Kübler, 2017) and discontinuous structures (cf. Vilares and Gómez-Rodríguez, 2020). Also, all of these results are obtained for standard language like newspaper text. For non-standard data, performance drops must be expected (Pinto et al., 2016; Jamshid Lou et al., 2019).

For historical German, so far, there have been experiments on chunking (Petran, 2012; Ortmann, 2021) and topological field parsing (Chiarcos et al., 2018; Ortmann, 2020). For chunking, the best results are observed for CRF-based sequence labeling with overall F_1-scores between 90% and 94% (Ortmann, 2021). For topological field identification, the application of a probabilistic parser yields overall F_1-scores >92% (Ortmann, 2020). In the present study, both of these approaches will be explored for the purpose of phrase recognition in historical German.

3 Data

The data sets for the experiments are taken from a previous chunking study (Ortmann, 2021).[2] The training data consists of two modern and two historical treebanks. The TüBa-D/Z corpus (Telljohann et al., 2017)[3] and the Tiger corpus (Brants et al., 2004)[4] contain modern German newspaper articles, whereas the Mercurius corpus (Demske, 2005)[5] and the ReF.UP corpus (Demske, 2019)[6] comprise Early New High German texts from the 14th to 17th century. All four data sets are annotated with constituency trees, but before they can be used to train a parser or extract phrase annotations for sequence labeling, a few modifications are necessary.

[2]`https://github.com/rubcompling/nodalida2021`

[3]Release 11.0, `http://www.sfs.uni-tuebingen.de/ascl/ressourcen/corpora/tueba-dz.html`

[4]Version 2.2, `https://www.ims.uni-stuttgart.de/forschung/ressourcen/korpora/tiger`

[5]Mercurius Baumbank (version 1.1), `https://doi.org/10.34644/laudatio-dev-VyQiCnMB7CArCQ9CjF3O`

[6]ReF.UP is a subcorpus of the Reference Corpus of Early New High German (Wegera et al., 2021), `https://www.linguistics.rub.de/ref`

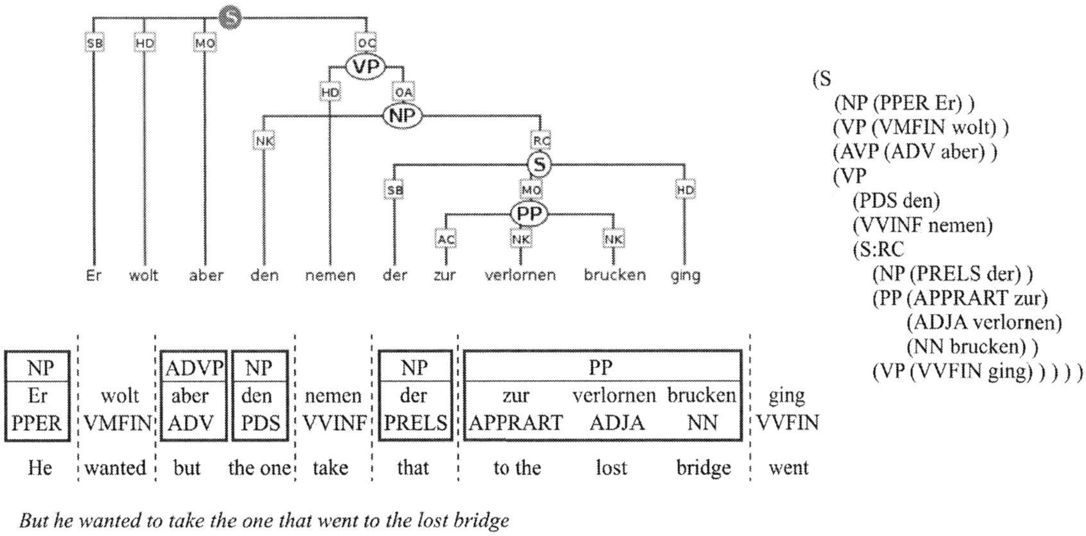

Figure 1: Example modification of a sentence from the ReF.UP corpus. At the top, the original constituency tree with discontinuous annotations according to the Tiger scheme is displayed. The bracket structure to the right represents the linearized version of the tree without crossing branches and grammatical functions. This format can be used to train a standard parser. At the bottom, the phrase annotation for the sentence is shown. The phrases have been extracted from the tree structure to the right and checked with a topological field parser to ensure that phrases do not cross field boundaries (indicated by dashed lines). The phrase annotations serve as training data for a sequence labeling tool and are also used for evaluation.

(i) The underlying annotation scheme of the Tiger corpus and the two historical treebanks allows for discontinuous annotations, which must be removed to enable the use of standard chunking and parsing methods. Here, a combination of the raising and splitting approaches described by Hsu (2010) is applied to the trees until no crossing branches remain.[7]

(ii) Since German exhibits a relatively free word order, grammatical functions like subject and object play an important role in the syntactic analysis of sentences, especially for the reduction of ambiguity (Fraser et al., 2013). For the purpose of phrase recognition, however, they are not relevant and, therefore, mostly excluded from the trees to reduce the size of the tagset and improve parsing performance (Rafferty and Manning, 2008; Dakota and Kübler, 2017).[8]

The modified trees can serve as training input for a parser, or they can be used to extract phrase annotations. Contrary to chunking studies, where the lowest non-terminal nodes are converted to chunks (Kübler et al., 2010; Ortmann, 2021), here, the highest non-terminal nodes of the relevant types correspond to the desired phrases.[9] Before the extracted phrases can be used for evaluation or to train a sequence labeling tool, another difference between the annotation schemes of the treebanks regarding topological fields must be taken into account, though.

(iii) While the TüBa-D/Z trees represent a combination of constituency and topological field annotations, the other three corpora that follow the Tiger scheme do not include topological fields. This means that constituents in the TüBa-D/Z data are already bound to the corresponding fields as required by the phrase

[7]Basically, discontinuous nodes are split and re-inserted into the tree based on the linear order of tokens in the sentence. The same holds for punctuation, which is appended to the same parent node as the next token to the left (or to the right for sentence-initial punctuation).

[8]The only exception are GFs that are needed to extract correct phrases from the trees. For the Tiger scheme, these are S:RC and S:OC. For TüBa-D/Z, the following GFs are preserved: KONJ, OS, R-SIMPX, NX:HD within PX, and NX:APP within NX. Also, one-word children of sentence nodes that only receive a grammatical function according to the Tiger scheme are assigned a phrase type `NP`, `PP`, `AP`, `AVP`, `VP`, or `SVP` based on their POS tag.

[9]Again, phrases of the four types are added for one-word constituents from Tiger-scheme trees based on the POS tag of the word.

	News1	News2	Hist	Mix
#Docs	3,075	1,863	28	1,891
#Sents	83,515	40,037	23,747	63,784
#Toks	1,566,250	727,011	569,854	1,296,865
#Phrases	388,531	162,336	152,866	315,202

Table 1: Overview of the four training sets. Only sentences with a gold parse are included, and the number of phrases refers to phrases of the four relevant types. The Mix set is a combination of the News2 and Hist sets.

Corpus	**#Docs**	**#Sents**	**#Toks**	**#Phrases**
TüBa-D/Z	364	10,488	196,630	49,329
Tiger	200	4,445	78,018	17,622
Modern	78	547	7,605	2,240
Mercurius	2	818	18,740	4,401
ReF.UP	26	2,173	54,005	15,355
HIPKON	53	342	4,210	1,146
DTA	29	608	18,515	4,068

Table 2: Overview of the test data. The number of phrases includes NP, PP, AP, and ADVP phrases as described in Section 1. Only sentences containing at least one of the four phrase types are considered.

definition in this study, whereas constituents in the other data sets may cross field boundaries. Therefore, phrases that are extracted from these data sets or identified by a parser that is trained on them are corrected with the help of a topological field parser (Ortmann, 2020).[10] Phrases that cross fields are split at the field boundary and replaced by the dominated sub-phrases to ensure that no phrase is located in more than one field.[11]

An example of the different modifications of the trees and extracted phrases can be found in Figure 1. The resulting data sets are used to build four distinct training sets: News1 corresponds to the TüBa-D/Z data, News2 is based on the Tiger treebank, Hist contains the historical data, and a joined set Mix includes all data sets that follow the Tiger annotation scheme. Table 1 gives a summary of the four training sets.

For evaluation, the test sections of the four treebanks[12] are processed in the same way as the training data, and phrases of the four types are extracted and split at topological field boundaries if necessary. In addition, the chunking study (Ortmann, 2021) provides three other test sets, which were annotated with phrases for the present paper: a corpus of modern non-newspaper data with texts from different registers and two historical data sets from the HIPKON corpus (Coniglio et al., 2014) and the German Text Archive DTA (BBAW, 2021) covering different genres and time periods. Table 2 gives an overview of the test data.[13]

Corpus	NP	PP	AP	ADVP
TüBa-D/Z	54.30	22.47	6.41	16.82
Tiger	55.28	27.55	6.09	11.07
Modern	61.88	17.72	5.94	14.46
Mercurius	50.44	26.68	5.23	17.66
ReF.UP	56.46	20.48	6.11	16.96
HIPKON	51.83	27.40	2.01	18.76
DTA	51.55	25.76	6.15	16.54

Table 3: Distribution of the four phrase types in the test data. Numbers are given in percent.

In Table 3, the distribution of the phrase types in the data sets is displayed. The most frequent phrase type are NPs with 50% to over 60% in the modern non-newspaper data, followed by PPs with 18% to 28%. ADVPs make up for 11% to 19%, while APs that are not dominated by other phrases are rare with 6% or less.

4 Methods

So far, the automatic syntactic analysis of historical German has been focused on the identification of chunks and topological fields. As described in Section 2, the best results for these tasks are reported for sequence labeling and statistical parsing. In the following, both approaches are applied to the recognition of phrases.

For sequence labeling, the neural CRF-based sequence labeling tool NCRF++ (Yang and Zhang, 2018) is selected. It achieves state-of-the-art performance for several tasks, including tagging, chunking, and named entity recognition in English (Yang et al., 2018). When POS tags are used as features, it also proves successful at identifying chunks in historical German with F_1-scores $>$90% (Ortmann, 2021). The default configuration consists of a three-layer architecture with a character and a word se-

[10] https://github.com/rubcompling/latech2020

[11] Theoretically, it would also be possible to merge the constituency trees with automatically created topological field annotations before training a parser on the merged trees. However, experiments indicate that this creates too many inconsistencies in the training data, e.g. due to errors in the automatic field annotation, and therefore leads to worse results than splitting the extracted phrase output at the field boundaries afterwards.

[12] While the Tiger corpus is provided with official training, development, and test sections, for the other three corpora, the same splits into training (80%), development (10%), and test set (10%) as in the chunking study (Ortmann, 2021) are used.

[13] The manually annotated data sets can be found in this paper's repository at https://github.com/rubcompling/konvens2021.

quence layer plus a CRF-based inference layer. For the present study, the toolkit is trained on the extracted phrases from the four training sets, where phrases are represented as BIO tags. POS tags are included as additional feature and, during training, the tool is also provided with the development sections of the training corpora. For every word, NCRF++ outputs the single most likely BIO tag, i.e. `B-XP` (beginning of phrase), `I-XP` (inside of phrase), or `O` (outside of phrase). For evaluation, the labels are converted to phrases, and the best result over five runs with different random seeds is reported.

For parsing, the unlexicalized Berkeley parser (Petrov et al., 2006)[14] is selected. It achieves a parsing F_1-score of 91.8% on the TüBa-D/Z corpus and 72% on the Tiger corpus (Dakota and Kübler, 2017) and has also been successfully applied to topological field parsing of historical German with overall F_1-scores >92% (Ortmann, 2020). In the present study, it is trained with default settings[15] on the four training sets, where the modified constituency trees are used as training input. For annotation, the parser is invoked in interactive mode[16] and given a sentence annotated with POS tags, it returns the single best parse. For evaluation, the constituency trees are then converted to phrases as described in the previous section.

5 Evaluation

To evaluate the performance of the selected approaches on the task of phrase recognition, the output of the trained systems is compared to the gold standard annotation. However, the evaluation of sequence annotations like phrases with standard metrics faces the problem of double penalties, meaning that one unit can count as two errors. For example, and adjective phrase that is recognized as adverb phrase would correspond to a false negative `AP` and, at the same time, a false positive `ADVP`. Similarly, if a system misses the initial preposition of a `PP` and instead annotates the rest as an `NP`, this would result in a false negative `PP` and a false positive `NP`. There have been different suggestions on how to deal with this problem. For word tokenization, Shao et al. (2017) argue that recall should be used as the only evaluation metric. While precision favors under-splitting systems, recall values clearly show the percentage of correctly recognized units that are relevant for higher-level tasks. However, in the case of segmentation tasks that include labeling, identifying entities with almost correct boundaries may also be useful (cf. Ortmann, 2021). For example, the studies on extraposition mentioned in Section 1 would still benefit greatly from the recognition of incomplete phrases, if not for a complete automatic analysis, then at least for an easier and faster compilation of much larger data sets (see also Eckhoff and Berdičevskis (2016) for a study on using automatic dependency parsing for pre-annotation of historical data to speed up manual annotation). Hence, precision values should not be disregarded entirely. Instead, in Ortmann (2021), I proposed a more fine-grained error analysis that takes into account different types of possible errors while at the same time circumventing the problem of multiply penalizing errors in a single unit.

In the following, this error analysis is adopted for the evaluation of phrase recognition and the output of the different methods and models is compared phrase-wise to the gold standard annotation, grouping phrases into one of seven classes: true positives (`TP`), false positives (`FP`), labeling errors (`LE`), boundary errors (`BE`), labeling-boundary errors (`LBE`) and false negatives (`FN`). In addition to the standard categories, labeling errors refer to phrases that cover the same token span but are labeled with a different phrase type. Boundary errors are phrases of the correct type but with incorrect boundaries, and labeling-boundary errors are a combination of the former two error types. Since the three error types indicate an existing and not a missing annotation, they are counted as false positives for the calculation of F-scores. Only sentences containing at least one of the four phrase types are evaluated, and punctuation at phrase boundaries is ignored.

Sequence labeling As already mentioned, the neural sequence labeling tool NCRF++ has been applied successfully to the identification of chunks in German, reaching F_1-scores between 90% and 94% for different historical data sets (Ortmann, 2021). As could be expected from previous studies (e.g., Petran, 2012), the accuracy for the recognition of phrases, i.e. longer units, with CRF-based sequence labeling is considerably lower. Table 4 gives a sum-

[14] `https://github.com/slavpetrov/berkeleyparser`

[15] `java -cp BerkeleyParser-1.7.jar edu.berkeley.nlp.PCFGLA.GrammarTrainer -treebank SINGLEFILE -out grammar.gr -path treebank.txt`

[16] `java -jar BerkeleyParser-1.7.jar -gr grammar.gr -maxLength 1000 -useGoldPOS`

Corpus	News1	News2	Hist	Mix
TüBa-D/Z	**85.18**	76.82	n.a.	n.a.
Tiger	78.93	**79.69**	n.a.	n.a.
Modern	**86.80**	83.10	n.a.	n.a.
Mercurius	**70.25**	67.83	9.05	8.93
ReF.UP	**70.62**	67.91	8.80	9.90
HIPKON	80.13	**81.18**	8.17	7.99
DTA	**72.02**	68.89	6.93	7.78

Table 4: Overall F_1-scores of the sequence labeling approach. Models trained on historical data are only applied to the historical test sets. The table reports the highest F_1-score over five runs and the best result for each corpus is highlighted in bold.

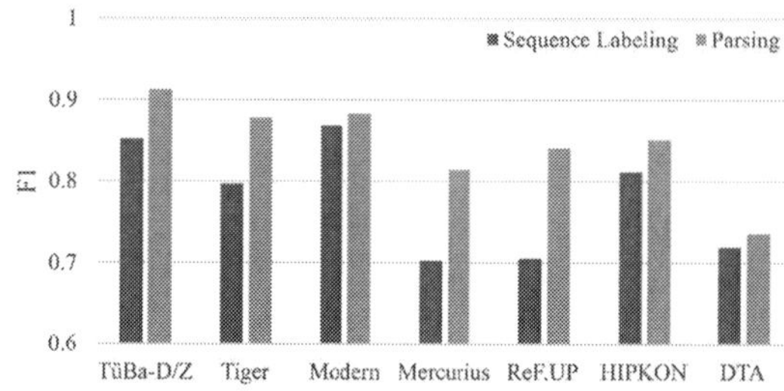

Figure 2: Comparison of the best F_1-scores for sequence labeling and parsing on the different test sets.

mary of the results for each of the four models.

Using gold POS tags as a feature, the two newspaper-based models still perform relatively well. Model News1 achieves the best results with F_1-scores between 70.3% and 86.8%. The results for the second modern model News2 also lie above 67% for all data sets. Contrary to the results for chunking (Ortmann, 2021), using historical training data does not improve the results on the historical test sets. Instead, the historical and mixed models do not reach F_1-scores $>10\%$ for phrase recognition, indicating that the tool was not successful at learning to identify the different phrase types based on the historical corpora. Possible reasons could be the high syntactic complexity of Early New High German sentences or too much variation in the training data, e.g. caused by the non-standardized spelling in historical German.

Parsing So far, the parsing approach has only been evaluated for topological field parsing of historical German with overall F_1-scores >92% (Ortmann, 2020). In Table 5, the results of the Berkeley parser for the recognition of phrases are given. On the modern data sets, the parser achieves F_1-scores of 87.8% to 91.3% with visible differences between the two modern models. While, unsurprisingly, each of them performs best on the test section of the corpus it was trained on, the News1 model also achieves the best results on the Modern data set and the DTA corpus, while the News2 model performs better on the other historical data sets.

Corpus	News1	News2	Hist	Mix
TüBa-D/Z	**91.30**	81.50	n.a.	n.a.
Tiger	82.73	**87.81**	n.a.	n.a.
Modern	**88.27**	84.44	n.a.	n.a.
Mercurius	60.32	65.72	**81.50**	81.06
ReF.UP	56.44	58.86	**84.15**	84.05
HIPKON	74.44	75.13	85.05	**85.12**
DTA	**73.66**	69.44	69.07	70.63

Table 5: Overall F_1-scores (in percent) for the four parser models on each data set. Models trained on historical data are only applied to the historical test sets, and the highest F_1-score for each corpus is highlighted in bold.

In contrast to the sequence labeling results, here, including historical training data improves the syntactic analysis of historical language, probably because the unlexicalized parser is unaffected by the non-standardized spelling or can better handle the complex sentence structures. For three of the four historical data sets, the Hist and Mix models outperform the modern models by ten percentage points or more. F_1-scores lie between 81.5% and 85.1% for the Mercurius, ReF.UP and HIPKON data, while the DTA is only analyzed with an F_1-score of 73.7%.

When compared to the sequence labeling tool, the parsing approach yields better results for the recognition of phrases. Figure 2 confirms that the best parser model outperforms the best sequence labeling model by up to 13.5 percentage points on each data set. Only for the modern non-newspaper data and the DTA, the results of the methods are similar. For the modern data, this could be due to the fact that the data set contains many non-complex phrases that are similar to chunks, e.g. simple noun phrases. 54% of the phrases in this data set consist of only one token, compared to 35%–50% in the other data sets, which makes it easier for the sequence labeling approach to identify them.

However, parser accuracy also declines for larger units (cf. Bastings and Sima'an, 2014). While the Berkeley parser reaches overall parsing F_1-scores of 92% and 86% for the modern data and 78%–79% for the historical data (cf. Table 6), F_1-scores heavily decline for larger constituents as well as phrases (see Figure 3). For constituents with more than five words, the average F_1-score of the four mod-

	News1	News2	Hist	Mix
TüBa-D/Z	**91.96**	n.a.	n.a.	n.a.
Tiger	n.a.	**86.42**	n.a.	n.a.
Mercurius	n.a.	52.27	**77.68**	77.44
ReF.UP	n.a.	45.15	78.97	**79.13**

Table 6: Overall labeled F_1-score for the four trained parser models on the test data, excluding virtual root nodes. Training and test trees are modified as described in Section 3, and models are only evaluated on test data that follows the same syntactic annotation scheme as the training data.

els is only about 70%. For phrases, the reduction is even larger with F_1-scores below 40% for phrases of twenty or more words. This observation may, in part, explain the lower results for the DTA because, proportionally, this data set contains about twice as many phrases of twelve or more words than the other corpora due to many dedications and very long phrases with coordinations and dominated sentences, e.g. in legal texts. A parser that performs better on larger constituents thus might be better equipped to analyze this data set.

Table 7 reports the parser results broken down by phrase types. Here, each category is evaluated separately and one unit may thus appear in two categories, e.g. as a false negative PP and a false positive NP as exemplified above. For most data sets, the highest F_1-scores are reached for adverb and noun phrases. While the former are usually very short and therefore easier to identify, noun phrases and prepositional phrases often contain pre- and/or post-nominal modifiers including longer constituents like relative clauses that lead to errors in the parser output. Adjective phrases are the least frequent phrase type and, although they tend to be short, also show the least accurate results for more than half of the data sets. Often they get mixed up with neighboring adverbs because a lexicalized model would be necessary to distinguish between pre-modifying adverbs as in example (3) and a separate adverb phrase in (4).

(3) Sie war [$_{\text{AP}}$ sehr/ADV glücklich/ADJD].
She was very happy.

(4) Sie war [$_{\text{ADVP}}$ gestern/ADV] [$_{\text{AP}}$ glücklich/ADJD].
Yesterday, she was happy.

Finally, Table 8 shows the distribution of error types for the best parser models. For all test sets, boundary errors are by far the most frequent error types with a proportion of 52% to 66%. The

Corpus	NP	PP	AP	ADVP
TüBa-D/Z	89.03	83.26	86.99	91.40
Tiger	86.60	79.28	75.80	82.35
Modern	87.35	76.37	80.60	79.94
Mercurius	77.96	70.47	62.61	82.59
ReF.UP	82.72	75.21	63.31	81.77
HIPKON	80.49	77.62	60.00	84.49
DTA	66.53	64.98	67.98	72.06

Table 7: Overall F_1-scores for each phrase type (in percent) for the best performing parser model on each data set.

Corpus	FP	LE	BE	LBE	FN
TüBa-D/Z	22.47	0.96	62.85	0.75	12.97
Tiger	20.15	1.08	59.22	1.15	18.41
Modern	19.12	1.99	64.34	0.40	14.14
Mercurius	26.84	1.23	51.94	1.49	18.50
ReF.UP	22.74	1.53	53.20	1.23	21.30
HIPKON	20.00	3.03	66.36	1.21	9.39
DTA	17.73	1.01	60.91	2.47	17.88

Table 8: Proportion of the five error types: false positives (FP), labeling errors (LE), boundary errors (BE), labeling-boundary errors (LBE), and false negatives (FN). Numbers are given in percent for the best parser model on each data set.

remaining errors are mostly traditional false positives and false negatives, while labeling and labeling-boundary errors are rare. Considering that the identification of phrases with almost correct boundaries may still satisfy the requirements of certain tasks as discussed above, this can thus be assumed for more than half of the errors. Furthermore, the results suggest great potential for improvement because the high percentage of boundary errors means that the parser already identified these phrases, and correcting boundaries could potentially lead to significant increases in precision.

6 Discussion

The present study has explored the automatic recognition of phrases in historical German. Two tools that proved successful in previous studies on chunking and topological field parsing were selected and trained on modern and historical treebanks. The evaluation has shown that the Berkeley parser outperforms the neural CRF-based sequence labeling tool NCRF++ on all data sets, reaching overall F_1-scores of 87.8% to 91.3% on modern German and 73.7%–85.1% on different historical corpora. Parsing results are most accurate for simple phrases while scores decline with increasing phrase length. Since the majority of errors turn out to be boundary errors, the results leave room for further improve-

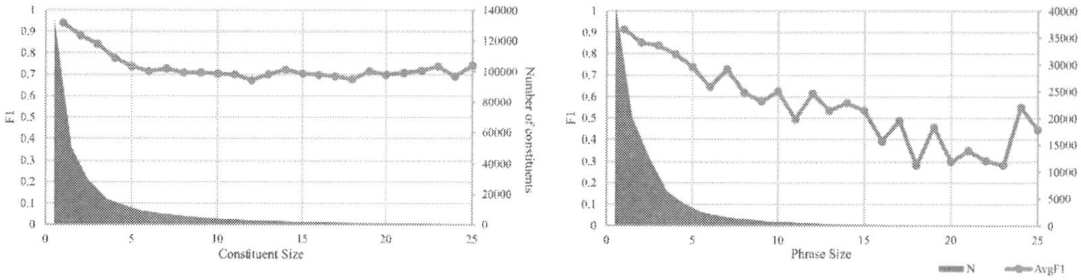

Figure 3: Average F_1-score of the four parser models for the recognition of constituents and phrases of sizes 1–25. The number of constituents includes all constituents of the given sizes in the test sections of the four training corpora. The number of phrases refers to phrases of the four types in the seven test sets.

ment of annotation precision.

Interestingly, the inclusion of historical training data improves the results of the parser, whereas the sequence labeling tool did not benefit from it. One possible explanation could be too much variation in the data due to the non-standardized spelling in historical German, which does not affect the unlexicalized parser. Future studies could experiment with spelling normalization, which was observed to improve the annotation results of modern NLP tools for parsing Middle English (Schneider et al., 2015) or tagging historical German (Bollmann, 2013) and Dutch (Tjong Kim Sang et al., 2017).

The normalized data could then also be used to explore lexicalized parsing, e.g. with the neural Berkeley parser (Kitaev and Klein, 2018). Although parsers do not necessarily need lexical information for good performance (Coavoux et al., 2019), studies on modern English show that the application of neural parsing methods in combination with pre-trained word embeddings can further improve the results (cf. e.g. Vilares and Gómez-Rodríguez, 2020). For morphologically more complex languages like German, this should be even more relevant (Fraser et al., 2013) and could also help in cases where lexical information is necessary to decide about the correct phrase boundaries.

Acknowledgments

This work was funded by the Deutsche Forschungsgemeinschaft (DFG, German Research Foundation) – Project-ID 232722074 – SFB 1102 (Project C6). I am grateful to the student annotators Anna Maria Schröter and Larissa Weber for the annotations. Also, I would like to thank the anonymous reviewers for their helpful comments.

References

Joost Bastings and Khalil Sima'an. 2014. All fragments count in parser evaluation. In *Proceedings of the Ninth International Conference on Language Resources and Evaluation (LREC-2014)*, pages 78–82, Reykjavik, Iceland. European Languages Resources Association (ELRA).

BBAW. 2021. Deutsches Textarchiv. Grundlage für ein Referenzkorpus der neuhochdeutschen Sprache. Berlin-Brandenburgische Akademie der Wissenschaften.

Marcel Bollmann. 2013. POS tagging for historical texts with sparse training data. In *Proceedings of the 7th Linguistic Annotation Workshop and Interoperability with Discourse*, pages 11–18, Sofia, Bulgaria. Association for Computational Linguistics.

Sabine Brants, Stefanie Dipper, Peter Eisenberg, Silvia Hansen-Schirra, Esther König, Wolfgang Lezius, Christian Rohrer, George Smith, and Hans Uszkoreit. 2004. TIGER: Linguistic interpretation of a German corpus. *Research on language and computation*, 2(4):597–620.

Jackie Chi Kit Cheung and Gerald Penn. 2009. Topological field parsing of German. In *Proceedings of the Joint Conference of the 47th Annual Meeting of the ACL and the 4th International Joint Conference on Natural Language Processing of the AFNLP: Volume 1 - Volume 1*, ACL '09, page 64–72, USA. Association for Computational Linguistics.

Christian Chiarcos, Benjamin Kosmehl, Christian Fäth, and Maria Sukhareva. 2018. Analyzing Middle High German syntax with RDF and SPARQL. In *Proceedings of the Eleventh International Conference on Language Resources and Evaluation (LREC 2018)*, Miyazaki, Japan. European Language Resources Association (ELRA).

Maximin Coavoux, Benoît Crabbé, and Shay B. Cohen. 2019. Unlexicalized transition-based discontinuous constituency parsing. *Transactions of the Association for Computational Linguistics*, 7:73–89.

Marco Coniglio, Karin Donhauser, and Eva Schlachter. 2014. HIPKON: Historisches Predigtenkorpus zum

Nachfeld (Version 1.0). Humboldt-Universität zu Berlin. SFB 632 Teilprojekt B4.

Daniel Dakota and Sandra Kübler. 2017. Towards replicability in parsing. In *Proceedings of the International Conference Recent Advances in Natural Language Processing, RANLP 2017*, pages 185–194, Varna, Bulgaria. INCOMA Ltd.

Ulrike Demske. 2005. Mercurius-Baumbank (Version 1.1). Universität Potsdam.

Ulrike Demske. 2019. Referenzkorpus Frühneuhochdeutsch: Baumbank.UP. Universität Potsdam.

Hanne Martine Eckhoff and Aleksandrs Berdičevskis. 2016. Automatic parsing as an efficient pre-annotation tool for historical texts. In *Proceedings of the Workshop on Language Technology Resources and Tools for Digital Humanities (LT4DH)*, pages 62–70, Osaka, Japan. The COLING 2016 Organizing Committee.

Alexander Fraser, Helmut Schmid, Richárd Farkas, Renjing Wang, and Hinrich Schütze. 2013. Knowledge sources for constituent parsing of german, a morphologically rich and less-configurational language. *Computational Linguistics*, 39(1):57–85.

Yu-Yin Hsu. 2010. Comparing conversions of discontinuity in pcfg parsing. In *Ninth International Workshop on Treebanks and Linguistic Theories*, pages 103–113.

Paria Jamshid Lou, Yufei Wang, and Mark Johnson. 2019. Neural constituency parsing of speech transcripts. In *Proceedings of the 2019 Conference of the North American Chapter of the Association for Computational Linguistics: Human Language Technologies, Volume 1 (Long and Short Papers)*, pages 2756–2765, Minneapolis, Minnesota. Association for Computational Linguistics.

Nikita Kitaev, Steven Cao, and Dan Klein. 2019. Multilingual constituency parsing with self-attention and pre-training. In *Proceedings of the 57th Annual Meeting of the Association for Computational Linguistics*, pages 3499–3505, Florence, Italy. Association for Computational Linguistics.

Nikita Kitaev and Dan Klein. 2018. Constituency parsing with a self-attentive encoder. In *Proceedings of the 56th Annual Meeting of the Association for Computational Linguistics*, Melbourne, Australia.

Sandra Kübler, Kathrin Beck, Erhard Hinrichs, and Heike Telljohann. 2010. Chunking German: an unsolved problem. In *Proceedings of the Fourth Linguistic Annotation Workshop*, pages 147–151, Uppsala, Sweden. Association for Computational Linguistics.

Caitlin Light. 2012. The information structure of subject extraposition in early new high german. *University of Pennsylvania Working Papers in Linguistics*, 18(1):20.

Frank Henrik Müller. 2005. *A finite-state approach to shallow parsing and grammatical functions annotation of German*. Ph.D. thesis, Seminar für Sprachwissenschaft, Universität Tübingen.

Katrin Ortmann. 2020. Automatic Topological Field Identification in (Historical) German Texts. In *Proceedings of the The 4th Joint SIGHUM Workshop on Computational Linguistics for Cultural Heritage, Social Sciences, Humanities and Literature*, pages 10–18.

Katrin Ortmann. 2021. Chunking Historical German. In *Proceedings of the 23rd Nordic Conference on Computational Linguistics (NoDaLiDa)*, pages 190–199.

Florian Petran. 2012. Studies for segmentation of historical texts: Sentences or chunks? In *Proceedings of the Second Workshop on Annotation of Corpora for Research in the Humanities (ACRH-2)*, pages 75–86.

Slav Petrov, Leon Barrett, Romain Thibaux, and Dan Klein. 2006. Learning accurate, compact, and interpretable tree annotation. In *Proceedings of the 21st International Conference on Computational Linguistics and 44th Annual Meeting of the Association for Computational Linguistics*, pages 433–440.

Alexandre Pinto, Hugo Gonçalo Oliveira, and Ana Oliveira Alves. 2016. Comparing the performance of different NLP toolkits in formal and social media text. In *5th Symposium on Languages, Applications and Technologies (SLATE'16)*, pages 3:1–3:16. Schloss Dagstuhl–Leibniz-Zentrum fuer Informatik.

Anna N Rafferty and Christopher D Manning. 2008. Parsing three german treebanks: Lexicalized and unlexicalized baselines. In *Proceedings of the Workshop on Parsing German*, pages 40–46.

Erik F. Tjong Kim Sang and Sabine Buchholz. 2000. Introduction to the CoNLL-2000 shared task: Chunking. In *Fourth Conference on Computational Natural Language Learning and the Second Learning Language in Logic Workshop*, pages 127–132.

Christopher D. Sapp. 2014. Extraposition in middle and new high german. *The Journal of Comparative German Linguistics*, 17(2):129–156.

Gerold Schneider, Hans Martin Lehmann, and Peter Schneider. 2015. Parsing early and late modern english corpora. *Literary and Linguistic Computing*, 30(3):423–439.

Yan Shao, Christian Hardmeier, and Joakim Nivre. 2017. Recall is the proper evaluation metric for word segmentation. In *Proceedings of the The 8th International Joint Conference on Natural Language Processing*, pages 86–90, Taipei, Taiwan.

Augustin Speyer. 2011. Die Freiheit der Mittelfeldabfolge im Deutschen. Ein modernes Phänomen. *Beiträge zur Geschichte der deutschen Sprache und Literatur*, 133(1):14–31.

Heike Telljohann, Erhard W. Hinrichs, Sandra Kübler, Heike Zinsmeister, and Kathrin Beck. 2017. *Stylebook for the Tübingen Treebank of Written German (TüBa-D/Z)*. Seminar für Sprachwissenschaft, Universität Tübingen, Germany.

Erik Tjong Kim Sang, Marcel Bollman, Remko Boschker, Francisco Casacuberta, FM Dietz, Stefanie Dipper, Miguel Domingo, Rob van der Goot, JM van Koppen, Nikola Ljubešić, et al. 2017. The clin27 shared task: Translating historical text to contemporary language for improving automatic linguistic annotation. *Computational Linguistics in the Netherlands Journal*, 7:53–64.

David Vilares and Carlos Gómez-Rodríguez. 2020. Discontinuous constituent parsing as sequence labeling. *arXiv preprint arXiv:2010.00633*.

Klaus-Peter Wegera, Hans-Joachim Solms, Ulrike Demske, and Stefanie Dipper. 2021. Referenzkorpus Frühneuhochdeutsch (Version 1.0).

Angelika Wöllstein. 2018. Topologisches Satzmodell. In Jörg Hagemann and Sven Staffeldt, editors, *Syntaxtheorien. Analysen im Vergleich*, 2., aktualisierte auflage edition, pages 145 – 166. Stauffenburg, Tübingen.

Jie Yang, Shuailong Liang, and Yue Zhang. 2018. Design challenges and misconceptions in neural sequence labeling. In *Proceedings of the 27th International Conference on Computational Linguistics (COLING)*, pages 3879–3889, Santa Fe, New Mexico, USA.

Jie Yang and Yue Zhang. 2018. NCRF++: An open-source neural sequence labeling toolkit. In *Proceedings of ACL 2018, System Demonstrations*, pages 74–79, Melbourne, Australia.

Automatically Identifying Online Grooming Chats Using CNN-based Feature Extraction

Svenja Preuß and **Tabea Bayha** and **Luna Pia Bley** and **Vivien Dehne**
Alessa Jordan and **Sophie Reimann** and **Fina Roberto** and **Josephine Romy Zahm**
and **Hanna Siewerts** and **Dirk Labudde** and **Michael Spranger**
University of Applied Sciences Mittweida
Mittweida, Germany
spranger@hs-mittweida.de

Abstract

With the increasing importance of social media in everyone's life, the risk of its misuse by criminals is also increasing. In particular children are at risk of becoming victims of online related crime, especially sexual abuse. For example, sexual predators use online grooming to gain the trust of children and young adults. In this paper, a two-step approach using a CNN to identify sexual predators in social networks is proposed. For the identification of a sexual predator profile an $F_{0.5}$ score of 0.79 and an F_2 score of 0.98 were obtained. The score was lower for the identification of specific line which initialized the grooming process ($F_2 = 0.61$).

1 Introduction

The importance of social networks in today's society is constantly growing. More and more children and young people are turning to digital forms of communication. Studies from Germany show that 71% of children between the ages of 6 and 13 actively use the Internet, and the trend is rising (Feierabend et al., 2020b). The situation is similar for young people between the ages of 12 and 19 (Feierabend et al., 2020a). In one study, 97% of the teenagers surveyed said they used the Internet every day or at least several times a week (Feierabend et al., 2020a). Those developments provide new opportunities for sex predators to gain access to minors, for example, through online grooming.

The Austrian Federal Criminal Police Office (Bundeskriminalamt, 2015) defines online grooming as the targeting of children and young people on the Internet with the aim of establishing sexual relationships. It is a special form of sexual harassment that can lead to physical and sexual abuse. The contact is initiated via the Internet, for example via social media or online video games.

In child online grooming an adult predator uses means of online communication in order to gain access to and trust from a minor in order use the minor for sexual purposes (Wachs et al., 2012).

In many countries, cyber grooming is legally considered a criminal offense. In the U.S., for example, 18 U.S. Code § 2422 criminalizes online grooming. In 2011, the European Parliament passed Directive 2011/92/EU, which obliges member states to enact corresponding legal regulations, including on criminal prosecution. In Germany the criminal law aspect was regulated in § 176/IV StGB.

In an effort to contain such sexual offenses software to identify potential predators is devised (Inches and Crestani, 2012). That kind of Software is supposed to be a preventive measure whose forensic/criminalistic benefit lies in assisting the day-to-day police work and even possibly preventing sexual offenses from happening. The goal is to reduce the expenditure of time needed to identify a potential sexual predator on social media. (Villatoro-Tello et al., 2012; Peersman et al., 2012)

In addition, to support law enforcement, the detection of chats with criminal content and the marking of relevant text lines is necessary. Therefore, this work will primarily focus on these two tasks. The first task is to detect suspicious chats and distinguish them from inconspicuous chats in order to identify the most likely sex offender within the suspicious chat. Subsequently, the offending lines can then be identified.

One contribution of this paper is classification approaches that enable both automatic detection of conversations and chats involving potential sexual predators, and conversation threads that exhibit distinct offender behavior. This is based on a two-stage approach that includes a CNN as a mechanism for selecting useful lexical features and an MLP as a classifier. It is shown that the use of the

CNN can significantly improve the results.

The development and evaluation of the presented approaches were based on the dataset provided as part of the International Sexual Predator Identification Competition at PAN-2012 (Inches and Crestani, 2012). In contrast to this competition, a main focus of this work is the detection of chats with potential sex offenders. Therefore, this dataset had to be annotated with additional annotations based on the tagged chat participants. In the absence of a suitable ground truth for developing a solution to detect the relevant lines within a chat, a gold standard was developed as an additional contribution to be made available for research purposes in collaboration with the owner of the data.

This paper is organized as follows: At first we present some related work in Section 2, followed by an overview of the data and methods used for this paper in Section 3 and 4. In Section 5 we discuss our results and finally conclude with Section 6.

2 Related Work

Sexual predator identification in social networks as a generic text classification problem is often solved by the use of machine learning. There are numerable publications related to grooming on social networks. Often, however, not the chat/conversation itself, but only the messages or the authors are classified (Villatoro-Tello et al., 2012; Pendar, 2007; Morris and Hirst, 2012; Mcghee et al., 2011; Eriksson and Karlgren, 2012).

Assuming that police investigators manually review all the results, the classification of conversations can reduce the amount of chats an investigator hast to read and, thus, reduces the time spent on the investigation. They would only have to reprocess a fraction of all the conversations, namely those that most likely contain a sexual predator. In previous works, if a chat classification was carried out, it represented only an intermediate step or a prefiltering in order to identify the predator (author) (Villatoro-Tello et al., 2012; Cardei and Rebedea, 2017).

In 2012 the Sexual Predator Identification competition, that was part of PAN [1], dealt with the identification of sexual predators in social networks. The best results were achieved by exercising a so-called Two-Step-Classification (Villatoro-Tello et al., 2012; Morris and Hirst, 2012; Peersman et al., 2012; Cardei and Rebedea, 2017). At first the Suspicious Conversation Identification (SCI) is used to sift out conversations featuring potential predators and, afterwards, the Victim from Predator Disclosure (VFP) is applied to classify the conversationalists (Villatoro-Tello et al., 2012). The winning paper by Villatoro-Tello et al. (Villatoro-Tello et al., 2012) tested both support vector machines (SVM) and neural networks (NN), each with a binary and tf-idf weighted Bag of Words (BoW) (with 117015 elements) as input. The SVM with a tf-idf weighting as SCI was able to achieve slightly better results on the validation data, with an $F_{0.5}$ measure of 0.9516, than a neural network (Villatoro-Tello et al., 2012). A later approach, also using an SVM, this time with a sequential minimum optimization, achieved an $F_{0.5}$ measure of 0.938, using a BoW with 1000 words as well as behavioral and interactive-behavioral features (Cardei and Rebedea, 2017).

This work differs from previous work in this area in particular in that it focuses primarily on chat and relevant line classification rather than author classification. To accomplish this, a multilayer perceptron (MLP) is used to classify the conversations, as this form of neural network has performed well in text classification in the past (Villatoro-Tello et al., 2012).

Generally, the examined features can be divided into lexical and behavioural features. Some approaches exclusively used lexical features (Pendar, 2007; Mcghee et al., 2011; Villatoro-Tello et al., 2012), most in form of a bag-of-words model (Villatoro-Tello et al., 2012; Morris and Hirst, 2012; Cardei and Rebedea, 2017) and sometimes extended through the tf-idf weight (Pendar, 2007; Villatoro-Tello et al., 2012; Morris and Hirst, 2012). For the purpose of extracting lexical features we utilized a convolutional neural network (CNN). Until now, in most cases, the terms and conditions of lexical features had to be initialized by the author, for example, in the form of dictionaries. Typically, these dictionaries contain terms that are unique for sexual predators. By using a convolutional layer to extract the lexical features, the network itself should learn which n-grams and phrases are relevant to distinguish between sexual predator and non-predator chats. In this way, not only terms from the vocabulary of sex offenders are learned, but also frequently used phrases of their chat partners and chats of non-offenders.

[1] A series of scientific events and shared tasks on digital text forensics and stylometry. https://pan.webis.de/

In order to improve the classification additional behavioral features were used (Morris and Hirst, 2012; Eriksson and Karlgren, 2012; Cardei and Rebedea, 2017), which ranged from the response time in conversations (Morris and Hirst, 2012) to the number of asked questions within a single message (Cardei and Rebedea, 2017). Results showed that lexical features are very important for identifying relevant conversations, while behavioral features have less of an impact (Cardei and Rebedea, 2017). In addition to the lexical features we surveyed different combinations of behavioral features, some of which are newly developed and others of which have been applied in previous works, including sentiment analysis (Liu et al., 2017).

In order to identify the suspicious lines in conversations, those that show a distinctive predator behavior, dictionaries were used primarily (Mcghee et al., 2011; Peersman et al., 2012). Another approach looked at the so-called predatoriness score, which is calculated from the summed weights of the uni and bi-grams contained in the message, determined by a linear SVM (Morris and Hirst, 2012). The best outcome for suspicious line detection so far was achieved through first classifying the authors and then, if they were flagged as a predator, returning all their lines, which resulted in an $F_{0.5}$ measure of 0.4762 (Popescu and Grozea, 2012). Another approach involved the use of a pre-trained classifier to sort the messages (Mcghee et al., 2011). In order to identify the distinctive lines in conversations we labeled each message to generate a gold standard and trained a CNN, besides testing a new "line-feature". To the best of our knowledge, no publicly available ground truth currently exists for the training data for this specific task. Therefore, providing a gold standard generated by two independent annotators is one of the new contributions of this paper. In order to drive research in this area, it will be made available in cooperation with the data's owner.

3 Data

The data used in this paper was provided by the 2012 Sexual Predator Identification competition (PAN) and together the data sets consist of 222,055 conversations. Within these conversations a sexual predator can communicate with a potential victim or non-predators can converse with each other. The former could resemble a suspicious message, which indicates a predator behavior, in composition or content. However, predators can also write about mundane topics. Therefore, the number of conversations with suspicious messages is limited to less than 4% in this data set to ensure a realistic scenario. (Inches and Crestani, 2012)

	number of conversations		
	overall	w/o pred.	with pred.
before	155,128	151,391	3,737
after	20,788	19,145	1,643
	number of authors		
	overall	w/o pred.	with pred.
before	218,702	218,448	254
after	35,023	34,794	229

Table 1: Test data before and after preprocessing

Preprocessing was used so as to counterbalance the dataset (Table 1).

3.1 Preprocessing of the Data

The reduction and normalization of the data set were required to further analyze the data. Therefore, all conversations who met at least one of the following conditions were removed from the data set:

- more than four participants (authors), because predators do not take part in such conversations
- only one participant (author) (Villatoro-Tello et al., 2012), since one-sided conversations seldom represent suspicious behavior
- each participant sent less than five messages (Villatoro-Tello et al., 2012), assuming that relevant predator behavior is better detectable after "getting acquainted"
- blank conversations, since no text can be analyzed

Additionally, all messages that contained images made from characters were removed as well (Villatoro-Tello et al., 2012) since they only create static and do not provide usable information. These messages include those which are longer than five rows and those whose ratio between symbols and letters is greater than 45%.

Normalizations were made in regard to spelling out abbreviations and the consistent uncapitalization of all letters (Eriksson and Karlgren, 2012). Emoticons were extracted through SoMaJo (Proisl and Uhrig, 2016) and Emot (Shah and Rohilla,

2018) and afterwards each existing emoticon was assigned an ID in the form of $[1-9]{3}-[a-z]{3}, which improved the detection as well as the differentiation of the individual emoticons. In addition, some preprocessing steps required a normalization of XML special characters.

3.2 Preprocessing of the CNN-input

The CNN-input requires the depiction of texts and words in a machine-readable format. Therefore, all words were lemmatized at first. Afterwards, a dictionary was compiled wherein every word got a corresponding ID and unknown words were assigned the ID null. Conversations or messages were portrayed as a list of one-hot vectors with minor density for each occurring word and brought to the same length by means of padding.

3.3 Preprocessing for the line identification

The data provided by the International Sexual Predator Identification competition at PAN-2012 did not include a ground truth for the identification of messages/lines. So, in order to test our supervised learning approach we had to generate our own ground truth by labeling the data manually. Therefore, the training data set was divided into multiple parts and assigned one of the following labels, which are inspired by Peersmann et al. (Peersman et al., 2012) and McGhee et al. (Eriksson and Karlgren, 2012):

0 - irrelevant

1 - sexual theme:

- (erogenous) body parts
- sexual acts
- sexual oriented adjectives, nouns or terms of endearment
- inquiries regarding clothing, especially underwear ("[...]what are you wearing", "what kind of panties do you have on?")

2 - paraphrasing sexual topics with non-sexual terms:

- characteristic words: "teach", "play", "learn"

3 - meeting in person:

- requests to meet in person, video-chat or call
- characteristic words: "meet", "call"

4 - requests for (personal) information:

- pictures, videos, phone number, webcam, address, ...
- characteristic words: "webcam", "cell", "pic", "address"

5 - inquiries about parents, friends, etc. or police:

- securing privacy, so that nobody finds out about the chat or planned actions
- (e.g., "you just cant tell anyone ok", "[...] make sure you delete this stuff", "who is home with you now")

6 - age references:

- child-oriented vocabulary and pet names (e.g., "cutie pie", "princess")
- statements about age or age differences (e.g., "you know im older")
- aware of the culpability (e.g., "your to young ill get in trouble lol") (Peersman et al., 2012)

This labeling process was repeated, so that each section was evaluated by two different persons and thus the unrelated assessments resulted in a Cohen's Kappa of 0.78742. In some cases, when the labels didn't concur, a third person had to reevaluate the messages.

4 Methods

The "Suspicious Conversation Identification", hereafter referred to as SCI, is the main focus of this paper. The SCI separates conversations depending on the participation of sexual predators. Since the data provided by the International Sexual Predator Identification competition at PAN-2012 is labeled on an author basis the following ground truth is applied to the SCI: Every conversation that contains a sexual predator is denoted as a predator-conversation. The "Victim from Predator Disclosure"(VFP) was tested as an addition. It takes the conversations, returned by the SCI, as input and is supposed to distinguish between sexual predators and other authors (e.g. potential victims). Therefore, author-conversation-pairs were created in order to behold each author in every one of his conversations. The VFP was trained on all the conversations that contained at least one predator. Finally, the amount of authors across all conversations that classified as a sexual predator constitutes the end result.

4.1 Classifier

The SCI/VFP classifier is made of two fundamental components, the feature extractor and the actual classifier (Figure 1).

The feature extractor is composed of a CNN which is trained to extract relevant n-grams for the following classification using temporal max pooling. The CNN input consists of texts in the form of one-hot vectors (Input_1). In order to display the similarity between words with regard to their context an embedding layer was integrated ahead of the convolutional layers. In this experimental setup always 40 of the 1-, 3-, 5- and 7-grams were extracted through an one-dimensional convolutional layer. Other lexical/behavioral features were used as an addition to this feature (cf. Subsection 4.2) (Input_2).

The actual classifier is an MLP that consists of two fully connected dense layers. The first dense layer had a size of 20 units, the second had only one unit and served as an output layer. At last the result was scaled to a value between 0 and 1 by a sigmoid function. As a manner of regularization a dropout layer was employed between the layers with a threshold of 0.5.

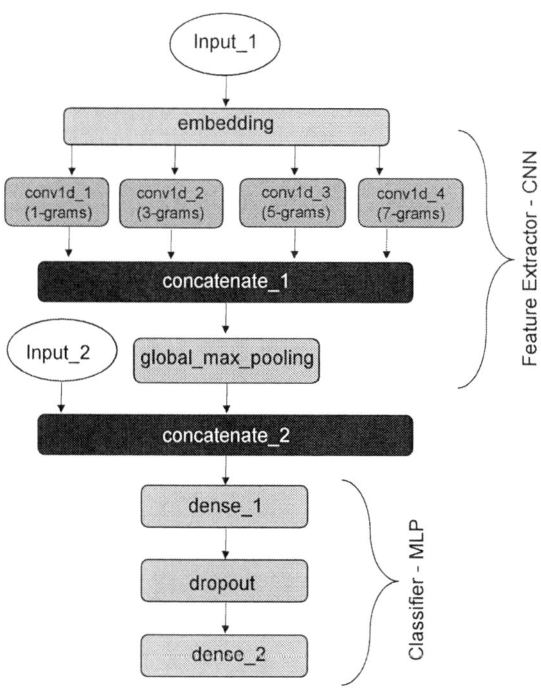

Figure 1: Classifier architecture.

4.2 Feature

The SCI as well as the VFP are based on lexical (LF) and behavioral or conversation based features (BF). The SCI relies on the first feature set (Table 2), which contains conversation-dependent attributes. The second feature set (Table 2) provides the foundation for the VFP. The latter contains similar features to the SCI, which were adjusted to be author-dependent rather than conversation-dependent.

The aforementioned features are based on the corresponding papers (cf. Table 2) and were implemented as follows:

Time of conversation start (TC): The time at which the conversation starts was represented as a figure that was rounded to the nearest whole hour. Every hour is represented two-dimensionally by an x- and y-coordinate in the unit circle so as to obtain a sound result during the change of days.

Duration of a conversation (DoC): For each conversation the duration of a conversation (in minutes) resulted from the difference between the time of the first and last messages.

Number of asked questions (NQ): The number of asked questions was made up of the percentage amount of messages per conversation (feature set 1) or else the amount of messages per author for each conversation (feature set 2) that contained questions. The amount of questions per author for every conversation was determined as well.

Number of messages (NoM): The total number of messages was defined as the amount of sent messages per conversation (feature set 1). In order to identify how dominant an author is in a conversation the percentage amount of messages per author for each conversation was determined (feature set 2).

Number of used emoticons (NoE): For each author the number of used emoticons was counted per conversation utilizing the emoticon-IDs. On the one hand the average number of emoticons per message was calculated for each author, on the other hand the amount of emoticons used by an author compared to the total amount of emoticons in the conversation was determined.

Response time (RT): The response time resulted from the difference between the point in time (in minutes) at which a message was sent and the moment the following message arrived in the conversation. For each conversation the mean response time was determined by calculating the sum over

feature set 1
time of conversation start
duration of conversation
# of asked questions (Morris and Hirst, 2012; Cardei and Rebedea, 2017)
# of messages (Morris and Hirst, 2012)
sentiment analysis (Liu et al., 2017)
feature set 2
# of asked questions (Morris and Hirst, 2012; Cardei and Rebedea, 2017)
# of messages (Morris and Hirst, 2012)
# of used emoticons (Morris and Hirst, 2012)
response time (Morris and Hirst, 2012; Cardei and Rebedea, 2017)
conversational initiation (Morris and Hirst, 2012; Cardei and Rebedea, 2017)
# of words per author (Morris and Hirst, 2012)
sentiment analysis (Liu et al., 2017)

Table 2: Used feature sets (behavioural)

all response times for all authors.

Conversational initiation (CI): The conversational initiation describes which author begins a conversation by sending the first message. Those authors got the value 1 assigned to this feature, other authors got the value 0.

Number of words per author (WA): The word count was defined by the average number of words used in a message by an author. In order to identify the level of participation in a conversation the word count for an author in a conversation was divided by the total word count for that specific conversation.

Sentiment analysis (SA): The sentimemt analysis feature was tested through four different approaches. The first attempt dealt with the Sentistrength tool (Thelwall et al., 2010a), a program that returns values between -1 (not negative) and -5 (very negative) or values between 1 (not positive) and 5 (very positive) in order to score the various sentiments. This entire analysis was based on a dictionary which also took misspelling and negations (e.g. "not nice") into consideration. In addition, a list of boost-words was integrated, whose words, like "very" or "extremely", could amplify the level of positivity/negativity of the sentiment (Thelwall et al., 2010b). The second attempt utilized a similar program, TextBlob, which was based on a dictionary as well. However, the returned score only regards the adjectives that were used and lies between -1 and 1 (Sohangir et al., 2018). The last two attempts did not apply premade tools and trained classifiers instead, by using a data set of 6.3 million tweets (Malafosse, 2019). Both were implemented according to two existing works. On the one hand, the classifier decided whether the sentiment was negative, neutral or positive, but not it's intensity (third approach) (Malafosse, 2019). On the other hand, the classifier was trained in Tensorflow (fourth approach) and returned four values (negative, neutral, positive, mixed) for each text input, which add up to 1 as shown by (Liu et al., 2017).

In this paper, the performance of all features (combined) was tested at first. Then, each feature was surveyed on its own. The features that obtained the best results on the training data were occasionally combined and analyzed again. The final results on the test data arise from those features and feature combinations that achieved the best performances on the training data.

4.3 Line identification

The analysis of lines that show a distinctive predator behavior was conducted under three different rudiments:

1. Usage of the pre-trained CNN from the VFP:
    - the CNN already learned distinctive word patterns in order to identify a sexual predator.
    - single messages from the test data were forwarded as input for the prediction.
2. Usage of a new CNN:
    - a new CNN, whose training was based on the generated ground truth, was created.
    - this classifier used a similar architecture to the SCI and VFP, but the second concatenate layer as well as the input were omitted.
3. Usage of the new CNN in combination with the line feature:

- in addition to the, through the CNN extracted, n-grmas a new feature (line feature) was tested.
- the line feature is based on the assumption that relevant messages are often found in the middle of a conversation. It refers to the message number in relation to the total number of messages in a respective conversation.
- the architecture of the classifier is the same as for the SCI/VFP.

5 Results and Discussion

For the purpose of detecting that epoch, which delivers the best results without overfitting, the overfitting-behavior was analyzed for each epoch for the SCI classifier.

5.1 Sentiment analysis

The sentiment analysis ensued in different manners (cf. Subsection 4.2). Our initial assumption, that conversations with a sexual predator should obtain positive sentiment scores more often than conversations without a predator, was confirmed through the sentiment analysis on a conversational basis. As can be seen in Figure 2, conversations with a sexual predator were to 65.97% positive and conversations without a predator only to 37.66%. Negative sentiment scores were more common for non-predator conversations with 41.62%.

Therefore, our next assumption was that a sexual predator would reach a sentiment score that was distinctly more positive than that of a non-predator (Liu et al., 2017), which couldn't be confirmed through the approach with Tensorflow. According to that the conversational partners of a sexual predator acquired positive scores in 505 conversations, the predators themselves only in 409 conversations. Thus the sentiment scores for predator/non-predator don't allow for a meaningful differentiation.

So far all the tested approaches were nearly indistinguishable. Therefore SentiStrength was used to attain the following results, because of it's easy handling and velocity.

5.2 SCI classification

Already, the lexical features, which were extracted through the CNN, yielded sound results on the validation data, which could be improved by joining the behavioral features. The combination of lexical

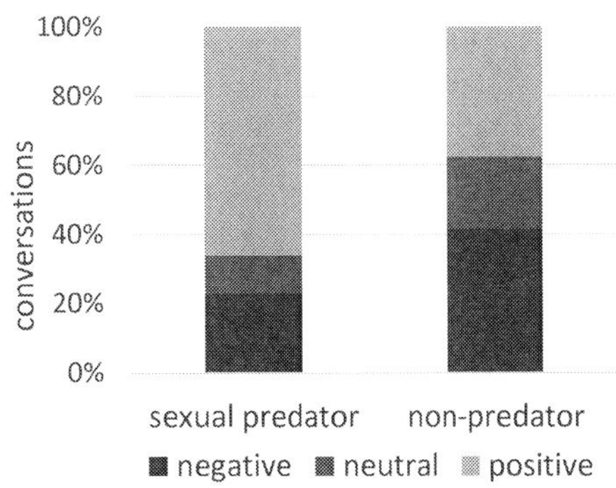

Figure 2: Sentiment values for predaror and non-predator conversations (third approach) (Malafosse, 2019).

features and sentiment scores (Table 3) resulted in an $F_{0.5}$ of 0.9935. All the results so far are based on a stratified 5-fold cross-validation.

Because of these findings a model that trained on lexical features and sentiment scores was reviewed on the test data. With a precision of 0.9982 and a recall of 0.9349 the following F-measures represent the best outcome for a classification of sexual predator chats to date: $F_{0.5}$ of 0.9723 and F_2 of 0.9469.

By reference to this procedure the number of apparently relevant conversations was reduced to 1567, which corresponds to roughly 1% of all the conversations that would have had to be screened manually. Thereby, only 30 conversations were classified as false-positives and 106 conversations were classified as false-negatives. Unfortunately by doing so 18 predators could not be identified. However, it is possible that the false negative classified conversations are attributable to the method, which was used to create the ground truth (cf. Subsection 4.1), where conversations with a sexual predator, that didn't show suspicious behavior, were labeled as relevant.

5.3 VFP classification

The data returned by the SCI created the foundation for the VFP, consisting of altogether 1537 predator conversations and 1567 non-predator conversations.

Similar to the SCI the lexical features constituted a great prerequisite for further analyses based on the training data results. In combination with one

Features	Precision	Recall	$F_{0.5}$
VT2012	-	-	0.9516
CR2017	0.9380	0.9380	0.9380
LF	0.9600	0.9322	0.9541
LF + BF	0.9826	0.9874	0.9835
LF + SA	**0.9935**	0.9891	**0.9926**
LF + TC	0.9881	0.9891	0.9882
LF + DoC	0.9881	**0.9907**	0.9886
LF + CQ	0.9891	0.9814	0.9875
LF + NoM	0.9934	0.9820	0.9910

Table 3: Results for the SCI classification on the training data compared to baseline results from (Villatoro-Tello et al., 2012) (VT2012) and (Cardei and Rebedea, 2017) (CR2017)

other behavioral feature significant improvements could be reached compared to the union of all features (Table 4). All results on the training data are based on a stratified 5-fold cross-validation.

The four most expressive behavioral features were then reviewed on the test data, either in combinations or alone with the lexical features (Table 5). Thereby, the conjunction of lexical features and all four of the aforementioned behavioral features achieved the best result with an $F_{0.5}$ measure of 0.9169 and an F_2 measure of 0.8916. 1466 author-conversation-pairs were returned as relevant, 109 of them were false positives and 179 couldn't be detected (false negatives). In order to identify sexual predators they have to be detected as such in at least one of their conversations. Therefore the end result is determined over all conversations to obtain the exact amount of authors, classified as predators (Table 6). Here the combination of lexical features and the four aforementioned behavioral features achieved the best result as well, with an $F_{0.5}$ measure of 0.7889 and an F_2 measure of 0.9221. The number of classified sexual predators was 213, an additional 70 were false positives and solely 5 predators could not be identified at all.

The obvious difference between the two F-measures is caused by the varying weight and the relatively low precision. Due to the imbalance of authors in the data set the 70 authors, who were incorrectly classified as predators, are a pretty small number compared to the overall 34,794 non-predators. Whereas, compared to the low total number of only 229 sexual predators, the 70 false positives carry a considerable weight, thus causing a low precision.

The usage of the two F-measures is justified through their computation which goes along with different assertions. *$F_{0.5}$-measure*: In order to optimize the expenditure of time that investigators need to find a potential sexual predator, it is better to only have the "right" suspects rather than returning every possible one (Inches and Crestani, 2012). *F_2-measure*: Since the investigators have to double-check the results given by the classifier anyways, it is better to have classified innocent authors as potential suspects (false positives) rather, than to miss out on an actual sexual predator. Therefore, it is important to increase the weight of the recall over the precision.

Features	Precision	Recall	$F_{0.5}$
LF	0.8689	0.8720	0.8693
LF + NoE	0.9279	0.9256	**0.9273**
LF + RT	**0.9302**	0.9147	0.9269
LF + CI	0.9297	0.9070	0.9249
LF + NoM	0.9290	0.9114	0,.252

Table 4: Best results for the VFP classification on the training data.

Features	Precision	Recall	$F_{0.5}$	F_2
LF + NoE	0.9042	0.8665	0.8964	0.8738
LF + CI	0.9201	**0.8841**	0,9127	0.8911
LF + RT	0.9162	0.8613	0.9047	0.8717
LF + NoM	0.9218	0.8750	0.9121	0.8840
all	**0.9256**	0.8835	**0.9169**	**0.8916**

Table 5: Results for the VFP classification on the test data

Features	Precision	Recall	$F_{0.5}$	F_2
VT2012	0.9804	0.7874	0.9346	0.8197
CR2017	1.0000	0.8180	0.9570	0.8489
LF + NoE	0.7241	0.9633	0.7620	0.9036
LF + CI	0.7276	0.9679	0.7656	0.9079
LF + RT	0.7376	0.9541	0.7727	0.9012
LF + NoM	0.7413	0.9725	0.7783	0.9154
all	**0.7527**	**0.9771**	**0.7889**	**0.9221**

Table 6: Final results for author classification over conversations compared to baseline results from (Villatoro-Tello et al., 2012) (VT2012) and (Cardei and Rebedea, 2017) (CR2017).

5.4 Identifying suspicious messages

The results for the line identification (Table 7) were determined by the given ground truth.

The third approach, a CNN that trained on the self-created ground truth, combined with the line feature (LiF), resulted in the best F_3 measure of

Features	Precision	Recall	F_3
PG2012	0.0915	0.8938	0.4762
CNN (VFP)	0.2472	**0.7247**	0.6074
CNN (GT)	0.4590	0.6971	0.6628
CNN + LiF (GT)	**0.4653**	0.7046	**0.6702**

Table 7: Final results for the line classification on the test data, comparing the CNN used for the VFP with the CNN trained on the self-created ground truth (GT) and with the baseline results from (Popescu and Grozea, 2012) (PG2012).

0.6702, with a precision of 0.4653 and a recall of 0.7046. The same CNN without the line feature (second approach) obtained a similar result with an F_3 measure of 0.6628. Those similarities imply that the assumption, that relevant messages occur more often in some paragraphs than in others, is true, however, no significant improvements could be reached.

The pre-trained CNN from the VFP (first approach) reached an F_3 measure of 0.6074. Because of its low precision with only 0.2472 and the greater weighting of the recall the latter has a larger impact on this F-measure.

The results of all three approaches show a greater recall, compared to the precision, which could be explained by the high count of messages that were returned as relevant, regardless of whether they were correctly classified or not. Nevertheless, the approaches that were based on the self-created ground truth (cf. Subsection 4.3) achieved a more balanced relation between precision and recall.

Due to the different approaches used to solve this task the results are difficult to compare. Notwithstanding the above, all three of the aforementioned approaches surpassed the existing results of the Sexual Predator Identification competition at PAN 2012.

6 Conclusion

Both the results of the sexual predator conversation identification and the identification of relevant messages have shown that a CNN can be of great use in extracting lexical features in the form of N-grams. With its help, the results known to us could be exceeded in both areas. The result of the SCI showed that a sentiment analysis in connection with the lexical feature is very well suited to the identification of sexual predator conversations and achieved an $F_{0.5}$ measure of 0.9723. Further tests with feature combinations have not yet been continued. The tests of the VFP showed, however, that the most successful features combined led to an improvement in the end result. Accordingly, a further step would be to combine features of the SCI and see whether this can lead to a further improvement. Especially with the knowledge that other features, such as the number of messages written by each author, showed similarly good results on the training data as the sentiment analysis.

A possible exploratory approach with regard to the VFP could be transfer learning based on the neural network trained for the SCI. The learned features of the SCI are used further and adapted and interpreted for the identification of a sexual predator.

When identifying the relevant messages, a newly tested line feature in conjunction with the lexical features was able to achieve the best results. The CNN that was used for the extraction of lexical features was trained on a self-created ground truth. When annotating the lines, it was particularly noticeable that some messages can be rated as relevant in one context and as irrelevant in another. Only the message "playing" in a sexual context would be a clear word for "paraphrase of sexual topics with non-sexual vocabulary" and thus relevant, but not to be considered relevant in connection with a hobby (sports). At the moment, each message was rated individually without knowing what was previously written. Another sequence-based network, such as an RNN, could possibly differentiate these messages better.

References

Bundeskriminalamt. 2015. Schutz vor (cyber-)grooming. Last accessed: August 14th, 2021.

Claudia Cardei and Traian Rebedea. 2017. Detecting sexual predators in chats using behavioral features and imbalanced learning. *Natural Language Engineering*, 23(4):589—-616.

Gunnar Eriksson and Jussi Karlgren. 2012. Features for Modelling Characteristics of Conversations—Notebook for PAN at CLEF 2012. In *CLEF 2012 Evaluation Labs and Workshop – Working Notes Papers, 17-20 September, Rome, Italy*. CEUR-WS.org.

Sabine Feierabend, Thomas Rathgeb, Hediye Kheredmand, and Stephan Glöckler. 2020a. Jim-studie 2020-jugend, information, medien-basisuntersuchung zum medienumgang 12- bis 19-jähriger. Last accessed: August 14th, 2021.

Sabine Feierabend, Thomas Rathgeb, Hediye Kheredmand, and Stephan Glöckler. 2020b. Kim-studie

2020-kindheit, internet, medien-basisuntersuchung zum medienumgang 6- bis 13-jähriger. Last accessed: August 14th, 2021.

Pamela Forner, Jussi Karlgren, and Christa Womser-Hacker, editors. 2012. *CLEF 2012 Evaluation Labs and Workshop – Working Notes Papers, 17-20 September, Rome, Italy*. CEUR-WS.org.

Giacomo Inches and Fabio Crestani. 2012. Overview of the International Sexual Predator Identification Competition at PAN-2012. In (Forner et al., 2012).

Dan Liu, Ching Yee Suen, and Olga Ormandjieva. 2017. A novel way of identifying cyber predators. *Computing Research Repository*, arXiv:1712.03903. Version 1.

Charles Malafosse. 2019. Fasttext sentiment analysis for tweets: A straightforward guide. Last accessed: February 25th, 2019.

India Mcghee, Jennifer Bayzick, April Kontostathis, Lynne Edwards, Alexandra Mcbride, and Emma Jakubowski. 2011. Learning to identify internet sexual predation. *International Journal of Electronic Commerce*, 15(3):103—-122.

Colin Morris and Graeme Hirst. 2012. Identifying Sexual Predators by SVM Classification with Lexical and Behavioral Features—Notebook for PAN at CLEF 2012. In (Forner et al., 2012).

Claudia Peersman, Frederik Vaassen, Vincent Van Asch, and Walter Daelemans. 2012. Conversation Level Constraints on Pedophile Detection in Chat Rooms—Notebook for PAN at CLEF 2012. In (Forner et al., 2012).

Nick Pendar. 2007. Toward spotting the pedophile telling victim from predator in text chats. In *International Conference on Semantic Computing (ICSC 2007)*, pages 235–241.

Marius Popescu and Cristian Grozea. 2012. Kernel Methods and String Kernels for Authorship Analysis—Notebook for PAN at CLEF 2012. In (Forner et al., 2012).

Thomas Proisl and Peter Uhrig. 2016. Somajo: State-of-the-art tokenization for german web and social media texts. In *Proceedings of the 10th Web as Corpus Workshop*, pages 57–62, Berlin. Association for Computational Linguistics.

Neel Shah and Shubham Rohilla. 2018. Open source emoticons and emoji detection library: Emot. Version 2.1.

Sahar Sohangir, Nicholas Petty, and Dingding Wang. 2018. Financial sentiment lexicon analysis. In *2018 IEEE 12th International Conference on Semantic Computing (ICSC)*, pages 286–289.

Mike Thelwall, Kevan Buckley, Georgios Paltoglou, Di Cai, and Arvid Kappas. 2010a. Sentiment strength detection in short informal text. *Journal of the American Society for Information Science and Technology*, 61(12):2544–2558.

Mike Thelwall, Kevan Buckley, Georgios Paltoglou, Di Cai, and Arvid Kappas. 2010b. Sentiment strength detection in short informal text. *Journal of the American Society for Information Science and Technology*, 61:2544–2558.

Esaú Villatoro-Tello, Antonio Juárez-González, Hugo Jair Escalante, Manuel Montes y Gómez, and Luis Villaseñor-Pineda. 2012. Two-step Approach for Effective Detection of Misbehaving Users in Chats—Notebook for PAN at CLEF 2012. In (Forner et al., 2012).

Sebastian Wachs, Karsten D. Wolf, and Ching-Ching Pan. 2012. Cybergrooming: risk factors, coping strategies and associations with cyberbullying. *Psicothema*, 24(4):628–633.

Who is *we*? Disambiguating the referents of first person plural pronouns in parliamentary debates

Ines Rehbein
Data and Web Science Group
University of Mannheim
ines@informatik.uni-mannheim.de

Josef Ruppenhofer
Archive for Spoken German
Leibniz Institute
for the German Language
ruppenhofer@ids-mannheim.de

Julian Bernauer
MZES
University of Mannheim
julian.bernauer@mzes.uni-mannheim.de

Abstract

This paper investigates the use of first person plural pronouns as a rhetorical device in political speeches. We present an annotation schema for disambiguating pronoun references and use our schema to create an annotated corpus of debates from the German Bundestag. We then use our corpus to learn to *automatically* resolve pronoun referents in parliamentary debates. We explore the use of data augmentation with weak supervision to further expand our corpus and report preliminary results.

1 Introduction

Personal pronouns are an important rhetorical device in political speeches that allow politicians to shape their message to appeal to specific audiences. Multiple functions of pronouns have been described, such as creating a feeling of unity with the audience (1.1), sharing responsibility (1.2) or criticising others (1.3) (Beard, 2000; Bramley, 2001; Håkansson, 2012).

Example 1.1. Members of Congress, we must work together to help control those costs (Bush 2004)

Example 1.2. We have increased our budget at a responsible 4 percent (Bush 2001)

Example 1.3. the more we get involved with other people, the more complicated our relationships get (B. Clinton 2002) [1]

Tyrkkö (2016) calls personal pronouns "one of the primary linguistic features used by political speakers to manage their audiences' perceptions of in-groups and out-groups". This makes them especially important for populist rhetoric where the speaker evokes a dichotomous view of society, *us-versus-them* (see, e.g., Mudde (2004); Mudde and Kaltwasser (2017)).

While the practice of *othering* might seem to be the most prominent feature of personal pronouns in political discourse, another important aspect also needs to be considered, namely their referential ambiguity (Tyrkkö, 2016; Wales, 1996). As stated by Allen (2007, pp.12),

> "Shifting identity through pronoun choice and using pronouns with ambiguous referents enables politicians to appeal to diverse audiences which helps broaden their ability to persuade the audience to their point of view. It is a scattergun effect —shoot broadly enough and you'll hit something".

While prior research on the interface between corpus linguistics, pragmatics, discourse studies and political science has presented empirical findings based on word frequencies (Vuković, 2012; Tyrkkö, 2016; Alavidze, 2017), only few studies have tried to systematically investigate this topic in more detail, i.e., by trying to measure the agreement between human annotators for disambiguating the referents of personal pronouns in political speeches, or by presenting large-scale studies of the use of personal pronouns beyond word frequencies.

This paper takes first steps in that direction by means of an annotation study in which we classify instancse of the first person plural pronoun *wir* 'we' in German parliamentary debates, using a classification scheme with 9 different classes. We report inter-annotator agreement for this highly subjective task and analyse our disagreements. We then present a preliminary analysis of our data where we look into differences in the use of *we/us* in political speeches, depending on (i)

[1] Two of the examples taken from Håkansson (2012).

the speaker, (ii) the topic, and (iii) the speaker's party affiliation.

In the second part of the paper, we undertake first experiments towards automatically predicting the referents of first person pronouns in parliamentary debates. For that, we make use of transfer learning, in combination with data augmentation based on weak supervision (Ratner et al., 2016, 2020). We show that our transfer learning approach brings substantial improvements over a majority baseline while pretraining the model on the larger, noisy data and fine-tuning it on our manual annotations yields only small improvements over training on the manual annotations only.

2 Related Work

First person plural pronouns from a linguistic perspective The reference of German *wir*, just like that of English *we*, is quite variable. Following the typology of Cysouw (2002), German *wir* as a first person plural (1PL) form has multiple distinct uses: (i) `minimal inclusive`, consisting of speaker and hearer (2.1); (ii) `augmented inclusive`, adding third parties beyond the minimal inclusive (2.2); (iii) `exclusive`, consisting of the speaker and third parties, but excluding the hearer (2.3).

Example 2.1. Sollen wir morgen telefonieren?
'Shall we talk on the phone tomorrow?'

Example 2.2. Kim kommt um 12 an. Sollen wir dann Mittag essen gehen?
'Kim will arrive at 11. Shall we go to lunch then?' [all three of us]

Example 2.3. Wir gehen ins Kino. Was habt ihr vor?
'We're going to the movies. What are your plans?'

In addition, special subtypes of uses may be recognized. For English, Quirk et al. (1985) discuss a set of special (sub)uses that also occur with German *wir*. For instance, a single author may nevertheless use 1PL pronouns to avoid appearing 'egotistical'. Doctors (among others) may use the 1PL pronoun in a a hearer-oriented way (e.g. *How are we feeling today?*). Of greatest relevance to our data are Quirk et al. (1985)'s generic uses and their class of rhetorical uses where the pronoun refers to a collective such as 'the party', 'the nation'.

While linguistic analyses of pronouns often simply view them as words with determinate reference to a deictically, anaphorically or cataphorically available entity, pragmatic and discourse-oriented studies of pronouns like ours focus on their conceptual emptiness and the fact that their referents must be inferred in context, with the possibility of (un)intentionally ambiguous uses, since individuals have multiple social, discursive and interactional roles.

Corpus studies of 1PL reference Very close in spirit to our work but operating on conversational interactions and with categories appropriate to that domain, Scheibman (2014) presents a study on the reference of *we* in relation to predicate patterns and pragmatic functions. The study coded instances of *we* from the Santa Barbara Corpus of Spoken American English for several features, among them (i) the inclusive vs exclusive distinction, (ii) type of referent (e.g. family member, couple, classmates, human beings, etc.), (iii) tense of predicate, (iv) modals present. The authors' findings suggest that different referential uses of first personal pronouns may be distinguishable based on contextual cues such as tense and modality.

Pronouns in political discourse Tyrkkö (2016) presents a diachronic study of the use of personal pronouns in political speeches over two centuries, showing shifts from a self-centric style (marked by frequent use of *I*) towards the more inclusive use of 1PL forms in the 1920s, which the author ties to the emergence of broadcast media. The study does not disambiguate 1PL forms but counts all of them as inclusive.

Íñigo-Mora (2004) studies the use of *we* in 5 Question Time Sessions of the British parliament, where MPs ask questions of government ministers. She distinguishes what she calls exclusive, inclusive, generic and parliamentary uses of *we* and examines their distribution across different combinations of interactants (opposition MP to member of government; member of government to opposition MP; member of government and supportive MP (in either direction)).[2] The frequency distribution is interpreted along two dimensions: (i) power and distance and (ii) identity, community and persuasion. Among the findings

[2]There is no generally agreed-upon terminology used to distinguish uses of *we*, either in general or in the political or parliamentary context. For Inigo-Mora the generic *we* refers to "a kind of patriotic "we" that embraces all British people". In the terminology of Quirk et al. (1985) this would be called a collective use. In our annotation scheme, the uses at issue would be labeled "COUNTRY".

is that exclusive uses of *we* constitue the most common type overall, accounting for 53.4% of all tokens. Exclusive *we* is at its most dominant in interactions from government supporting MPs to opposition MPs (76.1%) while it is hardly ever used in questions from opposition MPs to a member of government, which is taken to reflect the power dynamics. Inclusive uses of *we* were found to be much rarer overall, making up 14.5% of all tokens. None of these are uttered by opposition members speaking to members of government, while three quarters are produced between government supporting MPs and members of government, expressing shared identity. Opposition MPs mostly use generic and parliamentary *we*, thus affiliating themselves with the parliament as a distinct branch of government and the country at large, likely because that is where persuasion is most likely to succeed. It is unclear to what extent these results carry over to the plenary setting.

Non-parliamentary political discourse Studies of 1PL pronouns have also targeted other types of interactions. Bull and Fetzer (2006) analyze the use of *you* and *we* in tv interviews with British politicians that were broadcast during the 1997 and 2001 British general elections and just before the war with Iraq in 2003. The focus of the study was on question-response sequences in which politicians make use of pronominal shifts as a means of equivocation to effect shifts of accountability and responsibility. Proctor and Su (2011) examine the use of *we* by four (vice-)presidential candidates in debates and interviews around the time of the 2008 US election. The study focuses on which groups are the referents of *we* and which entities are picked out by possessive NPs of the form *our N*, considering the results in light of the candidates' political stature and targeted office as well as the differences between debate and interview settings.

Politeness Finally, we note that quite a lot of research on pronoun use exists in the area of politeness, though this typically targets pronouns of address. For instance, in a seminal study, Brown and Gilman (1960) discussed the differences in use between informal and formal second person pronouns (such as German *du* and *Sie*) as forms of address in terms of their association with the dimensions of power and solidarity between speakers. The authors argue that, while for a long

Party	#Tokens	#Annot	#Spk	per 1000
AfD	8,993	142	8	15.8
CDU/CSU	10,674	335	5	31.4
FDP	7,358	166	7	22.6
GRÜNE	7,457	136	5	18.2
LINKE	9,310	130	6	14.0
SPD	7,438	245	4	32.9
fraktionslos	797	9	1	11.3
Total	52,027	1,163	36	22.3

Table 1: Some statistics for the annotated testset (**#Spk**: no. of speakers per party; **per 1000**: no. of 1PL pronouns per 1000 tokens).

time the form chosen was mainly determined by power differentials, over time the choice came to depend more on the factor of solidarity.

3 Annotation Study

3.1 Data

The data we use in our study are parliamentary debates from the German Bundestag, covering a time period from Oct 24, 2017 to May 19, 2021.[3] The corpus includes over 330,000 sentences (>16,5 mio tokens), with political speeches by 777 different speakers.

From the XML files, we extracted the individual speeches and randomly selected a subset for manual annotation where we tried to collect roughly the same number of speeches/tokens for each party (see table 1). This resulted in a testset with 36 speeches by different speakers (52,027 tokens) where we manually disambiguated all instances of first person plural pronouns (*wir, uns, unser, unsere, unseren, unseres, unsre*) by classifying them into nine predefined classes. We describe our annotation schema below (§3.2).

3.2 Annotation schema

Table 2 and Table 10 in the appendix give an overview over our classification schema. We assume that references of *we/us* in parliamentary debates can be assigned to a small number of different categories, such as "we, the PARLIAMENT" or "our COUNTRY", or "our political PARTY". The schema has been designed in a bottom-up, data-driven fashion, using speeches from the European parliament and the German Bundestag for schema development. We test our classification schema in an annotation experiment and investigate a) how well human annotators agree when

[3]The data is available in XML format from `https://www.bundestag.de/services/opendata`.

Class	Description	Example
BOARD	Members of a board/ commission/committee	**Wir** haben heute im Untersuchungsausschuss erfahren
COUNTRY	references to Germany/ all Germans	**Wir** sind Weltmeister **Unser** Grundgesetz
GENERIC	generic uses that can be replaced by *one (de: man)*	Daran werden **wir uns** noch in 100 Jahren erinnern
GOVERN	members of the government	**Wir** haben die Arbeitslosigkeit bekämpft.
PARL	members of the parliament	**Wir** Abgeordnete... Lassen Sie **uns** diesen Antrag heute beschließen
PARTY	members of one specific party	**Wir** Liberale haben schon früher...
PEOPLE	groups of people defined by social variables (age, profession, religion and other shared characteristics ...)	Wie **wir** Älteren **uns** verhalten... **Wir** Steuerzahler, **Wir** Christen, **Wir** Pendler, ...
SPECPERS	groups of individuals or members of more than one group	**Wir** beide haben darüber diskutiert **Wir**, die deutsche und die israelische Regierung
UNION	geo-political groups on a supranational level (EU, NATO)	**Wir** in der EU... **Unsere** Europäische Union...

Table 2: Overview of the annotation scheme for 1PL references in parliamentary debates.

disambiguating 1PL pronouns in political speech; b) whether it is possible to automatically predict the intended reference of personal pronouns in parliamentary debates.

We expect that, as noted in section 2, a large part of vagueness and ambiguity in political speech is intended and will result in low IAA between some of the classes in our classification schema. However, we also expect that some classes (such as PARTY) are less ambiguous which should be reflected in a higher agreement between the annotators.

3.3 Annotation

The annotators, two computational linguists,[4] were presented with the speech texts where all instances of 1PL pronouns were highlighted. The task then consisted in assigning a label to each pronoun.[5] The annotators were only allowed to assign exactly one label per instance.

Inter-Annotator Agreement (IAA) We report Krippendorff's α and percentage agreement for two annotators on the 1,163 annotated instances. Inter-rater agreement was quite high with 0.82 α. Table 3, however, shows substantial differences in agreement between the individual classes. We obtained very high agreement for COUNTRY and PARTY (> 90% F1) and slightly lower but still reasonably high agreement for GOVERNMENT, PARLAMENT and UNION (between 78 – 87% F1). For GENERIC, PEOPLE and SPECIFIC_PERSONS, agreement was substantially lower (58–66% F1). Those classes are also less frequent in the data. The remaining class, BOARD, was too rare in our testset to report meaningful results (1 instance only).[6] We kept this class despite its low frequency in the Bundestag corpus, as we found it to be more frequent in speeches from the European Parliament.

Class	F1	Support
BOARD	0.0	1
COUNTRY	92.0	411
GENERIC	65.2	67
GOVERN	87.2	167
PARL	86.6	299
PARTY	90.6	103
PEOPLE	66.7	13
SPECPER	58.8	20
UNION	78.2	82
Total	86.1	1,163

Table 3: IAA (F1) and support (number of annotated instances in the gold standard) for individual classes.

After the annotation was completed, the two annotators discussed and resolved all disagreements to create a ground truth dataset that we used as evaluation data in our experiments (§6).

4 Data Analysis

We now present a preliminary analysis on our manually annotated dataset where we focus on differences in the use of 1PL pronouns across politicians and parties.

Table 1 shows that the governmental parties produce the most 1PL instances per 1000 words, which makes sense given that their members can choose between the greatest number of collective

[4]The data was annotated by the first two authors of the paper.

[5]We used INCEpTION (Klie et al., 2018) as annotaton tool.

[6]The confusion matrix for the annotations can be found in the appendix, Table 11.

Party	BOARD	COUNTRY	GENERIC	GOVERN	PARL	PARTY	PEOPLE	SPECP	UNION
AfD	0.0 (0)	6.0 (54)	0.6 (5)	0.0 (0)	5.1 (46)	3.4 (31)	0.4 (4)	0.2 (2)	0.0 (0)
CDU/CSU	0.0 (0)	11.4 (122)	2.1 (22)	9.6 (102)	5.0 (53)	0.5 (5)	0.3 (3)	0.4 (4)	2.2 (24)
FDP	0.0 (0)	5.7 (42)	1.6 (12)	0.0 (0)	6.1 (45)	5.2 (38)	0.0 (0)	0.5 (4)	3.4 (25)
GRÜNE	0.0 (0)	5.9 (44)	1.7 (13)	0.1 (1)	7.8 (58)	1.2 (9)	0.5 (4)	0.7 (5)	0.3 (2)
LINKE	0.1 (1)	7.1 (66)	0.9 (8)	0.0 (0)	3.7 (34)	1.7 (16)	0.2 (2)	0.0 (0)	0.3 (3)
SPD	0.0 (0)	10.6 (79)	0.9 (7)	8.6 (64)	8.1 (60)	0.5 (4)	0.0 (0)	0.4 (3)	3.8 (28)
frakt.los	0.0 (0)	5.0 (4)	0.0 (0)	0.0 (0)	3.8 (3)	0.0 (0)	0.0 (0)	2.5 (2)	0.0 (0)
Total	1	411	67	167	299	103	13	20	82

Table 4: Distribution of classes in the annotated testset (frequency per 1000 tokens and raw counts in brackets).

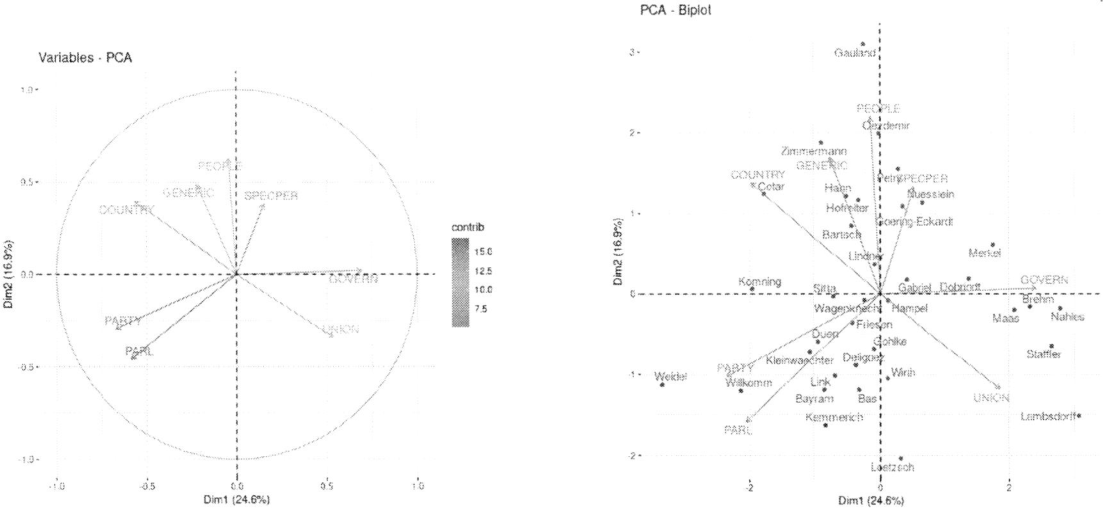

Figure 1: Principal Components Analysis (PCA): left figure shows the loadings for our class variables along the first two components (PC1, PC2), right figure also plots the speakers for PC1 and PC2.

identities.

Table 4 shows the distribution of the different classes across parties. As expected, only members of the CDU/CSU and SPD, the two parties involved in the government at the time of data collection, used *we* to refer to the government. Notably government MPs invoke their GOVERN identity substantially more than their PARTY identity. By contrast, members of the opposition parties refer more often to their own party, often to criticise the government and to distinguish their own policies from those of the government. This is particularly true for the FDP and the AfD, and to a lesser extent also for the LINKE and the GRÜNE.

All parties make frequent references to the parliament (PARL). The two parties in government, however, use many more references to COUNTRY than the opposition parties. This observation is in contrast to the findings of Íñigo-Mora (2004) (see Section 2) who found more pronoun references to the country from members of the opposition. We would like to stress that our data is not yet large enough to produce representative results. In addition, we would also expect an impact of interaction type on the use of pronouns. Íñigo-Mora (2004) investigated Question Time sessions in the British parliament while we focus on plenary speeches, which are longer, less interactive and always have a mixed audience of supporters and opponents, whereas Question Time (superficially) addresses only one or the other. These differences might be reflected in different communicative strategies and stylistic choices.

Another reason for the higher ratio of COUNTRY references in speeches by members of the governmental parties may be that their ranks include key office holders such as the minister of foreign affairs, whose topics tend to skew (inter)national. To investigate this, more data is needed so that we can control for the effects of office holders.

Figure 1 (left) shows the loadings for our class variables along the first two dimensions of a Principal Components Analysis (PCA), based on the normalised frequency counts for the different class variables for individual speakers. The first dimension (X axis) reflects 1PL pronoun references to the government on the right-hand side and to specific parties or the parliament as a whole on the left-hand side. This opposition separates politicians from the governmental parties from the ones from the opposition parties along the first dimension (Figure 1, right).

Figure 1 (right) also seems to show topical effects as Lambsdorff, a member of the FDP and the EU parliament, is positioned closest to the vector showing the loadings of the UNION variable. This might explain why he, as the only non-governmental politician, is also positioned at the right end of the first dimension. The politicians that are positioned left-most on the first dimension are Weidel (AfD), Willkomm (FDP), Komning (AfD) and Cotar (AfD). For the members of AfD, a nationalist and right-wing party deeply opposed to the European Union, it seems plausible that they are positioned not only at the opposite end of GOVERN but also of UNION. Further analysis is needed to investigate this.

Figure 1 (left) also shows that while the two classes PARTY and PARL are highly correlated and in opposition to GOVERNMENT, the more generic classes COUNTRY, GENERIC and PEOPLE also seem to cluster together. This again seems like a promising start for a more detailed analysis. Once more data has been annotated, it will be interesting to include the topic of the speeches in the analysis. This can be easily done, either based on the agenda of the debates or by using topic models. At the moment, however, our data is still too sparse for a more fine-grained analysis.

5 Training Data Augmentation

We now investigate whether and how well we are able to resolve ambiguities in 1PL pronoun references in parliamentary debates *automatically*, using our small annotated dataset to train a supervised ML system.

As our manually annotated dataset is too small to expect high accuracies for automatic prediction, we resort to data augmentation with weak supervision. Our approach proceeds as follows.

We first extract text segments from parliamentary debates from the German Bundestag (19th legislative term) and remove the debates in the test set from our unlabelled training corpus. Each segment consists of a paragraph with multiple

Class	#Pattern	#Hits	err/N
BOARD	1	7	0/7
COUNTRY	5	8,795	2/25
GENERIC	4	307	8/25
GOVERN	5	14,851	2/25
PARLIAMENT	4	3,339	2/25
PARTY	11	8,265	4/25
PEOPLE	1	230	19/25
SPECPER	4	106	3/25
UNION	4	540	3/25
TOTAL	40	36,433	43/203

Table 5: Distribution of distinct patterns per class used for training data creation and number of hits for each pattern. Last column shows no. of errors in N randomly sampled pattern instances.

sentences, as annotated in the xml files. Please note that we do not assign labels to segments but to *instances of 1PL pronouns* in the segments. We then apply a set of predefined patterns to identify instances of 1PL pronouns for each class in our annotation scheme. With the help of these patterns, we assign labels to the unlabelled training corpus and can now use this data to train a supervised ML system for pronoun disambiguation. Below we explain the different steps in more detail.

Patterns For pattern extraction, we make use of the spaCy DependencyMatcher which provides a flexible and efficient framework for defining search patterns over dependency trees.[7]

We combine the spacy DependencyMatcher with the Snorkel framework (Ratner et al., 2016, 2020), a programmatic approach to data augmentation without manual labelling effort. Instead, Snorkel provides an API that allows users to write labelling functions that target specific labels in the annotation scheme. Those functions can consist of simple string matches but can also include more sophisticated features by including the predictions of pretrained classifiers or information from external knowledge bases. While these labelling functions are expected to have low coverage and might also introduce a certain amount of noise, Snorkel addresses this problem by learning an unsupervised generative model over the output of the labelling functions, based on the (dis-)agreements between the predicted labels. This approach is similar in spirit to previous work on

[7]See `https://spacy.io/api/dependencymatcher`. To generate the trees, we use the German `de_core_news_sm` model also provided by spaCy.

quality estimation for annotations obtained from crowdsourcing (Hovy et al., 2013). The output of Snorkel is a set of probabilistic labels that can be used as input to any supervised ML classifier.

Table 5 shows the number of patterns used for each class and the number of hits, i.e., instances extracted by each pattern from the unlabelled training data. Please note that the number of patterns is not very informative on its own, as patterns can make use of regular expressions, lemma lists and syntactic patterns over dependency trees, thus allowing us to extract a larger variety of diverse training examples than could be obtained based on simple string matches.

As an example, consider the following patterns used to extract labelled data for the PARTY class. Our first pattern looks for instances of *wir, uns* (we, us) directly followed by a party name. This pattern can extract instances like *Wir Grüne* or *uns Liberale.* Another pattern looks for instances of *wir* as the subject of communication verbs like *kritisieren, hinterfragen* (criticize, question) etc., as those are usually statements refering to specific parties from the opposition. A third example relies on future forms of *werden* (will) in combination with verbs of action, such as *schaffen, durchführen, investieren* (accomplish, execute, invest) to detect instances from the GOVERNMENT class. This pattern would extract matches like *wir werden Arbeitsplätze schaffen* 'we will create jobs' or *Mindestens 2 Mrd. EUR werden wir in den sozialen Wohnungsbau investieren* 'We will invest at least EUR 2 billion in social housing construction'.

The result of our pattern-based approach is a silver standard corpus with more than 36,000 labelled instances. To get an impression of the quality of the patterns, we randomly extracted 25 instances per class and manually inspected them (last two columns in Table 5). While most patterns seem to produce only a small amount of noise, some categories were more problematic. We found it particularly difficult to produce reliable patterns for PEOPLE and GENERIC which is reflected in the low coverage and precision for the two classes (see §6, Table 9).

6 Experiments

We now explore the potential of our automatically created training set for disambiguating references of personal pronouns in political debates.

wform	class	support	DL
wir	PARL	(185/600)	9
unser	COUNTRY	(24/26)	2
Wir	COUNTRY	(65/240)	9
unserem	COUNTRY	(28/32)	4
uns	COUNTRY	(56/163)	8
unsere	COUNTRY	(25/42)	6
unserer	COUNTRY	(19/31)	7
unseren	COUNTRY	(7/11)	4
Uns	PARL	(1/2)	2
Unser	COUNTRY	(4/5)	2
Unsere	COUNTRY	(3/4)	2
unseres	COUNTRY	(6/6)	1
unsre	COUNTRY	(1/1)	1
Unsre	COUNTRY	(2/2)	1
Total		(426/1163) Acc=36.6%	

Table 6: Majority baseline, support and no. of distinct labels (DL) per pronoun word form in the test set.

For that, we report results for three baselines and then present transfer learning experiments where we use our automatically created dataset for pre-training and then fine-tune the model on the manually created dataset.

B1: Majority Baseline Our first baseline assigns each pronoun word form its most frequent label (Table 6). This results in an accuracy of 36.6%. The last column shows the number of distinct labels (DL) per pronoun word form in the test set. The three most frequent word forms can occur with nearly any class (*Wir, wir*: 9 DL, *uns*: 8 DL), thus showing the difficulty of this task.

B2: Rule-based Baseline Our second baseline is a rule-based system that simply applies our pre-defined patterns to the testset and labels all matches with the respective labels. We use Snorkel's generative model (see §5) for resolving ties between conflicting rules and report precision, recall and F1 for the rule-based approach. Table 8 (B2) shows that while we obtain a reasonable precision for some patterns (COUNTRY: 92%, PARL: 91%, PARTY: 72%), recall is a huge problem. For the two most difficult patterns, GENERIC and PEOPLE, we obtain not even one correct match.

B3: Feature-based Classification Our third baseline makes use of a conventional feature-based approach to text classification. For that, we consider the following features: (1) tf-idf ngram features (unigrams, bigrams, trigrams) for the left and right context of each 1PL pronoun, (2) the word form of the pronoun, and (3) named entities in the left and right context of the pronoun. We explored different settings for these features

setting	value
left/right context size	20 tokens
bow unigrams	yes
bow bigrams	yes
bow trigrams	no
tfidf	yes
lemmatisation	yes
stopwords	no
feature selection	yes (χ^2)
num features	300
NER in left/right context	no

Table 7: Feature settings used for B3 (feature-based classification, Table 7).

in a 5-fold cross-validation setup and observed best results for the feature values show in Table 7. We tested different classifiers (linear SVM, Ridge regression, SGD, decision trees, AdaBoost, Random Forests) and found that linear SVM gave us best results on our data (49.3% acc.).[8] Table 8 (B3) shows results for the linear SVM classifier. Results for other models and settings were in the range of 35-47% acc.

Transfer Learning Model Our model uses a simple transformer architecture, based on the sentence pair classifier implementation of Simpletransformers[9] and the pretrained `bert-base-german-dbmdz-cased` model.[10] For details on parameter settings, please refer to Table 12 in the appendix. The motivation behind modelling personal pronoun disambiguation as sentence pair classification is that we want to make the model aware of the pronoun's left and right context. For that, we split each instance into two sequences where the first sequence encodes the left context of the pronoun in question and the second sequence includes the pronoun and its right context (see figure 2 below). Please note that our instances encode paragraphs, not sentences, and that S1 and S2 can thus include more than one sentences. In cases where the 1PL pronoun is positioned at the beginning of the paragraph, S1 will be empty.

[8]The models have been implemented with scikit-learn: `https://scikit-learn.org/stable/supervised_learning.html`.

[9]`https://simpletransformers.ai`.

[10]The pretrained models are available from `https://github.com/dbmdz/berts`.

Members of Congress ,	<u>**we**</u> must work ...
S1	S2

Figure 2: Setup for transfer learning using sentence pair classification; S1 encodes the left context of the 1PL pronoun, S2 the pronoun and its right context.

Results for 5-fold cross-validation We now report cross-validation results on our small, manually annotated dataset (Table 9). As we do not have enough data to create a representative validation set for model selection, we report preliminary results for all models (T1, T2, T3) after 25 epochs of training. This procedure has to be taken with a grain of salt and will be addressed, once we have more annotated data.

The results show that even a small number of annotated instances yields substantial improvements over the majority baseline (Table 6) and accuracy increases from 36.6% to over 50%. The results, however, are only slightly higher than the ones for the SVM (Table 8, B2). Table 9, (T2) shows results for merging the hand-annotated data with the noisy labels. In order not to outweigh the manual annotations, we downsampled the additional training data to at most 300 new instances per class. This setting results in only minor improvements (from 50.2 to 50.9% acc.). In our third setting, we use the noisy labels for an additional pretraining step before fine-tuning the model on the hand-annotated data. This yields another small improvement and increases accuracy to 51.8%.

Discussion The somewhat disappointing results for our data augmentation strategy might have several reasons. First, it is conceivable that we need to put more effort into creating a) more precise and b) more diverse rules, and c) to improve coverage. Results on a held-out dataset, created by the same rule-based approach, show that our model is perfectly able to learn the annotations in the weakly supervised data, achieving an accuracy of 97.6% on the held-out data. This shows that despite our efforts to minimise lexical cues and rely more on syntactic patterns, our augmented training data is highly biased and does not enable the model to learn good generalisations for each class.

While improving coverage for the rule-based approach might ameliorate the problem, it is also possible that the pattern-based approach is more

Class	#Gold	#Hits	B2 TP	B2 Prec	B2 Rec	B2 F1	B3 Prec	B3 Rec	B3 F1
BOARD	1	0	0	0	0	0	0	0	0
COUNTRY	411	37	34	92	8	15	53	72	61
GENERIC	67	0	0	0	0	0	35	10	16
GOVERNMENT	167	53	23	45	15	22	41	35	38
PARLIAMENT	299	11	10	91	3	7	47	56	51
PARTY	103	17	13	76	13	22	49	30	37
PEOPLE	13	2	0	0	0	0	0	0	0
SPEC_PERSON	20	1	1	0	6	11	0	0	0
UNION	82	2	1	50	1	3	45	16	23
Total	1,163	123	83	Acc = 7.0%			Acc = 49.3%		

Table 8: Results for rule-based baseline (B2) and for the feature-based classification baseline (B3) (precision, recall and f1 for individual classes and acc. for all instances).

Class	#Gold	T1 Prec	T1 Rec	T1 F1	T2 Prec	T2 Rec	T2 F1	T3 Prec	T3 Rec	T3 F1
BOARD	1	0	0	0	0	0	0	0	0	0
COUNTRY	411	58	65	62	65	63	64	56	66	60
GENERIC	67	29	13	18	20	16	18	50	7	13
GOVERNMENT	167	40	36	38	40	47	43	40	4	7
PARLIAMENT	299	50	64	56	56	54	55	45	78	57
PARTY	103	56	36	44	52	54	53	43	32	36
PEOPLE	13	0	0	0	9	23	13	0	0	0
SPEC_PERSON	20	17	10	12	6	1	8	0	0	0
UNION	82	28	17	21	36	24	29	60	9	16
Total	1,163	Acc = 50.2%			Acc = 50.9%			Acc = 51.8%		

Table 9: Results for 5-fold cross-validation for 3 transfer learning settings. T1: training on testset only; T2: training on testset + augmented data; T3: pretraining on augmented data and fine-tuning on testset (precision, recall and f1 for individual classes and acc. for all instances).

suitable for less ambiguous classification tasks, such as spam detection or offensive language detection, where we only have a small number of classes that are more clearly divided and where it is easier to create patterns with a high precision and coverage.

7 Conclusions

In the paper, we investigated what kinds of collectives 1PL pronouns refer to in parliamentary debates. To this end, we developed an annotation scheme that assigned references to one of nine categories and explored how well human annotators agree when assigning those categories. Our annotation study showed a substantial agreement of $> 0.8\alpha$ between two human raters. We then presented a preliminary analysis of the use of 1PL pronouns as a rhetorical device and pointed to some crucial differences between the parties as well as between members of the government and opposition parties. We subsequently explored how well we are able to automatically resolve ambiguous 1PL pronouns in parliamentary debates, using transfer learning and data augmentation. While our preliminary results are promising, there is room for improvment before we can apply our work to large-scale analysis of pronoun references in political text.

In future work, we plan to improve the accuracy of 1PL pronoun resolution by creating more training data, but also by improving the model itself. Possible ways to do so include providing the model with more information on the speaker, such as the speaker's name, party affiliation or whether or not the speaker is part of the government. Other improvements might come from jointly modelling 1PL pronouns in context, instead of looking at them one at a time.

Acknowledgments

This work was supported in part by the SFB 884 on the Political Economy of Reforms at the University of Mannheim (projects B6 and C4), funded by the German Research Foundation (DFG).

References

Maia Alavidze. 2017. The use of pronouns in political discourse. *International Journal of Arts & Sciences,*

9(4):349–356.

Wendy Allen. 2007. Australian political discourse: Pronominal choice in campaign speeches. In *Selected Papers from the 2006 Conference of the Australian Linguistic Society, ed. by Mushin Ilana and Mary Laughren.*

Adrian Beard. 2000. *The Language of Politics.* London: Routledge.

Nicolette Ruth Bramley. 2001. *Pronouns of politics : the use of pronouns in the construction of 'self' and 'other' in political interviews.* Ph.D. thesis, Faculty of Arts and The Australian National University.

R. Brown and A. Gilman. 1960. The pronouns of power and solidarity. In T. A. Sebeok, editor, *Style in Language*, pages 253–276. MIT Press, Cambridge, Mass.

Peter Bull and Anita Fetzer. 2006. Who are we and who are you? the strategic use of forms of address in political interviews. *Text and Talk*, 26.

Michael Cysouw. 2002. The impact of an inclusive/exclusive opposition on the paradigmatic structure of person marking. In *Pronouns: Grammar and Representation*, pages 41–62. John Benjamins Publishing.

Jessica Håkansson. 2012. The use of personal pronouns in political speeches : A comparative study of the pronominal choices of two american presidents. School of Language and Literature, Linneaus University, Sweden.

Dirk Hovy, Taylor Berg-Kirkpatrick, Ashish Vaswani, and Eduard H. Hovy. 2013. Learning whom to trust with MACE. In *Human Language Technologies: Conference of the North American Chapter of the Association of Computational Linguistics, Proceedings, June 9-14, 2013, Westin Peachtree Plaza Hotel, Atlanta, Georgia, USA*, pages 1120–1130. The Association for Computational Linguistics.

Isabel Íñigo-Mora. 2004. On the use of the personal pronoun we in communities. *Journal of Language and Politics*, 3(1):27–52.

Jan-Christoph Klie, Michael Bugert, Beto Boullosa, Richard Eckart de Castilho, and Iryna Gurevych. 2018. The inception platform: Machine-assisted and knowledge-oriented interactive annotation. In *Proceedings of the 27th International Conference on Computational Linguistics: System Demonstrations*, pages 5–9. Association for Computational Linguistics.

Cas Mudde. 2004. The populist zeitgeist. *Government and Opposition*, 39:541–563.

Cas Mudde and Cristóbal Rovira Kaltwasser. 2017. *Populism: A very short introduction.* Oxford, UK: Oxford University Press.

Katarzyna Proctor and Lily I-Wen Su. 2011. The 1st person plural in political discourse – American politicians in interviews and in a debate. *Journal of Pragmatics*, 43(13):3251–3266.

Randolph Quirk, Sidney Greenbaum, Geoffrey Leech, and Jan Svartvik. 1985. *A Comprehensive Grammar of the English Language.* Longman, London.

Alexander Ratner, Stephen H. Bach, Henry R. Ehrenberg, Jason A. Fries, Sen Wu, and Christopher Ré. 2020. Snorkel: rapid training data creation with weak supervision. *VLDB J.*, 29(2-3):709–730.

Alexander J. Ratner, Christopher De Sa, Sen Wu, Daniel Selsam, and Christopher Ré. 2016. Data programming: Creating large training sets, quickly. In *Advances in Neural Information Processing Systems 29: Annual Conference on Neural Information Processing Systems 2016, December 5-10, 2016, Barcelona, Spain*, pages 3567–3575.

Joanne Scheibman. 2014. Referentiality, predicate patterns, and functions of we-utterances in American English interactions. In Theodossia-Soula Pavlidou, editor, *Constructing Collectivity: 'We' Across Languages and Contexts*, pages 23–43.

Jukka Tyrkkö. 2016. Looking for rhetorical thresholds: Pronoun frequencies in political speeches. *Studies in Variation, Contacts and Change in English*, 17.

Milica Vuković. 2012. Positioning in pre-prepared and spontaneous parliamentary discourse: Choice of person in the parliament of montenegro. *Discourse & Society*, (2):184–202.

Kate Wales. 1996. *Personal Pronouns in Present-Day English.* Cambridge: CUP.

A Appendices

Category	Description	Examples
COUNTRY	Refers to the country as a geo-political unit or to all citizens of this country. TEST: can be replaced by • "we Germans" • "our country" • "the German X"	**Wir** haben 2 Weltkriege verloren. **Wir** sind Exportweltmeister. **Wir** sind Papst. **Wir** als nationale Schicksalsgemeinschaft. **Wir** dürfen uns nicht vom Rest der Welt abschotten. **Unser** Grundgesetz / unsere Demokratie
PEOPLE	Refers to a (possibly large) group of people that are not defined by their nationality but by shared social variables or characteristics such as age, gender, class, religion, profession, ... Also used for references to society that are not limited to Germany as a geo-political unit.	wie **wir** Christen uns verhalten **Wir** als arbeitende Bevölkerung **Wir** Älteren, **Wir** Rentner **Wir** Steuerzahler, **Wir** Pendler
PARTY	Refers to members of a specific party (including coalitions of like-minded parties, e.g., on the supranational level)	**Unser** Antrag geht einen entscheidenden Schritt... **Wir** werden diese Regierung weiter kritisieren. **Wir** Liberale haben schon vor Jahren gesagt, ...
PARL	Refers to all members of the parliament (also references to both, government and opposition)	**Wir** Abgeordnete sind vom Volk gewählt. In diesem Haus debattieren **wir** heute... Lassen Sie **uns** diesen Antrag heute beschließen.
GOVERN	Refers to all members of the government	**Wir** haben entscheidende Schritte getan, um die Digitalisierung zu fördern. **Wir** haben Familien entlastet und die Arbeitslosigkeit bekämpft
UNION	Refers to geo-political groups on a supranational level, e.g., the EU, the NATO, etc.	**Wir** in der EU müssen zusammen einen Weg finden, wie wir unsere Sicherheitspolitik gestalten.
SPEC_PERS (GROUPS)	Refers to groups of specific individuals or members of more than one group	Sie haben die PKK und die YPG in einen Topf geworfen, **wir** sind aber nicht deckungsgleich. Frau Merkel und ich, **wir** haben darüber lange diskutiert. **Wir**, die deutsche und die israelische Regierung
GENERIC	Generic uses of *we/us* that can be replaced by *one/you* (German: man/es gibt) or *unser/e* can be replaced by *diese*. We assume a generic reading if *we/us* refers to the whole world/universe.	Das brauchen **wir** überall in der Welt → das braucht man überall... In den letzten Jahren haben **wir** viel über den Wandel der Gesellschaft gehört → hat man viel gehört über... Woran **wir** uns noch in 100 Jahren erinnern werden → Woran man sich noch in... die schwierigen Probleme **unserer** Zeit → dieser Zeit In einer Welt, in der **wir** über 222 gewaltsam ausgetragene Konflikte haben → in der es ... gibt
BOARD	Refers to members of a board / commission / committee /political organisation on the subnational level (subgroups of the parliament/government)	**Wir** haben im Untersuchungsausschuss viel diskutiert... Im Coronakabinett haben **wir** beschlossen... Im Agrarausschuss haben **wir** ...

Table 10: Overview of the annotation scheme for 1PL references in parliamentary debates.

A1 / A2	BOARD	COUNTRY	GENERIC	GOVREN	PARL	PARTY	PEOPLE	SPECPER	UNION
BOARD	0	0	0	0	0	0	0	0	0
COUNTRY	0	385	8	4	14	3	1	3	12
GENERIC	0	4	46	1	13	0	2	0	1
GOVERN	0	7	1	146	8	7	0	1	4
PARL	1	8	14	2	248	0	2	4	4
PARTY	0	1	0	2	5	96	0	0	1
PEOPLE	0	1	2	0	2	0	11	0	0
SPECPER	0	0	0	0	0	0	1	10	0
UNION	0	1	2	4	0	1	0	2	61

Table 11: Confusion matrix for the manual resolution of referents of ambiguous pronouns in parliamentary debates (A1: Annotator 1, A2: Annotator 2).

Name	Value
attention_probs_dropout_prob	0.1
hidden_act	gelu
hidden_dropout_prob	0.1
hidden_size	768
layer_norm_eps	1e-12
max_position_embeddings	512
num_attention_heads	12
num_hidden_layers	12
transformers_version	4.6.1
type_vocab_size	2
vocab_size	31102

Table 12: Parameters/settings used in our experiments.

Examining the Effects of Preprocessing on the Detection of Offensive Language in German Tweets

Sebastian Reimann
Uppsala University
Department of Linguistics
reimann.sebastian9483@gmail.com

Daniel Dakota
Uppsala University
Department of Linguistics
ddakota@lingfil.uu.se

Abstract

Preprocessing is essential for creating more effective features and reducing noise in classification, especially in user-generated data (e.g. Twitter). How each individual preprocessing decision changes an individual classifier's behavior is not universal. We perform a series of ablation experiments in which we examine how classifiers behave based on individual preprocessing steps when detecting offensive language in German. While preprocessing decisions for traditional classifier approaches are not as varied, we note that pre-trained BERT models are far more sensitive to each decision and do not behave identically to each other. We find that the cause of much variation between classifiers has to do with the interactions specific preprocessing steps have on the overall vocabulary distributions, and, in the case of BERT models, how this interacts with the WordPiece tokenization.

1 Introduction

The task of abusive language detection has become increasingly popular for a variety of languages (Zampieri et al., 2019; Basile et al., 2019; Al-Khalifa et al., 2020). German specifically has had two shared tasks on the topic, one in 2018 (Wiegand et al., 2018) and a second in 2019 (Struß et al., 2019).

Not only is offensive language detection somewhat subjective in nature, particularly in the need for contextual requirements, but is often examined through user generated mediums, creating another layer of complexity to successfully identify possible abusive language. Often, in order to create more useful features out of the text for the classifier, we must first treat the text to reduce the noise. While for standard feature generation via count vectors the impact is far more obvious (e.g. reduction of feature space), even when we feed a dense vector representations to a classifier (e.g. a sentence embedding), that embedding still represents the textual representation, simply in an alternative way. Thus, it too is influenced by individual alterations to the text. With languages that show large variation in dialect preferences and orthographic representations, this has been shown to be particularly important (Husain, 2020).

Twitter has proven to be a typical source for not only research on offensive language, but also necessitating additional preprocessing approaches given its different style of communication and lexicon. In this work we look to perform a set of ablation experiments in which we evaluate how different preprocessing techniques impact classifier behavior over three different approaches to classification when detecting offensive language in German Twitter. We seek to answer the following questions:

1. How do different preprocessing techniques influence performance across different classifiers?

2. Can we identify features within different preproccesing techniques that can help explain specific classifier behaviors?

2 Related Work

2.1 Data

Ross et al. (2016) introduced a Twitter corpus of offensive language detection, examining the 2015 refugee crisis. They predominantly focused on user's perceptions of hate speech and the reliability of annotations. They found that agreement among annotators was relatively low and that also the opinions of users asked in a survey diverge greatly and thus stress the necessity of specific guidelines. However, even with such guidelines, annotators can still show large differences (Nobata et al., 2016).

Task 2 of the GermEval 2018 shared task (Wiegand et al., 2018) focused on detecting offensive and non-offensive Tweets and was further examined in GermEval 2019 (Struß et al., 2019).

A different approach was taken by Zufall et al. (2019) who instead label offensive Tweets based on whether they may be punishable by law or not. This decision is based on two criteria: the type of target and the type of offense. A Tweet may be punishable if it is targeted at either a living individual or a specific group of people, and if it expresses either a wrong factual claim, abusive insults, or abusive criticism.

2.2 Classifiers

Abusive language detection in German has shown a great deal of variation across classifiers and feature thresholds (Steimel et al., 2019). In the 2018 shared tasks, SVMs were a popular choice (Wiegand et al., 2018), achieving effective results. Popular features include pre-trained word embeddings, mostly either fastText (Bojanowski et al., 2017) or word2vec (Mikolov et al., 2013), and lexical features based on polarity lexicons or lexicons on offensive language and effective results were achieved with only a few hundred features (De Smedt and Jaki, 2018). Other classifiers included standard Decision Trees or Boosted Classifiers, but tended to yield slightly worse performance (Scheffler et al., 2018).

The most effective approaches tended to use ensemble classifiers: CNNs with logit averaging (von Grünigen et al., 2018), a combination of RNNs and CNNs (Stammbach et al., 2018), or combination of Random Forest classifiers (Montani and Schüller, 2018).

With the introduction of BERT (Devlin et al., 2019), the 2019 shared task saw a different trend, with many participants submitting fine-tuned models (Struß et al., 2019). Paraschiv and Cercel (2019) pre-trained a BERT model on German Twitter data, obtaining the best reported macro F-score of 76.95. Other approaches included fine-tuning an ensemble of BERT models trained on different German textual sources (Risch et al., 2019).

SVMs continued to be a popular choice however, with some systems achieving results almost equal to BERT-based approaches by using word embeddings pre-trained on German Tweets and lexical features (Schmid et al., 2019).

2.3 Preprocessing

Angiani et al. (2016) experimented with the preprocessing methods of replacement of emoticons with a text representation, replacing negation contractions such as *don't* with *do not*, detection of spelling errors, stemming, and removal of stopwords for general sentiment analysis on Twitter data. Using a Naive Bayes classifier to classify whether the sentiment was positive, neutral or negative, most techniques yielded slight improvements over the baseline with little preprocessing.

While Risch et al. (2019) had a minimalistic approach to preprocessing and only normalized user names, Paraschiv and Cercel (2019), whose contribution performed best in the GermEval 2019 shared task, made use of a wide range of preprocessing methods when fine-tuning BERT. They replaced emojis with spelled-out representations; removed the #-character at the beginning of hashtags and split hashtags into words; transformed usernames, weblinks, newline markers, numbers, dates and timestamps to standard tokens; and manually corrected spelling errors. They however do not explicitly state how much this contributed to achieving a higher performance.

Schmid et al. (2019) lowercased and lemmatized words, while also removing the #-character of the hashtag and stop words when creating features for their SVM. Sentiment scores were also obtained for emojis through the sentiment ranking for emojis by Kralj Novak et al. (2015) and added to the sentiment scores obtained trough SentiWS (Remus et al., 2010) for all words in the sentence. Both scores were treated as separate features and ranged range from -1 to 1. Scheffler et al. (2018) also lemmatized and removed stop words, but did not explicitly state their treatment of hashtags and capitalization for their experiments involving SVMs, decision tree, and boosted classifiers. Moreover, they did not include emojis when modeling a sentiment score as one of their features.

3 Methodology

3.1 Data

For all experiments, we use the the dataset from the GermEval 2019 Task 2 (Struß et al., 2019). Tweets were sampled from a range of political spectrums and labeled as either OFFENSE or OTHER for the binary classification task (see Table 1 for data splits).

	OFFENSE	OTHER	Total
Train	1287	2709	3996
Test	970	2061	3031

Table 1: Train and Test Data Splits

3.2 Preprocessing

Base Methods Lemmatization is a relatively common preprocessing step applied in the shared task of Wiegand et al. (2018), examples include Scheffler et al. (2018) and Schmid et al. (2019), on which we base our experimental setup for our SVM and AdaBoost classifiers. Consequently, we lemmatize all words[1] for our AdaBoost and SVM experiments. A second base step, carried out in all experiments, including those when fine-tuning BERT for classification, is replacing user names with the token USER.

Emojis We try the approaches in the contributions to the GermEval 2019 shared task by both Paraschiv and Cercel (2019), who replaced emojis with textual representations, and Risch et al. (2019), who did not adress emojis in preprocessing, respectively. Additionally, we calculate for the non-neural classifiers an emoji sentiment score, also through the ranking of Kralj Novak et al. (2015), together with sentiment scores for words, through SentiWS (Remus et al., 2010). Unlike Paraschiv and Cercel (2019) however, who use English descriptions of emojis, we translate the descriptions into German.[2]

Hashtags We remove the #-character at the beginning of each hashtag. Additionally, we try splitting camel-cased hashtags as done by Paraschiv and Cercel (2019).

Capitalization We perform three strategies: retaining the original capitalization, lowercasing the entire text, and truecasing. Truecasing is "the process of restoring case information to raw text" (Lita et al., 2003). For German, this is beneficial since it keeps orthographic characteristics (e.g. all nouns are capitalized) but removes situational one (e.g. words capitalized only because they begin a sentence). Additionally, Risch et al. (2019) point out that in their experiments, for words written in Caps Lock, each letter is frequently recognized as a separate token. Additionally, truccasing has been shown to be useful for NLP on noisy data (Lita et al., 2003).

Truecasing the test and training data is performed by using the truecasing scripts from the Moses system (Koehn et al., 2007), which are normally used for statistical machine translation. We create a truecasing model by training on a large, cleaned, preprocessed German Wikipedia Text Corpus.[3] We use the SoMaJo tokenizer for German social media data (Proisl and Uhrig, 2016) to tokenize the Twitter data.

3.3 Classifiers

All hyperparameter optimization is performed using a 5-fold cross validation and results for all experiments are reported using macro-averaged F scores since the dataset is imbalanced and we wish to give equal weight to both the minority and majority classes.

SVM The features for the SVM (Boser et al., 1992) are similar to the ones used in the second system of Schmid et al. (2019), where pre-trained fastText vectors (Bojanowski et al., 2017) were used to create Tweet level vector representations. We initially experimented with a set of fastText vectors pre-trained on a smaller set of Twitter data as well as with different dimensions, but results were poor relative to other pre-trained fastText embeddings. We ultimately settled on on the default 300 dimensional fastText German embeddings (Grave et al., 2018), trained on the German CommonCrawl and Wikpedia, as they yielded the most stable performance.

We also add a binary feature which signals if a Tweet contains one or more German slurs from the slur dictionary of Hyperhero,[4] similar to that of Scheffler et al. (2018) and Schmid et al. (2019), although we do not manually create a lexicon of offensive terms as performed by the latter. The vectors plus the binary feature and the sentiment scores are concatenated and fed to the SVM.

We use a linear kernel and in order to reduce attributes with greater numerical ranges from dominating, we perform feature scaling (Hsu et al., 2008), and only hyperparameterize for the regularization parameter C.[5]

[1] We use spaCy.

[2] Translations are done using Google Translate.

[3] https://github.com/t-systems-on-site-services-gmbh/german-wikipedia-text-corpus

[4] http://www.hyperhero.com/de/insults.htm

[5] We only optimize C for 0.1, 1, 10 and 100

Iterators	10	50	100	500	
Learning Rate	0.0001	0.001	0.01	0.1	1

Table 2: Values for the grid search for hyperparameter tuning for the AdaBoost experiments

Epochs	2
Batch Size	32
Maximum Length	150
Learning Rate	2e-5
Optimizer	Adam
Loss Function	Cross-Entropy Loss

Table 3: Hyperparameters for fine-tuning BERT

AdaBoost Additionally, we experiment with AdaBoost (Freund and Schapire, 1996) as it was used by Scheffler et al. (2018). AdaBoost is a boosting technique that will combine multiple weak classifiers (in our cases tree stumps) by giving more weight to incorrectly classified training instances, importantly without large weight reduction to the correctly classified instances. We also hyperparameterize using grid search following values taken from Brownlee (2020).

BERT We use both the *bert-base-german-cased*[6] and the *dbmdz/bert-base-german-cased*[7], referring to them as DeepAI and dbmdz respectively hereafter. The DeepAI model was pre-trained on a German Wikipedia dump, the OpenLegal dump, a large data collection involving German court decisions, and 3.6 GB of news articles. This data was cleaned and segmented into sentences by the spaCy library. The dbmdz model was pre-trained on a collection of Wikipedia, the EU Bookshop corpus, Open Subtitles, CommonCrawl, ParaCrawl, and NewsCrawl. Both models make use of a WordPiece vocabulary which was created through the WordPiece tokenizer (Wu et al., 2016). As neither are pre-trained on any particular social media text, we assume that they are not well equipped to handle more common social media orthographic standards, such as hashtags and emojis. Following Risch et al. (2019) we fine-tune for two epochs using a batch size of 32 (see Table 3 for all hyperparameters).

4 Results

First we must note that we ran some BERT models with different initial seeds and noted instabilities in performance. Given this, results should not be viewed as entirely explained by the different preprocessing choices, rather and indication of the volatility of the models in interaction with preprocessing. We are more interested in highlighting the interaction and variation across BERT models and preprocessing than determining an optimal solution. For this reason, we only report scores using the default seed in order to allow a better analysis (see Section 5) in terms of linking observed differences to specific preprocessing choices, and interaction with both the WordPiece tokenization and the vocabulary distribution.

We first begin by establishing baselines for each classifier, in which minimal preprocessing is performed. For BERT, we only replaced user names with a USER token (baseline BERT in Table 4). For the SVM and AdaBoost we perform the former, but since we experiment with two different ways of treating emojis (replacement vs. inclusion in sentiment scores) and want to compare the results against an experiment where emojis are not taken into account at all, we additionally remove emojis in our baseline here and lemmatize all words (baseline SVM/AdaBoost in Table 4).

In Table 4 we present F-scores for our ablation experiments. We can see that AdaBoost tends to exhibit a degradation in performance in respect to performing only base preprocessing operations when any additional preprocessing techniques are applied. The only exception tends to be in experiments that have a combination of splitting hashtags and truecasing. This may simply be due a reduction of overall features, but it is not inherently clear what is causing the degradation.

The SVM tends to outperform AdaBoost overall, which is in line with Scheffler et al. (2018) though only in a couple of instances, shows any noticeable improvements. Lowercasing, as performed in Schmid et al. (2019), leads here to the biggest drop in performance. Surprisingly, the classification overall does not profit from the information offered by emojis, as both the experiment with emoji replacement as well as the experiment with only basic preprocessing and without emoji removal do not perform above the baseline. This also holds true for emoji replacement in combination with splitting hashtags since the performance here is slightly worse than for only splitting hashtags. Interestingly, we see that only truecasing the data yields the best performing model, and that, similar to AdaBoost, a

[6]https://deepset.ai/german-bert
[7]https://github.com/dbmdz/berts

Experiment	AdaBoost	SVM	DeepAI	dbmdz
emojis removed (baseline SVM/AdaBoost)	66.74	66.81	72.74	69.04
only basic methods (baseline BERT)	66.90	66.78	71.31	71.93
replacing emojis	66.39	66.23	71.34	72.60
splitting hashtags	66.20	66.90	68.62	**74.49**
only truecasing	66.09	**67.64**	73.25	69.13
replacing emojis + splitting hashtags + lowercasing	64.62	64.33	70.04	73.32
splitting hashtags + truecasing	**67.65**	66.74	**73.62**	71.85
replacing emojis + splitting hashtags	66.62	66.78	73.10	70.88
replacing emojis + splitting hashtags + truecasing	67.31	67.23	72.68	71.33

Table 4: F1-macro Scores for All Classifiers

combination of truecasing with emoji replacement and splitting hashtags led to improvments over the baseline as well, although here, splitting hashtags and truecasing without emoji replacement led to a slight decrease.

One striking difference is the performance of DeepAI vs dbmdz and their behaviors not only in respect to the preprocessing techniques, but also to each other. Firstly, we see that the baselines are slightly different and all applied preprocessing techniques benefit dbmdz, even if minimally, compared to DeepAI, where we some techniques result in worse performance relative to the baseline. Additionally, we can see that in some cases, the models actually have opposite behaviors. For example, simply splitting hashtags resulted in the best performance for dbmdz, yet was the worst performance for DeepAI. A counter example is only truecasing which yielded minimal performance gains for dbmdz but produced the second best results for DeepAI.

5 Analysis

While results for AdaBoost and the SVM do show some variation, the DeepAI and dbmdz exhibit much more noticeable changes. For this reason, we choose to examine only these two model in terms of how the minority and majority classes are behaving in order to try and glean insight into the underlying causes. Table 5 shows the precision and recall of classes for the these models. We can clearly see a great deal of volatility on the minority (OFFENSE) class, particularly on recall. This could again be because of a general instability but it may also suggest that, querying Tweets deemed offensive is far more sensitive to the preprocessing methods than labeling them correctly when the models are being fine-tuned. We perform a more in-depth analysis into possible reasons behind the variations between all classifiers and present the findings below.

5.1 Emojis

Without emoji replacement, the WordPiece tokenization used by the BERT models splits the unicode representations into single letters or chunks of two or three numbers. It can be assumed that these models cannot effectively make use of such representations. Replacing emojis with text on the other hand presents a way to retain the meaning of the emoji in the text, which seems to have helped DeepAI in particular in finding offensive tweets as all experiments with emoji replacement constantly outperform its baseline with respect to recall for the OFFENSE class.

One example is the case of the middle finger emoji, for which emoji replacement helps detect offensive Tweets. It occurs in 37 Tweets, 35 of which have the gold label OFFENSE. The DeepAI model trained on truecased data with emoji replacement managed to correctly label 13 of these without wrongly classifying posts that were labeled as OTHER. Table 6 shows how many of these 13 instances were detected DeepAI when different preprocessing methods were applied. This suggests that replacing emojis improves detecting offensive Tweets when the middle finger emoji is present. In the experiment with emoji replacement + hashtag splitting + lowercasing however, one of the two non-offensive Tweets was wrongly classified as offensive.

Replacing emojis also present some pitfalls. One such case for the DeepAI BERT classifier is related to the winking face emoji, which is not inherently associated with offensive behavior. However, the models trained on data where emojis were replaced

Experiment	DeepAI OFFENSE Prec.	DeepAI OFFENSE Rec.	DeepAI OTHER Prec.	DeepAI OTHER Rec.	dbmdz OFFENSE Prec.	dbmdz OFFENSE Rec.	dbmdz OTHER Prec.	dbmdz OTHER Rec.
emojis removed (baseline SVM/AdaBoost)	66.27	57.94	81.31	83.65	**84.09**	38.14	76.84	**96.60**
only basic methods (baseline BERT)	**78.62**	44.74	78.38	**94.27**	80.15	45.36	78.65	94.71
replacing emojis	58.51	**66.60**	**83.19**	77.78	73.36	50.82	79.78	91.31
splitting hashtags	75.78	40.31	76.98	93.93	72.27	**56.70**	**81.50**	89.76
only truecasing	69.49	55.88	80.99	88.45	82.31	38.87	76.95	96.07
replacing emojis + splitting hashtags + lowercasing	67.67	48.56	78.63	89.08	73.73	52.37	80.27	91.22
splitting hashtags + truecasing	77.24	50.72	80.03	92.96	77.49	46.49	78.81	93.64
replacing emojis + splitting hashtags	67.55	57.53	81.32	87.00	75.91	45.15	78.32	93.26
replacing emojis + splitting hashtags + truecasing	62.36	63.71	82.75	81.90	77.23	45.46	78.50	93.69

Table 5: Class Results for BERT DeepAI and dbmdz

Preprocessing	# of Tweets
emoji + splitting hashtags + lowercasing	10
truecasing	5
splitting hashtags + truecasing	3
baseline	2

Table 6: Number of Tweets classified as offensive by DeepAI BERT, out of the 13 Tweets with the middle finger emoji that were classified correctly in the experiment involving emoji replacement, hashtag splitting and truecasing

had a surprisingly high tendency to misclassify non-offensive Tweets containing this emoji with 9 (hashtag splitting + truecasing) and 15 (hashtag splitting + lowercasing) instances respectively wrongly considered to be offensive language. This suggests that they may have learned to associate the emoji in an unintended manner, especially as, in most cases, the emoji occurs in contexts without other elements that may potentially cause the classification as offensive.

Emoji replacing also helps the SVM classifier in detecting offensive Tweets that contain the middle finger emoji as in both the experiment with emoji replacement only and emoji replacement in combination with hashtag splitting and truecasing, 29 out of the 35 offensive Tweets with this emoji were classified as offensive. This in contrast to the experiment with only hashtag splitting and the experiment with neither emoji replacement nor hashtag splitting, in which 12 of these instances were not classified correctly. This may however be traced back to the fact that the middle finger emoji is not in the ranking of Kralj Novak et al. (2015). Their ranking of most frequent emojis was determined from Tweets collected between 2013 and 2015, while the middle finger emoji was only introduced in 2014. Given this, it is not surprising that the emoji was not in the top 750 most frequently used. This demonstrates a limitation of even newer external social media lexicons, as the medium of communication is rapidly evolving and even emojis can be time sensitive with the introduction of new ones, the discontinuation of older ones, or simply a decrease in usage.

Another interesting observation from the SVM experiments that included emoji replacement is the classification of Tweets containing the pig face emoji. While 14 Tweets contain the pig face emoji, only three have the gold label of OFFENSE. However, the SVM strongly prefers classifying Tweets with this emoji as offensive, as it does so in 11 cases. The classifier trained and tested on data where only hashtags were split but no emojis were replaced recognized the majority of the non-offensive instances correctly.

In the experiments with emoji replacement, this emoji was replaced with the word *Schweinegesicht* ("pig face"), which is included in Hyperhero's dictionary of German slurs. This results in Tweets with this specific replacement being marked as containing slurs, even if they are not labeled as OFFENSIVE. On the other hand, the sentiment score of the pig face emoji according to the ranking of Kralj Novak et al. (2015) was 0.375 and thus relatively neutral, which gives credence to the idea that emoji replacement was decisive for the wrong classifications.

Moreover, in the training data the word *Schwein* ("pig") occurs quite often in offensive Tweets. Given the use of character-level embeddings via fastText, there may be similarity between compound words that contain one or more subwords that may deemed offensive on their own, but not necessarily within the compound itself. Thus, it may be that the representations of *Schweinegesicht* and *Schwein* in the training data are inherently similar enough in vector space and are thus influencing their wrongly classified instances here.

	Basic	S-HT
Misclassified by Adaboost	95	80
Of which correct in Baseline	75	61
Misclassified by SVM	45	46
Of which correct in Baseline	4	5

Table 7: Tweets containing emoijs misclassified as offensive in two experiments with the AdaBoost classifier and the SVM classifier with Only Basic Methods (Basic) and Splitting Hashtags (S-HT)

For the AdaBoost classifier, similar patterns concerning the pig face emoji and the middle finger emoji are observed. Moreover, it seems that using sentiment scores for emojis in the AdaBoost experiments led to a general increase in the amount of Tweets with emojis being misclassified as offensive. Table 7 compared the misclassified examples that contain emojis in experiments, where emojis were turned to sentiment scores without hashtag splitting and with emoji scores and hashtag splitting, for both SVM and AdaBoost. It also shows how many of these wrongly classified instances were classified correctly in the respective baseline experiment. The numbers suggest that while the problem occurs also for the SVM classifier, it is not as pronounced and the differences between the two experiments under observation and the baseline are much less drastic.

5.2 Hashtags

For DeepAI, splitting hashtags and truecasing produced the best model. However, upon closer inspection, the impact of splitting hashtags does not seem to be as pronounced, albeit still positive. In the test set, only 147 Tweets require splitting of camel-cased hashtags, of which only 66 instances resulted in a different classification upon splitting (43 correctly classified, 23 incorrectly).

Instead, hashtag splitting results in a more natural tokenization by the WordPiece tokenizer used by each BERT model given its source data. For example, #HambacherForst (name of a German forest that was supposed to be cleared) is split correctly by DeepAI into ##Ham ##bacher Forst whereas when hashtag splitting is not performed, the tokenization is ##Ham ##bacher ##For ##st. The method of hashtag splitting however can produce errors. The abbreviation of the German party *AfD* for example is recognized as camel-cased and split into *Af* and *D* as separate tokens. Additionally, hashtag splitting is not always successful when one word in the hashtag is not written with a capital letter, such as #VerhöhnungderMaueropfer ("mockery of the victims of the Berlin Wall"), which is split into *Verhöhnungder*, the German word for *mockery* plus the article *(der)*, and *Maueropfer*.

Splitting hashtags leads in both cases to a lower number of subword tokens in terms of both the overall number of tokens produced as well as the number of individual token types present after a WordPiece tokenization is applied (see section 5.4 for more discussion on vocabulary distributions). This suggests that the WordPiece tokenizer for both models struggles in splitting hashtags into representative subwords, if hashtag splitting is not performed. This decrease in subword tokens is slightly higher for the dbmdz model, suggesting that without hashtag splitting, the the dbmdz WordPiece tokenizer creates more unwanted splits and thus, that the necessity for hashtag splitting may be greater for dbmdz than for the DeepAI.

Similarly, in the SVM experiments, hashtag splitting only had marginal effect. In most of the examples, the decision on whether the Tweet can be considered offensive or not was the same, regardless of where the hashtag was split hashtags, as no clear pattern emerged when examining Tweets that were classified differently.

5.3 Capitalization

No obvious positive effects could be observed when only changing the capitalization of the data before lemmatizing it in the experiments with AdaBoost, but a slightly positive effect is noted for the SVM. Indeed, a comparsion between the experiment involving base preprocessing and truecasing, shows that there are 27 offensive examples where truecasing changed the capitalization, and which were detected in the former but not in the latter setting. However, none of the truecased words in these examples seemed to be obviously decisive for the correct classification. Truecasing also seemed to have had a positive effect on the performance of DeepAI as seen in example (1):

(1) *seufz und bennent die WLAN SSID mal wieder in "FICKT LEISER!üm*"

sight and rename the WLAN SSID once again to "FUCK QUIETER!"

In experiments, where the original casing of the data remained untouched, the tag OTHER was used, whereas DeepAI trained on truecased text with emojis replaced and camel-cased hashtags split correctly labeled it as offensive.

The tokenizer of the baseline model tokenized it FI ##C ##K ##T L##E ##IS ##ER, thus treating almost each capital letter as a different subword unit. The crucial part that renders the sentence offensive was tokenized wrongly here, and the logical consequence is that it remained undetected. The truecased sentence on the other hand was split into f ##ickt lei ##ser. Even though, this tokenization is not completely in line with the intuitively correct one (fick##t leise##r), it seemingly made it easier for the model to recognize the offensive language.

The fact that even the tokenization for the truecased text does not seem to be ideal is underlined by the fact that, for example, the setting using only truecased text without replacing emojis or splitting camel-cased hashtags did not manage to classify this sentence as offensive, a decision which cannot be explained by the absence of the other two preprocessing steps.

However, the truecasing approach sometimes struggles with sentences that were entirely written in Caps Lock, where it simply did not change anything, as well as with English words since it was trained entirely on German data.

While lowercasing helped in the case of example (1) since it was also lowercased and the Tweet was labeled correctly, this is not always the case and at times, lowercasing is not helpful. In example (2), *Einzelheiten* was turned to *einzelheiten* and *Veranstaltung* to *veranstaltung*. A consequence of lowercasing was that the DeepAI struggled to recognize the nouns. Lowercased *einzelheiten* was then split into einzel ##heiten and *veranstaltung* resulted in *veranst* ##altung. For the truecased data, where the original capitalization was retained, the tokenizer recognized both nouns correctly.

(2) @dr0pr0w @kinzig9 Gibt es irgendwo mehr Einzelheiten yu der Veranstaltung?

@dr0pr0w @kinzig9 are there more details anywhere about the event?

Truecasing seemingly had a higher impact on the performance for DeepAI than dbmdz. A reason for this may lie in the way the respective WordPieces tokenizers for each model splits up words into subword units. In cases where non-capitalized words are written with sentence initialized capitalization, DeepAI splits these words up in an unnatural manner. The interrogative pronoun *Wozu* ("for what") at the beginning of a sentence is split into *Wo* and *zu*, the adverb *Gestern* ("yesterday") is split into *Gest* and *ern* and the verb *Geht* is split into *Geh* and *t*. When they are converted into their original, lowercased form, DeepAI does not split the words, while dbmdz, on the other hand, manages to recognize them correctly as one word without needing extra truecasing.

5.4 Vocabulary Distributions

We perform a high-level analysis on both the fastText and WordPiece coverage of the training data. For fastText, coverage ranges between 88.01-90.26% in terms of overall token coverage in the training data, with token types ranging from 69.72-71.40%, with the exception being the preprocessing setting of replacing emojis+splitting hashtags+lowercasing (which also had the lowest overall token coverage) yielding a type coverage of only 59.23%.

For DeepAI, a similar trend is seen with its WordPiece coverage. This specific setting shows over 3,000 fewer subtoken types after tokenization even though it produces overall more subtokens. These distributions may also explain the emojis+splitting hashtags+lowercasing results seen in Table 4, as this setting yields the worst performance for AdaBoost, the SVM, and DeepAI. It is also clear that while the other preprocessing distributions may yield similar coverage, the individual token distributions are not the same. These effects are evident in Table 5 in the high volatility of reported recall metrics for the OFFENSE class.

Similary however, the WordPiece tokenization by dbmdz yields a far lower number of token types in the emojis+splitting hashtags+lowercasing setting, and produces over 16000 more tokens, but does not show the same degradation in performance. Interestingly, dbmdz contains anywhere between 700-1000 more found token types in the training than its DeepAI counterpart for each preprocessing setting, and an average of 2-3% more overall total token coverage ($\approx$ 97% to 94% respectively). This just further emphasizes that the distributional coverage is not easily disentangled from the individual impact the combined feature sets (or even a single feature) have on classification, since the subtoken representations and distributions are not identical.

6 Conclusion

We have performed an in-depth analysis on the effects that preprocessing has on the performance of different classifiers on the detection of abusive language in German Tweets. While the fact that fine-tuned BERT models outperform more traditional machine learning approaches is not surprising, they however appear to be extremely sensitive to preprocessing decisions and different models behave somewhat unexpectedly, particularly when contrasted to each other. Standard preprocessing techniques, such as hashtag splitting, yield two very different behaviors from the the models, which, on the surface, is not intuitive.

Our analysis shows that the underlying word representations created by the various preprocessing techniques interact with the vocabulary coverage of fastText and the WordPiece tokenizer and plays a crucial role. Each individual preprocessing step is altering these distributions within the data which then derives slightly different sentence representations when generating sentence level embedding representations, the effects of which are not always clearly understood on the surface level. This is highlighted when some preprocessing steps, which would seem intuitively helpful, ultimately yield a degradation in performance.

Future areas of research include examining model stability with respect to preprocessing, and how preprocessing interacts with models that have been pre-trained on Twitter data with an updated WordPiece tokenizer. A deeper look at then identifying specific (sub)tokens that carry more decision making power through techniques, such as saliency (Li et al., 2016), would be of valuable insight.

References

Hend Al-Khalifa, Walid Magdy, Kareem Darwish, Tamer Elsayed, and Hamdy Mubarak, editors. 2020. *Proceedings of the 4th Workshop on Open-Source Arabic Corpora and Processing Tools, with a Shared Task on Offensive Language Detection*. European Language Resource Association, Marseille, France.

Giulio Angiani, Laura Ferrari, Tomaso Fontanini, Paolo Fornacciari, Eleonora Iotti, Federico Magliani, and Stefano Manicardi. 2016. A comparison between preprocessing techniques for sentiment analysis in twitter. In *Proceedings of the 2nd International Workshop on Knowledge Discovery on the WEB*, Cagliari, Italy.

Valerio Basile, Cristina Bosco, Elisabetta Fersini, Debora Nozza, Viviana Patti, Francisco Manuel Rangel Pardo, Paolo Rosso, and Manuela Sanguinetti. 2019. Semeval-2019 task 5: Multilingual detection of hate speech against immigrants and women in twitter. In *Proceedings of the 13th International Workshop on Semantic Evaluation*, pages 54–63.

Piotr Bojanowski, Edouard Grave, Armand Joulin, and Tomas Mikolov. 2017. Enriching word vectors with subword information. *Transactions of the Association for Computational Linguistics*, 5:135–146.

Bernhard E. Boser, Isabelle M. Guyon, and Vladimir N. Vapnik. 1992. A training algorithm for optimal margin classifiers. In *Proceedings of the Fifth Annual Workshop on Computational Learning Theory*, COLT '92, page 144–152, New York, NY, USA. Association for Computing Machinery.

Jason Brownlee. 2020. How to develop an AdaBoost ensemble in python.

Tom De Smedt and Sylvia Jaki. 2018. Challenges of automatically detecting offensive language online: Participation paper for the GermEval shared task 2018 (HaUA). In *Proceedings of GermEval 2018, 14th Conference on Natural Language Processing (KONVENS 2018)*, pages "27–32", Vienna, Austria.

Jacob Devlin, Ming-Wei Chang, Kenton Lee, and Kristina Toutanova. 2019. BERT: Pre-training of deep bidirectional transformers for language understanding. In *Proceedings of the 2019 Conference of the North American Chapter of the Association for Computational Linguistics: Human Language Technologies*, pages 4171–4186, Minneapolis, Minnesota.

Yoav Freund and Robert E Schapire. 1996. Experiments with a new boosting algorithm. In *icml*, volume 96, pages 148–156. Citeseer.

Edouard Grave, Piotr Bojanowski, Prakhar Gupta, Armand Joulin, and Tomas Mikolov. 2018. Learning word vectors for 157 languages. In *Proceedings of the International Conference on Language Resources and Evaluation (LREC 2018)*, pages 3483–3487.

Dirk von Grünigen, Ralf Grubenmann, Fernando Benites, Pius von Däniken, and Mark Cieliebak. 2018. spMMMP at GermEval 2018 shared task: Classification of offensive content in tweets using convolutional neural networks and gated recurrent units. In *Proceedings of GermEval 2018, 14th Conference on Natural Language Processing (KONVENS 2018)*, pages "130–137", Vienna, Austria.

Chih-Wei Hsu, Chih-Chung Chang, and Chih-Jen Lin. 2008. A practical guide to support vector classication.

Fatemah Husain. 2020. OSACT4 shared task on offensive language detection: Intensive preprocessing-based approach. In *Proceedings of the 4th Workshop on Open-Source Arabic Corpora and Processing Tools, with a Shared Task on Offensive Language*

Detection, pages 53–60, Marseille, France. European Language Resource Association.

Philipp Koehn, Hieu Hoang, Alexandra Birch, Chris Callison-Burch, Marcello Federico, Nicola Bertoldi, Brooke Cowan, Wade Shen, Christine Moran, Richard Zens, Chris Dyer, Ondřej Bojar, Alexandra Constantin, and Evan Herbst. 2007. Moses: Open source toolkit for statistical machine translation. In *Proceedings of the 45th Annual Meeting of the Association for Computational Linguistics Companion Volume Proceedings of the Demo and Poster Sessions*, pages 177–180, Prague, Czech Republic.

Petra Kralj Novak, Jasmina Smailović, Borut Sluban, and Igor Mozetič. 2015. Sentiment of emojis. *PLOS ONE*, 10(12):1–22.

Jiwei Li, Xinlei Chen, Eduard Hovy, and Dan Jurafsky. 2016. Visualizing and understanding neural models in NLP. In *Proceedings of the 2016 Conference of the North American Chapter of the Association for Computational Linguistics: Human Language Technologies*, pages 681–691, San Diego, California.

Lucian Vlad Lita, Abe Ittycheriah, Salim Roukos, and Nanda Kambhatla. 2003. tRuEcasIng. In *Proceedings of the 41st Annual Meeting of the Association for Computational Linguistics*, pages 152–159, Sapporo, Japan.

Tomas Mikolov, Ilya Sutskever, Kai Chen, Greg S Corrado, and Jeff Dean. 2013. Distributed representations of words and phrases and their compositionality. In *Advances in Neural Information Processing Systems*, pages 3111–3119.

Joaquín Padilla Montani and Peter Schüller. 2018. TUWienKBS at GermEval 2018: German abusive tweet detection. In *Proceedings of GermEval 2018, 14th Conference on Natural Language Processing (KONVENS 2018)*, pages 45–50, Vienna, Austria.

Chikashi Nobata, Joel Tetreault, Achint Thomas, Yashar Mehdad, and Yi Chang. 2016. Abusive language detection in online user content. In *Proceedings of the 25th International Conference on World Wide Web*, pages 145–153, Montréal, Canada.

Andrei Paraschiv and Dumitru-Clementin Cercel. 2019. UPB at GermEval-2019 task 2: BERT-based offensive language classification of german tweets. In *Proceedings of the 15th Conference on Natural Language Processing (KONVENS 2019)*, pages 398–404, Erlangen, Germany.

Thomas Proisl and Peter Uhrig. 2016. SoMaJo: State-of-the-art tokenization for German web and social media texts. In *Proceedings of the 10th Web as Corpus Workshop*, pages 57–62, Berlin.

Robert Remus, Uwe Quasthoff, and Gerhard Heyer. 2010. SentiWS - a publicly available German-language resource for sentiment analysis. In *Proceedings of the Seventh International Conference on Language Resources and Evaluation (LREC'10)*, Valletta, Malta. European Language Resources Association (ELRA).

Julian Risch, Anke Stoll, Marc Ziegele, and Ralf Krestel. 2019. hpiDEDIS at GermEval 2019: Offensive language identification using a german BERT model. In *Proceedings of the 15th Conference on Natural Language Processing (KONVENS 2019)*, pages 405–410, Erlangen, Germany. German Society for Computational Linguistics & Language Technology.

Björn Ross, Michael Rist, Guillermo Carbonell, Ben Cabrera, Nils Kurowsky, and Michael Wojatzki. 2016. Measuring the Reliability of Hate Speech Annotations: The Case of the European Refugee Crisis. In *Proceedings of NLP4CMC III: 3rd Workshop on Natural Language Processing for Computer-Mediated Communication*, pages 6–9.

Tatjana Scheffler, Erik Haegert, Santichai Pornavalai, and Mino Lee Sasse. 2018. Feature explorations for hate speech classification. In *Proceedings of GermEval 2018, 14th Conference on Natural Language Processing (KONVENS 2018)*, pages 51–57, Vienna, Austria.

Florian Schmid, Justine Thielemann, Anna Mantwill, Jian Xi, Dirk Labudde, and Michael Spranger. 2019. Fosil - offensive language classification of german tweets combining svms and deep learning techniques. In *Proceedings of the 15th Conference on Natural Language Processing (KONVENS 2019)*, pages 382–386, Erlangen, Germany.

Dominik Stammbach, Azin Zahraei, Polina Stadnikova, and Dietrich Klakow. 2018. Offensive language detection with neural networks for Germeval task 2018. In *Proceedings of GermEval 2018, 14th Conference on Natural Language Processing (KONVENS 2018)*, pages "58–62", Vienna, Austria.

Kenneth Steimel, Daniel Dakota, Yue Chen, and Sandra Kübler. 2019. Investigating multilingual abusive language detection: A cautionary tale. In *Proceedings of the International Conference on Recent Advances in Natural Language Processing (RANLP 2019)*, pages 1151–1160, Varna, Bulgaria. INCOMA Ltd.

Julia Maria Struß, Melanie Siegel, Josep Ruppenhofer, Michael Wiegand, and Manfred Klenner. 2019. Overview of GermEval task 2, 2019 shared task on the identification of offensive language. In *Proceedings of the 15th Conference on Natural Language Processing (KONVENS 2019)*, pages 354–365, Erlangen, Germany. German Society for Computational Linguistics & Language Technology.

Michael Wiegand, Melanie Siegel, and Joseph Ruppenhofer. 2018. Overview of the GermEval 2018 shared task on the identification of offensive language. In *Proceedings of the GermEval Workshop.*, pages "1–10", Vienna, Austria. Verlag der Österreichischen Akademie der Wissenschaften.

Yonghui Wu, Mike Schuster, Zhifeng Chen, Quoc V. Le, Mohammad Norouzi, Wolfgang Macherey, Maxim Krikun, Yuan Cao, Qin Gao, Klaus Macherey, Jeff Klingner, Apurva Shah, Melvin Johnson, Xiaobing Liu, Łukasz Kaiser, Stephan Gouws, Yoshikiyo Kato, Taku Kudo, Hideto Kazawa, Keith Stevens, George Kurian, Nishant Patil, Wei Wang, Cliff Young, Jason Smith, Jason Riesa, Alex Rudnick, Oriol Vinyals, Greg Corrado, Macduff Hughes, and Jeffrey Dean. 2016. Google's neural machine translation system: Bridging the gap between human and machine translation.

Marcos Zampieri, Shervin Malmasi, Preslav Nakov, Sara Rosenthal, Noura Farra, and Ritesh Kumar. 2019. SemEval-2019 task 6: Identifying and categorizing offensive language in social media (OffensEval). In *Proceedings of the 13th International Workshop on Semantic Evaluation*.

Frederike Zufall, Tobias Horsmann, and Torsten Zesch. 2019. From legal to technical concept: Towards an automated classification of German political Twitter postings as criminal offenses. In *Proceedings of the 2019 Conference of the North American Chapter of the Association for Computational Linguistics: Human Language Technologies*, pages 1337–1347, Minneapolis, Minnesota.

Neural End-to-end Coreference Resolution for German in Different Domains

Fynn Schröder*, **Hans Ole Hatzel***, and **Chris Biemann**
Language Technology Group
Universität Hamburg, Germany
{fschroeder, hatzel, biemann}@informatik.uni-hamburg.de

Abstract

We apply neural coreference resolution to German, surpassing the previous state-of-the-art performance by a wide margin of 10–30 points F1 across three established datasets for German. This is achieved by a neural end-to-end approach, training contextual word-embeddings jointly with mention and entity similarity scores. We explore the impact of various parameters such as language models, pre-training and computational limits with respect to German data. In an effort to support datasets representing the domains of both news and literature, we make use of two distinct model architectures: a mention linking-based and an incremental entity-based approach that should scale to very long documents such as literary works. Our code and ready-to-use models are publicly available.

1 Introduction

Coreference resolution is the task of resolving text spans in documents that refer to the same entities. These are grouped into mention-clusters with each cluster representing one entity. Figure 1 shows coreference annotations on a literary text with different entities being denoted by both subscripts and colors. Tasks such as question answering (Morton, 1999) or text summarization (Steinberger et al., 2007) can rely on coreference resolution as part of the language processing pipeline. Bamman et al. (2014) demonstrated that coreference resolution is also applicable to literary analysis. The task has recently seen large improvements as systems moved from rule-based (e.g. Roesiger and Kuhn, 2016; Lee et al., 2011) to neural approaches (e.g. Lee et al., 2017; Joshi et al., 2019). This advancement from a CoNLL-F1-score of 57.8, achieved by a rule-based system in the original CoNLL-2012 shared task (Pradhan et al., 2012), to 67.2 in the

[Alice]$_1$ was not a bit hurt, and [she]$_1$ jumped up on to [her]$_1$ feet in a moment: [she]$_1$ looked up, but it was all dark overhead; before [her]$_1$ was [another long passage]$_2$, and [the White Rabbit]$_3$ was still in sight, hurrying down [it]$_2$.

Figure 1: Coreference gold annotations for "Alice's Adventures in Wonderland" (annotations from Bamman et al., 2020)

first end-to-end neural system (Lee et al., 2017) has shown that neural systems are key to state-of-the-art performance.

Coreference resolution on German using neural networks has received little attention. There has, to our knowledge, no work been reported on German news datasets using neural networks yet. This work is also the first to use cross-task learning to improve performance on German literary datasets.

We apply and adapt exiting approaches to coreference on German, making our code and models publicaly available.[1] There are two approaches to neural coreference resolution that we consider: A mention-linking-based and an entity-linking-based approach. Both have an initial mention proposal step, finding text spans that are likely to represent mentions. In mention-linking approaches, out of the cross-products of mentions, those mentions with the highest likelihood are considered. Each such mention is connected to its highest-scoring antecedent with transitively connected mentions forming entities.

The entity-representation-based approach also involves the initial mention proposal step. However, rather then creating links on a per-mention basis, initial mentions are considered to be entity representations, with each subsequent mention be-

*denotes equal contribution

[1] https://github.com/uhh-lt/neural-coref/tree/konvens

ing compared to existing entity representations and assigned to those that match them best. This way memory usage and computational effort can be reduced, as it is proportional to the number of entities, rather than the square of the number of mentions.

2 Related Work

Relevant prior work can be put into two distinct categories: (a) Neural, state-of-the-art coreference resolution developed primarily on English (b) Coreference resolution applied to German.

Most neural coreference resolution models perform a ranking of antecedents based on the pairwise scores of mention candidates (Wiseman et al., 2015; Clark and Manning, 2016a; Lee et al., 2017), at this only relying on local decisions that may not be globally optimal to form coherent entities (Lee et al., 2018). This general architecture has been improved on in multiple ways.

To address the issue of global optimization, Clark and Manning (2016b) and Wiseman et al. (2016) create entity representations during the ranking step. Lee et al. (2018); Kantor and Globerson (2019) iteratively refine mention representations with associated antecedent information, performing what they refer to as higher-order inference.

While the end-to-end coreference model of Lee et al. (2017) uses a bidirectional LSTM (Hochreiter and Schmidhuber, 1997) to produce span representations, Lee et al. (2018) see a 3.2 F1 score increase on the English CoNLL-2012 shared task by additionally using ELMo (Peters et al., 2018) embeddings. Lee et al. (2018) also modify the model to perform coarse-to-fine antecedent pruning enabling an efficient computation and potentially allowing the processing of longer documents. Joshi et al. (2019) and Kantor and Globerson (2019) improve upon this by using BERT (Devlin et al., 2019) embeddings instead of the LSTM-based representations and gain another 3.3 F1 points.

Recently, Joshi et al. (2020) presented a model optimized for span representations named SpanBERT and saw another 2.5 point increase in F1 score, which has been reproduced by Xu and Choi (2020). Wu et al. (2020) have taken a different approach to coreference resolution; they outperform previous state of the art by 3.5 F1 points in part due to the ability to recover missed mentions by framing the task as a question-answering problem.

Toshniwal et al. (2020); Xia et al. (2020) both introduce incremental approaches to coreference resolution. Instead of comparing mention pairs like Lee et al. (2017), they compare mentions with entity representations, with the entity representations being produced from a linear combination of their mentions. Both approaches work by iteratively processing all mentions and scoring each mention with regard to a set of entities; as a result, an evaluation of the full cross-product of mentions is not necessary. The two approaches differ slightly in how they handle the introduction of new entities.

For coreference resolution on German texts, published work predates the age of neural networks in natural language processing. The CorZu system (Klenner and Tuggener, 2011; Tuggener and Klenner, 2014) is a rule-based incremental entity-mention model that has been extended with Markov Logic Networks for the antecedent selection.

Roesiger and Kuhn (2016) adapted the English system of Björkelund and Kuhn (2014) to German. A directed tree where each node represents a mention is used to model the coreferences in a document. For determining antecedents, both local and non-local handcrafted features are employed. They created the current state-of-the-art approach for German news datasets, evaluating their system on the SemEval-2010 shared task and on version 10 of the TüBa-D/Z dataset.

The domain of literature has, for both German and English, received increased attention in recent years with regard to coreference resolution. Roesiger et al. (2018) considered the domain specific challenges and phenomena of literature. Bamman et al. (2020) released an English dataset and Krug et al. (2018) released a German dataset (see Section 3.2 for details). While Krug (2020) performed coreference resolution on German literary data, Toshniwal et al. (2020) used the English dataset. Krug (2020) compare various approaches to coreference resolution on German historic novels using the DROC dataset (Krug et al., 2018). Their best-performing system in a gold-mention scenario uses a rule-based Stanford Sieve approach (Lee et al., 2011), iteratively applying rules starting from the most precise rule, going to less precise rules. When mention spans are generated by the model, the end-to-end neural network, based on the approach by Lee et al. (2017), performs about on par with the rule-based systems in conjunction with preprocessing pipelines.

Evaluation of coreference data presents a challenge, different proposed metrics emphasise different aspects of a model's performance. An average of the three metrics MUC, B^3, and $CEAF_{\phi_4}$ has been used in the CoNLL-2012 task (Pradhan et al., 2012). As these metrics are widely used we focus on them for reporting our results, including an average of the three, the CoNLL-F1 score.

3 German Coreference Datasets

3.1 News

The standard corpus for coreference resolution in German is TüBa-D/Z (Telljohann et al., 2017; Naumann and Möller, 2006), a manually annotated collection of newspaper articles released in multiple versions that incrementally add more documents. It was also used as the data source for the German part of the SemEval-2010 shared task on coreference resolution (Recasens et al., 2010).

To be comparable with previous work, we chose to use SemEval-2010 and TüBa-D/Z release 10.0 instead of the marginally larger 11.0 for most of our experiments. As there is no official split for the TüBa-D/Z, we use the same splits as previous work (Roesiger and Kuhn, 2016).[2]

While TüBa-D/Z does not contain singletons (on average 3.65 mentions per entity, 10.89 entities per article), these mentions are annotated in SemEval-2010 (on average 1.34 mentions per entity, 73.07 entities per article). Across the dataset, 84.6% of all entities and 64.1% of all mentions are singletons.

Compared to the standard English coreference corpus, OntoNotes (Weischedel et al., 2013), used in the CoNLL-2012 shared task on coreference resolution (Pradhan et al., 2012), TüBa-D/Z neither contains different genres of texts nor additional metadata such as speaker information. Regarding statistics such as average mentions per entity, mentions/sentence length and tokens/sentences/entities per document, German TüBa-D/Z 10.0 and English OntoNotes 5.0 are remarkably similar.

3.2 Literature

The DROC dataset (Krug et al., 2018) contains 90 coreference annotated literary documents where each document comprises one chapter with an average length of 4369.49 tokens. We use the splits established by Krug (2020), i.e. 58 training, 14 development and 18 test documents. There is a total of 51 797 mentions in 5365 clusters, 2409 of these are singleton clusters. As a result, while 45% of

[2]for corpus statistics, see Table 9 in the appendix

Mention-F1	MUC-F1	B^3-F1	CEAF$_{\phi_4}$-F1	CoNLL-F1
97.05	93.67	84.69	69.25	82.54

Table 1: Inter-annotator F1 scores for DROC as calculated using the scorer by Pradhan et al. (2012) based on the individual annotator's data by Krug et al. (2018).

clusters are singleton clusters, only 4.7% of mentions are singletons. Our calculations for the performance of human annotators on the subset of DROC are listed in Table 1, providing an upper bound for our performance expectations. In contrast to other datasets (e.g. Bamman et al., 2020), only mention heads are annotated, rather than whole nominal phrases. This means that in the sentence, "and [the driver] was none other than [that cursed Englishman]" (from the dataset by Bamman et al. (2020) "The Scarlet Pimpernel"), only the spans "Englishman" and "driver" would be annotated as coreferring instead. Thus, only spans up to a short length need to be considered in the mention proposal step. DROC also differentiates itself from other datasets in that it only annotates references to characters.

More generally, literary data, when compared to news texts, comes with the added challenge of document length. Longer documents tend to come with more mentions, DROC, for example, contains an average of 575.52 mentions per document whereas SemEval only has an average of 97.79. In general, increased document length lead to longer processing time, larger computational effort and higher memory requirements.

4 Model

In this section, we describe our German coreference resolution models in detail. We build on the widely adapted neural end-to-end architecture developed by Lee et al. (2017, 2018), improved by Joshi et al. (2019) and re-implemented in PyTorch (Paszke et al., 2019) by Xu and Choi (2020). Although the CorefQA system (Wu et al., 2020) is currently the top-performing system for English, we chose to not build upon it because it is more complex and requires vastly more computational resources than our chosen approach.

The general idea of our models is to first detect mentions and then to link them. Each document is processed individually during both training and inference; Figure 2 visualizes a single document being processed by both model variants. First, contextual ELECTRA (Clark et al., 2020) embeddings are obtained for each token and all possible

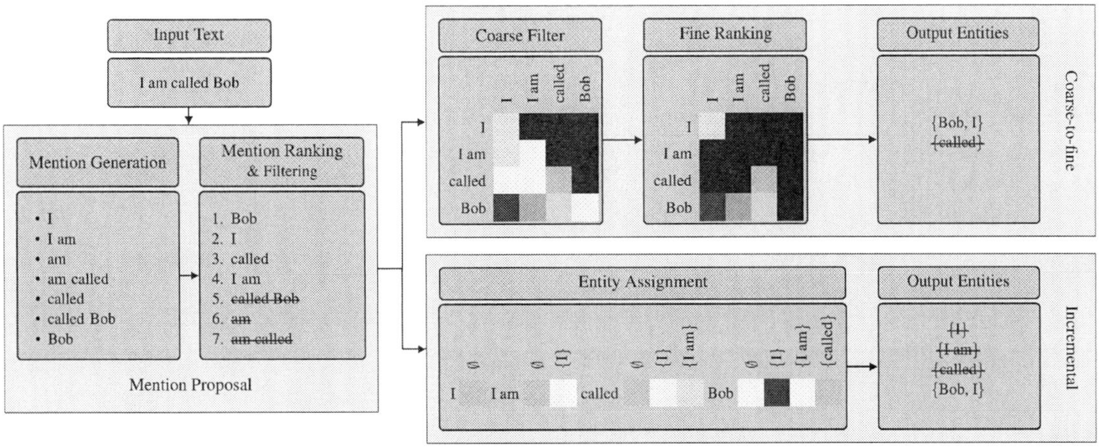

Figure 2: Conceptual visualization of our two end-to-end model variants processing an example document. Both models are based on the same mention proposal step. While the incremental model operates on an ever-growing set of entities, the coarse-to-fine model performs one comparison on the cross product of all mentions. Dark green color indicates a good match between mention and its assignment candidate, whereas black squares indicate that, due to filtering, no scoring was performed. All values are manually chosen for illustration purposes.

mention spans up to a configurable length are enumerated. Mention embeddings are created, containing start and end token embeddings and the attention-weighted average of all span tokens. In contrast to the English models, our models contain neither genre nor speaker embeddings as the German datasets do not supply this information.

A naïve approach of comparing each mention candidate with every other to find links between them raises computational issues, quickly becoming infeasible to compute as it requires $O(M^2)$ comparisons for $M = \text{max\_mention\_length} \cdot |D|$ mention candidates, for a document D where $|D|$ is the document length in word-piece tokens. To reduce computational effort over a naïve approach to find the best antecedent for each mention, we employ two established strategies: A coarse-to-fine and an incremental approach, with the incremental approach being able to handle documents of arbitrary length with limited memory.

4.1 Coarse-to-fine

Our model is based on the implementation by Xu and Choi (2020). For each mention span, the model learns a distribution over its antecedents based on how likely both individual spans are to be valid mentions and how likely they to refer to the same entity. Two pruning steps are used to make this mention linking computationally feasible.

To reduce the number of mentions, all mention embeddings are scored individually with a feed-forward neural network (FFNN). For each document D only the top $n = \min(4096, 0.4 \cdot |D|)$ mentions are kept after pruning. Instead of performing a pairwise comparison of all N mentions, only a fraction is used. Thus, removing obvious non-mentions and limiting the complexity to $O(n^2 \ll N^2)$, a step that we refer to as mention filtering.

In the coarse antecedent pruning step, the pairwise similarity scores of the remaining mention embeddings are summed with the individual mention scores. A subsequent fine-grained ranking is performed with the top $a = 64$ antecedents per mention; to this effect, pairwise mention-antecedent embeddings consisting of mention, antecedent and similarity embedding are created. These embeddings are scored with a FFNN and combined with scores from the coarse step resulting in scores for the top antecedents per mention. We do not use so-called higher-order inference as this effectively doubles the computational cost of the fine-grained antecedent scoring without improving the quality according to Xu and Choi (2020).

During training, the model learns to optimize the marginal log-likelihood of possibly correct antecedents for each mention, i.e. for each antecedent the score should be 1 if mention and antecedent belong to the same gold entity, 0 otherwise.

During inference, an undirected graph of mentions is created by connecting each mention with its highest-scoring antecedent. In this graph, each connected component of mentions forms an entity.

4.2 Incremental

The general approach of the incremental model follows Xia et al. (2020) and Toshniwal et al. (2020). Mention filtering is performed as in the course-to-fine model. We process the document iteratively, splitting the document into multiple windows for transformer language model inference. Unlike Toshniwal et al. (2020) but following Xia et al. (2020) we reuse all model weights, including both the transformer weights and all task-specific layers.

In a step we call entity assignment, every mention candidate chooses its entity in an iterative fashion. In our standard setup, this is modeled as a classification task with a dynamic number of classes and the initial set of classes, each class representing an entity $C_0 = \{\emptyset\}$. If, for any mention embedding m being processed, $\emptyset$ is selected as the class, the mention is added as a new class. Entity representations are tracked with $R(E_n)$ being set to m when the n-th entity is added. As a result, after the first mention is processed the set of classes is always extended: $C_1 = \{\emptyset, E_0\}$. Subsequently, new mentions E_x are added iteratively. Whenever any existing E_x is selected as the best fitting entity, its representation is updated using an update gate: $R(E_x) := (1-\alpha)m + \alpha R(E_x)$.

Training is done by means of cross entropy loss across all existing entities and the new entity class, with the gold class for each entity being its most recently assigned mention gold class. As a result, early in training many entity representations likely contain mentions that, from a gold label perspective, should not belong together. Toshniwal et al. (2020) use teacher forcing to address this issue and thereby reach earlier convergence; we test this approach in our setup, assigning each mention to its gold class for further computations, rather than relying on predicted classes.

The only way mention candidates can be discarded (either because they are not a mention or because they are singleton mentions) is by means of creating a new entity and never assigning any additional mentions to it, in postprocessing any such singleton entity would be removed, yielding the final output entities. To support detection of singleton mentions, we follow Xia et al. (2020) in adding an additional class representing the discarding of any given entity. In this "discard" scenario, singleton mentions are not removed in postprocessing since non-mentions are modeled explicitly.

Language Model	CoNLL-F1
BERT-Base, multilingual uncased	74.50
BERT-Base, multilingual cased	74.60
GBERT base, cased	75.35
GELECTRA base, cased	77.01
GNG_ELECTRA base, uncased	**77.86**
GBERT large, cased	79.05
GELECTRA large, cased	**79.24**

Table 2: TüBa-D/Z 10 development score of coarse-to-fine models with different language models (using 512 as segment size)

5 Experiments: News Domain

We perform preliminary experiments to select the best pre-trained German language model, its best context size and to optimize other hyperparameters. For the main experiments on the news datasets TüBa-D/Z 10 and SemEval-2010, we train and evaluate our coarse-to-fine model as it is easily capable of processing the typically rather short documents. We use the training, development and test splits as described in Section 3.1. The SemEval dataset contains singletons, but our coarse-to-fine model predicts only clusters of at least two entities. Following Roesiger and Kuhn (2016), we ignore singletons when scoring our systems' predictions.

5.1 Pre-trained Language Models

We evaluated multiple pre-trained language models for our coreference resolution model. As a baseline, we include the multilingual BERT-Base model (in both the cased and uncased variants) by Devlin et al. (2019). Chan et al. (2020) recently published German BERT and ELECTRA (cased, both base and large) denoted as GBERT / GELECTRA in Table 2. In addition, we included another ELECTRA model (uncased, base) by German-NLP-Group denoted as GNG_ELECTRA[3].

We find that all of the recent German language models perform better than the multilingual BERT. For the base models, ELECTRA outperforms BERT by a substantial margin. Using large models, ELECTRA performs marginally better. Based on the results shown in Table 2, we selected GNG_ELECTRA as the base and GELECTRA as the large model for our remaining experiments.

[3]Model description at `https://huggingface.co/german-nlp-group/electra-base-german-uncased`

Segment Length	F1 (base)	F1 (large)
128	75.69	76.28
256	76.56	77.29
384	77.01	78.51
512	**77.50**	**79.27**

Table 3: TüBa-D/Z 10 development score of coarse-to-fine models GNG_ELECTRA (base) and GELECTRA (large) with different segment lengths.

CoNLL-F1		News-Pretrain	
		✓	✗
Singletons	✓	61.66 ± 0.52	59.93 ± 0.33
	✗	$\mathbf{65.58 \pm 0.46}$	$\mathbf{64.26 \pm 0.51}$

Table 4: The effect of using pre-training on the DROC coarse-to-fine model on data with and without singletons. All results were averaged over 5 runs and the standard deviation is given.

5.2 ELECTRA Context Size

Following Joshi et al. (2019), we split documents into non-overlapping ELECTRA contexts, evaluating different splits for contexts as shown in Table 3. While Joshi et al. (2019) show that for English BERT-base/large a segment length of 128/384 is optimal, this does not hold true for our German models and dataset where larger segment lengths perform better. Our results are in line with the intuition that larger context sizes provide more contextual information for any given mention. Thus, we use a segment length of 512 in our models.

5.3 Hyperparameters

In general, parameters affecting computational limits have a large impact, all other parameters that we tested had only limited effect. Parameters controlling the pruning (top_span_ratio, max_top_spans and max_top_antecedents) have a strong negative effect when set too low, resulting in too aggressive pruning. Higher values increase evaluation scores with quickly diminishing returns; yet strongly increase computation time and memory.

To reduce GPU memory usage and computation time, we reduced the size of all feed-forward neural networks from 3000 used in previous work to 2048 without seeing distinct score changes on the TüBa-D/Z 10 development set. We also increased the size to 4096, resulting in more memory usage and slower computation, but negligible changes in evaluation performance.

6 Experiments: Literature Domain

For the literary dataset (DROC), we explore the use of both model variants. We initialize the incremental model with weights from the coarse-to-fine variant.

6.1 Coarse-to-fine Model

Given the relatively small size of the DROC dataset, we explore the impact of pretrained weights from the news tasks. We expected that while the different approaches to mention annotation (heads or entire noun phrases) would somewhat limit applicability of existing weights they would still lead to an improvement.

Table 4 shows the development set results for the DROC dataset, with the same set of initial weights that was pretrained on TüBa-D/Z 10 being used for all of our runs. Standard deviation for the ConLL-F1 scores are given, based on five runs with different random initializations. All layer weights, including task specific ones as well as language model ones were reused. The experiment was repeated for a variant of the DROC dataset with all singleton mentions removed.

Using Welch's t-test we can infer that the pertrained version does, on average, perform better for the no singleton variant ($p < 0.005$). As a result we will use the news-pretrained model variant in all our further experiments. This finding is also supported by the recent publication by (Xia and Durme, 2021) which establishes that, especially for short datasets, using pretrained weights is beneficial. We are unsure if further significant improvements could be gained by pre-training on additional datasets, for example GerDraCor (Pagel and Reiter, 2020), given that TüBa-D/Z is already a large dataset.

Table 5 shows how two configuration parameters affect the coarse-to-fine model's performance. The two options enable different features, where "segment info" describes how many BERT segments lie between the current and candidate mention while "token info" describes the token distance from the candidate mention to the document start. Further, "token info" encodes the length of the candidate mention span. This experiment was performed as

Distance Features			
Segment	Token	Coarse-To-Fine	Incremental
✗	✗	61.11 ± 0.57	**65.79**
✓	✗	$\mathbf{62.31 \pm 0.27}$	64.20
✗	✓	61.70 ± 0.22	62.57
✓	✓	59.93 ± 0.33	65.42

Table 5: Performance of the coarse-to-fine and incremental models with respect to two configuration parameters relevant to recency bias.

CoNLL-F1		Teacher Forcing	
		✓	✗
Discard	✓	63.92	**65.42**
	✗	58.52	57.27

Table 6: DROC incremental model configurations

we saw a recency bias in terms of connecting mentions in our early result explorations (see Section 7), an effect that could be caused by these distance based features. On average, the variant without token distance representation performs significantly better than the the one with both features enabled ($p < 0.001$). We attribute this to a greater mention recency bias that is encouraged by the additional features.

6.2 Incremental Model

The memory usage of the coarse-to-fine approach, while not prohibitive for the DROC dataset, will prevent its application to full length literary documents.

Table 5 illustrates the impact of the same configuration parameters that were used for the coarse-to-fine model. The impact of the parameters appears to be lessened in the incremental case.

Unsurprisingly, due to the possibility of handling singleton mentions, Table 6 clearly shows that the discard functionality is critical to model performance. Teacher forcing appears to have a negative impact on performance; this does come as a surprise but while convergence early in training was faster the final results were slightly worse.

6.3 Impact of Document Length

We seek to analyze how well incremental models fare as document length increases. To this end, we split DROC at the nearest sentence boundary into sub documents that are no longer than 512,

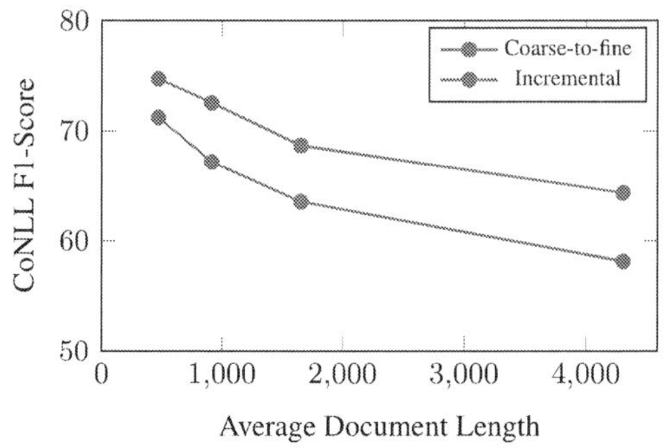

Figure 3: The performance of incremental systems compared to coarse-to-fine model as document lengths increases.

System	CoNLL-F1 TüBa	SE'10
German coarse-to-fine base	77.21	72.54
German coarse-to-fine large	**78.79**	**74.46**
IMS HotCoref	48.54	48.61
+ gold mentions	65.76	63.61
CorZu		45.82
+ gold mentions		58.11

Table 7: Results of our coarse-to-fine models and previous systems on the test set of TüBa-D/Z 10 and SemEval-2010 (without singletons). IMS HotCoref and CorZu scores as reported by Roesiger and Kuhn (2016). Full metrics in Table 10 in the appendix.

1024 and 2048 tokens. Previous work (Krug, 2020; Joshi et al., 2019) has established that, with longer documents, the performance of coreference systems drops. This can be interpreted as the inherent difficulty of the coreference task growing with document length. Figure 3 shows that for longer documents the gap in performance between the model variants increases slightly.

7 Results & Error Analysis

Our neural coarse-to-fine models outperform the previous state of the art by a large margin on both SemEval-2010 (+25.85 F1) and TüBa-D/Z (+30.25 F1) as shown in Table 7. In fact, even if the other systems are allowed to use gold mentions, our models still outperform them by more than 10 F1 points. Using ELECTRA large for contextual embeddings yields a small improvement over the base model (+1.58 F1 / +1.92 F1). Figure 4 shows an example of our systems prediction on an unseen document.

We manually analyze the predictions of our

[Bahn-Chef]$_1$ legt Statistik vor. Bisher keine Erklärung für [das Unglück von [Eschede]$_3$]$_2$ [Frankfurt]$_4$ (taz) - Der Eindruck, daß sich die Unfälle bei [der Bahn]$_5$ häuften, sei nur durch die " Berichterstattung der Medien " provoziert, erklärte [der Vorstandsvorsitzende [der Deutschen Bahn AG]$_5$, Johannes Ludewig (CDU]$_1$), gestern in [Frankfurt]$_4$. Zum bevorstehenden ersten Jahrestag [der ICE-Katastrophe von [Eschede]$_3$]$_2$ (3. Juni) verwies [Ludewig]$_1$ auf [die - bahneigene - Statistik]$_6$. [...]

Figure 4: Excerpt from a TüBa-D/Z 10 test set document (in total 438 tokens), where the shown output of our coarse-to-fine large model is identical to the human annotation (document score: 89.08 CoNLL-F1)

System	Model	F1 Score
Krug (2020) (with singletons)	Sieve	51.53
	CR	51.34
	E2E-NN	53.17
Ours (with singletons)	Incremental	**64.72**
	C2F	61.66
Ours (no singletons)	C2F	65.50

Table 8: Final results for the DROC dataset on the test set, with and without singleton mentions included.

coarse-to-fine model and find that it generally produces accurate coreference links both locally and document-wide. While entity assignment of mentions, identified in both prediction and gold data, is typically correct, missed and added mentions are more frequent errors. We assume that one reason is a contradicting training signal, i.e. while some mentions are annotated as such in the gold data, others are not because they are singletons or were missed in the annotation process.

Our incremental model on data including singletons outperforms the existing state of the art for DROC by 11.6 F1 points (see Table 8). Said results were achieved in a setup comparable to ours, with no gold information such as speakers or entity spans being used, except in the case of their end-to-end neural network (E2E-NN), where direct speech and speaker information were used.

We manually evaluate our model on entire literary texts. While we find local coreference relationships to be surprisingly accurate, when taking a

Es war einmal ein gar allerliebstes, niedliches Ding von einen [Mädchen]$_1$, [das]$_1$ hatte eine [Mutter]$_2$ und eine [Großmutter]$_2$, die waren gar gut und hatten das kleine [Ding]$_1$ so lieb. Die [Großmutter]$_2$ absonderlich, [die]$_2$ wußte gar nicht, wie gut sie ' s mit dem [Enkelchen]$_1$ meinen sollte [...]

(a) Model with token distance feature

Es war einmal ein gar allerliebstes, niedliches Ding von einen [Mädchen]$_1$, [das]$_1$ hatte eine [Mutter]$_2$ und eine [Großmutter]$_3$, die waren gar gut und hatten das kleine Ding so lieb. Die [Großmutter]$_3$ absonderlich, [die]$_3$ wußte gar nicht, wie gut sie ' s mit dem [Enkelchen]$_1$ meinen sollte, [...]

(b) Model without token distance feature

Figure 5: We observe a recency bias that appears to, in this case, be fixed by not including an explicit token distance feature. The term "Großmutter" (grandmother) is linked to the term "Mutter" (mother).[4]

more global view, some of our model's weaknesses are exposed. When searching the token "Holmes" in the German translation of "The Hound of the Baskervilles" [5] which should always refer to the same character we find the 212 tokens to occur in 31 different clusters with 4 mentions being assigned to no cluster. Our observation is that this often occurs after a long section of text without explicit mentions of the name, in fact the average distance from one mention of Holmes to the previous is 320.6 tokens whereas it is 655.3 for those cases where a new class is erroneously introduced. We suspect, that this could be attributed to the name taking less prominence in the entity representation after a while.

Figure 5a illustrates a recency bias in our model, "grandmother" and "mother" were erroneously combined into one entity, presumably because the distance between the "mother" and "grandmother" mentions were very small. On a larger scale this effect can be observable as long sequences of the same cluster forming, an effect that is especially prominent in our incremental models. This observation motivated our experiments with removing distance features (see Table 5), resulting in an improved model and, in this case (as seen in Figure 5b), an improved result. However, this par ticular model no longer detects "thing" (Ding) as a

[4]Text from: `https://www.projekt-gutenberg.org/bechstei/maerchen/chap053.html`

[5]`https://www.projekt-gutenberg.org/doyle/basker-1/`

valid mention which could both be a side effect of removing the distance features or an effect of the random initialization and training.

8 Conclusion

We apply recent developments in neural architectures for coreference resolution on German data and achieve a substantial improvement over the previous state of the art on all three established German datasets. We conducted experiments with two variants: a coarse-to-fine model suitable for rather short documents, and an incremental model that should scale to long documents. In our analysis we found that while the task of coreference resolution itself becomes more difficult as document sizes increase, the incremental approach scales worse than the course-to-fine approach in terms of accuracy. While we found local decisions to be accurate, shortcomings of the incremental model in global consistency and recency bias were explored.

In future work, we would especially like to address remaining challenges for the processing of long-form literary documents. In spite of the large improvements we achieved, there is still a considerable headroom for coreference resolution, as reflected by a large performance gap between the human baseline of 82.54 F1 and our best model with 64.7 F1 on the DROC dataset. On a more theoretic note, another extension worth pursuing in the future especially for the literary domain is the notion of subjective coreference. As an example, in the fairy tale "Little Red Riding Hood" (see Figure 5), the girl temporarily perceives a highly plot-relevant coreference between the grandmother and the big bad wolf, which is not reflected in objectivized models.

Acknowledgments

This work was, in part, supported by the DFG through the project "Evaluating Events in Narrative Theory (EvENT)" (grants BI 1544/11-1 and GI 1105/3-1) as part of the priority program "Computational Literary Studies (CLS)" (SPP 2207). This work was partly supported by the Cluster of Excellence CLICCS (EXC 2037), Universität Hamburg, funded through the German Research Foundation (DFG).

References

David Bamman, Olivia Lewke, and Anya Mansoor. 2020. An annotated dataset of coreference in English literature. In *Proceedings of the 12th Language Resources and Evaluation Conference*, pages 44–54, Marseille, France. European Language Resources Association.

David Bamman, Ted Underwood, and Noah A. Smith. 2014. A Bayesian mixed effects model of literary character. In *Proceedings of the 52nd Annual Meeting of the Association for Computational Linguistics (Volume 1: Long Papers)*, pages 370–379, Baltimore, Maryland. Association for Computational Linguistics.

Anders Björkelund and Jonas Kuhn. 2014. Learning Structured Perceptrons for Coreference Resolution with Latent Antecedents and Non-local Features. In *Proceedings of the 52nd Annual Meeting of the Association for Computational Linguistics (Volume 1: Long Papers)*, pages 47–57, Baltimore, Maryland. Association for Computational Linguistics.

Branden Chan, Stefan Schweter, and Timo Möller. 2020. German's next language model. In *Proceedings of the 28th International Conference on Computational Linguistics*, pages 6788–6796, Barcelona, Spain (Online). International Committee on Computational Linguistics.

Kevin Clark, Minh-Thang Luong, Quoc V. Le, and Christopher D. Manning. 2020. ELECTRA: Pre-training text encoders as discriminators rather than generators. In *8th International Conference on Learning Representations, ICLR 2020*, Addis Ababa, Ethiopia. OpenReview.net.

Kevin Clark and Christopher D. Manning. 2016a. Deep reinforcement learning for mention-ranking coreference models. In *Proceedings of the 2016 Conference on Empirical Methods in Natural Language Processing*, pages 2256–2262, Austin, Texas. Association for Computational Linguistics.

Kevin Clark and Christopher D. Manning. 2016b. Improving coreference resolution by learning entity-level distributed representations. In *Proceedings of the 54th Annual Meeting of the Association for Computational Linguistics (Volume 1: Long Papers)*, pages 643–653, Berlin, Germany. Association for Computational Linguistics.

Jacob Devlin, Ming-Wei Chang, Kenton Lee, and Kristina Toutanova. 2019. BERT: Pre-training of deep bidirectional transformers for language understanding. In *Proceedings of the 2019 Conference of the North American Chapter of the Association for Computational Linguistics: Human Language Technologies, Volume 1 (Long and Short Papers)*, pages 4171–4186, Minneapolis, Minnesota. Association for Computational Linguistics.

Sepp Hochreiter and Jürgen Schmidhuber. 1997. Long short-term memory. *Neural Computation*, 9(8):1735–1780.

Mandar Joshi, Danqi Chen, Yinhan Liu, Daniel S. Weld, Luke Zettlemoyer, and Omer Levy. 2020. SpanBERT: Improving pre-training by representing and predicting spans. *Transactions of the Association for Computational Linguistics*, 8:64–77.

Mandar Joshi, Omer Levy, Luke Zettlemoyer, and Daniel Weld. 2019. BERT for coreference resolution: Baselines and analysis. In *Proceedings of the 2019 Conference on Empirical Methods in Natural Language Processing and the 9th International Joint Conference on Natural Language Processing (EMNLP-IJCNLP)*, pages 5803–5808, Hong Kong, China. Association for Computational Linguistics.

Ben Kantor and Amir Globerson. 2019. Coreference resolution with entity equalization. In *Proceedings of the 57th Annual Meeting of the Association for Computational Linguistics*, pages 673–677, Florence, Italy. Association for Computational Linguistics.

Manfred Klenner and Don Tuggener. 2011. An Incremental Entity-Mention Model for Coreference Resolution with Restrictive Antecedent Accessibility. In *Proceedings of the International Conference Recent Advances in Natural Language Processing 2011*, pages 178–185, Hissar, Bulgaria. Association for Computational Linguistics.

Markus Krug. 2020. *Techniques for the Automatic Extraction of Character Networks in German Historic Novels*. Ph.D. thesis, Universität Würzburg.

Markus Krug, Lukas Weimer, Isabella Reger, Luisa Macharowsky, Stephan Feldhaus, Frank Puppe, and Fotis Jannidis. 2018. Description of a corpus of character references in German novels-DROC [Deutsches ROman Corpus]. *DARIAH-DE Working Papers*, 27.

Heeyoung Lee, Yves Peirsman, Angel Chang, Nathanael Chambers, Mihai Surdeanu, and Dan Jurafsky. 2011. Stanford's multi-pass sieve coreference resolution system at the CoNLL-2011 shared task. In *Proceedings of the Fifteenth Conference on Computational Natural Language Learning: Shared Task*, pages 28–34, Portland, Oregon. Association for Computational Linguistics.

Kenton Lee, Luheng He, Mike Lewis, and Luke Zettlemoyer. 2017. End-to-end neural coreference resolution. In *Proceedings of the 2017 Conference on Empirical Methods in Natural Language Processing*, pages 188–197, Copenhagen, Denmark. Association for Computational Linguistics.

Kenton Lee, Luheng He, and Luke Zettlemoyer. 2018. Higher-order coreference resolution with coarse-to-fine inference. In *Proceedings of the 2018 Conference of the North American Chapter of the Association for Computational Linguistics: Human Language Technologies, Volume 2 (Short Papers)*, pages 687–692, New Orleans, Louisiana. Association for Computational Linguistics.

Thomas S. Morton. 1999. Using coreference for question answering. In *Coreference and Its Applications*, pages 85–89, College Park, Maryland. Association for Computational Linguistics.

Karin Naumann and Vera Möller. 2006. Manual for the annotation of in-document referential relations. Technical report, Universität Tübingen.

Janis Pagel and Nils Reiter. 2020. GerDraCor-coref: A coreference corpus for dramatic texts in German. In *Proceedings of the 12th Language Resources and Evaluation Conference*, pages 55–64, Marseille, France. European Language Resources Association.

Adam Paszke, Sam Gross, Francisco Massa, Adam Lerer, James Bradbury, Gregory Chanan, Trevor Killeen, Zeming Lin, Natalia Gimelshein, Luca Antiga, Alban Desmaison, Andreas Kopf, Edward Yang, Zachary DeVito, Martin Raison, Alykhan Tejani, Sasank Chilamkurthy, Benoit Steiner, Lu Fang, Junjie Bai, and Soumith Chintala. 2019. Pytorch: An imperative style, high-performance deep learning library. In *Advances in Neural Information Processing Systems 32*, pages 8024–8035. Curran Associates, Inc.

Matthew Peters, Mark Neumann, Mohit Iyyer, Matt Gardner, Christopher Clark, Kenton Lee, and Luke Zettlemoyer. 2018. Deep contextualized word representations. In *Proceedings of the 2018 Conference of the North American Chapter of the Association for Computational Linguistics: Human Language Technologies, Volume 1 (Long Papers)*, pages 2227–2237, New Orleans, Louisiana. Association for Computational Linguistics.

Sameer Pradhan, Alessandro Moschitti, Nianwen Xue, Olga Uryupina, and Yuchen Zhang. 2012. CoNLL-2012 shared task: Modeling multilingual unrestricted coreference in OntoNotes. In *Joint Conference on EMNLP and CoNLL - Shared Task*, pages 1–40, Jeju Island, Korea. Association for Computational Linguistics.

Marta Recasens, Lluís Màrquez, Emili Sapena, M. Antònia Martí, Mariona Taulé, Véronique Hoste, Massimo Poesio, and Yannick Versley. 2010. SemEval-2010 task 1: Coreference resolution in multiple languages. In *Proceedings of the 5th International Workshop on Semantic Evaluation*, pages 1–8, Uppsala, Sweden. Association for Computational Linguistics.

Ina Roesiger and Jonas Kuhn. 2016. IMS HotCoref DE: A Data-driven Co-reference Resolver for German. In *Proceedings of the Tenth International Conference on Language Resources and Evaluation (LREC'16)*, pages 155–160, Portorož, Slovenia. European Language Resources Association (ELRA).

Ina Roesiger, Sarah Schulz, and Nils Reiter. 2018. Towards Coreference for Literary Text: Analyzing Domain-Specific Phenomena. In *Proceedings of the Second Joint SIGHUM Workshop on Computational Linguistics for Cultural Heritage, Social Sciences, Humanities and Literature*, pages 129–138, Santa Fe, New Mexico. Association for Computational Linguistics.

Josef Steinberger, Massimo Poesio, Mijail A. Kabadjov, and Karel Ježek. 2007. Two uses of anaphora resolution in summarization. *Information Processing & Management*, 43(6):1663–1680.

Heike Telljohann, Erhard W. Hinrichs, Sandra Kübler, Heike Zinsmeister, and Kathrin Beck. 2017. Stylebook for the tübingen treebank of written german (TüBa-D/Z). In *Seminar für Sprachwissenschaft, Universität Tübingen, Germany*.

Shubham Toshniwal, Sam Wiseman, Allyson Ettinger, Karen Livescu, and Kevin Gimpel. 2020. Learning to Ignore: Long Document Coreference with Bounded Memory Neural Networks. In *Proceedings of the 2020 Conference on Empirical Methods in Natural Language Processing (EMNLP)*, pages 8519–8526, Online. Association for Computational Linguistics.

Don Tuggener and Manfred Klenner. 2014. A Hybrid Entity-Mention Pronoun Resolution Model for German Using Markov Logic Networks. In *Proceedings of the 12th Edition of the Konvens Conference*, pages 21–29, Hildesheim, Germany. Universitätsbibliothek Hildesheim.

Ralph Weischedel, Martha Palmer, Mitchell Marcus, Eduard Hovy, Sameer Pradhan, Lance Ramshaw, Nianwen Xue, Ann Taylor, Jeff Kaufman, Michelle Franchini, et al. 2013. OntoNotes release 5.0 ldc2013t19. *Linguistic Data Consortium, Philadelphia, Pennsylvania*, 23.

Sam Wiseman, Alexander M. Rush, Stuart Shieber, and Jason Weston. 2015. Learning anaphoricity and antecedent ranking features for coreference resolution. In *Proceedings of the 53rd Annual Meeting of the Association for Computational Linguistics and the 7th International Joint Conference on Natural Language Processing (Volume 1: Long Papers)*, pages 1416–1426, Beijing, China. Association for Computational Linguistics.

Sam Wiseman, Alexander M. Rush, and Stuart M. Shieber. 2016. Learning global features for coreference resolution. In *Proceedings of the 2016 Conference of the North American Chapter of the Association for Computational Linguistics: Human Language Technologies*, pages 994–1004, San Diego, California. Association for Computational Linguistics.

Wei Wu, Fei Wang, Arianna Yuan, Fei Wu, and Jiwei Li. 2020. CorefQA: Coreference resolution as query-based span prediction. In *Proceedings of the 58th Annual Meeting of the Association for Computational Linguistics*, pages 6953–6963, Online. Association for Computational Linguistics.

Patrick Xia and Benjamin Van Durme. 2021. Moving on from OntoNotes: Coreference resolution model transfer. *CoRR*, abs/2104.08457.

Patrick Xia, João Sedoc, and Benjamin Van Durme. 2020. Incremental neural coreference resolution in constant memory. In *Proceedings of the 2020 Conference on Empirical Methods in Natural Language Processing (EMNLP)*, pages 8617–8624, Online. Association for Computational Linguistics.

Liyan Xu and Jinho D. Choi. 2020. Revealing the myth of higher-order inference in coreference resolution. In *Proceedings of the 2020 Conference on Empirical Methods in Natural Language Processing (EMNLP)*, pages 8527–8533, Online. Association for Computational Linguistics.

A Appendix

dataset	articles	sentences	tokens
SemEval-2010	1,235	26,098	455,046
- training	900	19,233	331,614
- develop.	199	4,129	73,145
- test	136	2,736	50,287
TüBa-D/Z 10.0	3,644	95,595	1,787,801
- training	2190	65,416	1,258,514
- develop.	727	15,593	276,635
- test	727	14,586	252,652
TüBa-D/Z 11.0	3,816	104,787	1,959,474
OntoNotes 5.0	3,493	94,269	1,631,995
DROC	90	18,161	393,164
- training	58	11,368	249,817
- develop.	14	3,570	72,258
- test	18	3,223	70,999

Table 9: Overview of the dataset releases referred to in this work.

	MUC			B^3			$CEAF_{\phi_4}$			CoNLL	LEA		
	R	P	F1	R	P	F1	R	P	F1	F1	R	P	F1
TüBa-D/Z 10.0													
German c2f base	81.92	79.90	80.90	77.41	73.52	75.41	75.16	75.50	75.33	77.21	74.98	70.82	72.84
German c2f large	82.85	81.61	82.23	78.41	75.73	77.05	76.75	77.44	77.09	**78.79**	73.25	73.25	74.67
IMS HotCoref										48.54			
+ gold mentions										65.76			
SemEval-2010													
German c2f base	76.64	76.08	76.36	71.18	69.12	70.14	71.83	70.45	71.13	72.54	67.88	65.7	66.77
German c2f large	79.07	76.51	77.77	73.88	70.48	72.14	74.79	72.21	73.47	**74.46**	70.69	67.18	68.89
IMS HotCoref										48.61			
+ gold mentions										63.61			
CorZu										45.82			
+ gold mentions										58.11			

Table 10: Recall, precision and F1 score on the test set of TüBa-D/Z 10 and SemEval-2010 (without singletons). Our coarse-to-fine (c2f) models use either ELECTRA base or large. IMS HotCoref and CorZu system scores as reported by Roesiger and Kuhn (2016).

How to Estimate Continuous Sentiments From Texts Using Binary Training Data

Sandra Wankmüller
Ludwig-Maximilians-Universität
Munich, Germany
https://orcid.org/0000-0002-4003-1704
sandra.wankmueller@gsi.lmu.de

Christian Heumann
Ludwig-Maximilians-Universität
Munich, Germany
chris@stat.uni-muenchen.de

Abstract

Although sentiment is conceptualized as a continuous variable, most text-based sentiment analyses categorize texts into discrete sentiment categories. Compared to discrete categorizations, continuous sentiment estimates provide much more detailed information which can be used for more fine-grained analyses by researchers and practitioners alike. Yet, existing approaches that estimate continuous sentiments either require detailed knowledge about context and compositionality effects or require granular training labels, that are created in resource intensive annotation processes. Thus, existing approaches are too costly to be applied for each potentially interesting application. To overcome this problem, this work introduces CBMM (standing for *c*lassifier-based *b*eta *m*ixed *m*odeling procedure). CBMM aggregates the predicted probabilities of an ensemble of binary classifiers via a beta mixed model and thereby generates continuous, real-valued output based on mere binary training input. CBMM is evaluated on the Stanford Sentiment Treebank (SST) (Socher et al., 2013), the V-reg data set (Mohammad et al., 2018), and data from the 2008 American National Election Studies (ANES) (The American National Election Studies, 2015). The results show that CBMM produces continuous sentiment estimates that are acceptably close to the truth and not far from what could be obtained if highly fine-grained training data were available.

1 Introduction

In natural language processing and computer science, the term *sentiment* typically refers to a loosely defined, broad umbrella concept: Feeling, emotion, judgement, evaluation, and opinion all fall under the term sentiment or are used synonymously with it (Pang and Lee, 2008; Liu, 2015). Interestingly, the broad notion of sentiment is very well captured by the psychological concept of an attitude (Liu, 2015). In psychology, scholars agree that an attitude is a summary evaluation of an entity (Banaji and Heiphetz, 2010; Albarracin et al., 2019). An attitude is the aggregated evaluative response resulting from a multitude of different (and potentially conflicting) information bases relating to the attitude entity (Fabringar et al., 2019). When putting the definition of an attitude as an evaluative summary into mathematical terms, an attitude is a unidimensional, continuous variable ranging from highly negative to highly positive (Cacioppo et al., 1997). This notion that attitudes are continuous is also mirrored in the sentiment analysis literature in which sentiments are devised to vary in their levels of intensity (Liu, 2015).

Despite this conceptualization, in an overwhelming majority of studies textual sentiment expressions are measured as instances of discrete classes. Sentiment analysis often implies a binary or multiclass classification task in which texts are assigned into two or three classes, thereby distinguishing positive from negative sentiments and sometimes a third neutral category (e.g. Pang et al., 2002; Turney, 2002; Maas et al., 2011). Other studies pursue ordinal sentiment classification (e.g. Pang and Lee, 2005; Thelwall et al., 2010; Socher et al., 2013; Kim, 2014; Zhang et al., 2015; Cheang et al., 2020). Here, texts fall into one out of several discrete and ordered categories.

If researchers would generate continuous—rather than discrete—sentiment estimates, this would not only align the theoretical conceptualization of sentiment with the way it is measured but also would provide much more detailed information that in turn can be used by researchers and practitioners for more fine-grained analyses and more fine-tuned responses.

For example, in the plot on the right hand side in Figure 1, the distribution of the binarized sentiment values of the tweets in the V-reg data set (Mohammad et al., 2018) is shown. If researchers and practitioners would operate only on this discrete sentiment categorization, the shape of the underlying continuous sentiment distribution would be unknown. In fact, all distributions shown on the left hand side in Figure 1 produce the plot on the right hand side in Figure 1 if the sentiment values are binarized in such way that tweets with a sentiment value of ≥ 0.5 are assigned to the positive class and otherwise are assigned to the negative class. Imagine that a team of researchers would be interested in the sentiments expressed toward a policy issue and they would only know the binarized sentiment values on the right hand side in Figure 1. The researchers would not be able to conclude whether the expressions toward the policy issue are polarized into a supporting and an opposing side, whether a large share of sentiment expressions is positioned in the neutral middle, or whether the sentiments are evenly spread out. Knowing the continuous sentiment values, however, would allow them to differentiate between these scenarios.

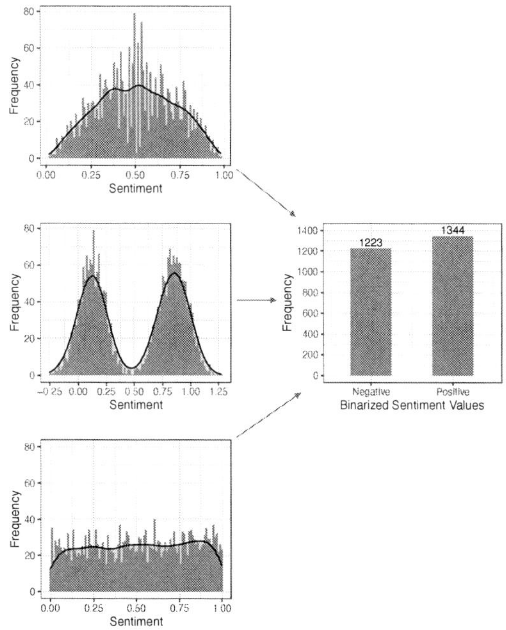

Figure 1: Continuous and Discrete Sentiment Distributions. Right plot: Binarized sentiment values of the tweets in the V-reg data set (Mohammad et al., 2018). Left plots: Histograms and kernel density estimates for three continuous distributions of sentiments that produce the plot on the right hand side if the continuous sentiment values are binarized such that tweets with values of ≥ 0.5 are assigned to the positive class and otherwise are assigned to the negative class. The unimodal distribution at the top is the true distribution of sentiment values but the other two distributions would generate the same binary separation of tweets into positive and negative.

As will be elaborated in Section 2, existing approaches that estimate continuous sentiment values for texts rely on (1) the availability of a comprehensive, context-matching sentiment lexicon and the researcher's knowledge regarding how to accurately model compositionality effects, or (2) highly costly processes to create fine-grained training data.

Sentiment analysis thus would benefit from a technique that generates continuous sentiment predictions for texts and is less demanding concerning the required information or resources. To meet this need, this work explores in how far the here proposed *c*lassifier-based *b*eta *m*ixed *m*odeling approach (CBMM) can produce valid continuous (i.e. real-valued) sentiment estimates on the basis of mere binary training data. The method comprises three steps. First, for each training set document a binary class label indicating whether the document is closer to the negative or the positive extreme of the sentiment variable has to be created or acquired. Second, an ensemble of J classifiers is trained on the binary class labels to produce for each of N test set documents J predicted probabilities to belong to the positive class. Third, a beta mixed model with N document random intercepts and J classifier random intercepts is estimated on the predicted probabilities. The N document random intercepts are the documents' continuous sentiment estimates.

In the following section, existing approaches that generate continuous sentiments are reviewed (Section 2). Then, CBMM is introduced in detail (Section 3) before it is evaluated on the basis of the Stanford Sentiment Treebank (SST) (Socher et al., 2013), the V-reg data set (Mohammad et al., 2018), and data from the 2008 American National Election Studies (ANES) (The American National Election Studies, 2015) (Section 4). A concluding discussion follows in Section 5.

2 Related Work

This work is concerned with the estimation of continuous values for texts in applications in which the underlying, unidimensional, continuous variable (e.g. sentiment) is well defined and the researcher seeks to position the texts along exactly this variable. Hence, this work does not consider unsupervised approaches (e.g. Slapin and Proksch,

2008) and only considers methods in which information on the definition of the underlying variable explicitly enters the estimation of the texts' values. Among these methods, one can distinguish two major approaches: lexicon-based procedures and regression models that operate on fine-grained training data.[1]

2.1 Lexicon-Based Approaches

An ideal sentiment lexicon covers all features in the corpus of an application and precisely assigns each feature to the sentiment value the feature has in the thematic context of the application (Grimmer and Stewart, 2013; Gatti et al., 2016). A major difficulty of lexicon-based approaches, however, is that even such an ideal sentiment lexicon will not guarantee highly accurate sentiment estimates. The reason is that sentiment builds up through complex compositional effects (Socher et al., 2013). These compositional effects either can be modeled via human-created rules or can be learned by supervised machine learning algorithms. Approaches that try to model compositionality via human-created rules range from simple formulas (e.g. Paltoglou et al., 2013; Gatti et al., 2016) to elaborate procedures (e.g. Moilanen and Pulman, 2007; Thet et al., 2010). Human-coded compositionality rules, however, tend to be outperformed by supervised machine learning algorithms (compare e.g. Gatti et al., 2016, Table 12 and Socher et al., 2013, Table 1). In the latter case, sentiment lexicons serve the purpose of creating the feature inputs to regression approaches—which are discussed next.

2.2 Regression Approaches

The second major set of approaches that generate real-valued sentiment estimates makes use of highly granular training data (e.g. as in the SST data set where each text is assigned to one out of 25 distinct values (Socher et al., 2013)). In these approaches, the fine-grained annotations are treated as if they were continuous and a regression model is applied.[2] Typically, the mean squared error (MSE) between the true granular labels and the real-valued predictions from the regression model is minimized. Regression approaches have shown to be able to generate continuous sentiment predictions that are quite close to the true fine-grained labels (Mohammad et al., 2018; Wang et al., 2018). Yet, the prerequisite for implementing such an approach is that fine-grained labels for the training data are available. Generating such granular annotations, however, is difficult and costly: Categorizing a training text into few ordinal categories is arguably a more easy task than assigning a text into one out of a large number of ordered values or even rating a text on a real-valued scale. As the number of distinct values increases, the number of inter- and intra-rater disagreements is likely to increase (Krippendorff, 2004). Hence, to produce reliable text annotations, it is advantageous to have each document rated several times by independent raters. The independent ratings then can be aggregated by taking the median or the mean of the ratings to obtain the final value (see e.g. Kiritchenko and Mohammad, 2017). The larger the number of raters for a document, the more reliable the final value assigned to the document. For this reason, generating reliable fine-grained labels for training documents via rating scale annotations requires a resource intensive annotation process.

The best-worst scaling (BWS) method in which coders have to identify the most positive and the most negative document among tuples of documents (typically 4-tuples), alleviates the problems of inter- and intra-rater inconsistencies (Kiritchenko and Mohammad, 2017). Yet, in order for the rankings among document tuples to generate valid real-valued ratings via the counting procedure implemented in BWS, it is essential that each document occurs in many different tuples such that each document is compared to many different other documents. This implies that a substantive number of unique tuples have to be annotated—which, in turn, demands respective human coding resources.

An alternative to the labeling of texts by human coders is the usage of already available information (e.g. if product reviews additionally come with numerical star ratings). The problem here, however, is that such information—if available at all—often comes in the form of discrete variables with only few distinct values (e.g. 5-star rating systems).

[1] Techniques for estimating continuous document positions on an a priori defined unidimensional latent variable also have been developed in political science. These methods either are at their core lexicon-based approaches (Watanabe, 2021) or require continuous values for the training documents (Laver et al., 2003)—and thus have the same shortcomings as either lexicon-based or regression approaches.

[2] Note that here, in correspondence with machine learning terminology, regression refers to statistical models and algorithms that model a real-valued response variable—which typically is assumed to follow a normal distribution.

To conclude, it is difficult and resource intensive to create or acquire fine-grained training data that is so detailed that it can be treated as if it were continuous. Not each team of researchers or practitioners will have the resources to create detailed training annotations and thus regression models cannot be applied to each substantive application of interest. Hence, the question that this work addresses is: Can one generate continuous sentiments with fewer costs in a setting where inter- and intra-rater inconsistencies are likely to be small? For example based on a simple binary coding of the training data?

3 Procedure

In the following, the three steps of the proposed CBMM procedure—(1) generating binary class labels, (2) training and applying an ensemble of classifiers, as well as (3) estimating a beta mixed model—are explicated. CBMM assumes that the documents to be analyzed are positioned on a latent, unidimensional, continuous sentiment variable. The aim is to estimate the test set documents' real-valued sentiment positions. The test set documents are indexed as $i \in \{1 \dots N\}$ and their sentiment positions are denoted as $\boldsymbol{\theta} = [\theta_1 \dots \theta_i \dots \theta_N]^\top$.

3.1 Generating Binary Class Labels

The CBMM procedure starts by generating binary class labels for the training set documents, e.g. via human coding. The coders classify the training documents into two classes such that the binary class label of each training set document indicates whether the document is closer to the negative (0) or the positive (1) extreme of the sentiment variable. Alternatively to human coding, binarized external information (such as star ratings associated with texts) can be used as class label indicators.

3.2 Training and Applying an Ensemble of Classifiers

In the second step, an ensemble of classification algorithms, indexed as $j \in \{1 \dots J\}$, is trained on the binary training data. The classifiers in the ensemble may differ regarding the type of algorithm, hyperparameter settings, or merely the seed values initializing the optimization process. After training, each classifier produces predictions for the N documents in the test set and each classifier's predicted probabilities for the test set documents to belong to the positive class are extracted. Thus, for each document i, a predicted probability to belong to class 1 is obtained from each classifier j, such that there are J predicted probabilities for each document: $\hat{\boldsymbol{y}}_i = [\hat{y}_{i1} \dots \hat{y}_{ij} \dots \hat{y}_{iJ}]$; whereby $\hat{y}_{ij}$ is classifier j's predicted probability for document i to belong to class 1.

3.3 Estimating a Beta Mixed Model

In step three, the aim is to infer the unobserved documents' continuous values on the latent sentiment variable from the observed predicted probabilities that have been generated by the set of classifiers. The approach taken here is similar to item response theory (IRT) in which unobserved subjects' values on a latent variable of interest (e.g. intelligence) are inferred from the observed subjects' responses to a set of question items (Hambleton et al., 1991). Central to IRT is the assumption that a subject's value on the latent variable of interest *affects* the subject's responses to the set of question items (Hambleton et al., 1991). For example, a subject's level of intelligence is postulated to influence his/her answers in an intelligence test. In correspondence with this assumption, the consistent mathematical element across all types of IRT models is that the observed subjects' responses are regressed on the unobserved subjects' latent levels of ability.

Here, there are documents rather than subjects and classifiers rather than question items. Yet, the aim is the same: to infer unobserved latent positions from what is observed. As in IRT, the idea here is that a document's value on the latent sentiment variable *affects* the predicted probabilities the document obtains from the classifiers. For example, a document with a highly positive sentiment is assumed to get rather high predicted probabilities from the classifiers. Consequently, the predicted probabilities are regressed on the documents' latent sentiment positions.

In doing so, it has to be accounted for that the predicted probabilities are grouped in a crossed non-nested design: In step 2, for each of the N documents, J predicted probabilities (one from each classifier) are produced such that there are $N \times J$ predicted probabilities. These predicted probabilities cannot be assumed to be independent. The J predicted probabilities for one document are likely to be correlated because they are repeated measurements on the same document. Additionally, the N predicted probabilities produced by one classifier also are generated by a common source. They come from the same classifier that might systematically differ from the others, e.g. produce systematically lower predicted probabilities.

Moreover, the data generating process is such that the documents are drawn from a larger population of documents. The population distribution of the probability to belong to class 1 might inform the probabilities obtained by individual documents. Similarly, the classifiers are sampled from a population of classifiers with a population distribution in the generated predicted probabilities that may inform an individual classifier's predicted probabilities. To account for this data generating process, a mixed model with N document random intercepts and J classifier random intercepts seems the adequate model of choice. (On mixed models see for example Fahrmeir et al. (2013, chapter 7)).

As the predicted probabilities, $\hat{y}_{ij}$, are in the unit interval [0,1], it is assumed that the $\hat{y}_{ij}$ are beta distributed. Following the parameterization of the beta density employed by Ferrari and Cribari-Neto (2004) the beta mixed model is:

$$\hat{y}_{ij} \sim B(\mu_{ij}, \phi) \quad (1)$$

$$g(\mu_{ij}) = \beta_0 + \theta_i + \gamma_j \quad (2)$$

$$\theta_i \sim N(0, \tau_\theta^2) \quad (3)$$

$$\gamma_j \sim N(0, \tau_\gamma^2) \quad (4)$$

In the model described here, $\hat{y}_{ij}$ (the probability for document i to belong to class 1 as predicted by classifier j) is assumed to be drawn from a beta distribution with conditional mean μ_{ij}. μ_{ij} assumes values in the range (0,1) and $\phi > 0$ is a precision parameter (Cribari-Neto and Zeileis, 2010). μ_{ij} is determined by the fixed global population intercept β_0, the document-specific deviation θ_i from this population intercept, and the classifier-specific deviation γ_j from the population intercept. As the documents are assumed to be sampled from a larger population, the document-specific θ_i are modeled to be drawn from a shared distribution (see equation 3).[3] The same is true for the classifier-specific γ_j. To ensure that the results from the linear predictor in equation 2 are kept between 0 and 1, the logit link is chosen as the link function $g(\cdot)$.[4]

Note that in the beta distribution $Var(\hat{y}_{ij}) = \mu_{ij}(1 - \mu_{ij})/(1 + \phi)$ (Cribari-Neto and Zeileis, 2010). This means that the variance of $\hat{y}_{ij}$ not only depends on precision parameter ϕ but also depends on μ_{ij}, which implies that the model naturally exhibits heteroscedasticity (Cribari-Neto and Zeileis, 2010). In the given data structure, documents that express very positive (or very negative) sentiments are likely to be easy cases for the classifiers and it is likely that all classifiers will predict very high (or very low) values. Documents that express less extreme sentiments, in contrast, are likely to be more difficult cases and the classifiers are likely to differ more in their predicted probabilities. This is, predicted probabilities are likely to exhibit a higher variance for documents positioned in the middle of the sentiment value range. To additionally account for this effect, the beta mixed model described in equations 1 to 4 can be extended with a dispersion formula describing the precision parameter ϕ as a function of document-specific fixed effects:[5]

$$h(\phi_i) = \delta_i \quad (5)$$

To keep $\phi_i > 0$, $h(\cdot)$ here is the log link (Brooks et al., 2017).[6] In the following, CBMM is implemented with and without the dispersion formula in equation 5. The variant of CBMM that includes equation 5 is denoted CBMMd.

With or without a dispersion formula, the θ_i describe the document-specific deviations from the fixed population mean β_0. Hence, the θ_i —in linear relation to β_0—position the documents on the real line and thus are taken as the CBMM and CBMMd estimates for the continuous sentiment values.

4 Applications

4.1 Data

The effectiveness of CBMM in generating continuous sentiments using binary training data is evaluated on the basis of four data sets:

The Stanford Sentiment Treebank (SST) (Socher et al., 2013) contains sentiment labels for 11,855 sentences [train: 9,645; test: 2,210] taken from movie reviews. Each of the sentences was assigned one out of 25 sentiment score values ranging from highly negative (0) to highly positive (1) by three independent human annotators.

[3]Note that the usually employed assumption is that the random effects are independent and identically distributed according to a normal distribution (Fahrmeir et al., 2013).

[4]Thus, equation 2 is $log(\mu_{ij}/(1 - \mu_{ij})) = \beta_0 + \theta_i + \gamma_j$.

[5]Note that the document-specific δ_i are fixed effects that are not modeled to be sampled from a shared population distribution. The reason is that current software implementations of mixed models that use maximum likelihood estimation only allow for inserting fixed effects but no random effects in the dispersion model formula (Brooks et al., 2017).

[6]Thus, equation 5 here is $log(\phi_i) = \delta_i$.

The V-reg data set from the SemEval-2018 Task 1 on "Affect in Tweets" (Mohammad et al., 2018) contains 2,567 tweets [train: 1,630; test: 937] that are likely to be rich in emotion. The tweets' real-valued valence scores are in the range (0,1) and were generated via BWS, whereby each 4-tuple was ranked by four independent coders.

Furthermore, *two data sets from the 2008 American National Election Studies (ANES)* (The American National Election Studies, 2015) are used. The feeling thermometer question, in which participants have to rate on an integer scale ranging from 0 to 100 in how far they feel favorable and warm vs. unfavorable and cold toward parties, is posed regularly in ANES surveys. In the 2008 pre-election survey, participants were additionally asked in open-ended questions to specify what they specifically like and dislike about the Democratic and the Republican Party.[7] Here, the aim is to generate continuous estimates of the sentiments expressed in the answers based on the binarized feeling thermometer scores. For the Democrats there are 1,646 answers [train: 1,097; test: 549]. This data set is named ANES-D. For the Republicans there are 1,523 answers [train: 1,015; test: 508] that make up data set ANES-R. For comparison with the other applications, the true scores from ANES are rescaled by min-max normalization from range [0,100] to [0,1].

To create binary training labels for the CBMM procedure, in all training data sets the fine-grained sentiment values are dichotomized such that the class label for a document is 1 if its score is ≥ 0.5 and is 0 otherwise. CBMM's continuous sentiment estimates for the test set documents then are compared to the original fine-grained values. Note that these four data sets are selected for evaluation precisely because they provide fine-grained sentiment scores against which the CBMM estimates can be compared to. In each of the four data sets, the detailed training annotations are the result of resourceful coding processes or—in the case of ANES—lucky coincidences. For example, around 50,000 annotations were made for the V-reg data set that comprises 2,567 tweets (Mohammad et al., 2018). Such resources or coincidences, however, are unlikely to be available for each potentially interesting research question. Thus, whilst these data sets are selected because they come with fine-grained labels that can be used for evaluating CBMM, the settings in which CBMM will be especially valuable are those in which external information that may serve as a granular training input is unavailable and the available amounts of resources are not sufficient for a granular coding of texts.

[7]The survey contains one question asking what the participant likes and a separate question asking what the participant dislikes about a party. For each respondent, the answers to these two questions are concatenated into a single answer.

4.2 Generating Continuous Sentiment Estimates via CBMM

Step 2 of the CBMM procedure consists in training an ensemble of classifiers on the binary training data to then obtain predicted probabilities for the test set documents. Here, for all four applications, a set of 10 pretrained language representation models with the RoBERTa architecture (Liu et al., 2019) are fine-tuned to the binary classification task. The 10 models within one ensemble merely differ regarding their seed value that initializes the optimization process and governs batch allocation.[8] As the seed values are randomly generated, this neatly fits with the assumption encoded in the specified mixed models that classifiers are randomly sampled from a larger population of classifiers. As a Transformer-based model for transfer learning, RoBERTa is likely to yield relatively high prediction performances in text-based supervised learning tasks also if—as is the case for the selected applications—training data sets are small.

In step 3 of CBMM, two different beta mixed models as presented in equations 1 to 5—one model with and the other without a dispersion formula—are estimated. In each mixed model, the estimate for θ_i is taken as the sentiment value predicted for document i.

Steps 1 and 3 of the CBMM procedure are conducted in R (R Core Team, 2020). The beta mixed models are estimated with the R package glmmTMB (Brooks et al., 2017). In step 2, fine-tuning is conducted in Python 3 (Van Rossum and Drake, 2009) making use of PyTorch (Paszke et al., 2019). Pretrained RoBERTa models are accessed via the open-source library provided by HuggingFace's Transformers (Wolf et al., 2020). The source code to replicate the findings is available at https://doi.org/10.6084/m9.figshare.14381825.v1.

[8]The 10 models applied for one application also have the same hyperparameter settings. In all four applications, a grid search across sets of different values for the batch size, the learning rate and the number of epochs is conducted via a 5-fold cross-validation. The hyperparameter setting that exhibits the lowest mean loss across the validation folds and does not suffer from too strong overfitting is selected.

4.3 Evaluation

4.3.1 Comparisons to Other Methods

The sentiment estimates from CBMM and CBMMd are compared to the following methods.

Mean of Predicted Probabilities [Pred-Prob-Mean]. For each document, this procedure simply takes the mean of the predicted probabilities across the ensemble of classifiers: $\hat{\theta}_i = \frac{1}{J}\sum_{j=1}^{J}\hat{y}_{ij}$.

Lexicon-Based Approaches. Two lexicons are made use of. First, the SST provides for each textual feature in the SST corpus a fine-grained human annotated sentiment value that indicates the feature's sentiment in the context of movie reviews. Hence, the SST constitutes an all-encompassing and perfectly tailored lexicon for the SST application and is employed as a lexicon here. Second, the SentiWords lexicon (Gatti et al., 2016), that is based on SentiWordNet (Esuli and Sebastiani, 2006) and contains prior polarity sentiment values for around 155,287 English lemmas, is used. For the SST and the SentiWords lexicons, the sentiment value estimates are generated by computing the arithmetic mean of a document's matched features' values. The procedures here are named SST-Mean and SentiWords-Mean.

Regression approaches, that make use of the true fine-grained sentiment values rather than the binary training data, are also applied. Note that the evaluation results for the regression-based procedures signify the levels of performance that can be achieved *if* one is in the ideal situation and possesses fine-grained training annotations. Hence, the regression approaches constitute a reference point against which the other approaches' performances can be related to.

Here, in all four applications, J = 10 RoBERTa regression models are trained on the training set and then make real-valued predictions for the documents in the test set such that there are J = 10 predictions for each test set document: $\hat{\boldsymbol{z}}_i = [\hat{z}_{i1} \dots \hat{z}_{ij} \dots \hat{z}_{iJ}]$; whereby $\hat{z}_{ij}$ is the real-valued prediction of regression model j for document i. To have a fair comparison to CBMM, the same procedures for aggregating the predicted values are explored. Thus, there are three different aggregation methods. First, the mean of the 10 models' predictions is taken such that the sentiment estimate is: $\hat{\theta}_i = \frac{1}{J}\sum_{j=1}^{J}\hat{z}_{ij}$ [Regr-Mean]. Second and third, a mixed model with and without a dispersion formula is estimated on the basis of the $\hat{z}_{ij}$. The estimates for the θ_i are extracted as the continuous sentiment predictions. Yet, to account for the data generating process of the $\hat{z}_{ij}$, a linear mixed model (LMM)—instead of a beta mixed model—is estimated:

$$\hat{z}_{ij} \sim N(\mu_{ij}, \sigma^2) \tag{6}$$

$$\mu_{ij} = \beta_0 + \theta_i + \gamma_j \tag{7}$$

$$\theta_i \sim N(0, \tau_\theta^2) \tag{8}$$

$$\gamma_j \sim N(0, \tau_\gamma^2) \tag{9}$$

This approach is named Regr-LMM. The LMM with a dispersion formula, Regr-LMMd, additionally has: $h(\sigma_i^2) = \delta_i$; with $h(\cdot)$ being the log link.

4.3.2 Evaluation Metrics

The generated continuous sentiment estimates are evaluated by comparing them to the original granular sentiment labels. Three evaluation metrics are used: the mean absolute error (MAE), the Pearson correlation coefficient r, and Spearman's rank correlation coefficient ρ. The evaluation metrics are selected such that there is a measure of the average absolute distance (MAE) as well as a measure of the linear correlation (r) between the original true sentiment values and the estimated values. Note that Spearman's ρ assesses the correlation between the ranks of the true and the ranks of the estimated values and thus evaluates in how far the order of documents from negative to positive sentiment as produced by the evaluated approaches reflects the order of documents according to the true scores.

4.4 Results

Table 1 presents the evaluation results across all applied data sets. Figure 2 visualizes distributions of the true and estimated sentiment values for the SST data. Across the four employed data sets (each with a different shape of the to be approximated distribution of the true sentiment values) the performance levels vary for all approaches. Yet, the main result remains consistent: the continuous sentiment estimates generated by CBMM correlate similarly with the truth and get only slightly less closer to the truth as the predictions generated by regression approaches that operate on fine-grained training data. At times, CBMM estimates even slightly outperform regression predictions. Hence, researchers that seek to get continuous sentiment estimates but do not have the resources to produce highly detailed training annotations can apply CBMM on binary training labels and thereby obtain estimated continuous sentiments whose performance is likely

	SST			V-reg			ANES-D			ANES-R		
	MAE	r	ρ	MAE	r	ρ	MAE	r	ρ	MAE	r	ρ
SST-Mean	0.190	0.554	0.574	0.171	0.437	0.487	0.242	−0.013	−0.033	0.252	0.059	0.058
SentiWords-Mean	0.201	0.428	0.429	0.177	0.429	0.475	0.254	0.067	0.079	0.289	−0.009	0.005
Regr-Mean	0.099	0.892	0.876	0.090	0.871	0.869	0.195	0.655	0.653	0.191	0.618	0.627
Regr-LMM	0.099	0.892	0.876	0.090	0.871	0.869	0.195	0.655	0.653	0.191	0.618	0.627
Regr-LMMd	0.099	0.892	0.876	0.090	0.872	0.870	0.195	0.655	0.653	0.192	0.618	0.627
Pred-Prob-Mean	0.216	0.859	0.856	0.198	0.804	0.844	0.202	0.646	0.649	0.218	0.624	0.613
CBMM	0.161	0.874	0.856	0.164	0.819	0.842	0.191	0.667	0.648	0.207	0.621	0.613
CBMMd	0.137	0.877	0.856	0.133	0.835	0.844	0.200	0.668	0.649	0.205	0.620	0.612

Table 1: Evaluation Results. For the SST, V-reg, ANES-D, and ANES-R test data sets, the mean absolute error (MAE), the Pearson correlation coefficient r, and Spearman's rank correlation coefficient ρ between the true and the estimated sentiment values are presented. The shading of the cells is a linear function of the approaches' level of performance. The darker the shading, the higher the performance. For computing the MAE, the predicted sentiment values are rescaled via min-max normalization to the range of the true sentiment values.

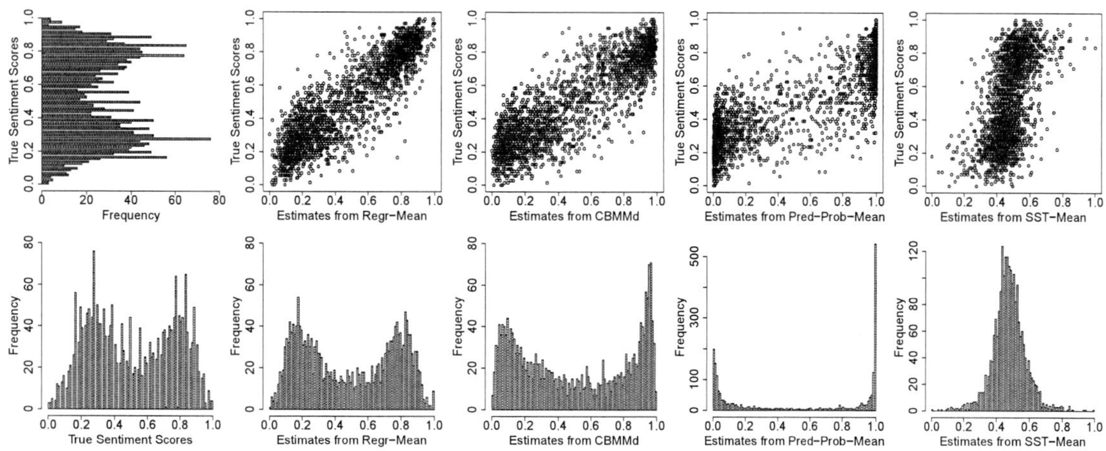

Figure 2: True and Estimated Sentiment Values for the SST Data. First column: Histograms of the true sentiment scores. Remaining columns, top row: Estimates from Regr-Mean, CBMMd, Pred-Prob-Mean, and SST-Mean plotted against the true sentiment values. Remaining columns, bottom row: Histograms of the estimates from Regr-Mean, CBMMd, Pred-Prob-Mean, and SST-Mean.

to be only slightly lower compared to predictions from regression models. Beside this main finding, the following aspects are revealed:

Lexicon-based approaches do not perform very well. The predicted sentiments are centered in the middle of the sentiment value range and changes in a document's sentiment are not strongly reflected in changes in the sentiment values predicted by the lexicons. (As an example see the most right column of Figure 2.) Consequently, the lexicon generated sentiment estimates exhibit relatively low levels of correlation with the true sentiment values. Especially the case of the SST lexicon for the SST data shows that it is not sufficient to have a lexicon that has a coverage of 100% and is perfectly tailored to the context it is applied to. In order to get valid sentiment estimates, one requires an aggregation procedure that accounts for the complex building up of sentiment in texts.

Regression Approaches. The continuous sentiment predictions generated by regression approaches tend to have the smallest distances to and the highest correlations with the true sentiment scores. Hence, the results demonstrate that *if* one has detailed training annotations available that can be treated as if they were continuous, regression approaches constitute an effective way to bring sentiment estimates as close as possible to the true sentiment values.

Across applications, the estimates obtained from Regr-Mean, Regr-LMM, and Regr-LMMd are highly similar. The reason is that the variance for the document-specific intercepts, τ_θ^2, is high relative to the error variance σ^2, and the classifier-specific variance τ^2_γ.[9] Thus, the LMM estimator is close to a fully unpooled solution in which a separate model for each document is estimated (Fahrmeir et al., 2013, p. 355-356). The sentiment predictions from Regr-LMM are therefore highly correlated with Regr-Mean that computes a separate mean for each document. Furthermore, adding a dispersion formula does not strongly affect the predictions from Regr-LMM.

Pred-Prob-Mean leads to acceptable results. Yet, the estimates from Pred-Prob-Mean still strongly mirror the binary coding structure (see the fourth column of Figure 2). Moreover, MAE tends to decrease and r tends to increase further if the predicted probabilities are aggregated via beta mixed models in CBMM.

CBMM produces continuous sentiment estimates that exhibit performance levels that are relatively close to those of the regression-based procedures. When considering the MAE and r, CBMMd tends to slightly outperform CBMM. As the predicted probabilities across all four data sets are characterized by a high degree of heteroskedasticity[10] additionally accounting for heteroskedasticity via the dispersion formula thus tends to further improve the estimates.

Interestingly, across the three approaches based on predicted probabilities (Pred-Prob-Mean, CBMM, CBMMd) Spearman's ρ nearly remains unchanged. This implies that the predicted order of documents on the latent sentiment variable is largely determined by the predicted probabilities from the ensemble of classifiers. Thus, whilst Pred-Prob-Mean, CBMM and CBMMd operate on the same order of documents,[11] it is the aggregation of the predicted probabilities by a beta mixed model—and the accounting for heteroskedasticity—that enables CBMM and CBMMd to alter the distances between the documents' positions on the sentiment variable such that the distribution of true sentiment values can be approximated more closely. (Compare the histograms of the values predicted by CBMMd and Pred-Prob-Mean in Figure 2.)

[9] Yet, across all evaluated data sets, a Restricted Likelihood-Ratio-Test (based on the approximation presented by Scheipl et al. (2008) as implemented in the RLRsim R-package) testing the null hypothesis that $\tau^2_\gamma = 0$, reveals that this null hypothesis can be rejected at a significance level of 0.01.

[10] To assess heteroskedasticity, Breusch-Pagan Tests (Breusch and Pagan, 1979) are conducted. For all applications and tested linear models, the Breusch-Pagan Test suggests that the null hypothesis of homoskedasticity can be rejected at a significance level of 0.01.

[11] Spearman's ρ between the estimates from Pred-Prob-Mean and CBMMd equals 0.999 across all applications.

5 Conclusion

This work introduced CBMM—a *c*lassifier-based *b*eta *m*ixed *m*odeling technique that generates continuous estimates for texts by estimating a beta mixed model based on predicted probabilities from a set of classifiers. CBMM's central contribution is that it produces continuous output based on binary training input, thereby dispensing the requirement of regression approaches to have (possibly prohibitively costly to create) fine-grained training data. Evaluation results demonstrate that CBMM's continuous estimates perform well and are not far from regression predictions.

CBMM here is applied in the context of sentiment analysis. Yet, it can be applied to any context in which the aim is to have continuous predictions but the resources only allow for creating binary training annotations.

References

Dolores Albarracin, Aashna Sunderrajan, Sophie Lohmann, Man pui Sally Chan, and Duo Jiang. 2019. The psychology of attitudes, motivation, and persuasion. In Dolores Albarracin and Blair T. Johnson, editors, *The Handbook of Attitudes*, pages 3–44. Routledge, New York, NY.

Mahzarin R. Banaji and Larisa Heiphetz. 2010. Attitudes. In Susan T. Fiske, Daniel T. Gilbert, and Gardner Lindzey, editors, *Handbook of Social Psychology*, pages 348–388. John Wiley & Sons, New York, NY.

Trevor S. Breusch and Adrian R. Pagan. 1979. A simple test for heteroscedasticity and random coefficient variation. *Econometrica*, 47(5):1287–1294.

Mollie E. Brooks, Kasper Kristensen, Koen J. van Benthem, Arni Magnusson, Casper W. Berg, Anders Nielsen, Hans J. Skaug, Martin Mächler, and Benjamin M. Bolker. 2017. glmmTMB balances speed and flexibility among packages for zero-inflated generalized linear mixed modeling. *The R Journal*, 9(2):378–400.

John T. Cacioppo, Wendi L. Gardner, and Gary G. Berntson. 1997. Beyond bipolar conceptualizations and measures: The case of attitudes and evaluative space. *Personality and Social Psychology Review*, 1(1):3–25.

Brian Cheang, Bailey Wei, David Kogan, Howey Qiu, and Masud Ahmed. 2020. Language representation models for fine-grained sentiment classification. *arXiv preprint*. arXiv:2005.13619v1 [cs.CL].

Francisco Cribari-Neto and Achim Zeileis. 2010. Beta regression in R. *Journal of Statistical Software*, 34(2):1–24.

Andrea Esuli and Fabrizio Sebastiani. 2006. SentiWordNet: A publicly available lexical resource for opinion mining. In *Proceedings of the Fifth International Conference on Language Resources and Evaluation (LREC'06)*, Genoa, Italy. European Language Resources Association (ELRA).

Leandre R. Fabringar, Tara K. MacDonald, and Duane T. Wegener. 2019. The origins and structure of attitudes. In Dolores Albarracin and Blair T. Johnson, editors, *The Handbook of Attitudes*, pages 109–157. Routledge, New York, NY.

Ludwig Fahrmeir, Thomas Kneib, Stefan Lang, and Brian Marx. 2013. *Regression*. Springer-Verlag, Berlin.

Silvia Ferrari and Francisco Cribari-Neto. 2004. Beta regression for modelling rates and proportions. *Journal of Applied Statistics*, 31(7):799–815.

Lorenzo Gatti, Marco Guerini, and Marco Turchi. 2016. SentiWords: Deriving a high precision and high coverage lexicon for sentiment analysis. *IEEE Transactions on Affective Computing*, 7(4):409–421.

Justin Grimmer and Brandon M. Stewart. 2013. Text as data: The promise and pitfalls of automatic content analysis methods for political texts. *Political Analysis*, 21(3):267–297.

Ronald K. Hambleton, Hariharan Swaminathan, and H. Jane Rogers. 1991. *Fundamentals of Item Response Theory*. Sage, Newbury Park, California.

Yoon Kim. 2014. Convolutional neural networks for sentence classification. In *Proceedings of the 2014 Conference on Empirical Methods in Natural Language Processing (EMNLP)*, pages 1746–1751, Doha, Qatar. Association for Computational Linguistics.

Svetlana Kiritchenko and Saif Mohammad. 2017. Best-worst scaling more reliable than rating scales: A case study on sentiment intensity annotation. In *Proceedings of the 55th Annual Meeting of the Association for Computational Linguistics (Volume 2: Short Papers)*, pages 465–470, Vancouver, Canada. Association for Computational Linguistics.

Klaus Krippendorff. 2004. *Content Analysis: An Introduction to Its Methodology*, 2nd edition. Sage Publications, Thousand Oaks.

Michael Laver, Kenneth Benoit, and John Garry. 2003. Extracting policy positions from political texts using words as data. *American Political Science Review*, 97(2):311–331.

Bing Liu. 2015. *Sentiment Analysis*. Cambridge University Press, New York.

Yinhan Liu, Myle Ott, Naman Goyal, Jingfei Du, Mandar Joshi, Danqi Chen, Omer Levy, Mike Lewis, Luke Zettlemoyer, and Veselin Stoyanov. 2019. RoBERTa: A robustly optimized BERT pretraining approach. *arXiv preprint*. arXiv:1907.11692v1 [cs.CL].

Andrew L. Maas, Raymond E. Daly, Peter T. Pham, Dan Huang, Andrew Y. Ng, and Christopher Potts. 2011. Learning word vectors for sentiment analysis. In *Proceedings of the 49th Annual Meeting of the Association for Computational Linguistics: Human Language Technologies - Volume 1*, pages 142–150, Portland, Oregon, USA. Association for Computational Linguistics.

Saif M. Mohammad, Felipe Bravo-Marquez, Mohammad Salameh, and Svetlana Kiritchenko. 2018. Semeval-2018 Task 1: Affect in tweets. In *Proceedings of International Workshop on Semantic Evaluation (SemEval-2018)*, New Orleans, LA, USA.

Karo Moilanen and Stephen Pulman. 2007. Sentiment composition. In *Proceedings of the International Conference on Recent Advances in Natural Language Processing (RANLP)*, pages 378–382, Borovets, Bulgaria.

Georgios Paltoglou, Mathias Theunis, Arvid Kappas, and Mike Thelwall. 2013. Predicting emotional responses to long informal text. *IEEE Transactions on Affective Computing*, 4(1):106–115.

Bo Pang and Lillian Lee. 2005. Seeing stars: Exploiting class relationships for sentiment categorization with respect to rating scales. In *Proceedings of the 43rd Annual Meeting of the Association for Computational Linguistics*, pages 115–124, Ann Arbor, Michigan, USA. Association for Computational Linguistics.

Bo Pang and Lillian Lee. 2008. Opinion mining and sentiment analysis. *Foundations and Trends in Information Retrieval*, 2(1-2):1–135.

Bo Pang, Lillian Lee, and Shivakumar Vaithyanathan. 2002. Thumbs up? Sentiment classification using machine learning techniques. In *Proceedings of the 2002 Conference on Empirical Methods in Natural Language Processing (EMNLP)*, pages 79–86, Philadelphia, Pennsylvania, USA. Association for Computational Linguistics.

Adam Paszke, Sam Gross, Francisco Massa, Adam Lerer, James Bradbury, Gregory Chanan, Trevor Killeen, Zeming Lin, Natalia Gimelshein, Luca Antiga, Alban Desmaison, Andreas Kopf, Edward Yang, Zachary DeVito, Martin Raison, Alykhan Tejani, Sasank Chilamkurthy, Benoit Steiner, Lu Fang, Junjie Bai, and Soumith Chintala. 2019. PyTorch: An imperative style, high-performance deep learning library. In Hanna Wallach, Hugo Larochelle, Alina Beygelzimer, Florence d'Alché Buc, Emily Fox, and Roman Garnett, editors, *Advances in Neural Information Processing Systems*, volume 32, pages 8024–8035. Curran Associates, Inc.

R Core Team. 2020. *R: A Language and Environment for Statistical Computing*. R Foundation for Statistical Computing, Vienna, Austria.

Fabian Scheipl, Sonja Greven, and Helmut Küchenhoff. 2008. Size and power of tests for a zero random effect variance or polynomial regression in additive and linear mixed models. *Computational Statistics & Data Analysis*, 52(7):3283–3299.

Jonathan B. Slapin and Sven-Oliver Proksch. 2008. A scaling model for estimating time-series party positions from texts. *American Journal of Political Science*, 52(3):705–722.

Richard Socher, Alex Perelygin, Jean Wu, Jason Chuang, Christopher D. Manning, Andrew Ng, and Christopher Potts. 2013. Recursive deep models for semantic compositionality over a sentiment treebank. In *Proceedings of the 2013 Conference on Empirical Methods in Natural Language Processing (EMNLP)*, pages 1631–1642, Seattle, Washington, USA. Association for Computational Linguistics.

The American National Election Studies. 2015. *ANES 2008 Time Series Study*. Inter-University Consortium for Political and Social Research, Ann Arbor, MI. https://electionstudies.org/data-center/2008-time-series-study/.

Mike Thelwall, Kevan Buckley, Georgios Paltoglou, Di Cai, and Arvid Kappas. 2010. Sentiment strength detection in short informal text. *Journal of the American Society for Information Science and Technology*, 61(12):2544–2558.

Tun Thura Thet, Jin-Cheon Na, and Christopher S.G. Khoo. 2010. Aspect-based sentiment analysis of movie reviews on discussion boards. *Journal of Information Science*, 36(6):823–848.

Peter D. Turney. 2002. Thumbs up or thumbs down? Semantic orientation applied to unsupervised classification of reviews. In *Proceedings of the 40th Annual Meeting on Association for Computational Linguistics*, pages 417–424, Philadelphia, Pennsylvania, USA. Association for Computational Linguistics.

Guido Van Rossum and Fred L. Drake. 2009. *Python 3 Reference Manual*. CreateSpace, Scotts Valley, CA.

Jin Wang, Bo Peng, and Xuejie Zhang. 2018. Using a stacked residual LSTM model for sentiment intensity prediction. *Neurocomputing*, 322:93–101.

Kohei Watanabe. 2021. Latent Semantic Scaling: A semisupervised text analysis technique for new domains and languages. *Communication Methods and Measures*, 15(2):81–102.

Thomas Wolf, Lysandre Debut, Victor Sanh, Julien Chaumond, Clement Delangue, Anthony Moi, Pierric Cistac, Tim Rault, Rémi Louf, Morgan Funtowicz, Joe Davison, Sam Shleifer, Patrick von Platen, Clara Ma, Yacine Jernite, Julien Plu, Canwen Xu, Teven Le Scao, Sylvain Gugger, Mariama Drame, Quentin Lhoest, and Alexander M. Rush. 2020. HuggingFace's Transformers: State-of-the-art natural language processing. *arXiv preprint*. arXiv:1910.03771v5 [cs.CL].

Xiang Zhang, Junbo Zhao, and Yann LeCun. 2015. Character-level convolutional networks for text classification. In *Proceedings of the 28th International Conference on Neural Information Processing Systems*, pages 649–657, Montreal, Canada. MIT Press.

forumBERT: Topic Adaptation and Classification of Contextualized Forum Comments in German

Ayush Yadav
International Institute
of Information Technology
Bangalore, India
yadavayush.ay42@gmail.com

Benjamin Milde
Language Technology Group
Dept. of Informatics
Universität Hamburg, Germany
milde@informatik.uni-hamburg.de

Abstract

Online user comments in public forums are often associated with low quality, hate speech or even excessive demands for moderation. To better exploit their constructive and deliberate potential, we present forumBERT. forumBERT is built on top of the BERT architecture and uses a shared weight and late fusion technique to better determine the quality and relevance of a comment on a forum article. Our model integrates article context with comments for the online/offline comment moderation task. This is done using a two step procedure: self-supervised BERT language model fine tuning for topic adaptation followed by integration into the forumBERT architecture for online/offline classification. We present evaluation results on various classification tasks of the public One Million Post dataset, as well as on the online/offline comment moderation task on 998,158 labelled comments from NDR.de, a popular German broadcaster's website. forumBERT significantly outperforms baseline models on the NDR dataset and also outperforms all existing advanced baseline models on the OMP dataset. Additionally we conduct two studies on the influence of topic adaptation on the general comment moderation task.

1 Introduction

Online user comments, such as those on journalistic content or product features are often associated with low quality, hate speech or even excessive demands for moderation. Automating this moderation or aspects of it can be considered to be of high practical interest. One of the key challenges of forum comment moderation is the specificity of category of classification. Forum comments have to be moderated for hate-speech, discrimination, spam among many other generally discussed classification tasks. Additionally comments on forum articles must also be moderated for relevance and contribution to the discourse.

Previous work by Schabus et al. (2017) and Schabus and Skowron (2018) introduces the idea of applied classification, wherein comments are annotated across multiple forum specific categories and classification models are created for each category. In this paper we focus on the more general "comment moderation task" on news forum comments. In this task, comments can be classified into one of two categories, either online or offline, where an online classification represents a comment that is accepted by the forum moderators and an offline classification represents comments that have been taken down by the forum moderators.

In recent years, the Natural Language Processing community has experienced a substantial shift towards using pre-trained models. Their usage on large corpora has proved to be beneficial in learning general language representations and has shown improvement in text classification and many other NLP tasks, which has also helped avoid training large language models from scratch. However, the lack of portability of NLP models to new conditions is a central issue in NLP. For many target applications like comment moderation on niche public forums, labelled data might be lacking and there might not be enough unlabelled data to train a general language model. These conditions press us to visit domain adaptation to improve the language model.

Therefore, in this paper we present forumBERT, a modification to the BERT architecture which uses two weight shared BERT models and a late fusion technique to better determine a comment's quality and relevance on a forum article. We also extend the work by Rietzler et al. (2020) and investigate the influence of a domain adapted BERT language model on the downstream comment moderation accuracy as a function of labelled downstream training examples. In particular, the contributions of our paper are:

- We present the forumBERT architecture to determine a comment's quality and relevance on a forum post.
- We introduce the NDR dataset which is used for the comment moderation task.
- We show that forumBERT outperforms baseline models on the comment moderation task. forumBERT achieves state of the art results on seven classification tasks on the One Million Posts Dataset.
- We analyse the influence of topic adaptation on the forumBERT architecture by varying the number of labelled datapoints in the comment moderation task.
- We also analyse the influence of the number of training steps of the BERT language model and the results on the downstream comment moderation classification task.

This paper has been structured in the following way: Section 2 introduces the BERT architecture and mentions existing comment moderation architectures and some relevant BERT model adaptations. Section 3 describes the NDR dataset and the NDR topic datasets. Section 4 introduces forumBERT and the training procedure followed. Section 5 evaluates forumBERT and BERT on the NDR dataset and the OMP dataset. Section 6 contains our topic adaptation experiments on the effectiveness of topic adaptation and the influence of topic adaptation as a function of labelled training examples.

2 Related Work

Pre-trained models using large corpora have dominated the task of text classification. This began with pre-trained word embeddings such as Word2Vec (Mikolov et al., 2013) and GloVe (Pennington et al., 2014) and now in the current paradigm, pre-trained models like ELMo (Peters et al., 2018), BERT (Devlin et al., 2019), GPT/GPT2 (Radford et al., 2019), XLNet (Yang et al., 2019), have achieved state of the art results in a wide spectrum of NLP taks including text classification.

BERT (Devlin et al., 2019) is an amalgamation of several key findings in NLP research such as contextualized word representations, sub word tokenization (Wu et al., 2016) and transformers (Vaswani et al., 2017). The main innovations are the unique learning methods adopted by BERT. The BERT language model is trained to optimize on two tasks, i.e Masked Language Modelling (MLM) and Next Sentence Prediction.
Masked language modeling is a fill-in-the-blank task, where a model uses the context words surrounding a [MASK] token to try to predict what the [MASK] word should be. Next Sentence Prediction is a classification task, in which the BERT model receives a pair of sentences as input and learns to predict if the second sentence in the pair is the subsequent sentence in the original document.

2.1 Comment Moderation Architectures and BERT Adaptations

Pavlopoulos et al. (2017a) introduced an RNN based method for the comment moderation task on a Greek news sports portal. This method was improved by Pavlopoulos et al. (2017b) to include dataset specific user-embeddings, generated by accounting for the number of accepted and rejected comments of every user on the sports portal. Risch and Krestel (2018) have proposed a semi-automatic approach to comment moderation using a comment, user and article information to create a high recall logistic regression model.

Large pre-trained BERT language models have been incorporated into many task specific architectures. Sentence-BERT (Reimers and Gurevych, 2019) is one such modification of the BERT network using Siamese and Triplet networks that is able to derive semantically meaningful sentence embeddings where semantically similar sentences are closer in the vector space. SentiBERT (Yin et al., 2020) is a BERT variant that effectively captures compositional sentiment semantics by incorporating BERT's contextualized representation with binary constituency parse tree to capture semantic composition.

However, in the current paradigm, pre-trained language models are generalized and their portability to new conditions still remains an issue. To this end, work by Rietzler et al. (2020) and Xu et al. (2019) shows that in the aspect target sentiment task, the performance of models that are pre-trained on a general language corpus can be improved by fine tuning the language model on a domain specific corpus. We build on this and in Section 6 show that even in the comment moderation task on niche forums, the performance of models that are pre-trained on a German general language corpus can be improved by finetuning the language model on each specific forum topic.

3 Datasets

To verify the topic adaptation capabilities in German news forum datasets, we procured the NDR dataset[1] which consists of almost one million labelled user comments and their adjoining articles from the NDR news website. This dataset can be obtained directly from NDR for academic and research use. To evaluate the performance of our forumBERT architecture on an already existing dataset, we use the One Million Posts Dataset (Schabus et al., 2017).

3.1 NDR Dataset

The NDR dataset consists of a collection of 998,158 labelled comments on 65,261 articles on the NDR website. All comments were collected between five and a half year span from 2014-05-09 to 2019-12-12. The dataset consists of the following attributes for every comment:

- Headline: The title of the article
- URL: A URL to the article on the NDR website
- Comment: The comment text
- Date: The date of posting the comment
- Label: A binary offline/online label, which represents the final status of the comment on the website. Offline labelled comments are considered non-desirable content on the forum.

On average the length of a comment on the NDR dataset is 59.15 words. The quartile comment lengths are shown in Table 1 and the distribution of comment lengths is plotted in Figure 1.

quartile	comment length
0.25	22
0.50	43
0.75	79
1.00	1308

Table 1: comment length at every quartile in the NDR dataset

[1] https://www.ndr.de/index.html

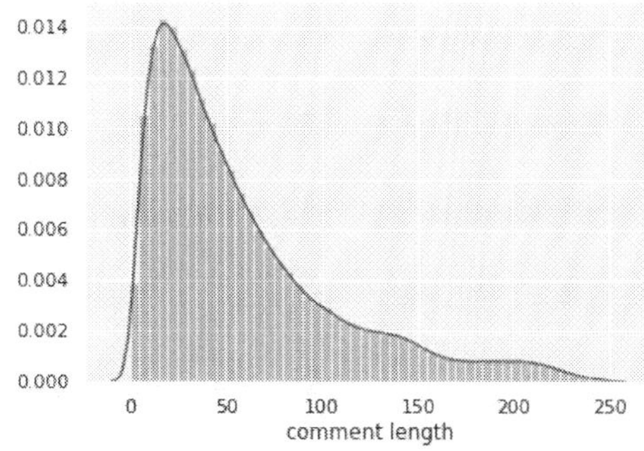

Figure 1: Distribution of comment length on the NDR dataset (clipped to a maximum comment length of 250 words.)

3.1.1 Topic Segmentation

News datasets are very general in nature where discussions range from politics, sports to technology and scientific news. Therefore, we used the URL attribute to segment the entire dataset into different topics for topic adaptation. Specifically, by splicing the URL attribute, topic information was obtained for each comment. For example, in "http://relaunch.ndr.de/sport/handball/bundesliga/" the url contains the topic of the article, which in this case is sport. This is used to segment the entire dataset into topics. The number of comments per topic are shown in Table 2.

Topic	online	offline	offline %
Nachrichten (News)	613061	215656	26.02%
Sport	73151	12258	14.35%
Kultur (Culture)	21231	5485	20.53%
Fernsehen (TV)	12218	2998	19.70%
Info	20020	5491	21.52%
Radio	1986	295	12.93%
Rest	11177	2996	21.11%

Table 2: number of online and offline examples in all topic forums

We applied topic adaptation (Rietzler et al., 2020) to two topics, "sport" and "kultur" (Culture), as both had among the most labelled training datapoints, as shown in Table 2). "Nachrichten" (News) is too general to be considered a forum topic and thus was omitted.

3.2 One Million Posts (OMP)

The One Million Posts dataset (OMP Schabus et al. (2017)) contains a selection of user comments posted to the Austrian Newspaper website "Der

Standard". The comments have been selected from a 12 month time span between 2015-06-01 and 2016-05-31. There are 11,773 freely labelled posts on nine categories (not all labelled comments are labelled in every category) and 1,000,000 unlabelled posts in the data set. The amount of labelled data for each of the nine categories has been mentioned in Table 3

Category	Does Apply	Does Not Apply	Percentage
Sentiment Negative	1691	1908	47%
Sentiment Neutral	1865	1734	52%
Sentiment Positive	43	3556	1%
Off-Topic	580	3019	16%
Inappropriate	303	3296	8%
Discriminating	282	3317	8%
Possibly Feedback	1301	4737	22%
Personal Stories	1625	7711	17%
Arguments Used	1022	2577	28%

Table 3: number of labelled examples in each category in the OMP dataset (Schabus et al., 2017)

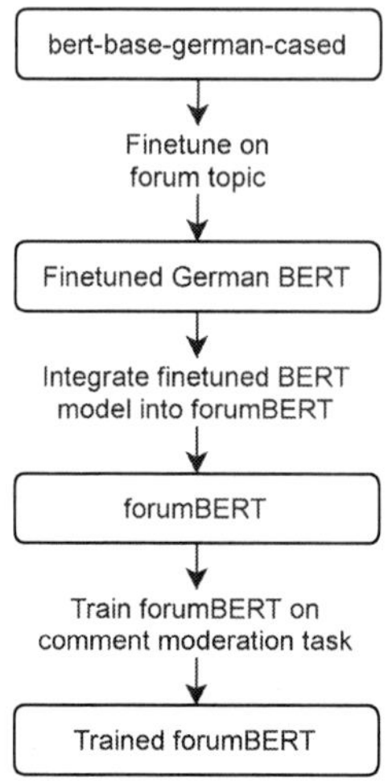

Figure 2: Schema diagram for the construction of forumBERT.

4 Methodology

This section presents forumBERT, which is an extension of BERT for contextual classification tasks like general comment moderation task. We use a German language pre-trained BERT language model as a basis and approach this task using a three-step procedure. In the first step we finetune the pre-trained weights of the language model in a self-supervised way on a topic-specific corpus. In the second step we incorporate this finetuned language model into the forumBERT architecture. The final step is the supervised training of forumBERT for the online/offline classification end-task. A schema for this process is depicted in Figure 2

In the following subsections, we discuss how we finetune the BERT language model and then the forumBERT architecture.

4.1 BERT: Language Model Finetuning and Topic Adaptation

To create our forumBERT model, our first step deals with finetuning a pretrained BERT language model using a topic specfic corpora. As described in Section 3.1.1 we split the NDR dataset into multiple topics. We adopt post-training of BERT (Xu et al., 2019) on a topic dataset which is algorithmically the same as pretraining the model. The Masked Language Modelling task is used to learn topic knowledge and remove any biases learnt from the pretraining datasets. Next Sentence Prediction helps BERT learn contextualized embeddings that are beyond word level. This is important since, at a high level we wish to generate similar embeddings for comments that are in the same context as it's adjoining article's context. Finetuning the language model helps mitigate the problem of having less labelled data, which is the case in many online forums. This finetuned language model is then incorporated into the forumBERT architecture.

Other than using the topic adapted BERT language model to create the forumBERT model, we also investigate the limitations of language model finetuning for the comment moderation task through two tasks described in Section 6.

4.2 forumBERT: A Weight Shared BERT Model

forumBERT is an extension of BERT for topic-knowledge learning and forum-comment classification. The model must be able to compare the article and the comment on the article to determine its quality and relevance on the forum. Inappropriate and discriminatory comments must be removed from the forum irrespective of the corresponding articles, but the model must also remove comments that are off-topic/irrelevant and digress too far from the topic of the article. To achieve this we use the forumBERT architecture.

We adapt the finetuned $BERT_{BASE}$ model for forum comment classification by using two finetuned $BERT_{BASE}$ models, one which takes in as input the headline of the article and another which takes the comment on the corresponding article as input. To mitigate the problem of a parameter explosion be-

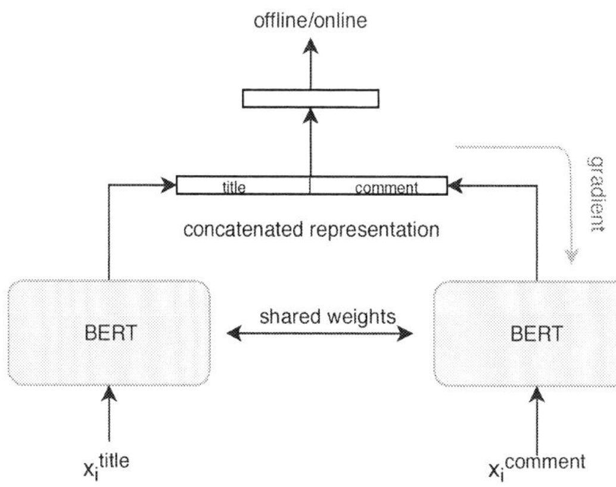

Figure 3: forumBERT architecture

cause of using 2 BERT models and to add implicit regularization we share the weight between the two BERT models (shown in Figure 3).

We follow Devlin et al. (2019) and consider the final hidden state corresponding to the [CLS] input token for both the BERT models. The pair of article and comment representations thus obtained are both of dimensions 768×1. The pair of embeddings are concatenated at the output of the BERT model (late fusion). Late fusion is preferred rather than concatenating the input tokens and passing them through the network, to allow the network to fully separate out the differences between the article and the comment. The dimensions of the concatenated vector is 1536×1. The fused vector is then passed through 2 fully connected layers with weights $W_t \in \mathbb{R}^{2n \times n}$ and $W_{t'} \in \mathbb{R}^{n \times k}$ respectively, where n is the dimension of the comment/headline embedding (n = 768) and k is the number of labels (k = 2). A softmax function is applied to the final k length vector.

$$\text{out} = \text{softmax}(W_{t'}(W_t(x))) \quad (1)$$

Here, x represents the fused representation vector. We optimize the cross-entropy loss.

4.3 Implementation Details

As a base for all our experiments we use the $\text{BERT}_{\text{BASE}}$ model which consists of 12 layers (transformer blocks), 12 attention heads 768 hidden dimensions per token amounting to a total of 110 million parameters. The parameters of this model are initialized using bert-base-german-cased[2], which has been pretrained on the German Wikipedia Dump (6 GB), the German OpenLegalData dump (2.4 GB) and German news articles (3.6 GB) and released by deepset.ai[3]. For the BERT language model finetuning we use 32 bit floating point computations using the Adam optimizer (Kingma and Ba, 2015). The batchsize is set to 8 while the learning rate is set to $3 \cdot 10^{-5}$. The maximum input sequence length is set to 512 tokens, which amounts to about 11 sentences per sequence on average. For all experiments except Experiment 6.1 we use a forumBERT model in which we integrate a topic adapted BERT language model which is trained for 13 epochs on the entire topic with a learning rate of $3 \cdot 10^{-5}$.

For the down-stream online/offline classification task we use 32 bit floating point computations and the Adam optimizer. The models are trained for 7 epochs, with a learning rate of $2 \cdot 10^{-6}$ for the two epochs and $6.31 \cdot 10^{-7}$ for the remaining 5 epochs. The validation accuracy converges after about 3 epochs.

For all experiments and results on the NDR dataset, we split the topic dataset in a 9:1 ratio. The larger portion of the dataset is used for language modelling and for training on downstream tasks and the smaller portion is used only for testing on downstream tasks.

5 Results

5.1 Comment Moderation Task on NDR Dataset

Meas.	BOW com.	D2V tit.+com.	BERT com.	BERT tit.+com.	fBERT tit./com.
Prec.	0.65	0.60	**0.73**	0.71	0.698
Rec.	0.27	0.15	0.38	0.42	**0.431**
F1.	0.38	0.24	0.50	0.527	**0.533**
Acc.	0.786	0.767	0.810	0.814	**0.819**

Table 4: Results of the comment moderation task on the entire NDR dataset (without any topic segmentation). Precision, Recall, F1-score are all computed on the minority class (offline).

For the comment moderation task, we compare the performance of forumBERT with following baseline models trained on the NDR sport and kulur topic datasets: 1) Logistic regression on count vectorizer (BOW model); 2) logistic regression on doc2vec[4] representation (D2V model); 3) 3 layer DNN (dense neural network) (3DNN model) built

[2]https://huggingface.co/bert-base-german-cased

[3]https://deepset.ai/german-bert

[4]The doc2vec document embedding (Le and Mikolov,

No. Training Ex.	1024			Sports Topic 8192			All Topic Data			
Model	Prec.	Rec.	F1	Prec	Rec	F1	Prec	Rec.	F1	Wins
log-reg (count)	0.222	0.639	0.329	**0.586**	0.212	0.311	**0.591**	0.212	0.311	2
log-reg (D2V)	0.203	0.618	0.305	0.220	0.649	0.328	0.428	0.046	0.083	0
3DNN (D2V)	0.131	0.496	0.207	0.141	0.460	0.216	0.290	0.241	0.263	0
BERT (comment)	0.267	0.633	0.375	0.318	0.692	0.435	0.584	0.369	0.452	0
BERT (title + comment)	0.283	0.650	0.394	0.337	0.689	0.452	0.571	0.406	0.475	0
forumBERT (title/comment)	**0.295**	**0.697**	**0.414**	0.328	**0.741**	**0.457**	0.483	**0.547**	**0.513**	7

No. Training Ex.	1024			Kultur Topic 8192			All Topic Data			
Model	Prec.	Rec.	F1	Prec	Rec	F1	Prec	Rec.	F1	Wins
log-reg (count)	0.264	0.617	0.370	0.331	0.678	0.445	0.513	0.327	0.339	0
log-reg (D2V)	0.210	0.637	0.316	0.253	0.636	0.362	0.578	0.056	0.102	0
3DNN (D2V)	0.193	0.636	0.296	0.202	0.607	0.302	0.292	**0.476**	0.362	1
BERT (comment)	0.319	**0.751**	0.447	0.318	**0.803**	0.455	0.552	0.417	0.475	2
BERT (title + comment)	0.358	0.652	0.462	**0.439**	0.638	**0.520**	0.650	0.363	0.465	2
forumBERT (title/comment)	**0.367**	0.643	**0.467**	0.398	0.643	0.468	**0.706**	0.375	**0.490**	4

Table 5: Comment moderation task results on the NDR sport topic dataset and the culture topic dataset. The results have been computed for three quantities of uniformly sampled training examples with the first two being 1024 and 8192. The final quantity is all training comments from that particular topic. Precision, recall and F1-score are computed on the minority class (offline).

on doc2vec representations; 4) two BERT models. For all models other than forumBERT and a BERT model, contextualized input of the form "TITLE [title] COMMENT [comment]", is provided as input. To test the importance of providing context, we also train a BERT model using only comment text as input.

We report performance measures on Table 5. forumBERT significantly outperforms all other models and has the highest F1 scores in both the sports and kultur topic datasets, even in few shot conditions (1024/8192 training examples). From this table, it can be seen that our approach significantly outperforms the standard BERT model, improving the F1 scores from 0.475 to 0.513 (8% increase) in the sports topic and an improvement from 0.465 to 0.490 (a 5.3% increase) in the kultur dataset. Also if we compare forumBERT to a standard BERT model with only comment input the F1 scores increase from 0.452 to 0.513 (a 13.4% performance gain) on the sport topic and an improvement from 0.475 to 0.490 (a 3.15% gain).

Table 4 represents the effectiveness of the design architecture of the forumBERT model. The forumBERT model considered here uses a pretrained BERT language model without performing topic adaptation. We see that forumBERT outperforms all other methods, giving the best recall value, F1 score and the best accuracy on the entire dataset.

5.2 Classification on the OMP Dataset

We also compare the performance of: 1) forumBERT; 2) BERT with contextualized input 3) BERT without contextualized input; 4) the baselines reported in Schabus et al. (2017); 5) advanced baseline for doc2vec (Le and Mikolov, 2014) (D2V) vector representation and a support vector machine (Cortes and Vapnik, 1995) with Radial Basis Function (RBF) kernel for classification as reported in Schabus and Skowron (2018). To compare with the published results, all results have been computed using stratified 10-fold cross validation. The forumBERT model considered here uses a pretrained BERT language model without topic adaptation. The results for each category are reported in Table 6.

From Table 6, it can be seen that for categories that do not require additional context from the article (i.e Sentiment Negative and Discriminating) "BERT with only input comment text" performs among the best. Providing contextualized input in the form of article title and comment dilutes the

2014) was first trained on the NDR dataset, prior to training any models for the comment moderation task.

information input to the model leading to worse predictions.

For categories that require contextualized input (i.e offtopic, inappropriate, Possibly Feedback and Personal Stories) it can be seen that "BERT with contextualized inputs" gives best results and slightly outperforms forumBERT in almost all categories to establish the state of the art results. Upon further investigation, we found that 10 articles account for a majority of the annotated comments in OMP. More precisely, 10 articles are the source of 72.1% of all "OffTopic" and "Inappropriate" annotated comments, 58.3% of all "Personal Stories" annotated comments and 45.1% of all "Possibly Feedback" comments. Without diversity in the article input to the forumBERT model, it tends to perform slightly worse than BERT. This was not the case with the NDR dataset, where there was enough diversity in the articles (65,261 articles) to promote better classification.

Nonetheless forumBERT exceeds all baseline and advanced baseline results and still offers competitive results on the OMP dataset.

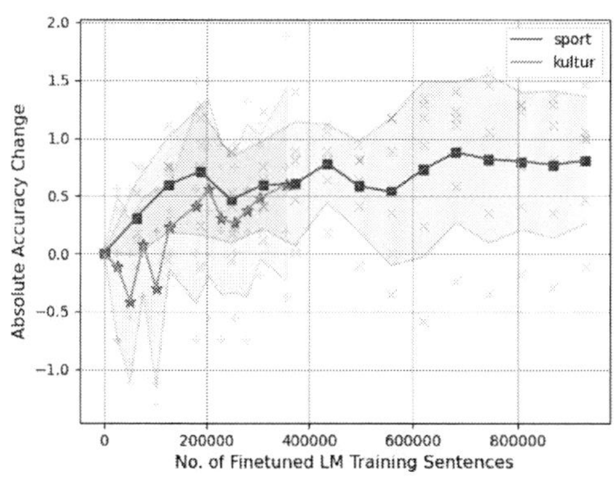

Figure 4: Absolute accuracy percentage improvements on the downstream offline/online classification task as a function of the number of training sentences the BERT language model was fine-tuned on. The ■ and ★ symbols represent the average over 6 runs of finetuning and classification on the "Sport" and "Kultur" topics of the NDR dataset (Section 3.1) respectively. The 'x' and the '+' represent individual runs. The filled-in portions represent the standard deviation over these 6 runs ($\mu + \sigma$). The absolute accuracy improvements are measured from 85.94% for the "Sport" topic and 81.64% for the "Kultur" topic.

Categ.	Meas.	BOW com.	D2V top.+com.	LSTM com.	BERT com.	BERT tit.+com.	fBERT tit./com.
Neg.	Prec.	0.552	0.621	0.534	0.664	0.663	**0.711**
	Rec.	0.510	0.483	**0.719**	0.642	0.709	0.646
	F1	0.530	0.544	0.613	0.654	**0.685**	0.677
Offtop.	Prec.	0.275	0.252	0.274	0.513	**0.537**	0.565
	Rec.	0.237	**0.453**	0.263	0.253	0.337	0.272
	F1	0.255	0.324	0.268	0.339	**0.415**	0.368
Inappr	Prec.	0.162	0.143	0.196	0.360	**0.411**	0.346
	Rec.	0.111	**0.412**	0.108	0.188	0.147	0.178
	F1	0.132	0.212	0.140	**0.247**	0.217	0.235
Disc	Prec.	0.184	0.154	0.113	**0.368**	0.325	0.304
	Rec.	0.102	**0.283**	0.141	0.112	0.052	0.112
	F1	0.132	0.200	0.126	**0.171**	0.089	0.163
Feed.	Prec.	0.655	0.531	0.630	0.741	**0.798**	0.792
	Rec.	0.580	0.735	0.628	0.698	**0.765**	0.762
	F1	0.616	0.617	0.630	0.719	**0.781**	0.771
Pers.	Prec.	0.698	0.589	0.638	0.836	**0.834**	0.832
	Rec.	0.592	0.850	0.665	0.828	**0.854**	0.841
	F1	0.640	0.696	0.651	0.832	**0.844**	0.836
Arg.	Prec.	0.610	0.545	0.568	0.716	**0.742**	0.733
	Rec.	0.512	0.763	0.645	0.733	0.754	**0.769**
	F1	0.526	0.636	0.604	0.725	0.748	**0.750**

Table 6: Classification results for multiple categories on the OMP dataset (Schabus et al., 2017). Precision, Recall and F1-score have been computed for the minority class for each category.

6 Experiments

We aim to answer the following research questions through our experiments:

Q1. How does the number of training iterations in the BERT language model finetuning stage influence the general comment moderation endtask performance on German topic forum datasets?

Q2. What is the influence of topic adaptation on the comment moderation endtask as a function of labelled endtask training examples?

6.1 Topic Adaptation

To answer Q1, we first split the topic datasets into a 9:1 ratio. The larger portion is used for BERT language model finetuning (topic adaptation) and the remaining is used for online/offline classification after every epoch of the language model finetuning. The results are shown in Figure 4.

Figure 4 and Table 2 empirically show that BERT is capable of learning topic specific forum comment knowledge even with less than 100,000 unlabelled training examples. We trained the BERT language model for 15 epochs individually on the sport and culture topic.

We also infer that topic based BERT language model finetuning improves the general downstream offline/online task. We see that the performance improves immediately in the case of the more specific sports topic, whereas for the more general

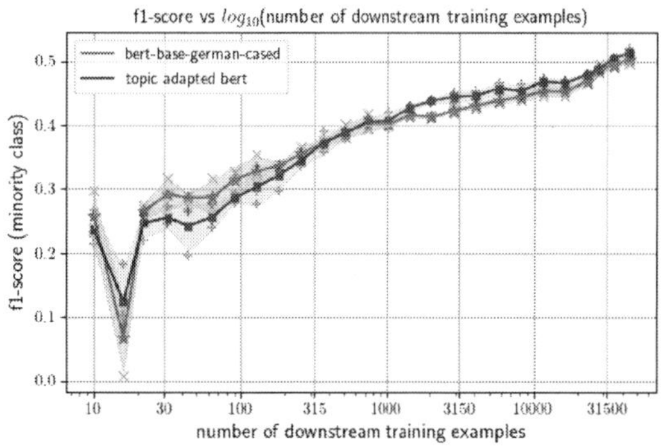

Figure 5: Average online/offline classification F1 score (for the minority "offline" class) computed on the sports topic using a pretrained forumBERT model (using bert-base-german-cased) and a sports topic adapted forumBERT model as a function of the number of downstream classification examples. The x-axis is represented on a log_{10} scale. The ■ and ★ symbols represent the average over 3 runs of online/offline classification on the sport topic of the NDR dataset (Section 3.1). The 'x' and '+' markers represent the individual runs. The filled-in portions represent the standard deviation over the 3 runs ($\mu \pm \sigma$)

culture topic, initially downstream classification performs worse (till 100,000 training sentences), but starts to see a steady gain in performance as it is trained after training on 150,000 sentences. Due to high variance in results, we average the results of 6 runs on each topic dataset and measure and plot the standard deviation to measure the improvements in performance.

6.2 Effectiveness of Topic Adaptation

To test the effectiveness of topic adaptation and answer Q2, we modelled the following experiment. We trained a pretrained forumBERT model and a sports topic-adapted forumBERT model on the comment moderation endtask using varying number of labelled endtask examples. Due to high variance in few shot results we average the results over 3 runs and measure and plot the standard deviation to generate reliable insights. The results of our experiment are shown in Figure 5.

From Figure 5 we see that the pretrained forumBERT model slightly outperforms the topic-adapted forumBERT model in very few shot learning situations (< 300 training examples). However, it can be seen that in the range of 315-1000 labelled training examples, the topic-adapted forumBERT model performs as well as the pretrained forumBERT model. Beyond this (> 1000 labelled training examples), the performance of topic adapted forumBERT clearly exceeds the pretrained forumBERT without topic adaptation. We also observe that the performance of both models starts converging beyond 10000 training examples.

From this experiment, we conclude that the effectiveness of topic adaptation reduces as the number of labelled training examples increase in the downstream task since labelled training examples consist of both task information and topic information, they provide much richer information to the model. As our experiment shows, with more than 10000 labelled training examples the advantage of using a topic adapted model diminishes.

7 Conclusion

In this paper, we introduced forumBERT, a simple architecture designed to determine comment's relevance in a discourse using 2 weight shared BERT models and a late fusion technique on BERT comment and article representations. Also, to mitigate the problem of portability of large NLP language models to niche language domains (in our case small news forums), we adopted a topic adaptation technique to learn better BERT representations.

We empirically showed that forumBERT outperforms all other baseline models on the NDR dataset. Our adaptation significantly outperforms the standard BERT model, improving the F1 scores from 0.475 to 0.513 (an 8% relative increase) on the sports topic dataset and an F1 score improvement from 0.465 to 0.490 (a 5.3% relative increase) on the culture topic dataset. The model also outperforms all existing advanced baseline results on the OMP dataset. Further analysis also shows the importance of topic adaptation as a function of labelled training examples. We would like to extend the application of forumBERT to other NLP tasks applications involving context dependent classification. Our implementation uses PyTorch (Paszke et al., 2019) and is publicly available.[5]

Acknowledgments. This work was partly funded by Hamburg's ahoi.digital program in the Forum 4.0 project. We would also like to thank German broadcaster Norddeutscher Rundfunk (NDR) for giving us access to an extensive collection of moderated NDR.de user comments.

[5]See `https://github.com/ayushyadav99/forumBERT`.

References

Corinna Cortes and Vladimir Vapnik. 1995. Support-vector networks. *Machine learning*, 20(3):273–297.

Jacob Devlin, Ming-Wei Chang, Kenton Lee, and Kristina Toutanova. 2019. BERT: Pre-training of deep bidirectional transformers for language understanding. In *Proceedings of the 2019 Conference of the North American Chapter of the Association for Computational Linguistics: Human Language Technologies, Volume 1 (Long and Short Papers)*, pages 4171–4186, Minneapolis, Minnesota. Association for Computational Linguistics.

Diederik P. Kingma and Jimmy Ba. 2015. Adam: A method for stochastic optimization. In *3rd International Conference on Learning Representations, ICLR 2015, San Diego, CA, USA, May 7-9, 2015, Conference Track Proceedings*.

Quoc Le and Tomas Mikolov. 2014. Distributed representations of sentences and documents. In *Proceedings of the 31st International Conference on International Conference on Machine Learning - Volume 32*, ICML'14, pages 1188–1196, Beijing, China.

Tomas Mikolov, Ilya Sutskever, Kai Chen, Greg S Corrado, and Jeff Dean. 2013. Distributed representations of words and phrases and their compositionality. In C. J. C. Burges, L. Bottou, M. Welling, Z. Ghahramani, and K. Q. Weinberger, editors, *Advances in Neural Information Processing Systems 26*, pages 3111–3119. Lake Tahoe, Nevada, USA.

Adam Paszke, Sam Gross, Francisco Massa, Adam Lerer, James Bradbury, Gregory Chanan, Trevor Killeen, Zeming Lin, Natalia Gimelshein, Luca Antiga, Alban Desmaison, Andreas Kopf, Edward Yang, Zachary DeVito, Martin Raison, Alykhan Tejani, Sasank Chilamkurthy, Benoit Steiner, Lu Fang, Junjie Bai, and Soumith Chintala. 2019. Pytorch: An imperative style, high-performance deep learning library. In *Advances in Neural Information Processing Systems 32*, pages 8024–8035. Vancouver, BC, Canada.

John Pavlopoulos, Prodromos Malakasiotis, and Ion Androutsopoulos. 2017a. Deep learning for user comment moderation. In *Proceedings of the First Workshop on Abusive Language Online*, pages 25–35, Vancouver, BC, Canada. Association for Computational Linguistics.

John Pavlopoulos, Prodromos Malakasiotis, Juli Bakagianni, and Ion Androutsopoulos. 2017b. Improved abusive comment moderation with user embeddings. In *Proceedings of the 2017 EMNLP Workshop: Natural Language Processing meets Journalism*, pages 51–55, Copenhagen, Denmark. Association for Computational Linguistics.

Jeffrey Pennington, Richard Socher, and Christopher Manning. 2014. GloVe: Global vectors for word representation. In *Proceedings of the 2014 Conference on Empirical Methods in Natural Language Processing (EMNLP)*, pages 1532–1543, Doha, Qatar.

Matthew Peters, Mark Neumann, Mohit Iyyer, Matt Gardner, Christopher Clark, Kenton Lee, and Luke Zettlemoyer. 2018. Deep contextualized word representations. In *Proceedings of the 2018 Conference of the North American Chapter of the Association for Computational Linguistics: Human Language Technologies, Volume 1 (Long Papers)*, pages 2227–2237, New Orleans, Louisiana. Association for Computational Linguistics.

Alec Radford, Jeff Wu, Rewon Child, David Luan, Dario Amodei, and Ilya Sutskever. 2019. Language models are unsupervised multitask learners.

Nils Reimers and Iryna Gurevych. 2019. Sentence-BERT: Sentence embeddings using Siamese BERT-networks. In *Proceedings of the 2019 Conference on Empirical Methods in Natural Language Processing and the 9th International Joint Conference on Natural Language Processing (EMNLP-IJCNLP)*, pages 3982–3992, Hong Kong, China.

Alexander Rietzler, Sebastian Stabinger, Paul Opitz, and Stefan Engl. 2020. Adapt or get left behind: Domain adaptation through BERT language model finetuning for aspect-target sentiment classification. In *Proceedings of The 12th Language Resources and Evaluation Conference*, pages 4933–4941, Marseille, France.

Julian Risch and Ralf Krestel. 2018. Delete or not delete? semi-automatic comment moderation for the newsroom. In *Proceedings of the First Workshop on Trolling, Aggression and Cyberbullying (TRAC-2018)*, pages 166–176, Santa Fe, New Mexico, USA. Association for Computational Linguistics.

Dietmar Schabus and Marcin Skowron. 2018. Academic-industrial perspective on the development and deployment of a moderation system for a newspaper website. In *Proceedings of the Eleventh International Conference on Language Resources and Evaluation (LREC-2018)*, Miyazaki, Japan. European Languages Resources Association (ELRA).

Dietmar Schabus, Marcin Skowron, and Martin Trapp. 2017. One million posts: A data set of german online discussions. In *Proceedings of the 40th International ACM SIGIR Conference on Research and Development in Information Retrieval (SIGIR)*, pages 1241–1244, Tokyo, Japan.

Ashish Vaswani, Noam Shazeer, Niki Parmar, Jakob Uszkoreit, Llion Jones, Aidan N Gomez, Ł ukasz Kaiser, and Illia Polosukhin. 2017. Attention is all you need. In I. Guyon, U. V. Luxburg, S. Bengio, H. Wallach, R. Fergus, S. Vishwanathan, and R. Garnett, editors, *Advances in Neural Information Processing Systems 30*, pages 5998–6008. Long Beach, CA, USA.

Yonghui Wu, Mike Schuster, Zhifeng Chen, Quoc Le, Mohammad Norouzi, Wolfgang Macherey, Maxim Krikun, Yuan Cao, Qin Gao, Klaus Macherey, Jeff Klingner, Apurva Shah, Melvin Johnson, Xiaobing Liu, ukasz Kaiser, Stephan Gouws, Yoshikiyo Kato, Taku Kudo, Hideto Kazawa, and Jeffrey Dean. 2016. Google's neural machine translation system: Bridging the gap between human and machine translation.

Hu Xu, Bing Liu, Lei Shu, and Philip Yu. 2019. BERT post-training for review reading comprehension and aspect-based sentiment analysis. In *Proceedings of the 2019 Conference of the North American Chapter of the Association for Computational Linguistics: Human Language Technologies, Volume 1 (Long and Short Papers)*, pages 2324–2335, Minneapolis, Minnesota. Association for Computational Linguistics.

Zhilin Yang, Zihang Dai, Yiming Yang, Jaime Carbonell, Russ R Salakhutdinov, and Quoc V Le. 2019. XLNet: Generalized autoregressive pretraining for language understanding. In *Advances in Neural Information Processing Systems 32*, pages 5753–5763. Vancouver, BC, Canada.

Da Yin, Tao Meng, and Kai-Wei Chang. 2020. SentiBERT: A transferable transformer-based architecture for compositional sentiment semantics. In *Proceedings of the 58th Annual Meeting of the Association for Computational Linguistics*, pages 3695–3706, Online.

Robustness of end-to-end Automatic Speech Recognition Models – A Case Study using Mozilla DeepSpeech

Aashish Agarwal and **Torsten Zesch**
Language Technology Lab
University of Duisburg-Essen
Duisburg, Germany

Abstract

When evaluating the performance of automatic speech recognition models, usually word error rate within a certain dataset is used. Special care must be taken in understanding the dataset in order to report realistic performance numbers. We argue that many performance numbers reported probably underestimate the expected error rate. We conduct experiments controlling for selection bias, gender as well as overlap (between training and test data) in content, voices, and recording conditions. We find that content overlap has the biggest impact, but other factors like gender also play a role.

1 Introduction

Automatic Speech Recognition (ASR) has made striking progress in recent years with the deployment of increasingly large deep neural networks (Zhang et al., 2017; Sperber et al., 2018; Chang et al., 2019; Zhang et al., 2020). Now when you see a shiny new model with an error rate reported to be below 10%, are you likely to get the same error rate on your data? Many reported results probably underestimate the word error rate (WER) to be expected when a model is applied outside of its exact training conditions (Likhomanenko et al., 2020)

For example, in many datasets, there is a large imbalance between male and female voices (usually not enough female data). When evaluating only within such a dataset and not controlling for gender, the model can optimize overall WER by performing worse for females (Tatman, 2017). If the model is eventually applied in a setting where males and females are equally likely to use the system, WER will be much higher.

Other issues that might lead to underestimating error rate are overlaps between the train and test sets regarding content, voices or recording conditions. Another issue to be considered is selection bias when the training process can select samples for training and testing.

A really robust model should generalize beyond these factors, but we find that current models trained on the available datasets do not. We argue that this is partly due to the focus on reporting improvements in a within-dataset setting. It just sounds better to report a 4.3% WER on the standard dataset instead of a more realistic number (which we show can be several times higher). However, as most real-world applications are unlikely to directly reflect the properties of a specific dataset, most users would be better off with more robust models and a realistic estimate.

Most of the end-to-end speech recognition systems for English use the Librispeech (Panayotov et al., 2015) corpus, which has pre-defined data splits trying to avoid the issues discussed above.[1] For German data, standard splits are not fully established leading to large differences in WER between datasets, e.g. Agarwal and Zesch (2019) report WER in the range between 15 and 79.

We argue that this is also a challenge for other languages, where standard data splits are not defined, including Arabic (Menacer et al., 2017), Kazak (Mamyrbayev et al., 2019), Bengali (Islam et al., 2019), and Russian (Adams et al., 2019).

We thus perform experiments investigating the relative impact of dataset properties in order to give practical advice on how to train the models. This might also have consequences for the way speech datasets are collected. For data-rich languages like English, these issues can somewhat be offset by using more training data, so that a model might still be able to generalize well across different conditions. We thus perform our experiments

[1] However, note that over time fixed data splits lead to overfitting the methods on the dataset.

on German, which –at least when it comes to the amount of publicly available, transcribed speech data– has to be counted as an under-resourced language. We perform our experiments using the end-to-end speech recognition toolkit Mozilla DeepSpeech.[2] Our results probably generalize to other neural architecture similar to DeepSpeech.

We make our experimental setup publicly available (URL removed for review).

2 Dataset Properties

As we argue that dataset properties play such a big role, we will first have a look at the available training data collections. While for English or Chinese quite large datasets are publicly available, all German datasets are of limited size (see Table 1).

However, only focusing on the overall size is misleading anyway as e.g. even one million hours of one person reading the same sentence over and over again would not result in a usable model. We thus also look at other properties. A dataset like M-AILABS with very few voices is unlikely to generalize well to new voices. On the other hand, a dataset like Mozilla Common Voice (MCV) with thousands of voices easily reaches the largest overall size in our set, but as most voices repeat the same sentences, the dataset does not capture the same breadth of lexical material. As a consequence, the size of unique content in the MCV dataset is rather small, but not as small as the TUDA-De dataset where each sample is recorded by 5 different microphones bringing the unique size down to 7 hours (from 184 hours in total).

We thus argue that the question *Can I train a robust model with [XYZ] hours of data?* cannot be answered without estimating the relative influence that each of these factors is going to have on the training process.

2.1 Voice Gender

As we are not aware that the gender balance of the available German datasets has been analyzed in detail before, we provide the statistics in Table 2. We found that across almost all the datasets, except M-Ailabs, the number of male voices is predominantly high. For example, in TUDA-De, male to female ratio is 3:1 and in MCV it is 9:1. This means that male voices form the majority of the corpora. Thus such corpora might not be able to generalise well in realistic settings. Projects

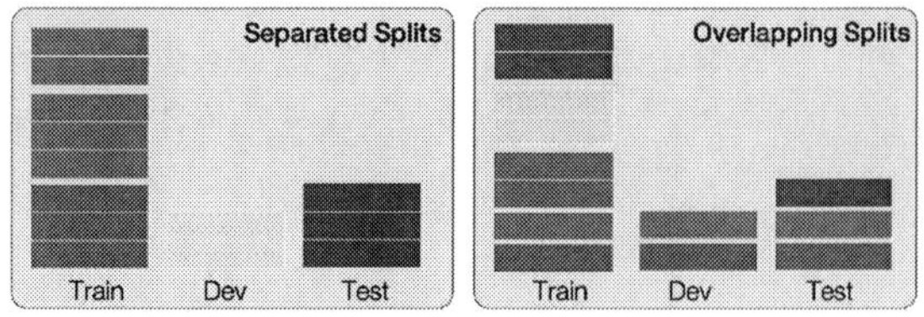

Figure 1: Visualization of data split issue

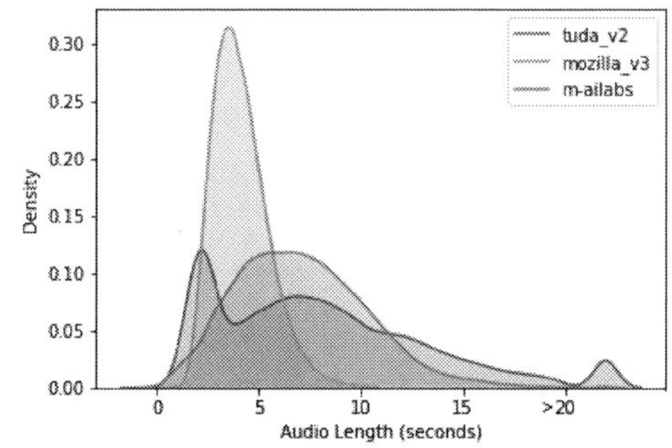

Figure 2: Distribution of sample length

collecting speech samples from volunteers should try to recruit more women and in general a more diverse set of dialects etc. When designing a speech corpus, keeping diversity (not only regarding gender) in mind would be beneficial.

2.2 Data Splits

Having a dataset with multiple voices, varied recording conditions, and little content redundancy does not automatically guarantee a robust model. Care has to be taken to separate cases between train, validation and test. Figure 1 visualizes the issue in a general way. A fixed data split (left) should separate dimensions are as much as possible, e.g. not have the same voices or the same content in train and test (right).

Of course, the severity of the issue depends on the usage scenario. If all one wants to do is recognizing spoken digits from 0 to 10, there is no harm with having samples of all digits in train and in the test, as in the application scenario those digits are all to care about. However, if the goal is a robust, domain-independent model, we need to control for overlap in sentences between train and test in order to obtain a realistic error rate estimate.

2.3 Selection Bias

An issue indirectly related to dataset properties is that frameworks often perform some kind of preprocessing and might filter out some samples in the process. For example, in Figure 2 we

[2] https://github.com/mozilla/DeepSpeech

Dataset	Domain	Number of Mics	Number of Voices	[h] Total	[h] Unique
TUDA-De (v2)	Wikipedia, Europarl, Commands	5	179	184	7
Mozilla Common Voice (MCV) v3	Wikipedia	many	4850	321	24
M-AILABS	Audiobooks (LibriVox, Project Gutenberg), Speeches, Interviews	?	~5	233	233

Table 1: German datasets used in this study

Gender	TUDA-De #	TUDA-De [h]	MCV #	MCV [h]	M-AILABS #	M-AILABS [h]
Male	129	123	1555	215	1	40
Female	50	61	173	33	4	147
Unknown	-	-	3122	73	?	46
male:female	3:1	2:1	9:1	7:1	1:4	1:4

Table 2: Dataset analysis regarding gender of voices

Train	Test	WER
TUDA-De	*TUDA-De (v2)*	*14.9*
	MCV (v3)	79.3
	M-AILABS	79.7
MCV	*MCV (v3)*	*26.8*
	TUDA-De (v2)	54.6
	M-AILABS	43.7
M-AILABS	*M-AILABS*	*17.5*
	TUDA-De (v2)	84.9
	MCV (v3)	68.3

Table 3: Cross-domain results

Dataset	[h]	Baseline	No content
TUDA-De	184	14.9	66.9
MCV	321	26.8	43.9
M-AILABS	233	17.5	17.1

Table 4: WER without content overlap

show the length distribution of samples in each dataset. Without looking at other dataset properties it might look useful to get rid of very short or very long samples and to only train (and test!) a model using samples close to the peak of the distribution. However, this might introduce a selection bias, where we reduce WER by simply discarding all the hard cases. This leads to excellent within-dataset results, but poor cross-dataset results.

3 Experiments & Results

For our experiments, we used the latest released version of Mozilla DeepSpeech (v0.6.0).[3] We choose the best hyperparameters[4] as described in (Agarwal and Zesch, 2019). The models are trained and tested on a compute server having 56 Intel(R) Xeon(R) Gold 5120 CPUs @ 2.20GHz, 3 Nvidia Quadro RTX 6000 with 24GB of RAM each. The typical training time on a single dataset under this setup was in the range of 2 hours. We ran our experiments for approximately 200 hours, which is equivalent to about 50 kg of CO_2.[5]

3.1 Baseline: All data, random split

As a baseline, we simply take all data and randomly split the data into train/dev/test, i.e. we do not take any of the dataset properties discussed above into account. This is the setup that is most likely used whenever not discussed differently in a paper. Table 3 gives an overview of the WER obtained in that way (rows in italics). Given the limited amount of training data, the results are in the expected range and generally similar to previously reported results (Agarwal and Zesch, 2019). However, as noted above, those numbers are probably underestimating the true error rate.

We thus also conduct cross-domain experiments, as testing on a dataset different from training is a natural way of checking the model robustness without any overlap at all. If the WER reported on the dataset itself is a realistic measure of performance, we should see cross-domain results that are similar. However Table 3 shows that WER always dramatically rises – mostly to the point that the model is not being useful anymore. MCV seems to generalize somewhat better than TUDA-De or M-AILABS, which indicates that many voices are more important for model robustness than more unique training samples.

In the remainder of this section, we explore which other factors are influencing results the most.

[3] https://github.com/mozilla/DeepSpeech/releases/tag/v0.6.0

[4] Batch Size - 24, Dropout - 0.25, Learning Rate - 0.0001

[5] https://www.rensmart.com/Calculators/KWH-to-CO2

Dataset	Total Size [h]	Number of Voices		WER		
		Train	Dev, Test (each)	No Content	No Voice	No Content & Voice
TUDA-De	184	145	15	66.9	37.2	74.1
M-AILABS	186	3	1	17.8	72.1	75.2

Table 5: Results with No Voice and No Sentence Overlap

3.2 Content overlap

Table 4 compares the baseline results with the setup when there is no content overlap (i.e. exact same utterance) between the data splits. Note that we use the same amount of data in both conditions, only the splits are different.

M-AILABS is not affected, as there is no content overlap to begin with.[6] This nicely shows that the results obtained for a specific dataset are replicable in general. The other datasets are heavily effected showing that content overlap is the main reason for underestimating the true error rate. As the MCV dataset has many voices and microphones, the 43.9 WER is probably already a robust estimate (cf. cross-domain results in Table 3).

3.3 Voice overlap

Table 5 first shows the results without content overlap (these are the same numbers as in Table 4) and then the results without voice overlap. The WER on M-AILABS, that only has very few voices, goes up to over 70% well into the unusable range. Results for TUDA-De go down, but only as we are not controlling for content overlap anymore. This is another piece of evidence that content is actually more important than voices, as it has a relatively larger impact. If we control for both (last column), all models perform approximately on the same abysmal level.

3.4 Recording conditions

TUDA-De is the only dataset where we can easily control recording conditions in the form of microphones used.[7] We can use 88h for this experiment and use 3 mics for training and 1 for dev and test each. Without content overlap, we obtain a WER of 73.8, while without mic overlap it is 53.1. Content overlap is thus the much more important factor. Consequently removing content and mic overlap only slightly increases WER to 77.4.

[6]The small difference is due to the independent randomization when re-running an experiment.

[7]Actually 'recording conditions' is a much wider variable, but not present as meta-data in most datasets.

3.5 Gender

As we have shown, the influence of content overlap is rather strong and likely to overshadow any gender effect to be found in the data. We thus isolate the gender variable by creating a sub-corpus where there is not content overlap between train and test and where the test set for male and female voices contains the same sentences. We find that training on male yields 63.5 WER for males and 87.4 for females showing the expected gender gap. If we train only on female voices, we get 55.2 WER for females and 88.3 for males.

4 Summary

Our study shows that the robustness of end-to-end speech recognition models heavily depends on dataset splits. Content overlap is the main reason for underestimating the true error rate. Especially in datasets that are collected in a crowd-sourced fashion, where many voices read the same sentences, or when multiple microphones are used, extra care has to be taken to avoid information leakage from train to test. However, other factors like gender balance or recording conditions are also contributing to the effect.

References

Oliver Adams, Matthew Wiesner, Shinji Watanabe, and David Yarowsky. 2019. Massively multilingual adversarial speech recognition.

Aashish Agarwal and Torsten Zesch. 2019. German end-to-end speech recognition based on deepspeech. In *Proceedings of the 15th Conference on Natural Language Processing (KONVENS 2019)*, pages 111–119, Erlangen, Germany. GSCL.

Xuankai Chang, Wangyou Zhang, Yanmin Qian, Jonathan Le Roux, and Shinji Watanabe. 2019. Mimo-speech: End-to-end multi-channel multi-speaker speech recognition.

J. Islam, M. Mubassira, M. R. Islam, and A. K. Das. 2019. A speech recognition system for bengali language using recurrent neural network. In *2019 IEEE 4th International Conference on Computer and Communication Systems (ICCCS)*, pages 73–76.

Tatiana Likhomanenko, Qiantong Xu, Vineel Pratap, Paden Tomasello, Jacob Kahn, Gilad Avidov, Ronan Collobert, and Gabriel Synnaeve. 2020. Rethinking evaluation in ASR: are our models robust enough? *CoRR*, abs/2010.11745.

Orken Mamyrbayev, Mussa Turdalyuly, Nurbapa Mekebayev, Keylan Alimhan, Aizat Kydyrbekova, and Tolganay Turdalykyzy. 2019. Automatic recognition of kazakh speech using deep neural networks. In *Intelligent Information and Database Systems*, pages 465–474, Cham. Springer.

Mohamed Amine Menacer, Odile Mella, Dominique Fohr, Denis Jouvet, David Langlois, and Kamel Smaili. 2017. An enhanced automatic speech recognition system for Arabic. In *Proceedings of the Third Arabic Natural Language Processing Workshop*, pages 157–165, Valencia, Spain.

Vassil Panayotov, Guoguo Chen, Daniel Povey, and Sanjeev Khudanpur. 2015. Librispeech: An ASR corpus based on public domain audio books. In *2015 IEEE International Conference on Acoustics, Speech and Signal Processing, ICASSP 2015*, pages 5206–5210. IEEE.

Matthias Sperber, Jan Niehues, Graham Neubig, Sebastian Stüker, and Alex Waibel. 2018. Self-attentional acoustic models.

Rachael Tatman. 2017. Gender and dialect bias in YouTube's automatic captions. In *Proceedings of the First ACL Workshop on Ethics in Natural Language Processing*, pages 53–59, Valencia, Spain.

Qian Zhang, Han Lu, Hasim Sak, Anshuman Tripathi, Erik McDermott, Stephen Koo, and Shankar Kumar. 2020. Transformer transducer: A streamable speech recognition model with transformer encoders and rnn-t loss.

Ying Zhang, Mohammad Pezeshki, Philemon Brakel, Saizheng Zhang, Cesar Laurent Yoshua Bengio, and Aaron Courville. 2017. Towards end-to-end speech recognition with deep convolutional neural networks.

Effects of Layer Freezing on Transferring a Speech Recognition System to Under-resourced Languages

Onno Eberhard and **Torsten Zesch**
Language Technology Lab
University of Duisburg-Essen, Germany
onno.eberhard@stud.uni-due.de
torsten.zesch@uni-due.de

Abstract

In this paper, we investigate the effect of layer freezing on the effectiveness of model transfer in the area of automatic speech recognition. We experiment with Mozilla's DeepSpeech architecture on German and Swiss German speech datasets and compare the results of either training from scratch vs. transferring a pre-trained model. We compare different layer freezing schemes and find that even freezing only one layer already significantly improves results.

1 Introduction

The field of automatic speech recognition (ASR) is dominated by research specific to the English language. There exist plenty available text-to-speech models pre-trained on (and optimized for) English data. When it comes to a low-resource language like Swiss German, or even standard German, only a very limited number of small-scale models is available. In this paper, we train Mozilla's implementation[1] of Baidu's DeepSpeech ASR architecture (Hannun et al., 2014) on these two languages. We use transfer learning to leverage the availability of a pre-trained English version of DeepSpeech and observe the difference made by freezing different numbers of layers during training.

2 Transfer Learning and Layer Freezing

Deep neural networks can excel at many different tasks, but they often require very large amounts of training data and computational resources. To remedy this, it is often advantageous to employ transfer learning: Instead of initializing the parameters of the network randomly, the optimized parameters of a network trained on a similar task are reused. Those parameters can then be fine-tuned to the specific task at hand, using less data and fewer computational resources. In the fine-tuning process many parameters of the original model may be "frozen", i.e. held constant during training. This can speed up training and improve results when less training data is available (Kunze et al., 2017). The idea of taking deep neural networks trained on large datasets and fine-tuning them on tasks with less available training data has been popular in computer vision for years (Huh et al., 2016). More recently, with the emergence of end-to-end deep neural networks for automatic speech recognition (like DeepSpeech), it has also been used in this area (Kunze et al., 2017; Li et al., 2019).

Deep neural networks learn representations of the input data in a hierarchical manner. The input is transformed into simplistic features in the first layers of a neural network and into more complex features in the layers closer to the output. If we assume the simplistic feature representations are applicable in similar, but different, contexts, layer-wise freezing of parameters seems like a good choice. This is further reinforced by findings from image classification (Yosinski et al., 2014), where the learned features can additionally be nicely visualized (Zeiler and Fergus, 2014).

As for automatic speech recognition, the representations learned by the layers is not as clear-cut as within image processing. Nonetheless, some findings, for example that affricates are better represented at later layers in the network (Belinkov and Glass, 2017), seem to affirm the hypothesis that the later layers learn more abstract features and earlier layers learn more primitive features. This is important for fine-tuning, because it only makes sense to freeze parameters if they don't need to be adjusted for the new task. If it is known that the first layers of a network learn to identify "lower-level"-features, i.e. simple shapes in the context of

[1] https://github.com/mozilla/DeepSpeech

	Dataset	Hours	Speakers
Pre-training	English	>6,500	?
Transfer	German	315	4,823
	Swiss German	70	191

Table 1: Overview of datasets

image processing or simple sounds in the context of ASR, these layers can be frozen completely during fine-tuning.

3 Experimental Setup

In our experiments, we transfer an English pre-trained version of DeepSpeech to German and to Swiss German data and observe the impact of freezing fewer or more layers during training.

3.1 Datasets

We trained the models for (standard) German on the German part of the Mozilla Common Voice speech dataset (Ardila et al., 2020). The utterances are typically between 3 and 5 seconds long and are collected from and reviewed by volunteers. This collection method entails a rather high number of speakers and quite some noise. The Swiss German models were trained on the data provided by Plüss et al. (2020). This speech data was collected from speeches at the Bernese parliament. The English pre-trained model was trained by Mozilla on a combination of English speech datasets, including LibriSpeech and Common Voice English.[2] The datasets for all three languages are described in Table 1. For inference and testing we used the language model KenLM (Heafield, 2011), trained on the corpus described by Radeck-Arneth et al. (2015, Section 3.2). This corpus consists of a mixture of texts from the sources Wikipedia and Europarl as well as crawled sentences. The whole corpus was preprocessed with MaryTTS (Schröder and Trouvain, 2003).

3.2 ASR Architecture

We use Mozilla's DeepSpeech version 0.7 for our experiments. The implementation differs in many ways from the original model presented by Hannun et al. (2014). The architecture is described in detail in the official documentation[3] and is depicted in Figure 1. From the raw speech data, Mel-Frequency Cepstral Coefficients (Imai, 1983) are

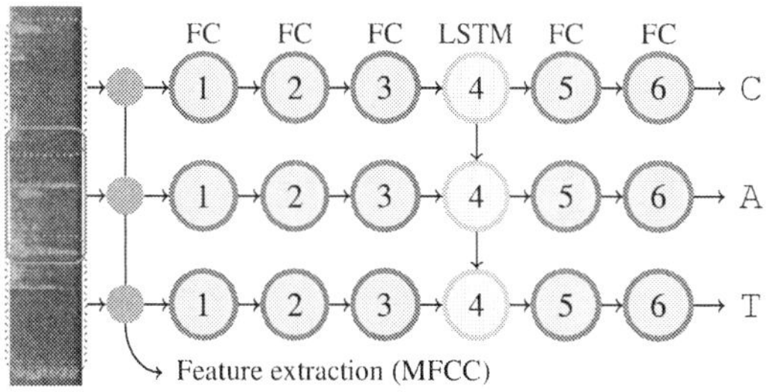

Figure 1: DeepSpeech architecture. The fully connected (FC) layers 1 – 3 and 5 are ReLU activated, the last layer uses a softmax function to compute character probabilities.

extracted and passed to a 6-layer deep recurrent neural network. The first three layers are fully connected with a ReLU activation function. The fourth layer is a Long Short-Term Memory (LSTM) unit (Hochreiter and Schmidhuber, 1997); the fifth layer is again fully connected and ReLU activated. The last layer outputs probabilities for each character in the language's alphabet. It is fully connected and uses a softmax activation for normalization. The character-probabilities are used to calculate a Connectionist Temporal Classification (CTC) loss function (Graves et al., 2006). The weights of the model are optimized using the Adam method (Kingma and Ba, 2014) with respect to the CTC loss.

3.3 Training Details

As a baseline, we directly train the German and Swiss German model on the available data from scratch, without any transfer (hereafter called "Baseline"). To assess the effects of layer freezing, we then re-train the model based on weight initialization from the English pre-trained model.[4] In this step, we freeze the first N layers during training, where $N = 0, \ldots, 5$. For $N = 4$ we additionally experiment with freezing the 5th layer instead of the LSTM layer, which we denote as "Layers 1-3,5 Frozen". We do this because we see the LSTM as the most essential and flexible part of the architecture; the 5th and 6th layer have a simpler interpretation as transforming the LSTM hidden state into character-level information. This stage should be equivalent across languages, as long as the LSTM hidden state is learned accordingly, which is ensured by not freezing the LSTM. For all models, we reinitialize the last layer, because of the different alphabet sizes of German / Swiss German and

[2] https://github.com/mozilla/DeepSpeech/releases/tag/v0.7.0

[3] https://deepspeech.readthedocs.io/en/latest/DeepSpeech.html

[4] https://github.com/mozilla/DeepSpeech/releases

English (ä, ö, ü), but don't reinitialize any other layers (as done e.g. by Hjortnaes et al. (2020)). The complete training script, as well as the modified versions of DeepSpeech that utilize layer freezing are available online[5]. The weights were frozen by adding `trainable=False` at the appropriate places in the TensorFlow code, though some other custom modifications were necessary and are described online[5]. For Swiss German, we do not train the network on the German dataset first and transfer from German to Swiss German, as this has been shown to lead to worse results (Agarwal and Zesch, 2020).

	German		Swiss	
Method	WER	CER	WER	CER
Baseline	.70	.42	.74	.52
0 Frozen Layers	.63	.37	.76	.54
Layer 1 Frozen	.48	.26	.69	.48
Layers 1-2 Frozen	**.44**	**.22**	**.67**	**.45**
Layers 1-3 Frozen	**.44**	**.22**	.68	.47
Layers 1-4 Frozen	.45	.24	.68	.47
Layers 1-3,5 Frozen	.46	.25	.68	.46
Layers 1-5 Frozen	**.44**	.23	.70	.48

Table 2: Results on test sets (cf. Section 3.3)

3.4 Hyperparameters & Server

In training each model, we used a batch size of 24, a learning rate of 0.0005 and a dropout rate of 0.4. We did not perform any hyperparameter optimization. The training was done on a Linux machine with 96 Intel Xeon Platinum 8160 CPUs @ 2.10GHz, 256GB of memory and an NVIDIA GeForce GTX 1080 Ti GPU with 11GB of memory. Training the German language models for 30 epochs took approximately one hour per model. Training the Swiss German models took about 4 hours for 30 epochs on each model. We did not observe a correlation between training time and the number of frozen layers. For testing, the epoch with the best validation loss during training was taken for each model.

4 Results & Discussion

Results of our baselines are very close to the values reported for German by Agarwal and Zesch (2019) and Swiss German by Agarwal and Zesch (2020) using the same architecture.

The test results for both languages from the different models described in Section 3.3 are compiled in Table 2. Figures 2 and 3 show the learning curves for all training procedures for German and Swiss German, respectively. The epochs used for testing (cf. Table 2) are also marked in the figures.

For both languages, the best results were achieved by the models with the first two to three layers frozen during training. It is notable however, that the other models that utilize layer freezing are not far off, the learning curves look remarkably similar (in both plots, these are the lower six curves). For both languages, these models achieve much better results than the two models without layer freezing ("Baseline" and "0 Frozen Layers"). The results seem to indicate that freezing the first layer brings the largest advantage in training, with diminishing returns on freezing the second and third layers. For German, additionally freezing the fourth or fifth layer slightly worsens the result, though interestingly, freezing both results in better error rates. This might however only be due to statistic fluctuations, as it can be seen in Figure 2 that on the validation set, the model with 5 frozen layers performs worse than those with 3 or 4 frozen layers. For Swiss German, the result slightly worsens when the third layer is frozen and performance further drops when freezing subsequent layers. Similar results were achieved by Ardila et al. (2020), where freezing two or three layers also achieved the best transfer results for German, with a word error rate of 44%. They also used DeepSpeech and a different version of the German Common Voice dataset.

The results don't show a significant difference between freezing the fourth or the fifth layer of the network ("Layers 1-4 Frozen" vs. "Layers 1-3,5 Frozen"). This indicates that the features learned by the LSTM are not as language-specific as we hypothesized. It might even be that, in general, it does not matter much which specific layers are frozen, if the number of frozen parameters is the same. It might be interesting to see what happens if the last instead of the first layers are frozen (not necessarily with this architecture), thereby breaking the motivation of hierarchically learned features, with later layers being more task-specific.

It is interesting that the models with four or five frozen layers, i.e. only 2 or 1 learnable layers, still achieve good results. This indicates that the features extracted by DeepSpeech when trained on

[5] https://github.com/onnoeberhard/deepspeech

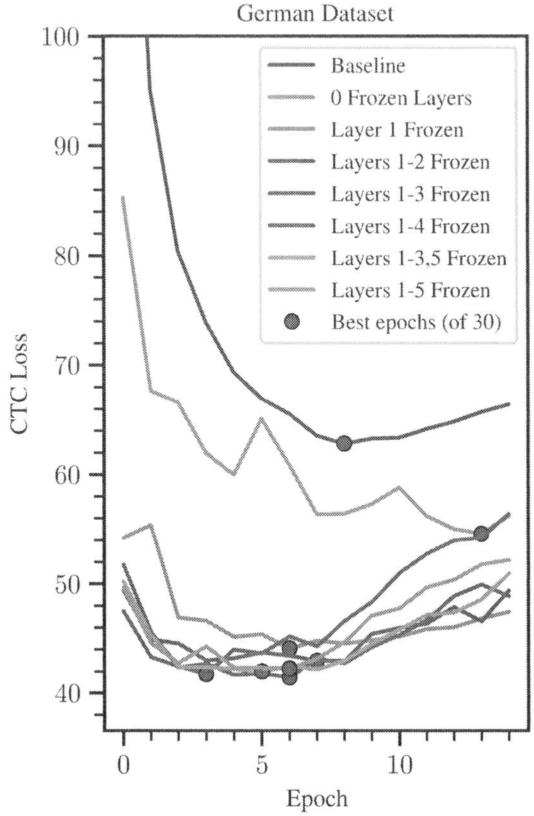

Figure 2: Learning curves (validation loss) on the German dataset. Layer freezing has a noticeable impact, but how many layers are frozen does not seem to make much of a difference. See Section 3.3 for details.

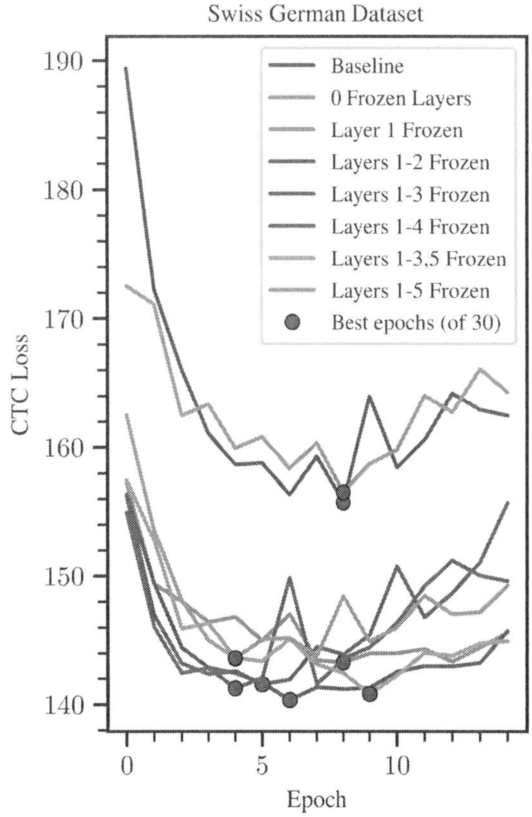

Figure 3: Learning curves (validation loss) on the Swiss German dataset. Compare with Figure 2.

English are general enough to really be applicable for other languages as well. It is probable that with a larger dataset the benefits of freezing weights decrease and better results are achieved with freezing fewer or no layers. For both languages it is evident that the transfer learning approach is promising.

Limitations Our experiment is limited to a transfer between closely related languages. For example, when just transcribing speech there is no need for such a model to learn intonation features. This might be a problem when trying to transfer such a pre-trained model to a tonal language like Mandarin or Thai. There might also be phonemes that don't exist or are very rare in English but abundant in other languages.

5 Summary

We investigate the effect of layer freezing on the effectiveness of transferring a speech recognition model to a new language with limited training data. We find that transfer is not very effective without layer freezing, but that already one frozen layer yields quite good results. The differences between freezing schemes are surprisingly small, even when freezing all layers but the last.

Acknowledgements

We want to thank Aashish Agarwal for valuable help in setting up DeepSpeech and for providing preprocessing scripts as well as the hyperparameters we used for training.

References

Aashish Agarwal and Torsten Zesch. 2019. German end-to-end speech recognition based on deepspeech. In *Proceedings of the 15th Conference on Natural Language Processing (KONVENS 2019): Long Papers*, pages 111–119, Erlangen, Germany. German Society for Computational Linguistics & Language Technology.

Aashish Agarwal and Torsten Zesch. 2020. Ltl-ude at low-resource speech-to-text shared task: Investigating mozilla deepspeech in a low-resource setting.

Rosana Ardila, Megan Branson, Kelly Davis, Michael

Kohler, Josh Meyer, Michael Henretty, Reuben Morais, Lindsay Saunders, Francis M. Tyers, and Gregor Weber. 2020. Common voice: A massively-multilingual speech corpus. In *Proceedings of The 12th Language Resources and Evaluation Conference, LREC 2020, Marseille, France, May 11-16, 2020*, pages 4218–4222. European Language Resources Association.

Yonatan Belinkov and James Glass. 2017. Analyzing hidden representations in end-to-end automatic speech recognition systems. In *Advances in Neural Information Processing Systems*, volume 30, pages 2441–2451.

Alex Graves, Santiago Fernández, Faustino Gomez, and Jürgen Schmidhuber. 2006. Connectionist temporal classification: labelling unsegmented sequence data with recurrent neural networks. In *Proceedings of the 23rd international conference on Machine learning*, pages 369–376.

Awni Hannun, Carl Case, Jared Casper, Bryan Catanzaro, Greg Diamos, Erich Elsen, Ryan Prenger, Sanjeev Satheesh, Shubho Sengupta, Adam Coates, and Andrew Y. Ng. 2014. Deep speech: Scaling up end-to-end speech recognition.

Kenneth Heafield. 2011. KenLM: Faster and smaller language model queries. In *Proceedings of the Sixth Workshop on Statistical Machine Translation*, pages 187–197, Edinburgh, Scotland. Association for Computational Linguistics.

Nils Hjortnaes, Niko Partanen, Michael Rießler, and Francis M. Tyers. 2020. Towards a speech recognizer for Komi, an endangered and low-resource uralic language. In *Proceedings of the Sixth International Workshop on Computational Linguistics of Uralic Languages*, pages 31–37, Wien, Austria. Association for Computational Linguistics.

Sepp Hochreiter and Jürgen Schmidhuber. 1997. Long short-term memory. *Neural computation*, 9(8):1735–1780.

Minyoung Huh, Pulkit Agrawal, and Alexei A. Efros. 2016. What makes imagenet good for transfer learning?

Satoshi Imai. 1983. Cepstral analysis synthesis on the mel frequency scale. In *ICASSP'83. IEEE International Conference on Acoustics, Speech, and Signal Processing*, volume 8, pages 93–96. IEEE.

Diederik P. Kingma and Jimmy Ba. 2014. Adam: A method for stochastic optimization.

Julius Kunze, Louis Kirsch, Ilia Kurenkov, Andreas Krug, Jens Johannsmeier, and Sebastian Stober. 2017. Transfer learning for speech recognition on a budget. In *Proceedings of the 2nd Workshop on Representation Learning for NLP, Rep4NLP@ACL 2017, Vancouver, Canada, August 3, 2017*, pages 168–177. Association for Computational Linguistics.

Bryan Li, Xinyue Wang, and Homayoon S. M. Beigi. 2019. Cantonese automatic speech recognition using transfer learning from mandarin. *CoRR*.

Michel Plüss, Lukas Neukom, and Manfred Vogel. 2020. Germeval 2020 task 4: Low-resource speech-to-text.

Stephan Radeck-Arneth, Benjamin Milde, Arvid Lange, Evandro Gouvea, Stefan Radomski, Max Mühlhäuser, and Chris Biemann. 2015. Open Source German Distant Speech Recognition: Corpus and Acoustic Model. In *Proceedings Text, Speech and Dialogue (TSD)*, pages 480–488, Pilsen, Czech Republic.

Marc Schröder and Jürgen Trouvain. 2003. The german text-to-speech synthesis system mary: A tool for research, development and teaching. *International Journal of Speech Technology*, 6(4):365–377.

Jason Yosinski, Jeff Clune, Yoshua Bengio, and Hod Lipson. 2014. How transferable are features in deep neural networks? In *Advances in Neural Information Processing Systems 27: Annual Conference on Neural Information Processing Systems 2014, December 8-13 2014, Montreal, Quebec, Canada*, pages 3320–3328.

Matthew D. Zeiler and Rob Fergus. 2014. Visualizing and understanding convolutional networks. In *Computer Vision – ECCV 2014*, pages 818–833. Springer International Publishing.

DeInStance: Creating and Evaluating a German Corpus for Fine-Grained Inferred Stance Detection

Anne Göhring, Manfred Klenner, Sophia Conrad
Department of Computational Linguistics
University of Zurich, Switzerland
goehring,klenner,conrad@cl.uzh.ch

Abstract

We introduce **deInStance**, a corpus of 1000 politicians' answers in German (**de**) containing sentences labeled with explicitly expressed and **in**ferred **stance**s - pro and con relations - by 3 annotators. They achieved an acceptable inter-rater agreement given the inherent subjective nature of the task. A first baseline, a fine-tuned BERT-based token classifier, achieved F_1-scores of around 70% . Our focus is on the difficult subclass of sentences comprising only non-polar words, but still with an (implicit) pro or con perspective of the writer.

1 Introduction

When people are asked about their position with regard to a certain topic, they typically answer by elaborating an argumentation in favor or against this topic. Argument mining is concerned with the structure of such arguments and the classification of each part. This happens at the clause level: a clause might be a claim, the support of a claim, etc. But what about the entities and events within the different parts of a clause? What can the reader infer from the writer's perspective on these different subtopics contained in the author's text? In this work, we present a new resource together with a first neural sequence labeling model of such inferred fine-grained stances. The goal is to find all those entities (called targets) in a text that the writer approves (*pro*) or disapproves (*con*), explicitly or implicitly. These targets might be aspects of the overall topic of the text, but also any entity mentioned in the text towards which the writer seems to bear a positive or negative attitude. Among these non-aspect targets are entities reflecting the writer's moral convictions, political views, and all sorts of other preferences.

2 Corpus Annotation

As a starting point, we took the German part of the freely available xstance[1] corpus. The original corpus contains politicians' stances consisting of an explicit position (from strongly/weakly against to weakly/strongly in favor) together with a comment as answer to given questions from different topics. We annotated a subcorpus[2] of 1000 answers where each word receives a label: *pro* (in favour of), *con* (against) or *none* (neutral). A *pro* relation indicates that the writer approves (i.e. is in favor of) the denoted entity or event; correspondingly for *con*.[3]

2.1 Objective of the Annotation

In order to clarify the annotation task and to show the differences to aspect-based sentiment analysis, take the following question: *Do you support the introduction of minimum wage for employees?* One answer is: *Another unhelpful blanket proposal from the mothballs of socialism, which would further weaken our country's competitiveness.* Socialism (text author is against it) and the competitiveness (author is in favour) are somehow related to the question, but they are not aspects in the sense of aspect-based sentiment analysis. Aspects are strongly correlated categories of an item (e.g. the price of a product). Another writer puts it in the following way: *This would be the breaking of a promise.* The author is against such a *break of a promise*, which again is not an aspect (of *minimum wage*). This characterization of our setting shows that we cannot reduce the task to a mere aspect-based sentiment analysis.

[1] https://github.com/ZurichNLP/xstance (Vamvas and Sennrich, 2020)

[2] The data is available on request.

[3] We only labeled the dependency heads of the corresponding target phrases with pro's and con's, all other words are *none*.

2.2 Annotation Guidelines

Our annotation guidelines are brief. Annotate those *pro/con* relations of the text author that (1) explicitly state his/her stance or (2) implicitly bears or must bear towards the entities mentioned in his/her comment. It is crucial to be aware that the borderline between these cases sometimes is fuzzy. When does an opinion starts to become stated explicitly? We thus decided not to annotate the implicit/explicit distinction. We just annotated the writer's attitude : *pro* or *con*.

Guideline (1) is plain. Given *I have welcomed the liberalizations that have been implemented*, there is a *pro* relation of the writer towards *liberalizations*. There are a number of linguistic indicators for an explicit assertion of stance:

1. a personal statement (first person pronoun) with a verb of (dis)approval: *I approve it*
2. predicative statements: *Liberalization is good*
3. modal constructions: *Liberalization should be carried out*
4. verb-based inference schemata: *It prevents a solution to other problems*

(1) most explicitly states that the writer is in favor of *it* and the positive evaluation in (2) immediately gives rise to a *pro* relation of the writer towards liberalization. (3) expresses the need to have liberalization. This again points out that he/she is in favor of liberalization. In (4), *prevent* casts a *con* relation between its logical subject (*it*) and the theme role (*solution*). A contra relation towards a positively connotated theme indicates a negative subject and suggests that the writer stands in *con* relation towards it (here *it*).

The second annotation objective is concerned with relations that are not directly asserted or stated by the linguistic means from above, but either must hold as a kind of presupposition or do hold because they follow from some conventional pragmatic reasoning. Take the following examples:

1. *After liberalization the employees are paid even less*
2. *The quality of education should not depend on the income*
3. *This is what the constitution says*

The pragmatically used particle *even* in (1) together with world knowledge (less pay is bad) indicates that the writer regarded it as negative, if the employees got less money. This, in turn, means that she/he must be (maybe only in a situation-specific way) in favor of the employees - not a particular subset of but the group of employees in general. He/She cares about their situation. Also, she/he is against the mentioned liberalization, which is not explicitly stated but inferred.

(2) is a response to the following question: Should the government be more committed to equal educational opportunities? Only if he/she is in favor of education, the answer can be understood as an approval: education must be one of his/her values. However, there is no *pro* nor *con* relation with respect to *income*.

The question underlying the answer in (3) is: Should the government increase its support for nonprofit housing construction? The comment (just this sentence) is an example of an implicature trigger. We cannot give the whole implicature chain, but in principle it goes like this: The constitution is in favor of it, I, the writer, cite this authority and it thus is an authority of mine and I hereby indicate that I am in favor of it as well. Thus, the writer can be understood as being in favor of the constitution, this is the annotation goal here.

Such attitudes depend on the subjective understanding and reasoning of the annotators. However, it is a worthy goal to not only be able to identify the writer's directly stated stance, but also to fix her obligations, values, preferences that become visible in what is semantically/pragmatically implied.

2.3 Annotation Results

The 1000 comments containing 32,274 tokens in 2183 sentences were manually labeled by 3 trained raters. We performed independent harmonization at various progress points, each annotator checking the differences between the others' annotation and their own, adjusting it if needed.

As a simple concrete example, the sentence '*In the long term, Switzerland belongs to the EU.*' is labeled by all three annotators as:

Langfristig	*gehört*	*die*	*Schweiz*	*zur*	***EU***
none	none	none	none	none	**pro**

Although annotators A1 and A3 tend to label more tokens (around 12.5%) than A2 (10.5%), our annotations are sparse. The proportion of *pro* and *con* labels is approx 70-75% and 25-30%, respectively (see Table 1). This imbalance probably deteriorates the results for the *con* label.

To evaluate the reliability of our annotations, we calculate Cohen's kappa for the agreement and

annotator	pro	con	none
A1	2986	1132	28156
A2	2412	974	28888
A3	2870	1141	28263

Table 1: Label distributions for each annotator (A1-A3). Tokens are either labeled as *pro* (in favor of) or as *con* (against), or they are not (none).

Krippendorff's alpha for the disagreement between the different raters. On the whole corpus, the inter-rater reliability measured by Krippendorff's alpha is above the acceptability threshold of 0.667. The pairwise kappa coefficients show a higher agreement between annotators A1 and A3 (0.8578); annotators A1 and A2 disagree most (0.7229).

3 Experiments

Attention-based models are the current architecture of choice for many natural language processing tasks. For training the stance labeling models, we used the self-attentional transformer (Vaswani et al., 2017) implementation provided by HuggingFace (Wolf et al., 2020): the class BertForTokenClassification is defined as a token classification model on top of a language model, i.e. a linear classification layer on top of the tokens' hidden state output. We chose the pretrained German BERT model from DBMDZ[4] to train our models.

3.1 Configurations

The experiment settings vary for the datasets used, but the model parameters are fix throughout the runs (see Appendix A). On the data configuration side, we take each rater's labeled dataset separately and mix these annotations in various ways:

- Major: majority label per token
- Inter: intersection label (same or *none*)
- Concat: concatenation of all annotations

The setting *Major* means that we took those annotations that two or all raters have tagged, whereas in *Inter* only those are taken that all raters have selected. To simulate a weighted average, we also simply concatenated the labeled data from the three annotators to form one larger *Concat* set. We trained models also with the individual annotations (models M1-M3) in order to see whether the annotations are reasonable (i.e. reproducible).

[4]https://huggingface.co/dbmdz/bert-base-german-cased

3.2 Results

All our models achieve modest though reasonable F_1-scores given the challenging task. To mitigate the anecdotal character of a single evaluation, we randomly shuffle the annotated comments into 10 different dataset splits, and run the training and evaluation on each split (cross-validation). For instance, given the annotations of annotator $A1$, we trained a model (called M1) on a train set split, used it to predict labels for the test set split and evaluated this with respect to the annotations of $A1$ for that test set split (see Table 2).

model	acc	F_1	pro		con	
			prec	rec	prec	rec
M1	93.2	69.2	70.0	71.0	67.8	63.7
M2	93.6	66.4	66.3	68.5	65.5	63.4
M3	93.4	69.7	70.0	71.0	68.5	66.2
Major	93.7	**70.4**	70.5	**73.0**	68.3	66.3
Inter	**94.4**	64.2	64.5	67.2	63.1	58.1
Concat	93.4	**70.4**	**71.3**	71.1	**70.0**	**67.3**
C_{fair}	93.1	68.1	68.3	71.7	64.8	62.5

Table 2: Accuracy, F_1, precision, and recall results of the different models: models for individual annotators (M1-M3), majority (Major), intersection (Inter), and concatenation (Concat and C_{fair}).

On average, these baseline models attain an overall accuracy of 93-94%, achieve better precision and recall for *pro* than for *con* labels, from the lowest *con* recall of 58% to the highest *pro* precision of 71%. The high accuracy is due to the high number of (word) instances of the none class (i.e. a word that is neither *pro* nor *con*). There is no clear best setting, but *Major* is better reproducible with respect to F_1 than *Inter*. It is therefore a good choice for a gold standard generation strategy in our case.[5]

All these results are evaluated within each data configuration, e.g. the intersection model on the intersection test data. This does not allow for a direct comparison of the models. We thus run cross-configuration evaluations, where we created a single test set from the annotations of A1 and evaluated with respect to it (see Table 3). For instance, a model trained on the majority (*Major*) data applied to this test set has a accuracy of 92.9% (second line of the table).

[5]Note that, for a fair comparison with the other settings, the concatenation of the same data annotated by 3 different raters, i.e. the fact that training data is tripled is compensated at training time by the number of epochs divided by 3 (C_{fair}).

model	acc	F_1	prec	rec
M1	93.2	69.1	70.7	67.5
Major	92.9	67.9	70.0	65.9
Inter	92.6	62.7	**77.2**	52.7
Concat	**93.3**	69.0	74.9	64.0
C_{fair}	93.1	**69.5**	68.7	**70.4**

Table 3: Cross-configuration results

The comparison with the manual annotations of A2 and A3 (not with the predictions of their models, M2 and M3!) represents the upper-bound of "human models": the resp. F_1 scores are 73.5% and 86.7%. The accuracy and F_1 scores of A1's model *M1* (i.e. an intra-configuration evaluation) come close to human performance, but the gap is substantial: 69.1% versus 73.5% and 86.7% (both *Concat* models contain part of A1 and performs on par with *M1*). So either *Concat* or *Major* are the natural choice for producing the final gold standard.

3.3 Discussion

About 20% of the annotated sentences do not contain any explicit polar words, according to a per se limited lexical resource[6], of course. Are these "non-polar" sentences harder for a model to tag than the "polar" sentences?

Splitting the non-polar sentences from the polar ones, we trained a polar model on A1's annotations and evaluated it once on the non-polar, i.e. exclusive subset from the same annotator (see Table 4). Comparing these results to the individual intra-configuration results for M1-M3 shown in Table 2, we can observe similar tendencies for *pro* and *con* labeling quality levels. Although further evaluations are needed to confirm these preliminary results, this could indicate that baseline BERT models can bridge the gaps remaining in polar lexicons.

label	F_1	prec	rec
pro	0.68	0.71	0.66
con	0.66	0.66	0.67

Table 4: F_1, precision and recall of A1's polar model P1 evaluated on the non-polar subset

Apart from some cases where such non-polar words are just (polarity) lexicon gaps, there are some challenging examples of sarcasm and underlying world knowledge. For example, the words *Umwelt* (environment) and *Landschaft* (landscape) have no explicit polarity, though they may have a positive connotation, but the author of the following sarcastic comment *'Umwelt und Landschaft kann man nur einmal kaputt machen.'* (*'Environment and landscape can be destroyed only once.'*) reveals a *pro* position towards both terms. As a further example, consider the word *Atomkraftwerk* (nuclear power plant) and its two different labels (pro, none) in the following sentence: *Darum ist es sicherer wenn die Schweiz eigene Atomkraftwerke*$_{\textbf{pro}}$ *besitzt als Strom aus ausländischen Atomkraftwerken*$_{\textbf{none}}$ *zu beziehen.* ('That is why it is safer for Switzerland to have its own nuclear power plants than to buy electricity from foreign nuclear power plants.')

4 Related Work

As far as we know, there is no prior work on fine-grained stances in German texts.

Luo et al. (2020) analyse the opinions in the highly topical and controversial debate of climate change. Their BERT-based classifier achieves 75% accuracy for the stance detection of global warming. The main differences to our work concern the language, the granularity of the labeled units, and the number, i.e. diversity of topics. While they label whole English sentences with stance on one topic, we detect all possible targets at token-level in German politicians' comments on various issues.

Allaway and McKeown (2020) specify a connotation lexicon that includes the cultural and emotional perspectives of the writer. Although many words do have a context independent connotation, in our texts a word often switches its polarity depending on the context.

5 Conclusion

In texts expressing stance, we not only find explicitly communicated opinions that comprise a person's overall opinion towards the target, but also his/her implicitly given preferences and values which establish common ground for the reader's understanding of the argumentation. We have introduced **deInStance**, a corpus on such a fine-grained level and carried out experiments with a baseline BERT model showing a reasonable performance. Predicting fine-grained stance could be beneficial for overall stance detection, but it also could be used to get closer to an author's personal profile.

[6]We use the Polart lexicon (Klenner et al., 2009) available from the IGGSA webpage.

References

Emily Allaway and Kathleen R. McKeown. 2020. A unified feature representation for lexical connotations. *CoRR*, abs/2006.00635.

Diederik P. Kingma and Jimmy Ba. 2015. Adam: A method for stochastic optimization. In *3rd International Conference on Learning Representations, ICLR 2015, San Diego, CA, USA, May 7-9, 2015, Conference Track Proceedings*.

Manfred Klenner, Angela Fahrni, and Stefanos Petrakis. 2009. PolArt: A robust tool for sentiment analysis. In *Proceedings of the 17th Nordic Conference of Computational Linguistics (NODALIDA 2009)*, pages 235–238, Odense, Denmark. Northern European Association for Language Technology (NEALT).

Yiwei Luo, Dallas Card, and Dan Jurafsky. 2020. DeSMOG: Detecting stance in media on global warming. In *Findings of the Association for Computational Linguistics: EMNLP 2020*, pages 3296–3315, Online. Association for Computational Linguistics.

Jannis Vamvas and Rico Sennrich. 2020. X-Stance: A multilingual multi-target dataset for stance detection. In *Proceedings of the 5th Swiss Text Analytics Conference (SwissText) & 16th Conference on Natural Language Processing (KONVENS)*, Zurich, Switzerland.

Ashish Vaswani, Noam Shazeer, Niki Parmar, Jakob Uszkoreit, Llion Jones, Aidan N Gomez, Ł ukasz Kaiser, and Illia Polosukhin. 2017. Attention is all you need. In *Advances in Neural Information Processing Systems*, volume 30, pages 5998–6008. Curran Associates, Inc.

Thomas Wolf, Lysandre Debut, Victor Sanh, Julien Chaumond, Clement Delangue, Anthony Moi, Pierric Cistac, Tim Rault, Rémi Louf, Morgan Funtowicz, Joe Davison, Sam Shleifer, Patrick von Platen, Clara Ma, Yacine Jernite, Julien Plu, Canwen Xu, Teven Le Scao, Sylvain Gugger, Mariama Drame, Quentin Lhoest, and Alexander M. Rush. 2020. Huggingface's transformers: State-of-the-art natural language processing.

A Appendices

Appendix A. Model settings

Regarding the model settings, we fine-tune the pre-trained cased German model from DBMDZ while training our token classifier, i.e. all the weights are updated, not only the classifier's weights. We train models on a single GPU (NVIDIA GeForce GTX TITAN X) for 3 epochs without early stopping. We use the Adam optimizer (Kingma and Ba, 2015) with default epsilon=1e-08. We use a learning rate of 5e-5 for all experiments with a training batch size of 32, with no gradient accumulation. We set the random seed to 1, the maximum sequence length to 256. As the number of examples varies between 1720 and 1765 training sentences in the different data splits, the optimization process runs through 162 to 168 steps.[7]

[7] multiplied by 3 for the concatenation configuration: 5160 to 5295 training sentences, processed in 486 to 498 optimization steps.

Combining text and vision in compound semantics: Towards a cognitively plausible multimodal model

Abhijeet Gupta[†] **Fritz Günther**[*] **Ingo Plag**[†] **Laura Kallmeyer**[†] **Stefan Conrad**[†]
[†]Heinrich-Heine-Universität Düsseldorf
{abhijeet.gupta, ingo.plag, kallmeyer, stefan.conrad}@uni-duesseldorf.de
[*]University of Tübingen
fritz.guenther@uni-tuebingen.de

Abstract

In the current state-of-the art distributional semantics model of the meaning of noun-noun compounds (such as *chainsaw, butterfly, home phone*), CAOSS (Marelli et al. 2017), the semantic vectors of the individual constituents are combined, and enriched by position-specific information for each constituent in its role as either modifier or head. Most recently there have been attempts to include vision-based embeddings in these models (Günther et al., 2020b), using the linear architecture implemented in the CAOSS model. In the present paper, we extend this line of research and demonstrate that moving to non-linear models improves the results for vision while linear models are a good choice for text. Simply concatenating text and vision vectors does not currently (yet) improve the prediction of human behavioral data over models using text- and vision-based measures separately.

1 Introduction

The meaning and interpretation of noun-noun compounds, i.e. the combination of two words to form a new word (as in *chainsaw, butterfly, home phone*), is a contested area of study. In both theoretical linguistics and psycholinguistic circles one of the central questions is the contribution of the individual constituents in the construction of a compound's meaning (see, e.g., Bauer et al. 2013; Bell and Schäfer 2016; Schmidtke et al. 2018, ch. 20 for recent discussion).

Some psycho-computational approaches use distributional semantic models to produce representations of compound meanings. In the current state-of-the art model CAOSS (Marelli et al. 2017) the semantic vectors of the individual constituents are combined, and enriched by position-specific information for each constituent in its role as either modifier or head (e.g. *chain* as modifier in words like *chainsaw, chain mail, chain reaction, chainsaw, chain-smoking*)[1]. This enrichment is achieved by a linear architecture in which each constituent vector is first multiplied with a position-specific matrix before adding the two constituent representations to derive the compound representation.

Another aspect of compound meaning has only recently begun to attract attention, namely the role of visual information in creating and processing individual concepts and their combination. Research on embodied cognition revealed that concepts are not only based on linguistic experience, but are also grounded in perceptual experience (e.g. Barsalou 1999). In the field of neuro-psychological learning (e.g. Devereux et al. 2018), deep learning networks have been implemented in the learning of word meaning. Similarly, visual information should also play a major role in conceptual combination, at least for concrete concepts. The first study to show the effects of vision-based information in conceptual combination has been (Günther et al., 2020b).

In that study the authors compared two parallel implementations of the CAOSS model: one using text-based embeddings (henceforth *text embeddings*), the other picture-based semantic embeddings (henceforth *vision embeddings*). These embeddings (more specifically, the cosine similarities between the compound embeddings and their constituent embeddings) were then quite successfully used to predict behavioral data from experiments with human participants (i.e. reaction times in different experimental tasks). Importantly, considering information from vision embeddings in addition to text embeddings leads to significantly better predictions of human behavior. This work raises two important questions that merit further exploration. The first is about the modeling architecture, the second about the combination, instead of the

[1]See Mitchell and Lapata (2010) for another approach of dealing with asymmetric models of constituents and, Li et al. (2020); Köper and im Walde (2017) for other interesting and similar work on related phenomena.

comparison, of the two kinds of vector spaces.

Günther et al. (2020b) have used a linear architecture as implemented in the CAOSS model. In the present paper, we will explore whether non-linear architectures are better-suited to construct compound meaning representations. Our second aim is to test whether the combination of vision embeddings and text embeddings is a better basis for predicting human behavior rather than considering text embeddings and vision embeddings separately.

2 Method

2.1 Outline

We started out with pretrained sets of text and vision embeddings for compounds and their single components from (Günther et al., 2020b), which were kindly provided by the authors. We trained different machine learning architectures towards predicting the compound embeddings from their constituents.

2.2 Models

In our approach, we use a supervised learning task with the aim to assess whether the estimation of distributional meaning representations of noun-noun compounds (both, text and vision based) benefits from adding non-linearity to the models.

We compare two generic model architectures: A simple linear regression (LR) model predicting the compound embedding, and a feed-forward neural network (NN) model. Both types of model are built with the Keras toolkit (Chollet, 2015) with a TensorFlow back-end (Géron, 2019).

The LR model is inspired by Günther et al. (2020b), but does not use the position matrices of the CAOSS model. It has no hidden layers, thus treating all features as independent. In our experiments, we use the LR model as the baseline instead of the CAOSS model for two reasons: 1) In terms of architecture, the two models are analogous; however, 2) CAOSS does not train and test on distinct datasets, which potentially inflates the evaluation results (due to model memorization, Levy et al. 2015) [2]. The NN model, on the other hand, has 1 or more hidden layers that model non-linear relationships between the input and output, and facilitate interactive behavior between the input features. We experimented with 1-4 hidden layers, and report results up to 3 due to a decline in model performance beyond 3 hidden layers.

For both text and vision compound estimations, we employ the same set of model architectures, using text-based embeddings for the former and picture-based embeddings for the latter (Section 2.3). For each datapoint, the input is a function of the embeddings $\vec{c_1}$, $\vec{c_2}$ of the constituents of the compound, $f(\vec{c_1}, \vec{c_2})$, and the output is the embedding of the compound. f can be any operation; we experiment with concatenation, addition and multiplication.

Hyperparameters. The number of units in each hidden layer of the NN models is optimized for each model separately. We consider a step-size of 50 between a range of 250 to 750 hidden units in a hidden layer. All hidden layers use *tanh* as activation function and *tanh* or *sigmoid* as the activation function for the final output layer. To avoid over-fitting, we add a dropout layer in front of each hidden layer with a standard dropout value of 0.5 (Baldi and Sandowski, 2013). We use *mean-squared-error* as the loss function and an additional L_2 weight regularization in the range $[10^1, 10^{-3}]$ at the time of loss computation to further optimize over any parameters that might be outliers. For model optimization we experimented with SGD and Adadelta (Zeiler, 2012).

2.3 Datasets for the compound embeddings

Semantic Spaces. The 400-dimensional text and 300-dimensional vision pretrained embeddings were obtained *as-is* from Baroni et al. (2014) and Günther et al. (2020b) respectively.

Datasets [3]. The training datasets are obtained from Günther et al. (2020b). The dataset for the text models contains 5988 datapoints with 2387 unique constituents and 5988 compounds, the dataset for the vision models 1577 datapoints with 942 constituents and 578 compounds. Since we evaluate model performance on both text and vision data against human behavioural measures (Section 3), we create a test dataset where: 1) for each datapoint, the constituents have an overlap in the text and vision semantic spaces[4]; and, 2) the datapoints in the test set do not overlap with the training datasets. This dataset contains 352 datapoints with

[2]Our datasets are designed towards minimizing memorization.

[3]The datasets are publicly available at `https://doi.org/10.17026/dans-xdp-3qhj`.

[4]It is not necessary to also have text and vision embeddings for the compounds in the test sets since these are not required by the current evaluation, see below.

321 unique constituents and 352 compounds.

We introduce three different ways to combine the two input constituents – the modifier (M) and head (H): 1) Concatenation (Con) ($\vec{M} \oplus \vec{H}$) – allows the model to freely combine the information of the two embeddings; 2) Addition (Add) ($\vec{M}+\vec{H}$); and, 3) Multiplication (Mul) ($\vec{M} \odot \vec{H}$) – both variants make the dimension-wise correspondence between two embeddings comparatively explicit. In addition to the above datasets, we generate in parallel another set of datasets (identical to the above) where the semantic spaces have been normalized via L_2 normalization. We choose this overhead to ensure that the compound prediction models are not confounded by outlier values.

3 Evaluation

The empirical performance of all models was assessed with five behavioral data sets, consisting of participant ratings from Gagné et al. (2019), and reaction times as used by Günther et al. (2020b): 1) **rC1:** ratings as to what extent the meaning of the *first* constituent (modifier) is retained in the compound meaning; 2) **rC2:** to what extent the meaning of the *second* constituent (head) is retained in the compound meaning; and, 3) **rcmp:** to what extent the meaning of the compound is predictable from *both* constituents (i.e., compositionality ratings). 4) **TS:** timed sensibility task, in which participants have to judge whether a given compound has a meaningful interpretation (Günther et al., 2020b); and, 5) **LDT:** lexical decision task, in which participants have to judge whether a given word is a real English words or not (Balota et al., 2007).

For each of these data sets, we initially identified an optimal linear mixed-effects regression model predicting these behavioral measures from a set of control variables (constituent frequencies and family sizes, compound length and frequency) using step-wise backwards model selection. We then added to each model as additional predictors the cosine similarities between the compound embeddings produced by the model and their respective constituent embeddings. These similarities have been identified as the main predictors of human behavioral data in previous empirical studies (Günther and Marelli, 2019; Günther et al., 2020a). In a semantically transparent compound we expect the embeddings of a constituent (or of both constituents) to be more similar to the embedding of the compound than in a semantically opaque compound. For instance, we expect a low cosine similarity between *lady* and *ladybug* since meaning-wise there is little of 'lady' in *ladybug*. As shown in numerous empirical studies, more compositionally-transparent compounds receive higher compositionality ratings (e.g. Gagné et al. 2019) and are processed faster (e.g. Günther et al. 2020b).

We obtained the conditional variance explained (r^2) of the mixed-effects regression models as our index of goodness-of-fit (using the R package *MuMIn*; Barton 2018). For each of the five data sets, we determined the rank order of these r^2 values for all models under evaluation, and calculated as an overall measure of a model's performance its mean rank across all five data sets.

4 Results & Discussion

Table 1 gives our main results. We start by predicting the text and the vision compound embeddings independently (columns 1-3, and 4-6, resp.). For each model: *Norm* – indicates whether the semantic space has been L_2 normalized (or not), *Input* – the type of input representation (Sec. 2.3) and *Arch* – the model architecture along with the number of hidden layers and units, if applicable (Section 2.2). For evaluation, we combine the text and vision model outputs for each datapoint in our test set in two different ways (column 7): a) **Mono** – we compute the cosine similarities between the predicted compound embedding and the constituent embeddings separately for the text embeddings and the vision embeddings (in all, 4 values); and, b) **Multi** – we compute the cosine similarities between the concatenation of the two predicted compound embeddings (text and vision) and the concatenations of the respective constituent embeddings (text and vision), i.e., we operate on multi-modal representations of compounds and constituents (in all, 2 values). Columns 8-12 give the evaluation scores as described in Sec. 3. Column 13 gives the order of the mean ranks for each text-vision model as computed on the basis of the r^2 values. Table 1 shows our top 5 *Mono* and *Multi* models from a rank-ordered list. The last line is the baseline model i.e., the LR model nearest to CAOSS (Sec. 2.2).

Two important points emerge from Table 1. First, we see that the best text models are all LR models (column 3), and that the vision models are all NN models (column 6). It appears that, in the case of a picture-based semantic space, predicting compounds effectively is a non-linear problem and

Table 1: Rank ordered list of top 5 Mono and Multi (NN) models along with the baseline model (BL). Best r^2 scores for each evaluation metric for both *Mono* and *Multi* in bold.

Text Models			Vision Models			Type	r^2					Rank
1	2	3	4	5	6	7	8	9	10	11	12	13
Norm	Input	Arch	Norm	Input	Arch	Type	TS	LDT	rC1	rC2	rcmp	
-	Add	LR	L_2	Add	NN 450-350	Mono	0.357	0.479	0.652	0.489	0.444	1
-	Add	LR	L_2	Con	NN 650-550	Mono	**0.358**	0.477	**0.654**	0.490	**0.446**	2
-	Add	LR	-	Add	NN 450	Mono	0.355	**0.483**	0.650	**0.492**	0.428	3
-	Add	LR	L_2	Con	NN 350-250	Mono	**0.358**	0.479	0.652	0.474	0.438	4
-	Con	LR	L_2	Add	NN 450-350	Mono	0.356	0.479	0.651	0.482	0.441	5
L_2	Con	LR	L_2	Con	NN 550-450-400	Multi	0.341	0.481	0.651	0.475	0.456	1704
L_2	Con	LR	L_2	Con	NN 450-350	Multi	**0.342**	0.478	0.652	0.475	0.457	1807
L_2	Con	LR	L_2	Add	NN 700-600-500	Multi	0.340	**0.485**	0.650	**0.489**	0.460	4993
L_2	Con	LR	L_2	Con	NN 350-250	Multi	0.341	0.478	0.657	0.477	0.468	6436
L_2	Con	LR	L_2	Add	NN 450-350	Multi	0.340	0.475	**0.663**	0.483	**0.477**	9302
-	Add	LR	-	Add	LR	BL	0.352	0.463	0.621	0.467	0.401	415874

should be treated as such. The vision-based space is a comparatively richer space (than text) in terms of features (Deng et al., 2009), and requires a more complex architecture for an effective treatment of compounds and constituents. The text semantic space (normalized or otherwise), on the other hand, is known to work well with straightforward inputs (Baroni et al., 2012) and to that effect our results are in line with the previous works.

Second, we see that the *Mono* models outperform the *Multi* models (column 7). In an ideal scenario, the multi-modal representations should resonate better with cognitive data as compared to those generated from individual semantic spaces. This is because language users do not primarily learn word meanings from reading texts, but by encountering new words in situations that involve and necessitate the integration of various kinds of information present. Combining vision embeddings and text embedding is thus an important step towards a more realistic model of meaning construction by language users. The worse performance of our combined embeddings does not bear this out. This may mean that the simple concatenation of text and vision features is not optimal and seems to blur information contained in the single text and vision embeddings. A more promising way to combine text and vision semantic spaces might be to encode the two into one and use the resultant multi-modal space as input for the compound prediction. Given the data we currently have, this is however difficult since the number of compounds for which we have text and vision embeddings both for constituents and compound is rather low.

Looking at the r^2 scores between *Mono* and *Multi*, none of the models outperforms the others in all criteria. However, except for (Multi - TS) all our models score considerably better than our LR baseline analogous to (Günther et al., 2020b). We see an improvement that is between the range of 0.6 to 7.6 percentage points, which is substantial for this kind of behavioral data: In the mixed-effect models for our TS and LDT data sets, most frequency effects (the most robust predictors of response times) explain between 1 and 15 percent of variance, and in the rating studies these values range between 1 and 5 percent.

5 Conclusion

Our results confirm that the modelling of compound semantics that is aimed at emulating human cognition, does indeed benefit from the use of non-linear models. While in this work the vision semantic space was the main benefactor from non-linearity, it remains to be seen if hyperparameter tuning over a broader range might also improve the contribution put forth by the text models. The natural next step in further developing such models is to give combined text and vision information at input rather than at output level and to allow the models to freely select the best features from both semantic spaces for compound prediction. This would presumably also be a step closer towards human cognition. We aim to achieve this in our ongoing experiments by either utilizing an existing multi-modal space for such modelling tasks or by encoding spaces of different modality into one.

References

Pierre Baldi and Peter Sandowski. 2013. Understanding dropout. In *Proceedings of Advances in Neural Information Processing Systems*, pages 2814–2822.

David A Balota, Melvin J Yap, Keith A Hutchison, Michael J Cortese, Brett Kessler, Bjorn Loftis, James H Neely, Douglas L Nelson, Greg B Simpson, and Rebecca Treiman. 2007. The English Lexicon Project. *Behavior Research Methods*, 39:445–459.

Marco Baroni, Raffaella Bernardi, Ngoc-Quynh Do, and Chung-chieh Shan. 2012. Entailment above the word level in distributional semantics. In *Proceedings of the 13th Conference of the European Chapter of the Association for Computational Linguistics*, pages 23–32. Association for Computational Linguistics.

Marco Baroni, Georgiana Dinu, and Germán Kruszewski. 2014. Don't count, predict! a systematic comparison of context-counting vs. context-predicting semantic vectors. In *Proceedings of the 52nd Annual Meeting of the Association for Computational Linguistics (Volume 1: Long Papers)*, pages 238–247.

Lawrence W Barsalou. 1999. Perceptual symbol systems. *Behavioral and brain sciences*, 22(4):577–660.

Kamil Barton. 2018. *MuMIn: Multi-Model Inference*. R package version 1.40.4.

Laurie Bauer, Rochelle Lieber, and Ingo Plag. 2013. *The Oxford reference guide to English morphology*. Oxford University Press, Oxford.

Melanie J. Bell and Martin Schäfer. 2016. Modelling semantic transparency. *Morphology*, 26(2):157–199.

François Chollet. 2015. keras. `https://github.com/fchollet/keras`.

Jia Deng, Wei Dong, Richard Socher, Li-Jia Li, Kai Li, and Li Fei-Fei. 2009. Imagenet: A large-scale hierarchical image database. In *2009 IEEE conference on computer vision and pattern recognition*, pages 248–255. Ieee.

Barry J Devereux, Alex Clarke, and Lorraine K Tyler. 2018. Integrated deep visual and semantic attractor neural networks predict fmri pattern-information along the ventral object processing pathway. *Scientific reports*, 8(1):1–12.

Christina L Gagné, Thomas L Spalding, and Daniel Schmidtke. 2019. Ladec: the large database of english compounds. *Behavior Research Methods*, 51(5):2152–2179.

Aurélien Géron. 2019. *Hands-on machine learning with Scikit-Learn, Keras, and TensorFlow: Concepts, tools, and techniques to build intelligent systems*. O'Reilly Media.

Fritz Günther and Marco Marelli. 2019. Enter sandman: Compound processing and semantic transparency in a compositional perspective. *Journal of Experimental Psychology: Learning, Memory, and Cognition*, 45:1872–1882.

Fritz Günther, Marco Marelli, and Jens Bölte. 2020a. Semantic transparency effects in german compounds: A large dataset and multiple-task investigation. *Behavior Research Methods*, 52:1208—-1224.

Fritz Günther, Marco Alessandro Petilli, and Marco Marelli. 2020b. Semantic transparency is not invisibility: A computational model of perceptually-grounded conceptual combination in word processing. *Journal of Memory and Language*, 112:104104.

Maximilian Köper and Sabine Schulte im Walde. 2017. Complex verbs are different: Exploring the visual modality in multi-modal models to predict compositionality. In *Proceedings of the 13th Workshop on Multiword Expressions (MWE 2017)*, pages 200–206.

Omer Levy, Steffen Remus, Chris Biemann, and Ido Dagan. 2015. Do supervised distributional methods really learn lexical inference relations? In *Proceedings of the 2015 Conference of the North American Chapter of the Association for Computational Linguistics: Human Language Technologies*, pages 970–976.

Gen Li, Nan Duan, Yuejian Fang, Ming Gong, and Daxin Jiang. 2020. Unicoder-vl: A universal encoder for vision and language by cross-modal pre-training. In *Proceedings of the AAAI Conference on Artificial Intelligence*, volume 34, pages 11336–11344.

Marco Marelli, Christina L. Gagné, and Thomas L. Spalding. 2017. Compounding as Abstract Operation in Semantic Space: Investigating relational effects through a large-scale, data-driven computational model. *Cognition*, 166:207–224.

Jeff Mitchell and Mirella Lapata. 2010. Composition in distributional models of semantics. *Cognitive science*, 34(8):1388–1429.

Daniel Schmidtke, Christina L Gagné, Victor Kuperman, Thomas L Spalding, and Benjamin V Tucker. 2018. Conceptual relations compete during auditory and visual compound word recognition. *Language, cognition and neuroscience*, 33(7):923–942.

Matthew D. Zeiler. 2012. Adadelta: An adaptive learning rate method. In *CoRR, abs/1212.5701*.

MobIE: A German Dataset for Named Entity Recognition, Entity Linking and Relation Extraction in the Mobility Domain

Leonhard Hennig **Phuc Tran Truong** **Aleksandra Gabryszak**

German Research Center for Artificial Intelligence (DFKI)
Speech and Language Technology Lab
{leonhard.hennig,phuc_tran.truong,aleksandra.gabryszak}@dfki.de

Abstract

We present MobIE, a German-language dataset, which is human-annotated with 20 coarse- and fine-grained entity types and entity linking information for geographically linkable entities. The dataset consists of 3,232 social media texts and traffic reports with 91K tokens, and contains 20.5K annotated entities, 13.1K of which are linked to a knowledge base. A subset of the dataset is human-annotated with seven mobility-related, n-ary relation types, while the remaining documents are annotated using a weakly-supervised labeling approach implemented with the Snorkel framework. To the best of our knowledge, this is the first German-language dataset that combines annotations for NER, EL and RE, and thus can be used for joint and multi-task learning of these fundamental information extraction tasks. We make MobIE public at https://github.com/dfki-nlp/mobie.

1 Introduction

Named entity recognition (NER), entity linking (EL) and relation extraction (RE) are fundamental tasks in information extraction, and a key component in numerous downstream applications, such as question answering (Yu et al., 2017) and knowledge base population (Ji and Grishman, 2011). Recent neural approaches based on pre-trained language models (e.g., BERT (Devlin et al., 2019)) have shown impressive results for these tasks when fine-tuned on supervised datasets (Akbik et al., 2018; De Cao et al., 2021; Alt et al., 2019). However, annotated datasets for fine-tuning information extraction models are still scarce, even in a comparatively well-resourced language such as German (Benikova et al., 2014), and generally only contain annotations for a single task (e.g., for NER CoNLL'03 German (Tjong Kim Sang and De Meulder, 2003), GermEval 2014 (Benikova et al., 2014); entity linking GerNED (Ploch et al., 2012)). In addition, research in multi-task (Ruder, 2017) and joint learning (Sui et al., 2020) has shown that models can benefit from exploiting training signals of related tasks. To the best of our knowledge, the work of Schiersch et al. (2018) is the only dataset for German that includes two of the three tasks, namely NER and RE, in a single dataset.

In this work, we present MobIE, a German-language information extraction dataset which has been fully annotated for NER, EL, and n-ary RE. The dataset is based upon a subset of documents provided by Schiersch et al. (2018), but focuses on the domain of mobility-related events, such as traffic obstructions and public transport issues. Figure 1 displays an example traffic report with a *Canceled Route* event. All relations in our dataset are n-ary, i.e. consist of two or more arguments, some of which are optional. Our work expands the dataset of Schiersch et al. (2018) with the following contributions:

- We significantly extend the dataset with 1,686 annotated documents, more than doubling its size from 1,546 to 3,232 documents
- We add entity linking annotations to geo-linkable entity types, with references to Open Street Map[1] identifiers, as well as geo-shapes
- We implement an automatic labeling approach using the Snorkel framework (Ratner et al., 2017) to obtain additional high quality, but weakly-supervised relation annotations

The dataset setup allows for training and evaluating algorithms that aim for fine-grained typing of geo-locations, entity linking of these, as well as for n-ary relation extraction. The final dataset contains 20,484 entity, 13,104 linking, and 2,036 relation annotations.

[1] https://www.openstreetmap.org/

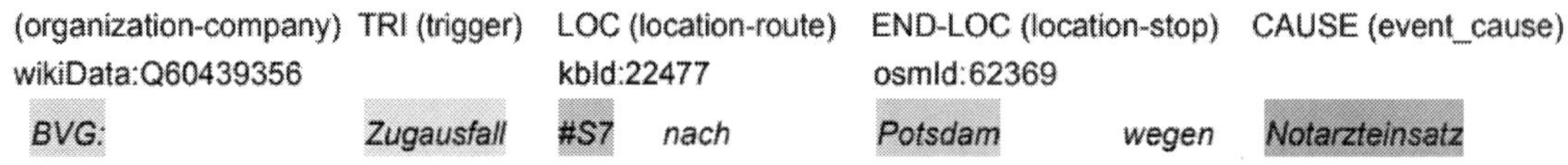

Figure 1: Traffic report annotated with entity types, entity linking and arguments of a *Canceled Route* event

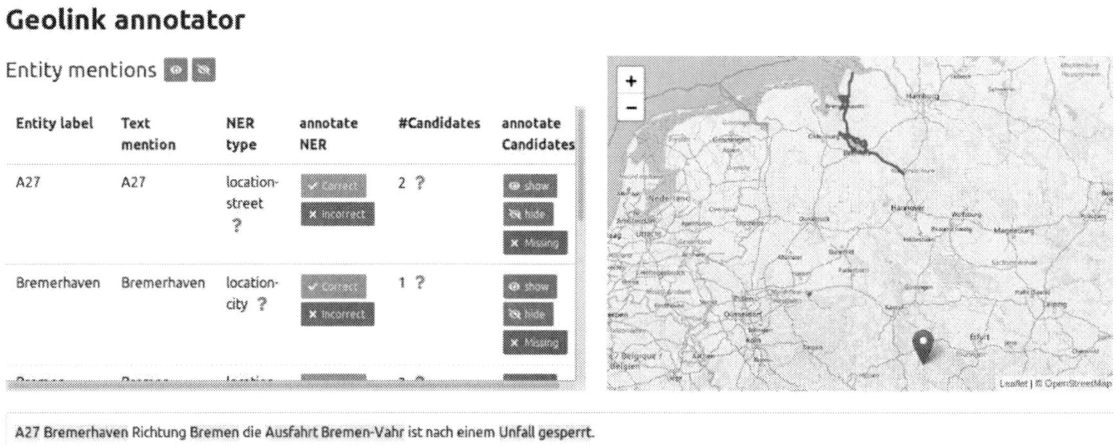

Figure 2: Geolinker: Annotation tool for entity linking

2 Data Collection and Annotation

2.1 Annotation Process

We collected German Twitter messages and RSS feeds based on a set of predefined search keywords and channels (radio stations, police and public transport providers) continuously from June 2015 to April 2019 using the crawlers and configurations provided by Schiersch et al. (2018), and randomly sampled documents from this set for annotation. The documents, including metadata, raw source texts, and annotations, are stored with a fixed document schema as AVRO[2] and JSONL files, but can be trivially converted to standard formats such as CONLL. Each document was labeled iteratively, first for named entities and concepts, then for entity linking information, and finally for relations. For all manual annotations, documents are first annotated by a single trained annotator, and then the annotations are validated by a second expert. All annotations are labeled with their source, which e.g. allows to distinguish manual from weakly supervised relation annotations (see Section 2.4).

2.2 Entities

Table 3 lists entity types of the mobility domain that are annotated in our corpus. All entity types except for *event_cause* originate from the corpus of Schiersch et al. (2018). The main characteristics of the original annotation scheme are the usage of coarse- and fine-grained entity types (e.g., *organization*, *organization-company*, *location*, *location-street*), as well as trigger entities for phrases which indicate annotated relations, e.g., *"Stau" ("traffic jam")*. We introduce a minor change by adding a new entity type label *event_cause*, which serves as a label for concepts that do not explicitly trigger an event, but indicate its potential cause, e.g., *"technische Störung" ("technical problem")* as a cause for a *Delay* event.

2.3 Entity Linking

In contrast to the original corpus, our dataset includes entity linking information. We use Open Street Map (OSM) as our main knowledge base (KB), since many of the geo-entities, such as streets and public transport routes, are not listed in standard KBs like Wikidata. We link all geo-locatable entities, i.e. *organizations* and *locations*, to their KB identifiers, and external identifiers (Wikidata) where possible. We include geo-information as an additional source of ground truth whenever a location is not available in OSM[3]. Geo-information is provided as points and polygons in WKB format[4].

[2] avro.apache.org

[3] This is mainly the case for *location-route* and *location-stop* entities, which are derived from proprietary KBs of Deutsche Bahn and Rhein-Main-Verkehrsverbund. Standardized ids for these entity types, e.g. DLID/DHID, were not yet available at the time of creation of this dataset.

[4] https://www.ogc.org/standards/sfa

Relation	Arguments
Accident	DEFAULT-ARGS, delay
Canceled Route	DEFAULT-ARGS
Canceled Stop	DEFAULT-ARGS, route
Delay	DEFAULT-ARGS, delay
Obstruction	DEFAULT-ARGS, delay
Rail Repl. Serv.	DEFAULT-ARGS, delay
Traffic Jam	DEFAULT-ARGS, delay, jam-length

Table 1: Relation definitions of the MobIE dataset. DEFAULT-ARGS for all relations are: location, trigger, direction, start-loc, end-loc, start-date, end-date, cause. Location and trigger are essential arguments for all relations, other arguments are optional.

Figure 2 shows the annotation tool used for entity linking. The tool displays the document's text, lists all annotated geo-location entities along with their types, and a list of KB candidates retrieved. The annotator first checks the quality of the entity type annotation, and may label the entity as *incorrect* if applicable. Then, for each valid entity the annotator either labels one of the candidates shown on the map as correct, or they select *missing* if none of the candidates is correct.

2.4 Relations

Table 1 lists relation types and their arguments. The relation set focuses on events that may negatively impact traffic flow, such as *Traffic Jams* and *Accidents*. All relations have a set of required and optional arguments, and are labeled with their annotation source, i.e., human or weakly-supervised. Different relations may co-occur in a single sentence, e.g. *Accidents* may cause *Traffic Jams*, which are often reported together.

Human annotation. The annotation in Schiersch et al. (2018) is performed manually. Annotators labeled only explicitly expressed relations where all arguments occurred within a single sentence. The authors report an inter-annotator agreement of 0.51 (Cohen's κ) for relations.

Automatic annotation with Snorkel. To reduce the amount of labor required for relation annotation, we explored an automatic, weakly supervised labeling approach. Our intuition is that due to the formulaic nature of texts in the traffic report domain, weak heuristics that exploit the combination of trigger key phrases and specific location types provide a good signal for relation labeling. For example, *"A2 Dortmund Richtung Hannover 2 km Stau"* is easily identified as a *Traffic Jam* relation mention due to the occurrence of the *"Stau"* trigger in combination with the road name *"A2"*.

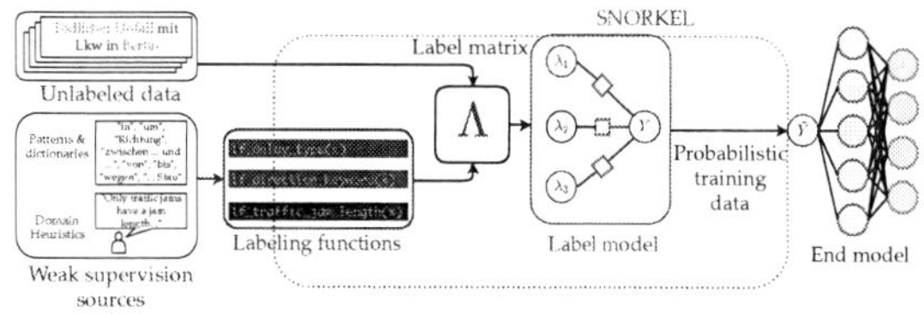

Figure 3: Snorkel applies user-defined, 'weak' labeling functions (LF) to unlabeled data and learns a model to reweigh and combine the LFs' outputs into probabilistic labels.

We use the Snorkel weak labeling framework (Ratner et al., 2017). Snorkel unifies multiple weak supervision sources by modeling their correlations and dependencies, with the goal of reducing label noise (Ratner et al., 2016). Weak supervision sources are expressed as labeling functions (LFs), and a label model combines the votes of all LFs weighted by their estimated accuracies and outputs a set of probabilistic labels (see Figure 3).

We implement LFs for the relation classification of trigger concepts and role classification of trigger-argument concept pairs. The output is used to reconstruct n-ary relation annotations. Trigger classification LFs include keyword list checks as well as examining contextual entity types. Argument role classification LFs are inspired by Chen and Ji (2009), and include distance heuristics, entity type of the argument, event type output of the trigger labeling functions, context words of the argument candidate, and relative position of the entity to trigger. We trained the Snorkel label model on all unlabeled documents in the dataset that contained at least a *trigger* entity (690 documents). The probabilistic relation type and argument role labels were then combined into n-ary relation annotations.

We verified the performance of the Snorkel model using a randomly selected development subset of 55 documents with human-annotated relations. On this dev set, Snorkel-assigned trigger class labels achieved a F1-score of 80.6 (Accuracy: 93.0), and role labeling of trigger-argument pairs had a F1-score of 72.6 (Accuracy: 83.1). This confirms our intuition that for the traffic report domain, weak labeling functions can provide useful supervision signals.

3 Dataset Statistics

We report the statistics of the MobIE dataset in Table 2. The majority of documents originate from Twitter, but RSS messages are longer on average,

	Twitter	RSS	Total
# docs	2,562	670	3,232
# sentences	5,409	1,668	7,077
# tokens	62,330	28,641	90,971
# entities	13,573	6,911	20,484
# linked	8,715	4,389	13,104
# events	1,461	575	2,036

Table 2: Dataset statistics per source

and typically contain more annotations (e.g., 10.3 entities/doc versus 5.3 entities/doc for Twitter). The annotated corpus is provided with a standardized *Train/Dev/Test* split. To ensure a high data quality for evaluating event extraction, we include only documents with manually annotated events in the *Test* split.

Table 3 lists the distribution of entity annotations in the dataset, Table 4 the distribution of linked entities. Of the $20,484$ annotated entities covering 20 entity types, $13,104$ *organization** and *location** entities are linked, either to a KB reference id, or marked as NIL. The remaining entities are non-linkable types, such as time and date expressions. The fraction of NILs among linkable entities is 43.1% overall, but varies significantly with entity type. *Locations* that could not be assigned to a specific subtype are more often resolved as NIL. A large fraction of these are highway exits (e.g. "*Pforzheim-Ost*") and non-German locations, which were not included in the subset of OSM integrated in our KB. In addition, candidate retrieval for *organizations* often returned no viable candidates, especially for non-canonical name variants used in tweets.

The dataset contains $2,036$ annotated traffic events, $1,280$ manually annotated and 756 obtained via weak supervision. Table 5 shows the distribution of relation types. *Canceled Stop* and *Rail Replacement Service* relations occur less frequently in our data than the other relation types, and *Obstruction* is the most frequent class.

	Twitter	RSS	Total
date	434	549	983
disaster-type	78	18	96
distance	37	175	212
duration	413	157	570
event-cause	898	116	1,014
location	887	1,074	1,961
location-city	844	1,098	1,942
location-route	2,298	324	2,622
location-stop	1,913	1,114	3,027
location-street	634	612	1,246
money	16	3	19
number	527	198	725
org-position	4	0	4
organization	296	121	417
organization-company	1,843	46	1,889
percent	1	0	1
person	135	0	135
set	18	37	55
time	683	410	1,093
trigger	1,614	859	2,473

Table 3: Distribution of entity annotations

	# entities	# KB	# NIL
location	1,961	703	1,258
location-city	1,942	1,486	456
location-route	2,622	2,138	484
location-stop	3,027	1,898	1,129
location-street	1,246	1,036	210
organization	417	0	417
organization-company	1,889	192	1,697

Table 4: Distribution of entity linking annotations

	Twitter	RSS	Total
Accident	316	80	396
Canceled Route	259	75	334
Canceled Stop	25	42	67
Delay	337	48	385
Obstruction	386	140	526
Rail Replacement Service	71	27	98
Traffic Jam	67	163	230

Table 5: Distribution of relation annotations

4 Conclusion

We presented a dataset for named entity recognition, entity linking and relation extraction in German mobility-related social media texts and traffic reports. Although not as large as some popular task-specific German datasets, the dataset is, to the best of our knowledge, the first German-language dataset that combines annotations for NER, EL and RE, and thus can be used for joint and multi-task learning of these fundamental information extraction tasks. The dataset is freely available under a CC-BY 4.0 license at `https://github.com/dfki-nlp/mobie`.

Acknowledgments

We would like to thank Elif Kara, Ursula Strohriegel and Tatjana Zeen for the annotation of the dataset. This work has been supported by the German Federal Ministry of Transport and Digital Infrastructure as part of the project DAYSTREAM (01MD19003E), and by the German Federal Ministry of Education and Research as part of the project CORA4NLP (01IW20010).

References

Alan Akbik, Duncan Blythe, and Roland Vollgraf. 2018. Contextual String Embeddings for Sequence Labeling. In *Proceedings of the 27th International Conference on Computational Linguistics*, pages 1638–1649, Santa Fe, New Mexico, USA. Association for Computational Linguistics.

Christoph Alt, Marc Hübner, and Leonhard Hennig. 2019. Improving Relation Extraction by Pretrained Language Representations. In *Proceedings of AKBC 2019*, pages 1–18, Amherst, Massachusetts.

Darina Benikova, Chris Biemann, and Marc Reznicek. 2014. NoSta-D Named Entity Annotation for German: Guidelines and Dataset. In *Proceedings of the Ninth International Conference on Language Resources and Evaluation (LREC'14)*, pages 2524–2531, Reykjavik, Iceland. European Language Resources Association (ELRA). ACL Anthology Identifier: L14-1251.

Zheng Chen and Heng Ji. 2009. Language specific issue and feature exploration in Chinese event extraction. In *Proceedings of Human Language Technologies: The 2009 Annual Conference of the North American Chapter of the Association for Computational Linguistics, Companion Volume: Short Papers*, pages 209–212, Boulder, Colorado. Association for Computational Linguistics.

Nicola De Cao, Gautier Izacard, Sebastian Riedel, and Fabio Petroni. 2021. Autoregressive Entity Retrieval. In *Proceedings of ICLR 2021*. ArXiv: 2010.00904.

Jacob Devlin, Ming-Wei Chang, Kenton Lee, and Kristina Toutanova. 2019. BERT: Pre-training of deep bidirectional transformers for language understanding. In *Proceedings of the 2019 Conference of the North American Chapter of the Association for Computational Linguistics: Human Language Technologies, Volume 1 (Long and Short Papers)*, pages 4171–4186, Minneapolis, Minnesota. Association for Computational Linguistics.

Heng Ji and Ralph Grishman. 2011. Knowledge Base Population: Successful Approaches and Challenges. In *Proceedings of the 49th Annual Meeting of the Association for Computational Linguistics: Human Language Techologies*, pages 1148–1158, Portland, Oregon, USA. Association for Computational Linguistics.

Danuta Ploch, Leonhard Hennig, Angelina Duka, Ernesto William De Luca, and Sahin Albayrak. 2012. GerNED: A German corpus for named entity disambiguation. In *Proceedings of the Eighth International Conference on Language Resources and Evaluation (LREC'12)*, pages 3886–3893, Istanbul, Turkey. European Language Resources Association (ELRA).

Alexander Ratner, Stephen H. Bach, Henry Ehrenberg, Jason Fries, Sen Wu, and Christopher Ré. 2017. Snorkel: Rapid Training Data Creation with Weak Supervision. *Proceedings of the VLDB Endowment*, 11(3):269–282. ArXiv: 1711.10160.

Alexander J Ratner, Christopher M De Sa, Sen Wu, Daniel Selsam, and Christopher Ré. 2016. Data programming: Creating large training sets, quickly. In *Advances in Neural Information Processing Systems*, volume 29. Curran Associates, Inc.

Sebastian Ruder. 2017. An Overview of Multi-Task Learning in Deep Neural Networks. *arXiv:1706.05098 [cs, stat]*. ArXiv: 1706.05098.

Martin Schiersch, Veselina Mironova, Maximilian Schmitt, Philippe Thomas, Aleksandra Gabryszak, and Leonhard Hennig. 2018. A German corpus for fine-grained named entity recognition and relation extraction of traffic and industry events. In *Proceedings of the Eleventh International Conference on Language Resources and Evaluation (LREC 2018)*, Miyazaki, Japan. European Language Resources Association (ELRA).

Dianbo Sui, Yubo Chen, Kang Liu, Jun Zhao, Xiangrong Zeng, and Shengping Liu. 2020. Joint Entity and Relation Extraction with Set Prediction Networks. *arXiv:2011.01675 [cs]*. ArXiv: 2011.01675 version: 2.

Erik F. Tjong Kim Sang and Fien De Meulder. 2003. Introduction to the conll-2003 shared task: Language-independent named entity recognition. In *Proceedings of the Seventh Conference on Natural Language Learning at HLT-NAACL 2003*, pages 142–147.

Mo Yu, Wenpeng Yin, Kazi Saidul Hasan, Cicero dos Santos, Bing Xiang, and Bowen Zhou. 2017. Improved Neural Relation Detection for Knowledge Base Question Answering. In *Proceedings of the 55th Annual Meeting of the Association for Computational Linguistics (Volume 1: Long Papers)*, pages 571–581, Vancouver, Canada. Association for Computational Linguistics.

Automatically evaluating the conceptual complexity of German texts

Freya Hewett [1,2]
[1] Humboldt Institute for Internet and Society, Berlin, Germany
freya.hewett@hiig.de

Manfred Stede [2]
[2] Applied Computational Linguistics
University of Potsdam, Germany
stede@uni-potsdam.de

Abstract

Conceptual complexity is concerned with the background knowledge needed to understand concepts within a text and their implicit connections (Hulpuș et al., 2019). In the present study, a recently proposed framework from Hulpuș et al. (2019), which assesses the conceptual complexity of English newspaper articles, is replicated and adapted to German lexica entries aimed at three different age groups. The final results on the corpus of 885 German texts improve upon the original study in both a pairwise classification task and a ranking task, showing that the framework transfers well to a different language and a different genre. We release the dataset used, as well as an extended version with a total of ca. 3000 texts.

1 Introduction

Text simplification aims to reduce the complexity of a text whilst retaining the main informational content. Conceptual complexity is concerned with the background knowledge needed to understand concepts within a text, and the implicit connections between the concepts that contribute to understanding a text (Hulpuș et al., 2019). The present study aims to evaluate the conceptual complexity of German texts, by recreating a recent study from Hulpuș et al. (2019) in which they assess the conceptual complexity of English language newspaper articles from the Newsela corpus (Xu et al., 2015), which contains articles at five different levels of complexity. To do this, they develop a framework which is based on psycholinguistic theories on reading comprehension, in particular *priming*, which states that words are recognised faster if preceded by words related in meaning (Collins and Loftus, 1975).

In the present study, this framework is directly applied to German texts from three lexica designed for beginner readers, children and adults. The framework is then slightly adapted to account for nuances specific to the German language, such as compound words. The results show that the model adapts well to German texts and works well across domains. We also release the lexica dataset to foster research on German text simplification, and a script to build the dataset as the lexica grow.[1]

2 Background

The main hypothesis in Hulpuș et al.'s (2019) study is that the more priming in a text, the lower the conceptual complexity. A spreading activation (SA) framework (Quillian, 1962, 1967; Collins and Loftus, 1975) is used to illustrate the priming process. The framework compares concepts to nodes in a network, with the properties of concepts represented as labelled relational links from the node to other concept nodes. Whenever a concept is mentioned in a text, it activates other neighbouring concepts in the graph (Collins and Loftus, 1975). The amounts of activation generated by this process are used to symbolise the amount of priming in the text.

The rest of this section provides a summary of the model proposed by Hulpuș et al. (2019). The model is implemented using the DBpedia knowledge graph (Lehmann et al., 2014), which converts information from Wikipedia into a graph structure. The texts are first annotated with concepts from DBpedia using an entity linker. The SA process for each of these concepts is then calculated and consists of three functions: an input, output and activation function. Each iteration in the SA process is called a *pulse*, denoted by p. $A^{(p)}(c)$ denotes the amount of activation that node c has after pulse p. Whenever a concept is mentioned in a text, referred to as a seed concept, its activation is set to 1.0, and all other nodes are set to 0.0. At pulse 1, the SA

[1] https://doi.org/10.5281/zenodo.5196030

process is triggered and activations flows from the seed concept. The **output function** adjusts the activation according to two parameters; α is a *distance decay parameter*, which decays the activation outputted by a node at every pulse. A *firing threshold* β is also used, which limits the concepts which can fire in the next pulse. The function is defined as follows:[2]

$$A_{out}^{(p+1)}(c) = \alpha \cdot f_\beta(A^{(p)}(c)) \quad (1)$$

where $f_\beta(x) = x$ if $x \geq \beta$; 0 otherwise. The **input function** collates the activation that flows in to a target node from neighbouring (source) nodes and takes two aspects into account, the popularity and the exclusivity. The popularity is measured by how many neighbouring nodes a concept has, the exclusivity measures the semantic relatedness between two nodes by using the types of relation that connect the two nodes.[3] These two factors multiplied together are termed *accessibility*. The **input function** is defined as follows:

$$A_{in}^{(p+1)}(c) = \sum_{r \in \rho(c)} A_{out}^{(p+1)}(n_r(c)) \cdot \overline{acc}_r(c) \quad (2)$$

where $\rho(c)$ refers to the set of relations of concept c, $n_r(c)$ the neighbours of concept c through the relation r, and $\overline{acc}_r(c)$ the normalised accessibility of concept c through relation r.[4] The **activation function** computes the activation of a concept as a sum of its activation at p and its incoming activation at $p+1$:

$$A^{(p+1)}(c) = A^{(p)}(c) + A_{in}^{(p+1)}(c) \quad (3)$$

The SA process finishes when there are no more concepts which have not already fired and have an activation value higher than the β threshold. In a next step, a function (denoted as $\phi(SA(c))$) is applied to the activations that the nodes have at the last pulse of the SA process and the resulting activation scores are then subject to a forgetting process. ϕ^A uses the activation from the SA process, except for the seed concept, where the popularity score is used instead. ϕ^1 is a constant function in which all concepts which become active during the SA process receive a score of 1.

[2]Functions are taken from Hulpuș et al. (2019).

[3]The functions for popularity and exclusivity can be found in Appendix A.1 and A.3.

[4]The function for normalised accessibility can be found in Appendix A.3.

Cumulative activation (CA) calculates the SA values after they have been subject to forgetting:

$$CA^{(i)}(c) = \sum_{k=0}^{i} \gamma_{k,i}\phi(SA^{(k)}(c)) \quad (4)$$

where $CA^{(i)}(c)$ denotes the CA of a concept c at the time of reading word i. γ represents the forgetting process and is the product of three set decay factors which decrease the activation of the concepts at each encountered word, sentence and paragraph. Scores can also increase if concepts are repeated or if related concepts are mentioned later in the text. The final scores for a text are calculated at the moment the concept is encountered (AE), at the end of sentences (AEoS), paragraphs (AEoP) or the sum of all three (All). The inverse of the average of these scores is used as the conceptual complexity score for the text. The scores are used for two tasks: a pairwise classification task (i.e. which text of two texts is more conceptually complex) evaluated by calculating the percentage of pairs that are classified correctly over all the pairs in the corpus, and a ranking task (i.e. correctly ordering the texts on one topic in order of conceptual complexity) evaluated by comparing the model's ranking to the gold-standard using Kendall's tau-b, which is on a scale from -1 to +1 (Kendall, 1945).

3 Related work

Conceptual complexity. An earlier study, also by Štajner and Hulpuș (2018), on the automatic assessment of conceptual complexity uses knowledge graph based features, such as the number of neighbours a node has and the length of the shortest path connecting two nodes. They build on this work by introducing shallow and surface features based on the output of an entity linker, such as the number of unique entities in a sentence or the average distance between consecutive mentions of entities (Stajner and Hulpuș, 2020).

Feng et al. (2010) evaluate the features which best predict readability, using magazine articles designed for primary school children of different ages in a classification task. They use "discourse features" such as the density of named entities and proper nouns across a sentence or text, or the length of chains of semantic relations (such as synonym or hypernym) from an entity, based on the hypothesis that the density of named entities and proper nouns introduced in a text relates to the burden placed on the readers' working memory and therefore the complexity level of a text.

For texts in German, Weiß and Meurers (2018) evaluate a large feature set of complexity indicators on a dataset of news subtitles and scientific articles and their counterparts aimed at children. Some of the most informative features were frequency measures calculated using different lexicons and corpora as well as content overlap within sentences. vor der Brück et al. (2008) develop a readability checker for German texts called DeLite and build so-called semantic networks for sentences, in which the word-class functions of the words and the relations between them are represented as a graph. Using 500 German texts from the municipal domain they compare human judgements on readability to automatic and conclude that indicative features include inverse concept frequency, the number of reference candidates for a pronoun and the number of propositions in a sentence.

Knowledge graphs. Knowledge graphs (KGs) have been used in a wide variety of tasks such as computing the semantic similarity of concepts (Zhu and Iglesias, 2017), finding relevant tokens in text (Bronselaer and Pasi, 2013), in recommendation systems (Joseph and Jiang, 2019) and for calculating document similarity (Paul et al., 2016). Using KGs in language-based tasks as a proxy for background knowledge is not a novel idea, and has been done in the context of argumentation mining with reasonable success (Kobbe et al., 2019; Botschen et al., 2018).

4 Data

The main data for the present study comes from a total of 885 articles from three Wiki-based lexica in German language: MiniKlexikon, Klexikon and Wikipedia. Klexikon is aimed specifically at children aged between 6 and 12 (Dunemann, 2016) and MiniKlexikon is designed for children who are beginner readers, and is therefore an even simpler version of the Klexikon. We make the assumption that the three different sub-corpora represent three different levels of conceptual complexity due to the target groups they are written for: younger children, children and adults. Children have less prior knowledge so therefore a text written for them should require less background knowledge; this aspect is explicitly mentioned in the guidelines for writing articles for the MiniKlexikon.[5] As Wikipedia articles can be extremely long, in comparison to the other two lexica, only the introduction or abstract was taken for the purposes of the current study. Any Klexikon articles longer than 2800 characters were excluded, as well as any articles where parallel topics did not exist across all sub-corpora. This resulted in 295 texts for each level. The different sub-corpora will be referred to hereafter as level 0 (MiniKlexikon), level 1 (Klexikon) and level 2 (Wikipedia). Table 1 shows that the level 1 sub-corpus contains the longest articles, but the average sentence length gets longer as the complexity level increases. Examples from the corpus can be seen in Table 2.

Sub-corpus	Texts	Avg. AL	Avg. SL
Level 0	295	134.86	9.57
Level 1	295	305.45	13.29
Level 2	295	169.89	18.41

Table 1: Average length of articles (AL) and average sentence length (SL) in the three sub-corpora (tokens).

5 Experiments

The system from Hulpuş et al. (2019) was first replicated, adapted only by changing the language of the DBpedia graph to German. As in the original study, different parameters were experimented with: the extent of the forgetting process, γ, – the so-called type of decay – and the ϕ function, which is the function applied to the values which result from the SA process. The distance decay parameter α and the firing threshold β, two parameters which control the amount of nodes activated in each SA step, were not experimented with and the best performing values from the original study were used, 0.25 and 0.01 respectively. The system was then applied to all 885 texts in the lexica corpus. The results can be seen in Table 3: the average accuracy for pairwise classification using the best parameters from the original study (as documented in (Štajner et al., 2020)) was .86, which is the same as the original system for English texts. The best parameters for the German texts – as can be seen in the right-hand side of Table 3 – increased the average accuracy for the pairwise classification to .89. In both cases the AEoS score provided the best results.

[5]`https://miniklexikon.zum.de/index.php?title=Hilfe:Regeln&oldid=23440`

Level 2	Simplified (level 0/1)	Simplification
The name Allosaurus **is derived from the Greek language and** translates to 'different lizard'.	The name Allosaurus means something like 'different lizard'.	removal of non-essential concepts that demand more background knowledge
Amsterdam is the capital city and the **most populous** city in the **Kingdom of** the Netherlands.	Amsterdam is the capital city of the Netherlands. Amsterdam is also the **biggest** city in the Netherlands.	replacement of non-essential demanding concepts with more commonly known ones
Furthermore, **astronomy strives to understand** the universe as a whole, its origins and its development.	Astronomers investigate how space originated.	avoidance of abstract concepts

Table 2: Translated examples of conceptual simplification from the lexica corpus created for the present study. The types of simplification are taken from (Štajner and Hulpuş, 2018).

decay	medium decay, ϕ^1				strong decay, ϕ^A			
score	**AE**	**AEoS**	**AEoP**	**All**	**AE**	**AEoS**	**AEoP**	**All**
0-1	.56	**.93**	.89	.92	.58	.87	.82	.88
0-2	.35	.88	.69	.79	.52	**.94**	.82	.91
1-2	.30	.76	.48	.59	.48	**.87**	.62	.76

Table 3: The accuracy scores for the pairwise classification task with the parameters from the original study (Hulpuş et al., 2019). The scores on the left use the best parameters for the Newsela corpus, the scores on the right use the best parameters for the lexica corpus. The highest accuracy for each pair of levels is highlighted in bold.

5.1 Adaptations

Manual inspection of the concepts annotated by the entity linker, DBpedia Spotlight (Mendes et al., 2011), revealed some inaccurate annotations, particularly at a confidence level of 0.35, which is the level used by Štajner et al. (2020). Nouns with capitalised articles are often tagged as films or bands that go by the same name such as *the depth* (*Die Tiefe*). We experimented with different confidence levels (0.35 to 0.65, at intervals of 0.05) and with an alternative entity linker for German, TagMe, with the same amount of the equivalent confidence levels (Ferragina and Scaiella, 2010, 2012). Whilst the accuracy of the tagged concepts did appear to improve, neither the confidence values nor the TagMe entity linker improved the scores for either task. Another approach was taken to try and improve the accuracy of the entity linker for the specific task of solely tagging concepts. In the context of the present model, a concept is simply defined, by proxy, as a node in the DBpedia KG. By analysing the texts in the corpus, this definition could be elaborated upon to say that concepts are nodes in the DBpedia KG that are also nouns, verbs, adjectives, adverbs or cardinal numbers. The whole corpus was tagged with Part-of-Speech tags using TreeTagger (Schmid, 1999) and entity annotations were removed that did not fit this definition. This reduced the amount of concepts tagged by approximately 15%.

Another challenge that the entity linkers have to deal with, that is somewhat unique to the German language, is the high presence of compound words such as *Pumporgan*: literally pump organ, "heart". *Pumporgan* does not have its own DBpedia page which implies it is a somewhat novel compound. Most novel compounds are transparent, as it can be assumed that the reader is seeing them for the first time, so they have to be able to be understood by the context and the meaning of the constituents (Smolka and Libben, 2017). In this way, annotating *Pumporgan* with the individual concepts *Pump* and *Organ* would reflect the process that a reader goes through when processing a novel compound, and would be the ideal behaviour for the entity linker. To facilitate the tagging of such compounds, a compound splitter (Ziering and van der Plas, 2016) was applied to the level 2 data before the entity linking stage. According to the MiniKlexikon guidelines[6], unusual compounds should be hyphenated and so the splitter was not used on levels 0 and 1, and instead hyphenated words were separated.

We also experimented with different ϕ functions. ϕ^U refers to *unchanged*, so taking the SA scores as is, ϕ^{red} refers to *reduced* so simply applying the forgetting process to the entity linker output, leaving out the SA process completely and ϕ^{pop} refers to *popularity*, and also leaves out the SA process whilst including the popularity scores of the tagged concepts. The equations for these ϕ functions can be found in Appendix A.2. We also introduced an **AEoD** score which sums up the score for the whole document, and tried out different combinations of calculating the **All** score.

[6]https://miniklexikon.zum.de/index.php?title=Hilfe:Regeln&oldid=20790

System	ϕ	Decay	AA	tau-b
original framework, English texts	ϕ^1	medium	.86+	.82*
framework replication, German texts	ϕ^A	strong	.89	.79
PoS based outlier removal	ϕ^A	strong	.89	.78
compound splitting, just level 2	ϕ^A	strong	.89	.79
compound splitting, all levels	ϕ^A	strong	.70	.41
AEoD score	ϕ^A	strong	.52	.04
All + AEoD	ϕ^A	strong	.81	.62
AEoS + AEoP	ϕ^A	strong	.87	.74
unchanged scores	ϕ^U	medium	**.91**	**.83**
entity linker + forgetting	ϕ^{red}	medium	**.91**	**.83**
entity linker + popularity + forgetting	ϕ^{pop}	strong	.85	.70

Table 4: The average accuracy (AA) for the pairwise classification task and tau-b for the ranking task using the AEoS scores for various models, with different ϕ and decay parameters (only the best-performing combinations for each system are shown). +From Štajner et al. (2020). *From Hulpuș et al. (2019): the tau-b results are calculated using an entity linker which is not publicly available; a direct comparison is therefore not possible.

5.2 Results & discussion

The results on the lexica corpus can be seen in Table 4. The best accuracy and tau-b score is for the model with unchanged scores from the SA process (ϕ^U) and the model which just uses the seed concepts and a forgetting process (ϕ^{red}). This second model, ϕ^{red}, also has the advantage of being much more efficient than the models which involve the spreading activation process. This is an improvement of 5 percentage points on the original study, although it is worth mentioning that the results can not be directly compared due to the different nature of the datasets. The lexica corpora used in this study are on 3 different levels (as apposed to the Newsela corpus which has 5 levels) and the texts do not necessarily represent parallel translations.

As can be seen in Table 1, the average sentence lengths of the different levels of the corpus increase as the complexity increases. In fact, using average sentence length as a sole feature for the ranking task results in a tau-b score of .87. However, for downstream tasks such as automatic simplification or summarisation, a content based classification of complexity – such as the conceptual complexity value – could prove to be a lot more informative. Another use case for conceptual complexity is for texts that may not conform to this pattern of shorter sentences for less complexity. For example, when simplifying complex sentences by including examples or extra clauses that explain difficult terms, the sentence length will increase as the complexity level decreases.

As the success of a framework that uses a specific KG as a proxy for long-term memory is obviously highly dependent on the quality of the KG, a manual inspection of the DBpedia KG was carried out. This showed that nodes are not always linked to each other in an intuitive way, with many nodes completely isolated. A random sample of 30 results from the popularity function showed that the node *multiplication* scores 0, as it has no neighbours, and *Helgoland* and *Calligra Suite* score higher than *ruler* or *hair*, which may not correspond to an average reader's level of familiarity. Working with a different KG or calculating the popularity or familiarity of concepts in an ontology-independent way could yield more accurate results; we leave this to future work.

6 Conclusion & outlook

In this study, the conceptual complexity of German lexicon entries was examined by replicating and adapting a spreading activation framework proposed by Hulpuș et al. (2019). When compared to the results from the study using the same entity linker (Štajner et al., 2020), the current implementation improves the average accuracy score for pairwise classification by 5 percentage points. This shows that the adapted framework also works with shorter texts and can be adapted to work with languages other than English. We release the main dataset used and a script to continually update it. An interesting direction for future research would be a closer examination of the way concepts are connected on a text level, implicitly and explicitly, and how the discourse structure affects complexity.

Acknowledgments

Thank you to the anonymous reviewers for their very helpful comments. This research is funded by the German Federal Ministry of Education and Research (BMBF).

References

Teresa Botschen, Daniil Sorokin, and Iryna Gurevych. 2018. Frame- and entity-based knowledge for common-sense argumentative reasoning. In *Proceedings of the 5th Workshop on Argument Mining*, pages 90–96. Association for Computational Linguistics.

Antoon Bronselaer and Gabriella Pasi. 2013. An approach to graph-based analysis of textual documents. In *8th Conference of the European Society for Fuzzy Logic and Technology (EUSFLAT 2013)*, pages 634–641. Atlantis Press.

Tim vor der Brück, Sven Hartrumpf, and Hermann Helbig. 2008. A Readability Checker with Supervised Learning using Deep Syntactic and Semantic Indicators. *Informatica*, 32:429–435.

Allan Collins and Elizabeth Loftus. 1975. A Spreading Activation Theory of Semantic Processing. *Psychological Review*, 82:407–428.

Tabea Dunemann. 2016. Ins Netz gegangen: Klexikon.de. Wenn Wissen mitmachen lässt. *tv diskurs*, 76:112–113.

Lijun Feng, Martin Jansche, Matt Huenerfauth, and Noémie Elhadad. 2010. A Comparison of Features for Automatic Readability Assessment. In *Proceedings of the 23rd International Conference on Computational Linguistics: Posters*, pages 276–284. Association for Computational Linguistics.

Paolo Ferragina and Ugo Scaiella. 2010. TAGME: On-the-Fly Annotation of Short Text Fragments (by Wikipedia Entities). In *Proceedings of the 19th ACM International Conference on Information and Knowledge Management*, pages 1625–1628. Association for Computing Machinery.

Paolo Ferragina and Ugo Scaiella. 2012. Fast and Accurate Annotation of Short Texts with Wikipedia Pages. *IEEE Software*, 29(1):70–75.

Ioana Hulpuş, Narumol Prangnawarat, and Conor Hayes. 2015. Path-Based Semantic Relatedness on Linked Data and Its Use to Word and Entity Disambiguation. In *The Semantic Web - ISWC 2015*, pages 442–457, Cham. Springer International Publishing.

Ioana Hulpuș, Sanja Štajner, and Heiner Stuckenschmidt. 2019. A Spreading Activation Framework for Tracking Conceptual Complexity of Texts. In *Proceedings of the 57th Annual Meeting of the Association for Computational Linguistics*, pages 3878–3887. Association for Computational Linguistics.

Kevin Joseph and Hui Jiang. 2019. Content based News Recommendation via Shortest Entity Distance over Knowledge Graphs. In *Companion of The 2019 World Wide Web Conference, WWW 2019*, pages 690–699. ACM.

Maurice G. Kendall. 1945. The treatment of ties in ranking problems. *Biometrika*, 33:239–251.

Jonathan Kobbe, Juri Opitz, Maria Becker, Ioana Hulpus, Heiner Stuckenschmidt, and Anette Frank. 2019. Exploiting background knowledge for argumentative relation classification. In *2nd Conference on Language, Data and Knowledge (LDK 2019)*, volume 70, pages 8:1–8:14. Schloss Dagstuhl - Leibniz-Zentrum für Informatik.

Jens Lehmann, Robert Isele, Max Jakob, Anja Jentzsch, Dimitris Kontokostas, Pablo Mendes, Sebastian Hellmann, Mohamed Morsey, Patrick Van Kleef, Sören Auer, and Christian Bizer. 2014. DBpedia - A Large-scale, Multilingual Knowledge Base Extracted from Wikipedia. *Semantic Web Journal*, 6:1–29.

Pablo N. Mendes, Max Jakob, Andrés García-Silva, and Christian Bizer. 2011. DBpedia Spotlight: Shedding light on the web of documents. In *Proceedings of the 7th International Conference on Semantic Systems*, pages 1–8. Association for Computing Machinery.

Christian Paul, Achim Rettinger, Aditya Mogadala, Craig Knoblock, and Pedro Szekely. 2016. Efficient Graph-Based Document Similarity. In *The Semantic Web. Latest Advances and New Domains*, pages 334–349. Springer, Cham.

Ross Quillian. 1962. A revised design for an understanding machine. *Mechanical Translation*, 7:17–29.

Ross Quillian. 1967. Word concepts: A theory and simulation of some basic semantic capabilities. *Behavioral Science*, 12:410–430.

Helmut Schmid. 1999. *Improvements in Part-of-Speech Tagging with an Application to German*, pages 13–25. Springer Netherlands.

Eva Smolka and Gary Libben. 2017. 'Can you wash off the hogwash?' : semantic transparency of first and second constituents in the processing of German compounds. *Language, Cognition and Neuroscience*, 32(4):514–531.

Sanja Štajner and Ioana Hulpuș. 2018. Automatic Assessment of Conceptual Text Complexity Using Knowledge Graphs. In *Proceedings of the 27th International Conference on Computational Linguistics*, pages 318–330. Association for Computational Linguistics.

Sanja Stajner and Ioana Hulpuș. 2020. When shallow is good enough: Automatic assessment of conceptual text complexity using shallow semantic features. In *Proceedings of the 12th Language Resources and Evaluation Conference*, pages 1414–1422, Marseille, France. European Language Resources Association.

Sanja Štajner, Sergiu Nisioi, and Ioana Hulpuș. 2020. CoCo: A Tool for Automatically Assessing Conceptual Complexity of Texts. In *Proceedings of*

The 12th Language Resources and Evaluation Conference, pages 7179–7186. European Language Resources Association.

Zarah Weiß and Detmar Meurers. 2018. Modeling the Readability of German Targeting Adults and Children: An empirically broad analysis and its cross-corpus validation. In *Proceedings of the 27th International Conference on Computational Linguistics*, pages 303–317. Association for Computational Linguistics.

Wei Xu, Chris Callison-Burch, and Courtney Napoles. 2015. Problems in Current Text Simplification Research: New Data Can Help. *Transactions of the Association for Computational Linguistics*, 3:283–297.

Ganggao Zhu and Carlos A. Iglesias. 2017. Computing semantic similarity of concepts in knowledge graphs. *IEEE Transactions on Knowledge and Data Engineering*, 29(1):72–85.

Patrick Ziering and Lonneke van der Plas. 2016. Towards Unsupervised and Language-independent Compound Splitting using Inflectional Morphological Transformations. In *Proceedings of the 2016 Conference of the North American Chapter of the Association for Computational Linguistics: Human Language Technologies*, pages 644–653. Association for Computational Linguistics.

A Appendices

A.1 Popularity function

The popularity function is defined as follows:

$$pop(c) = \frac{log(D(c))}{log(|V| - 1)} \tag{5}$$

where $D(c)$ denotes the number of neighbours of concept c, and $|V|$ the total number of concepts in the KG.

A.2 ϕ functions

Functions for ϕ^A and ϕ^1 as described in Section 2, taken from Hulpuș et al. (2019):

$$\phi^A(SA(c)) = \begin{cases} SA(c), & \text{if } SA(c) < 1.0 \\ pop(c), & \text{if } SA(c) \geq 1.0 \end{cases} \tag{6}$$

$$\phi^1(SA(c)) = 1 \quad \text{if} \quad SA(c) > 0.0 \tag{7}$$

Additional functions for ϕ^U, ϕ^{red} and ϕ^{pop}:
ϕ^U, which refers to *unchanged* and simply takes the values as-is from the SA process and is defined as follows:

$$\phi^U(SA(c)) = SA(c) \tag{8}$$

ϕ^{red}, which refers to *reduced*, which just takes the seed concepts and applies forgetting, and is defined as follows:

$$\phi^{red}(SA(c)) = \begin{cases} 0.0, & \text{if } SA(c) < 1.0 \\ SA(c), & \text{if } SA(c) \geq 1.0 \end{cases} \tag{9}$$

ϕ^{pop}, which refers to *popularity*, which just calculates the popularity for activated concepts and applies forgetting, which is defined as follows:

$$\phi^{pop}(SA(c)) = pop(c) \quad \text{if} \quad SA(c) > 0.0 \tag{10}$$

A.3 Differences to original study (Hulpuș et al., 2019)

Our replicated framework was tested with a subsample of 25 Newsela texts (Xu et al., 2015). Using the original rankings as published here[7] as gold standard, our replicated system had a tau-b of .9.

The reasons for this slight difference could be due to the following reasons: Štajner et al. (2020) use a different exclusivity calculation (cf. 12), the Newsela texts used for the present study are formatted slightly differently and do not have paragraph information, two equations (11, 6) were adjusted as the original equations in (Hulpuș et al., 2019) do not fully match the descriptions in the accompanying paper. In addition to this, Štajner et al. (2020) do not specify if they use a support parameter when using the entity linker DBpedia Spotlight. This slightly limits the pool of neighbouring nodes which is returned. In the present study we use a support value of 20.

The normalised accessibility function:

$$\overline{acc}_r(c) = \frac{acc_r(c)}{(acc_r(c) + \sum_{r' \in \rho(n_r(c))} acc_{r'}(n_{r'} \circ n_r(c)))} \tag{11}$$

The exact equation for exclusivity was not listed in the paper, and at the time of replicating the framework, no further information was available. The following function was used, adapted from the function in (Hulpuş et al., 2015):

$$excl(r) = \frac{1}{|* \xrightarrow{T} x \xrightarrow{T} *| + |* \xrightarrow{T} y \xrightarrow{T} *| - 1} \tag{12}$$

[7] https://github.com/ioanahulpus/cocospa/blob/master/results/newsela.csv

WORDGUESS
Using Associations for Guessing, Learning and Exploring Related Words

Cennet Oğuz[1], André Blessing[2], Jonas Kuhn[2], Sabine Schulte im Walde[2]
[1]German Research Center for Artificial Intelligence (DFKI), Saarland Informatics Campus
[2]Institute for Natural Language Processing, University of Stuttgart
ceog01@dfki.de,
{blessiae,jonas,schulte}@ims.uni-stuttgart.de

Abstract

This paper presents WORDGUESS, a game-with-a-purpose vocabulary training where –in order to guess a target word (such as ***snow***)– the player is offered associations of that target word (such as *winter, white, cold*). The game relies on existing association norms and co-occurrence information to establish an entertaining way of deepening the player's learning and understanding of vocabulary and of associative relatedness between words in the vocabulary. WORDGUESS comes with data in English and German and can be extended with data from further languages. From an application-oriented point of view the players' data enables us to induce conditions and weights for word association and to quantify contextual relationships, which is useful for many NLP purposes such as ontology induction and anaphora resolution.

1 Introduction

Games-with-a-purpose (GWAP) offer enjoyable entertainment to players and at the same time allow researchers in Natural Language Processing (NLP) to collect and explore cognitive and (computational) linguistic facets of human-generated data. While the term GWAP has been coined by Von Ahn and Dabbish (2008), the underlying idea has been pursued across linguistic levels and across NLP purposes for much longer. To provide a few examples across research fields, the adventure and interactive fiction games by Gabsdil et al. (2002) rely on natural-language question-answering dialogues to explore inference systems with reference resolution, syntactic ambiguities, and scripted dialogues; Chamberlain et al. (2008) exploit collaborative work to identify relationships between words and phrases in web data; *OntoGame* (Siorpaes and Hepp, 2008) matches classes in an ontology with Wikipedia articles; Hladká et al. (2009) propose a gamified annotation approach for coreference resolution; Guillaume et al. (2016) design *ZombiLingo*, a game for syntactic dependency annotation.

We present a GWAP-style game implementation called WORDGUESS[1] where associations of a target word are offered to players in order to guess the target word. For example, associations such as *winter, white, cold* provide hints to players when guessing the target word *snow*. Our game is a web-based and mobile-based application whose aim is to learn and understand word-association and word-context relationships: previous research has shown that associations and corpus co-occurrence are related (Church and Hanks, 1990; de Deyne and Storms, 2008a; Schulte im Walde et al., 2008, i.a.); we plan to explore their connections and differences in more depth. In this vein, (i) we vary associations obtained from humans, and context-based words induced from corpus co-occurrence; (ii) we provide a multilingual gaming environment in order to understand the conditions across languages and relational patterns between native and second languages; and (iii) we offer the players to choose between levels of difficulty (i.e., providing more or less cues). The obtained data enables us to induce conditions and weights for word association and to quantify contextual relationships, taking native language, age and gender into account.

Regarding the technical setup, we use *Angular*, a TypeScript-based open-source web application framework, for the implementation of the user interface (UI), while *MongoDB*, a cross-platform document-oriented database program, is utilized for storing and organizing the game constituents (e.g., defined games, users, and played games). We also provide a responsive UI design in order to make the game usable on different devices such as phones, tablets and computers.

[1]https://wordguess.ims.uni-stuttgart.de

2 Related Work

Gamification is a common way to make a wide variety of tasks entertaining in NLP. In the following, we provide an overview of NLP-oriented games for data collection, language learning and linguistic analysis, which are the purposes closest to ours.

Data Collection Lafourcade (2007) proposes a gamification approach by making people play with associative words in order to memorize associations with *JeuxDeMots*, a two-player game based on agreement. Kuo et al. (2009) present an interactive community-based game for collecting question-answering data in order to provide a report about data quality, collection efficiency, player retention, concept diversity, and game stability for future community-based games. Lafourcade et al. (2017) use games to create and enrich weighted lexical resources from crowdsourced data by investigating existing rich lexical networks that can be used to infer linguistic coercion.

Language Learning Advances in NLP techniques have been used to investigate students' learning situations and behaviour patterns in a wide range of learning practices and studies. Mart (2012) claims that guessing new words presented in isolation is hard but words in context help learners to deduce meaning from the context, whereas Crow and Quigley (1985) demonstrate that an approach to vocabulary studies based on semantic organization is productive. These theories indicate that computer games are powerful tools for educational aims (Malone, 1980). Therefore, we suggest our game for vocabulary learning in both the native and a second language to attract user motivation.

Many games aim to improve teaching methods for language learning and other educational environments. Jung and Graf (2008) build a word-association game and show that word association supports more effective and attractive vocabulary learning. Madge et al. (2019) offer a text-tagging and language-learning game for enhanced syntactic annotation and language resources.

Linguistic Analysis NLP techniques have also helped to identify students' behaviour and learning models by explaining complex linguistic patterns that occur in the games' language data in order to provide enhanced education methodologies. Goodman (2014) uses a guessing game in order to understand whether reading is a series of guesses informed by graphic, semantic and syntactic cues while substituting the words. Picca et al. (2015) show NLP utilization for understanding children's language development by gathering data from a pedagogical *Serious Game* which is designed for a primary purpose other than pure entertainment.

We offer a novel gamified approach that is inspired by (Goodman, 2014; Jung and Graf, 2008) for word guessing by using word-association and word-context pairs. Our game aims to create opportunities for both players and researchers: players go for it for learning and entertaining purposes, while researchers may analyze the cognitive and linguistic inferences.

3 WordGuess: Motivation, Design, Architecture

Motivation Associations, i.e., words spontaneously called to mind by a stimulus word, have served as a tool in cognitive science research for decades to investigate the mechanisms underlying semantic memory, making use of the implicit notion that associates reflect meaning components of words. Accordingly, a large number of data collections of associations is available, such as the *Edinburgh Association Thesaurus* (Kiss et al., 1973), the University of South Florida norms (Nelson et al., 2004), the *Database of Noun Associations for German* (Melinger and Weber, 2006), norms for German nouns and verbs (Schulte im Walde et al., 2008) and for Dutch words (de Deyne and Storms, 2008b), and the *Small World of Words* norms (de Deyne et al., 2019), among others.

For many NLP purposes such as ontology induction and anaphora resolution, it is crucial to define and induce semantic relations between words or contexts, and according to the *co-occurrence hypothesis* (Miller, 1969; Spence and Owens, 1990) semantic association is related to the textual co-occurrence of stimulus-associate pairs. Therefore, a number of studies have exploited the connection between co-occurrence distributions and semantic relatedness, and used association norms as a test-bed for distributional models of semantic relatedness (Church and Hanks, 1990; Rapp, 2002; de Deyne and Storms, 2008a; Schulte im Walde et al., 2008, i.a.).

Game Idea The aim of WordGuess is to exploit a gamification environment in order to deepen the understanding of associative relatedness. Differently to previous approaches, we do not directly

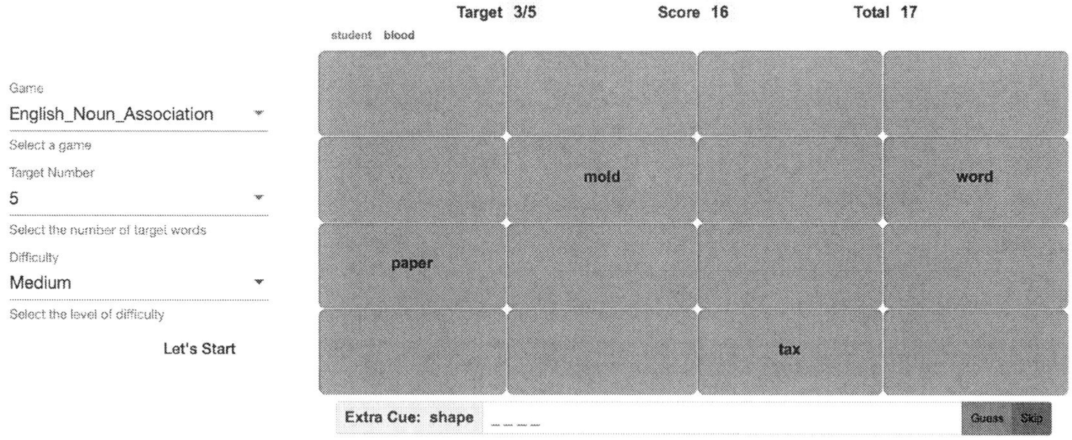

Figure 1: Sample page views of the game: (a) On the left you can see the decision page where the player can choose a predefined game, the number of targets and the difficulty level. (b) On the right you can see a game page at some point during the game where (top row: left to right) the player is currently working on the third out of five targets (3/5), currently scores 16 for this target (out of a maximum of 20) because four cue words have been selected already, and currently holds a total score of 17 from the past two target word guesses. On the bottom left we see an extra cue word (*shape*) and five underscores _ _ _ _ _ to indicate that the target word is five characters long; this information corresponds to the medium difficulty level. The player can either write a guess and press "Guess" or give up on this target at any point and press "Skip" (bottom right). The red+green words above the grid refer to previously guessed (green) or not guessed (red) target words.

analyse and quantify existing norms of human association in comparison to corpus co-occurrence. Rather, we investigate their relatedness by *utilising* them alternately in the same gaming environment and under the same conditions, so that comparing the ease or difficulty of players can inform us indirectly about their similarities and differences.

In this vein, the game relies on existing association norms and co-occurrence data across languages to establish an entertaining way of collecting human associations. The players see a grid with empty cells which they can click in any order (see Figure 1). Each click reveals a cue. The less cues the player needs to guess the correct target word, the higher the score; a wrong guess decreases the score by three.

For each player who is registered[2] we keep track of the order of the chosen cues, the correct and wrong guesses, and the required time for a correct guess. In addition, we can relate those parameters to the players' profile including age, gender and native language. The underlying cues are either based on existing association norms or on corpus-induced co-occurrences, so that we can use the data to obtain a clearer picture for association-target relations, co-occurrences and the interplay of both.

[2]Players can choose between playing with or without an account. We only keep track of players who create an account.

Game Implementation WORDGUESS works in two different modes: (1) the *project mode* for the researcher to set up a new game, and (2) the *player mode* for the player to play a game from the available set of games in the project mode.

In the project mode, a researcher defines a game and specifies the game properties. Our system accepts data collections in JSON file format. Each file corresponds to a game setup, i.e., the data is read from a file and establishes a new game. Each target-association pair is presented as a JSON object with *target*, *context*, and *score* ⟨key,value⟩ pairs. After uploading the game file, the researcher defines the game settings, such as the name of the game, target order, context order, context number, cue selection and game definition (see examples in Appendix). The name of the game is the attribute seen by the player for the game selection. Target–context pairs may be selected according to their order, or randomly. In addition, the context number defines how many contexts are provided to the players; the cue selection determines the choice of extra cues (random, highest, lowest, none).

The player mode presents the game to the players. A player may register for playing a game, or alternatively skip the registration and play the game anonymously for entertainment and learning. The registration is performed as explicit agreement between researcher and player to provide data. Without that agreement, the player is able to play the game without sharing any information. Game-related functions are not affected by this decision. Before starting the game the player has to determine the game's attributes. As can be seen from Figure 1 (left), the decision page represents the game-related options such as game, target number, and difficulty level. Afterwards, the player can start playing the game according to the selected options. WORDGUESS currently offers two game languages: German and English. At the same time, target words distinguish between two word classes, nouns and verbs. The player can select the number of target words to guess as either five or ten. We present two different types of cues, i.e., target cues and context cues for each target word to guess. *Target cues* are derived from the target word. In the easy mode, we provide the number of characters of the target word together with one of the characters (e.g., __r_ for *farm*), whereas in the medium mode we only show the target's character count (e.g., ____). We do not show any target cue in the hard mode. *Context cues* for target words are the main focus of our game and research, either human associations or corpus co-occurrence words. They are shown to the player in the grid, as illustrated in Figure 1 (right), plus one bonus cue (bottom left corner). The extra context cue which is the most associated context word of the target is available right from the beginning when the context cues in the grid are still hidden. The player clicks the boxes in the grid one by one to find the context cues, and tries to guess the target. Previous correct and wrong guesses for the current target word are displayed on the same page. At the same time, the player is able to skip a target word and to move on to guessing the next target word. The game continues for the chosen number of target words, and at the end of the game the player sees a summary of wrong and correct answers, and their scores. Registered players can track their scores and vocabulary development across games on their profile page.

Technical Setup We utilize Angular (v9.2.3) as the application framework as well as TypeScript (v3.2.4) as the programming language. MongoDB (v4.2.3), a document-oriented database program, is used for managing the stored data. Additionally, Express (v4.16.1) is exploited as the server framework for Node (v14.2.0) which is our runtime application environment.

Motivating Users Malone (1980) indicates that players are willing to master long-term activities (challenge), pursue informative games (curiosity), and let games invoke their imagination (fantasy). Challenges require a maximum level of difficulty whereas curiosity needs an optimum level of complexity in the game. WORDGUESS enables vocabulary improvement abilities as an informative reason to activate curiosity during the game, as well as different difficulty levels to enable a challenge.

We provide a very simple user interface to the players to keep their attention to only the game. Additionally, the necessary actions to play the game are not complicated or tiring such as long reading, learning additional techniques, or checking the accuracy of the current knowledge. We use harmonious colors to create serious perception whereas simple actions (to click the boxes) make the application game-like.

Data Privacy and Ethics As mentioned before, the player registration is performed as explicit agreement between researcher and player to provide data. Without that agreement, the player is able to play the game without sharing any information. Game-related functions are not affected by this decision. Information about age range, gender, and native language are kept if the player registers to the system. Furthermore, we encode the usernames by applying hashing algorithms. Players are able to delete their accounts whenever they want.

4 Conclusion and Future Works

This paper presented WORDGUESS, a game-with-a-purpose vocabulary training where associations of a target word are offered to players in order to guess the target word. From an application-oriented point of view, the gamification provides data that enables us to induce conditions and weights for word association and to quantify contextual relationships, which is useful for many NLP purposes such as ontology induction and anaphora resolution.

As regards future work, we plan to implement age-based user interfaces like colorful pages for children. The multiplayer, score-based competitions with enriched context based on descriptive information are on the agenda as well. Finally, data from further languages will be added to enable cross-lingual studies.

Acknowledgments

We thank the three anonymous reviewers for feedback on the game and on the paper. Furthermore, Cennet Oğuz was supported by the CRETA center funded by the German Ministry for Education and Research (BMBF), FKZ 01UG1601 and FKZ 01UG1901; André Blessing was supported by funding from the German Research Foundation (Deutsche Forschungsgemeinschaft, DFG) through MARDY (Modeling Argumentation Dynamics) within SPP RATIO.

References

Jon Chamberlain, Massimo Poesio, and Udo Kruschwitz. 2008. Phrase detectives: A web-based collaborative annotation game. In *Proceedings of the International Conference on Semantic Systems*, pages 42–49.

Kenneth W. Church and Patrick Hanks. 1990. Word association norms, mutual information, and lexicography. *Computational Linguistics*, 16(1):22–29.

John T. Crow and June R. Quigley. 1985. A semantic field approach to passive vocabulary acquisition for reading comprehension. *Tesol Quarterly*, 19(3):497–513.

Simon de Deyne, Danielle J. Navarro, Amy Perfors, Marc Brysbaert, and Gert Storms. 2019. The "Small World of Words" English word association norms for over 12,000 cue words. *Behavior Research Methods*, 51:987–1006.

Simon de Deyne and Gert Storms. 2008a. Word associations: Network and semantic properties. *Behavior Research Methods*, 40(1):213–231.

Simon de Deyne and Gert Storms. 2008b. Word associations: Norms for 1,424 Dutch words in a continuous task. *Behavior Research Methods*, 40(1):198–205.

Malte Gabsdil, Alexander Koller, and Kristina Striegnitz. 2002. Natural language and inference in a computer game. In *Proceedings of the 19th International Conference on Computational Linguistics*, pages 1–7.

Kenneth S Goodman. 2014. Reading: A psycholinguistic guessing game. In *Making Sense of Learners Making Sense of Written Language*, pages 115–124.

Bruno Guillaume, Karën Fort, and Nicolas Lefebvre. 2016. Crowdsourcing complex language resources: Playing to annotate dependency syntax.

Barbora Hladká, Jiří Mírovský, and Pavel Schlesinger. 2009. Play the language: Play coreference. In *Proceedings of the ACL-IJCNLP 2009 Conference Short Papers*, pages 209–212.

Jaeyoung Jung and Sabine Graf. 2008. An approach for personalized web-based vocabulary learning through word association games. In *2008 International Symposium on Applications and the Internet*, pages 325–328.

George R. Kiss, Christine Armstrong, Robert Milroy, and James Piper. 1973. An associative thesaurus of English and its computer analysis. In *The Computer and Literary Studies*. Edinburgh University Press.

Yen-ling Kuo, Jong-Chuan Lee, Kai-yang Chiang, Rex Wang, Edward Shen, Cheng-wei Chan, and Jane Yung-jen Hsu. 2009. Community-based game design. In *Proceedings of Human Computation*, pages 15–22.

Mathieu Lafourcade. 2007. Making people play for lexical acquisition with the jeuxdemots prototype. In *Proceedings of the 7th International Symposium on Natural Language Processing*.

Mathieu Lafourcade, Bruno Mery, Mehdi Mirzapour, Richard Moot, and Christian Retoré. 2017. Collecting crowd-sourced lexical coercions for compositional semantic analysis. In *LENLS: Logic and Engineering of Natural Language Semantics*.

Chris Madge, Richard Bartle, Jon Chamberlain, Udo Kruschwitz, and Massimo Poesio. 2019. Making text annotation fun with a clicker game. In *Proceedings of the 14th International Conference on the Foundations of Digital Games*, pages 1–6.

Thomas W Malone. 1980. *What makes things fun to learn? A study of intrinsically motivating computer games*. Ph.D. thesis, ProQuest Information & Learning.

Çağrı Tuğrul Mart. 2012. Guessing the meanings of words from context: Why and how. *International Journal of Applied Linguistics and English Literature*, 1(6):177–181.

Alissa Melinger and Andrea Weber. 2006. Database of Noun Associations for German. URL: http://www.psycholing.es.uni-tuebingen.de/nag/.

George Miller. 1969. The organization of lexical memory: Are word associations sufficient? In George A. Talland and Nancy C. Waugh, editors, *The Pathology of Memory*, pages 223–237. Academic Press, New York.

Douglas L. Nelson, Cathy L. McEvoy, and Thomas A. Schreiber. 2004. The University of South Florida free association, rhyme, and word fragment norms. *Behavior Research Methods, Instruments, & Computers*, 36(3).

Davide Picca, Dominique Jaccard, and Gérald Eberlé. 2015. Natural language processing in serious games: A state of the art. *International Journal of Serious Games*, 2(3):77–97.

Reinhard Rapp. 2002. The computation of word associations: Comparing syntagmatic and paradigmatic approaches. In *Proceedings of the 19th International Conference on Computational Linguistics*, Taipei, Taiwan.

Sabine Schulte im Walde, Alissa Melinger, Michael Roth, and Andrea Weber. 2008. An empirical characterisation of response types in German association norms. *Research on Language and Computation*, 6(2):205–238.

Katharina Siorpaes and Martin Hepp. 2008. Ontogame: Weaving the semantic web by online games. In *Proceedings of the European Semantic Web Conference*, pages 751–766.

Donald P. Spence and Kimberly C. Owens. 1990. Lexical co-occurrence and association strength. *Journal of Psycholinguistic Research*, 19:317–330.

Luis Von Ahn and Laura Dabbish. 2008. Designing games with a purpose. *Communications of the ACM*, 51(8):58–67.

A Appendix: Project Setup for English/German & Example Grid/End for German

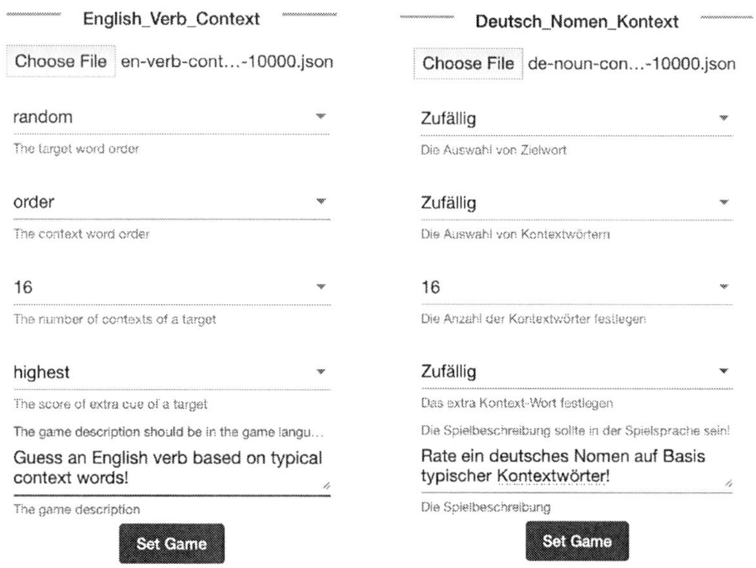

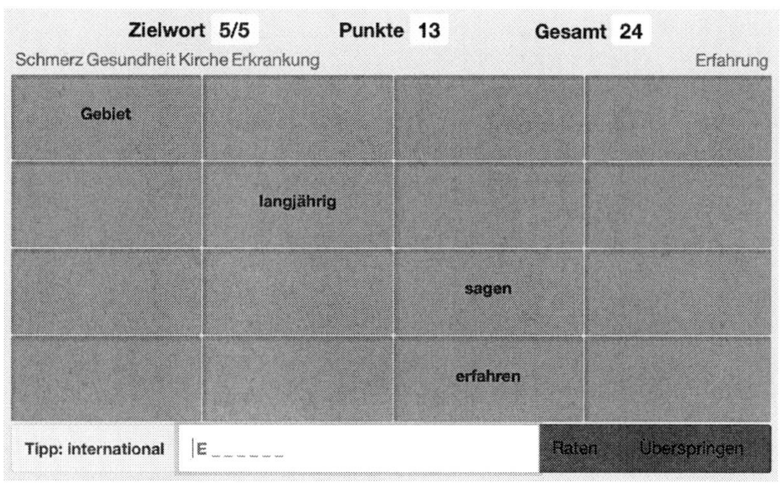

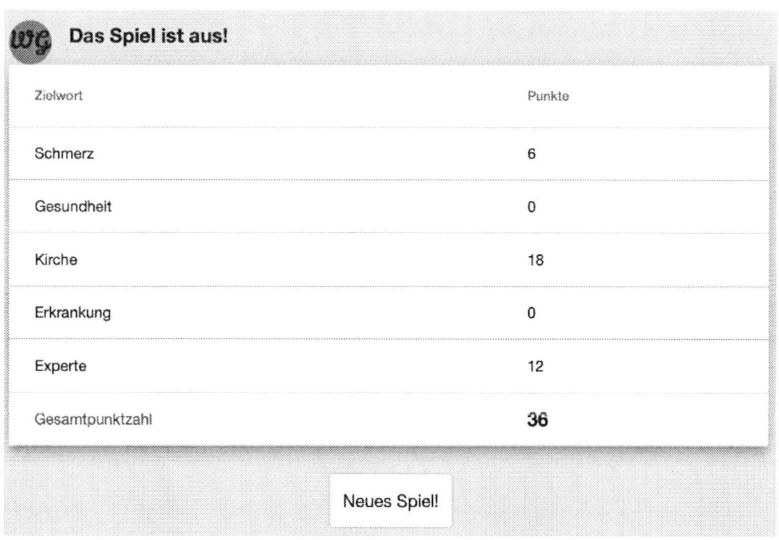

Towards a balanced annotated Low Saxon dataset for diachronic investigation of dialectal variation

Janine Siewert
University of Helsinki
janine.siewert@helsinki.fi

Jörg Tiedemann
University of Helsinki
jorg.tiedemann@helsinki.fi

Yves Scherrer
University of Helsinki
yves.scherrer@helsinki.fi

Abstract

We describe a new annotated dataset for Low Saxon with the intention to complement existing corpora. This corpus covers the period from the 15th to the 21st century and is annotated with PoS and morphosyntactic tags as well as century and region information. This dataset will be used for diachronic dialectometry, but can lend itself to other NLP tasks as well. The target size is around 2000 sentences per dialect and century and at the time of writing, 798 texts have been selected for inclusion in the corpus. They will be gradually added as the annnotation progresses.

1 Introduction

We present a dataset for Low Saxon,[1] a Germanic minority language spoken by roughly five million people in Northern Central Europe (Moseley, 2010). Despite its relatively large number of speakers, there are hardly any annotated corpora for this language, hampering corpus-based research into more modern varieties and causing a lack of well-functioning NLP tools.

The dataset is part of our research into the diachronic development of the internal variation in Low Saxon and builds upon the Reference Corpus Middle Low German/Low Rhenish (1200-1650) (ReN-Team, 2019) (henceforth *ReN*) and the LSDC dataset (Siewert et al., 2020) attempting to fill the gap between them. Therefore, it covers both historical and contemporary Low Saxon dialects from the Veluwe in the western corner of the language area to the Lower-Prussian dialects in the east.

Our ultimate goal with this new dataset is to perform analyses of the internal variation within Low Saxon and its change over time. Questions of interest are, for instance, the frequency and geographical spread of features like two-part conjunctions (*dārümme dat*, *êr dat*), double negation, and whether the perfect tense of modal verbs requires the main verb to occur in the infinitive or the perfect participle. These relate to the larger topic of inter-dialectal contact and how stable syntactic structures are when the speaker community is under constant exposure to a closely related more prestigious language and under pressure of language shift.

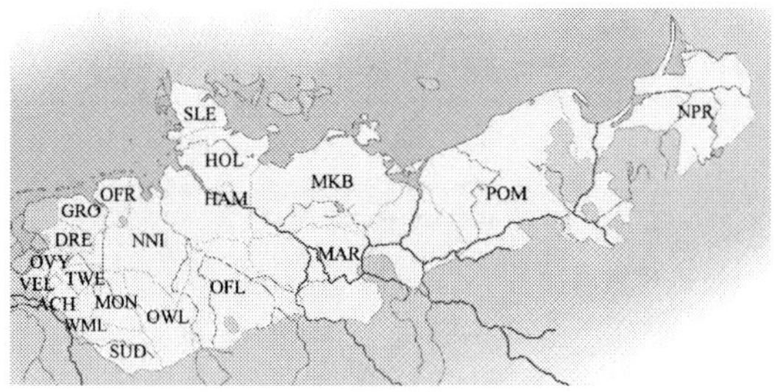

Figure 1: The Low Saxon dialects to be covered in the corpus.

2 Background

Low Saxon belongs to the western branch of the Germanic languages and is traditionally spoken mainly in Northern Germany and the North-Eastern Netherlands with official recognition in both countries. The eastern dialects Pomeranian (POM) and Low Prussian (NPR) shown in Figure 1 were spoken in these regions prior to WW II.[2]

When the Hanseatic League lost its status in the 16th and 17th century, the Middle Low Saxon literary language was replaced by southern varieties.

[1] Also called *Low German*, referring here to the varieties protected under the European Charter for Regional and Minority Languages as *Nedersaksisch* in the Netherlands and *Niederdeutsch* in Germany as well as extinct eastern varieties.

[2] The Baltic dialects previously spoken north of the Low Prussian area and included in the ReN will not form part of our corpus, as although e.g. in Estonia, Low Saxon had survived as a spoken language until the 19th, probably even until the early 20th century, (Ariste, 1981, 97–98) the amount of written post Middle Low Saxon sources preserved seems too small for meaningful analyses.

While Low Saxon survived in oral communication and occasional Low Saxon texts continued to be produced, German and Dutch became the dominant written languages (Gabrielson, 1983).

Despite its official recognition and usage in e.g. the media and school education today, no interregional standard language has been introduced so far, resulting in a tendency for Low Saxon speakers to follow regional writing traditions or come up with systems of their own, both of which are often based on the majority language orthography of the respective country.

The creation of NLP tools for modern Low Saxon thus requires a large annotated corpus representing this dialectal and orthographic variation.

3 Resources available

The main resources already available are the ReN and the LSDC. The ReN comes with HiNTS tags[3], morphological annotation and lemmatisation for the major regions of the northern dialects (North Low Saxon, East Elbian, Baltic Low Saxon), Westphalian, Eastphalian including Elbe Eastphalian, and South Marchian (*Südmärkisch*) spanning the time from ca. 1200 to 1650 (Peters and Nagel, 2014). The 146 annotated texts contain around 1.4 million tokens and the 89 transcribed (i.e. not annotated) ones ca. 900,000 tokens.

The LSDC dataset contains ca. 2 million tokens in ca. 100,000 sentences representing 16 dialects from the 19th century onward (Siewert et al., 2020). It covers a different set of dialects than the ReN, is smaller and includes neither PoS or morphological tags, nor lemmatisation.

Limitations of these datasets are, for instance, that the ReN excludes the dialects from today's Netherlands and that the LSDC dataset is only annotated for century and dialect, but does not include morphosyntactic annotation. In addition, the LSDC dataset is not very balanced, meaning that not all dialects are equally well represented in all of the three centuries covered.

The ASnA (*Atlas spätmittelalterlicher Schreibsprachen des niederdeutschen Altlandes und angrenzender Gebiete*) is based on a large collection of transcriptions of Middle Low Saxon documents excluding the eastern language area but including varieties from today's Netherlands (Peters, 2017). However, this dataset is not publicly available.

In addition to these, there is a thus far unpublished dataset from the University of Groningen / Centrum Groninger Taal en Cultuur for the Gronings dialect used by de Vries et al. (2021), which contains around 50k tokens, PoS tags and lemmatisation to standard Dutch, and might serve as additional training data for our tagging task.

A few larger corpus collections, such as OPUS or the Wikipedia dumps, contain Low Saxon data as well, but since generally no information on the dialect is provided, we decided to exclude them.

4 Data collection and selection

We are striving to gather at least 2000 sentences per dialect and century. Preferably, these should represent a variety of writers, genres and different places within the dialect region. For a somewhat balanced representation, the size of the geographical regions should at least be roughly comparable. Whereas in the LSDC dataset, the Westphalian group was subdivided into several subdialects both on the German and the Dutch side, our intention is to treat German Westphalian as one group and Dutch Westphalian as another one. More detailed information on the origin of the texts, e.g. the birth place of the writer or the printing place, will nonetheless be provided if available.

For German Low Saxon, we primarily collect data from the period between the middle of the 17th and the early 19th century, since this time span is covered by neither the ReN nor the LSDC; however, for Dutch Low Saxon it has been necessary to start our data collection from the 15th century. The LSDC provides a sufficiently large amount of sentences for some dialects and centuries, but most dialects still require additional data.

As we ultimately plan to perform syntactic analyses, we prefer prose, but the lack of data for various dialects, particularly in the 17th and 18th century, might necessitate an inclusion of poetry. In that case, genres will be labelled as well.

We have started to compile our own set of older Dutch Low Saxon data where the Middle Low Saxon data from Groningen and Drenthe mostly originate from the Cartago website,[4] from Twente from the Twentse Taalbank.[5] In addition, we also gather digitised data from local archives.

The German Low Saxon data mainly consists

[3] *Historisches-Niederdeutsch-Tagset*, adapted for Middle Low Saxon based on the HiTS (Historical Tagset for German) and explained by Barteld et al. (2018)

[4] `http://cartago.nl/nl/`

[5] `http://www.twentsetaalbank.nl/`

of digitised data from German university libraries and Google Books. Our search largely relies on Hansen's literature catalogue (Hansen, 2021), which strives to list all German Low Saxon authors as well as all books and other media published in German Low Saxon from 1473 onward.

Table 1 shows the number of texts collected so far. These texts differ largely in size, the shortest ones consisting of only one or a few pages and the longest ones being complete books with several hundreds of pages.

The data selection for older Dutch Low Saxon is not always straightforward. Even medieval writings from this area often contained both eastern (= Low Saxon) and western (= Dutch) traits (Niebaum, 1997, 63), and in contrast with the switch to the clearly distinct German in the areas further east in the 16th and 17th century the written language in the Dutch Low Saxon regions gradually shifts towards the comparatively similar one used in the Western Netherlands (Kremer, 2008, 43). Consequently, the question arises which texts are still sufficiently Low Saxon and which ones should instead by classified as Dutch and excluded from the corpus. A possible solution could be to base this on orthographic criteria. On the other hand, for the regions in Germany, it is generally easy to determine if a text is written in Low Saxon or German.

	15th	16th	17th	18th	19th
GLS			39	88	194
DLS	197	206	5		69

Table 1: Number of texts per group (*GLS* 'German Low Saxon' and *DLS* 'Dutch Low Saxon') and century.

The first version of the dataset will contain 200 sentences with manually corrected PoS and morphological annotation representing four dialects (Eastphalian, Holsatian, Marchian/Brandenburgish and Mecklenburgish - West Pomeranian) of German Low Saxon with 50 sentences each. The Mecklenburgish - West Pomeranian data stems from the second half of the 17th century, the Marchian/Brandenburgish data from the 18th century and the Holsatian and Eastphalian data from the first half of the 19th century. We will continuously update the dataset and add more sentences as the annotation progresses.

5 Preprocessing and annotation

Text acquisition Many of the digitised texts from the 17th, 18th and 19th century are only available as scans, while 59 of them include raw OCR. We have begun manual corrections of the raw OCR for training specialised models with Transkribus[6].

Sentence splitting General sentence splitting tools tend to work well on modern Low Saxon texts, but this is not the case for Early Modern Low Saxon and even less so for medieval texts, since punctuation does not follow the modern conventions. In the ReN, sentence splitting was based on the occurrence of inflected words. As a result, the corpus consists in large parts of sentence fragments instead of more complex sentence structures. While this might be an appropriate solution for the context of the Reference Corpus, it does not suit our goal of diachronic comparison of syntactic structures. Furthermore, this might pose difficulties to tagging, as disambiguation would often make it necessary to look across sentence fragment boundaries.

Morphosyntactic tagging The ReN serves as the basis for automatising the annotation process. We have converted the PoS and morphological tags in the ReN to the UD standard with a replacement script followed by manual corrections, since the correspondences do not always match one-to-one. For instance, the ReN often shows no distinction between conjunction and subjunction, and in several cases different usages of the same lemma are given the same PoS tag, such as only ADV in case of *of* 'if, or' even though it can function as both an adverb and a conjunction. Furthermore, following the ReN annotation, we have added extra labels for marking strong and weak declension, which do not belong to UD's universal features.

The converted ReN data is then used for training a full morphological tagger to annotate both the remainder of the ReN and the Middle Low Saxon data from the Netherlands. In a preliminary experiment with a small manually corrected Dutch Low Saxon dataset, a BiLSTM tagger (Scherrer and Rabus, 2019) trained on ReN data achieved a morphological tagging accuracy of around 85%.

We will manually correct a few hundred sentences of the automatic annotation and use those for fine-tuning. This process will be repeated step-by-step with data from the following century until

[6]`https://readcoop.eu/transkribus/?sc=Transkribus`

```
# sent_id = NDS_010_HOL_1910_as-noch-de-trankrusel-brenn
# text_orig = Ja, wo is de Knieptang?
# text = Ja, wår is de knyptange?
1  Ja         ja         INTJ   _  _                        0  root   _  lemma[gml]=jâ^1|SpaceAfter=No
2  ,          ,          PUNCT  _  _                        3  punct  _  _
3  wår        wår        ADV    _  _                        1  conj   _  lemma[gml]=wôr(e)
4  is         weasen     AUX    _  Number=Sing|Person=3     3  cop    _  lemma[gml]=wēsen^2
5  de         de         DET    _  Gender=Fem|Number=Sing   6  det    _  lemma[gml]=dê^1
6  knyptange  knyptange  NOUN   _  Gender=Fem|Number=Sing   3  nsubj  _  lemma[gml]=knîptange|SpaceAfter=No
7  ?          ?          PUNCT  _  _                        3  punct  _  _
```

Figure 2: Example of the UD annotation with reduced morphological features.

the contemporary period.

UD annotation Aside from the basic corpus, we have also started to select sentences to be included in a separate dataset for Universal Dependencies[7]. Mostly, these sentences originate from public domain texts included in the LSDC dataset, but we make use of our additional resources as well. This UD dataset will cover the Modern Low Saxon period, contain roughly the same amount of sentences per dialect and, in addition to PoS and morphological tags[8], it will feature dependencies and lemmatisation.

Due to the lack of an interregional standard, there is not one single obvious choice for lemmatising a dataset for Low Saxon covering several centuries and regions. As a compromise, we have opted for double lemmatisation: The main lemma will be given in the *Nysassiske Skryvwyse* – an interregional spelling used by e.g. the Dutch Low Saxon Wikipedia which is based on a historically motivated abstract set of common phoneme distinctions instead of a particular local pronunciation[9] – while a second lemma will be provided in normalised Middle Low Saxon following Lasch et al. (1928 ff) if the word was already attested at that stage of the language, cf. the tenth column in Figure 2.

6 Challenges

A few morphological issues require further discussion in relation to the annotation, since we need to take into account that we annotate language change in process. We will illustrate two of these issues here.

Differing number of inflectional categories Mergers of inflectional categories have occurred in different dialects at different points in time and to a different extent. For example, the distinction between dative and accusative still present in Middle Low Saxon has been lost in most modern dialects (Lindow et al., 1998, 144). Since the corpus contains both varieties with and without this distinction, our approach is to annotate as if the distinction had been preserved in all of the dialects. When, however, the local variety clearly shows a different inflection, i.e. if an accusative-like form is used instead of the expected dative, the regional annotation will be given in the tenth column in the form *Case[regional]=Acc*.

Change in pronoun usage The data we have collected shows that while it is not uncommon to still encounter the old 2nd person singular *dû* in Dutch Low Saxon texts from the 19th century, this pronoun has faded out of use in most dialects at the latest by the 21st century. With the exception of Groningen, North Drenthe and parts of Twente and the Achterhoek, Dutch Low Saxon dialects today have usually lost the *dû* (Bloemhoff, 2008, 101–103) and instead adopted the Standard Dutch system for the 2nd person using the counterparts of Dutch *jij* and *jullie* for the singular and plural respectively.

Due to the fact that the original pronoun of the second person plural *gî* was (and partly still is) also used as a polite address, one cannot always tell from the context if *gî* as referring to a single person is to be interpreted as a politeness marker or whether it already has replaced the *dû* as the default 2nd person singular. In such unclear cases, we refrain from annotating for number or politeness. By default, the *gî* and its agreeing verbs will nevertheless be annotated as plural in the sixth column with divergent regional developments being marked in the tenth column as *Number[regional]=Sing*.

[7] `https://raw.githubusercontent.com/UniversalDependencies/UD_Low_Saxon-LSDC/master/nds_lsdc-ud-test.conllu`

[8] The morphological tags are still missing in the first version, but will be included in the second one.

[9] `https://skryvwyse.eu/`

7 Access

The dataset can be accessed via our Helsinki NLP GitHub page[10]. The first release is published under a CC BY-NC licence, but as more data is added, different parts of the dataset might be published with separate licences depending on the licences the original files were provided with.

8 Conclusion

Our new balanced dataset for Low Saxon will cover the whole Modern Low Saxon period as well as late Middle Low Saxon from the Dutch side, and include not only annotation for dialect and century, but also PoS and morphological tags.

This novel resource will thus facilitate investigations into dialectal variation across time and, in addition, offer new possibilities to the development of NLP tools for this low-resource language.

References

Paul Ariste. 1981. *Keelekontaktid.* Valgus, Tallinn, Estonia.

Fabian Barteld, Sarah Ihden, Katharina Dreessen, and Ingrid Schröder. 2018. HiNTS: A tagset for middle low German. In *Proceedings of the Eleventh International Conference on Language Resources and Evaluation (LREC-2018)*, Miyazaki, Japan. European Languages Resources Association (ELRA).

Henk Bloemhoff. 2008. Klank- en vormleer. In Henk Bloemhoff, Jurjen van der Kooi, Hermann Niebaum, and Siemon Reker, editors, *Handboek Nedersaksische Taal- en Letterkunde*, page 65–112. Van Gorcum, Assen, Netherlands.

Artur Gabrielson. 1983. Die Verdrängung der mittelniederdeutschen durch die neuhochdeutsche Schriftsprache. In Gerhard Cordes and Dieter Möhn, editors, *Handbuch zur niederdeutschen Sprach- und Literaturwissenschaft*, pages 119–153. Erich Schmidt Verlag, Berlin, Germany.

Peter Hansen. 2021. Die niederdeutsche Literatur.

Ludger Kremer. 2008. Geschiedenis van de Nedersaksische taalkunde. In Henk Bloemhoff, Jurjen van der Kooi, Hermann Niebaum, and Siemon Reker, editors, *Handboek Nedersaksische Taal- en Letterkunde*, page 23–51. Van Gorcum, Assen, Netherlands.

Agathe Lasch, Conrad Borchling, Gerhard Cordes, and Dieter Möhn. 1928 ff. *Mittelniederdeutsches Handwörterbuch.* Wachholz Verlag, Neumünster, Germany.

Wolfgang Lindow, Dieter Möhn, Hermann Niebaum, Dieter Stellmacher, Hans Taubken, and Jan Wirrer. 1998. *Niederdeutsche Grammatik.* Verlag Schuster, Leer, Germany.

Christopher Moseley, editor. 2010. *Atlas of the World's Languages in Danger*, 3 edition. UNESCO Publishing, Paris. Online version: `http://www.unesco.org/culture/en/endangeredlanguages/atlas`.

Hermann Niebaum. 1997. Ostfriesisch-groningische Sprachbeziehungen in Geschichte und Gegenwart. In Volkers F. Faltings, Alastair G.H. Walker, and Ommo Wilts, editors, *Friesische Studien III*, page 49–82. Odense University Press.

Robert Peters. 2017. *Atlas spätmittelalterlicher Schreibsprachen des niederdeutschen Altlandes und angrenzender Gebiete (ASnA).* De Gruyter, Berlin and Boston.

Robert Peters and Norbert Nagel. 2014. Das digitale 'Referenzkorpus Mittelniederdeutsch / Niederrheinisch (ReN)'. *Jahrbuch für Germanistische Sprachgeschichte*, 5(1):165–175.

ReN-Team. 2019. Referenzkorpus Mittelniederdeutsch/Niederrheinisch (1200-1650). Archived in Hamburger Zentrum für Sprachkorpora. Version 1.0. Publication date 2019-08-14.

Yves Scherrer and Achim Rabus. 2019. Neural morphosyntactic tagging for Rusyn. *Natural Language Engineering*, 25(5):633–650.

Janine Siewert, Yves Scherrer, Martijn Wieling, and Jörg Tiedemann. 2020. LSDC - a comprehensive dataset for Low Saxon dialect classification. In *Proceedings of the 7th Workshop on NLP for Similar Languages, Varieties and Dialects*, page 25–35, Barcelona, Spain (Online). International Committee on Computational Linguistics (ICCL).

Wietse de Vries, Martijn Bartelds, Malvina Nissim, and Martijn Wieling. 2021. Adapting monolingual models: Data can be scarce when language similarity is high.

[10] `https://github.com/Helsinki-NLP/LSDC-morph`

German Abusive Language Dataset with Focus on COVID-19

Maximilian Wich*, **Svenja Räther***, **and Georg Groh**
Technical University of Munich, Department of Informatics, Germany
maximilian.wich@tum.de, svenja.raether@tum.de, grohg@in.tum.de

Abstract

The COVID-19 pandemic has had a significant impact on human lives globally. As a result, it is unsurprising that it has influenced hate speech and other sorts of abusive language on social media. Machine learning models have been designed to automatically detect such posts and messages, which necessitate a significant amount of labeled data. Despite the relevance of the COVID-19 topic in the field of abusive language detection, no annotated datasets with this focus are available. To solve these shortfalls, we target to create such a dataset. Our contributions are as follows: (1) a methodology for collecting abusive language data from Twitter with a substantial amount of abusive and hateful content, and (2) a German abusive language dataset with 4,960 annotated tweets centered on COVID-19. Both the methodology and the dataset are intended to aid researchers in improving abusive language detection.

1 Introduction

Hate speech is a serious challenge that social media platforms are currently confronting (Duggan, 2017). However, it is not limited to the online world. According to a study, there is a link between online hate and physical crime (Williams et al., 2020). As a result, it is critical to combat hate speech and other forms of abusive language on social media platforms to improve the conversation atmosphere and prevent spillover.

Owed to the large amounts of content created by billions of users, it is inefficient to detect this phenomenon manually. Therefore, its automatic detection is an essential part of the fight against this. Machine learning is a promising technology that aids in the training of classification models for detecting hate speech.

The success of a classification model depends largely on its training data. It requires data to learn patterns that can be used for solving the task. Large amounts of labeled data are required in the context of hate speech because hate speech is multifaceted and diversified (e.g., misogyny, racism, anti-Semitism) (Rieger et al., 2021). As a result, researchers have published many abusive language datasets in recent years (Vidgen and Derczynski, 2020; Wich et al., 2021b; Schmidt and Wiegand, 2017). The majority of the datasets are in English, and only a small portion is in German. Another shortcoming of the existing datasets is that, with some exceptions, they do not cover COVID-19-related hate (Vidgen et al., 2020; Alshalan et al., 2020; Ziems et al., 2020). COVID-19, however, has become a popular topic in the hate and extremist communities (Guhl and Gerster, 2020; Velásquez et al., 2020), making it a suitable topic in the hate speech detection community as well. Our research goal is to develop a German abusive language dataset with an emphasis on COVID-19 to solve both shortcomings.

Contribution:

- With a topical focus, we present a methodology for collecting abusive language from Twitter.
- We report a 4,960-tweet German abusive language dataset with an emphasis on COVID-19. The labeling schema comprises two classes: *ABUSIVE* (22%) and *NEUTRAL* (78%).

2 Related Work

German abusive language datasets can be found in the literature. Ross et al. (2016) published a 469 tweets dataset on anti-refugee sentiment. Bretschneider and Peters (2017) published a dataset

*These authors contributed equally to this work.

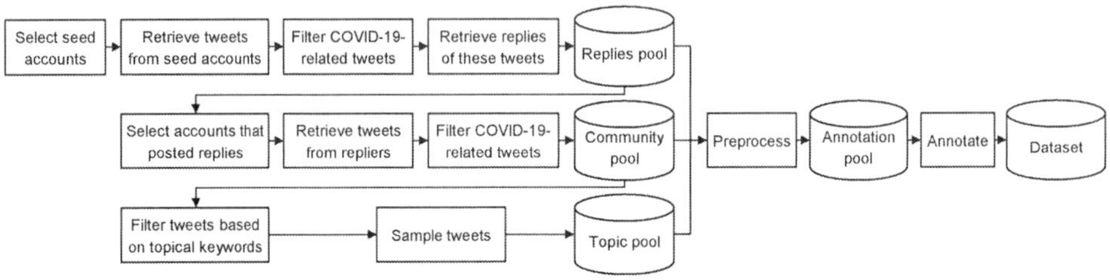

Figure 1: Dataset creation process adapted from Räther (2021)

of 5,836 Facebook posts on anti-foreigner prejudices. Two abusive language datasets have been reported as part of GermEval, a series of shared tasks focusing on the German language (Wiegand et al., 2018; Struß et al., 2019). The dataset from 2018 contains 8,541 tweets and the one from 2019 7,025. Both utilized the same labeling schema. Based on the interpretation of the data collection, the tweets do not seem to have a topical focus (Wiegand et al., 2018; Struß et al., 2019). Two additional German datasets were reported as part of the multilingual shared task series "Hate Speech and Offensive Content Identification in Indo-European Languages" (HASOC) (Mandl et al., 2019, 2020). The German dataset from the shared task contained 4,669 posts from Twitter and Facebook in 2019 (Mandl et al., 2019); 3,425 posts from YouTube and Twitter in 2020 (Mandl et al., 2020). The only German dataset that comprises posts from the COVID-19 period is from Wich et al. (2021a). However, the authors did not concentrate on COVID-19 content.

Several researchers have published abusive language datasets that directly tackle the COVID-19 topics, nevertheless, they are small in number. Vidgen et al. (2020) published an English Twitter dataset about East Asian prejudice from 20,000 posts collected during the pandemic. Ziems et al. (2020) collected tweets related to anti-Asian hate speech and counter hate. They annotated 2,400 tweets and utilized these tweets to train a classifier and detected "891,204 hate and 200,198 counter hate tweets" (Ziems et al., 2020, p.2). However, to the best of our knowledge, no one has reported a German abusive language or hate speech dataset with attention on COVID-19.

3 Methodology

The dataset creation process comprised three parts. The first one dealt with the data gathering and selection approach we employed to retrieve data from Twitter with a high portion of abusive content. Subsequently, the selected data is annotated by three annotators. Finally, we assessed the newly developed dataset based on dataset metrics and compared it with other German abusive language datasets.

3.1 Collecting Data

Figure 1 demonstrates the data collection process that we report in the following. The tweets to be annotated are sampled from the *annotation pool* equally fed by three other pools—*replies pool, community pool*, and *topic pool*. Ensuring a topical concentration on COVID-19 and a high portion of hateful content is the reason for this approach.

The starting point of the data collection for all pools was a set of three seed accounts. These accounts originate from a study conducted by Richter et al. (2020), in which the authors have described influential Twitter accounts sharing misinformation about COVID-19. The accounts were selected by the authors based on the following criteria (Richter et al., 2020): (1) At least 20,000 accounts follow the account. (2) The account has shared or reported misinformation about COVID-19. (3) The account was active as of May 20, 2020. These accounts were chosen as seeds because hateful content often coincides with misinformation (Guhl and Gerster, 2020).

From these accounts, we retrieved the tweets that they published between 01.01.2020 and 20.02.2021 through the Twitter API. Subsequently, we filtered out the tweets that are related to COVID-19. We used a list of 65 keywords for this purpose (see Table 1). It comprised stemmed terms from a glossary about the current pandemic[1] and some additions. Next, we retrieved the replies to these tweets through the Twitter API—a reply is a tweet that refers to another tweet. These replies were stored in the *replies pool*. To ensure the quality and quantity of hateful content, two annotators analyzed a sample of 100 tweets.

[1] www.dwds.de/themenglossar/Corona

The *community pool* comprised COVID-19-related tweets from the accounts that replied to the seed accounts' tweets. We utilized a similar approach as in the previous phases. We retrieved the tweets from the accounts, limiting the maximum number of tweets per account to 500 and considering only tweets posted beyond 01.01.2020. The retrieved tweets were then filtered based on the 65 COVID-19-keywords. A sample of 100 tweets undergoes the same quality inspection as in the previous phase.

The third and last pool was the *topic pool*, whose purpose was to increase the prevalence of hateful content and topical diversity. It consists of tweets related to topics that coincide in the context of hate speech and COVID-19 (sCAN, 2020). Table 2 illustrates the topics provided by sCAN (2020) and the associated keywords that we employed for filtering the tweets. To balance the different topics, we limited the number of filtered tweets per keyword to 1,000.

After filling the data pools, we applied two preprocessing phases to the data. First, all tweets holding less than two textual tokens were removed. Second, close and exact duplicates were removed by using locality-sensitive hashing with Jaccard similarity (Leskovec et al., 2020). Third, account names appearing in the tweets are masked to reduce annotator bias created by account names recognition. The *annotation pool* was then created by sampling the pools equally.

3.2 Annotating Data

The annotation schema for the sampled tweets comprised two classes:

- *ABUSIVE*: The tweet comprised any form of insult, harassment, hate, degradation, identity attack, and the threat of violence targeting an individual or a group.
- *NEUTRAL*: The tweet did not fall into the *ABUSIVE* class.

The data is annotated by three non-experts (two female, one male; all between 20 and 30 years old). To prepare them for the annotation process, they received training that contained a presentation of the annotation guidelines and a discussion among all annotators to define the task. Since the annotators are non-experts, we permitted them to skip tweets if they are indifferent (e.g., due to unclear cases or missing context information). This is to prevent the impairment of the quality of labels. The label indifference was handled as a missing label in the further course. Owing to limited resources, 275 tweets were annotated by two or three annotators to assess the inter-rater reliability with Krippendorff's alpha (Krippendorff, 2004). All other tweets received only one annotation from any of the annotators. We employed `doccano` as an annotation tool (Nakayama et al., 2018).

3.3 Evaluating Dataset

We compared our dataset with the GermEval and HASOC datasets by investigating the cross-dataset classification performance. For this purpose, we trained each dataset on a binary classification model for abusive language and assessed the models on all test sets. This is possible because the binary labels of all datasets are compatible. The objective of this assessment is to investigate how well our dataset generalizes and how well classifiers that were trained on a dataset without any COVID-19 content performed on our dataset. The classification model employed the German pre-trained BERT base model `deepset/gbert-base` as a basis (Chan et al., 2020). Before training the model, we removed all user names and URLs. The models were trained for 6 epochs with a learning rate of 5×10^{-5}. Evaluation was conducted after each epoch and the model with the highest macro F1 was selected. The validation set is 15% of the training set.

4 Results

At the end of the data collection process, we obtained 768,419 unique tweets from 7,629 users in our overlapping pools. The final dataset sampled from these pools without duplication, and anno-

Table 1: COVID-19-related keywords for filtering

covid, corona, wuhan, biontech, pfizer, moderna, astra, zeneca, sputnik, abstandsregel, aluhut, antikÃűrpertest, ansteck, asymptomatisch, ausgangssperre, ausgehverbot, ausreisesperre, balkonien, beatmungsgerät, besuchsverbot, desinf, durchseuchung, einreisesperre, einreiseverbot, epidemi, existenzangst, fallzahl, gesichtsvisier, gesundheitsamt, grundrechte, hygienedemo, hygienemaÃ§nahme, immun, impf, infekt, influenza, inkubationszeit, intensivbett, inzidenz, kontaktbeschrÃd'nkung, kontaktverbot, lockdown, lockerungen, mundschutz, mutation, maske pandemie, pcr, pharmaunternehmen, präventionsmaÃ§nahme, plandemie, querdenk, quarantäne, reproduktionszahl, risikogruppe, sars-cov, shutdown, sicherheitsabstand, superspreader, systemrelevant, tracing-app, tröpfcheninfektion, übersterblichkeit, vakzin, virolog, virus

Table 2: Hate- and COVID-19-related topics and keywords (column Topic taken over word for word from sCAN (2020))

Topic (sCAN, 2020)	Keywords
"Anti-Asian racsim"	asiat, chines, ccp, wuhan, chinavirus
"Misinformation and geopolitical strategy"	amerika, militär, biowaffe
"Resurgence of old antisemitic stereotypes"	jude, jüdisch, pest, schwarze tod
"New world order, «anti-elites» speech and traditional conspiracy theories"	elite, #nwo, weltordnung, deepstate, plandemie
"Fear of the «internal enemy», exclusion of the foreigner and scapegoating mechanisms"	greatreset, muslim, illegal, migrant

Table 3: Classification metrics of COVID-19 classifier on its test set in percent

Class	Precision	Recall	F1
NEUTRAL	92.4	93.7	93.1
ABUSIVE	74.7	70.8	72.7
Macro avg.	83.5	82.2	82.9

Table 4: Cross-dataset classification performance (macro F1 in percent) – CD = COVID, GE = GermEval, HC = HASOC

	CD-19	GE 18	GE 19	HC 19	HC 20
CD-19	82.9	72.8	76.7	67.8	68.0
GE 18	73.4	76.9	74.6	65.4	65.4
GE 19	73.3	75.2	75.3	62.5	73.0
HC 19	60.8	63.4	63.9	66.4	64.6
HC 20	54.0	59.9	53.1	48.6	80.5

tations by our three annotators comprised 4,960 tweets. 22% of the tweets were labeled as *ABUSIVE* by our annotators, whereas 78% were labeled as *NEUTRAL*. The annotated tweets were created by 2,662 accounts—on average 1.86 tweets per account (min: 1; max: 41). All tweets were posted between January 2020 and February 2021.

Krippendorff's alpha of the three annotators is 91.5%, which is a good score for inter-rater reliability. Only 275 tweets were annotated by two or three annotators owing to limited resources.

Table 3 demonstrates the classification metrics of the classifier trained and assessed on our COVID-19 dataset. The train set contained 3,485 tweets, the validation set 735, and the test set 740. We ensured that an author appeared only in one of the three sets. Without any architecture optimization or hyperparameter search, we obtained a macro F1 score of 82.9%. Considering the metrics for the *ABUSIVE* class, we can see that there is still room for improvement. However, this study does not aim to develop the latest state-of-the-art model. This classifier is intended to serve as a baseline for future studies utilizing our new COVID-19 dataset.

To compare our dataset with another German abusive language dataset, we investigated the cross-dataset classification performance. As indicated in Table 4, the rows correspond to the classifiers, whereas the columns to the test sets. We observed that the model trained on the COVID-19 dataset demonstrated similar performance as the ones from the GermEval datasets. Its macro F1 score is in the same range as the ones from GermEval and it performed similarly on the other test sets. The classifiers from the HASOC datasets step out of line. The HASOC 2020 classifier seemed to concentrate on a different type of abusive language. It performed quite well on its dataset but scored lower on all other test sets. Even if the GermEval classifiers scored higher results on the COVID-19 test set, they did not achieve the same F1 score as the COVID-19 classifier. This indicates that abusive language in the domain of COVID-19 varies from what it was before the pandemic.

5 Conclusion

We created a German abusive language dataset that focuses on COVID-19. It contains 4,960 annotated tweets from 2,662 accounts. 22% of the tweets are labeled as *ABUSIVE*, 78% as *NEUTRAL*. Due to limited resources, not all documents were annotated by two or more annotators. We prioritized holding a variety of tweets equivalent to the size of related German datasets. Furthermore, the high inter-rater reliability for the overlapping annotations indicates that the annotation behavior of the three annotators was well aligned. Also, the generalizability of the dataset demonstrates that our COVID-19 dataset has an equivalent cross-dataset classification performance.

Our second contribution is a dataset creation methodology for abusive language. We indicated that it aids in the creation of a dataset with a significant portion of abusive language.

We consider both our dataset and the dataset creation methodology noteworthy contributions to the hate speech detection community.

Resources

Code and data are available under `github.com/mawic/german-abusive-language-covid-19`.

Acknowledgments

This paper is based on a joined work in the context of Svenja Räther's master's thesis (Räther, 2021). The research has been partially funded by a scholarship from the Hanns Seidel Foundation financed by the German Federal Ministry of Education and Research. This material is based upon work supported by Google Cloud.

References

Raghad Alshalan, Hend Al-Khalifa, Duaa Alsaeed, Heyam Al-Baity, and Shahad Alshalan. 2020. Detection of Hate Speech in COVID-19–Related Tweets in the Arab Region: Deep Learning and Topic Modeling Approach. *J Med Internet Res*, 22(12):e22609.

Uwe Bretschneider and Ralf Peters. 2017. Detecting offensive statements towards foreigners in social media. In *Proceedings of the 50th Hawaii International Conference on System Sciences*.

Branden Chan, Stefan Schweter, and Timo Möller. 2020. German's next language model. In *Proceedings of the 28th International Conference on Computational Linguistics*, pages 6788–6796, Barcelona, Spain (Online). International Committee on Computational Linguistics.

Maeve Duggan. 2017. *Online harassment 2017*. Pew Research Center.

Jakob Guhl and Lea Gerster. 2020. Krise und Kontrollverlust - Digitaler Extremismus im Kontext der Corona-Pandemie. Institue for Strategic Dialogue.

K. Krippendorff. 2004. *Content Analysis: An Introduction to Its Methodology*. Content Analysis: An Introduction to Its Methodology. Sage.

Jure Leskovec, Anand Rajaraman, and Jeffrey David Ullman. 2020. *Finding Similar Items*, 3 edition, pages 78–137. Cambridge University Press.

Thomas Mandl, Sandip Modha, Anand Kumar M, and Bharathi Raja Chakravarthi. 2020. Overview of the HASOC Track at FIRE 2020: Hate Speech and Offensive Language Identification in Tamil, Malayalam, Hindi, English and German. In *Forum for Information Retrieval Evaluation*, FIRE 2020, pages 29–32, New York, NY, USA. Association for Computing Machinery.

Thomas Mandl, Sandip Modha, Prasenjit Majumder, Daksh Patel, Mohana Dave, Chintak Mandlia, and Aditya Patel. 2019. Overview of the HASOC Track at FIRE 2019: Hate Speech and Offensive Content Identification in Indo-European Languages. FIRE '19, pages 14–17, New York, NY, USA. Association for Computing Machinery.

Hiroki Nakayama, Takahiro Kubo, Junya Kamura, Yasufumi Taniguchi, and Xu Liang. 2018. doccano: Text Annotation Tool for Human. Software available from https://github.com/doccano/doccano.

Svenja Räther. 2021. Investigating techniques for learning with limited labeled data for hate speech classification. Master's thesis, Technical University of Munich. Advised and supervised by Maximilian Wich and Georg Groh.

Marie Richter, Chine Labbé, Virginia Padovese, and Kendrick McDonald. 2020. Twitter: Superspreader von Corona-Falschinformationen.

Diana Rieger, Anna Sophie Kuempel, Maximilian Wich, T. Kiening, and Georg Groh. 2021. Assessing the Prevalence and Contexts of Hate Speech in Fringe Communities: A Case Study of Alt-Right Communities on 8chan, 4chan, and Reddit. In *Proceedings of 71st Annual ICA Conference*.

Björn Ross, Michael Rist, Guillermo Carbonell, Benjamin Cabrera, Nils Kurowsky, and Michael Wojatzki. 2016. Measuring the Reliability of Hate Speech Annotations: The Case of the European Refugee Crisis. In *Proceedings of NLP4CMC III: 3rd Workshop on Natural Language Processing for Computer-Mediated Communication*, volume 17 of *Bochumer Linguistische Arbeitsberichte*, pages 6–9, Bochum.

sCAN. 2020. Hate speech trends during the Covid-19 pandemic in a digital and globalised age. SCAN project – Platforms, Experts, Tools: Specialised Cyber-Activists Network. `scan-project.eu/wp-content/uploads/sCAN-Analytical-Paper-Hate-speech-trends-during-the-Covid-19-pandemic-in-a-digital-and-globalised-age.pdf`.

Anna Schmidt and Michael Wiegand. 2017. A survey on hate speech detection using natural language processing. In *Proceedings of the Fifth International Workshop on Natural Language Processing for Social Media*, pages 1–10, Valencia, Spain. Association for Computational Linguistics.

Julia Maria Struß, Melanie Siegel, Josef Ruppenhofer, Michael Wiegand, Manfred Klenner, et al. 2019. Overview of GermEval Task 2, 2019 shared task on the identification of offensive language. In *Proceedings of the 15th Conference on Natural Language Processing (KONVENS 2019)*, pages 354–365.

Nicolás Velásquez, R Leahy, N Johnson Restrepo, Yonatan Lupu, R Sear, N Gabriel, Omkant Jha, B Goldberg, and NF Johnson. 2020. Hate multiverse spreads malicious COVID-19 content online beyond individual platform control. *arXiv preprint arXiv:2004.00673*.

Bertie Vidgen and Leon Derczynski. 2020. Directions in abusive language training data, a systematic review: Garbage in, garbage out. *Plos one*, 15(12):e0243300.

Bertie Vidgen, Scott Hale, Ella Guest, Helen Margetts, David Broniatowski, Zeerak Waseem, Austin Botelho, Matthew Hall, and Rebekah Tromble. 2020. Detecting East Asian prejudice on social media. In *Proceedings of the Fourth Workshop on Online Abuse and Harms*, pages 162–172, Online. Association for Computational Linguistics.

Maximilian Wich, Melissa Breitinger, Wienke Strathern, Marlena Naimarevic, Georg Groh, and Jürgen Pfeffer. 2021a. Are your Friends also Haters? Identification of Hater Networks on Social Media: Data Paper. In *Companion Proceedings of the Web Conference 2021 (WWW'21 Companion)*.

Maximilian Wich, Tobias Eder, Hala Al Kuwatly, and Georg Groh. 2021b. Bias and comparison framework for abusive language datasets. *AI and Ethics*.

Michael Wiegand, Melanie Siegel, and Josef Ruppenhofer. 2018. Overview of the germeval 2018 shared task on the identification of offensive language. In *Proceedings of the 14th Conference on Natural Language Processing (KONVENS 2018)*.

Matthew L Williams, Pete Burnap, Amir Javed, Han Liu, and Sefa Ozalp. 2020. Hate in the Machine: Anti-Black and Anti-Muslim Social Media Posts as Predictors of Offline Racially and Religiously Aggravated Crime. *The British Journal of Criminology*, 60(1):93–117.

Caleb Ziems, Bing He, Sandeep Soni, and Srijan Kumar. 2020. Racism is a Virus: Anti-Asian Hate and Counterhate in Social Media during the COVID-19 Crisis. *arXiv preprint arXiv:2005.12423*.

Comparing Contextual and Static Word Embeddings with Small Philosophical Data

Wei Zhou
Institute for Natural Language Processing
University of Stuttgart
weizhou14330@gmail.com

Jelke Bloem
Institute for Logic, Language and Computation
University of Amsterdam
j.bloem@uva.nl

Abstract

For domain-specific NLP tasks, applying word embeddings trained on general corpora is not optimal. Meanwhile, training domain-specific word representations poses challenges to dataset construction and embedding evaluation. In this paper, we present and compare ELMo and Word2Vec models trained/finetuned on philosophical data. For evaluation, a conceptual network was used. Results show that contextualized models provide better word embeddings than static models and that merging embeddings from different models boosts task performance.

1 Introduction

Statistical distributions of terms in context can be used to characterize their semantic behavior (Lenci, 2018). This is the fundamental idea that distributional models of language are built upon. When trained on large corpora, these models can provide valid word representations which can be further utilized in various downstream NLP tasks. Two common models are Word2Vec's skipgram model (W2V, Mikolov et al., 2013) and the ELMo model (Peters et al., 2018). Although word embeddings pretrained on large corpora provide good meaning representations, using them in domain-specific tasks does not achieve good results (Nooralahzadeh et al., 2018). This is because the semantic space of a certain domain can be different from that of general language. For instance, the word *substance* refers to matter in ordinary language but in philosophical contexts it is a technical term from metaphysics pertaining to entities (Robinson, 2020).

Contextualized models like ELMo address this problem to some extent, but require a lot of domain-specific data to obtain a tailored model, while such datasets are typically smaller. The main contributions of this paper are:

- We trained and finetuned ELMo models with a philosophical corpus.
- We examined and compared models with contextual embeddings and static embeddings with intrinsic evaluations.
- We experimented with combining finetuned W2V and pretrained ELMo embeddings for representations of philosophical terms.

2 Related work

Efforts have been made in the following directions with regards to creating domain-specific word embeddings. Firstly, the construction of domain-specific corpora. Roy et al. (2017) appended manual annotations (predicate-argument structure) to training data in the field of cybersecurity. The additional annotation makes the original dataset more suited to the task of training cybersecurity embeddings. Secondly, refinement can be carried out on existing embeddings. Boukkouri et al. (2019) combined W2V embeddings trained on a small domain-specific corpus with ELMo embeddings and evaluated them on a clinical entity recognition task. They found combined embeddings outperformed embeddings trained on large corpora in the medical domain. Lastly, one can also explore suitable models for training with small amount of data. Herbelot and Baroni (2017) proposed a refined W2V model called Nonce2Vec (N2V), which learns word meanings from tiny data. The N2V model takes a high-risk learning approach with heightened learning rate and larger window size to process contexts greedily. Besides N2V, simple additive models have also proven to work well on small data (Lazaridou et al., 2016; Bloem et al., 2019).

As for evaluations of domain-specific word embeddings, the usual approach is to design in-domain tasks (Nooralahzadeh et al., 2018) or ground truths (Betti et al., 2020; Oortwijn et al., 2021). However, many domains lack such evaluation data. Bloem et al. (2019) proposed a general evaluation metric of *consistency*, based on the idea that a stable model could provide similar word embeddings given the same term across similar sources.

3 Task Description

The overall goal of this paper is to examine and compare different models by evaluating word embeddings trained on a small philosophy corpus.

3.1 Dataset

We used the dataset from Bloem et al. (2019), consisting of version 0.4 of the QUINE corpus (Betti et al., 2020) and evaluation terms. This corpus is made up of all philosophical texts written by the author Willard Van Orman Quine, consisting of 228 articles, books and bundles. The corpus consists of OCR-processed, manually corrected text and contains about 2 millions tokens after tokenization.

3.2 Model

ELMo We trained two ELMo models of different sizes and finetuned one. For training, we used the above dataset with a split of training data (17000 sentences) and testing data (5016 sentences). For finetuning, we continued training a pre-trained ELMo model[1] on the philosophical texts. Key training parameters for the three ELMo models can be found in Appendix A. The learning rate was set to default (0.2) for all models.

Word2Vec We trained Word2Vec skipgram models in the Gensim (Rehurek and Sojka, 2011) implementation with our data based on a pretrained-256 dimensional embedding model: the Nonce2Vec background model (Herbelot and Baroni, 2017) trained on Wikipedia data. We used consistency (Bloem et al., 2019) as a metric to choose the best hyper-parameters. It is measured as cosine similarity between two vectors of the same seed word. Our seed words were chosen from general philosophical terms[2] (Appendix B), excluding target terms from the Quine dataset used for evaluation (Appendix D). We abandoned terms ending with -ism and multi-token terms and selected terms whose frequency is over 50 in our corpus. We selected sentences containing seed words, divided each selected set into two parts and combined each part with the rest of the corpus. As a result, we have three corpora in total: the whole corpus and two sub-corpora. The model with the background semantic space is most consistent with a learning rate of 0.005 and led to 0.97 cosine similarity.

Nonce2Vec We trained a Nonce2Vec (N2V) model with consistency as the metric for tuning hyper-parameters. Unlike the W2V models, N2V only changes the embeddings of targeted terms, with the remaining semantic space frozen. We measured consistency with seed words, as we did with W2V. Since N2V is designed to be trained on "tiny data", we limited the contexts of each target term to up to 10 sentences both during tuning and model training. With the best selected hyperparameters, the model has a 0.97 consistency score.

3.3 Combined Embeddings

According to Boukkouri et al. (2019), combining contextualized word embeddings with their static counterparts works better on downstream tasks than merely using contextualized or static ones. The combination methods used in their paper were concatenation and addition. In our study, we further explored whether assigning weight works better than simply adding the two types of embeddings. The new embeddings are defined as $E_{mix} = \alpha * E_{elmo} + (1 - \alpha) * E_{w2v}$, where α is the weight assigned to the ELMo embeddings and $(1 - \alpha)$ the W2V. We experimented 11 values from 0 to 1 for α with an interval of 0.1.

3.4 Evaluation

We evaluated models based on word embeddings of specific terms. These terms were proposed by Oortwijn et al. (2021) as a ground truth for evaluation. They constructed a conceptual network of all relevant index terms of Quine's *Word and Object* (1960). The index terms were categorized by domain experts into one of the six clusters they defined (language, ontology, reality, mind, metalinguistic and relational terms, reproduced in Appendix D. We generated word embeddings for the 73 terms in the first five categories. 30 of these terms have a frequency less than 100 in the corpus ($n < 100$), 9 terms over 1000 ($n \geq 1000$) and 34 in between ($100 \leq n < 1000$). For ELMo, type embeddings were generated by averaging token embeddings for the same type in different contexts. For multi-token terms that were not in the model's

[1] `https://github.com/allenai/bilm-tf`

[2] source1 URL, source2 URL

vocabulary, we used the averaged embeddings to represent the whole. This is done for all models and evaluations and no other multiword term processing takes place (e.g. on the corpus). The embeddings were evaluated by the following metrics:

Cluster similarity Following Oortwijn et al. (2021), for each term, we sampled a term in the same category and a term in the different category and compared their similarity with the original term. We then calculated the probability that the cosine similarity between the same category terms was higher than that of a different category. We performed the sampling process 100 times for each terms and averaged the scores as our final scores.

Rank For each target term, we find the top 5 nearest (besides itself) terms by cosine similarity. Each term accounts for 0.2 score if it is in the same category as the target term. The highest score for a target term is therefore 1. We then added up the scores for all target terms as the rank score. There are 73 terms in total. However, the highest rank score is not 73, but 71.4: in the category *Mind*, there are only two terms, which means for each term in *Mind*, the highest score is 0.2 rather than 1.

Dunn index is used to measure how well embeddings of terms in the same category cluster (following e.g. Huang et al., 2016). A higher number suggests better clustering, which means a small variance between members of a cluster, and large differences between means of each cluster.

Gap is similar to cluster similarity, except that we consider pairs of all terms in this case. We calculated the cosine similarity between each two terms. We then averaged the overall similarity of the terms from the same sets and from the different sets and got their gaps.

4 Results

The main results are shown in Table 1. Our results show that, except for the pretrained ELMo model, ELMo models generally provide better embeddings than the W2V model. This might be attributed to the sequential structure of ELMo, which encodes neighbouring information based on contexts. To better understand the performance scores, we divided the results of rank score and cluster similarity into two conditions, namely the single-token terms and multi-token terms. Table 2 shows the results. The rank score and cluster similarity of the W2V model are lower than those of the ELMo small model in both single and multi-token terms' cases. However, we found that in the single-token terms case, there is a bigger difference of the rank (2.8 versus 0.8) and cluster similarity (0.13 versus 0.04) between the two models. This might be because the meaning of multi-token terms are less context dependent. Since we averaged the embeddings for each subtoken within the multi-tokens, the final representation of the multi-tokens already encodes some neighbouring information. By contrast, for single-token terms, ELMo is better in incorporating neighbouring information than the W2V model.

As for the combined models, we found that the rank score performance increased greatly from 39.4 (only ELMo) to around 44 (combined). However, there is nearly no difference between the combined models and the finetuned W2V. This suggests our finetuned W2V model already provides a reasonable semantic space for the Quine data, and adding additional information does not improve it. We also experimented with merging the embeddings from both models. The results for the rank score and cluster similarity are shown in Figure 2. Contrary to our expectation that increasing the portion of pretrained ELMo decreases both scores, there is

Model	Sim	Rank	Dunn	gap
E_s	0.69	**49.2**	0.44	0.08
E_m	0.69	46.6	0.37	0.07
E_pre	0.65	39.4	0.41	0.05
E_ft	**0.74**	48.0	0.40	0.10
W2V_ft	0.65	45.6	0.39	0.07
N2V	0.67	43.2	**0.52**	**0.14**
E_preW_ft+	0.66	44.8	0.43	0.06
E_preW_ftc	0.67	44	0.42	0.05

Table 1: Evaluation results. E = ELMo, s = small, m = medium, pre = pretrained, ft = finetuned. The last two models provide combined embeddings, where + = addition, c = concatenation. All models have dim=256 except for E_m and E_preW_ftc with dim=512.

Term	**single-token**		**multi-token**	
Model	**Rank**	**Sim**	**Rank**	**Sim**
E_s	23.2	0.69	26	0.79
W2V_ft	20.4	0.56	25.2	0.75
Δ	**2.8**	**0.13**	0.8	0.04

Table 2: Results of single and multi-token terms on rank and cluster similarity. For Sim, only the original terms were considered, instead of resampled ones.

a peak for both scores when the portion of W2V embeddings is around 0.3-0.4. It seems that combining pretrained language model embeddings with W2V needs to be examined carefully to find the sweetest point. Non-linear combination could also be explored in future work.

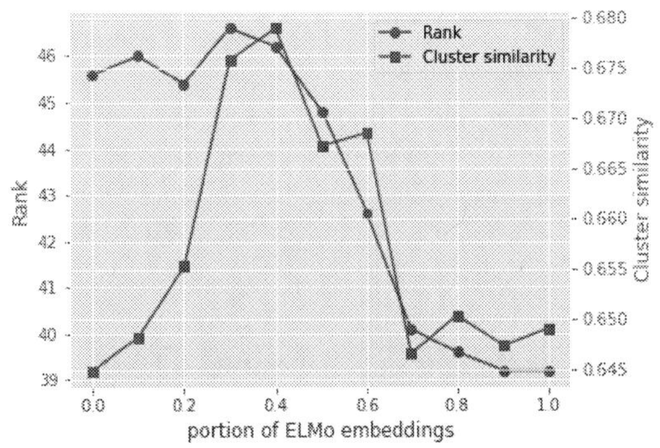

Figure 1: Rank score and cluster similarity of the merged embeddings as the portion of ELMo embedding is increased from 0 to 1.

From Table 1 and consistent with Oortwijn et al. (2021), we observed that the N2V model provides the highest Dunn index (0.52). When we scale the distance numbers to the same level for all models, we observe that the maximal intra-cluster distance in N2V is smaller than in other models. One reason could be that due to limited contexts and increased learning rate, the N2V model aggressively learns new meanings so the new meanings encode less noisy information, such as old meanings or contextual meanings. This enables outliers to be closer to their cluster centroids, resulting in a lower maximal intra-cluster distance used in Dunn index calculation. A higher intra-cluster similarity could also explain why the N2V model has a higher gap score.

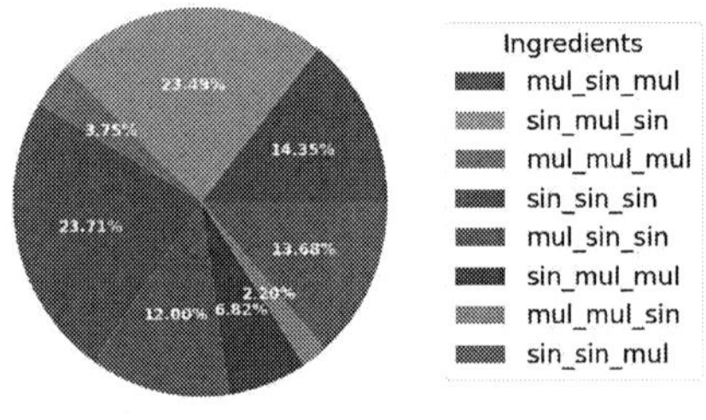

Figure 2: Distributions of eight types of errors from ELMo small model. Mul = multi-token, sin =single-token. The order of the token type corresponds to: original terms, same-cluster terms, different-cluster terms.

Semantic error analysis of terms in this dataset can only be performed by Quine domain experts. However, we can examine some superficial features. From Table 2, we observed different performance from single-token and multi-token terms. To examine the influence of single/multi-token terms on evaluation scores, we took both the correct and incorrect cases from cluster similarity and categorized them into 8 types (2*2*2) based on the token type (single or multi) of original terms, sampled-same-group term and sampled-different-group term. Figure 2 shows the results for the error case. The all-single-term case which accounts for the largest portion, nearly one fourth of all errors. The next two biggest error sources are confusion between the single and multi-token terms: in the sin_mul_sin case, instead of predicting the original term (sin) and same-cluster term (mul) to be more similar, the model predicted the original term and different-cluster terms (sin) as more similar. The same observation can be found in the mul_sin_mul case. When we look at the mul_mul_sin and the sin_sin_mul types from the correct case, we found they together account for nearly a half of all correct cases. This indicates that terms of the same type (single/multi) have the tendency to be closer, which could be the result of averaging subtoken embeddings in ELMo, comparable to the *sum effect* observed by Kabbach et al. (2019). We present the term distribution from the ELMo small model in Appendix C. We conclude that full multi-token term processing would be preferable but small datasets may not provide enough instances of each. N2V should be less affected by this due to its training on contexts of the full multi-token term even if it is low-frequent.

5 Conclusions

In this study, we pretrained/finetuned ELMo and W2V models with a small corpus of philosophical texts and compared them using intrinsic evaluation methods. We also explored combining the two kinds of embeddings. Our main conclusions are: 1) ELMo models provide better embeddings than the finetuned W2V model despite the small data size, except a pretrained model without tuning, which performs worse. 2) Concatenating and adding embeddings does not bring extra value in this study; however, when merging embeddings from different models, performance can be gained by tuning the contribution of each model.

References

Arianna Betti, Martin Reynaert, Thijs Ossenkoppele, Yvette Oortwijn, Andrew Salway, and Jelke Bloem. 2020. Expert concept-modeling ground truth construction for word embeddings evaluation in concept-focused domains. In *COLING 28*, pages 6690–6702, Barcelona, Spain (Online). International Committee on Computational Linguistics.

Jelke Bloem, Antske Fokkens, Aurélie Herbelot, and Computational Lexicology. 2019. Evaluating the consistency of word embeddings from small data. In *RANLP*.

Hicham El Boukkouri, Olivier Ferret, Thomas Lavergne, and Pierre Zweigenbaum. 2019. Embedding strategies for specialized domains: Application to clinical entity recognition. In *ACL*.

Aurélie Herbelot and Marco Baroni. 2017. High-risk learning: acquiring new word vectors from tiny data. In *EMNLP*.

Jian Huang, Keyang Xu, and V.G.Vinod Vydiswaran. 2016. Analyzing multiple medical corpora using word embedding. *2016 IEEE International Conference on Healthcare Informatics (ICHI)*, pages 527–533.

Alexandre Kabbach, Kristina Gulordava, and Aurélie Herbelot. 2019. Towards incremental learning of word embeddings using context informativeness. In *Proceedings of the 57th Annual Meeting of the Association for Computational Linguistics: Student Research Workshop*, pages 162–168, Florence, Italy. Association for Computational Linguistics.

Angeliki Lazaridou, Alexander Peysakhovich, and Marco Baroni. 2016. Multi-agent cooperation and the emergence of (natural) language. *arXiv preprint arXiv:1612.07182*.

Alessandro Lenci. 2018. Distributional models of word meaning. *Annual Review of Linguistics*, 4(1):151–171.

Tomas Mikolov, Ilya Sutskever, Kai Chen, Gregory S. Corrado, and Jeffrey Dean. 2013. Distributed representations of words and phrases and their compositionality. In *NIPS 2013.*, pages 3111–3119. Neural Information Processing Systems Foundation, Inc.

Farhad Nooralahzadeh, Lilja Øvrelid, and Jan Tore Lønning. 2018. Evaluation of domain-specific word embeddings using knowledge resources. In *LREC*.

Yvette Oortwijn, Jelke Bloem, Pia Sommerauer, Francois Meyer, Wei Zhou, and Antske Fokkens. 2021. Challenging distributional models with a conceptual network of philosophical terms. In *NAACL*, pages 2511–2522, Online. ACL.

Matthew Peters, Mark Neumann, Mohit Iyyer, Matt Gardner, Christopher Clark, Kenton Lee, and Luke Zettlemoyer. 2018. Deep contextualized word representations. In *NAACL*, pages 2227–2237, New Orleans, Louisiana. ACL.

Radim Rehurek and Petr Sojka. 2011. Gensim–python framework for vector space modelling. *NLP Centre, Faculty of Informatics, Masaryk University, Brno, Czech Republic*, 3(2).

Howard Robinson. 2020. Substance. In Edward N. Zalta, editor, *The Stanford Encyclopedia of Philosophy*, Spring 2020 edition. Metaphysics Research Lab, Stanford University.

Arpita Roy, Youngja Park, and Shimei Pan. 2017. Learning domain-specific word embeddings from sparse cybersecurity texts. *ArXiv*, abs/1709.07470.

A ELMo hyper-parameters

	LSTM		Char cnn		Data	
Model	**Output dim**	**Hidden dim**	**N char**	**Embed dim**	**Type**	**Token**
ELMo s	256	1024	261	16	philosophy	1.6M
ELMo m	512	2048	261	16	philosophy	1.6M
Pretrained	256	1024	261	16	miscellaneous	800M
Finetuned	256	1024	261	16	combined	combined

B Seed words

inference	deductive	argument
analytical	antecedent	necessary
effect	cause	epistemology
extension	intension	extensional
formal	freedom	identity
argument	hypothetical	induction
categorical	infinity	intension
extension	justice	logical
moral	truth	ontology
perceptual	relativity	identity
premise	reason	theoretical
property	reasoning	extension
proposition	practical	relation
nature	analysis	disposition
subjective	analytic	critical
substance	appearance	experience
synthetic	belief	empirical
analytic	concept	formal
knowledge	practical	reason
logical	pure	standpoint
maxim	reality	subject
objective	rational	subjective
perspective	real	system
existence	perspective	spirit
fallacy	paradox	verification
meaning	science	symbol
analogy	paradox	intuition
inference	predicate	judgment
essential	sense	synthetic
extension	simplicity	theoretical
illusion	state	understanding
deductive	hypothetical	will
intensional	ideology	being
fact	imagination	use
mention	valid	

C Term distribution from ELMo small model

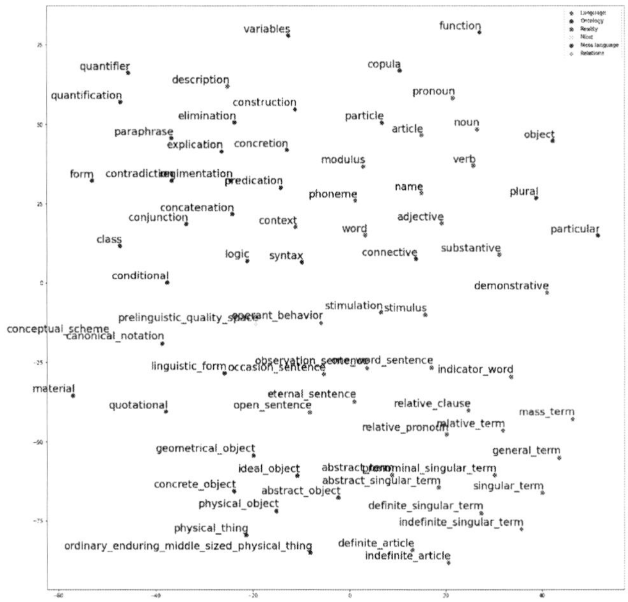

Term distribution after t-SNE dimension reduction for the ELMo small embeddings. Note that the Dunn index for the clusters after dimension reduction is 0.05 (down from 0.44), so there is a large information loss and this visualization does not fully represent the 256-dimensional model.

D Target terms

Language	Ontology	Reality	Mind	Metalinguistic
Pronominal singular term	Ordinary enduring middle sized physical thing	Operant behavior	Prelinguistic quality space	Canonical notation
Abstract term	Class	Modulus	Conceptual scheme	Paraphrase
Adjective	Concrete object	Stimulation		Variables
Article	Physical object	Phoneme		Concatenation
Definite article	Ideal object	Stimulus		Concretion
Indefinite article	Geometrical object	Context		Conditional
Mass term	Material			Conjunction
Demonstrative	Object			Connective
Description	Abstract object			Construction
General term	Particle			Contradiction
Singular term	Particular			Copula
Definite singular term	Physical thing			Form
Indefinite singular term				Function
Eternal sentence				Quantification
Indicator word				Quantifier
Name				Quotational
Noun				Predication
Relative term				Plural
Substantive				Regimentation
Observation sentence				Elimination
Occasion sentence				Explication
Open sentence				Linguistic form
Pronoun				Logic
Abstract singular term				Syntax
Relative clause				
Relative pronoun				
One word sentence				
Word				
Verb				

Association for Computational Linguistics
209 N. Eighth Street
Stroudsburg, Pennsylvania 18360

ISBN 978-1-7138-3697-1

CURRAN ASSOCIATES INC.
proceedings.com